A Textbook of Cultural Economics

Ruth Towse

Professor of Economics of Creative Industries, CIPPM, Bournemouth University
Professor Emerita, Erasmus University Rotterdam

CAMBRIDGE
UNIVERSITY PRESS

CAMBRIDGE
UNIVERSITY PRESS

University Printing House, Cambridge CB2 8BS, United Kingdom

Published in the United States of America by Cambridge University Press, New York

Cambridge University Press is part of the University of Cambridge.

It furthers the University's mission by disseminating knowledge in the pursuit of education, learning and research at the highest international levels of excellence.

www.cambridge.org
Information on this title: www.cambridge.org/9780521717021

First published 2010
Reprinted 2013

Printed in the United Kingdom by the CPI Group Ltd, Croydon CR0 4YY

A catalogue record for this publication is available from the British Library

ISBN 978-0-521-88872-1 Hardback
ISBN 978-0-521-71702-1 Paperback

For Mark

week1: chpt 16, 17, 25, 28

Contents

Figures

Tables

Boxes

Abbreviations

A&R	artist and repertoire
ACE	Arts Council of England
AEI	average earnings index (UK)
AR	average revenue
AVMS	Audiovisual Media Services (EU directive)
BBC	British Broadcasting Corporation
CBA	cost–benefit analysis
CBC	Canadian Broadcasting Corporation
CD	compact disc
CNC	Centre National de la Cinématographie (France)
CPB	Corporation for Public Broadcasting (US)
CTEA	Copyright Term Extension Act
CV	contingent valuation
DCMS	Department for Culture, Media and Sport (the United Kingdom's ministry for culture)
DJ	disc jockey
DRM	digital rights management
DVD	digital versatile disc
EC	European Commission (executive arm of the European Union)
FCC	Federal Communications Commission
GATS	General Agreement on Trade in Services
GDP	gross domestic product
GNP	gross national product
GVA	gross value added
IFACCA	International Federation of Arts Councils and Culture Agencies
IFPI	International Federation of Phonographic Industries
IP	intellectual property (patents, copyright, trademarks, etc.)

IPR	intellectual property right
ISIC	International Standard Industrial Classification
IT	information technology
MFN	most favoured nation
MPAA	Motion Picture Association of America
MPB	marginal private benefit
MPC	marginal private cost
MR	marginal revenue
MSB	marginal social benefit
MSC	marginal social cost
NAICS	North American Industrial Classification System
NBC	National Broadcasting Company (US)
NEA	National Endowment for the Arts (the arts council of the United States)
NPV	net present value
OECD	Organisation for Economic Co-operation and Development
PI	Pareto improvement
PLR	public lending right
PPI	potential Pareto improvement
PPP	purchasing power parity
PPS	purchasing power standard (used in the European Union)
PRS	Performing Rights Society (UK)
PSB	public service broadcasting
ROH	Royal Opera House (UK)
RPE	relative price efficiency
RPI	retail price index (UK)
SIC	Standard Industrial Classification
SOC	Standard Occupational Classification
SOCAN	Society of Composers, Authors and Music Publishers of Canada
TPMs	technological protection measures
TRIPS	Trade-Related Aspects of Intellectual Property Rights (WTO)
TV	television
TVWF	Television without Frontiers (EU audio-visual directive)
UN	United Nations
UNCTAD	UN Conference on Trade and Development
UNDP	UN Development Programme
UNESCO	UN Educational, Scientific, and Cultural Organization

VAT	value added tax (the sales tax used throughout the European Union)
VCR	video cassette recorder
VoD	video on demand
WCT	WIPO Copyright Treaty
WIPO	World Intellectual Property Organization
WPPT	WIPO Performances and Phonograms Treaty
WTO	World Trade Organization
WTP	willingness to pay

Preface

This book is written as an introduction to cultural economics; it assumes no knowledge of economics, even of supply and demand, and each economic concept is explained as it is introduced in the text. The book represents my kind of cultural economics, and my motive for writing this book is to expand cultural economics beyond its earlier scope to include the creative industries and the issues of copyright law that relate to them. The creative economy/ creative industries approach is not just a fad in cultural policy (though it is certainly also that), and it encompasses many economic features that are important for the study of cultural economics. Nowadays, the term 'creative industries', which is widely used in government and international organisations, includes all cultural economics' 'traditional' subjects of the arts and heritage along with the cultural industries; as the book shows, copyright in the creative industries is an aspect of that too.

The other motive for writing the book is to make it as international as possible in terms of illustrations and experience. I have worked for ten years in the Netherlands at Erasmus University Rotterdam and have also taught from time to time at the University of Catania in Italy, and doing so has made me aware of just how differently students with different backgrounds think about cultural economics and policy; this is not surprising, because every country has a different history and set of institutions. Meeting this aim of international coverage is inevitably biased by my own experience and limitations, however. Even though there are now very good information sources about many countries in English available online, information in English on some things is still not easy to get or interpret. As it happens, the Netherlands is one of the countries that excels in both the collection and analysis of considerable amounts of data on the cultural sector and it translates a great deal of it into English; the United Kingdom now also produces good data and research on the cultural sector and the creative industries, and naturally I tend to know more about the United Kingdom. Data are not always easy to read even for UK citizens such as myself, however (is it for England and Wales? Is Northern

Ireland included? Data relating to the United Kingdom as a whole should cover England, Wales, Scotland and Northern Ireland.) and monetary figures are in pounds sterling. I am conscious, therefore, that my efforts to illustrate various points are biased towards the United Kingdom and the Netherlands. International comparisons are made more difficult by the presence of different currencies whose values fluctuate over the years; where necessary, I have indicated the rough equivalent in euros or US dollars, but caution should be exercised in reading these figures.

Having said that, information on the cultural sector in the twenty-seven countries of the European Union and Canada is now accessible in euros via the concerted efforts of the Council of Europe and the European Institute for Comparative Cultural Research (ERICarts). I have used a lot of data from this source, and I would recommend every reader to look at individual country data, which are also listed by topic; the reference is Council of Europe/ERICarts, 'Compendium of cultural policies and trends in Europe', 10th edition 2009; see www.culturalpolicies.net. For the United States, the National Endowment for the Arts (NEA) publishes research reports on federal government statistics that are available online, and the governments of Australia, Canada and New Zealand also provide considerable information and data online on their cultural activities. International organisations, especially UNESCO (the United Nations Educational, Scientific, and Cultural Organization) and WIPO (the World Intellectual Property [IP] Organization), the United Nations agency for IP, also provide good information on the creative industries and on copyright.

My own career in cultural economics began in the 1980s with comparative data analysis on the finance of the arts for the Council of Europe; I have retained my interest (and scepticism) of data since then and believe that an understanding of the sources, mode of collection and analysis of data constitute one of the most important aspects of studying economics – hence the considerable amount of data in the book and discussions, as in chapter 12, on details of how research is carried out. I do not think it has ever been so easy to do research as it is today, with Wikipedia and online sources of all kinds, many of which are excellent, though you do need to exercise judgement as to the validity of websites. I also believe, however, that data do not speak for themselves, and without theoretical hypotheses, or at least a theoretical framework for analysing them, just having the data does not mean anything. Therefore, this book outlines and explains the basic economic theories that have been used and continue to be used in cultural economics with which the reader needs to become familiar in order to read the professional literature in this field – whether in the *Journal of Cultural Economics*, which is the international academic journal specialising in cultural economics, or other publications, including those of governments and international organisations.

Many students and others are scared by economics and feel that it is inaccessible because of the techniques and 'mathematics' needed (in fact, it is only a bit of elementary geometry and algebra; if it required much more, I would not be able to be an economist either!). Throughout the book, whenever anything technical is explained (and there is not that much of it), illustrations from the cultural sector are used to lighten the burden and to make the material relevant. If you persist, you should have learned quite a bit of economics by the time you have read the book. The 'further reading' that I suggest is at the same level as this textbook; there is much, much more besides, but you can discover that for yourself! Apart from reading articles and book reviews in the *Journal of Cultural Economics*, there is the massive (2006) *Handbook of the Economics of Art and Culture*, edited by Victor Ginsburgh and David Throsby, which is intended as a definitive collection of essays representing the state of professional level cultural economics, written by experts whose names crop up all the time in cultural economics; I recommend reading some chapters of this volume, and others can be used to access literature even if you find them hard to read. I have edited *A Handbook of Cultural Economics* (Towse, 2003a), which has sixty-one short chapters, most six to ten pages long, that are intended to introduce readers to a range of topics in cultural economics; reference is made throughout this book to the chapters in this handbook according to the topic.

How the book is organised

The book is organised in five parts and consists of twenty chapters. Part I deals with general issues – the data and theories used in cultural economics and the economic organisation of the creative industries – and consists of seven chapters. Chapter 1 is an introductory chapter that sketches out many of the topics that are analysed in the rest of this book and provides a brief history of cultural economics; an appendix summarises the main types of economic theories used throughout the book and is intended as a reference source. Chapter 2 presents an economic profile of the cultural sector while chapter 3 sketches the organisation of markets for cultural products. Chapter 4 describes the economic organisation of the creative industries, chapter 5 deals with the theory of production, costs and supply of cultural goods and services, and chapter 6 analyses audiences, participation and the demand for cultural goods and services. This is followed by chapter 7 on the theory of welfare economics and public finance and how they are applied in cultural economics. Together, these chapters provide the background of the historical and institutional aspects of the present-day economic organisation of the creative industries and the theory of production and consumption that cultural economics uses in analysing markets in the creative economy.

Part II covers the 'traditional' arts and heritage. Chapter 8 is a long chapter on the economics of the performing arts, a topic on which there has been a lot of work in cultural economics. Chapter 9 is on the economics of museums and built heritage, while chapter 10 provides an evaluation of cultural policy from the point of view of cultural economics. This chapter forms the conclusion to what can be thought of as the scope of 'traditional' cultural economics, and chapters 1 to 10 could form the basis of a one-semester course in cultural economics.

Part III mixes work in cultural economics on artists' labour markets with that on the economics of copyright. Chapter 11 applies labour economics, including human capital theory, to markets for artists' services and chapter 12 summarises empirical work by cultural economists on artists' labour markets. Chapter 13 introduces the reader to the economics of copyright and the impact that digitalisation is having on artists and the markets they supply, including those in the creative industries. Putting together these chapters is where the author's own research interests are centred, and the role of copyright has not previously been included in this way in texts on cultural economics. Part III could be used in conjunction with Parts I and II as an extended course in cultural economics. Alternatively, Part III could be used in conjunction with Part IV.

Part IV is a detailed treatment of the economics of creative industries. Chapter 14 starts the subject off by discussing the definition and notion of the creative industries and policies relating to them. It is followed by the work in cultural economics on the individual industries: chapter 15 on the economics of the music industry; chapter 16 on the economics of the film industry; chapter 17 on the economics of broadcasting; chapter 18 on the economics of the book publishing industry and reading; and chapter 19 is on the economics of festivals, creative cities and cultural tourism. Part IV of the book, combined with chapter 11 could be used as a one-semester course on the economics of cultural industries.

Finally, Part V, which consists of a single chapter, chapter 20, reviews the whole book, offering some conclusions about the strengths and weaknesses of cultural economics and suggesting areas in which further work might be done.

Throughout the book, theory and empirical research in cultural economics are interwoven and evidence is provided from a range of international sources on the topics covered. Some topics and information of special interest are put into boxes separate from the main text; some contain short biographical sketches of important figures in cultural economics while others are particular pieces of information or data. At the end of each chapter there is recommended further reading, in addition to the references from the work cited in the chapter; this is reading that I know from experience students find stimulating. A set of questions and exercises for students that are drawn from my own teaching is also provided; the examination and essay questions have been used before and work well as assessment and as discussion topics.

A note on terms and references

During the three years I have been writing this book there has been a switch in terminology, towards the ideas of the 'creative economy' and 'creative goods and services' in place of what were (and still are in some quarters) called the 'cultural economy' and 'cultural products'; the term 'creative industries' was already well established, however, though criticised by many social scientists. There is no need to worry too much about all this because any list of industries demonstrates what is being discussed, and these definitions are dealt with in the text. In any case, I have chosen to write about a subset of these industries – the performing arts, heritage, the music, film, broadcasting and publishing industries – with the addition of a chapter on festivals, creative cities and cultural tourism that covers a variety of 'industries' because these are the ones for which there is a literature by cultural economists. What it does mean is that you may find different terms applied to the same idea; in other words, I have not necessarily been consistent – and nor have other writers!

One more term that is often bothersome: 'billion' in this book means a thousand million (ten to the power nine).

Another change that has taken place over the last few years is that national governments and international organisations publish a great deal of information online, sometimes without there being a 'paper' version. Moreover, permission to use the information may be specifically given on the website, provided that the correct referencing is used. That is what I have done throughout this book. It is important always to check that up on websites, however, which also change from time to time. I checked the availability of online sites for data and other information before this book went to the publisher, but it may well happen that some items have subsequently changed.

My thanks

No one can write a textbook without becoming aware of how great a debt is owed to others, both those whose work we know and those whom we know in person. I have led a charmed life as far as my academic career is concerned. I was introduced to economics at my excellent girls' school, Nottingham High School for Girls, where Mrs Edwards taught A level economics and managed to make us feel like grown-ups; at the University of Reading, my beloved tutor Dr Eric Budden opened up the world of academia to me; my MSc(Econ.) course at the London School of Economics frightened me to death it was so hard, but at the same time it gave me the intellectual basis that has lasted me a lifetime, and led to my first appointment as a lecturer at the age of twenty-three at what is now Middlesex University. I also met my husband, Mark Blaug, in those heady days. I taught 'general' economics – introductory micro and macro, location economics, economics of social policy – and began to research and publish in the economics of the arts, the forerunner to cultural economics, in the 1980s. I worked briefly with Alan Peacock, now an old friend, whose path-breaking work in the subject has been so influential for many others besides myself. My really lucky break, though, was to be invited by Arjo Klamer to join the vakgroep Kunst- en CultuurWetenschappen at Erasmus University Rotterdam, where I spent nine years until my retirement in 2008, specialising in teaching and research on cultural economics and the economics of copyright, with generous colleagues who made me abundantly welcome and put up with my English ways. Together we started up the masters course in cultural economics and cultural entrepreneurship, which over the years attracted many fine Dutch and foreign students of the kind that makes teaching a pleasure.

Anyone in cultural economics owes a huge debt to Will Baumol, who, besides being the founder of our subject and one of the greatest all-round living economists, is also a warm and generous friend and colleague; when I edited his work on the cost disease it was just amazing to see how much he had written and how creative it was. Other friends-cum-revered-colleagues are David Throsby and Bruno Frey. I have always said how lucky cultural economics is to have such excellent all-round economists working in the field, and they both typify that. There are many more on their way up the professional ladder, and that ensures the future success of our subject. I am glad to say one of them is my PhD student, Christian Handke, who kindly produced the figures in this book and helped me with various technical problems.

I could not have got started on this book without a year's sabbatical at the Netherlands Institute for Advanced Studies (NIAS) in Wassenaar, which provides a calm environment for writing and research. A sabbatical also imposes on one's colleagues, and I am grateful to them for their indulgence. In addition, of course, my greatest debt is to my husband Mark, to whom this book is dedicated and to whom I have been married for forty years. Among all the other things, he has given me enormous encouragement throughout my career and has been my most constructive critic and adviser, including for this book.

Part I

General issues in cultural economics

Introduction

Chapters 1 to 7 introduce the subject matter of cultural economics. Chapter 1 is a general introduction to the topics covered in the book and the history of cultural economics. Chapter 2, on the economic profile of the cultural sector, is concerned with the definition and measurement of the creative economy. Chapter 3 investigates the working of the market economy in the cultural sector. Chapter 4 is on the economic organisation of the creative industries. Chapter 5 deals with the production and supply of creative goods and services, and chapter 6 similarly deals with the consumption, participation and demand aspects. Chapter 7 looks at the way cultural economics analyses policy using welfare economics. These chapters therefore lay the foundation for analysing and understanding the creative industries studied in subsequent chapters.

1 Introduction to cultural economics

This chapter introduces cultural economics and explains how cultural economists set about analysing the cultural sector – the arts (performing arts, visual arts and literature), heritage (museums and built heritage) and the creative industries (the music, publishing and film industries, broadcasting, and so on). It provides a guide to the terms used throughout the book and prepares the way for the concepts and subject matter of subsequent chapters.

What is cultural economics about?

Ten questions we ask and answer

What determines the price of a pop concert or an opera? Why is there a star system in the arts? Why are many artists poor? Why does Hollywood dominate the film industry? Can we predict the success of a film or record? Does illegal downloading damage the record industry? Does free entry to museums bring in more visitors? Why does the government support the arts? How much are we willing to pay to protect the cultural heritage? What are the reasons for public service broadcasting? These are ten of the many questions that cultural economists have asked and tried to answer. This book asks and answers them through the lens of cultural economics.

Cultural economics

Cultural economics studies these (and other) questions using economic analysis. As a discipline, economics uses theory – economic principles – to analyse problems and it also uses empirical evidence – the use of statistical data – to try to answer them. Cultural economics uses this analysis and applies it to the cultural sector; it confronts theoretical hypotheses about the production and consumption of cultural goods and services with empirical research.[1] Cultural economics is a branch of economics but it is also part of the wider investigation of the world of the arts and culture by other related disciplines, especially the sociology of culture and arts management; there is considerable overlap of subject matter with media economics as well, especially in the area of the broadcasting, audiovisual and publishing industries.

Why 'cultural' economics?

Why *cultural* economics and not just 'economics'? One reply is that there are many areas of applied economics each with its own designation, such as the economics of education, the economics of health and environmental economics (each, by the way, having some affinity with cultural economics). Any applied area requires a knowledge of the specific features of the sector it studies: you cannot look at the economics of the electricity industry without some understanding of the technology of the generation and distribution of electrical power and you cannot do cultural economics without some understanding of the performing and visual arts, museums and heritage and the media industries such as film and broadcasting, as well as of creativity and the training of artists. It is not just a matter of being well informed about these things, however; it is also that economic ideas have to be adapted where necessary to take into account issues that are distinctive to the cultural sector. Just using 'ordinary' economic theory of labour markets is not enough for understanding artists' economic behaviour, for example. Cultural economics adapts economic ideas to the specific features of the cultural sector.

What economics is and does

Economics is a well-developed and, in many ways, powerful discipline but it has its limitations and drawbacks. At its best, it studies the reaction of people and organisations to incentives, such as rewards or benefits (such as income or profit, but also satisfaction), and to disincentives, such as raising the price or being made to pay a charge. These reactions are co-ordinated through the institution of the marketplace, mostly using the medium of money, and result in the production and supply of goods and services that are sold to people who

---

[1] The term 'services' covers a wide range of items, including financial services such as banking and insurance down to everyday items such as haircuts and car repairs. In the cultural sector, a theatrical performance and a museum visit are services, while a book and a CD are goods.

are willing to pay for them. Markets are both real and virtual: online buying and selling, such as downloading a track on iTunes or buying a book online, is just as much a market as a car boot sale or a shop. Not all goods and services are sold for a price, though: a few are made available to people without payment and their supply is provided by some organisation that is financed not by the money from sales but from a source such as taxes or gifts. Entry to a national museum may not be charged for, nor is going to school, but these services are not free, because their production takes up resources that have other uses, and therefore the question of how much of them to produce and how much to spend in doing so is an economic one.

Opportunity cost

This brings us to what is probably the most powerful single idea in economics: opportunity cost. Even if things do not have a price, resources are used up in producing them – people's time (labour), money and equipment (capital) and, for some things, space or land. While time and other resources are being spent producing one thing, they are not available for use in producing another; when you spend money from your budget on one thing, it cannot be used to purchase another. Opportunity cost means that people and organisations have to make choices, and that is why economics is sometimes described as the science of making choices (and also why it is called the 'dismal science'!).

Social choice and welfare economics

It is not only individual consumers and producers who have to make choices, however. Governments have to make choices too: how much of people's incomes and profits to take in taxes, how much to spend on education or the arts or heritage or on health or defence. Public finance is the branch of economics that studies these matters, and cultural economics uses a lot of the ideas from it. Public choice theory studies how government officials and politicians behave – for example, what influences their decisions about how to distribute tax funds to the many arts and heritage organisations or in listing heritage sites.

Economists use the notion of social welfare as the basis for analysing economic decisions for the whole of a society, such as a nation state, and think in terms of overall social benefits and social costs as well as in terms of private benefits and costs to individuals. It is assumed that the aim of good government and of society in general is to improve social welfare – the utilitarian concept of the greatest happiness for the greatest number. Welfare economics is used to rationalise state intervention in the market mechanism, whether through laws or other regulation, financial subsidy (subvention) or the direct provision of goods and services. Chapter 7 goes into these topics in detail and chapter 10 uses these theories to evaluate cultural policy.

Proven through Test [handwritten]

Unable to proof (opinions) [handwritten]

Positive and normative economics

One of the strengths of economics as a discipline is that it makes a distinction between 'positive' and 'normative' analysis. Positive statements are ones that can be tested by evidence; the statement that downloading music without payment damages the music industry can be tested by seeing if there is a relationship over time between an estimate of the number of tracks downloaded illegally and the number of tracks sold or the number of record companies in existence. (Notice that the statement has to be translated into a testable hypothesis.) Normative statements cannot by their nature be tested because they revolve essentially around a matter of opinion. 'People ought not to download music without paying for it' is a value judgement, and it is a question of whether or not you believe it or agree with it. Often, two things get confused: you might say 'Why shouldn't people download music without paying for it?' and get the answer 'Because it damages the music industry'. If you can show by using empirical evidence that the second statement is not true, then you have invalidated the reason they give; but, while it may be the wrong explanation, you still have not proved that it is or is not morally wrong.

E.g. Using Utils to estimate welfare [handwritten]

Value judgements and economics   *~ Unable to Judge all values* [handwritten]

One thing economists try to be very careful about is making the distinction between positive and normative statements but it can be difficult for even the most dedicated to do this all the time, and one of the strongest criticisms of economics is that it does not and cannot succeed in wiping out all value judgements. This view has been put forward in cultural economics and we shall explore it later on. You may already have spotted a value judgement or two in the text above. One area in which most economists agree that it is not possible to get away from value judgements is welfare economics: the utilitarian belief in happiness as the gauge of welfare is a value judgement. So, say the critics, is the idea that people respond rationally to incentives, and others say that, especially in the arena of the arts and culture, people do not act just as individuals but are strongly influenced by what others in their society do: that tastes are not given, but are learned from these others they admire and want to copy or join in with. Another value judgement that is widely used in economics is that consumers best understand their own needs and wants and demand goods accordingly – the so-called doctrine of consumer sovereignty. These are some of the underlying beliefs of economists that are not always made transparent.

Limitations of economics

There are limitations to the use of economics in general and specifically in relation to the arts and culture; an obvious example is artists' production: few would say that artists are motivated to supply works of art just for the money. Nevertheless, economic analysis, even of the 'traditional' kind, does throw light on artists' labour markets and highlight how artists differ from other workers in their supply decisions; moreover, empirical research by cultural economists has been able to map out and analyse information about artists' earnings and hours of work. It would be a serious mistake, however, to think that economics can provide all the answers, and many cultural economists are content to offer their analysis without making such claims. Some critics dwell a lot on these problems in order to highlight alternative approaches that they favour. Criticism is important to keep a discipline vibrant and 'on its toes' but it is not always easy for beginners in the field to sift out the valid criticisms. In particular, some critics make much of the limitations of 'neoclassical' economics in the arts – some features of which were criticised in the preceding paragraph – but it is important to understand that cultural economists in fact use a range of different approaches, not only the neoclassical one. In the appendix to this chapter, some of the approaches used by cultural economists are briefly summarised as a guide to the reader.

Rich culture • tourism = Economic growth

Relation of cultural economics to other disciplines

Cultural economics does not have a monopoly of the study of economic phenomena in the cultural sector. Cultural sociologists study some of the same topics that cultural economists do. It can fairly be said that they have displayed far more interest in the cultural industries than economists have. Sociologists have also studied artists' labour markets and participation in the arts, for instance. Because of their different intellectual backgrounds, economists and sociologists may draw different implications from their research; for example, the study of artists' career development in sociology relates it to the role of professionalism, whereas the economist might relate it to the study of incentive structures. Arts management has emerged as a specialist subject over the last ten years, studying the internal management of individual arts organisations and their environment. Some topics, such as performance indicators (see chapter 10), bring cultural economics and arts management close together. Within arts management, marketing the arts relates to a joint interest in participation in the arts and in taste formation. The latter topic can also be studied by psychologists and by cultural anthropologists, who 'observe' cultural consumption and production.

Economic geographers and urban analysts are interested in the location of cultural facilities and in the distribution of employment. The role of the arts in urban development and the role of 'cultural clusters' come close to work on economic impact in cultural economics and in urban economics. On a global level, the cultural sector is viewed as a means of economic development in South countries, not only for its tourist potential but also because cultural industries are regarded as dynamic and important sources of economic growth. Chapter 19 of this book looks at the economic literature on these topics.

A brief history of cultural economics

What we now call cultural economics started life as the economics of the arts, and in recognition of that some authors still use the term 'economics of the arts (or art) and culture'. The first systematic work that stimulated the birth of cultural economics was that by William Baumol and William Bowen on the performing arts.

Baumol and Bowen's book *Performing Arts: The Economic Dilemma*

The origin of present-day cultural economics is widely held to be the publication in 1966 of Baumol and Bowen's book *Performing Arts: The Economic Dilemma*. There had been some previous interest in economic aspects of the arts and museums before then by a few economists (particularly Lionel Robbins; see below) but this was not yet recognised as belonging to a coherent body of work. Baumol and Bowen presented a thoroughly researched, systematic empirical study of finance, costs and prices in theatre, orchestras, opera and ballet, and also of payments to and employment of performing artists in the United States (with some comparative material from the United

Box 1.1 Professors William Baumol and William Bowen

William Baumol (1922–), Professor of Economics at New York University (NYU) (and affiliated with Princeton University), is one of the most prolific and creative economists and his work in many branches of economics is widely recognised. These include welfare economics and the theory of regulation, environmental economics, contestable markets and entrepreneurship as well as his work on the cost disease, which he applies not only to the arts but also to other labour-intensive sectors of the economy. He is also an artist and wood carver. He is still active as a teacher and researcher in economics and is director of the Centre for Entrepreneurship at NYU. He is joint author with Alan Blinder of one of the main introductory textbooks in economic principles.

In cultural economics, besides applying the cost disease analysis to the performing arts, the mass media and libraries, he also pioneered the use of econometrics (the statistical analysis of economic hypotheses) to the rate of return on works of art; in addition, he has published several important articles on the economic history of the arts, on Athenian and Elizabethan theatre and on musical composition in Mozart's Vienna.

Professor William Bowen was a younger colleague of Baumol's at Princeton in the 1960s when they agreed to collaborate on the research project. Bowen subsequently became president of Princeton University and published in the economics of education; he did not publish anything further on cultural economics.

The research project that resulted in the book *Performing Arts: The Economic Dilemma* was initiated by the Twentieth Century Fund. It lasted over three years and involved obtaining and analysing data from several hundred organisations and 150,000 questionnaires to audiences at over 100 performances in several US cities and in London. Baumol's role was the overall design of the research and to set the project's objectives while Bowen organised the collection and analysis of the data. Baumol wrote most of the book and developed the cost disease theory.

Source: Baumol (1997).

Kingdom), and they evolved the theory that has come to be called the 'cost disease' in the arts (see chapters 5 and 8 in this book). The combination of novel empirical data (at the time, almost nothing was known about the 'arts economy') and a theoretical hypothesis that explained the observed increasing costs of producing the performing arts was what stimulated further research on these topics in the United States and in other countries. Box 1.1 introduces the research by Baumol and Bowen; it is analysed in detail in chapter 8 of this book.

The case for subsidy to the arts?

Baumol and Bowen's book aroused tremendous interest among arts administrators and policy-makers because they saw in it justification for their own experience of rising costs, due not to internal bad management in arts organisations but instead to external and unstoppable economic forces. What we now call the 'cost disease' was also called 'Baumol's law', endowing the theory with a scientific quality of inevitability. Rising costs of supplying the arts would mean prices having to be increased, thus reducing demand and leading to a shortfall of revenues from sales of tickets. This was called the 'earnings gap', and it would have to be made up by state subsidy or private patronage if the arts were to survive at contemporary levels of quantity and quality in terms of the output of the performing arts; if not, there would be an 'artistic deficit' due to the need to economise on production standards.

For their part, however, Baumol and Bowen had not advocated government subsidy as a necessity, because, as professional economists, they were concerned with positive results rather than normative policies. Instead they used the arguments of welfare economics, that the benefits of the arts are enjoyed by the whole of society, not only the individuals who attend them; as we see later, welfare economics now provides the 'standard' economic argument for government subsidy (chapter 7). In so doing, Baumol and Bowen were appealing to objective economic theory rather than to subjective advocacy of the arts. Unfortunately, though, many of those who took up the cudgels did not make that distinction, particularly those working in the arts, and, indeed, Baumol and other cultural economists occasionally stepped over the positive/ normative divide. Moreover, that can be very difficult to maintain in relation to welfare economics, as will be explained later.

History of economic thought on the economics of the arts and heritage

To get an idea of the novelty of Baumol and Bowen's contribution, it is interesting to look at how economists had treated the arts and heritage previously. In fact, even the earliest economists had referred obliquely to the arts, typically questioning whether they obeyed ordinary economic laws or were exceptional types of goods and services; historians of economic thought as well as cultural economists have also searched their writings for their views on the role of the state in relation to the finance of the arts.

Adam Smith

Smith (1723–90), author of the *Wealth of Nations*, published in 1776, is held to be the founder of modern economics; he wrote at a time in which the private market for the performing arts and creative arts was flourishing, and he saw no reason for intervention by the state (in fact, he deplored the licensing of theatres and censorship). He lived at the time of the founding of two cultural institutions: the British Museum, in 1753, financed by a private lottery to house a private collection from the estate of Sir Hans Sloane that the English parliament had unwillingly purchased; and the Royal Academy, in 1768, financed by a loan from the king (which had to be repaid). The Royal Academy remains a private organisation to this day and it was only long after Smith's death that the British Museum came to be owned by the state. These events did not elicit his comment, however, although he was involved in a private initiative to found an art academy in his native Scotland.[2] He did remark on what we now call the superstar system in the performing arts, commenting on the 'exorbitant rewards' of opera singers and dancers at a time when some opera singers, especially the castrati, were treated like modern pop stars and, similarly, became very rich; he treated those rewards in the same way as he did the wages of other labour, however (see box 11.1). Though he perceived the case for some state intervention in education because of what we would now call its 'public goods' qualities, he did not extend this reasoning to the arts, even though he thought them essential to civilised life; indeed, he seems to have opposed the idea of state involvement in the arts.

William Stanley Jevons

The first recognition of the 'public goods' aspects of the arts seems to have been by the nineteenth-century British economist Jevons (1835–82), who saw the need for open-air musical concerts alongside a number of other public works and for the public provision of public libraries. He advocated state finance of the performing arts and libraries as a kind of social investment, on the grounds that it would amply be repaid over the years by the reduction of the number of the poor receiving the 'dole' and by a reduction in crime.

John Maynard Keynes

Keynes (1883–1946) is widely acknowledged as the leading macroeconomist of the twentieth century and as having had enormous influence on economic policy in Britain in the inter-war period and during the Second World War. Keynesian economics is recognised worldwide and is frequently evoked as a solution to recessions. Keynes was also a major figure on the arts scene and became the first chairman of the Arts Council of Great Britain when it was founded in 1945 (a position he held for only a short time until his death the next year). Although he did not write explicitly on the economics of the arts,

---

[2] De Marchi and Greene (2005).

he left a record of his views on the role of the state and the role of markets in the arts in speeches and writings, from which it can be seen that he saw the role of subsidy to the arts as boosting market supply and demand as a temporary measure; Keynes believed that, if it was successful in its mission of raising the quality of the arts and making them accessible throughout the country, the Arts Council could cease to exist and the market alone would sufficiently support the arts. He therefore saw deficiency of demand on the market as being the main problem, and he believed that greater prosperity would solve it.

John Kenneth Galbraith

[handwritten: → Arts & Economics are not related at all]

Galbraith (1908–2006) is probably best known for his book *The Affluent Society*, published in 1958, with its message of 'private affluence' and 'public squalor'; it was immensely popular and sold well beyond the confines of the economics profession. He spent most of his academic career at Harvard University, retiring in 1975. He appears to have run what was probably the first seminar on the arts and economics there in the 1960s, though it was not particularly well received, however.[3] In a paper for the Arts Council of Great Britain, he put forward the view that economics had nothing to say about the arts. He regarded the arts as 'exceptional' – that is, not like other economic goods – because they are produced by 'artisan' methods rather than being mass-produced by the big business he abhorred and inveighed against in his many writings.

Lionel (Lord) Robbins

[handwritten: → Arts should be treated like science degree]
[handwritten: → Arts have economic impact]

Like Keynes, Robbins (1898–1984) was an important figure in the world of British arts, having been the chairman of the boards of the National Gallery and the Courtauld Institute of Art, a director of the Royal Opera House, Covent Garden, and a member of the board of the Tate Gallery. He was professor of economics at the London School of Economics for forty-five years and in the early 1960s wrote two articles that may be said to be the first deliberate application of economics to art and to museums. He advocated the public patronage of national art galleries (art museums) on the same grounds as those on which the state also supported 'high excellence' in science and learning; and, in analysing the political economy of museums, he took the line that, like education, the arts confer collective benefits on society. He also believed, however, that public support for these things was more a question of the values of a civilised society and state than of economics. It was left to his

---

[3] Goodwin (2006).

younger colleagues Alan Peacock and William Baumol (who, incidentally, did his PhD with Robbins on welfare economics) to analyse these points more formally using the apparatus of welfare economics.

Are the arts exceptional?

It can be seen from the brief (and partial) sketches of what economists had had to say about the arts prior to the publication of the Baumol and Bowen book in 1966 that there was no consensus as to whether the arts are amenable to economic analysis. Clearly, Baumol and Bowen and the later tribe of cultural economists did not think so! It is fair to say, however, that it is a question that lurks in the mind of some cultural economists to this day.

Development of cultural economics from the 1970s

Tibor Scitovsky (1910–2002), another welfare economist who studied and taught at the London School of Economics, moving later to the United States as professor of economics, where he taught at Berkeley, Stanford and Yale, published his book *The Joyless Economy: An Inquiry into Human Satisfaction and Consumer Dissatisfaction* in 1976. Like Galbraith, he was critical of consumerism and the lifestyle of most Americans (Scitovsky was Hungarian by birth and retained many of his cultured east European attitudes), and he argued that consumer behaviour could be explained not only by the satisfaction of existing wants but by the craving for novelty. He was far ahead of his time in believing that economics could learn much from behavioural psychology, a novel concept in the 1970s but accepted by many economists now, and his emphasis on the search for novelty chimes well with the current interest in the creative industries.

It was also in the 1970s that John Michael Montias carried out pioneering research on the art market (see box 3.3). Alan Peacock (see box 6.1) initiated the first economic analysis of museums and of built heritage; he also investigated the finance of broadcasting on behalf of the British government, producing a report on the financing of the British Broadcasting Corporation (BBC), known as the 'Peacock Report', in 1986 (remarkably, broadcasting, or, rather, the BBC, had already been subjected to economic analysis in 1950, by Ronald Coase (see box 5.4)). In Australia, David Throsby and Glenn Withers researched the performing arts in the late 1970s, developing some of the theoretical models that have been widely adopted in cultural economics; Throsby (see box 11.2) has worked continuously in cultural economics over the last thirty or so years, making a major contribution in all aspects of cultural economics. Bruno Frey and the late Werner Pommerehne contributed a European perspective on cultural economics in their 1989 book *Muses and Markets*; Frey has also made a major contribution to cultural economics, particularly in relation to the economics of museums (see, for example, box 4.1). These are all individuals who keep cropping up in this book, and their work has had a fundamental influence on the development of present-day cultural economics.

All this early work was published in a variety of publications[4] but, with the founding of the *Journal of Cultural Economics* in 1977, cultural economics acquired a forum for the publication of articles on a range of topics now perceived as belonging to an identifiable, distinct field of study. It seems that the term 'cultural economics' was chosen partly as a parallel to cultural sociology and partly because the term 'the arts' was too narrow a concept to cover what had come to be the study of museums and heritage as well as the cultural industries (music, film, broadcasting, publishing, and so on) in addition to the performing arts.

Augustin Girard, head of the studies and research department of the French Ministry of Culture, drew attention to the cultural industries in the 1970s and there were scattered articles by economists on one or another of the industries in the 1980s. It was not until the 1990s, however, that interest in the economics of this branch of cultural production really developed.

Cultural economics and the creative industries

A new twist in the story of cultural economics was the development of research on what are now increasingly called the creative industries. This term came into use in the last years of the twentieth century with the almost simultaneous publication in 2000 of the book *Creative Industries: Contracts between Art and Commerce* by Richard Caves, a well-known US economist specialising in the field of industrial organisation (see chapters 5 and 13), and the seemingly unrelated broadening of interest in the previously designated 'cultural' or 'media' industries on the part of policy-makers, particularly in the United Kingdom. In 1998 the UK Department for Culture, Media and Sport (DCMS) produced its first *Creative Industries Mapping Document*, which laid down a list of the industries included in this new way of conceptualising the arts and heritage. They included:

[4] Many early articles are reprinted in Towse (1997).

- advertising;
- architecture;
- art and antiques markets;
- computer and video games;
- crafts;
- design;
- designer fashion;
- film and video;
- music;
- performing arts;
- publishing;
- software; and
- television and radio.

Creative Industries

This list (which, notably, does not include museums or the built heritage) is very similar to the industries analysed by Caves, give or take an item. What was significant in both these developments was that they bundled together the 'high' and 'low' arts and subjected them to the same treatment.

The role of intellectual property   → *Artists' Soundtracks* → *Architects Blueprints*

The underlying analytical approach to the concept of the creative industries is very different as between that of Caves and the DCMS. Caves' way of defining them was already present in the subtitle to his book and focused on the fact that creators of works of art must collaborate with what he called 'humdrum inputs' – a commercial enterprise – in order to get their work produced, publicised and marketed. By contrast, the DCMS and, later, other policy-making bodies used a somewhat different analytical basis for their concept of the creative industries:

The creative industries are those that are based on individual creativity, skill and talent. They also have the potential to create wealth and jobs through developing and exploiting intellectual property.[5]

The difference is the emphasis on the role of intellectual property (IP), mainly copyright and related rights but also design rights, trademarks and patents. IP law thus becomes an important aspect of cultural policy. Chapters 13 and 14 go into copyright and its role in the creative industries in detail.

Things moved one step further in the IP direction with the work on the creative industries by the World Intellectual Property Organization (WIPO), UNESCO (the United Nations [UN] Educational, Scientific, and Cultural

---

[5] See www.culture.gov.uk/about_us/creativeindustries.

Organization) and UNCTAD (the UN Conference on Trade and Development). The creative industries also feature in the work of the World Trade Organization (WTO) with its TRIPS (Trade-Related Aspects of IP Rights) agreement and policy. All these organisations are concerned with the size of the creative industries sector and with their role in economic growth and development, and are interested in cultural economics as a field of study and in what economics has to say about the role of IP, especially copyright law. In chapter 2, the problem of defining and measuring the creative industries is analysed.

Market forces in the creative industries

One of the chief features of commercialised culture is the fact that it relies heavily upon market forces. This means that private entrepreneurs, who are in business to make profits, get to decide what creative work is produced and consumers, perhaps without having a lot of knowledge or experience of what is good art, decide what succeeds on the market through their choice of what to buy or attend. Many people in the arts deplore this principle, arguing that we need expert judgement to decide what is worthwhile art and government subsidy to finance it, because consumers are not well informed enough or willing to pay enough to sustain it through the market. Economists, however, regard consumer sovereignty – (the belief that consumers are the best judges of their wants – as the main determining factor in consumption.)

As economists, we have to be careful to distinguish positive and normative issues here. The market may be able in some circumstances to provide high-quality cultural goods; it is argued that, especially with the internet, niche markets in affordable specialised cultural products are developing. Globalisation and international trade also expand markets for producers and reduce prices to consumers; it is debatable whether they increase or decrease cultural diversity. Economists do not believe that we should make normative judgements about what people should or should not want to consume; if people want to pay for lap dancing but not for ballet, we may deplore their taste, but it would be interference in their right to make that choice as long as what they do is legal. Many of us would say the best policy is to offer good education and opportunities to experience the arts and hope that people come to enjoy them. Of course, if prices are too high to allow them to attend the arts, that is something that can be investigated, and it may be remedied by subsidies to cultural suppliers that enable them to reduce prices, but it should not be assumed that it is inevitably so. People pay high prices for pop concerts and football games when they want to! This is the principle of consumer sovereignty, and freedom of choice for consumers is an article of faith of economics.

Markets are not inhabited solely by hard-nosed commercial suppliers and not all production via the market is motivated by the desire for commercial gain. Private non-profit organisations, many of which are not directly subsidised, play an important role in the markets for the arts and culture. As we shall see later on, many countries have a 'mixed' economy in which state-subsidised, private non-profit and commercially orientated organisations all coexist. Variety *is* the spice of life!

These themes are taken up throughout this book, with chapters 3 and 4 developing the theme of the role of markets in cultural production.

About the book

The aim of this book is to expand cultural economics beyond its earlier emphasis on the performing arts and heritage to include the economics of the creative industries and of the copyright issues that relate to them. The creative industries approach may be just a fad in cultural policy but it also presents challenges to cultural economics that it has not fully met so far.

Analysis of the contemporary creative economy requires some shifts away from more traditional thinking. First, it is no longer possible to draw the line in any meaningful way between what were once called the 'high arts' and the 'popular arts'. It used to be thought that that distinction could be made on the basis of whether or not the art form was subsidised by the state or not but studies of international comparisons of state subsidies to the cultural sector in various countries have shown that this is no safe guide: pop music gets subsidy in the Netherlands and opera gets none in Japan. It is now a world in which film directors learn their trade making advertisements for television and opera singers make a living by singing jingles for advertisements.

Second, there have also been developments in economic theory that influence the way cultural economists approach their work. In the forty or so years of its existence, cultural economics has taken on board analytical changes in economics, such as the development of principal agent theory, information economics, transaction cost economics and the theory of property rights analysis (see the appendix to this chapter for a brief description of these theories), which have transformed the way economists analyse economic relationships. Third, technological progress has profoundly influenced the media industries and has also impacted on all the creative industries in one way or another, altering costs and prices and the way consumers access cultural products and how producers supply them.

All these developments have had their impact on cultural economics.

Further reading

Two excellent introductory essays are those by Bruno Frey in his (2000) book *Arts and Economics*: 'Economics of art: a personal survey' (chapter 1) and 'Art: the economic point of view' (chapter 2); I recommend nearly every chapter in this book, as you will see in the 'Further reading' sections in the following chapters of this book. David Throsby's (2001) book *Economics and Culture* also has an interesting introductory chapter (chapter 1), in which he presents his point of view on the subject. You could also read the 'Introduction' in the Towse (2003a) *Handbook of Cultural Economics*.

Appendix: Brief introductions to the economic theories used in cultural economics

Though cultural economics is defined as the application of economic theory to the cultural sector, the subject can be approached from different points of view, reflecting different approaches within economics as a discipline. Sometimes, students worry about which theory is being used and how that matters. Moreover, some authors explicitly promote or reject one approach or 'school of thought' over another, and this can be confusing to students and non-specialist readers. In this section, the various theoretical approaches that have been taken by cultural economists are identified and briefly explained. They are macroeconomics; neoclassical economics – focusing on microeconomic theory of price theory and welfare economics; public choice theory; and transaction cost economics and property rights theory. These thumbnail sketches are included here for reference purposes and each approach is explained in more detail as it is used in the context of later chapters.

Macroeconomics

Macroeconomics is the study of aggregate economic variables, such as the size and growth of national income, employment and inflation, and it deals with economy-wide policies to achieve economic growth. Macroeconomics is involved in the measurement of the size of the cultural sector and the contribution to national income of the creative industries (see chapter 2). Macroeconomics provides the theoretical basis for Baumol's cost disease, which is a result of differential growth in the economy.

Neoclassical economics

Neoclassical economics is what most people learn when they first study economics and most elementary textbooks, without necessarily saying so, adopt the neoclassical position.[6]

Neoclassical economics does not lend itself easily to a precise definition but it includes the following points:

- the assumption that individual producers and consumers rationally calculate all alternatives when making their choices and they have sufficient information for doing so; consumers seek to maximise satisfaction from the goods and services they buy and producers are motivated by the desire to maximise profits;
- producers and consumers are able to anticipate and allow for ('discount') future income and expenditures when making a decision in the present;
- resources can be switched between uses in response to changes in prices;
- markets work in the sense that supply and demand respond to prices and to competition and prices therefore act as signals as to what to produce.

Many economists question one or more of these statements, and also the focus on the self-seeking individual ('economic man') who ignores social behaviour and concern with public life. Welfare economics uses the features of neoclassical economics to analyse social well-being rather than private satisfaction, applying microeconomic theory in the context of society as a whole.

Microeconomics

Microeconomics is concerned with the economic behaviour of the individual producer and consumer. It uses a neoclassical approach and has its focus on price theory – the study of demand decisions by consumers and of the supply decisions of firms (costs of production, revenues and pricing policy). Traditionally, neoclassical analysis has assumed that firms maximise profits; microeconomic analysis is also applied to non-profit organisations, however, which may maximise other objectives, such as attendances or membership. Microeconomic theory is used in chapters 5, 6, 7 and 11 in this book.

---

[6] The term 'neoclassical' is to be understood as succeeding 'classical' economics, as developed by Smith in 1776 and his followers in the subsequent 100 years or so.

Welfare economics

Welfare economics is probably the most widely used approach in cultural economics. Welfare economics analyses the conditions for achieving maximum social efficiency from the use of resources in every market in the economy, adopting the approach of neoclassical economics. It considers the conditions for welfare-improving policies and therefore forms the basis for government intervention in the market economy. It does so by analysing 'market failure', a situation in which the market cannot be expected to be self-correcting and, therefore, intervention by regulation and/or financial subsidy by the government is called for to achieve maximum welfare – for instance, the regulation of monopoly.

Cost–benefit analysis and contingent valuation

Welfare economics provides the theoretical basis for the cost–benefit analysis (CBA) of long-term investments, such as building a theatre or museum. Information about expected costs, revenues and the wider benefits over the lifetime of the project is assessed and this forms the basis of the decision whether to go ahead. CBA is a widely used and accepted method of government decision-making. CBA is also used in economic impact studies, which measure the costs and benefits of a cultural project to a city or region.

CBA is being complemented and to some extent replaced in cultural economics by a recent and fast-growing literature on contingent valuation (CV) analysis, also firmly rooted in welfare economics, which uses surveys of people's subjective estimates of the value they place on public projects as a basis for decision-making. These methods of decision-taking attempt to provide 'positive' empirical evidence of economic and cultural variables.

Welfare economics is the subject of chapter 7, and its justification of cultural policy of support for the arts and heritage features in chapter 10. Market failure is discussed in chapters 7, 10, 13 and 17 and economic impact studies are to be found in chapters 10 and 19. Chapters 6 and 9 explain the use of contingent valuation theory.

Public choice theory

Public choice theory adopts an economic approach to political decision-making. It concentrates on the incentives that influence the choice of policies –

for example, why politicians support the arts and how they use the arts to gain political support for themselves, on the one hand, and, on the other, how cultural lobbyists influence arts policy. Public choice theory may be thought of as offering another approach to welfare economics: welfare economics takes the choice of policies as given, whereas public choice theory looks at how policies are made. Principal–agent analysis is relevant here; it considers the kind of policies or incentive structures that the 'principal', for example, the grant-giver, can offer the agent, the arts organisation in receipt of the grant, to fulfil the principal's intentions. Public choice theory has been applied in cultural economics to the heritage (chapter 9) and it also crops up in various other places in the book.

Principal–agent analysis and asymmetric information

Fundamental to public choice theory are two concepts that interact: principal–agent analysis and asymmetric information. In the political arena, the principal is the voter or taxpayer on whose behalf a certain policy is being put into practice by the agent, say a cultural organisation. Asymmetric information is the situation in which those on one side of a bargain have more information than the other parties to it and they are likely to use that for their own advantage.

Generally speaking, voters and politicians have less information than the enterprises (arts organisations or for-profit producers of cultural products) they are trying to influence about what can be achieved. So, for example, voters may support a policy of evening opening of museums, but managers of museums can find many reasons why that is not possible, at least without more funding.

It is an important economic insight to realise that, if people have an advantage they can exploit, whether in the private or the public sector, they are likely to do so, and this will affect the way resources are used; this is called 'opportunistic behaviour' and it is important in transaction cost economics.

Transaction cost economics

Transaction cost economics provides an alternative way of understanding the way firms and industries are organised to the neoclassical approach. Instead of being governed entirely by relative prices, the transaction cost approach dwells on the costs of using the market economy, because that involves various kinds of costs, such as the costs of finding information, making deals and enforcing contracts, and so on. This is where opportunistic behaviour can become relevant, because it increases transaction costs. Transaction cost economics explains the role of firms as reducing these costs. This topic is explained in chapter 5 and in box 5.4.

Property rights approach (contract theory)

The property rights approach is loosely connected to transaction cost economics and looks at the transfer of property rights when transactions take place. It may also be called contract theory, because it analyses the type of contracts that occur between the parties concerned so that the incentives exist for each to complete the deal satisfactorily. Property rights include intellectual property rights, such as copyright, which exist in almost every cultural good. Information problems also exist here, and the transaction costs are what prevent the perfect contract from being feasible. Caves uses contract theory and the property rights approach in his theory of the economic organisation of the creative industries (see chapters 5 and 14).

2 Economic profile of the cultural sector

This chapter investigates various aspects of building an economic profile of the cultural economy and introduces a theme that is taken up, one way or another, in every chapter of the book, namely the role of the private and public sectors in the provision of cultural or creative goods and services. Though the term 'creative economy' has become increasingly used, it nevertheless typically covers a broader scope of industries than the arts, heritage and cultural industries as studied in cultural economics, including, as in the *Creative Economy Report 2008* published by UNCTAD (2008), scientific and technical – even economic – creativity. This is still emerging terminology and there is as yet no one settled definition of the scope of the term. To make matters more specific, therefore, the term 'cultural sector' is used here unless specifically talking about the creative industries. The chapter also introduces the use of empirical data to present a description of the cultural sector: data sources and descriptive statistics, and how the size of the sector is measured.

In the chapter, we look at several related topics that provide an economic profile of the sector: the role of public and private ownership; cultural policy and public finance; statistics on the cultural sector; and, finally, measuring the size of the cultural sector in countries using published data and national income accounting, international trade in cultural products and international comparisons of the cultural sectors in several countries, rounding off with a discussion of the use and abuse of statistics. The emphasis is on the practicalities of drawing up a profile of the cultural economy.

Public and private ownership in the cultural sector

One of the main features that shapes the cultural sector is the fact that both public institutions and private organisations are involved to a greater or lesser extent in the production of cultural goods and services. Every country in the world has some form of public broadcasting (radio and television) and, usually, there is public ownership of some heritage items, such as archaeological remains or national edifices, for example royal palaces. Many countries have publicly owned museums even when other parts of the cultural sector, such as the performing arts (music, theatre, opera, dance, and so on), the visual arts, literature and film, are privately supplied. It is not uncommon in European countries to find performing arts facilities, such as orchestras, opera and theatres, being wholly financed by the state and staffed by management and technical employees as well as by singers and players with civil servant status. This happens in Austria, Germany, France, the Netherlands and Sweden to name a few, and it is quite hard to grasp for people from Australia, Canada, Japan, the United Kingdom and the United States.

The typical model that we deal with in cultural economics (and in this book), however, is that of a mixed economy of public and private ownership and supply, in which many arts and heritage suppliers are non-profit organisations supported to a greater or lesser extent by public expenditure. This is the model that characterises the cultural sector of all developed countries, and of many developing countries too. What differs between countries is the balance of public and private ownership, how much public finance is devoted to the cultural sector and how that is provided.

Various types of government intervention

Modes of finance of cultural facilities vary between countries; some are owned outright by the state and managed by the public administration, others are supported by direct grants of financial subsidy and/or by indirect financial means, such as reduced taxation. Regulation – the use of rules and laws – is also used to steer the way the private market works. Regulation is widely used in preserving built heritage while copyright and other intellectual property laws apply in all the creative industries. These differences make it difficult to generalise about how the arts and culture are financed and organised, but it also means that there is a rich source of experience that can be compared and evaluated, and international comparison is one of the ways in which cultural economists have studied the cultural sector.

Public and private goods

True public goods have a combination of two necessary conditions: 'non-rivalry' and 'non-excludability'; private goods are ones that are used up in consumption (rival) and where the owner (or buyer) can capture all the benefits by excluding others. Non-rivalry means that the enjoyment of a good by one person does-not reduce what is there for others to enjoy, and non-excludability means it is not possible (at least without excessive expense and difficulty) to stop people gaining access to them. These features make it unlikely that private for-profit firms will produce public goods, because 'free-riding' by consumers makes it impossible for producers to charge for them; by contrast, suppliers of private goods can control the sale of the goods and services they produce and obtain revenue from selling them at the market price. Some goods are 'quasi-'public goods that have one or other feature of a 'pure' public good: for example, a radio signal is non-rival, but it can be made excludable and charged for directly or a charge can be made for use of the receiver (such as a licence fee).

One of the problems that digitalisation has given rise to is that many 'information goods' are effectively public goods once they are available on the internet, and property rights, mostly copyright, cannot be protected easily.

Because of these features, public goods are mostly produced collectively, often by the government but also by non-profit organisations. Some properties of the arts and culture are true public goods in the economic sense, such as shared history, cultural heritage and language, but far and away the majority of goods and services in the cultural sector are not public goods; they are rival (the more for you, the less for me) and access to them can be limited to those who have paid an entry charge or subscription (they are excludable). Of course, a cultural organisation can choose to let some people in for free, say children, or to give their product away (such as a 'free' newspaper). Even if 'free' goods and services are supplied by a public organisation, though, they are nevertheless 'private' goods in the economic sense unless they have the specific combination of non-rivalry and non-excludability, and it is important to distinguish publicly supplied goods from public goods. Conversely, some privately owned items, such as buildings and gardens, provide 'external' benefit to the public because viewing them cannot always be prevented.

Even pure public goods do not necessarily have to be publicly owned, however; they can be provided by non-governmental organisations or private clubs. In the United Kingdom, a great deal of the built heritage is owned and managed by the National Trust, which is a private membership organisation (see box 2.1). In the Netherlands, there is a similar model of

Box 2.1 The National Trust in the United Kingdom

The National Trust in England, Wales and Northern Ireland (there is also a National Trust for Scotland) is a private, non-profit membership organisation that has existed for over 100 years and that performs a significant role in preserving heritage (built and natural). It buys and renovates properties, opens them to the public and provides a range of visitor services. It owns over 300 historic properties. In terms of built heritage, it specialises in great houses ('stately homes'), castles and other buildings of historic and architectural interest, and it also owns gardens and parks and areas of outstanding natural beauty. Its finance comes from the membership fees of its over 3 million members, from entrance fees and from its trading activities (car parks, restaurants, shops, publishing, rental of properties, and so on). The National Trust is therefore a private organisation providing heritage services that in many countries would be provided by the state; this is an example of the private provision of goods with public goods characteristics by a non-profit, membership organisation.

membership organisations that manage public service broadcasting licences (see chapter 17).

Why ownership matters

One question economists are interested in is the different incentives and outcomes resulting from public and private ownership. There are several reasons why it matters whether a cultural good is provided by a public body or by a private enterprise, such as a non-profit organisation or a private firm (see box 2.1 for an example). Publicly owned organisations are financed through public funds, usually generated by taxes paid by the population of a state or country (or maybe through a supranational body, such as the European Union). This usually means that there must be public policy about how taxes are spent and rules about what the arts organisation has to achieve with public funding. This is also the case when private cultural organisations get subsidies from public sources. Much of this book is devoted to the public finance of the arts and culture and to the economic aspects of cultural policy that determine how public expenditure is allocated (see below and chapters 7 and 10).

One area in which ownership has been very important is in the media industries – broadcasting and the press. Television and radio originated in public ownership in many countries but have now been privatised. This has had an impact on cultural content, as commercial practices produce a very different constellation of broadcast material from what the state monopoly public service broadcasters used to. The ownership of media, especially newspapers and television stations, is also a matter of concern when the market becomes highly concentrated. This is discussed in detail in chapter 17.

Property rights and ownership

It is worth considering what is actually meant by ownership. When you own something, you may do what you like with it (subject sometimes to restrictions imposed by public authorities); but you can also acquire property rights to use certain items without owning them. For example, you do not own the copyright to a song by Madonna, but you can purchase a licence that allows you to listen to it; but that is all: you may not play it in public or do a host of other things with it (read the licence conditions!). When you buy a painting or a photograph, you own the object but you do not own the copyright; that stays with the artist. Many cultural goods and services, especially with digitalisation, are controlled by licences rather than by ownership, and people pay a rental fee for them for a limited period of time instead of a price that entitles the purchaser to own the item outright with no time limit. Ownership and control are therefore very different things.

Ownership and control

In general, the greater the proportion of public funding an organisation receives, the less control it will have over its management decisions regarding what it produces, its pricing policy and even perhaps where it is located. In many European countries, however, the so-called policy of privatisation of cultural facilities has taken place, whereby a facility that was owned by the state is reorganised into a non-profit organisation with managerial control, while the state still owns the capital elements, such as the building and, in the case of museums and art galleries, the collection. For example, the collections of formerly state-managed museums in the Netherlands and the United Kingdom are still owned and financed by the state but are now managed by specially created autonomous non-profit organisations.

Non-profit and for-profit organisations

Non-profit organisations are enterprises whose main objective is to provide financial support or to provide goods and services for non-commercial purposes; they are managed by people who may not own or have an economic interest in the enterprise. Any profit – that is, the excess of revenues over costs – must be reinvested in the organisation in accordance with its mission. This is in contrast to for-profit enterprises (usually called firms in economics), which seek to make maximum profit and distribute profits to owners and shareholders or reinvest them in order to make higher profits in the future. Non-profit organisations, which in some contexts could include government-owned providers, tend to dominate the 'high' arts, where profits are not made and where foundations and charitable organisations, often financed by private philanthropists or contributions by members and other supporters, seek to spread the enjoyment and execution of the arts or to support ventures that need financial assistance to promote less popular or high-quality work. Chapter 5 analyses the different pricing and output decisions of for-profit and non-profit enterprises.

Charitable status

Some countries, notably the United Kingdom and the United States, have a history of involvement of non-profit organisations in the provision of the arts and culture that, for items such as libraries and museums, goes back 200 years or so (and for schools and hospitals far longer than that). Charitable status, which means that they fall under charity law, confers tax advantages to the organisations and requires that they appoint responsible persons to sit on the board of management who are held accountable for financial rectitude.

Public choice issues

Public choice theory analyses the incentives to politicians and bureaucrats to behave in certain ways. It explains why public employees act in their own interests rather than those of the public they are supposed to be serving. The public ownership and control of cultural provision, the granting of public subsidies and regulatory controls all enable politicians and bureaucrats to exercise their power and influence. This can explain some otherwise seemingly anomalous behaviour: for example, public museums all over Europe close on Mondays to suit the needs of the employees rather than those of visitors. An interesting contrast is the privately owned Royal Academy of Arts in London, which stayed open throughout the night during its extremely popular Monet exhibition a few years ago.

Summary

This section has shown that ownership and control are likely to shape the profile of the cultural sector; typically, both public and private enterprises and for-profit and non-profit organisations coexist in a 'mixed' economy. Cultural economists expect to find different incentives and outcomes at play when comparing publicly owned and managed arts and heritage organisations with the private sector. Different institutional arrangements and practices therefore have to be taken into account, and, accordingly, we would expect these arrangements, and cultural policy as well, to vary from country to country.

Cultural policy

Cultural policy plays a fundamental role in shaping the economic profile of the cultural sector, and cultural economists have had a considerable interest in how cultural policy works. Cultural policy seeks to achieve certain goals by guiding the direction of the cultural sector, often by counteracting market outcomes. Governments can do this by public expenditure and by regulation. Governments may finance cultural organisations either because they can achieve policy goals that way or because private finance is deemed to be insufficient or, perhaps, inappropriate.

Policy goals and evaluation

The goals of cultural policy are determined by politicians, and the role of economics in policy-making is confined to providing an analysis of possible outcomes, such as the projected costs and benefits of various policy options, rather than advising on what the policy goals should be – that is, they give 'positive' as opposed to 'normative' advice. Another important role for cultural economists is the evaluation of the success or otherwise of policies and this has to be carried out in relation to the goals of the policy. Frequently this is difficult to do, either because goals are not clearly stated or because there are multiple goals, such as raising the quality and increasing access to a particular art form. The goals of cultural policy in many countries are quite general, such as promoting interest in the arts and heritage or enabling young people and those with disadvantages to participate in cultural experiences. Cultural economists have therefore attempted to encourage governments to be more explicit in their policy-making. In particular, they have had an influence on the generation of statistics that can be used to evaluate policies. This may seem obvious now, but twenty-five years ago it was very difficult to find out even the most basic information about, for example, the amount of public expenditure on the subsidised arts or which sections of the population were benefiting from it.

Later on in this chapter, I investigate cultural statistics and discuss how they can be used – and misused!

Policy measures

Governments have a range of policy measures at their disposal: they can levy taxes on incomes, goods and services, property and profits; they can have discriminatory taxes with lower or zero rates of taxation on certain items – for example, in the United Kingdom, books are exempt from VAT (value added tax on sales); they can give subsidies directly to private (almost always non-profit) cultural organisations by giving them sums of money or they can subsidise them indirectly by waiving the tax on gifts that individuals or business sponsors give them; finally, they can directly own and finance arts and heritage organisations. These are all economic measures; some can be used only by national governments while others can be applied by regional or local governments. Regulation as a policy measure is discussed later on.

Public finance

Public finance is the area of economics that specialises in analysing government taxation and expenditure.

Taxation

Governments raise taxes in order to finance their public spending commitments. Taxes mean that consumers and businesses have less to spend, so, for example, income tax (a direct tax) reduces the amount a taxpayer can spend on the arts and entertainment. Taxes on goods and services (indirect taxes) make them more expensive, which reduces people's ability to consume them, and they therefore also reduce the revenue that the supplier receives. Economists study the effects of taxation on the distribution of income between people in the population; the 'incidence' of taxes on richer and poorer people is both a matter of the efficiency of taxes and of their equity or fairness. It is generally agreed, at least in developed countries, that taxes should be proportional to income and that the very well off should pay proportionately more than the less well off through progressive tax rates; similarly, there is broad consensus that indirect taxation should not fall on necessities, thus penalising poor people more than richer ones.

Redistribution of income

The same type of thinking applies to the recipients of public expenditure. Many societies redistribute tax revenues from rich to poor. We want certain goods and services to be available to everyone because, as a society, we believe they are important. These are called 'merit goods'. Education is a good example: we believe that a society functions better when everyone has a minimum level of education; educated people commit less crime and are more likely to vote in elections, for instance. Some people regard the arts and heritage as merit goods and believe that a cultured society is a better one; other economists object to the idea of merit goods on the grounds that their provision overrides consumer sovereignty (see box 2.2). These beliefs may be based on altruism (wanting things for others for their own benefit) but it may also be in a person's self-interest to live in a well-ordered society. Other broad policy objectives for government expenditure are equality of opportunity, and provision of the arts and heritage, either directly or by subsidy, may be intended to give everyone access to them.

Subsidies in the cultural sector

One of the questions that economists study in public finance is what the most effective ways are of distributing government expenditures, and this has been an important topic in the public finance of the arts and heritage. As things stand in most countries, subsidies are typically granted to cultural organisations rather than given to consumers (see chapter 6). Subsidies to cultural organisations are also mostly given for general purposes, such as to provide high-quality programmes, instead of specifying target outcomes, such as the proportion of new visitors, though that approach is now being used in cultural policy in some countries (see chapters 8 and 10). Therefore, cultural economists look at the socio-economic characteristics of people who benefit from public expenditure on the arts and heritage and at the redistributive effects of subsidy.

Box 2.2 Richard Musgrave and merit goods

The concept of merit goods was introduced by Richard Musgrave (1910–2007) in the late 1950s. Like a number of other economists who made significant careers in US universities, Musgrave was born in Europe (Germany) and moved to the United States, where he became Professor of Political Economy at Harvard University. He is regarded as having revolutionised the study of public finance with the publication of his book *The Theory of Public Finance* (1959), and his book co-authored with his wife, Peggy Brewer Musgrave, *Public Finance in Theory and Practice* (1973), was for many years the standard textbook in the field.

Musgrave saw merit (or demerit) goods as cutting across the traditional distinction between private (rival) and public (non-rival) goods because they stem from the acceptance by individuals of community values even if they differ from personal preferences. He cited concern for the maintenance of historical sites, respect for national holidays and regard for the environment, learning and the arts as cases of merit goods. In such cases, he believed consumer sovereignty should be replaced by the norm of community preferences. This would involve the state in redistributive activity using public finance but Musgrave also recognised that private donorship was, essentially, the attempt of the donor to impose his or her values on the donee.

Despite Musgrave's significant influence on public finance, far from all public finance economists accept this concept, notably Alan Peacock, whose work on cultural economics has repeatedly rejected merit goods, while, however, recognising the role of public goods in heritage preservation. Nevertheless, the notion of the arts as merit goods often crops up in cultural economics and it is far from dead.

Source: Musgrave (1987).

Chapter 6 goes into participation in the arts, and the subject is also analysed in relation to each of the cultural sectors in Parts II and III of the book. Chapter 7 goes into detail on public finance.

Regulation

Governments use regulation as a means of implementing policies either to prevent some undesirable outcome or to encourage a positive one. Regulation may be combined with economic measures, such as a fine for non-compliance or a grant to promote compliance. Regulation can therefore shape the profile of the cultural sector.

Some regulations, such as health and safety rules at work and competition laws, affect all sectors of the economy, and they raise the costs of production; for instance, the requirement to have an attendant at every exit of a theatre adds to the costs of running theatres. The media industries are subject to specific regulation over ownership: along with rules about the concentration of ownership within one subsector, such as newspapers, there are also cross-media ownership rules (for example, the ownership of newspapers and television); these rules are discussed in chapter 17. Other regulations target the cultural sector directly, such as restrictions on altering heritage buildings (see chapter 9) or copyright laws that have an impact on the supply and consumption of cultural goods as well as on the distribution of revenues to rights holders (chapter 13). Regulations therefore have economic effects without being specifically economic in nature. Lately, cultural economists have started to look more and more at regulatory measures in the cultural sector, often in the context of public choice theory.

Statistics on the cultural sector

For the remainder of this chapter, statistics relating to the cultural sector and the ways they are used to build up its profile are discussed in detail.

One of the main themes of cultural economics since its inception has been the call for greater clarity in policy-making and the development of cultural statistics to aid the evaluation of policy measures. Particularly when public expenditure from taxes is involved, there has to be accountability to taxpayers and voters in a democracy as to how public money is spent and how effectively policies have been carried out. In order to study these various aspects of public finance, statistics on public expenditure are needed, and, in the case of the cultural sector, they have not always been easy to find. In the past there has been a certain resistance to treating the arts and heritage like other goods, and arts bureaucrats and arts organisations have tended to take the view that they know best (see chapter 10). The tide has now turned, as the creative industries are regarded as a high-growth sector of the economy, and this view has led to a considerable effort to co-ordinate data-gathering and categorisation, in part to make that case. These efforts have taken place at the national level for internal policy purposes but also at the international level: the European Union has stimulated a lot of inter-country comparison of cultural statistics for various purposes, both economic and cultural, and UNESCO, the international organisation of the United Nations for education, science and culture, has done the same on a worldwide basis. Therefore, far more information on the economic profile of the cultural sector is now available than when Baumol and Bowen set out to obtain it (as shown in box 1.1).

Although considerable progress has been made in assembling data, the picture is by no means complete, however, even in countries where cultural policy is regarded as important, and, as policies and cultural practices vary between countries, it has proved difficult to find common definitions and categories. Data on important subsections of the cultural sector, notably artists' labour markets, are still far from satisfactory even in countries that have a good cultural statistics, and data on the private for-profit cultural industries have proved difficult to obtain.

The purpose here is to lay out some of the issues surrounding statistics on the cultural sector and look at the data themselves and their interpretation. Throughout the following chapters, data on the various aspects of the production and consumption of cultural goods and services are presented, and, as a cultural economist, I place great emphasis on fact-finding and interpretation. It should always be borne in mind that facts do not speak for themselves and data can be misused as well as used to good purpose. The correct use of data in conjunction with well-specified hypotheses is the ideal goal of empirical economic analysis.

Statistics on what?

Statistics on the cultural sector may be divided into two basic types: those on culture and those on the cultural or creative economy. In terms of culture, data on the provision of the arts and heritage, the diversity of cultural products available, the location of cultural facilities, information about artists, and so on are collected. Economic data include the economic size of and employment in the whole sector and its component parts, private consumer spending and government expenditure.

In addition to the data themselves, trends in these categories over time are needed to be able to see, for example, if audiences have increased or if the sector has grown. For evaluation purposes, it is necessary to combine different pieces of information; for example, expressing the amount of government expenditure per head of the population or per region enables comparisons to be made.

Sources of data

During the 1970s considerable efforts were made in Europe to obtain consistent and comparable data on the finance of the cultural sector and cultural provision in the different countries. That proved to be a slow process, but now the Council of Europe maintains an excellent website, www.culturalpolicies. net, that gives a detailed overview of the cultural sector for many (though not all) European countries and for Canada, using compilations of national government statistics. As discussed below, it is still difficult to make definite international comparisons within Europe, as countries have different concepts and practices, and some countries have their own currencies, necessitating awkward calculations of value; for those with the euro as their currency, however, the direct comparison of financial data is now possible. In 2007 Eurostat, the official statistics office of the European Union, produced a 'pocketbook' on comparable European statistics for the twenty-seven member states; this does not supersede the Council of Europe's efforts, which are more detailed, but it is a very useful addition to it.[1]

For the United States, the National Endowment for the Arts (NEA) provides data and research reports drawing on other government statistical sources, available at www.nea.gov. These data relate to the creative and performing arts and to some heritage facilities, particularly museums. For Australia, data on the cultural sector are published by the Australian Bureau of Statistics, available at www.abs.gov.au, and by the Australia Council for the Arts, available at www.ozco.gov.au.

The data in this book have been chosen to illustrate the various points made throughout rather than to give a complete overall picture. That would in any case not be possible, as, inevitably, only some countries produce comprehensive cultural statistics. As far as possible, the intention is to avoid comparative financial data that require converting currencies (something that is in any case a specialised operation – see below). Some conversion is necessary to give a rounded view, however, and, for that, data on the arts and heritage in Australia, the United Kingdom and the United States are also included despite the problems of different currencies. Data sources on each of the cultural industries are analysed separately in Part IV.

UNESCO has a division on culture with a website, www.unesco.org/ culture, that has several subdivisions dealing with cultural diversity, world heritage, tangible and intangible heritage, the arts, museums, and cultural industries and cultural tourism, as well as a communication and information division, one of whose remits is the media. Both research and publish reports on all these topics from time to time, as does the UNESCO Institute for Statistics. UNCTAD also published its first *Creative Economy Report* in 2008, which is a collaborative effort between several UN agencies for

---

[1] Eurostat (2007).

trade, economic development and intellectual property, containing detailed worldwide data on a broad range of themes, including the size and growth of creative economies and international trade in cultural goods and services.[2]

Despite these and several other data sources, the hope that comprehensive and comparable data on international cultural facilities, production and consumption can be assembled is still a vain one; much can be done using partial data, however, as this book tries to do. In what follows, some of the most serious problems of describing and analysing the cultural sector that are generally encountered are discussed.

Measuring the size of the cultural sector

There are several aspects to measuring the size of the cultural (or any other) sector of the economy. One is what to include; second, activities have to be allocated to a specific classification so as to avoid 'double-counting' – counting an item more than once; then a method of measurement has to be adopted. National income accounting is the method used for all official economic statistics; it avoids double-counting by using the concept of value added. Each of these terms is explained in what follows. Though they sound daunting, it will be seen that they are really no different in principle from ordinary household accounts!

What to include?

The first step is to draw up a list of what is deemed to constitute the cultural sector, and this may be controversial. The areas of the arts and heritage that have been mentioned in previous sections are obvious candidates: literature, the visual arts, the performing arts, museums and built heritage. Then there are the cultural industries: according to the UNESCO web page on cultural industries,

It is generally agreed that this term applies to those industries that combine the creation, production and commercialisation of contents which are intangible and cultural in nature. These contents are typically protected by copyright and they can take the form of goods or services... The notion of cultural industries generally includes printing, publishing and multimedia, audio-visual, phonographic and cinematographic productions, as well as crafts and design.[3]

---

[2] UNCTAD (2008).

[3] See http://portal0.unesco.org/culture/admin/ev.php?URL_ID=18668&URL_DO=DO_TOPIC&URL_SECTION=201&reload=1189846616 (accessed 15 September, 2007). This page was no longer accessible on 2 January 2009.

With the publication of the *Creative Economy Report* in 2008, however, matters have moved on somewhat, and the report has three pages discussing different conceptualisations and definitions of the creative industries and of the creative economy. The UNCTAD definition of the creative industries is more all-encompassing:

The creative industries:
- are the cycles of creation, production and distribution of goods and service that use creativity and intellectual capital as primary inputs;
- constitute a set of knowledge-based activities, focused but not limited to arts, potentially generating revenues from trade and intellectual property rights;
- comprise tangible products and intangible intellectual or artistic services with creative content, economic value and market objectives;
- are at the cross-roads among the artisan, services and industrial sectors;
- constitute a new dynamic sector in world trade.

(UNCTAD, 2008: 13)

This clearly goes well beyond the previous conceptualisation and could include a far broader range of goods and services. The danger is that too broad a definition cannot be operationalised and lends itself to different interpretations, thus weakening the main reason for adopting a standardised version in the first place. Chapter 14 looks at the problems specific to the cultural industries of finding a workable list. In the end, however, any list has to be arbitrary. One point is obvious, though, and that is that the broader the classification and the more items that are included in it, the bigger the size of the cultural sector!

Standard classification of industries

Governments get the 'raw' data from tax returns and from surveys of enterprises, asking the respondent to itemise their economic activities; this is the starting point for measuring the size or total output of the whole economy. Each economic activity is put into a standardised classification that avoids the problem of double-counting, and the production of goods and services is designated into industry groupings according to what they produce. This is done by a system of 'Standard Industrial Classification' (SIC) operated by national governments that is now standardised worldwide by the United Nations statistics division[4] as the International Standard Industrial

---

[4] See http://unstats.un.org/unsd/class/family/historical/isic/default.htm (accessed 15 September 2007). There is also the North American Industrial Classification System (NAICS); see www.census.gov/eos/www/naics.

Classification (ISIC) of all economic activities. All economic activities are put into one ISIC or another and their output and contribution to national income (the sum of all incomes within a national boundary) are then calculated (see national income accounting below). Broad categories are used for convenience, such as the service industries, manufacturing, agriculture, mining, and so on. The cultural sector, does not fit into one of these broad categories, however: for example, live music performances are 'Services' while the production of CDs is 'Manufacturing'. As we see in chapter 12, many artists are not easily classified into one activity because they do several types of work; in addition, new products and processes can also make it difficult to use old classifications, and this has been a problem for the classification of activities in the cultural sector.

ISIC classifications for cultural goods and services

There are several tiers of classifying industries, however, and every economic activity large and small must be pigeonholed into one or another at the most detailed level of classification. These levels are identified as one-digit, two-digit, three-digit and four-digit levels, and at each level there is greater detail. It is not unlike the system used by libraries for classifying books and journals, which every student is familiar with. Box 2.3 illustrates how it works.

National income accounting

Having eliminated the possible double-counting of economic activities by allocating them to a specific classification, the process of adding up the contribution each makes to the economy as a whole can then begin. The aim is to measure national income in value terms, and it may be done by the 'income' method, the 'expenditure' method or the 'output' method (and they should all produce the same result).

- The income method measures national income by adding up all sources of income – wages and salaries, profits, interest and rent.
- The expenditure method measures national income by adding up all expenditures by households, firms and government departments.
- The output method measures the value of the output of every economic activity by individual producers to large corporations; this is called gross domestic product (GDP). When income earned abroad from exports is added to it, it then becomes gross national product (GNP).

Box 2.3 ISIC classification of performing arts

Say you want to look up the classification of 'theatre': you have to start by looking down the list for the most likely sectoral grouping.

- ISIC classification: section 'O' for 'Other community, social and personal service activities'.
- This includes the two-digit level: 'Division: 92 – Recreational, cultural and sporting activities'.
- This is further broken down at the three-digit level into:
    1. 921 'Motion picture, radio, television and other entertainment activities';
    2. 922 'News agency activities';
    3. 923 'Library, archives, museums and other cultural activities'; and
    4. 924 'Sporting and other recreational activities'.
- 921 has as a four-digit-level classification 9214: 'Dramatic arts, music and other arts activities'.
- Further breakdown yields: 'Production of live theatrical presentations, concerts and opera or dance productions and other stage productions; activities of groups or companies, orchestras or bands; activities of individual artists such as actors, directors, musicians, authors, lecturers or speakers, sculptors, painters, cartoonists, engravers, etchers, stage-set designers and builders etc.; operation of concert and theatre halls and other arts facilities; operation of ticket agencies; restoring of works of art such as paintings etc.'
- Nonetheless, it specifically does not include, for example, 'casting activities', which is 9249; therefore, that activity in a theatre would have to be classified separately from its other functions.

Source: http://unstats.un.org/unsd/cr/registry/regcs.asp?CI=17&Lg=1&Co=9214
(accessed 15 December 2008).

Of course, whichever of the three methods is used, the result should be the same; this is because, in accounting terms, income and expenditure must be equal. Avoidance of double-counting is achieved by measuring 'gross value added' (GVA), a term that means the value in monetary terms added by an activity to the production process.

How measurement by value added works

There is a chain of production in every production process that starts from zero, so that the whole value of first stage of the production process is the value added; then, at the next stage, the value of the output is converted into value added by deducting the value added at the first stage from the value of the output at the second stage, and so on until the final product reaches the retail price and the consumer. So, to give an example: an author writes a manuscript for a novel as the first stage in a chain of production; all the payment to the author is the value added at the first stage of creation. Then the novel is printed and marketed as a book; the value added of these activities is the value of the wholesale price of the sale of the book by the publisher to a bookshop *minus* the payment to the author and the costs of the printing and marketing. The bookshop sells the book at a retail price and its value added is the difference between the retail and wholesale prices.

Once the gross value added of an industry or sector of the economy has been measured, its percentage contribution to GDP can easily be calculated. Moreover, once there are data for several years, the growth of the sector can be calculated and compared with the growth of GDP for the whole economy. Some data for Europe are presented in box 2.4.

Problems of measuring the cultural sector

As mentioned above, measuring the cultural sector requires a great deal of manipulation of data from different ISICs, for individual artists and for enterprises producing cultural goods and services. Industrial classification is slow to respond to new industries: sectors such as agriculture and mining that were once the mainstays of a developed country's economy nowadays contribute very low percentages to GDP but they are still detailed categories in national income accounts; service industries now exceed manufacturing in value added but their breakdown is not so detailed. The current interest in the economic profile of the cultural sector and in data on the creative economy is part of the recognition of the changing nature of the economy.

One of the problems that beset early measures of the economic contribution of the arts and cultural industries was that there were no official data on value added and, instead, turnover figures were used, often supplied by trade associations that had an interest in exaggerating the importance of their sector by inflating the data. Turnover simply measures the value of output without removing the double-counting of production costs. It is an indicator of the level of economic activity, but value added is by far preferable as a true measure of the contribution to the economy. National income accounting cannot be used in some situations, however: it requires circumstances in which economic activity is organised formally, with workers being paid a wage and goods being traded at a price; it also relies on producers co-operating

Box 2.4 Contribution of the cultural and creative sector to the European economy, growth and employment, 2003–5

Turnover in 2003: €654.3 billion.

Value added to European GDP in 2005: 2.6 per cent.

Growth of cultural and creative sector from 1999 to 2003: 19.7 per cent. That was 12.3 percentage points higher than growth in the general economy over the four-year period.

Employment in 2004: a minimum of 5.8 million people worked in the cultural and creative sector (including cultural tourism), equivalent to 3.1 per cent of the active employed population in the EU25 countries.

The sectors analysed:

- the arts field, including visual arts (crafts, painting, sculpture, photography) and performing arts (theatre, dance, circus);
- heritage (museums, arts and antiques market, libraries, archaeological activities, archives);
- cultural industries, including film and video, radio and television broadcasting, video games, book and press publishing and music; and
- creative sectors, including design (fashion design, interior design, graphic design), architecture and advertising.

Sources: KEA European Affairs (2006) and UNCTAD (2008).

with the government to provide the necessary information. Many activities in developing countries are produced in the informal economy, such as crafts, and may well not get into the national accounts. There are numerous similar examples and circumstances that may obstruct a meaningful measure of the size of the cultural sector.

Other methods than national income accounting can be used to get a measure of the economic importance of a sector of the economy; for example, how many people are employed in it, or even just how many people work in it. In box 2.4 data for the European Union in 2003–5 are presented, using turnover figures as well as value added and employment data; turnover is measured by the value of total sales.[5]

Americans for the Arts, a non-profit organisation, has provided data on the economic profile of the cultural sector of the United States, including both

---

[5] Data for the individual countries are to be found in UNCTAD (2008), which also includes similar data on Australia, Canada and the United States.

for-profit enterprises and non-profit cultural organisations, in a report for the US Congress.[6] The categories are very similar to the European ones in box 2.4, with the addition of 'Art schools and services', though the report uses a far more detailed eight-digit SIC classification. The focus is on the number of enterprises and employees in 'arts-centric' businesses, however, not on value added, and therefore the data are not directly comparable to the European data in box 2.4. Using that definition, it was found that the creative industries constitute 4.4 per cent of all businesses and account for 2.2 per cent of all employment in the United States – making them, as the report says, 'a formidable industry in the US'.

Exports and imports of creative goods and services

The creative industries' contribution to the domestic economy is measured in terms of value added to GDP; in international trade, income also flows into and out of national income via exports and imports. International trade is measured in terms of both the balance of trade between countries (the volume of products imported and exported) and the balance of payments (the revenue flows from imports and exports). The balance of payments measures the value of exports and imports between countries; when the value of exports is equal to the value of imports, the balance of payments is zero. Net exports of goods and services – meaning that the value of exports is greater than the value of imports so the balance of payments is positive – contribute to national income.

International trade figures are collected and analysed by several organisations, namely UNCTAD, UNDP (UN Development Programme) and UNESCO, and data from these sources are now combined in UNCTAD's *Creative Economy Report 2008*. Data on international trade in cultural goods and cultural services are divided into two components: cultural goods include items such as sound-recording equipment and TV sets; international trade in cultural services, such as films and sound recordings, appear as services, and payments for them are royalties and licence fees (this topic is discussed in detail in chapter 14). International trade data are denominated in US dollars, which make comparisons between countries easy.

Over the last twenty years or so world trade in cultural goods has grown significantly; between 1980 and 1998 annual world trade of printed matter,

[6] Americans for the Arts (2005); see also Americans for the Arts (2008).

literature, music, visual arts, cinema, photography, radio, television, games and sporting goods grew fourfold. This trade essentially took place between a very few trading partners, however; Japan, the United States, Germany and the United Kingdom were the biggest exporters, with 55 per cent of total exports. Imports were also highly concentrated, with the United States, Germany, the United Kingdom and France accounting for nearly a half of all imports. The high concentration of exports and imports of cultural goods among a few countries did not change substantially in the 1990s, though, by 1998, China was the third most important exporter, and the new 'big five' were the source of 53 per cent of cultural exports and 57 per cent of imports.[7] This may seem strange, but it is a normal pattern in world trade that developed countries are both importers and exporters of the same goods. When it comes to trade in cultural services, however, the only net exporters are the United States and the United Kingdom (see tables 14.2 and 14.3 for detailed statistics).

How to use statistics

Data on the creative industries are becoming increasingly available from national governments and international sources, and that means they are likely to be as accurate as possible. Nevertheless, when it comes to using the data, researchers have to check up on what definitions and categories were used in their collection and classification in order to be sure the data are relevant for the purpose to which they are going to be put. It is also possible that even official data are 'massaged' to create an impression; there has been a considerable amount of hype surrounding the creative industries, and data have been used to make striking claims. The Americans for the Arts data cited earlier are presented in those terms and the United Kingdom's Department for Culture, Media and Sport has the same tendency to crow over the size and growth of the creative industries. Apart from that, some data are collected on items that cannot be precisely defined, such as 'art' and 'artists', and, as chapter 12 shows, it is particularly important to know how the data on artists are collected in order to interpret them.

Having data is one thing and knowing how to use them is another. One of the most common operations with data is to look at trends over time: first of all, the researcher needs to make sure that the data are collected in the same way year

---

[7] UNESCO (2000b).

on year; then a choice has to be made as to which years to select for making the comparison and that can be manipulated to get a desired result. For example, the Ministry of Culture wants to know if museum visits are rising: imagine a situation in which visits to a museum are the same every year except one, in which they rise (say, because there is a special exhibition that year). An illustration can demonstrate how data can be manipulated: say that in year 1 there are 100 visits, year 2 there are 100, year 3 there are 110, year 4 there are 100. If you compare year 4 and year 1, there was no change; if you compare year 3 and year 1, visits have risen; if you compare year 4 and year 3, they have fallen. That is how data can be used for strategic reasons.

Another elementary error that can also be misleading is to report financial figures in monetary rather than 'real' terms (that is, taking inflation into account). If expenditure increases by 5 per cent but the inflation rate is also 5 per cent, there has been no real increase; if the rate of inflation were higher, real expenditure would have fallen. This elementary mistake is often made by non-economists, and to correct it you need to know exactly which years the data are for and use an index of prices to take account of inflation. The 'accounting year' can also vary between organisations (and countries), so, again, this information is needed to make a fair comparison. These are a few of the problems of using statistics and it is important to be aware of them.[8] One of the ways in which statistics have been used and misused is in international comparisons of cultural data.

International comparisons

International comparisons of data on the arts suffer from all these, and even more, problems. One way they have frequently been used is to compare public expenditure in different countries to 'prove' that one country is somehow deficient. The comparison is far from straightforward, however, and is probably never fully meaningful, as is explained in what follows. Outside a common currency area, such as the Eurozone, exchange rates have to be used to convert financial data into commensurable units. The correct way of doing this is to use the 'purchasing power parity' (PPP) exchange rate, which takes into account differences in income levels and prices in different countries.[9] This is also known as the 'purchasing power standard' (PPS) and is used

---

[8] This section only touches on a subject that requires a systematic course on research methods.

[9] See www.oecd.org/dataoecd/61/56/39653523.xls for purchasing power parity rates in thirty-four countries from 1980 to the present computed by the Organisation for Economic Co-operation and Development (OECD).

Table 2.1 Public cultural expenditure per capita in selected countries

Country	Amount	Year	Currency
Germany	99	2003	euro
Italy	118	2000	euro
Netherlands	163	2004	euro
Spain	109	2003	euro
Canada	234	2003	Canadian dollar
Australia	276	2005	Australian dollar

Sources: Council of Europe/ERICarts (2008) and Australian Bureau of Statistics (2008).

by Eurostat.[10] For example, a ticket for a pop concert that costs €30 in Finland would be more expensive in real terms in Romania, because average incomes are lower there, so the ticket represents a higher proportion of expenditure out of income. It is such differences that the PPS evens out.

One of the most obvious differences between countries is their size, and population size has an enormous impact on the size of national income and expenditure. That can easily be dealt with by expressing statistics in per capita (per head of population) terms, because that 'standardises' the data. Table 2.1 shows public expenditure per capita for a few countries: note the different years and currencies – those in euros are not in PPS terms.

The figures in Table 2.1 differ considerably – but what are we to make of that? Can we conclude that one country does the right thing and others do not? Some arts lobbyists have used such data to 'prove' to their governments that they are not spending enough on the arts! Similarly, we need to ask what league tables of large economic size and high growth mean. To answer these questions we have to look at what a society perceives the benefits of the arts, heritage and creative industries to be. If creativity and novelty are valued very highly, then it would not matter if they lead to high or low economic growth.

Conclusion

This chapter has covered two broad topics in an introductory way: various features that influence institutional arrangements, such as the proportion of public and private finance in the cultural sector, and the use of data to provide a profile of the cultural economy. Institutional arrangements include patterns

[10] See Eurostat (2007).

of ownership, government intervention through public finance and regulation and the cultural policy they are intended to promote. One way of evaluating that policy is through the collection and analysis of data on the creative economy. It has taken a long time to develop reliable cultural data, and that has made it possible to use them to flesh out a profile of the main economic features of the cultural sector in a country and to make comparisons between countries. It is important that cultural economists know how to access data and assess the pitfalls of how they are used, especially when they are being used for advocacy. It is all too easy to slip between the 'positive' statement about, say, how many people are employed in the arts and the 'normative' one of whether or not this is good for the economy.

There is considerable interest in inter-country comparisons, particularly within the European Union, and it is important to ask oneself what is really gained by this. Can the economic profile of one country's cultural sector ever be fully comparable to another's? Data may be collected and correctly analysed but the fact remains that each country has a different set of cultural institutions and values, and data can never take those into account. It is important that cultural economists know how to draw up a profile of the cultural sector, and it is also important that they recognise the limitations of what may be inferred from it.

Further reading

Using a dictionary of economic terms can be very helpful when you come across technical terms for the first time (and even the second time!). There are a number on the market that can be bought in bookshops or second-hand and there are also online dictionaries. In addition, introductory textbooks in economics deal with topics such as public goods and national income accounting; take a look at the one by William Baumol and Alan Blinder (2006), *Essentials of Economics: Principles and Policy*, with applications for the US economy. Also on the United States, Tyler Cowen's 2006 book *Good and Plenty* is a good read.

A Handbook of Cultural Economics (Towse, 2003a) has two chapters that relate to the material here: chapters 20 on 'Cultural industries' (Towse, 2003b) and 21 on 'Cultural statistics' (Goldstone, 2003) cover these topics. Having read this chapter, though, you should be able to tackle the 'professional' literature, and two sources come to mind. First, the UNCTAD publication *Creative Economy Report 2008*, which I used for this chapter, is very informative on economic concepts and statistics and is thorough and readable. Second, the website www.culturalpolicies.net, which is maintained by experts from all over Europe under the auspices of the Council of Europe/ERICarts: their 'Compendium of cultural policies and trends in Europe', on its tenth edition in 2009, has country profiles under various headings with descriptions of cultural policy and a host of data on everything from finance to participation. As you will see, I have used it frequently for my own research in writing this book.

3 Markets for cultural goods and services

In this chapter, we first define the operations of the market economy for cultural products – what economists mean by markets, how markets work in theory and the role of the price mechanism. Few markets in any sector of the economy work entirely without some form of regulation, however, and intervention in the market is widespread; this is especially true of the cultural sector, and it is another aspect of the mixed economy model mentioned in the previous chapter. The second part of the chapter goes on to consider the historical development of markets for various cultural products; this shows the emergence of the role of markets, some of which continue to function in much the same way today. Finally, the main features are outlined of the industries that make up the present-day cultural sector, which are analysed in detail in Part IV of the book. This chapter also paves the way for chapters 5 and 6, which go in depth into the theory of supply and demand in the context of the creative industries, and for chapters 7 and 10, in which intervention in the working of the market economy by government is discussed.

The market economy

Why look at markets for cultural products?

One of the chief topics in cultural economics is whether the market economy can meet the demands of society for cultural products. Should it fail to do so, the government may intervene to try to ensure that the aims of cultural policy are met. This may be achieved by financial subsidies to producers and/or consumers, by regulating markets to alter the way they work through economic incentives or by replacing the market altogether with state-run institutions. As we saw in chapter 1, however, this point of view is that of present-day cultural economics, and it was developed only during the last half of the twentieth century; even now it is not accepted by some cultural economists,

---

Box 3.1 Tyler Cowen, *In Praise of Commercial Culture*

Tyler Cowen is Professor of Economics at George Mason University, Virginia, where he is also director of the Mercatus Center and of the James M. Buchanan Center for Political Economy. He has written five books, in which he examines different aspects of the power of markets to supply cultural products of all kinds: *In Praise of Commercial Culture, What Price Fame?, Creative Destruction: How Globalization is Changing the World's Cultures, Good and Plenty: The Creative Successes of American Arts Funding* and *Markets and Culture Voices: Liberty vs. Power in the Lives of the Mexican Amate Painters.* His latest book is an offbeat introductory text in economics entitled *Discover Your Inner Economist: Use Incentives to Fall in Love, Survive Your Next Meeting, and Motivate Your Dentist.* He also runs a daily blog, 'The marginal revolution'. He likes the following description of himself sufficiently to put it on his website: 'Tyler Cowen is an economist, culture vulture, restaurant critic and the best blogger in the world.' His books do not use what might be called conventional cultural economics; instead, he uses his wealth of knowledge about cultural production worldwide, both historically and in the present, combined with his insights as an economist, to offer a broad picture of the role of markets in national and international trade in cultural products.

Source: www.gmu.edu/jbc/Tyler.

---

who believe markets can be left to work in the cultural sector as they do in other sectors of the economy. Tyler Cowen is one such economist (see box 3.1).

What all economists do agree on is that cultural goods and services are economic goods, in the sense that they use resources (land, labour, capital and other inputs) that have alternative uses, and therefore there is always an opportunity cost to producing them. Equally, consumers have limited means (income and wealth) in relation to all their wants and therefore have to make choices about which goods and services to buy and in what quantity. These considerations alone make the case for an economic analysis of the production and consumption of cultural products and naturally lead to questions about what determines supply, demand and prices; in other words, we need to understand how market forces operate in the cultural sector before deciding if they can meet private and social aspirations and requirements.

The market economy and the price mechanism

The market economy can be defined simply as a social system in which goods and services are bought and sold; sellers offer goods and services in return for a payment, and buyers purchase the items they want by paying for them. Trade takes place when sellers who have produced goods or who own items that they want to sell and buyers who need or want the goods on offer are able to agree on a price. The price need not be an amount of money – it could be some agreed amount of another good or service, like a swap or barter – but, in most societies, money is used because it is an easy way of establishing the relative prices of different goods in a common unit of value. Money itself is significant only for what it can buy. Prices are determined by a combination of the quantities of goods that sellers have to offer and the strength of buyers' willingness and ability to pay for them. Some goods and services are provided free at the point of consumption (entry to museums is free in some places, for instance) but there is still an underlying 'shadow price', meaning the amount that is spent by the government or other organisation to finance production of the good or service that represents the equivalent of a price for untraded goods.

Supply and demand and the equilibrium price

The price mechanism is fundamental to the market economy and it is no surprise that the analysis of supply and demand is the first formal economic theory that people learn. Figure 3.1 represents the market for a particular good or service; here the example is of concert tickets, and so the horizontal axis, labelled Q, refers to the number (quantity) of concert tickets available at any one time. Suppliers are expected to supply more of their products as the market price goes up (the line S in figure 3.1a) and consumers are expected to buy less of a good as the price goes up (the line D in figure 3.1a). The market price is where the quantity of tickets offered for sale (the quantity supplied) is taken up by buyers demanding them (the quantity demanded) at the same price. That is the equilibrium price, P_e, and, at that price, Q_e is the quantity bought and sold; the market is said to be in equilibrium at the point where the supply schedule (S) crosses the demand schedule (D), with the subscript 'e' denoting the equilibrium position in which there is no impetus for change.

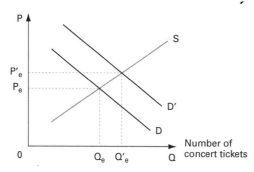

Figure 3.1a   Effect on a market of an upward shift in demand

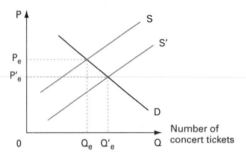

Figure 3.1b   Effect on a market of a downward shift in supply

Excess demand and excess supply

Changes do occur, however. Equilibrium would be disturbed if, for example, fans hear a rumour that this could be the last concert by a band; ticket sellers would raise prices because they know fans will offer more for tickets. The supply of tickets is limited, however; therefore, there is 'excess demand', and prices go up until they get so high that fans stop buying the tickets. This is pictured in figure 3.1a as an outward shift of the demand schedule, D to D'. A new equilibrium comes about when P_e rises to P'_e, at which the new quantity sold is Q'_e. Notice that how many more tickets are bought and sold and how much the price rises are determined by the slopes of the D and S schedules; in chapters 5 and 6, the significance of this is discussed in detail, as the 'elasticity' or responsiveness of supply and demand to price changes. It is easy to see, however, that if S were fixed in amount – the number of tickets is limited by the number of seats at the venue – the shift in D to D' could cause only greater excess demand and a higher price. In figure 3.1a, there is some increase in the supply of concert tickets, for example, from adding more seating or standing room.

Supply could shift too; if it shifted out to the right, from S to S', that would indicate that sellers are willing to supply more of a good or service at every price (see figure 3.1b); this is very important in cultural economics, because subsidy to an arts organisation is intended to do just that. As sellers offer a greater quantity for sale, there is 'excess supply' at the equilibrium price and price has to fall to the new (lower) equilibrium price, P'_e, to induce buyers to buy the extra quantity supplied – Q'_e in figure 3.1b. Again, notice that how much price falls and quantity rises depends upon the size of the shift in S but, crucially, also on the slope of D, the responsiveness of demand to price changes.

Price signals

Prices play a crucial role in sending signals to buyers and sellers about how plentiful or scarce supplies are in relation to demand. When there is a glut of a good on the market, its price will fall and suppliers will stop producing the good; when there is a shortage, its price will rise and induce suppliers to produce more of the good. The price therefore moderates the quantity supplied and the quantity demanded. Market forces work in this way when there is competition between buyers and sellers for relatively scarce goods and services. Besides 'rationing' goods via prices, the price system also governs the use of resources, and determines how they are used to produce goods and services and which goods and services enterprises would do well to supply. The market mechanism works for inputs as well as for output: chapters 11 and 12 of this book are about the labour market for artists; one of the main conclusions of work by cultural economists on artists' labour markets is that they are characterised by excess supply – too many artists chasing too few work opportunities and pay (see figure 11.1).

The allocation of resources

The term used by economists to signify the amount and types of resources that are used to produce particular products and which products are produced is the 'allocation of resources', meaning how resources are apportioned. The mix of inputs and the mix of output are both determined by market incentives – the desire of sellers to get the highest possible return (profit) for their investment in production and the desire of buyers to use their income or budget in the most effective way to achieve the greatest satisfaction or 'utility', depending upon their likes and dislikes (tastes). Chapters 5 and 6 explain these aspects of the theories of supply and demand in more detail.

Specialisation and market exchange

Trading in markets is 'as old as the hills' and there is archaeological evidence of trade in both necessities, such as flint tools, and in ornaments (beads, shells, and so on) taking place thousands of years ago. Trade allows people to specialise and to use resources more efficiently than would be the case if each were self-sufficient; this gives rise to the division of labour or specialisation of tasks, famously written about by Adam Smith (see box 3.2). Smith emphasised the spontaneity of the market and of the division of labour, which he saw as mutually intertwined, and the wealth-enhancing power of trade. Not all trade is spontaneous, though, and not all is just for the sake of improving wealth; ritual trade and gift-giving take place in many societies, and custom often influences where and how goods are traded; some cultural economists have applied these motives to the production of art.

Box 3.2 From Adam Smith, *The Wealth of Nations*

This division of labour, from which so many advantages are derived, is not originally the effect of any human wisdom, which foresees and intends that general opulence to which it gives occasion. It is the necessary, though very slow and gradual consequence of a certain propensity in human nature, which has in view no such extensive utility; the propensity to truck, barter, and exchange one thing for another (bk. 1, ch. 2: 25).

As it is the power of exchanging that gives occasion to the division of labour, so the extent of this division must always be limited by the extent of that power, or, in other words by the extent of the market (bk. 1, ch. 3: 31).

Source: Smith (1776/1976).

What (or where) is a market?

At one time a market was – and, indeed, may still be – a physical place in which traders congregated to attract buyers. A sale or auction is an example of that type of market and, in such a situation, buyers make their offers of price and compete directly with each other with the items going to the highest bidder. The present-day eBay works the same way, except that buyers and sellers do not meet in a real place or in real time, but that serves to demonstrate that markets can be organised 'virtually'. In some markets, mostly nowadays in less developed countries, each price is arrived at by 'higgling and haggling' in the market – that is, there are no posted prices that you can see to guide you as you decide whether or not to buy. Even so, there is bargaining over many prices or payments; artists often have to bargain over prices and fees, though they may prefer to leave it to an agent – and we all instinctively understand that the greater the competition there is between buyers for a good, the greater the bargaining power of the seller and the higher the price will be, whereas, if there is competition between sellers, prices are likely to be lower. For the last 100 or so years people in developed countries have become accustomed to buying the goods they want in shops and supermarkets at fixed prices. They are also 'markets' in which exchange – of money for goods – takes place.

Economists' use of the term 'the market'

Economists use the term 'the market' in several of the senses mentioned above. We still use the term 'marketplace' on occasion, even if there is no physical place where trade takes place. When we speak of the role of the markets in the arts, that means the market economy in a generic sense as compared, say, to state provision. When we speak of the contemporary art market, what is meant is the network of buyers and sellers throughout the world who are in contact with each other and who exchange physical works of art and information about them, including about prices. When we speak of the market for singers, we mean the 'virtual' market in which the services of singers (for operas and musicals, concerts, sound recording work, choirs, TV shows, etc.) are supplied and demanded and fees or wage rates are arranged; for some singers, this could be an international market, such as the one for top stars; for others, it could be supply and demand in their local area market.

'Thick' and 'thin' markets

Adam Smith recognised that the degree of specialisation, the division of labour, was limited by the extent of the market (box 3.2). While this statement has been interpreted in several ways, it obviously implies that there are markets of differing 'density'. An example from the world of the arts is provided by theatres: many small towns do not have a theatre, and unless there is a large population of theatre-goers the one theatre in a larger town has to offer a range of productions; in major centres, however, such as Broadway and the West End of London, a large number of theatres can coexist and even specialise in one type of drama or other entertainment. This also allows specialisation to develop for actors and other cultural workers, and in dependent trades, such as costume hire. The 'thick' market for musicians has also developed in these major centres, with ample opportunities for short-term contracts for singers and players in recording sessions and with 'scratch' orchestras; these activities are serviced by ancillary specialist facilities, such as booking agents and diary services.

Market-makers

In highly developed markets, there is a great deal of information and a strong organisational structure of 'market-makers' – people and institutions that match up buyers and sellers with each other. In the world of opera singers, for instance, there are well-organised systems of agents, who look for work for the singers they have taken on and who arrange their fees and performance schedules. In the art world, there is a hierarchy of dealers and gallery owners representing and marketing artists' work to the public and to museums, who negotiate prices for the sale of artists' works. In the world of book publishing, there are literary agents who negotiate deals with publishers on behalf of authors. The more developed the market is, the greater the specialisation that can develop. Thus the bigger the market, the 'thicker' it is in terms of specialised tasks within it, and the better it functions in terms of competitive pricing and product differentiation; globalisation of trade maximises specialisation. A less developed 'thin' market means that there is less scope for specialisation and prices may be higher and productivity lower.

The 'law of one price'

In a competitive 'thick' market, price differences between suppliers will be eroded because some entrepreneur has the incentive to make a profit by 'buying cheap and selling dear', an activity known as 'arbitrage'. International money markets in currencies are among the most highly organised markets there are and it is possible to make profits through arbitrage by playing on tiny differences in exchange rates at different times of the day and night in different centres (New York, London, Singapore, and so on). This is easy to do with money, because there is no need to move it around physically. Even when the movement of goods or people is necessary for trade to take place, however, arbitrage can still pay if there are significant price differences between markets for the same or similar goods and services. Arbitrage therefore brings about what the classical economists used to call the 'law of one price' – that effective competition forces prices to be the same everywhere. As we shall see later on, entrepreneurship often consists of finding opportunities for trade where price differentials exist. The market economy works through competition – that is, rivalry – and the incentive of making a gain gets prices down to the lowest possible level: this process works in the cultural economy too, especially in the private sector.

Price discrimination

By contrast to the competitive price, a monopoly seller who is the sole supplier in a market may be able to sell the same good or service at different prices in order to increase revenue and profit; this is 'price discrimination', and it will be worthwhile when consumers have different responses to price. The supplier must be able to control to whom the good is sold and it must also be possible to keep different 'segments' of the market apart so that arbitrage cannot take place. There are several standard ways of doing this that are widely used by arts and heritage organisations: charging lower prices to young people or senior citizens based on age (which can be verified by an identity card); charging different prices for different parts of a theatre by having numbered seats and tickets and preventing movement between seats; and charging different prices (including free entry) for different days of the week, which is done by some museums. Price discrimination can also be easily used for online sales when the seller can differentiate between buyers, say, by identifying who are enthusiasts and charging them more.

Because price discrimination can be practised only by monopolists it has been regarded as undesirable, but it can also improve welfare by enabling people who are willing to pay a higher price to do so. The ultimate example of the use of price discrimination is, of course, an auction, at which each item is sold separately and for a different price. Willingness to pay is investigated further in chapter 6 and the use of price discrimination is discussed in a number of places throughout the book.

Regulated markets

The notion of the market economy governed by only the price mechanism conjures up an image of an economic free-for-all. There are many circumstances and situations in which markets are not left to work freely, however, and, instead, market forces are controlled or regulated. Indeed, historically, marketplaces themselves were controlled by the state; in England in medieval times, only towns and cities with a royal charter conferred as a privilege by the king were allowed to hold produce markets, and markets for valuable metals such as gold and silver were highly regulated to ensure the quality of the metals and to protect their prices.

Many economists support the regulation of markets, while believing that private incentives working through the price mechanism and the market economy are the best way to achieve maximum economic growth and welfare. There are, needless to say, differing views on the strength and extent of regulation and its economic effects; a current battleground concerns the appropriate strength of copyright law (see chapter 13 for a full analysis).

Types of regulation

Governments use regulation as a means of implementing policies either to prevent some undesirable outcome or to encourage a positive one. Regulation may be combined with economic measures, such as a fine for non-compliance or a grant to promote compliance. Some regulations affect all sectors of the economy, though they can have different impacts in different sectors, and other regulations target specific sectors. Here only a suggestive list of regulations that impact on the cultural sector is given; regulation in specific industries is dealt with in the relevant chapter.

- Health and safety rules at work – affect the whole economy.
- Minimum wage legislation – affects the whole economy.
- Training qualifications – there may be specific requirements for different sectors.
- Censorship and decency laws – mostly affect cultural sector (film, live performance); some cultures have tighter control and a narrower sense of what is decent.
- Media ownership rules – affect newspapers and television.
- Cultural content rules – mostly affect radio and television.
- Protection of heritage – affects built heritage and international trade in artefacts.
- Protection of intellectual property – affects the whole economy; copyright law is most relevant to the cultural sector.
- Competition laws – affect the whole economy but have specific effects in the cultural sector.

Some of these laws and regulations have been in place for centuries and they have shaped the way that the market for cultural products worked in the past, with a continued influence on the present. As may be seen, some were designed to protect the state and others to protect its citizens.

Regulatory institutions

Guilds

The medieval guild system was strictly regulated to ensure that the supply of specific products was produced by properly trained craftsmen and so was of a certain quality, but it also enabled guilds to control prices. The apprenticeship system controlled the number of trained master craftsmen coming on to the market so that there was little competition on the supply side that would threaten the incomes of the craftsmen by lowering prices. It also protected trade secrets and acted as a type of control of the use of intellectual property.

The guild system applied to artists and craftsmen of all kinds – painters, sculptors, tile painters, stained glass makers, printers, map-makers. The Stationers' Company in England controlled the publishing of books and almanacs, the latter being generally more profitable. The Guild of St Luke was the guild to which painters belonged. Box 3.3 reports on research by John Michael Montias on the seventeenth-century Dutch painter Vermeer's membership of the guild in Delft.

Box 3.3 John Michael Montias and the Guild of St Luke

John Michael Montias (1928–2005) was a Professor of Economics at Yale University who collected Dutch art of the 'golden age', in the seventeenth century. He pioneered the economic history of art markets and made a particular study of the Guild of St Luke in Delft, to which the painter Johannes Vermeer belonged. His research into Dutch and Flemish archives revealed details of Vermeer's life and parentage that were previously unknown. Studying the records of the guild, he found that its members included painters, glass makers, book printers and sellers, art dealers (who were often also painters), embroiderers, faiencers and sculptors. In addition, Montias was one of the first scholars to estimate the number and output of Dutch master paintings in the seventeenth century – perhaps as many as 100,000, of which only a few thousand survive – and to research the economic and social status of artists. He published *Artists and Artisans in Delft: A Socio-economic Study of the Seventeenth Century* in 1982 and *Vermeer and His Milieu: A Web of Social History* in 1989. Montias' work was widely recognised beyond cultural economics and was cited as a source for the novel by Tracy Chevalier, *Girl with a Pearl Earring* (1999), on which the film with the same title was based.

The guild system lasted in some countries well into the eighteenth century; in Italy, for example, there were over 1,000 guilds in 1700. Guilds were one of the objects of Smith's antagonism in 1776, along with state monopolies. It is perhaps somewhat surprising to realise that traditional guilds still exist in some places; performers of Japanese Noh and Kabuki theatre and Bunraku puppet players are still required to be guild members and belong to one of the guild families. There are also other guilds that still have some influence; for example, the Screen Actors' Guild of America and the Writers' Guild operate strict rules for members and impose them on the film and television industry, though they do not have full monopoly control of the market.

Monopolies

Besides the monopolies of the guilds, other monopolies existed through Crown or state grants that controlled national and international trade. A monopoly was a licence or privilege allowed by the Crown (for a fee) to an individual or organisation for the sole production or buying and selling of a specific good or service. Monopolies also protected international trade; for example, the Dutch East India Company (founded in 1602) was granted a monopoly by the Dutch state to control the spice trade. Monopolies reached a peak in England in the reign of Elizabeth I (1558–1603) and thereafter were controlled by the 1623 Statute of Monopolies, which formed the basis eventually of intellectual property law (see below). Monopoly is nowadays regulated through competition law (see below).

Theatres and companies of actors needed state-granted licences to perform in Elizabethan England, one company being the King's Men, to which Shakespeare belonged. These grants of monopoly did not necessarily inhibit competition if enough of them were issued and the licence also had a role of censorship. Elizabethan theatre was, in fact, quite a competitive business (see below). Theatres and many other places of entertainment still need licences for public performances, which are mostly issued by local authorities, mainly to ensure safety standards for workers and audiences. It is an interesting question in cultural economics as to the extent to which local theatres, orchestras, museums, and so on are monopolies today in the economic sense of being a sole supplier of a particular good or service in their locality.

Trade unions and professional associations

In some respects trade unions and professional associations are the modern equivalent of guilds; they exist to protect their members from excessive exploitation in terms of payment and conditions of work. In some countries, particularly those in Europe in which artists are employed in state-run arts organisations, trade unions and professional associations are integrated into the process of setting payments to artists. In the cultural sector, there are trade unions for performers (actors, singers, dancers, musicians, radio and TV announcers, stuntmen, and so on), for technical personnel (cameramen and other film crew, theatre technicians, and the like) and for creative artists (writers, composers, visual artists). These organisations typically negotiate agreements on conditions of work and minimum payments with employers, such as theatre management, film companies and recording studios, that prevent competition from beating fees and wages down. A significant aspect of trade unions is the extent to which they are able to control the supply of specific skills; in some countries, there have been formal 'closed shop' agreements with employers whereby only members are accepted for employment. This practice may be outlawed as anti-competitive but it often persists by tacit agreement. Like guilds, some trade unions and professional associations accept as members only those who have already some professional level training or work experience, and they therefore offer some degree of reassurance that their members are professionally competent.

Certification

One of the economic functions of the guilds was to ensure the quality of the products their members produced, as well as regulating prices; a master craftsman had to have completed a long apprenticeship and received the requisite training and also had to demonstrate his (and, rarely, her) skill before admittance to membership of the guild. This kind of certification solved the information problem for the consumer, who lacked the knowledge to assess the quality and price of a work, and therefore fulfilled the role of certifying value for money.

One of the biggest problems for producers and consumers alike in the world of the arts is information about quality. Buyers do not want to buy fake art or hire an architect who is not professionally competent and record labels do not want to hire unskilled studio musicians. Certification of quality can be achieved in many ways: the most widespread is probably educational qualifications, such as a diploma or degree, showing that a worker has completed a training course, but this is a far cry from the type of guaranteed quality offered by the guild system. Regulation by the state in cultural professions is very weak compared, say, to that in medicine and teaching, and even self-regulation is not common. These points are discussed further in chapters 11 and 12.

The need on the part of consumers and employers for some form of certification of quality gives rise to the presence of middlemen and intermediaries in the markets for art and artists, mentioned above, to overcome the problem of 'asymmetric information' – the situation in which the one party to a deal (say the supplier) knows more about the quality of the product than the other (say the customer). This topic is a prevalent problem in the arts, and is discussed throughout the book in one or another context.

Copyright and other intellectual property law

Intellectual property law that establishes and protects copyrights, patents and trademarks has considerable influence on markets for cultural products. What are recognised as the first patents were issued in Venice in the fifteenth century. The English Statute of Anne (1710) is regarded as the first copyright legislation. In general, IP law grants the creator (the author) the exclusive right to control his or her works and reputation. In that sense, IP rights confer monopoly control to the author or inventor; the degree of control over the relevant market that the IP makes possible varies, however, and, in the case of copyright in works of art, that monopoly is limited. Copyright applies work by work, so anyone writing a love poem or photographing a view has the copyright on his or her work, but, equally, anyone else writing a very similar love poem and photographing the identical view has copyright on his or her work too; the only requirement is that the work was not copied. Copyright law is used to protect the owners of works in copyright and its purpose is to ensure that the owner is paid for his or her work. Probably the most familiar restriction nowadays is that copyright law makes it illegal to play music and films in public or make them available to others without the permission of the copyright holder.

The role of trademarks is somewhat different: they offer consumers some form of quality assurance as they give the holder of the trademark an incentive to maintain the quality of their output. Trademarks and trade names are used by many businesses in the creative industries, especially fashion; in addition, film companies and pop groups also use copyright and trademarks to protect merchandise associated with their images.

Droit de suite (artists' resale right) specifically targets visual artists and awards them a share of the increase in the price of a work of art sold by an artist to a buyer when it is resold, usually in a public sale. Copyright and droit de suite are dealt with at length in chapter 13 of this book.

Antitrust/competition law

Monopoly is nowadays regulated through competition law (known as anti-trust law in the United States) in most developed countries, and the law has been evoked to control the mergers of firms that would give them too great a share of the market and to prevent price-fixing. The so-called 'Paramount case' in 1948 is probably one of the best-known examples of the control of monopoly in the cultural sector, whereby the US antitrust authorities forced the movie studios to divest themselves of their cinemas on the ground that they used their ownership to prevent competition from independent movie-makers (see box 4.3). Competition law has also been applied in the present century to control mergers in the music business and to control the activities of copyright collecting societies (see chapters 13 and 15).

The above topics are all types of regulation that control the outcomes of a free market economy. It can be seen that most limit the effect of unbridled competition; competition law does the opposite, however: it tries to promote competition in the face of monopoly as a market outcome. Monopoly and competition are discussed at length from the theoretical point of view in chapter 5 and then later on in Part IV of the book. Regulations that affect markets for cultural products are also discussed later in the book in specific contexts; for example, ownership rules for media companies preventing the monopolisation of television channels and newspapers are discussed in chapters 14 and 17, and film regulation is to be found in chapter 16.

Economic history of the arts

As the work of Montias has demonstrated (box 3.3), much can be learned from studying the economic history of markets for cultural products, and there is a body of work in cultural economics on the economic development of various art forms over the last few centuries. Besides being interesting and informative in its own right, the study of economic history reminds us that our present-day economic organisation of cultural production (varied though it is throughout the world) has historical origins that have influenced it, and that gives us a perspective on alternative models and ways of doing things.

Patronage

It is worth reminding ourselves that state support for the arts and other cultural production is both an old and a new phenomenon; in its older version, it took the form of private patronage by royalty and the rich that financed the production of works of art, museum collections and the performing arts for their own enjoyment, and access to these works was limited to the court and upper echelons of society. The wealthy and aristocratic also collected works of art and curiosities and showed them to others of their social milieu, but access to museums by the public is relatively recent; when the British Museum opened, in 1753, the entry price was made high enough to keep out 'ordinary' people as there were fears that they would break the items! Present-day state patronage of the arts and culture is dedicated to enhancing and preserving our cultural heritage and making it available to the whole society. Throughout history, however, what we now call the performing arts in the form of music, song, dance, puppetry, drama and storytelling were available via the market to people of all walks of life.

Private enterprise in cultural production

It is interesting to consider that the production of many cultural goods and services has always been dependent upon the market, and they are still entirely produced by private enterprise in the cultural industries (except perhaps in countries with totalitarian regimes); examples are art markets, book and newspaper publishing and music publishing. The performing arts and museums also have a long history of being supported by the market, and, indeed, commercial theatre and musicals are still run by private enterprise, as are circuses and popular entertainment.

The art market

The art market flourished in the Low Countries (Flanders and Holland) as the increasingly wealthy middle class of the seventeenth-century 'golden age' bought paintings and etchings, hand-painted tiles and books with engravings for their homes. Works of art were created for sale on the market as well as being commissioned and the significance of this demand is that it had nothing to do with court or aristocratic patronage. Some artists were very entrepreneurial and not only ran workshops producing a huge output of works of art but also were dealers in other artists' works. Rembrandt ran a workshop and was an art dealer, as was Rubens. Rubens went one further: his workshop in Antwerp (now in Belgium) had assistants doing all the 'routine' work, not only of mixing the paints but also of applying them as background in an early form of mass production; in addition, he built his studio so that the public could view him at work – a privilege for which he charged. Moreover, many paintings were only based on his compositions and were made entirely by his assistants, with Rubens giving the paintings no more than a 'final touch'; interestingly, these paintings sold at lower prices.

The art market was 'global', with considerable trade and movement of artists between the Low Countries, Italy and Germany. Artists followed the money: in the seventeenth century that was in Holland, by the eighteenth century England, and by the nineteenth and twentieth centuries France and the United States were the leading markets for art.

Museums

Museums – or 'cabinets of curiosities', or *Wunderkammer*, as they were first known – began as private collections assembled by individual men of science, travellers and explorers or on behalf of a monarch, starting from around the 1600s. Some of these collectors were neither rich nor royal; some collected for their own interest, but there was already a market in antiques and curiosities by the end of the sixteenth century. Collections consisted of all sorts of items designed to cause wonder and amazement – books, coins, weapons, costumes, taxidermy, minerals, and so on, as well as botanical specimens. The Tradescant collection of natural and man-made objects, dating from the 1620s and located in a building known as the Ark, became the *Musaeum Tradescantianum*, the first public museum in England; later, the collection was passed on to the Ashmolean Museum at Oxford University, the world's first university museum, built in 1677. Botanical collections started around the middle of the sixteenth century and were attached to the universities of Pisa, Padua, Florence and Bologna, and later to many others throughout Europe. Later collectors, such as Pieter Teyler, the eighteenth-century cloth merchant and banker who lived in Haarlem (Holland) and founded the Teyler Museum, also included works of art – old master prints and drawings; others collected musical instruments, clocks, furniture, sculpture, and so forth.

The 'Grand Tour', whereby young men from wealthy families from northern Europe toured France and Italy and, for the bolder, Greece, in search of classical antiquity and enlightenment, was the source of many items for the family collection, many of which have ended up in museums. Museums, of course, have always bought private collections and items on the open market to add to their existing collection. The 'new rich' could also buy a whole collection, just as they bought books 'by the yard' for their libraries. Collecting and buying art continued into the twentieth century, and several famous private American museums were founded that way. Over the centuries museums have become more specialised, though 'universal' collections are still very important: special collections include archaeology, anthropology, crafts, natural history, science, space, maritime, military history and children's museums; art museums (art galleries) may also be housed separately.

The first public museum is acknowledged to be the Kunstmuseum in Basle, which the city founded in 1671 based on the purchase of the Amerbach Cabinet. Other early public museums include the Uffizi Gallery in Florence, founded by Cosimo I, Grand Duke of Tuscany in the mid-sixteenth century; the gallery had been open to visitors by request beforehand, but in 1765 it was gifted to the government of Tuscany and officially opened to the public. By the middle of the eighteenth century the royal collections began to be transferred to public museums and made widely available for the edification of, at least, the middle class, if not (yet) the masses.

Book publishing

There was already a trade in books in ancient Greece and Rome, and the rich had private libraries; the Ancient Library of Alexandria was founded around 300 BC. The so-called 'Islamic golden age', which stretched from the eighth to the thirteenth centuries, encouraged copying, selling and dealing in books throughout the Islamic world, with centres in Baghdad, Damascus and Córdoba, in Spain. The market for books developed in northern Europe (especially Burgundy and Flanders) before the advent of printing in the mid-fifteenth century. Illuminated manuscripts were produced by entrepreneurial master craftsmen 'on spec' and were bought by rich families and by the Church (individual churches, monasteries and nunneries); the trade was highly organised and specialised, with some craftsmen specialising in lettering, others in gold inlay, others in flower painting, and so on.

Book publishing and bookselling became 'industrialised' with the introduction to Europe of the metal movable printing press, for printing on vellum and paper, by Johannes Gutenberg, a goldsmith by training, born in Mainz, Germany; the so-called Gutenberg Bible, the first printed book in Europe, was published in Vulgate Latin in an estimated 180 copies in 1455. Though movable type printing had been invented 400 years earlier in China and was in use in Korea in the mid-thirteenth century, the techniques had not been exported to Europe. The main location of the early printing industry, however, was in Venice, where the city authorities encouraged the import of printing presses and the immigration of printers by issuing letters patent.

It is not known how many people in Europe at the time were able to read. Muslims and Jews did so because of their need to read holy scriptures but the tradition of individual reading in Christian Europe developed only when the Bible was translated into vernacular languages – English in 1526 (by William Tyndale, who was burnt at the stake for heresy for so doing), German in 1534 (with the publication of the Luther Bible) and eventually into many other languages. Reading literacy was relatively high in northern Europe by the middle of the seventeenth century. With universal primary education nowadays in developed countries, literacy (meaning the ability to read and write) is widespread (though far from 100 per cent); UNESCO estimates present-day literacy to be 80 per cent worldwide. Nevertheless, there is a considerable difference between the ability to read and write a simple sentence and the functional literacy needed to read books and other printed matter.

Booksellers were both printers and publishers and were the focus of censorship in England in the sixteenth century, mainly for religious reasons. The Worshipful Company of Stationers and Newspaper Makers (usually known as the Stationers' Company), which had been founded in 1403, received a royal charter in 1557, according to which the company was legally empowered to seize books that were offensive to the Church and to the Crown. It was the Stationers' Company that petitioned for the first copyright law, the Statute of Anne (which was passed in 1709 and came into force the following year), when it had lost its earlier monopoly. In 1666, when Samuel Pepys observed the Great Fire of London, he reported the considerable loss of books in the fire as it reached St Paul's Cathedral Yard, where all the booksellers had stalls (and he also reported that many harpsichords and other large musical instruments were hastily removed from homes at risk from the fire). As the market for published material grew, the functions of printing and bookselling had become separate by the nineteenth century.

Printing and book publishing was also well established in the Low Countries by the 1600s, Antwerp, Leiden and Utrecht being centres. Printing was introduced into the United States in the seventeenth century, but even by the mid-1850s half the authors of published books were British. The US constitution of 1787 authorised the introduction of patents and copyright '[t]o promote the Progress of Science and useful Arts, by securing for limited Times to Authors and Inventors the exclusive Right to their respective Writings and Discoveries'; in the United States copyright applied only to works by American authors, however, and there was widespread piracy by American publishers because they did not have to pay a royalty to British authors. Nonetheless, some publishers did pay a fee; for example, Dickens was paid well for a tour of the United States to promote his works in the 1860s (a fact that was at one time used by economists to argue that copyright law is not necessary as payment can be arranged by contract). Piracy was in fact beneficial to some authors: when part 1 of Cervantes' *Don Quixote*, often regarded as the first modern novel, was published in 1605 it was immediately pirated and thereby gained hugely in popularity, leading to five printings in its first year of publication – a clear case of what economists call 'network effects'.

Newspapers and periodicals

Though there is some debate about it, the first modern newspaper is believed to have been the *Courante uyt Italien, Duytslandt, &c*, published in 1618 in Amsterdam. There were news pamphlets of various kinds in England but the *Daily Courant*, founded in 1702, is credited as the first regular daily newspaper. In 1704 the *Boston News-letter* was the first continuously published newspaper in the United States. The *Halifax Gazette*, started in 1751, was the first newspaper in Canada; the *Pennsylvania Evening Post* became the first American daily in 1783; *The Times* of London began publication in 1785 and *Le Figaro* was founded in France in 1826. Broadsheet newspapers might have begun in the eighteenth century but it was not until the early nineteenth century that advances in printing newspapers facilitated daily mass circulation. By 1814 *The Times* of London was able to make 1,100 impressions per minute using new printing technology.

The eighteenth century also saw the founding of a host of periodicals that were published monthly, weekly or even several times a week: *The Spectator* magazine was founded in 1711 and published daily in London, even though it was not a newspaper; *The Gentleman's Magazine* was a monthly magazine started in Britain in 1731 that eventually had a worldwide circulation until its demise in 1907. In the United States, *The Atlantic Monthly* was started in 1851, and published contemporary literature until 2005, when it stopped doing so in regular issues (it now publishes as an annual fiction issue); since 2008 it has been freely accessible online.

Music publishing

Music printing and publishing developed somewhat later than the printing of books and did not entirely replace hand copying. The first music printing and publishing benefited from the Venetian patent in the sixteenth century. In England, William Byrd and Thomas Tallis were granted a Crown monopoly in 1575 to print music, and volumes of both sacred and secular music were published; these were sold for household music-making – consort playing and singing and also for dancing. By the seventeenth century the German publisher Breitkopf was publisher to the Bach family; the company Breitkopf and Härtel continues to publish music by most of the leading German and Viennese composers, such as Mozart, Beethoven, Schumann, Liszt, Wagner and Brahms (see box 5.3). Sales of sheet music for performance in the home throughout Europe and in America remained an important source of revenue right up to the spread of radio in the early twentieth century and reached bestseller proportions, with up to a million copies being sold worldwide of very popular works. Large-scale instrumental and choral music were initially performed only in royal courts or chapels, but during the nineteenth century public concerts gradually began to be organised by private concert societies. Beethoven's famous Ninth Symphony was commissioned in 1817 by the privately run membership organisation, the Philharmonic Society of London (and published by Breitkopf and Härtel).

Copyright in printed music gradually became established throughout Europe during the nineteenth century but piracy was a serious threat; it was a financial threat to the authorised publisher rather than to the composer, however, who, like a literary author, was usually paid an upfront fee. Composers worried more about the quality of pirated published music, which was often badly edited and printed. Some copying was in fact an established perk of the printer or copyist. Enforcing copyright in music required collective action, and copyright collecting societies were established by the music profession to collect royalties (see chapter 13).

Opera and ballet

Composers made their living either producing music for the Church or in opera – and there was no problem about doing both in Italy, where, for instance, Vivaldi composed more than forty operas and produced over 500 concertos. Mozart followed a similar path in Austria. Well into the nineteenth century it was the convention that the composer also conducted or led the orchestra and coached the lead singers for the first performances. The organisation of opera in Italy (and, indeed, worldwide, as Italian opera was exported to Russia and Argentina and all countries in between) is in fact an object lesson in the spontaneous role of the market: the *impresarii*, those cultural entrepreneurs par excellence, supplied operatic works newly composed to a specially commissioned libretto, along with the singers, costumes and scenery, to every Italian opera house for the two main performing seasons of the year, Lent and Michaelmas, dealing with different states, currencies, customs and appalling transport conditions, all on market principles, for a period of nearly 200 years. The opera theatres themselves were usually financed by the rental of boxes to personages who spent practically every evening there during the performing seasons, being served dinner there by their servants and entertaining; gambling at the theatre was a common activity, and the concession was a lucrative additional source of finance for the opera theatre. When there was a financial deficit it was made up by gifts from wealthy patrons. In some cases, opera theatres were owned by the city or state; nevertheless, the *impresarii* bore the financial risk and financed the whole cost of the production until the opera had been performed, when they were paid the fee. In the eighteenth and early nineteenth centuries Italian opera dominated courts in London, Paris, Vienna and St Petersburg. In France, Lully developed opera at the court of Louis XIV, but, elsewhere, national traditions of opera took a long time to emerge.

Opera also changed as an art form over the centuries, from masques in which royal patrons, such as Louis XIV in France and Charles II in England, danced alongside professional dancers to the mainly vocal art it is today; ballet developed within this framework and only really became an independent art form in the late nineteenth century, and often it is tied to the same theatre as the opera. The Imperial Russian Ballet, the Royal Danish Ballet and the Royal Swedish Ballet were also founded under royal patronage in the eighteenth century. In 1909 the Ballets Russes was established as a private company in Paris by the Russian Sergei Diaghilev with Russian dancers; later it moved to Monte Carlo. It became one of the most famous contemporary ballet companies, with choreography by Petipa, Fokine and Massine, music by Debussy, Ravel, Satie, Prokofiev and Stravinsky and sets by Braque, Matisse, Miró and Picasso, to name but a few of the now famous artists whose work Diaghilev commissioned. Balanchine also worked with the Ballets Russes before moving to New York as co-founder and ballet master of the New York City Ballet.

Theatre

There was a market in plays and performances in England from the sixteenth century on even before theatre buildings were built in London in the last quarter of the century; several notable theatres were built, only one of which was the Globe, so famously associated with Shakespeare. Part-owner, manager and resident playwright (and sometime actor) at the Globe, Shakespeare had quite a few rivals in all these capacities; there was a significant number of competing theatre buildings, companies of actors and playwrights. Elizabethan theatre was popular with all levels of society and was financed by the box office until, in 1642, the Puritans closed the theatres for religious reasons; their popularity resumed when they were reopened in 1660 with the restoration of the monarchy. In the following century John Gay's *Beggar's Opera*, which opened in 1728, ran for sixty-two nights and was one of the most successful plays of all time (though that figure pales into insignificance in comparison with *The Mousetrap* by Agatha Christie, which had had over 23,000 performances in the course of its nearly fifty-six-year run in London's West End by August 2008!). The theatre tradition of satire and comic opera continued with vaudeville and music hall until it was displaced by cinema in the 1930s.

Similar trends were to be found in other countries. In mid-seventeenth-century France, Molière, both a playwright and an actor, founded his own theatre company, and, in eighteenth-century Italy, Goldoni created both plays and opera libretti in the tradition of Molière's comedy of manners; both were hugely popular. The Italian tradition of travelling players of the *commedia dell'arte* only finally ended with the advent of cinema. Other popular performing arts with long histories are the circus, which is still popular in Russia and in many developing countries, and Chinese opera, which flourished in China until the Cultural Revolution in the 1960s, when over 5,000 troupes were disbanded.

What do we learn from studying the economic history of the arts?

The brief and very partial summaries above give a flavour of the economic history of some of the creative industries. They present a picture of the development of markets in the Renaissance emerging from the control of guilds and a system of monopolies; this took longer in some countries than others, but it was a universal trend. In some of the creative industries, private markets survive with little institutional change, and, even in the performing arts, which rely to a greater or lesser extent on state support, vestiges of their economic histories are still to be seen today (see chapter 4).

What the study of the economic history of the arts shows can be equally briefly summarised:

- the market economy was a major supplier of a range of cultural goods and services, the production and consumption of which thrived in centres of wealth;
- specialisation has taken place as markets grew;
- production and consumption were globalised, even from an early period;
- there was a big divide between the entertainment of royal and princely courts, not only in access but also in the art forms themselves; this is most apparent in the performing arts, notably opera and ballet; and
- regulation in the form of censorship and intellectual property law has very long roots in history.

The study of the economic history of cultural production can prove very instructive to contemporary art lovers who think that adequate levels of cultural provision can be achieved only with considerable state intervention. It is a reminder that this is essentially a post-Second-World-War outlook that went hand in hand with the growth of the welfare state.

Economic history raises another important question for economists, however: is it just market forces that have moulded the historical development of the production and consumption of cultural goods and services, or have the institutions and regulatory regimes played a determining role? This is known as 'path dependency', and it has been a major dispute within economics and economic history. As an instance, think of the development of copyright: the roots of copyright law in England (and thereby to many other countries, including the United States) are in the guild system. As that broke down, the economic monopoly of printers and publishers of books and the control the state was able to exercise over what was published began to wane, until, eventually, the publishers (but not the authors of the day, who apparently foresaw the consequences and resisted the change) lobbied parliament for legislation to protect their property; and that is the basis of the law we have today. In Europe, however, the development of authors' rights was very different and emphasised the creativity of the author rather than the commercial interest of the publishers.

Perhaps path dependency in arts provision is nowhere more apparent than in Germany, where the many states and principalities had their own court theatres, now owned and managed by the state or city authorities. Present-day Berlin is an extreme example of this with no fewer than four opera companies, each with its own theatre, now maintained by the city.

Conclusion

This chapter has introduced the way economists use the notion of the market economy and the basic analytics of supply and demand in a market. The role of the price mechanism was explained in terms of the way prices act both as signals to producers and consumers and as a source of revenue to producers. It was pointed out that there are, in practice, few totally free markets, and many operate under regulations of various kinds. This is true of the cultural economy, which, in addition, has its own set of regulations.

The chapter ended with brief economic histories of a selection of the creative industries. It demonstrated that, both now and in the past, cultural products 'high' and 'low' alike have been supplied both through the market, financed by revenues from sales, and by the state provision of facilities and/or finance. In fact, like most other goods in developed countries, cultural products are traded in a mixed economy, meaning that there is a combination of provision by state-owned organisations, state-subsidised private non-profit organisations and private enterprise profit-making firms, and these markets were in the past, and are often in the present, regulated. The combination of these variously financed sources of supply is different in different countries and in different art forms, however.

The modern welfare state in Europe, as well as in Australia, Canada and to a certain extent also in the United States, includes provision of the arts and heritage as part of its service to its citizens. That was also the case in communist countries, and some of the former Soviet bloc countries are still in the process of finding a balance between state and market provision. The next chapter takes up the same theme for the present-day economic organisation of the creative industries.

Further reading

The best book to read in connection with this chapter is Tyler Cowen's *In Praise of Commercial Culture* (1998). It is a deliberately provocative book that argues for the strength of the market and uses much fascinating economic history to show how markets for the arts developed. For those with special interests, John Michael Montias' 1989 book *Vermeer and His Milieu: A Web of Social History* is recommended on the history of art markets; for music markets, F. M. Scherer's chapter in the 2006 Ginsburgh and Throsby *Handbook of the Economics of Art and Culture* (chapter 4) is recommended; on books, I found Mark Rose's book *Authors and Owners: The Invention of Copyright* fascinating; for film, John Sedgwick's book *Popular Filmgoing in 1930s Britain* (2000) can be recommended. In the performing arts, John Rosselli's work on the economic history of markets in opera is especially interesting; see his article 'From princely states to the open market: singers of Italian opera and their patrons 1600–1850', reprinted in Towse (1997) and Mary Oates and William Baumol's article in the same volume on Renaissance theatre in London.

4   Economic organisation of the creative industries

In this chapter, the present-day economic organisation of production in the creative industries is briefly described using the concepts introduced in the previous chapters: public or private finance, for-profit and non-profit enterprise, pricing policy, free or regulated markets, specialisation and integration in the chain of production. The chapter provides a background for the detailed analysis of the industries in Parts II and IV. It does not aim to cover all the creative industries, only the ones that are included in this book, and the focus is on the topics that have been dealt with in cultural economics: the art market, museums, publishing, the music industry, the performing arts and film.

Economic organisation refers to the way that firms and industries are structured and to the effect this has on markets – for example, whether there is monopoly or competition in the market, which in turn influences the price at which goods and services are supplied. Supply to a market involves a chain of production from the creation of the content through the production process, marketing and finally, delivery to consumers; in some industries these activities are vertically integrated, while in others there is less integration and more specialisation in markets for particular goods and services. Some industries have been subject to considerable technological change while others have not. Following on from chapter 3 and the economic history of cultural production, it can be seen that the past has had an influence on present-day economic organisation, although that influence is stronger in some industries than in others.

The art market

In many ways, the art market has changed very little over the centuries, though it has become more globalised. Artists produce works of art that are sold on the market for a price that the market will bear. Artists nowadays typically work alone, though they may share studio space with others; some do their own marketing and organise their own outlets, such as fairs, at which they sell their work direct to buyers. By and large, though, artists rely on the services of private galleries or art dealers to sell their work. Galleries and dealers are private for-profit enterprises, though many of them make very little profit despite charging artists very high commission on sales, and there is a considerable turnover of entry and exit in art dealing. Prices of works of art in this market depend upon a number of features, including the reputation of the artist, the type of medium and the subject. The revenue from the sale of their work is a source of income, though few artists are able to support themselves just from their art work and many do other jobs to make a living (see chapter 12). In some countries, state grants are available to individual artists for limited periods of time or for specific projects; in the Netherlands, for instance, there is long-tem income support (see box 11.5).

The art market, for all the cultural importance of the works of art that are bought and sold in it by private individuals and public institutions, including museums, is a private for-profit institution. How the art market works has been of considerable interest to cultural economists, especially over recent years. Works of art are extremely heterogeneous: they vary by the artist, its provenance, the genre, when they were created, what the subject is, what the condition of the work is and many other features. This diversity alone would make the art market different from the market for other more homogeneous goods, in which substitutability between one item and another in that market is relatively easy. For homogeneous goods, economists expect one price to be charged in a competitive market – the 'law of one price'. For diverse works of art, though, buyers need a great deal of information in order to make a satisfactory purchase and sellers want to reach as many buyers as possible to get the best price for the sale of their unique work(s).

Primary and secondary markets

A distinction is made between the primary and secondary markets for works of visual art (paintings, drawings, etchings and lithographs, sculpture, photographs, and so forth). The primary market is where work by living artists is bought and sold, and market supply depends upon the number of artists and the individual artists' current output. It is the market for the first sale of newly created works of art, and works are sold mostly through private art dealers or direct by the artist to a buyer. There is often excess supply even at low prices.

The secondary market deals with works of art, almost always by deceased artists (although that trend has changed recently, for example with auctions of works by Damien Hirst), that are being sold on by an owner through a sale or auction or by a private dealer. In this market, the stock of works is more or less fixed, but high prices may attract a flow of supply as people offer works they own for sale. Sales are often organised as auctions but private dealers also work in the secondary market, selling to private buyers, to business organisations and to art museums and galleries. Prices depend upon the willingness to pay of buyers in what is a highly organised, 'thick' international market. Museums also buy on this market to enhance their collections and they have to compete with each other and with wealthy private individuals for high-quality and rare works.

What has interested cultural economists most has been the operation of art auctions. Items sold include many other types of work, including prints and photographs and other collectibles and antiques in addition to paintings, drawings, and so on. The auction market is dominated by a few houses in the art world; the two leading international auction houses are Christie's and Sotheby's, and they form a duopoly (a two-firm 'monopoly') whose independence in terms of their willingness to compete with each other, especially over fees, has been questioned.

Art auctions

Auctions are interesting to economists because they are a particular type of market. Sellers bring their items for sale to the auction house on a specific date and buyers gather to buy them or bid through intermediaries, including by telephone, and now by internet, with the process co-ordinated by an auctioneer. Art auctions utilise the English auction method of taking the highest bid offered by buyers as the final price – the 'hammer' price, as the auctioneer bangs a surface with his gavel, or small hammer, to indicate that the sale of the item is over. English auctions are used for many goods, such as farm animals, land and property. Auctions for some goods – fish and flowers, for example – are sold by the Dutch auction method, whereby the auctioneer starts at a high price and lowers it until a buyer accepts the price being indicated by shouting 'Mine' and the sale is concluded. Economists have been interested in the question of whether these methods yield the same prices and, in the case of the art market, whether it is 'efficient' in setting prices for works of art – i.e. satisfactory to both buyer and seller.

Auction prices

Sellers of works of art often set a minimum price with the auctioneer below which they will not sell, and this is called the reserve price; for obvious reasons, this is not made known, and the auctioneer goes to lengths not to reveal it by his starting price. The reserve price protects sellers from having to sell at a low price if there is insufficient interest among buyers. With the stock of works of art available at a sale being fixed, the hammer price depends upon the strength of demand for the works being sold at any one time. Auction houses make their income from the premium paid by the buyer (typically 10 per cent of the sale price) and from a commission paid by the seller (5 per cent) as well. Auction houses therefore have an incentive to see prices rise. Besides the big international houses there are also national auction houses, and, with private dealers also acting as intermediaries, sellers have some choice where to sell their works of art. It is estimated that about a quarter of works of art are sold at auction; cultural economists have concentrated on the auction market, however. The main art markets are in London, Paris and New York; dealers tend to specialise in certain types of works of art, and auctions are arranged for specific groupings of artworks, such as European or American works, Impressionists, landscapes, and so on. Some studies have shown that where a work is sold influences the price obtained for it, suggesting that the international market is not fully efficient.

Is buying art a good investment?

A question that has interested cultural economists is whether works of art are a good investment compared to financial assets – does the rate of return on a work of art match that on, say, government bonds? This has led to a great deal of complex econometric work analysing trends in art prices, and one reason for the focus on auctions is that auction prices are published whereas those of private sales are not. (It is an interesting question as to whether private sale prices and auction prices are comparable for similar works of art, and there is some disagreement among cultural economists on the answer.) Using what are called 'repeat sales' data for individual works that have been repeatedly sold over a period of years (or even centuries), an index of prices can be constructed. Alternatively, the so-called 'hedonic' method is used, in which the price depends upon the characteristics of specific works. The rate of return on these works of art can then be calculated and compared with rates of return from stocks and shares as financial assets. In general, the results seem to show that investment in art produces a lower rate of return than financial assets; this is in part because art works are not as 'liquid' as financial assets, which can be sold quickly and easily; in addition, there are the 'transaction costs' of selling, such as commission fees, that are relatively high, and there are other expenses, such as insurance. It may also be, however, because works of art are enjoyed for consumption reasons, and owners want the pleasure of owning works of art as well as a financial return from them.

Finally, although the art market itself is unregulated, many countries have laws that control the movement of works of art of national importance, and owners of 'heritage' art are not free to sell without some restriction; in the United Kingdom, that means that, before such a work can be exported, it must obtain a licence and show that a domestic buyer cannot meet the market price. This reflects the fact that many important works of art and other collectible items, such as furniture, are owned by private owners in what are called 'stately homes' – the country houses of the (former) landowning nobility and other wealthy people. These are an important part of the built heritage in all European countries, most of which have similar regulation of the export of works of art. Other laws that relate specifically to art markets are artists' resale rights or droit de suite, as they are known in Europe. These are intended to enable artists to gain a share of the profits from rising prices of their work when it is sold by another owner. This is related to copyright law, and is dealt with in chapter 13.

Craftwork

Craftwork of all kinds (furniture, pottery, decoration, jewellery, embroidery, cloth, leather, fancy goods and many other hand-worked items) is often sold in very much the same way as works of art, with shops, craft centres and fairs selling the ongoing supply produced by living craftspeople in the primary market, and the secondary market dealing in antiques. Designers and makers of high-quality goods are given state support in some countries and a state-run body may gather information about works produced and also assist with marketing. In general, craftspeople rely on the marketplace and on revenues for sales as income from their work. 'Artisanal products' are promoted by UNESCO for developing and transitional countries through prizes and support for trade fairs, and the skills of craftspeople are recognised as part of the intangible heritage. UNESCO has adopted this definition:

Artisanal products are those produced by artisans, either completely by hand, or with the help of hand tools or even mechanical means, as long as the direct manual contribution of the artisan remains the most substantial component of the finished product. These are produced without restriction in terms of quantity and using raw materials from sustainable resources. The special nature of artisanal products derives from their distinctive features, which can be utilitarian, aesthetic, artistic, creative, culturally attached, decorative, functional, traditional, religiously and socially symbolic and significant.[1]

Many countries have museums devoted to craftwork and to design whose collection has been bought on the open market or donated. Craftspeople are included in work by cultural economists on artists' labour markets (chapters 11 and 12), but otherwise there has been little research specifically on the economics of crafts. Crafts are protected to some extent by intellectual property law – copyright and design rights, trade names and trademarks – but the extent of coverage is controversial; nor do crafts fit into standard industrial classification systems, and international trade in craft products is believed to be hampered thereby.[2]

Museums

Types of museums

Museums or art galleries are where the most highly prized works of art and craft eventually end up. One thing to be noted about museums, though, is that they are very disparate. Cultural economists have been mostly concerned with art and other 'cultural' museums; it is worth mentioning, however, that many countries do not distinguish in their policies or financial data between types of museums. The website 'Museums USA' lists over twenty types of museums ranging from anthropological museums to zoos. In Australia, where natural and built heritage are reported together, many of these museums are parks or nature centres and so seem to be part of the natural heritage. Others – art museums, children's museums, culture

---

[1] See http://portal.unesco.org/culture/en/ev.phpURL_ID=35418&URL_DO=DO_PRINTPAGE&URL_SECTION=201.html (accessed 1 December 2008).
[2] UNCTAD (2008).

museums – are more easily associated with the cultural sector; historic houses and the like belong more to what we call the built heritage. Besides the architectural importance of the building, they often house important collections of works of art and craft. Museums devoted to science, planetaria and space, natural history, the military, maritime and other special interests all form part of the museum sector and often many of these categories form part of the collection of a 'mixed' museum typical of the 'national' museum.

Distribution of museums and their collections

The US data also demonstrate the uneven geographical distribution of museums; for example, there are 228 art museums in Illinois and five in Kansas. In other countries, the concentration of museums – or, at least, of the major ones – is often in the capital city with much less on offer in the provinces. Some countries have a policy of distributing museums and parts of the national collection around the country, however. The Netherlands is an example of this: there are national museums (*rijksmusea*) distributed between various cities, and museums can be required to transfer items from their collection to other museums – a policy of 'deaccessioning'[3] within the country. Another model is the 'branch' museum, whereby a museum in one part of the country, say the capital, has regional extensions; the Tate Gallery in England has two regional branches, one in Liverpool and the other in St Ives in Cornwall. The Solomon R. Guggenheim Museum in New York has a SoHo extension in New York City. This policy is beginning to cross national borders with branches and franchises: the Guggenheim has branches in Berlin, Bilbao and Venice; France's national Louvre has an agreement to open a 'satellite' museum in Abu Dhabi;[4] and the St Petersburg Hermitage has branches in Amsterdam and London.

Another development that extends the scope of the museum is the online museum, using digitalisation of the layout of the building and the collection that is available on the internet. The United Kingdom even has

---

[3] Deaccessioning usually implies the sale of items from the collection (see below); in the Netherlands, items are moved elsewhere rather than sold.

[4] This is a deal to rent the name of the Louvre, some of its art treasures and its expertise for a new museum to be built on Saadiyat Island off Abu Dhabi. The rental fee is reported to be just under $1 billion (Alan Riding, *International Herald Tribune*, 12 January 2007; see also chapter 19).

a twenty-four-hour 'virtual museum' that exists only online. These developments are likely to be more widely adopted and they raise problems of intellectual property ownership: they are difficult to charge for and are typical public goods, being non-excludable and non-rival, and are mostly publicly financed. These remarks apply with equal force to archives and national library collections.

Ownership of the museum and its collection

Many museums, or at any rate their collections, are state-owned by national, regional and local government, and in many countries they may also be managed by state bureaucracies. World-famous national museums such as the Louvre, the British Museum, the Prado and the Berlin Museums Island are all state-owned. There are some prominent museums that are both privately financed and privately owned, however: famous private museums include the Thyssen Bornemisza Museum in Madrid, housed in a building given by the Spanish state, the Museu Calouste Gulbenkian in Lisbon and the Royal Academy in London. There are many privately owned and financed museums in the United States, some of the more famous being the Solomon R. Guggenheim Museum and the Frick Collection in New York, the Isabella Stewart Gardner Museum in Boston and the J. Paul Getty Museum in Malibu, California. Accordingly, within the museum sector, there is a mixture of private and public finance for non-profit organisations and direct provision for state-owned and -managed museums.

Museums usually charge entry fees, though the price may not be cost-covering. In some countries there is a free entry day or entry to national collections is free (as in the United Kingdom); prices are often reduced for young people and for senior citizens (price discrimination). Many publicly financed museums now hold what have come to be called 'blockbuster' exhibitions, with special exhibits, often assembled from other museums and private collections, that are put on for a limited period of time. These have become very popular with the public, and museums can charge very much higher prices for entry than are charged for visiting the regular collection. A novel feature of these exhibitions is selling 'timed' tickets, which limit entry according to a timetable. Such exhibitions have become a basis for cultural tourism nationally and internationally (see chapters 9 and 19).

The collections of museums, however, typically remain in state ownership, and often restrictions are placed on what may be done with them, regulating or preventing sales, particularly abroad. The state also assists in the acquisition of items by accepting works of art in lieu of death duties (tax on estates of the deceased).

Deaccessioning

One of the topics in the economics of museums that has particularly attracted attention is deaccessioning – the sale of items from the museum collection. Cultural economists have long argued that museums do not act rationally in managing their collections because they do not (and do not have to) place a financial value on them (Montias (box 3.3) was a prominent proponent of deaccessioning). While it is understood that it may not be possible to place a meaningful valuation on a whole collection, it is nevertheless possible to value individual items, for example by comparing them to similar items that have been sold on the market. There are two results from this stance: museum managers do not perceive the opportunity cost of the items in their collections; and they deprive the public of the chance to view many items in the collection for which there is not exhibition space and which then remain in the vaults unseen by visitors.

Deaccessioning may not be an option for publicly owned collections, however, because the state may not allow items to be sold, on the grounds that they belong to the nation. Nor is it only state-owned museums that have these restrictions: some private museums are also unwilling, or even unable by the terms of the bequest, to sell or alter the collection; for example, the Isabella Stewart Gardner Museum in Boston, Massachusetts, cannot alter any aspect of the museum. That is also the case with the private Beyeler Museum in Basle, Switzerland, which has been studied by Frey and Meier (see box 4.1) as a case study in the significance of the particular institutional arrangement – the combination of mainly private finance with some public support. Other topics that have been studied in the economics of museums are the multi-product nature of the output of a museum and pricing; chapter 9 explores these topics further.

Box 4.1 Professor Bruno Frey on the institutional culture of museums

Bruno Frey is Professor of Economics at the University of Zurich and research director of the Centre for Research in Economics, Management and the Arts, Switzerland. He is one of the most prominent and extensively cited economists working in Europe and has published on an extraordinarily broad range of topics, applying his view of economics to them. As he says on his web page, he 'seeks to extend economics beyond standard neo-classics by including insights from other disciplines, including political science, psychology and sociology'. His recent work has been on the economics of happiness, terrorism, awards and honours, and democracy and federalism; it would be hard to find another economist writing with expertise on so many seemingly unrelated topics. The common thread running through them all is his belief in the importance of institutions and incentives and a behavioural approach; nevertheless, he retains the outlook of an economist in terms of applying rational maximising behaviour. He has applied this approach to various topics in the economics of the arts and culture and, in the present context, to museums. Frey is one of the most important contributors to cultural economics, and several of his books and many of his articles are 'required reading' in the subject.

Frey has been a critic of museum culture for some time, pointing out that museums are often run for the convenience of the employees instead of the public (for example, every continental European museum closes on Mondays and has opening times that suit museum staff, not visitors). Moreover, the laws and rules in Switzerland, as elsewhere in Europe, governing state-owned museums (examples of 'institutional arrangements') prevent deaccessioning and encourage the hoarding of works of art in the vaults; public museums have no incentive to increase their earned income by providing better visitor facilities, such as shops or cafés, because the bureaucracy that manages them would just absorb any profit and, equally, would finance any deficit.

In a recent working paper entitled *Museums between Private and Public: The Case of the Beyeler Museum in Basle*, Frey and co-author Stephan Meier investigate as a case study the difference it made to the way the museum behaves with respect to deaccessioning, special exhibitions and visitor amenities that it is a privately funded museum, albeit with some state support (estimated to be 14 per cent of the total budget). Their analysis uses Frey's favoured institutional approach to cultural economics.

The Beyeler Museum opened in 1997 and since then has become the most visited museum in Switzerland; it has an important modern art collection donated by art gallery owners Hildy and Ernst Beyeler, who also financed the building, designed by Renzo Piano. It is acknowledged to be the most successful museum in Switzerland in terms of numbers of visitors. As Frey and Meier expected, the museum offered improved visitor amenities, such as more flexible opening hours and an excellent restaurant, and devoted much time, effort and attention to continuous special 'blockbuster' exhibitions with the focus on the number of visitors. Its collection policy does not differ from that of a public museum, however: there is no deaccessioning; the collection is not valued in monetary terms; and any borrowing and lending takes place by barter.

Sources: Frey (2000), www.bsfrey.ch/index.html and http://papers.ssrn.com/sol3/papers.cfm?abstract_id=316698.

The publishing industry

Moving now to the world of literature, this is discussed in cultural economics in the context of literary publishing. The publishing industry consists of the production of books, newspapers and magazines. Traditionally, publishing referred to the printing and distribution of works such as books, newspapers, magazines and other such matter on paper, such as maps. With digitisation and the internet, however, publishing has expanded beyond paper to include electronic sources, such as the electronic versions of all these items, and electronically generated content, such as blogs, websites, and so on.

Publishing is mostly a private enterprise and attracts little subsidy, with the exception of some literary magazines, though there are schemes in some countries (especially in northern Europe) for supporting authors and translators of books and providing grants to assist them with publication; Sweden has had subsidised newspaper publishing and distribution since the 1970s, however. There is considerable international trade in published material, especially books, and, unsurprisingly, the United States and the United Kingdom dominate the industry worldwide (see chapter 18). This creates concern about domestic production in countries with relatively small populations and 'minority' languages, for which the preservation of cultural diversity in publishing is a significant aspect of cultural policy.

Apart from the 'fixed book price' that exists in many European countries (but not the United Kingdom or Ireland) and in Japan, there is no specific regulation of book or magazine publishing (unless for the purposes of censorship in those countries that have it). Copyright is very important in the publishing industry, however, for authors of books, for journalists and for publishers. In addition, libel, defamation, decency and invasion of privacy laws apply in particular to newspapers, and there is sufficient concern in the United States about freedom of expression for there to be a 'Freedom to Read' Committee of the Association of American Publishers; in the United Kingdom, the Press Council is a system of voluntary regulation by the industry. Regulation regarding media ownership applies to newspapers but not to magazines and books, and is discussed in detail in chapter 18.

Book publishing

Like the art market, the market for books has changed little in the way it works, despite considerable technological progress, though the ownership of publishing houses has become a great deal more concentrated over the last century.

There is a tremendous supply of titles by potential authors and the market for new book production is very well organised, with literary agents acting as intermediaries in contact with editors in publishing houses. Their role is to sift out potentially marketable work by assessing its merit. Books that are thought to have very high potential as best-sellers are auctioned by agents to publishers. Books are mostly written by freelance authors who have a royalty contract with a publisher; the publisher edits and has the book printed and markets it. Books are sold through bookshops or online retailers and book clubs, but also in supermarkets and other retail outlets.

The book market is very diverse, consisting of both literary and commercial works; the book trade therefore deals with a huge and heterogeneous array of output. This is illustrated in box 4.2 for the book trade in the United Kingdom.

Box 4.2 Profile of the UK book market

UK publishers produced 119 million titles in 2001, of which 11 per cent were adult fiction, 9 per cent were children's, 26 per cent were non-fiction and the remainder academic, scientific and technical books and school textbooks. The United Kingdom produced 45 per cent of all books published in the English language. There were 2,280 publishers in 2006.

UK publishers sold an estimated 787 million books in 2006, with an invoiced value of £2.81 billion; of these, 60 per cent were sold on the home market and 40 per cent exported. In 2006 the value of the UK home book market was £1,814 million and the export market value was £999 million. The United Kingdom is both the second largest exporter and importer of books in the world, according to UNESCO statistics. The United States is the single largest destination for UK book exports, with sales of £215.6 million; the Republic of Ireland was the second largest destination (£133.3 million), followed by Germany (£92.2 million) and Australia and the Netherlands (£80 million each). The United Kingdom imported books worth $1,273 million in 2002.

Consumers aged twelve to seventy-four spent an estimated £2.3 billion on books in 2006 and libraries (the British Library and university, public and school libraries) spent £160.7 million. Public expenditure on libraries (all) was £441 million.

The Booksellers' Association in the United Kingdom had 4,410 outlets in membership in 2006, an increase of 34 per cent compared to April 1997. In contrast, the number of independent booksellers in membership had declined by 22.6 per cent, from 1,839 in 1997 to 1,424 in 2007, with a decline of 4 per cent in the last ten months due mainly to stores ceasing trading.

Sources: Publishers Association (2006) and UNESCO Institute for Statistics (2005).

The market is almost all private, though there is subsidy for special categories of books, such as poetry, and, in countries that have a policy of promoting their language(s), grants are made to authors as mentioned above, sometimes for very long periods, to support the writing of new books. The fixed book price system, which allows publishers to fix the price of books with booksellers, is intended to promote diversity of titles and access by consumers to bookshops, though it raises the price for book buyers (see chapter 18). Besides the market for new books, there is also a thriving second-hand market, which is well organised through shops, dealers and online selling. E-books are developing rapidly at the time of writing, with access to online delivery becoming possible for a wide selection of titles.

Newspapers and magazines

Individual newspapers have come and gone but most countries have a selection of national and regional or local titles that reflect different political and other interests. Circulation figures are regarded as the measure of output and success, helping to attract advertising, which is a vital source of finance. *The New York Times* has a daily circulation of 1.2 million (1.6 million on Sundays); *USA Today* has 2.3 million, while the popular UK national newspaper *The Sun* has 3.2 million and it has strong competitors. Most major newspapers now have an online version.[5]

Present-day magazines are an offshoot of periodicals, some of which are learned journals and the rest are publications supplying information and comment on a wide range of topics, from high-quality literary magazines down to TV listings. For example, *The Economist*, founded in 1843 and still running, had an international circulation of 1.2 million in 2007; *Entertainment Weekly* has a circulation of 1.7 million; the German magazine *Der Spiegel* has a circulation of over 1 million.

Periodicals and magazines have over the years been very important in literary publishing and were a source of income to many famous authors: to give some famous examples, Dickens published 'Sketches by Boz' in the *Morning Chronicle* (for which he worked as a reporter) and several of his most famous novels were published in monthly instalments before being made into books; Conan Doyle published many Sherlock Holmes stories in the *Strand Magazine*. Edgar Allan Poe, reputedly the first American author to

---

[5] See Küng, Picard and Towse (2008).

live by writing alone, also worked for and published in a succession of periodicals and magazines. Periodicals and magazines now, as in the past, offer employment to a host of correspondents, reporters and general writers as well as to editors, and an enormous number are published worldwide.

Many newspapers, periodicals and magazines were founded and owned by individual entrepreneurs. All parts of the publishing industry now, however, are highly concentrated and owned by large international corporations (for instance, see box 14.3 on Rupert Murdoch's News Corporation). Newspapers and magazines in the United States get a significant part of their finance from advertising (80 and 56 per cent respectively), and that leads in the case of newspapers to two-thirds of their content being advertisements,[6] though they also raise revenue from sales and subscriptions. In recent years free newspapers, financed by advertising, have become a serious threat to the established newspaper market. The internet is also a strong competitor for advertising revenues, and the resulting fall in income to newspapers is causing smaller ones to close down.

The economics of newspapers and magazine publishing falls more into the field of media than of cultural economics; what little work there is in cultural economics on publishing has concentrated on books (see chapter 18).

The music industry

In contrast to publishing, all aspects of the music industry have been studied in cultural economics. The music industry is complex and varied. It consists of musical composition and publishing, live performance and sound recording. It is both an old industry and a new industry, and has experienced many changes of taste, technique and technology, from the troubadours of medieval Europe to the iPod. Current catalogues of recorded music and of live performance include world music of peoples from Australia to Zaire, Asian classical music, European music for the Church, the courts and concert halls from the devotional music of twelfth-century Hildegard of Bingen and the dances of the Renaissance duchy of Burgundy, to the whole canon of baroque, classical, jazz, contemporary classical and popular music from Europe, North and South America – in other words, serious and popular music of every genre, past and present. Some of this music was composed and published, some exists only in sound recordings; some pieces require huge forces of performers and

---

[6] See Vogel (2001).

instruments while other music calls for only one performer (and electronic music requires neither!). Therefore, it is necessary to consider many aspects of this industry, starting from the creation of music by composers, songwriters, lyricists and performers, and moving through the chain of production to music publishing, performance organisations and venues, the production of musical instruments, the sound recording industry and, finally, the distribution of music in all these branches of the industry through sales outlets and downloading services.

It is not difficult to see that there are many different economic aspects of this varied cultural output; on the one hand, there are the individuals who create and perform it, whether for payment or love; on the other, the 'industry' – meaning the record or sound recording industry – is large, concentrated, vertically integrated and globalised. It has been in the forefront of demands for protection by copyright law and has been subject to several technological revolutions, some initiated within the industry itself and others from outside it, especially digitisation and the internet, which have so profoundly altered the production of music.

There are many stages in the chain of production of music: musical composition is a creative activity of individual composers and songwriters; music publishing is a specialist task undertaken by private enterprise; the live performance of pop and classical music (in clubs, concerts, festivals, theatres, and so on) may be financed privately or with public subsidy; sound recording used to be a specialist task but now it is easy to produce good-quality recordings without a dedicated sound studio and trained sound engineers; distribution takes place via sales of CDs and other sound carriers (DVD, cassette) through specialised record shops and other high street retail outlets and, increasingly, through the online supply of tracks as downloads (legal and illegal). These production and distribution activities are in the hands of different types of economic agents, though there is vertical integration (ownership of the different stages in the chain of production) in the music business, particularly between music publishing and sound recording, which has become increasingly concentrated in the last few decades.

Musical composition

Musical composition is done by composers and songwriters. When words are involved, they are created by lyricists, and sometimes a partnership between composer and lyricist is vital to artistic success (think of Gilbert and Sullivan and Rodgers and Hammerstein) while other composers write their own lyrics

(Wagner, Bob Dylan, the Beatles) or set existing words to music. Composition is a very broad field and includes musicals and opera, 'classical' song and pop music of all kinds, music for film and TV programmes, jingles for advertising and ringtones for mobile phones. In some circumstances, the composer is commissioned or hired by an organisation or firm that is going to use his or her work; in other cases, the composer may perform the works him- or herself. There is also a range of possibilities as to who owns the copyright and all the rights to use the music; the copyright rests in the first instance with the composer unless the work was undertaken during employment (called work made for hire), when it belongs to the employer. For some commercial purposes, however, composers are required as part of a contract to transfer the copyright (see chapters 13 and 15 for more detail). Composers often have an agent who manages negotiations with 'buyers'. For contemporary classical music, there are grants for composers, either to the individual or through the organisation commissioning the work (say a symphony or set of songs).

Music publishing

Like book publishing, music publishing is almost always a private enterprise, and nowadays it is often an arm of a private corporation whose other activities include sound recording and maybe film production. There are still famous old firms in music publishing that go back centuries, however; for example, in Germany, Breitkopf and Härtel (mentioned in chapter 3) and, in Italy, Ricordi – Verdi's publisher and, to some extent, mentor. Music publishers perform a range of tasks: they print the notes and lyrics on paper for sale as sheet music or for hiring out to performing organisations, such as orchestras and music theatres; they license the performing and mechanical (recording) rights to performers and record companies; and they negotiate the use of the works they publish for use in films, TV programmes, and suchlike. They also commission recordings of some works and hire them out in a sound library to advertisers or film-makers who want a specific sound.

Much of the role of the music publisher has moved from being responsible for the printing of music to managing musical rights for composers and songwriters. Publishers with a roster of composers on whose works copyright has expired can still control their use in two ways: first, by the old established system whereby the music is printed in orchestral parts for the different instruments with the only full score being that used by the conductor (though 'pocket scores' are also sold to the public); and, second, by commissioning new performing editions of a work or of a composer's output, thereby creating a 'new' copyrightable version. Copyright collection societies are particularly important in the music industry for managing some aspects of copyright, such as public performance rights of composers and publishers. Music publishing continues to be a profitable area of the music industry, despite the decline in sound recording revenues. Music shops are the outlet to consumers of sheet music and they are often owned by the publishers or are small privately owned enterprises selling items such as musical instruments.

Sound recording

Sound recording is a for-profit part of the music business, with 80 per cent of the world sound recording market in the hands of four international corporations: Universal Music Group, Sony BMG, EMI and Warner Music Group. They represent the trend over the twentieth century of frequent mergers and takeovers of record labels. Sound recordings in the form of CDs, DVDs and cassettes are produced and sold under the name of the record label and cover the whole range of world music. Record sales of popular works run into the millions; only about one in ten sound recordings is profitable, however. Although originally record companies ran their own sound studios (such as the EMI Abbey Road Studio in London, of Beatles fame), most recording studios are now separate enterprises, and the recording process is managed by a sound engineer selected by the group of musicians.

In terms of copyright, record companies have to acquire the right to make the sound recording from the composer and they then control the rights in the sound recording. The 'signed' performers have a royalty contract with the record label and the 'backing' performers are paid a studio fee for the time they spent in recording. (Recently all performers have acquired new rights in their performances, something that is discussed in detail in chapter 13.) Many instrumental musicians and singers work in 'scratch' bands and choruses on short-term contracts, often just for a three-hour 'session' – hence the term 'sessions' musicians. In order to help the musicians obtain the maximum amount of work, there are diary services in the busiest markets for recorded music that keep a performer's diary and book his or her recording sessions (you can't answer the phone during a recording!); this is another example of specialist market-making in a 'thick' market. Top performers are all represented by agents and many also have a manager. There is considerable excess supply of potential performers and the market is very well organised, with managers and agents acting as middlemen in contact with record labels. They also act as 'gate-keepers' to identify potentially marketable work in a field that is dominated by the star system, as we see in chapter 15.

Distribution of sound recordings

Sound recordings are sold direct to the public in a variety of outlets, including supermarkets, petrol stations and bookshops, as well as in music stores dedicated to their sale, some of which are owned by record labels. Increasingly, there are online sales of records of commercial sound recordings produced by the majors or the 'indies' (independent record labels), and also direct sales from the performers themselves, including orchestras and other groups and ensembles that now market their own sound recordings. The online distribution of music is not in the hands of the record industry but with specialised companies, iTunes, Pressplay, and so forth, which are middlemen for the rights and provide the technical facilities for downloading tracks made by record labels. Radio and TV stations are extremely important in the public performance and dissemination of recorded music and they have to pay composers, performers and record labels for the use of their work in broadcasts. The same is true for the use of recorded music in film and other uses, such as advertising or ringtones. Music videos have become an important offshoot of sound recording and are used both as promotion of the band and as entertainment in their own right on TV.

Performing arts

The previous chapter gave a brief economic history of the performing arts, from which it could be seen that, as Baumol has claimed in the context of the cost disease (see box 1.1), little has changed in economic terms. Live performance of music, opera, dance and spoken theatre has indeed changed little in some respects, and some considerable proportion of performances are of works that have been in the repertoire going as far back as the times of Shakespeare and Johann Sebastian Bach. The repertoire is being added to, however, with newer works being produced, and technological developments have enabled performances to larger audiences; of these, perhaps the amplification of sound and the use of sound recording have had the greatest economic impact; the former has enabled concerts to take place in large auditoria and the latter has reduced reliance on large forces of live players.

Live performance of music

Orchestras, chamber ensembles, choirs, musical theatre and opera companies, ensembles, bands, groups and individual soloists perform every sort of music for live audiences in a host of venues, from theatres and churches to cafés and ships to football stadia. Groups vary from the several hundred singers and orchestral players on a regular contract with an established performing arts organisation to individual instrumentalists and singers who work on short-term contracts moving from band to band. Many small groups in all genres have no formal organisation. Concerts are promoted by many different types of publicly and privately financed organisations, and audiences vary very much in size. There is usually price discrimination in concert and music theatre tickets and prices can range from very high to very low, with some members of the audience willing to pay considerable amounts for tickets – for example, for top festival tickets or for top performers. Festivals are important in offering live performances and are increasingly popular. Bands often go on live tours to promote a new recording or even to sell reissues, and these are increasingly organised by the record label or, as a recent trend, by concert promoters who deal with merchandising as well as concert promotion. Many small ensembles, however, from string trios to jazz bands, promote their own concerts and rely on the revenues from ticket sales for finance and to get by in the private market. Radio and TV also play a role in broadcasting live performances and many of the bigger publicly financed radio stations employ their own orchestras. The larger 'classical' orchestras usually are in receipt of state subsidies, grants from foundations, business sponsorship and gifts from private patrons. In many European countries, a city or state owns and manages an orchestra, employing the musicians more or less as civil servants. Live performance of music is therefore a mixture of those performers who rely on the market for making a living and those who are financed publicly.

Opera

Nowadays, Germany probably supports more opera companies than any other country with over 150 publicly owned theatre companies. The leading companies operate in their own theatres while the others share the city's theatre with spoken drama and other uses. The typical German opera company tends to offer a broader repertoire than would be found in opera houses in other countries, regularly performing operetta and musicals with their 'classically' trained singers;

all salaried performers, principals, chorus and orchestral musicians are employed by either the state or the city, and enjoy the same job protection and conditions of work as other state employees. This model is typical of a number of European countries. By contrast, opera houses in the United States and the United Kingdom have developed as private non-profit organisations that are in receipt of a mixture of public subsidy, patronage and sponsorship; in these countries, there is an active marketplace for singers, conductors, directors and set designers working freelance with contracts relating to a specific production.

There are two basic systems by which opera performances are organised – 'stagione' or repertory. The stagione (meaning literally the 'season') is the classic Italian system, whereby one opera is given a certain number of performances (usually six to ten) over several weeks, followed by a rehearsal period for the next opera (during which the theatre may also be used for ballet, orchestral performances and chamber music), after which that opera is performed for its run, and so on. Over the performing season from late autumn to the end of spring, perhaps six or eight operas are produced sequentially. This system is still followed in most of the thirteen opera houses in Italy (at least, those that are still open). Under the stagione system, principal singers are hired by the opera for the rehearsal period and the run of performances, usually three or four performances of the opera per week, which enables the singers to rest the voice in between performances. This is costly, because it results in many 'dark' nights in the opera house, and also the resident orchestra is not used much during the rehearsal period, other than for ballet or concerts.

The repertory system of opera performance, like its spoken theatre equivalent (see below), has nightly alternating performances of several operatic works in the repertory over the performing season or year. This system is to be found in most German opera houses. It demands either a great deal from the company of singers or a larger company. It facilitates more performances (of each opera and, probably, of more operas), some portion being revivals from previous performing seasons. Many opera houses in fact operate a mixed system of stagione and repertory, meaning that an opera enters the repertoire for a season and is performed alternately with several others over a period of time. This calls for a greater use of guest artists to supplement company principal singers, and possibly also a much larger chorus.

Though thousands of operas have been written, many of which are even in performing editions, only a very small fraction of them is performed at all, and of those there is a canon of the most commonly performed operas that are the mainstay of opera houses. *La Bohème, Madama Butterfly, La Traviata,*

Carmen, Il Barbiere di Siviglia and *Le Nozze di Figaro* are regularly to be found in the performance schedule of every opera house in the world. When a 'modern' work is performed, audience size drops dramatically.

Nowadays, very few opera companies survive without significant state support, though even in this most expensive of art forms it does happen, typically in the form of the opera festival; examples are the Bayreuth Festspiele, Glyndebourne Festival Opera (a private company in the United Kingdom), the Arena di Verona, the Rossini Festival in Pesaro, the Santa Fe Opera Festival and the Wexford Opera Festival (in Ireland). Festivals run for a short period of the year, often the summer. Even if they do not receive direct public funding, however, they rely on sponsorship and gifts that in some countries, at least, are tax-deductible (see chapter 7), and on recording deals and broadcasting fees.

Dance

The story with dance is rather different; ballet, like opera, rarely survives on the market but, on the other hand, other dance forms part of popular performing arts that do. Musicals often employ choreographers and dancers, including dancers who can sing; musicals such as *Cats* or *West Side Story* could not exist without them and musicals, at least in New York and London, are entirely dependent upon the market.

A ballet company is often tied to an opera company, sharing the use of the stage and orchestra. When choreographers create the structure of a ballet or modern dance, it can be set down in notation or recorded on video and used for teaching dancers their moves. If anything, ballet is even more tied than opera to 'warhorses', the standard repertoire that is repeatedly performed, such as *Swan Lake* and *The Nutcracker*. Choreographers are also involved in a range of other art forms that require structured performances by people, such as music videos and ice shows. Choreographers may be employed or work as freelancers. They are usually paid a fee and they have copyright on their work, so they are paid royalties for a work's performance. Choreographers are also frequently working dancers. The copyright of a ballet rests with the choreographer, unless he or she was employed by the dance company to create the work.

Dance is promoted in a range of venues, mostly theatres. Dance companies vary quite a lot in size and type, from subsidised national ballet companies with a large *corps de ballet*, with the dancers on long-term contracts, to the many small groups of independent dancers who work together when finances allow it. Dance companies specialise in various types of dance, including various schools of contemporary dance and ethnic dance.

Ticket prices for ballet and modern dance performances tend to be lower than for opera but they may also be raised when there is a star performer. In some countries dance is very popular, and features in film (especially in India) and on television; in Russia, ballet is often televised. Amateur dance competitions have become a popular television format. The economic aspects of opera and dance are discussed at length in chapter 8.

Theatre

The word 'theatre' has two meanings: it can be the building in which performances of several art forms take place and it can be the art form of spoken drama itself. Theatre ownership is an interesting topic that has received almost no attention from cultural economists.

The theatre as a building

Theatre buildings in most continental European countries are owned by the state, either the national or state government, if the theatre was originally part of the court, or the municipality. By contrast, in the United Kingdom and the United States theatre ownership was and still is to a remarkable degree a private enterprise, and this is crucial to the flourishing New York Broadway and London's West End theatre systems, because there are theatres for almost every type of performance, ranging from large ones with an orchestra pit to small ones with very limited facilities, that can be hired for long or short runs of plays, musicals, dance, operas, and so on. The theatre building provides a range of front-of-house and backstage facilities as well as the stage and the auditorium and the personnel who deal with them – the technicians and stagehands, ushers, ticket sellers and the rest are employed by the theatre itself. Their services are typically hired along with the theatre.

Theatre as drama

Spoken theatre or drama is the performance of plays created by playwrights, who have copyright in their work and are paid a royalty or fee for its use in a public performance. New plays are sometimes commissioned but, perhaps more typically, most performances are of existing plays. Plays may be published and put on sale to the public. Theatrical companies are a mixture of publicly supported and privately financed organisations dependent upon the market. For-profit theatre exists in larger cities with a cast hired for the planned run of the play; if the play is a success, other actors may have to be hired to replace those leaving. In London's West End, the same play is performed up to eight times a week (six days a week with two performances on Saturdays and Wednesdays). Reliance on the market means that prices have to cover the costs of putting on the play; all theatres price-discriminate according to seating in the theatre in order to increase revenues.

An interesting difference between customs regarding prices for theatrical performances in different countries, particularly for the publicly financed provincial theatres, is that, in many, an *abonnement* system is the norm, whereby the regular audience member buys a ticket for the whole performing season (and for a range of performing art forms playing in the same building) either for every performance or for a selection. This system has never caught on in the United Kingdom, however, where tickets are sold individually per performance.

As with music and dance performing companies, the non-profit theatrical company may be either a permanent company of actors on long-term contracts (in Europe, as mentioned earlier, they may be employed by the state) or an ensemble of actors on short-term contracts gathered together for the run of the production of a specific play. Some theatre is 'repertory', meaning that the same company of actors performs in a different play throughout the performance season: a famous example of a repertory company is the United Kingdom's Royal Shakespeare Company, which offers productions of four or five different plays per season. The number of performances of a play in the typical theatre in a provincial city depends on how the stage is shared out between other performing organisations, such as resident opera and dance companies and visiting performing groups.

The film industry

Film production is similar to theatrical performance, in that it requires directors, actors and technical personnel working together at appointed times, and film exhibition also takes place at specific times, as with live performance. The market for film is highly complex and consists of film production, film distribution, theatrical exhibition in cinemas and transmission on television. Films are also shown in private clubs and can be bought or rented in DVD or video format by consumers, and, with digitisation, films can be downloaded from legal and illegal sources on the internet, causing the film industry the same concerns over copyright protection as the music industry. All these activities are now undertaken by different enterprises, though in the early days of the film industry they were all done by the same studio under

Box 4.3 The Hollywood studio system

The Hollywood studio system is the name given to the fully integrated mode of production and distribution in the film industry that operated in Hollywood from the 1920s – the so-called golden age – until a stop was put to it by the US antitrust authorities in 1948 under the Sherman Act. With the studio system, a film company combined ownership of a production studio with a distribution division and ownership of a cinema (movie theatre) chain, and, in addition, had performers and film-making personnel on strict long-term contracts requiring them to work exclusively for that company. The Hollywood 'majors' were five fully vertically integrated corporations, including Paramount Pictures, against which the antitrust case was brought, leading to it sometimes being called the 'Paramount case'. The case was about the restrictive practices of the distribution arm, which did not allow independent film producers access to theatrical exhibition due to the practice of the exclusive booking by movie theatres of their own films, and the result was that, by decree of the Supreme Court, film companies were required to cease these exclusive dealing arrangements; this led the studios to sell their cinema chains – an example of 'disintegration' in economic organisation.

what was known as the Hollywood studio system (see box 4.3). Markets for film tend to be differentiated by language but the market area for different languages varies substantially; English, Spanish and Arabic are languages with large market areas. Dubbing and subtitles can expand the market and there is considerable international trade in films.

Film-making is now a worldwide industry, with many countries producing films. Even though the industry is mostly in private ownership and seeks to make profit, many governments support their film industries with various types of state intervention, including state subsidy. Commercial film production is concentrated in Hollywood and Bollywood (the Indian film industry in Mumbai, the city formerly called Bombay), and China and Russia have growing film industries. At the start of the twenty-first century half the world's production of films was in Asia, Europe produced 28 per cent, the United States produced 15 per cent, South America produced 3 per cent, Canada under 2 per cent and the remainder originated in the Middle East and Africa.[7] Hollywood films nevertheless still dominate markets everywhere. Besides cinema exhibition, showing films on television is an important source of revenue.

---

[7] Korean Film Council, cited in Choi (2006).

Films are the target of regulations to protect the national or regional industry, as in Canada and the European Union, by having quotas on the television exhibition of 'foreign' films, which in practice mean that showing US films is restricted; exhibition in cinemas (movie theatres) is regulated only by censorship (rating), however, to protect the public, especially (but not only) children.

Film production

Getting finance is the first stage of film production, and that in itself is a specialised occupation. Production starts with a film script, which then leads on to the choice of directors, location and scenery, designer and cameraman. One indication of how complex all this is can be deduced from reading the credits at the end of the film! Not surprisingly, there is a great deal of specialisation in the film business, with agencies and other companies dealing with searches for location, hiring the cast and extras. Editing the film is done post-production and has become a highly specialised process, which digitisation has to some extent altered. There has been a constant stream of technological advance in film-making and exhibition over the years, of which digitisation is the latest step. Special effects and stunts are also highly specialised, as are the composition, performance and dubbing of the music for the film, which is usually specially composed. The director has the copyright as an author of the film and, in some countries, the producer also has copyright.

Film distribution and cinema

The finished version of the film is distributed to cinemas and/or formatted into videos and DVD for retail distribution for sale or for rental. Commercially organised distribution of film over the internet has not yet become widespread (and there is plenty of illegal copying) but, as broadband develops, it is expected that the downloading of film will increase. Distribution to cinemas is a specialised activity and is done on a country-by-country basis, since copyright, distribution and exhibition rights are nationally based. Cinemas pay a rental fee for the film; multiplex cinemas may show the same film at different times as well as several films over the same period. Multiplexes are now far more common than the grand old cinemas of the mid-twentieth century. Cinemas are mostly privately owned and operated on a for-profit basis, though film clubs and art cinemas operating on a non-profit basis coexist with private enterprise. Prices for cinema showings vary by release date and the location of the cinema but there is no longer price discrimination within theatres.

Broadcasting

Broadcasting by radio and television is a means of distributing culture in a wide sense: both media offer programmes on the arts and entertainment as well as news and other information. Over-the-air broadcasting signals that audiences accessed through radio receivers and TV sets constituted the first technology for distributing broadcast programmes, and this is still an important means of delivery; later came cable and satellite distribution and now the internet is also a means of access. Although it is not strictly correct to call all these technologies 'broadcasting', it is a common way of referring to the industry.

Both radio and television distribution have changed very considerably in line with technical developments over the last twenty years or so. Until the 1980s the typical ownership of radio and, later, of TV stations was by a national, state-run broadcasting monopoly, and that continues to be the case in many less developed countries. Commercial radio and TV financed by advertising developed in competition with public service broadcasting (PSB) and that is the typical position in most countries at present; consumers do not have to pay for advertiser-financed broadcasts but they do pay by taxes or a licence fee for PSB.

The state owns the electromagnetic spectrum, which it licenses in bands to broadcasters, public and private. Mobile phones also use part of the spectrum but do not compete with broadcasters for it, though they do compete as platforms for the delivery of broadcasts. Consumers mostly access broadcasts by radio and TV sets, which they buy as ordinary consumer goods in shops. Increasingly, broadcasts are streamed over the internet and can be accessed without a licence. The 'price' of the traditional over-the-air broadcasting is a combination of the cost of the licence fee or tax paid to the broadcaster and the cost of the set to its owner. Cable and satellite services are sold as subscriptions for a period of time. Pay-per-view television enables the supplier to charge per programme by means of a set-top box. Whatever system is used, there is a combination of public and private provision – the public service broadcasts being nowadays for reasons of policy more than of economic necessity, as was the case when the only transmission was that of the state monopoly. There is now considerable competition in what is essentially a private market that is state-regulated.

Digitisation has now made reception of radio and television possible on a host of platforms besides the traditional sets – the internet, mobile phones, Blackberries, and so on. The switchover to digital broadcasting imposes costs on listeners, who have to buy new sets to receive it. Chapter 17 goes into detail on the financing of TV and radio, with the focus on PSB.

Internet

The internet is the newest medium for the dissemination of cultural goods and services; it has been enabled by digital production technology and the spread of cheap personal computers. Apart from blogs, 'amateur' sites such as Facebook and YouTube and some online newspapers, at the time of writing the internet was only beginning to create new cultural material, although it has been extremely important in its ability to advertise and provide online consumption; Wikipedia as a free resource is breaking new ground, however (no doubt this will be out of date by the time this book is published!). Digitisation and the effect of the internet are discussed in relation to each chapter in Part IV but there is not yet sufficient research in cultural economics to form the basis of a dedicated chapter. The same is true of the ever-growing games industry.

Conclusion

These sketches of the present-day economic organisation of the creative industries provide an introduction to the way economists analyse the production and consumption of cultural products. These topics now constitute the next two chapters of the book; chapter 5 provides the analytical basis for understanding the economics of production – the supply side of the market – and chapter 6 does the same for consumption – the demand side of the market. One of the trends that this chapter demonstrated is the increasing intervention in the creative industries by the state through subsidy and regulation. The 'older' industries, particularly the performing arts and museums, have more and more come to be publicly financed, though the public institutions coexist with some notable private ones. The 'newer' media, such as recorded music and film, were developed as and still are private enterprises, though some types of film are increasingly subsidised in many countries; television and radio have a mixed economy, with public service and private enterprise commercial channels coexisting and competing. The internet has developed through the market (though with an initial boost from government); it is privately financed and remains largely unregulated.

Further reading

My *Handbook of Cultural Economics* (Towse, 2003a) comes into its own for further reading on this chapter, as there are quite a few chapters that provide good introductions to the economic organisation of the various markets and industries. First the art market: there are several different topics here – the organisation of the market, how auction sales work and what determines dealer prices: on the organisation of the market and dealers, see Olav Velthuis (chapter 60 on 'Visual arts'), Martin Shubik (chapter 24, 'Dealers in art') and Dominique Sagot-Duvauroux (chapter 5 on 'Art prices'); on the mechanism and conduct of art auctions, the chapter (3, 'Art auctions') by Orley Ashenfelter, who is the leading expert on this subject, is an excellent introduction for the uninitiated. On museums, there is a chapter by Peter Johnson in the same *Handbook* on the economics of museums (chapter 41, 'Museums'); and Bruno Frey has two highly readable essays in his book *Arts and Economics* (2000): chapter 3, 'For art's sake – open up the vaults!', and chapter 4, 'Superstar museums: an economic analysis'. On the performing arts and back to *A Handbook of Cultural Economics*, there are chapters by Jörg Schimmelpfennig (chapter 10, on ballet), Bill Luksetich (chapter 42 on 'Orchestras') and by myself on 'Opera' (chapter 41). For film and music and books, see Darlene Chisholm (chapter 40, 'Motion pictures'), Andrew Burke (chapter 42, on 'Music business') and Marja Appleman (chapter 29, 'Fixed book price'). Finally, chapter 8 of Küng, Picard and Towse's *The Internet and the Mass Media*, by Ala-Fossi, Bakker, Ellonen *et al.* (2008), provides short sketches of the impact of the internet on the media industries (newspapers, broadcasting and publishing). That completes a rather long reading list!

5 Production, costs and supply of cultural goods

This chapter deals with the supply of cultural goods and services and with the economic aspects of their production. The first stage of production in the creative industries is creativity, and that may be generated by individuals or by enterprises; in economic terms, though, we can also regard artists and others involved in 'primary' creative activity as producers. Supply to the market is made up of individual producers deciding how much to supply at different prices; what influences their decisions affects supply. The most important economic factor affecting supply is the cost of production and, in the chapter, various types of costs are analysed. Some producers are motivated only by profit, others are non-profit firms with other objectives; some have a monopoly position in the market while others operate in a competitive market. All these factors affect supply, the prices of cultural goods, which goods and services are produced, firms' revenues and, ultimately, how creators are rewarded.

Creativity

The starting point for all cultural supply is something we can call 'creativity'. The people who create new work can be called 'artists' as a general term.[1] Creativity may be defined in many ways and much has been written about it by social psychologists, philosophers, art historians, musicologists, critics, and so on, and lately by the authors of the UNCTAD (2008) *Creative Economy Report 2008*. They adopt a broad definition that covers artistic, scientific and economic creativity with 'technological creativity' at the core:

---

[1] The creative industries 'industry' has spawned the word 'creatives', which certainly overcomes the problem that all creators are not artists in the usual sense. I prefer the word 'artists', because it tallies with work in cultural economics on artists' labour markets, which has typically taken a very broad view of 'artists'.

Definition
- Artistic creativity involves imagination and a capacity to generate original ideas and novel ways of interpreting the world, expressed in sound, text and image;
- scientific creativity involves curiosity and a willingness to experiment and make new connections in problem-solving; and
- economic creativity is a dynamic process leading towards innovation in technology, business practices, marketing etc., and is closely linked to gaining competitive advantages in the economy.

(UNCTAD, 2008: 9)

This is a very broad definition that recognises the interaction of both the artistic and the commercial, the latter being more or less the definition of entrepreneurship in economics (see below), and, as the report notes, however creativity is defined, it is fundamental to defining the scope of the creative economy. As we saw in chapter 2, the broader the scope, the larger the size of the cultural sector, or the creative economy, as the UN now calls it. Creativity has thus come to be seen as the contemporary equivalent of innovation in the industrial age; and in the so-called 'post-industrial' economy or 'information age', 'knowledge economy', even 'weightless' economy – all titles that convey the increased economic role of ideas – copyright now plays the role that patents were supposed to have had in encouraging the technological progress that drove manufacturing industry.

The motivation of creative supply

Two aspects of creative activity that are of interest to cultural economics are, first, what motivates artistic creativity and, second, how artists get their work to market – that is, how it reaches the audience. Cultural economists believe the way to understand these industries is to study the motivation and organisation of the individual artists, firms and organisations whose business it is to supply creative goods and services. Accordingly, the industrial organisation of the creative industries is analysed using the same economic tools as would be applied to any industry. That analysis has to take into account the specific features of creative goods and services, however, which differ in some respects from other products, and this is particularly true of those information goods and services that have been created digitally.

Supplying the market requires there to be co-ordination of resources and management of marketing and/or production by commercial entrepreneurs. How artists fare in this process will determine the supply of new work upon which the creative industries depend, and that has led cultural economists to study artists' labour markets, the subject of chapters 11 and 12. This chapter, however, deals with the economic factors influencing the supply of cultural products from the point of view of the theory of the firm and the factors that affect the size of enterprises in the creative industries.

Entrepreneurship

The starting point of the organisation of production is the entrepreneur. The entrepreneur may be a single individual or the top level of management of a large corporation. The entrepreneur sees and seizes an opportunity to bring a new good to the market or to squeeze in with a new way of doing things. Entrepreneurship is therefore essential to both the working of markets and to competition. The motivation for entrepreneurship in the capitalist economy is economic success, either in terms of short-run profits or the long-run growth of the enterprise. Entrepreneurship need not be confined to profit-making, though; a non-profit organisation is 'entrepreneurial' if it introduces new ways of doing things. The essential features of entrepreneurship are therefore imagination, the ability to perceive and seize opportunities and the ability to co-ordinate the finance and management of the production and distribution of goods. Entrepreneurship may be thought of as the creative end in the world of business, and that is clearly what is recognised in the definition of creativity cited above.

Cultural entrepreneurship is currently much touted as a concept in arts organisations and it is therefore important to understand exactly what is meant by the term. What it should not be confused with, however, is good management; in economics, these are distinct functions. Nor is the entrepreneur the supplier of capital, though he or she may be so in a small organisation. Typically, entrepreneurs take risks with other people's investment! Box 5.1 catalogues just a few of the long list of famous cultural entrepreneurs.

Sources of finance

Where do entrepreneurs in the arts and entertainment or in any other business get their finance from? Like artists, at the start they often have to finance themselves by working for nothing or doing other jobs to pay the rent and rely on family gifts for support. Once they have managed to establish themselves and set up a legally constituted company, they may be able to get a bank loan, sell shares on the stock exchange or attract venture capital. Loans are at an agreed rate of interest and repayment must be made over a specified

Box 5.1 Entrepreneurs in the arts

Entrepreneurship in the arts is hardly something new and the list is very long indeed, especially if you include entertainment industry entrepreneurs such as Walt Disney and Rupert Murdoch. Here are just a few! Shakespeare could be considered one of them: he built and owned a theatre and managed a company of actors while, of course, writing plays for them to perform. Later actor-managers in English theatre were David Garrick and Henry Irving. Garrick can even lay claim to having started cultural tourism to Stratford-upon-Avon and the 'Shakespeare industry' there; Stratford had completely ignored its most famous son until Garrick's arrival there in 1745 with a crowd of worshippers from London! Richard D'Oyly Carte not only founded an opera company and commissioned Gilbert and Sullivan to write operettas for it, he also ran a concert agency (representing the singer Patti and the author Oscar Wilde) and with the profits, financed the building of the Savoy Theatre and Hotel. Sergei Diaghilev, creator of the *Ballets Russes*, is undoubtedly an entrepreneur by any standard! Not only did he create the company and organise its tours, he commissioned a roster of composers – Debussy, Ravel, Satie, Prokofiev and most famously Stravinsky – hired Fokine as choreographer and legendary dancers (Nijinsky, Pavlova) and kept the company going until his death.

In our own day, Andrew Lloyd Webber (Baron Lloyd-Webber of Sydmonton) was listed as the eighty-seventh richest Briton in 2006 based on his musicals and the Really Useful Theatre Company, which owns a number of West End theatres in London, as well as companies holding the musical rights, publishing and making recordings and films of his theatrical productions. In the Netherlands, Joop van den Ende is a Dutch billionaire theatre producer and media tycoon, co-founder of Endemol (and owner of the TV rights to *Batman*), and with John de Mol he has the distinction of having invented the *Big Brother* reality TV format.

period of time; shares, however, are an entitlement to a share in the profits made by the company, and it is this feature that causes economists to think that the pursuit of profit is the motive of commercial for-profit organisations. Profit is the excess of revenue from sales over the costs of the operation (of which the interest on any loan is one). For-profit firms are assumed by economists to aim for the maximum possible rate of profit so as to ensure their continued ability to raise financial capital on the stock exchange, where they have to compete for funds with all the other firms in all the other industries that are also seeking finance. They publicise their profitability in order to attract shareholders. So, for instance, the Dutch-founded international entertainment corporation Endemol NV is owned by a consortium consisting of Goldman Sachs Capital Partners, Mediaset Group and Cyrte Group. Its financial results for the first half of 2007 are posted on its website: net income attributable to the shareholders €56.6 million (8.8 per cent of turnover); 13.6 per cent growth compared to the first half year of 2006; earnings per share €0.45.[2]

Non-profit organisations may also make profits but they are not allowed to distribute them and therefore cannot issue shares on the stock exchange. They may borrow money in the form of loans but they mostly rely on grants, gifts and other such finance that is not motivated by the desire for financial gain. Like for-profit organisations, they finance themselves internally from sales receipts and other sources of revenue, but they do not set prices so as to make the maximum profit.

The 'angel' system

As a footnote to this section, a system for financing private theatre in the United Kingdom is worth a mention: people known as 'angels' ('Be an angel, darling!') put up finance for productions without much expectation of a return on their money, apparently because they get pleasure from so doing. These are not gifts – it is a business-like and well-organised system that just happens not to pay! A scheme to encourage the public to make small investments is organised by the Theatre Investment Fund. The UK tax authorities even have special instructions on the taxation of 'angels'' profits and losses.[3]

Organisational goals

While the motives of for-profit firms are assumed to be the maximisation of profit and the survival and growth of the firm, the motives of non-profit organisations are less easy to generalise. All organisations have goals and they are embodied in their articles of incorporation. For non-profit organisations these goals are usually the pursuit of high-quality provision of a specific good or service, and the mission to increase access to it by the public or a particular group of people. In the arts, this would include a statement of artistic goals; for example, a museum would have the preservation, research on and display of its collection as its goals and a desire to offer the public the best possible opportunity for enjoying and learning from it as its mission. Management is concerned with the implementation of these goals and with strategies for future development.

The relevance for economics of these goals is that they determine decisions about prices and the size of the output to be supplied, on the one hand, and, on

[2] See http://212.153.67.148/Uploads_com/070726%20H1%202007.pdf (accessed 9 December 2008).
[3] See www.hmrc.gov.uk/manuals/bimmanual/bim66601.htm (accessed 19 December 2008).

the other, how to evaluate the success of the enterprise. For for-profit firms, their policy is to set a profit-maximising price, and the valuation of the firm, its profitability and growth are all measures of success. Non-profit organisations set prices and output in accordance with the objectives for which they were set up and their ability to achieve those objectives can be evaluated in many ways, one of which is the ability to attract donations and voluntary support; those in receipt of public subsidy or expenditure are evaluated in accordance with the conditions for which the grant was awarded, for example to attract more visitors. The evaluation of success in the arts and cultural industries is discussed in detail in chapters 7, 10 and 14. For the rest of this chapter, I concentrate on the microeconomics of supply and the analysis of economic organisation of the creative industries.

Theory of supply

Price-takers and price-makers

The theory of supply was developed in its neoclassical form by Alfred Marshall at the end of the nineteenth century. Supply forms one of the 'scissors' of the standard picture of the market, with demand as the other; the interaction of supply and demand determines what price will come about in the market for a particular good or service (this was explained in chapter 3). In a competitive market, all the firms supplying the same or very similar goods will be forced to charge a similar price or their customers will move to another supplier. A monopoly as the sole supplier of a good can set its own price, however, as long as there is some demand for its product. Thus a firm in a competitive market is a 'price-taker' and a monopoly or oligopoly is a 'price maker' (an oligopoly is a situation in which a few firms dominate the market). In between is 'monopolistic competition', where there is competition but the firm has some freedom to set its price, depending upon how easy it is to substitute one supplier's product for that of another. So, prices and the type of market structure or economic organisation of an industry are very much interrelated.

The supply schedule

The firm's supply schedule represents its willingness to offer different quantities of a good for sale at various prices and, typically, the higher the price the greater the quantity it will be prepared to offer. The market supply schedule is the combined quantities of a good that all firms in an industry are willing to supply at various prices. As the price rises, firms expand to produce a greater level of output and new, less efficient firms enter the market; when the market price falls, firms contract their output and less efficient firms make losses and leave the market. In general, the willingness to supply depends upon the cost of producing the good or service that increases with output. Costs are explained in detail below.

The supply schedule can be written as $Q_S = f(C, P)$, where Q_S is the quantity of the good supplied, C are costs and P is the price of the good. The f represents the functional relation, which is typically drawn as a straight line in diagrams. A supply schedule has both an intercept (its starting point) and a slope. The intercept could be just above the origin of the schedule at point 0; this indicates that the good can be produced at very low prices. When there are high fixed costs of production, the intercept of the supply schedule is significantly above point 0.

Shifts and movement along the supply schedule

A change in the cost of production would result in a shift in the supply schedule; if costs rise, say because wages rise, the supply schedule would shift up to the left, indicating that Q_S is lower at every price (and that a given level of Q_S requires a higher price). However, if a cost-saving technology is introduced, the supply schedule would shift down to the right, or, as depicted in figure 3.1b (in chapter 3), a subsidy to production was shown to shift the supply schedule down to the right. A change in the market for the good, due, say, to a shift in demand, would cause the price to change and that causes a movement along the supply schedule; if the price rises with an upward shift in demand, to P'_e in figure 3.1a, a greater Q_S would be offered on the market.

Elasticity of supply

The slope of the supply schedule shows the response of Q_S to the change in price, and this is measured by the elasticity of supply. The elasticity of supply is defined as the percentage change of the quantity supplied due to a percentage change in the price. So, for example, if a 10 per cent rise in price leads to a 20 per cent increase in supply, then elasticity of supply is 2 and that shows a strong response to the price rise, and supply is said to be 'elastic'; if, by contrast, the quantity supplied rises only by 5 per cent, elasticity of supply is 0.5 and supply is not very responsive, and it is said to be 'inelastic'. Elasticity varies along the supply schedule and therefore has to be measured at specific points along it. Elasticity can be measured for the firm's supply schedule and for the market supply schedule, though the latter is more usual.

Knowing the elasticity of supply is fundamental to many aspects of the creative industries. We would like to know what will induce a greater supply of creative output; but, unless producers (artists, organisations, and so forth) respond to price incentives, policies such as subsidy to arts organisations and copyright law are not likely to work. At present there is insufficient understanding of the elasticity of supply of creative work by artists to be confident that, for example, changing the terms of copyright encourages them to produce more. An estimate of the response of the supply of artists' labour to the wage rate was made by David Throsby and is presented in box 5.2; as explained in chapter 11, markets apply to labour just as they do to goods – the wage rate is the price of an hour of labour and workers supply hours of work.

Box 5.2 David Throsby's research on the supply of artists' labour

David Throsby is Professor of Economics at Macquarie University in Sydney. He has worked on cultural economics for over thirty years and has published several books and many articles on the subject. His first book on cultural economics (with Glenn Withers), *The Economics of the Performing Arts*, was published in 1979, and it is a model of rigorous theoretical and empirical research in cultural economics. His 2001 book *Economics and Culture* has been both popular and influential and has been translated into several languages. It summarises his view that the pursuit of cultural value must be taken into account in understanding markets for art and the labour market for artists.

Throsby has carried out a number of surveys of artists' labour markets in Australia and he has consistently found that artists of all kinds typically do both arts and non-arts work. Using data from his survey of Australian artists (see box 11.2), he estimated the hours of labour supplied as a function of earnings from both arts and non-arts sources (such as teaching). He found that the supply of artistic labour rose with earnings from both sources, indicating both an own elasticity of supply due to income from arts work and a positive cross-elasticity – when artists earn more from *non-arts* work, they devote more time to *arts* work. Chapters 11 and 12 go into this in detail.

Stocks and flow of supply

A stock is the total quantity of a particular good in existence at a given moment in time; the flow of supply takes place over a period of time, such as a month or year. When the stock of the good is fixed, as is the case, for example, with back-catalogue sound recordings, old master paintings and other heritage items (historic buildings, ancient objects, and so forth), the elasticity of supply is very low. Even when the stock is fixed in quantity, however, high prices may encourage owners to sell, so that there is a flow of items onto the market and elasticity is not zero.

The *flow* of supply, by contrast, is when new work or adaptations of older work that responds to changes in prices are produced. There have been reissues of a number of works (sound recordings, films, books) and, in the heritage sector, renovation or excavation may increase the supply. The balance between the stock and flow of supply in some areas is very important in the market, and new technologies, such as digitisation, are changing the relation of the stock and flow of supply of goods in many areas of the arts.

Short-run and long-run supply

A standard way in which economists think about the world is in terms of short-run and long-run tendencies. What is rather irritating about this distinction is that it is never exact! Keynes jokingly once said: 'In the long run we are all dead'! However, there is a clear definition in the theory of the firm: the short run is the period in which the capital equipment and land of an enterprise cannot be changed, while, in the long run, all inputs to the production process for all output can be expanded or contracted. The long run and the short run also impact on elasticity: elasticity of supply is expected to be greater in the long run, when the producer has been able to adjust the scale of the enterprise to output that is appropriate to market conditions, than it is in the short run with a fixed scale for the operation. As we see below, this ties up with the structure of costs.

Measuring output

Though it is easy to lay down general rules about measuring responsiveness to price, it is not always so easy in practice to figure out exactly what the quantities are in which output should be measured. In some of the creative industries, there are standard measures of output – for example, the number of film or record titles or hours of broadcasting – but, even here, there may well be ambiguity and for some purposes another measure might be more appropriate, say the number of CDs or the size of the audience for a TV programme. A producer of CDs might think in terms of the number of CDs produced per year and, if we wish to measure the effect of downloading on the output of the record industry, changes in the number of CDs produced per year would be the figure to use. If the issue is, say, the effect of mergers in the record industry, however, a competition authority might take the number of titles or tracks into account, and that would certainly be relevant to achieving cultural diversity.

Moreover, what is the 'output' of, say, an orchestra? Is it the number of performances per year or the number of people attending? If the same people regularly attend the performances of a particular orchestra, the number of tickets sold does not accurately measure the number of people attending. This is discussed in more detail in chapter 6. For some purposes, it could be more interesting to know what type of works the orchestra is performing. Sometimes, a composite measure of output is used, such as the number of attendances per performance or the proportion of new works performed per year. It is obvious from this that the measurement of output is very much tied up with performance indicators (a topic dealt with in chapter 10).

Multi-product firms and organisations

An even greater complication is the fact that many suppliers, private enterprise firms and non-profit organisations alike, often do not produce a single product. A film is accompanied by a website and, maybe, the sale of the soundtrack on CD, a game and other merchandise, such as toys. These are joint products and they are likely to be protected by trademarks and copyright law. Other cultural suppliers produce several products: a museum produces a service for the public (education, entertainment) as well as maintaining its collection for future generations; it may also research special aspects of its collection and restoration. In the theory of supply, economists simplify these details by speaking of a single product in order to lay down general rules about supply. These are useful tools of analysis but, when they are put into practice, details like these cannot be ignored.

Costs and the theory of supply

The most important determinant of the entrepreneur's willingness to supply various quantities of a good or service at particular prices is the cost of producing the output. Any production process requires some combination of inputs to produce the output, and the amount and the unit costs of those inputs determine the total costs. Most production requires the input of labour, and in the cultural sector labour costs are likely to be higher than in, say, manufacturing industry, especially for the performing arts. Input requirements for producing a particular good or service are seen by economists in terms of the 'production function'; the production function is then matched up with the prices of inputs, and results in the cost function. These concepts are explained in turn.

The production function

The entrepreneur combines different factors of production – capital, labour, materials and other inputs – in order to produce various quantities of output. So, for example, a potter needs capital equipment in the form of a wheel, a kiln, a drying rack and various tools, clay as a material and his or her labour time in order to produce pots of one type or another. Some processes, such as making pottery, are very old and have not fundamentally changed with technical developments but, for many other production processes, the relationship of inputs and output depends upon the technology at the time, and that changes over the years. An example of frequent technological change is that of the materials used in producing a sound recording: the first gramophone records were on wax, followed by shellac (78 rpm), then vinyl (singles and long-players), then CDs and now using digital technology, which enables anyone to produce a reasonable quality of recorded sound in his or her home (in the garage!), while twenty years ago a fully equipped recording studio and engineer were needed. On the other hand, some production techniques do not lend themselves to technological development, such as playing the violin; indeed, most great violinists prefer to play a Stradivarius violin made in the eighteenth century!

The production function can be written simply as $Q = f(K, L, M, t)$, summarising the points made above: Q is the output of a particular good or service, K is capital, L is labour hours, M is the quantity of material and t means the level of technology. The f represents the functional relationship, stating that the level of output depends upon the quantities of inputs utilised. Most production functions assume that there is complementarity between K, M and L – that is, that some capital equipment, some materials and some labour are needed for production to take place. The ratio of one to the others depends upon the ease of substitutability between them, however. Once the possible input or factor combinations have been ascertained, the final decision is determined by the relative prices of each item.

Substitutability of factors of production

The production function lays out the technically possible combinations of inputs that can be used in the production process for a given state of technical knowledge. Before the invention of sound recording or radio, every café and hotel had a live band playing, but now canned music has been substituted for live (though in the United States one does hear a piano player in shops and hotel bars). In many production processes, improved technology enables capital machines to do what people's labour once had to do, and this is also true to some extent in the arts and heritage. Theatre scenery no longer has to be hauled up and down by hand with ropes; instead, it is controlled by computer; museums use surveillance cameras instead of security guards – there are many such examples of substituting capital for labour. Although substitution between factors of production may be technologically possible, however, whether it is economically desirable will, of course, depend upon costs and prices. If labour is very cheap and capital equipment very dear, then it will not be worth a theatre's while to computerise its sets. Therefore, the extent of factor substitutability depends upon both the state of technology and the relative prices of factors of production.

Prices of factors of production

All production requires the use of resources that could be employed in producing many different types of goods. Therefore, the price for factors of production – the wage rate for labour, the rate of interest on capital and the prices of materials and other inputs – are determined by demand and supply in their respective markets. So, for instance, an electrician could work with a pop group or for a film company or in a theatre, or for a construction company that has nothing to do with the cultural sector; the wage rate for electricians will depend upon demand and supply in the market for electricians as a whole. Thus, when a theatre wants to hire an electrician, it has to compete with other potential employers and pay a wage in line with what the others would pay. It is a 'price-taker' in the market for factors of production. The same goes for capital: as mentioned earlier, firms have to compete for financial capital with all other firms in all other industries, both nationally and internationally. If the enterprise has a bank loan, the rate of interest it must pay is the same as other competing users: the going rate charged by the bank, and all banks are likely to charge similar rates of interest. Capital equipment, however, is less flexible than labour, and once it is in place it will have to last for the period over which the return on it was planned; any investment in capital, whether your computer or a theatre's computerised lighting system, has to pay for itself over its planned lifetime.

Total, average and marginal costs

In this section, the cost structure of the individual firm is analysed. It should be noted that the analysis does not distinguish between for-profit and non-profit enterprises, because costs are determined by technology and the market for factors of production, and these are the same for all types of enterprise.

Total cost

Total cost is simply the price per unit of the factor of production times the quantity of the factors that are utilised in producing a given level of output of a good or service. Thus, the wage rate (w) times the number of hours of labour (L) plus the price per unit of materials (P_M) times their quantity (M) plus the payment (r) for the capital equipment (K) is total cost (TC). This can simply be written as

$$TC = wL + P_M M + rK$$

In formal terms, total cost is a function of factor prices and the quantities of the factors of production (inputs), and when the cost function is drawn in diagrammatic form it is called the cost curve. From total cost are derived two much-used concepts in economics: average cost (AC) and marginal cost (MC). Average total cost (ATC) is, quite simply, total cost averaged over the output (Q), or TC/Q; this is also called the 'unit cost'. Box 5.3 presents what seems to be the earliest use of the concept of average total cost, not by an economist but by the music publisher Gottfried Härtel, somewhere around 1800.

Variable and marginal cost

Average total cost includes the fixed costs incurred in setting up the production process before any units of output are produced – the capital equipment, land and building – and variable costs. 'Variable' cost means all those items that vary with the level of output: there can be total variable and average variable costs – if K is fixed, then the variable costs consist of $wL + P_M M$ in the equation above. Marginal cost is the increase in variable cost due to the production of one more unit of output. So, to return to the example of the

Box 5.3 Average total cost in music publishing: the choice of technology

F. M. (Mike) Scherer, Professor of Public Policy and Corporate Management at the Harvard Kennedy School, is a widely acknowledged expert on industrial economics and the economics of technological change. He is also an expert on the history of the music business (see Scherer, 2006). In the course of his research on music publishing, he discovered what he believes to be the first calculations, dating from around 1800, that compared average total cost for the two technologies then used in printing sheet music, engraving and typeset.

In 1796 Gottfried Härtel bought the German music publishing firm Breitkopf, which there-after became known (and to this day) as Breitkopf and Härtel, publishers of music by Beethoven, Haydn, Mendelssohn, Schumann, Liszt, Wagner and Brahms, among others. In order to ensure a profit, Härtel calculated the average costs per sheet of music of engraving and typesetting, finding that typesetting had, overall, lower unit costs. Using Härtel's data for engraving and typesetting, Scherer constructed ATC curves, and found they followed the familiar shape, falling sharply for the first 200 sheets and then more gradually up to 1,000 sheets. Typesetting had higher fixed set-up costs (900 pfennigs per sheet) and constant marginal and average costs of 5 pfennigs per sheet. Engraving he calculated to have fixed costs of 750 pfennigs and marginal costs that were 4.25 pfennigs for the first 100 to 1,200 sheets and 2.50 for the range of 800 to 1,000 sheets.

Source: Scherer (2001).

pottery, the marginal cost is the cost of labour and materials used in producing one more pot. What is more difficult to grasp is the relationship between average and marginal costs: when average cost is falling, marginal cost is below average cost; and, when AC is rising, MC is greater than AC.[4] Figure 5.1a shows short-run average costs (SAC) and short-run marginal costs (SMC) and Figure 5.1b shows long-run average costs (LAC) and long-run marginal costs (LMC).

To make things easier, consider a situation in which every unit of output of a production process costs exactly the same to produce; then MC = AC and, instead of a cost curve, there would just be a horizontal line with the intercept on the vertical axis at that particular amount. As explained later in the context of competitive markets, the level of output at which AC = MC at output level Y in figure 5.1a is the optimal one in the short run for the firm in

---

[4] The following example may help to understand the relation between average and marginal. Take the average height of all the people in a room; let's say it is 1.75 metres. Now a new person comes into the room who is 1.8 metres tall: this 'marginal' person is taller than the average, so he or she raises the average. The average is rising and the marginal is higher than the average.

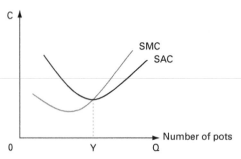

Figure 5.1a   Short-run cost curves

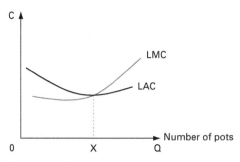

Figure 5.1b   Long-run cost curves

perfect competition, and point X in figure 5.1b is the optimal output in long-run perfect competition. In long-run equilibrium, points Y and X would coincide.

There are reasons to believe, however, that AC is not equal to MC except where they cross, because of two sets of circumstances: in the short run, the law of diminishing returns to a factor can be expected to come into force; and, in the long run, economies of scale are present.

The law of diminishing returns to a factor

As stated above, in the short run, when the amount of capital equipment and space are fixed so the scale of production cannot be changed, output can be altered only by varying the amount of labour and materials used in the production process. There are limits to how great an increase in output more workers or hours of work can produce, however, and this is expressed in economics as the 'law of diminishing returns to a factor'. This law states that the rate of increase in the productivity of labour (the output per unit of labour) will decline as more of it is employed to work with the fixed factors of production. This is because workers need capital equipment and space to work in and the extra output they can produce without an increase in that equipment is limited; under these conditions, the increase in the output they produce will get smaller and smaller. If a small pottery with one kiln for firing the pots hires more potters, it will at some point get more and more congested and the contribution each extra potter can make to increasing output will decline; this is what is meant by diminishing returns to labour as a factor of production. Bearing in mind that every extra hour of labour has to be paid for, either at the same wage or even at a higher wage rate, at some level of output, such as point Y in figure 5.1a, it becomes uneconomic to increase the hours of labour time as labour productivity or output per person falls.

Short-run costs

Initially, as the variable factors of production are increased, the short-run average cost of producing the good or service falls, but it will flatten out and eventually begin to rise as the capital constraint holds back the ability to produce ever more output with more labour and materials. This is why short-run average cost curves are drawn with a U shape. As explained above, MC < AC when AC is falling, and MC > AC when AC is rising. At the bottom of the U, there is a level of output at which SMC = SAC, at point Y in figure 5.1a.

In figure 5.1a, the example of the pottery is represented. Output is the number of pots produced; capital (the kiln and so on) is fixed in the short run and labour is the only variable factor of production. In accordance with the law of diminishing returns (in this case, to labour), SAC begins by falling as more labour (the number of potters working in the pottery) is added, reaches a minimum point Y and then starts to rise as congestion in the use of the capital (the kiln) sets in. At point Y, SAC is at a minimum, and so that represents the output at which the pottery is most efficient in the short run; at that point, that is the lowest SAC or unit cost for producing pots.

Economies of scale (returns to scale)

By contrast, in the long run, the scale of the whole enterprise (the firm) can be changed by adding or reducing the amount of space and capital equipment – say by investing in another kiln and expanding the workspace of the pottery – and there will be a long-run optimal size for the enterprise such that the potters can work efficiently. While the size of the pottery is small it could become more efficient if it expanded, but it is also likely that, eventually, it could become unmanageably big. This phenomenon is referred to as 'economies of scale' and 'diseconomies of scale'. When the scale of the operation increases and output increases more than in proportion to the increase in the quantity of factors used, we say there are increasing returns to scale; conversely, when the output grows at a lower rate than the factors used, there are decreasing returns to scale. In between is what in many circumstances would be the optimally efficient level of output, when an increase in inputs is matched by an equal increase in output – so-called constant returns to scale. This occurs at point X in figure 5.1b.

Returns to scale and costs

Returns to scale are reflected in the long-run average cost curve. When there are economies of scale (increasing returns), LAC falls; when there are diseconomies of scale (decreasing returns), LAC rises. Point X in Figure 5.1b is the minimum LAC at which the firm is deemed to be operating at its most efficient level of output, and the firm would therefore plan to produce that output in the long run.

Short run, long run and elasticity of supply

Short- and long-run costs also affect the supply price and therefore the elasticity of supply: the short-run elasticity of supply is lower (less responsive to price changes) than the long-run elasticity of supply. This is, simply, because the increase in output is limited by the capital and space constraint in the short run.

Fixed costs, sunk and historic costs

In economics, a distinction is made between fixed and sunk costs: sunk costs are the cost of capital equipment that cannot be 'amortised', meaning that there is no possibility of recouping the outlay on the investment by selling it to another user if the firm has to close down or cut back hard on production. A film set built for a particular film is a big investment that is very unlikely to be usable for another film, though the studio could be. Therefore, the cost of the film set is a sunk cost, but that of the studio a fixed cost.

Sunk costs are thought to be increasingly important in the production of information goods and feature prominently in theories about the size of firms (dealt with later on in the chapter). The significance of all this is that economists hold that fixed or sunk costs incurred in the past, called historic costs, should not be taken into account in calculating the cost of supplying a good; this doctrine of historic costs is very different from the way accountants think about costs, and it becomes important in thinking about the price at which the individual producer is willing to supply the market. As we see in what follows, it is marginal costs that determine supply, and marginal cost pricing is held to be the most efficient rule for setting the price and output of an enterprise.

Structure of the market: industrial organisation

In neoclassical economics, the emphasis is on how the price and output decisions of an individual enterprise are modified by the market it supplies through the price mechanism. The presence or absence of competition determines the economic structure of the industry. The theory is developed for profit-maximising enterprises and may not be relevant for non-profit organisations. I consider that later.

The monopolist firm

It seems reasonable to assume that all entrepreneurs would like to have a monopoly of the market so that they can control the market and set the price they wish to, though they are constrained in that by consumers' demand. What prevents firms from maintaining a monopoly position in the market is effective competition from other suppliers producing the same product. A firm supplying a new product that is first to the market may have a short-term monopoly before other competitors catch up: this is called 'first-mover advantage' or 'lead time' in the market. At one time this could be sufficient to prevent effective competition; for example, printing a book required setting up the type, and that was a considerable sunk cost that acted as a deterrent to anyone copying the book. This has been used as an argument against the need for protection by copyright law but, as the lead time has been considerably shortened with new copying technologies, the argument no longer carries the same conviction. Therefore, the question is not whether there is any element of monopoly but how persistent it is – can it be competed away by rival firms?

The neoclassical theory of monopoly can be summed up in a diagram. The firm's costs are depicted as AC and MC curves, as in figure 5.1 above. As the sole supplier to the market for this particular good, say of brand-name

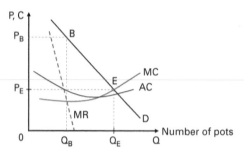

Figure 5.2   Supply of a monopoly compared with a competitive market

designer pottery, the market demand and the firm's demand schedule are the same thing – D in figure 5.2. Related to demand is marginal revenue (MR), which is the increase in total revenue as one more unit of output is sold. The firm has the objective of maximising profit, where profit is the excess of revenue over costs, and it therefore chooses the output at which the difference between total revenue and total cost is greatest. This is where marginal cost (MC) is equal to marginal revenue, and, in figure 5.2, that corresponds to output Q_B. At Q_B, we can see from D that the price at which Q_B will sell is P_B.

If the market consisted of competing firms, say ones producing identical pots, instead of a monopoly supplier of designer pots, point E would be the result, with a market price P_E and market supply of Q_E. At point E, the MC = MR rule also applies to competitive firms, but now marginal revenue is the price per item because each pot sells at the same price (see the explanation for the competitive firm below). This comparison of the two positions shows that the price (P_E) would be lower and the output (Q_E) greater in a competitive market than in a monopoly, and it is used to show the 'social cost' of monopoly; in this case, the monopoly is due to brand names of designer pots, but it could be due to a copyright or trademark or to other 'barriers to entry'. The demonstration that consumers are worse off with monopoly is the basis for the promotion of competition by economists, and this is achieved by the regulation of monopoly (antitrust) by competition law (as in the 'Paramount case'; see box 4.3).

Contestable markets

A 'contestable' market is one in which the monopoly of one firm can be challenged by new entrants when there is 'free entry', meaning that there are no 'barriers to entry'. The factors that might prevent freedom of entry are very high fixed costs or some legal impediment, such as patents and copyrights that constitute barriers to entry. As long as a market is contestable, the monopolist will not be able to exploit the consumer for long by charging a higher price, and that may be sufficient guarantee of protection for the consumer without the need for state regulation.

The firm in a competitive market

The neoclassical ideal is the competitive market, in which the forces of competition work freely to achieve the best use of resources and enable consumers to exercise the maximum choice of goods and services. Consumer sovereignty will rule as entrepreneurs seek to satisfy consumer tastes and demand. This ideal situation comes about because competition forces 'unfit' high-cost firms out of the market, leaving only low-cost, price-taking producers that are able to supply the market at the going equilibrium price. The price is the lowest possible that allows firms to survive and make sufficient profit to stay in production and meet market demand. The firm can adjust its level of output according to the market price in both the short and long run and the overall result is that the profit-maximising firm achieves its own equilibrium position at its most efficient level of production. This is illustrated in figure 5.3.

Figure 5.3 shows the long-run equilibrium position for a profit-maximising firm in a competitive market, where the market price is P_E. The firm is a price-taker and can sell any amount of its pots at the market price P_E but nothing if its price is higher than the market price; this is because it is producing a standard product and consumers do not see a difference between one firm's pots or another's. In those circumstances, the marginal revenue is the same as price or average revenue; thus $P = MR$. Profit maximisation indicates that the firm will choose the output at which $MC = MR$, and this also means that $MC = P$. In figure 5.3, in long-run equilibrium, the firm supplies Q_X number of pots at price P_E. Total revenue (TR) = $Q_X \times P_E$ and

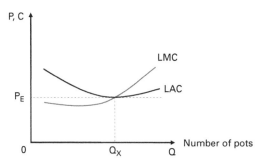

Figure 5.3   Long-run equilibrium output for a firm in a competitive market

total cost (TC) = Q_X x AC at point Q_X. Therefore, TR = TC and the firm breaks even, making what is called 'normal' profit.

At output Q_X, average cost (LAC) is at its minimum, and this is where marginal cost (LMC) is equal to LAC. This is also the point where the firm experiences constant returns to scale (at point X in figure 5.1b). Therefore, everything comes conveniently together, and the market price P_E covers not only the cost of producing an extra unit (LMC) but also the average costs (LAC), so the outcome is mutually beneficial for consumer and producer.

If the market price were to rise above P_E, the firm would make 'supernormal' profit, because TR would be greater than TC, but that would encourage entry by other firms and so the market supply schedule would shift down to the right (as in figure 3.1b) and cause the market price to fall back until all firms are just making normal profit at P_E. If the price falls below P_E, the firm would make a loss, as TR would be less than TC, and so it would have to leave (exit) the market.

With all firms in the market in long-run equilibrium, the sum of the output of each one constitutes the market supply. With the firm setting P = MC, the firm's MC curve is effectively its supply schedule.

So, to be clear: figure 5.2 represents the market in which a single monopoly firm charging P_B can be compared to what would be the case if the market consisted instead of competing firms, in which case the long-run equilibrium price would be P_E. Figure 5.3 analyses the output by a firm in a competitive market that is a price-taker at P_E, the long-run equilibrium price in the competitive market.

Marginal cost pricing

Marginal cost pricing, where the firm sets price equal to marginal cost as above, is crucial to much of neoclassical economics, including welfare economics. Marginal cost pricing is held by economists to be the best outcome for consumers, because setting price at marginal cost represents the lowest possible price at which enterprises can supply the market and when P = MC = AC – that is, in long-run equilibrium – competitive firms cover costs and make normal profit. This is not always feasible, however, and the case of 'natural monopoly' is particularly important in the creative industries as most enterprises are believed to be natural monopolies because of their high fixed costs.

Natural monopoly

It was argued earlier that there is a limit both in the short and long run to the efficient size and output capacity of the firm and that the cost of production per unit eventually rises, even in the long run (as in figure 5.1b). This is not the case in a certain category of enterprise known as a 'natural monopoly' – the situation in which there are economies of scale (increasing returns) and decreasing costs (falling LAC) over all conceivable levels of output. Such enterprises are expected to have very high fixed costs but also very low marginal costs. A natural monopoly was traditionally associated with industries in which there are networks, such as electricity and water utilities and cable TV; many of the creative industries and other information industries are now believed to share these characteristics, however, especially with digitisation, which has typically reduced marginal costs to almost zero (see chapter 14). This has significant implications for the regulation of these industries by competition authorities, and, as explained in what follows, for subsidy to cultural organisations.

The monopoly is 'natural' as there is no possibility of contestability through the market, for two basic reasons: one, the high fixed (or sunk) costs act as a barrier to entry; and, second, competitive firms would have to set P = MC, but that would not allow them to recoup the high fixed costs, since MC is less than ATC (see figure 5.4). Moreover, breaking up a natural monopoly by a regulator would increase unit costs, because economies of scale would not be fully exploited and therefore the consumer would have to pay a higher price.

The best outcome for a regulated natural monopoly is marginal cost pricing combined with some method of covering fixed costs; however, this may have to be imposed by government intervention. One such solution is to subsidise the fixed costs; another is to charge a certain amount to cover the fixed cost – the so-called 'two-part tariff', with two prices, one set at marginal cost and one to cover the fixed cost. A water or cable connection charge is a classic example of such a charge for a private for-profit utility; subsidy is common for non-profit organisations in the arts and heritage, as illustrated in figure 5.4. This is discussed further in chapter 7.

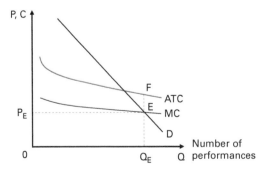

Figure 5.4   Natural monopoly with a two-part tariff

Figure 5.4 illustrates the situation in which a natural monopolist, say a theatre, is encouraged to use marginal cost pricing. With increasing returns to scale, MC is always below average total cost since it is falling, and so setting P = MC at E and producing output Q_E will not cover total costs; however, a subsidy of EF per unit would cover the fixed-cost element in ATC and enable marginal cost pricing at output Q_E and price P_E to be used to raise the revenue $0P_EEQ_E$ from sales. Total revenue would therefore be $0P_EEQ_E$ + EF x Q_E. Subsidy would be paid only to a non-profit firm but, in fact, exactly the same analysis applies to a for-profit firm, such as a cable television company; in this case, EF x Q_E could be financed by advertising and each programme would have a price according to MC.

The point about a regulated natural monopoly is that consumers are better off because they pay the marginal cost of the item they use as they would if there were a competitive market, but, if the natural monopoly were broken up into smaller competing firms, they would not have such low costs as with the increasing returns/falling costs case, and so prices would be higher.

Comparison of a profit-maximising (for profit) and a non-profit monopoly

It has been suggested several times in this chapter that the supply and pricing policy of a non-profit organisation would be different from that of a for-profit firm. In order to make the contrast, assume that both the for-profit and the non-profit firm are natural monopolies and that they face the same costs of production. ATC, average total cost, falls as the output Q increases; thus MC is below ATC, as in figure 5.4. Figure 5.5 contrasts these two types of price-setting behaviour; B is a for-profit theatre and N is a non-profit theatre. The only difference between them is that the profit-maximising enterprise B (commercial theatre, film-maker, and so on) sets its price and output so as

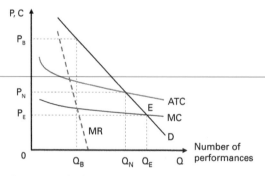

Figure 5.5   Comparison of a for-profit and a non-profit theatre

to get the maximum profit at output Q_B by choosing the level of output at which equates MC = MR (as in figure 5.2). By contrast, it is expected that the non-profit theatre N aims to reach as great an audience as possible, and that can be achieved by setting the price so that average cost is just covered by average revenue (the price per unit), which is represented by D, the demand schedule; thus output is chosen where ATC = D, at output Q_N.

Figure 5.5 shows that the profit-maximising theatre would set its output at Q_B and charge price P_B. The non-profit theatre chooses Q_N and P_N. Theatre B will play to much smaller audiences than theatre N and its prices are much higher, so it can be assumed that only better-off people go to that theatre. Notice, however, that neither theatre would produce at point E, where P = MC, without either public subsidy or private donations or sponsorship. Therefore, subsidy to a non-profit organisation would achieve a lower price, P_E, than the enterprise could achieve itself. This is explained in chapter 7 (see figure 7.4).

Other forms of industrial structure

Between the extremes of monopoly and perfect competition lie two other market forms: monopolistic competition and oligopoly. These are more likely to be found in practice in the cultural sector than in the economy at large. Monopolistic competition combines the downward-sloping demand schedule of monopoly with the presence of competition; the monopoly is not very strong because there is the possibility for the consumer of substituting between suppliers of a similar but not identical good or service; thus a local theatre or cinema has a local monopoly, but, if one charges a much higher price than the neighbouring theatre or cinema, consumers would switch to that instead. Monopolistic competition also applies to products such as book, film and record titles; each is different but consumers may find it easy to substitute between film or books of the same genre, for example. Economists treat the copyright 'monopoly' in terms of monopolistic competition because copyright does not prevent competition with similar items, just the copying of one particular item.

Oligopoly is a situation in which there are only a few firms in the market; they behave like monopolists in terms of being price-makers but are restricted by the policies of their rivals, with which they compete for a share of the market. They are believed to act in such a way as to avoid an all-out price war by mimicking each other in terms of the price and quality of their products. The sound recording industry is a prominent example in the cultural sector of an oligopoly as the four 'majors' dominate the industry (see chapter 15).

Price collusion – agreeing to charge the same price, for instance – is illegal, being contrary to competition law, but it can be hard to prove, and the fact that different firms charge the same or very similar prices for similar goods is, in itself, no proof of collusive behaviour.

Summing up on the neoclassical theory of supply

The apparently simple law of supply that the quantity supplied by the market rises as price increases turns out to be a complex story at the level of the individual firm: it involves the interaction of the underlying conditions of production and technological constraints (as determined by the production function), the costs of production (as determined by supply and demand in the markets for factors of production), the objectives of the firm as to profit-making and the contestability of the market by competitors.

The neoclassical theory of the firm assumes that market pressures working through the price mechanism are the most important influence on the firm's decision-taking and that this is what determines the structure of the industry.

The neoclassical view of the firm has been challenged on various grounds, as we now go on to discuss. Nevertheless, there are prominent economists who believe it is relevant for understanding the cultural sector and the creative or 'information' economy, and most economists, whatever their persuasion, use the essential notions of economies of scale and the law of diminishing returns to a factor. In addition, some of the results associated with the neoclassical paradigm, in particular marginal cost pricing, are fundamental to the broader view of the market economy that is taken in welfare economics and in many other applications, such as the economics of copyright and competition law. It therefore has a wider significance than just as a theory of firm behaviour.

Other approaches to industrial organisation

The main criticism of the neoclassical economic theory of the firm is that it has nothing to say about management decisions of firms or the internal organisation of firms – that is, about how real firms behave. It stresses instead the influence of market prices, to which the firm can only respond but cannot control, and the constraints of the production function; it also assumes that entrepreneurs are fully and costlessly informed about all market prices and transactions. Thus, in that theory, the role of the entrepreneur is extremely limited. Managerial economics, developed early on by William Baumol (see box 1.1), and transaction cost theory, associated with Ronald Coase and Oliver Williamson (see box 5.4), seek to remedy the absence of an economic theory of firm behaviour. Two aspects are dealt with briefly here: the so-called 'make-or-buy' decision and transaction costs. Bear in mind that what all these different theories are getting at is to explain the size of firms in an industry and therefore the extent of competition in the market – that is, the economic organisation of industries. This in turn determines the choice of products available to consumers, their prices and the size of firm in which workers are employed.

Integration of firms

The size of an enterprise is influenced not only by its costs of production and technology but also by the management choices it makes with respect to integration with other firms. Integration is achieved through mutually agreed mergers but also by acquisitions, when one firm buys another, possibly in a hostile takeover. The purpose of integration is typically to expand operations by economies of scale and scope and to increase profitability.

There are two basic types of integration: horizontal and vertical. Horizontal integration is when firms merge with or acquire competitors (an example being mergers between record labels in the music industry – see chapter 15). In vertical integration, an 'upstream' firm supplies to a 'downstream' firm. This reflects the fact that most goods go through various stages of production – the 'chain of production', discussed in chapter 4 – before they are sold to the final consumer (an example is integration between music publishers and record labels).

Mergers and acquisitions can result in very large dominant firms and therefore may be subject to regulation by competition authorities. Integration is an important aspect of the creative industries, and it is discussed in Part IV.

Make or buy?

One big decision the firm has to make is whether to make all the component parts in its chain of production itself or to buy them in from independent suppliers via the market. If it makes all components, it can control the process, delivery dates, quality, and so forth but it may sacrifice the efficiency gains from specialisation; it may also become large and unwieldy and suffer from diseconomies of scale in management. If instead the enterprise buys in its component parts (inputs), however, it puts itself in the hands of the suppliers, which might exploit its dependence on them by threatening to hold up production, increase their prices or reduce the quality of their product. On the other hand, buying inputs on the open market means that there are benefits of specialisation in terms of lower costs that even a large integrated firm could not achieve internally. It is also less likely that a large enterprise is able to adopt new technologies speedily.

The make-or-buy decision is regarded by economists as one of the most important problems to be tackled by the manager of an enterprise, and it is one of the main determinants of the structure of an industry, since the degree of integration determines the size of the firm. The decision is faced by non-profit as well as for-profit firms; for example, a museum must decide whether to undertake its own restoration work or whether to buy in the services from another museum or specialist restorer. It might also decide to organise its own shop and print its own posters and other merchandise rather than get an outside firm to do so.

As we see in what follows, the make-or-buy decision has significant implications for the cost of the transactions involved as well as for the management structure of the firm.

Transaction cost theory of the firm

When the enterprise buys in its inputs from other firms on the open market, it must have a contract with them that lays down the conditions of sale – the agreed price, quantity, quality, delivery date, and so on. Negotiating contracts takes time and the expenditure of resources and therefore has costs. Such costs are called 'transaction costs', and the importance of these costs in the strategic decisions of the firm has given rise to the so-called 'transaction cost theory' of the firm, first introduced by Ronald Coase and developed by Oliver Williamson (see box 5.4). According to this theory, the firm seeks to minimise transaction costs in taking its make-or-buy decision, and this is what determines the size of the enterprise.

Transaction costs include various kinds of costs that arise because entrepreneurs do not have full information about conditions in the market and about the intentions of those with whom they make contracts; they need to search out possible suppliers and buyers and obtain information about prices in the market; there are also bargaining costs involved in drawing up and agreeing contracts with their workers and with suppliers of other inputs and in monitoring the costs of enforcing contracts, checking the quality of materials supplied, and so on. Box 5.4 explains this in more detail.

Box 5.4 Transaction cost theories of Ronald Coase and Oliver Williamson

Ronald Coase (1910–), a British-born economist who spent much of his career in the United States, is the Clifton R. Musser Professor Emeritus of Economics at the University of Chicago Law School. He won the Nobel Prize in Economics in 1991 for, essentially, two path-breaking articles, both of which have had a profound effect on the development of economics over the last fifty years or so. His first article, 'The nature of the firm', published in 1937, barely attracted notice until much later; it asked the seemingly strange question: why are there firms at all? As anyone can in principle assemble the necessary inputs to produce the goods they want, why do firms exist? Coase's answer, unlike Adam Smith's on specialisation, was that the cost of using the market – searching out sources of inputs, comparing prices, and so on – uses up resources, and when these activities are co-ordinated by a hierarchical organisation with an internal command structure – that is, a firm – transaction costs are minimised.

Coase's second article, 'The problem of social cost' (1960), revolutionised thinking about 'market failure' – situations in which the legitimate actions of one person impose costs upon others. Coase put forward the proposition that market failure need not be corrected by government intervention through taxes and subsidies, as was at the time believed (and, to some extent, still is – see chapter 7 of this book), as long as property rights were fully specified and clearly assigned; when that is so, any dispute over damage can be negotiated or, if necessary, resolved through the courts. What prevents that in practice is the presence of the transaction costs of so doing. Therefore, in what has come to be called 'the Coase theorem', it is transaction costs that prevent property rights from solving such problems; if transaction costs were zero, the initial assignment of property rights would not matter, as they could be traded on the market costlessly and would go to the owner who could make best use of them. With this analysis, Coase also laid the foundation of the discipline of law and economics. He also did the earliest work on the economics of broadcasting – a 1950 book on the United Kingdom's BBC and a famous article criticising the operation of the US Federal Communications Commission in its policy of licensing the electromagnetic spectrum, putting forward the sale of property rights as a more efficient method of allocating spectrum to users.

Oliver Williamson (1932–) was a student of Ronald Coase and is now the Edgar F. Kaiser Professor Emeritus at the Haas School of Business at the University of California at Berkeley. His contribution to the theory of the firm was to extend transaction cost theory by arguing that the existence of the firm is due to its having 'specific assets' that are unique to it and that have much lower value outside the context of that firm.[a] (An example from the world of the arts is a string quartet; when one member leaves it can be very difficult to find a replacement, but, equally, that member's value is higher with that quartet than playing with other musicians.) If these specific assets are separately owned, there will be opportunities for costly hold-ups and even cheating, so that combining ownership overcomes such problems of what Williamson called 'opportunism' – hence the existence of the firm.

[a] Williamson was a Nobel Laureate in 2009.

These transaction costs have given rise to a whole theory of the firm – transaction cost economics – that explains the existence of the firm as a means of reducing those costs that would arise if producers had to contract with each other for every input. Within the firm, managers can order actions to be taken rather than having to negotiate agreement on every transaction. Thus the firm is managed or 'governed' within in a different way in this theoretical framework.

The property rights approach

In a similar vein, the scope and size of the firm can also be analysed in terms of what is called the property rights approach. In this approach, the firm is understood to be a 'bundle of property rights'. Recognition of the role of property rights has swept through economics, and especially law and economics, over the last twenty years, largely thanks to Coase and the Coase theorem (see box 5.4).

In the information economy, property rights are especially important in relation to non-tangible goods and to services. If a firm supplies tangible goods, it can control their use by withholding them from the market: if you do not pay for a bicycle, the supplier does not let you take it away. If someone is not paid for the work he or she has done, he or she does not work for the employer again and the law will support his or her claim for recovering payment. With intangible 'goods', such as the creation of a novel or a song, copyright law establishes the property right (hence the term 'intellectual property'), without which the rights owner would easily lose control of the work and the payment due to it. The main point about property rights is that the ownership of the power to control something can be divorced from the physical control of it; so, for example, the video formatting of a film is done by the transfer of a specific set of rights in a film to the video firm. It is these rights that are transacted in contracts, and the problem of specifying them in sufficient detail so as to avoid the possibility of misunderstanding is what lies at the back of transaction costs. The widespread use of contracts has led to this branch of theory being also called 'contract theory' by some economists; this is used by Richard Caves in his important book on the economics of the creative industries, which is discussed at length in chapter 14.

Summary and conclusion

This chapter has provided an overview of the theory of supply and the role that costs play in it. Supply to the market for a product is the quantity of the good or service that all enterprises in the market are willing to supply at various prices. A number of factors influence the individual firm's supply decisions, in particular costs of production and transaction costs. Furthermore, the decision of the individual enterprise (for-profit and non-profit) whether or not to integrate and control the whole chain of production and distribution (upstream and downstream) is what determines the structure of the market – that is, if the industry is competitive or a monopoly or oligopoly. In fact, as we shall see in chapter 14, there is a strong tendency in some of the creative industries towards oligopoly, and, given the unique nature of most cultural products, monopolistic competition predominates in others. Antitrust and competition authorities, however, may break up firms that become too dominant in the market to protect consumers from being exploited.

Two schools of thought on the factors influencing the firm's supply were presented: neoclassical theory, which emphasises the constraints of technology and the pressure of the market on the firm via price, while the transaction cost and property rights theories look for managerial explanations for the size of the firm and analyse its structure via theories of contracting. Contract theory is developed fully in chapter 14.

As a conclusion, it can be said that there is not necessarily any incompatibility between these theories of firm behaviour and the theory of supply. Each stresses a different feature of the firm's experience. Considerable technological change or turbulence can alter the structure of property rights and even make some unenforceable; this has happened with the advent of digital technologies. Monopolies can develop and then be quickly destroyed in the process of capitalistic creative destruction that comes with dynamic growth and innovation. Small firms with clever entrepreneurs can find gaps in the market that they can exploit with little or no external finance; most go to the wall but some grow to become giants. In the final analysis, that is the way the market economy works.

Further reading

The neoclassical theory of supply is to be found in any elementary textbook of economics, such as chapters 7 to 10 of the Baumol and Blinder (2006) textbook mentioned earlier. My preference in elementary textbooks is John Sloman's (2006) *Economics*, which has its own workbook and editions for various countries as well as its own website; chapters 5, 6 and 8 cover the material of this chapter. An article that students have often found useful is by

Oliver Hart (1989), which contrasts the neoclassical, transaction cost and property rights approaches. A simple exposition of transaction cost economics is on Wikipedia under 'transaction cost'. For those interested in a more detailed treatment, the article by Matthias Klaes (2008) in *The New Palgrave Dictionary of Economics* is worth reading and accessible. This dictionary can be found in the reference section of the library; not every article is easy to read but it is interesting to browse in it a bit.

6 Consumption of cultural goods and services

This chapter deals with the demand side of the market – the consumption of cultural goods and services. In economic terms, the buyers, audiences, visitors and viewers of the whole range of cultural products of the creative industries can be thought of as 'consumers' when they buy an item such as a ticket to go to a concert or to visit a monument or when they buy a book. Two aspects of the consumption of cultural products are analysed: patterns of consumption as revealed by consumers' purchases of cultural goods and services, and the theory of demand, which seeks to explain the choices consumers make. Consumer spending is the source of revenue for producers; for for-profit suppliers it is their sole source, and for subsidised non-profit organisations it represents some proportion of their income. Understanding consumer behaviour is also achieved by analysing participation in cultural activities by looking at the socio-economic profiles of consumers.

Participation and demand

Participation in the arts and heritage may take place with or without payment for admission, and the characteristics of participants, such as age and family background, are important information for policy-makers. The theory of demand seeks to explain consumer behaviour in terms of the economic factors that affect consumer decision-making, in particular price and income. Studies of participation are complementary to the theory of demand because they provide a picture of consumers that economic variables alone cannot. Studies of demand for and participation in cultural activities form the basis for marketing cultural products for both for-profit and non-profit suppliers.

Participation and cultural policy

Cultural policy aims to broaden participation in the arts and culture, and one of the main means of implementing policy is by subsidising arts organisations so that they can charge lower prices. It is important to know if this policy works. If, say, it transpired that all participants in an art form were well off and willing to pay a price that covered the full cost of producing it, not only would there be little point to subsidy but, to make matters worse, less well off taxpayers would be financing the consumption of the better off. The question, though, is whether people can be persuaded by lower prices to participate; if people do not have the taste for something, no matter how low the price, they may not want to consume it whether they are rich or poor. The theory of demand studies the interaction of consumers' tastes and economic variables, and, even though we cannot observe people's tastes, consumption behaviour is an indicator of their tastes and preferences.

Consumption of cultural goods and services

Data on consumption are typically gathered by national statistical offices and published on a regular basis. They include the consumption of cultural goods and services. Different categories are used by the various national offices. Table 6.1 shows average consumer spending in the United States on a selection of items.[1] Notice that they include goods and services, 'hardware' and 'software'.

Analysis of trends in the consumption of these items from 2001 to 2005 showed that total consumer expenditure in real terms (i.e. taking inflation into account) on the performing arts had risen less than the increase in both GDP and spending on recreation; spending on movies had fallen, however (see table 6.2).

Table 6.1 Average consumer spending in the United States, 2004 (US dollars)

All entertainment	2,218
Admissions to movies, theatre, opera, ballet	92
Video game hardware and software	18
Video cassettes and discs	43
Radios and sound equipment	135
All reading	130
Books	50
Newspaper subscriptions	42
Magazine subscriptions	15

Source: US Department of Labor, Bureau of Labor Statistics, Consumer Expenditure Survey: selected entertainment categories.

[1] NEA (2006).

Table 6.2 Percentage change in real GDP and consumer spending on cultural goods and services, 2001–5

GDP	11.7
Personal consumption spending	13.5
Recreation consumption spending	31.1
Admissions to performing arts events	1.9
Admissions to movie theatres	−6.9
Books and maps	19.6
Magazines, newspapers and sheet music	14.0
Video and audio goods	52.1
Commercial amusements	21.6

Source: US Department of Commerce, Bureau of Economic Analysis.

Table 6.3 Average weekly household expenditure on cultural goods and services in Australia, 2003/4 (Australian dollars)

Literature	8.43
Music	1.65
Performing arts	1.59
Visual arts and crafts	1.66
Broadcasting, electronic media and film	7.87
Other arts	1.86
Heritage	0.39
Other culture	12.94
Total	36.40

Source: Australian Bureau of Statistics (2008).

European data on consumption expenditure on cultural goods and services cover similar but not the same items and they are expressed both in terms of euros and PPS, the purchasing power standard that reflects the differing levels of GDP and prices within the European Community (explained in chapter 2). In 1999 the share of cultural expenditure in total expenditure was 4.5 per cent for the EU-15; Sweden and Denmark had the highest, with 5.6 per cent, and Greece and Lithuania the lowest, at 2.7 per cent.[2]

In 2003/4 Australian households spent 4 per cent of their total expenditure on cultural goods and services.[3] Table 6.3 shows average weekly expenditure by Australians on the arts and culture; like the US data, they include items such as musical instruments and television sets.

[2] Eurostat (2007).
[3] Australian Bureau of Statistics (2008). In 2003/4 the Australian dollar was roughly equivalent to US$ 1.3.

Participation studies

Participation in the arts and culture is usually measured through surveys that collect data on attendance at a range of cultural activities and also amateur participation in them, such as acting in plays, playing a musical instrument, taking photographs, reading books, and so on. Some of these studies are carried out by organisations that exist to promote the arts but they are also done as part of wider social surveys of consumption patterns of goods and services by government statistical offices and people's use of time (see time budget surveys below). Respondents to the surveys are asked what types of items they participated in over a set period, usually a year, and how often they undertook the activity – how many visits they made to the theatre, a museum, how many books they bought or read, and so forth. As with previous data, countries adopt different categories and may also survey different age groups. Ireland has a particularly detailed survey on attendance (see table 6.4); in addition, 19 per cent of those surveyed said they had taken part in at least one type of arts activity in the last year.

Socio-economic characteristics

Participation surveys may also include questions on socio-economic variables, such as income, occupation, family size, age, gender, ethnic origin, and so on, that provide a profile of the typical participant. Eurostat collects such data for the twenty-seven countries of the European Union (EU-27) and presents them in terms of gender, age and level of education and by eight socio-economic occupational groupings (managers, other white-collar, self-employed, manual, students, unemployed, house persons, retired). Table 6.5 shows the percentage of the population of the EU-27 participating in cultural activities at least once a year for some groups – women, manual workers and retired persons.

Participation and consumption

Participation in the arts and heritage is sometimes inferred from attendances or ticket sales. Not every attendee has to buy a ticket; some people may also have access without paying, perhaps because they are eligible for free entry (children, senior citizens) or even because entry is free to all (as in some national museums). Thus the total of attendances may exceed the number of consumers. Conversely, a frequently made mistake in the context of using participation data is to make claims about the popularity of the arts by

Table 6.4 Attendance at arts activities in Ireland, 2006 (percentage of population that attended)

Category of event	2006
Mainstream film	57
A play	30
Rock or popular music	28
Open-air street theatre/spectacle	19
Traditional Irish or folk music	19
Stand-up comedy	18
Musical	17
Variety show/pantomime	16
Art exhibitions	15
Circus	13
Country and western music	10
Traditional/folk dance	8
Jazz/blues music	7
Classical music concert or recital	7
Arthouse film	5
World music	5
Readings (e.g. literature/poetry)	5
Opera	4
Contemporary dance	3
Ballet	2
Other live music performance	17
Other dance performance	7

Source: Council of Europe/ERICarts (2008): Ireland.

Table 6.5 EU-27 participation in cultural activities, 2007 (percentage)

	All	Women	Manual workers	Retired
Visited historical monuments (palaces, castles, churches, gardens, etc.)	54	53	53	42
Been to the cinema	51	50	57	20
Visited museums or galleries	41	41	35	31
Been to a concert	37	36	35	25
Visited a public library	35	37	28	23
Been to the theatre	32	34	24	25
Seen a ballet, a dance performance or an opera	18	19	13	15

Source: Eurostat (2007).

inferring the number of *people* participating from the number of tickets sold by arts organisations over a period of time. Many people who attend one thing (a concert, for instance) are strongly disposed to visit another (say a museum). If it is the same people going to everything, the number of attendances overestimates the number of people involved. Participation surveys may also ask respondents about multiple 'omnivore' attendances and analyse the combination of cultural products that they buy.

Time budget studies

Time budget studies provide data on how people from a given population (such as a national state) spend their time. They are now carried out by many countries and can be very detailed. They measure in hours the use of time spent on a range of activities, including the arts and culture; for instance, data for Canada show that, for persons aged fifteen and older participating at least once a year in cultural activities, average daily cultural activity time use in 2005 was:

- 135 minutes watching television;
- 13.5 minutes reading books;
- 9.8 minutes reading newspapers;
- 3.2 minutes surfing the internet;
- 2.3 minutes going to a movie; and
- 2.2 minutes reading magazines.[4]

Audience/visitor surveys

The above data relate to national average participation in a range of cultural activities. Audience surveys are surveys undertaken by individual arts organisations in order to understand the characteristics of their audiences and visitors for purposes such as marketing and making a case for financial support. Museums seem to have been most diligent in this, and there are multitudes of surveys of museum visitors. For example, London's Tate Modern, which opened in May 2000, had 21.5 million visitors in its first five years. Surveys found that the most popular visiting hour at the Tate Modern was Saturday between 2 p.m. and 3 p.m., with over 2,000 visitors; visitors typically stayed one and three-quarter hours; just over a half of all visitors were male and 60 per cent of visitors were under thirty-five years of age; 40 per cent

---

[4] Council of Europe/ERICarts (2008).

were repeat visitors and 40 per cent came from abroad.[5] This information is obviously important for the organisation's marketing and planning purposes.

Demand and revenue

All the above data represent people's choices but they do not tell us what economic factors influence their decisions to consume one item or another. Demand theory analyses consumers' choices in terms of the relative prices of goods and services, consumers' incomes and their tastes and preferences. The demand schedule may be drawn up for an individual or for the market; market demand was shown in figure 3.1 as the relation between the quantities of a good that would be bought at various prices: when the price is high, fewer consumers will buy the good, and, when it is low, more will buy it.

The revenue to the enterprise from sales of the good is the other side of the coin. In chapter 5, the demand schedule was shown also to represent the average revenue to the seller. In the cultural sector, sales revenues are not necessarily the only source of income, and a private enterprise supplier is likely to be far more reliant on sales than a non-profit organisation that also has income from grants and donations. Consumers are not just a source of income, however; they are also participants who are signalling their satisfaction with a product or a visit. Their participation is an indicator of the success of a product. Economists are able to go further than the mere fact of participation and look at the degree of satisfaction as evidenced by the willingness to pay for it – the sensitivity of demand to prices. Understanding consumers' demand decisions, therefore, is an important aspect of cultural economics. This is especially so for policy purposes, since the main thrust of subsidy to the arts is to reduce prices to consumers. We shall also see that the standard economic theory of consumer behaviour needs to be extended to deal with cultural products, and that demand as expressed in the marketplace falls short of the full extent of society's willingness to support the arts and heritage and some elements of other creative industries.

Sales and revenue

As with supply, it is necessary to measure the units of the quantity demanded of the good or service in question, such as the number of books or CDs or the

[5] Tate (2005).

number of tickets to a museum or performance. Sales are the number of items sold, and total revenue is simply the quantity sold times the price that is paid. When there is price discrimination there is demand at the different prices for the same good or service, say a seat in a theatre, and then the demand for the performance would be the number of tickets sold at each price and total revenue that number times the price paid. Price discrimination is dealt with in more detail below.

Demand schedule

The quantity demanded (Q_D) can be expressed as a function of the price of the good (P), the price of other goods (P_Z), the consumer's income (Y) and tastes and preferences (T); later on, each of these variables is discussed in turn. This can be written as follows:

$$Q_D = f(P, P_Z, Y, T)$$

The relation between Q_D and P is negative and, accordingly, the demand schedule, D, which shows the relation between them, slopes down.

Movements along and shifts in the demand schedule

As P changes, Q_D changes, and this is a movement along the demand schedule. The other variables cause a shift in the demand schedule. The relation between Q_D and P_Z, the price of other goods, is complex. Some goods and services are complements, meaning that the consumer likes to consume both goods together (for example, an iPod and iTunes); then, if the price of the complement goes up, Q_D goes down, and that is represented as a shift to the left of the demand schedule. On the other hand, when goods are substitutes (say CDs and online music services) and their prices rise, Q_D would increase as consumers switch to the cheaper option, causing a shift to the right of the demand schedule, D.

Income is assumed to have a positive effect on Q_D and people will consume more as Y increases, and if people's tastes, T, change in favour of the good they will buy more at each price; both these effects would shift the demand schedule out to the right.

A shift in the demand schedule can be read in two equivalent ways: that more of the good will be bought at each price or that consumers are willing to pay a higher price for each quantity of the good.

Table 6.6 Imaginary demand for theatre tickets

Q (number of tickets)	P (price in euros)
100	40
200	35
300	30
400	25
500	20
600	15
700	10

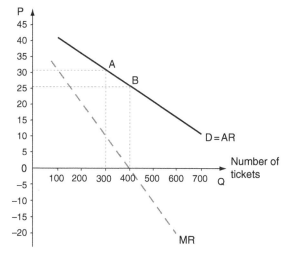

Figure 6.1   Demand, average revenue and marginal revenue

A numerical example

We can use some figures involving an imaginary demand schedule for theatre tickets to illustrate. Figure 6.1 plots the data in table 6.6 as a diagram. In figure 6.1, starting with the highest price of €40, 100 tickets are demanded; at price €35, 200 tickets are demanded; at a price of €30, the quantity demanded is 300; and so on. This results in the demand schedule marked D, the demand facing the theatre. Demand is also the same as average revenue (AR) – that is, total revenue (TR) averaged over the quantity bought.

Individual demand and willingness to pay (WTP)

The demand schedule can represent an individual person's demand, showing how much he or she is willing to pay for various quantities of a good, thereby reflecting the satisfaction or 'utility' he or she has for the good; if someone has a very strong preference for a particular good, he or she would be willing to pay more and maybe give up something else in order to be able to afford it. The strength of an individual's preferences cannot be directly observed, however; all we know from the demand function is that Q_D is the result of the interaction between all the variables in the equation, and the demand schedule maps the influence of the price of the good, P, holding the other variables constant. This is interpreted as willingness to pay, a concept that is very important in cultural economics.

Consumer surplus

Figure 6.1 can also be used to explain WTP and the concept of 'consumer surplus'. One of the contributions of economics is to point out that, if a single price is set below the WTP of some consumers, potential revenue is lost to the enterprise (the theatre in the above example). This is called consumer surplus, and it is the area under the demand schedule above the price that is being charged. For instance, in figure 6.1, let us say the theatre decided to charge a single price of €30, corresponding to point A. Consumer surplus is then the triangle above the horizontal line at A. Anyone willing to pay more than €30 is better off; that is the consumer surplus. It is possible to calculate by how much they are better off in terms of WTP: each of the people willing to pay €40 are better off by €10 and those willing to pay €35 are better off by €5. So the theatre has 'lost' 10 x 100 = €1,000 plus 5 x 200 = €1,000, a total of €2,000 that it could have taken in revenue if it had charged those prices.

Price discrimination

We can now be more precise about the advantages to an enterprise of price discrimination as compared to charging a single price. Notice that, by the same logic as the above, buyers whose WTP is less than €30 do not buy a ticket at that price; therefore, potential buyers to the right of point A on the demand schedule 'drop out' of the market. If, however, the theatre is able to set a range of prices that perfectly matches WTP, it could eliminate the consumer surplus and capture it as its revenue. With the same demand data as table 6.6, we can compare total revenue with and without price discrimination.

With a single price of €30, the number of tickets sold is 300 and total revenue is €9,000. If the theatre were to divide up its seats into sections with 100 seats in each and sell 100 tickets at €40, 100 at €35 and 100 at €30, it would generate revenues of €10,500 (4,000 + 3,500 + 3,000). This price discrimination taps the different willingness to pay and maximises revenue – compare that to the total revenue of €9,000 at a price of €30. Notice that, even if it charges a lower single price of €25, it would still not achieve the maximum revenue and would just increase consumer surplus.

Price discrimination is possible, however, only if the enterprise is a price-maker with monopoly power in the market. If the market is perfectly competitive, that would result in a single equilibrium price ruling the market, and each enterprise would have to supply at that price or lose all trade to competitors. There will always be some consumer surplus and lost potential revenue in a competitive market. In the case of a theatre, it seems likely that it would have some degree of monopoly, because it presents a different play with different actors. If its prices are far out of line with those of other theatres, however, it could lose audiences to them.

Price discrimination is not worthwhile unless the buyers can be separated so that there is no arbitrage (in a theatre there are numbered seats), and there also has to be a different elasticity of demand for each group. This is explained below.

Marginal revenue (MR)

Before turning to elasticity of demand, we need to define marginal revenue. MR is the increase in revenue to an enterprise that results from the sale of one more unit of output, in this example a theatre ticket. When the price is the same for each unit sold (as in perfect competition), then marginal revenue and price are the same (see figure 5.3). When the demand schedule is downward-sloping, however, indicating that the quantity demanded rises as the price falls, marginal revenue is different at every point. So, referring to table 6.7,

Table 6.7 Total revenue and marginal revenue

Q (number of tickets)	P (price in euros) = AR	TR (total revenue)	MR (marginal revenue)
100	40	4,000	
200	35	7,000	30
300	30	9,000	20
400	25	10,000	10
500	20	10,000	0
600	15	9,000	−10
700	10	7,000	−20

when the number of tickets demanded rises from 300 to 400, corresponding to a fall in price from €30 to €25, total revenue rises by €1,000. Marginal revenue is the change in total revenue divided by the change in quantity, which is 100 tickets. So, as the price falls from €30 to €25 and TR rises by €1,000, MR = 1,000/100 = 10. This is illustrated in table 6.7, which uses the data from table 6.6 along with the figures for TR and MR. The fourth column in table 6.7 shows MR as Q_D and P change, and this is illustrated in figure 6.1.

Price elasticity of demand

Like elasticity of supply, elasticity of demand measures the percentage change in quantity due to a change in price, but this time it is quantity demanded. Moreover, since there is a negative relationship between price and demand, elasticity of demand is a negative number. The important thing, however, is the actual number in absolute terms: if the figure is greater than one, then demand is elastic (greater than −1); this means that a reduction in the price will result in a more than proportionate increase in the quantity demanded.

The formula for calculating elasticity of demand is:

percentage (proportionate) change in Q_D ÷ percentage (proportionate) change in P

A numerical example of how to calculate this using the figures in table 6.7 is as follows.

- Starting from the point P = 30 and Q_D = 300, let price fall to €25.
- As P falls from €30 to €25, Q_D rises from 300 to 400.
- At P = 30, the proportionate change (fall) in price is −5/30 = −1/6.
- At Q_D = 300, the proportionate change in quantity demanded is 100/300 = 1/3.
- Therefore the elasticity of demand is 1/3 / −1/6 = −2.

This shows that the demand schedule at that point is elastic. Notice that this is calculated at one point on the demand schedule; in fact, elasticity of demand varies at every point on the demand schedule (as a quick calculation using table 6.7 data will prove); it is important therefore to calculate the elasticity of demand around a particular P and Q_D point.

Relation of elasticity of demand to revenue

There is a straightforward mathematical relation between elasticity of demand and revenue that can be explained fairly easily from the starting point of what is called unit elasticity of demand – that is, when elasticity of demand is equal to -1. When the percentage (proportionate) change in Q_D is equal to percentage (proportionate) change in P, elasticity of demand is equal to -1 (unit elasticity). At that point, there is no change in the total revenue and so marginal revenue = 0. This is shown at point B in figure 6.1. So, if a 10 per cent reduction in P results in a 10 per cent increase in the number of tickets demanded, TR is unchanged. This provides a very useful benchmark for a general rule about the relation between elasticity of demand and revenue: when demand is elastic (> -1) a reduction in the price will result in an increase in TR (MR > 0) and an increase in price will reduce it; thus P and TR move in opposite directions. If demand is inelastic (< -1), a reduction in price reduces TR and an increase in price increases TR (so P and TR move in the same direction). Point B in figure 6.1 corresponds to the point on the horizontal axis (measuring Q) at which MR = 0, the point at which TR is at its maximum. Thus anywhere to the left of point B on the demand schedule is relatively elastic.

This rather technical-seeming point has considerable implications for both the management of an enterprise and for cultural policy, because once the elasticity of demand is known we can see what the effect of a change in price will be. For the enterprise, it tells the management if reducing prices is going to result in more or less revenue: for a for-profit firm, that would affect its profit, and, for a non-profit firm, revenue is important as a source of income. For a government using subsidy to an enterprise to help it reduce prices, it is also vital information on two counts: first, if consumers are not sensitive to price changes, then a policy of reducing prices to encourage greater participation will not achieve its goal; second, if consumers are sensitive to price changes, the enterprise can increase its earned income by reducing prices, thus reducing the amount of subsidy a non-profit organisation would need to encourage greater participation. This explains why economists are so keen on the subject of price elasticity of demand!

Income elasticity of demand

Things are never that simple, unfortunately, and price is not the only economic variable that influences consumers' demand decisions: income is also a factor, and in the case of cultural products it has a strong influence. (Box 18.2 provides a numerical example of the relative effects of price and income elasticities.) Income elasticity of demand is simply defined as the percentage change in quantity demanded due to a percentage change in consumer income, and it is positive; the question is: how great is the effect? As we see in the later part of this chapter, cultural economists have attempted to measure both price and income elasticities for precisely the reasons given above.

Cross-elasticity of demand

As explained earlier, when considering the demand for one good or service, the consumer also takes into account his or her preferences and the prices of other goods and services P_Z, some of which are complements and some substitutes. A complementary good enhances the satisfaction from consuming the good in question while a substitute offers an alternative. Some items are close substitutes (one film rather than another film) and others are not so close (going to the cinema instead of watching TV). Economists analyse these choices in terms of prices using the notion of cross-elasticity: the effect on the quantity demanded of one good of a change in the price of another good – the percentage change in the quantity of good M that is demanded due to the percentage change in the price of good N. If M and N are complements (such as iPods and iTunes) cross-elasticity is negative (if the price of iPods goes down you buy more tracks from iTunes), and if they are substitutes the cross-elasticity is positive (if the price of CDs goes down you buy less online music). The size of the cross-elasticity tells you the strength of the complementarity or substitutability between the goods.

Tastes and preferences in demand theory

Economists do not think that prices and incomes are the only influence on demand, as the demand function showed earlier; the strength of the consumer's taste for a good or service and preference for one item over another obviously play a significant role. Economists are not good at dealing with how tastes are formed, however – why do some people like one thing and not another? Traditionally, that problem has been left to social psychologists and marketing experts to analyse. Cultural economists have attempted to go further into the matter, however, because changing people's tastes is often a goal of cultural policy. An example can illustrate how tastes and economic variables interact: you go to the opera and pay €100 for the seat and so does the person sitting next to you. All we know about you both is that you have paid €100 to go to the opera. In fact, you are a struggling PhD student, but you just had to see this great performance once in your lifetime – you have a very strong taste and very little income and you saved up all year for it. What about the person next to you? Is she an opera buff like you, or just a rich person who goes to see her friends at the opera and does not care that much about it? The point is that willingness to pay a particular price is consistent with both of these possibilities. We reveal our preferences by our consumption patterns and demand behaviour but no one can tell from it the strength of our taste from economic variables alone.

Shifts in the demand schedule

Going back to the demand function $Q_D = f(P, P_Z, Y, T)$, we can now see that a change in P_Z, Y and T will shift the demand schedule. An increase in Y, a rise in the price of a substitute or a fall in the price of a complement, and a change in T in favour of the good being analysed will all shift the demand schedule out to the right and vice versa.

Vouchers for the arts

One way in which cultural economists have advocated increasing participation in the arts is by means of vouchers distributed to less well off people and/or to specific groups of people in the population, such as students. A voucher entitles the holder to a ticket for a performance or museum either without payment or with a reduced ticket price. The voucher encourages consumption by effectively increasing the holder's real income, thus shifting the market demand schedule out to the right; this enables the supplier to move up the supply schedule, supply more and charge a higher price – how much depends upon both the amount of the voucher and on the elasticity of supply, the responsiveness of the producer to a change in price (see figure 3.1a).

Vouchers empower the consumer to make more effective choices by increasing the ability to pay. Economists favour this way of increasing participation in the arts because it allows the consumer to signal which art form and which arts organisation he or she wants to attend; the voucher makes the consumer sovereign. Demand-side subsidy channels the subsidy through the consumer to the arts organisation of his or her choice. By contrast, supply-side subsidy, whereby the arts organisation gets the subsidy, puts the arts organisation in the position of deciding what to offer consumers.

With a voucher scheme, the arts organisation can turn in the vouchers it receives to the government office responsible and collect the value of the voucher as revenue. Proponents of vouchers believe that arts organisations

Box 6.1 Professor Sir Alan Peacock and vouchers for the arts

Professor Sir Alan Peacock (1922–) has worked in cultural economics for nearly forty years, and it was he who pioneered much of what is now the core subject matter of the field. Given his considerable output of academic work and practical participation in cultural economics, it is amazing to realise that it was essentially a sideline to a long and distinguished career as professor of economics in four UK universities, specialising in public finance, welfare economics and public choice theory. He was appointed chairman of the Committee on Financing the BBC, for which he was knighted in 1987, and was chairman of the Scottish Arts Council from 1986 to 1992 (and a member of the Arts Council of Great Britain). His 1993 book *Paying the Piper* provides a unique insight into the tensions between economics and the complexities of distributing grants to arts organisations.

As early as 1969 Peacock had argued for the use of vouchers in the arts, as a way of overcoming problems of access for poorer consumers (as had Baumol and Bowen). The economic rationale for vouchers is that they achieve a redistribution of spending power without altering the allocation of resources, as is the case with subsidies to producers. Vouchers as a way of delivering arts subsidy have several advantages for a 'classical liberal', such as Peacock: in particular, they put the power of deciding what art is in the hands of consumers rather than in those of a 'paternalistic cultural monopoly' (such as the Arts Council), partly overcoming a persistent problem with subsidy to the arts, which is that the high-culture arts appeal to better-off consumers, who therefore benefit more from tax transfers than do poorer taxpayers. In addition, arts organisations are freed from having to please the funding body in order to qualify for a grant, because vouchers enable them to charge consumers a commercial price; the organisation at which the voucher is spent cashes in the value of the voucher from the issuing agency and thus obtains its subsidy. As a result, arts organisations become viable only if their product is appealing to the consumer. The voucher scheme can be restricted to a list of certified arts organisations, the certification being a mark of recognition that aids the consumer. The issue of vouchers can be restricted to a target group, for example young people or senior citizens. This has been done for schoolchildren in the Netherlands via schools.

Peacock came to accept that there are serious problems with the administration of vouchers for the arts, especially with transferability: if consumers do not want to go to arts events at any price (even for nothing), they can sell their vouchers, contravening their purpose. Peacock also came to realise from his contact with arts councils and the like, however, that their main objection to vouchers essentially arises from their loss of power to dispense patronage to arts organisations directly (Peacock, 1993: 128–30) – an observation entirely consistent with his interest in public choice theory.

Sources: Peacock (1993) and Towse (2005).

therefore have to respond to consumers' tastes in order to have access to the subsidy, while, on the demand side, people issued with vouchers will inform themselves about the arts, and so vouchers lead to the cultivation of tastes (see box 6.1 on Alan Peacock and vouchers for the arts).

Limitations of demand theory in cultural economics

The demand analysis presented in the previous section is neoclassical theory that makes several assumptions:

- consumers are able to order their preferences for goods and services rationally;
- tastes are given and constant;
- consumers are fully and costlessly informed about the market; and
- relative prices are the main determinant of consumption choices, subject to the constraint of income.

These assumptions do not tie up fully with observed behaviour in cultural markets, and, in addition, the theory needs modification in order to apply to cultural goods and services, which in some respects differ from 'ordinary' goods. What is different about the arts and culture is that they deal with novelty and new experiences, about which consumers cannot be fully informed, and people do not rely just on their own judgement but listen to experts and/or follow the crowd. There is also the question as to how tastes for new products are formed.

Rational individual behaviour

In cultural economics, the emphasis on individual choice has been questioned on several grounds: one is that people do not think everything out for themselves but are strongly influenced by what other people choose; this creates a 'snowball' or 'bandwagon' effect (see below), whereby, once a product has caught on, more and more people want to buy it. Some writers believe there is a tendency in the cultural sector to 'conspicuous consumption' – that is, buying an item to show off (e.g. going to the theatre to be seen there, or wearing the clothes of certain fashion houses). Another more serious point is that culture is a shared good and therefore reflects common values. I come back to the implications of this point in more detail in chapter 7.

Experience goods

The term 'experience goods' is often used in connection with cultural goods and services, especially the so-called 'high arts'. Unfortunately, there is some confusion about what the term means, and it seems to be used differently by different analysts. It can be interpreted to mean (1) that enjoyment increases with experience; (2) that you need to experience the good in order to have information about it and judge its quality; and (3) that you buy the good for the experience it gives you. The last-mentioned is not how the term is used in cultural economics, though it is used with that meaning in marketing.

The first interpretation is uncontroversial; it implies that people's willingness to pay for cultural products increases with age and experience. Some cultural economists have made this point even more strongly, by calling a growing taste for the arts 'rational addiction' – the more you have the more you want. The second interpretation is more controversial and, in my opinion, can be taken too far: not all art is too difficult for a consumer to fathom (though some may be). Once people have read a book or been to a film, they surely know what to expect in general terms: they understand the experience of reading a book and watching a film. Knowing whether they will like a particular book or film is a different matter, but they can judge that for themselves based on their experience and tastes. In this respect, cultural consumption is no different from trying a new exotic fruit or going on holiday to a new country. People do not have to be certain about everything they purchase – just able to judge whether they will like it, or not, when they have done so. Some writers have suggested that a reason for state involvement in the arts is to overcome consumers' lack of experience of quality; that is valid up to a point but it cannot justify subsidy for established art forms and 'ordinary' cultural products. Of course, the more information consumers have, the more likely they are to be satisfied with their purchases.

Consumption capital

Experience in consuming builds up what has been called 'consumption capital', meaning the consumer invests in knowledge about culture and develops his or her taste so that he or she becomes more and more adroit at making good decisions. As with all capital, this investment costs time and money and is therefore treated with care; it also lasts, but requires renewing so as not to be outdated. Some authors have referred to this as 'learning by consuming'.

Tastes and taste formation

The question of taste and taste formation is a controversial one in neoclassical economics. The phrase *de gustibus non est disputandum* (roughly translated as 'there is no accounting for tastes') has been evoked by economists to make the point that tastes are not an economic phenomenon; tastes are given and preferences are stable and constant, and choices about which goods to consume and a willingness to pay for them are based only on relative prices and income (see box 6.2).

Box 6.2 The dispute over 'De gustibus non est disputandum'

The 1977 article 'De gustibus non est disputandum' by George Stigler (1911–91) and Gary Becker (1930–) has been a source of dispute ever since it was written. Both Stigler and Becker are Nobel-Prize-winning economists from the University of Chicago. The article states the proposition that 'one may usefully treat tastes as stable over time and similar among people'. Further, they state: 'We take categories of behavior commonly held to demonstrate changes in tastes or to be explicable only in terms of such changes, and show both that they are reconcilable with our assumption of stable preferences and that the reformulation is illuminating' (Stigler and Becker, 1977: 77). They do so using what has come to be called the 'household production function', in which households maximise a utility function of commodities that they can produce themselves or buy on the market (analogous to the make-or-buy decision of firms explained in chapter 5). This has formed the basis of the economics of the family, which has been very contentious, especially with feminist economists. The household has a real 'full' income that consists of both money income and the value of the time that it can devote to producing goods and services for its consumption – for instance, making music at home rather than going out to a concert or buying a record. Stigler and Becker use this approach to analyse the 'addictive' consumption of music (that the more good music one hears, the greater one's appreciation of it) in terms of the time that is devoted to consuming music and building consumption capital – that is, knowledge about music. They explain it in terms of the lower 'time cost' that results from the investment that has previously been made.

This theory has been criticised on the grounds that it does not make propositions that can be tested empirically and, in addition, that all it does is push the explanation of the development of taste or 'addiction' to music one stage further back; it is essentially dogmatic and seeks to show that economics can explain everything. In doing so, it suggests that people respond robotically to changes in prices over which they have no control.

Source: Stigler and Becker (1977).

Cultural economists find the approach outlined in box 6.2 problematic for a more pragmatic reason: where does it leave policies adopted by governments either to encourage consumption of the arts and culture or to overcome the limitations of the market by providing public goods? In fact, cultural economists have investigated taste formation for the arts and found that the strongest predictor of later consumption is childhood participation, especially outside the school. Tastes form over a lifetime and build up into adulthood. Taste formation is therefore what economists call a 'dynamic' process, meaning that it takes place over time. Of course, income also increases with age, and so does the ability to spend time on cultural pursuits, as older people have more leisure time and less responsibility for children, so all these factors come into play and influence demand and participation in cultural activities. These factors are important for marketing cultural products as well as for understanding economic behaviour.

Search and information costs

As we saw in chapter 5, using the market is not costless and has transaction costs for producers; this is also the case for consumers, who have to spend time and other resources obtaining information about products and learning if they enjoy them. This was referred to above as building consumption capital. As with transaction costs, consumers try to reduce these costs, and they are able to do so in various ways: by experience, by learning, by getting expert opinion and by observing the choices of others.

'Nobody knows'

Extreme information problems about creative, especially new, products not only lead to uncertainty on the part of the producer as to the reception of the product, they also cause problems for consumers. The statement 'Nobody knows' reflects the inherent uncertainty in the consumption as well as in the production of novelty.

Supplier-induced demand

Lack of information is a serious problem when the ordinary consumer simply cannot acquire sufficient knowledge to make an informed decision and requires expert assistance to do so. Cultural economists have applied this notion to the arts, where it puts the professional art expert to the fore in informing people what great art is and what is worth consuming. If the expert is in a position to control resources, such as grants of public finance, he or she may impose his or her choices on others and reduce consumer sovereignty. Note that this is not the same idea as merit goods: it is not saying that people *should* experience the arts, but that, if they want to, then they need expert help in so doing.

Gate-keepers and critics

One way that people obtain information about cultural products (and other goods too) is through intermediaries. Magazines, newspapers and radio programmes and the like give accounts of the content of films, records, books, plays, and so on and publish reviews by experts. Critics assess the quality of performers and performances, TV programmes, and so on. All these are what are called 'gate-keepers', and they perform an important role in providing information and forming consumers' tastes for all sorts of cultural products. They sift out items from a huge potential stock of products that consumers choose from; consumers therefore have to find an intermediary they trust to make a selection that suits them. Shops can perform that function: you might go to a certain shop, say to get clothes that suit your taste, because you know you like the selection it stocks. Particular critics or blogs whose opinions you share are also 'gate-keepers' you can rely on.

Bandwagon and snowball effects

The terms 'bandwagon effects' and 'snowball effects' essentially mean that consumers follow the crowd and make choices that are influenced by those of others; they do not make individualistic decisions, as envisaged by neoclassical demand theory. Fads, crazes and fashions fit into this category and are easily observable in connection with the sudden popularity of pop stars, best-sellers and the like. This behaviour may be rational, as it reduces the individual's search costs.

Network effects

Not unrelated to the underlying idea of the snowball or bandwagon effect is the concept of 'network effects'. Again, this is a term that can mean different things in a different context. In relation to consumption, what it refers to is that some goods and services are more valuable to the consumer the more people there are using them – that is, the bigger the network, the greater each individual's utility. E-mail and SMS (short message service) are examples, as are P2P (peer-to-peer) sites: the more people use them, the better the service for each user. These are what economists call 'external effects' of the individual's behaviour: it is not that the individual seeks to improve the service for others, just that others benefit from his or her self-interested behaviour. We see in chapter 7 how externalities are very important in discussions about public policy for the arts and heritage.

Judging quality by price

One aspect of consumer behaviour that is very problematic for economics is if people use the decision rule that the higher the price, the better the quality. This is something people do when they have no other information. It is obviously common knowledge that this rule usually works: if you want to know which the best tickets are for a concert, buy the most expensive ones. This could lead to people demanding more at higher prices – the reversal of the usual negative demand relation of quantity and price. Ultimately, incomes constrain this from happening on a large scale.

Willingness to pay and non-market demand

The theory of demand in combination with the theory of supply provides an explanation of how trade takes place in a market: a good is supplied to the market by a producer, consumers buy it at the price that is determined in the market by the interaction of buyers and sellers, and the revenue from the sales provides income for the seller. Buyers have expressed their desire for the good by their willingness to pay and in purchasing the good. It is this scenario that leads economists to conclude that the price paid for a good expresses both WTP and the satisfaction or utility that the consumer gets from it.

Standard economic theory of demand therefore tells us that consumers reveal their wants via market prices and signal to the supplier what goods and services to produce; the main exception to this rule is public goods, for which there is no functioning market. In cultural economics, however, while it is recognised that market demand is a significant expression of consumers' wishes, there are other circumstances in which market demand falls short of total WTP for cultural products, for which people are willing to contribute taxes to finance their production without actually taking part in the market themselves; in addition, unborn generations are not able to express their WTP via the market, but it is believed that they will value certain goods and services in the future. These sources of WTP are called (respectively) option demand and demand by future generations, and they are relevant to decisions about the amount of subsidy that is appropriate for supporting the provision of some goods and services; later in the book, this is applied to the preservation of the built heritage and to public service broadcasting. They are also discussed in the context of welfare economics in chapter 7, and option demand is discussed below in relation to contingent valuation studies.

Applications of demand theory

I now turn to two of the main ways that demand theory can be applied in practice in cultural economics: empirical estimates of elasticities and contingent valuation (CV) studies.

Estimates of elasticity of demand

Estimating elasticity is a complex econometric task that requires demand data on numbers of tickets sold (for example) at various prices in combination with information about consumers' income and other factors that affect demand. It is not easy to obtain the necessary data; though arts organisations have data on daily ticket sales, and they may also have carried out audience surveys that include a question on attendees' income, they would not be likely to have information on the purchase and prices of other complementary or substitute goods, which would have to be found from other sources (such as participation surveys and published price data). As a result, not many reliable studies have been done and there is no consensus on the results. The jury is still out on the question as to whether the demand for the performing arts (demand for ballet, theatre and orchestral concerts have all been studied in various countries – see chapter 8) is elastic or inelastic with respect to the price. Income elasticity is always positive, though it has not always been found to be very great. Recent studies of price and income elasticities of demand for books have found that demand is price-elastic and income elasticity is high, suggesting that they are a luxury good. A few studies have also considered the cross-elasticity of demand, for instance between theatre and cinema prices. Research estimating elasticities is discussed in subsequent chapters in the book in relation to specific cultural products.

Implications of measures of elasticity

As argued above, these estimates of elasticity are important because they can tell a cultural enterprise if it could increase its sales revenue by altering its prices. Sensitivity to prices as measured by elasticity also indicates to government whether policies to reduce prices can achieve their purpose of attracting greater participation; if price elasticity of demand for the arts is low, other policies should be adopted. Countries that have a policy of fixed book prices in an attempt to ensure the survival of small bookshops could be damaging readership and revenues by making books more expensive.

Contingent valuation

Contingent valuation is a method used for estimating demand when market demand is not the only indication of willingness to pay, as with option demand and provision for future generations, which cannot be expressed directly through entry prices. In these circumstances, WTP has to be measured indirectly, and CV methods and CV studies are used because the only way that the strength of this demand can be expressed is via surveys.[6] CV can also be used to measure a population's WTP for a good that is not provided through the market, either because it has not yet been offered for sale or because it is a public good provided without charge by the community. In the latter case, CV measures what people would pay in taxes to have the good or service.

CV was first developed for use in valuing natural heritage and damage to wilderness and it continues to be used widely in environmental economics. In cultural economics, it has been used in connection with the built heritage – for example, the restoration and maintenance of individual buildings or groups of buildings, even a whole city – to discover the willingness to pay for items that are not priced in the marketplace either by users or non-users. CV studies can be used as part of the planning process in order to decide how much to spend on a particular project. The study is typically carried out by the use of questionnaires and interviews of visitors at the site, while others – the non-users – are sampled by various means, such as random telephone interviews.

Some economists have questioned the accuracy of CV as a way of measuring WTP. People are asked to reply to a questionnaire with the researcher informing them about the proposal and how much it will cost. Despite all the care that researchers take in presenting surveys, there is still the worry that it is hard to get respondents to assess their WTP accurately in an abstract setting. It can be counter-argued, though, that having an indication of the public's WTP gives policy-makers information they would otherwise not have, and that is bound to improve decision-making. For policy purposes, however, it has to be taken into account that good-quality CV surveys are expensive to conduct.

Conclusion

The consumption of cultural goods and services has several dimensions to it: aggregate expenditure data indicate the amount of spending by consumers and the proportion of income they have chosen to spend on cultural products. Participation studies provide information about the type of culture people choose and on their socio-economic characteristics, without indicating their expenditure or willingness to pay, and demand studies analyse consumers'

---

[6] Experimental economics adopts a laboratory setting for similar studies using applied game theory but this has not yet been done in cultural economics.

choice with respect to price and WTP. Demand translates into revenue for producers, and elasticity of demand shows how that is affected by consumers' sensitivity to prices. Price alone does not tell the whole story, however; incomes, level of education, age, and so on, as well as the consumption choices of others, can also influence demand.

This chapter has exposed both the strengths and weaknesses of economics when analysing consumer behaviour in the cultural sector and it has shown that cultural economists are trying to adapt these models to the special features of the arts and culture. What we have seen is that demand is complex, and studies of participation and attendance are also useful in establishing patterns of consumption of cultural products.

Some cultural economists regard the arts as having such strong public goods characteristics that price alone cannot measure value; some also believe that individual preferences do not express the value of creative goods because they have meaning only in a communal context, and what people pay is not a true measure of the cultural value they experience. Contingent valuation studies have been widely used in cultural economics to try to overcome some of these problems, though they have also been regarded with a certain amount of suspicion. In the chapters that follow, all these ideas are explored further in the context of the different creative industries.

Further reading

I recommend for a start that you look at some of the data sources listed as sources to the tables in this chapter. If you are interested in US arts participation and consumer spending, look at NEA (2003) and NEA (2006); both are available online. Also online is the NEA Report no. 36, *Effects of Arts Education on Participation in the Arts* (NEA, 1995). The Bureau of Labor Statistics compiles time budget studies with the American Time Use Survey (available online at www.bls.gov/tus/home.htm#related).

For European data, see the Eurostat pocketbook *Cultural Statistics: 2007 Edition* (Eurostat, 2007), which explains data sources, and www.culturalpolicies.net for country-by-country data and sources (including Canada). Also on Europe, Rick van der Ploeg's chapter 'The making of cultural policy: a European perspective', in the Ginsburgh and Throsby *Handbook of the Economics of Art and Culture* (2006), discusses participation and demand.

The Australia Bureau of Statistics (2008) and the Australia Council produce copious data online, the latter at www.australiacouncil.gov.au/research/

dance/facts_and_figures/attendance_at_performing_arts_events and www.australiacouncil.gov.au/research/arts_funding/facts_and_figures/government_funding. Finally, for a discussion of contingent valuation and the concept of value in culture, see Throsby (2001, ch. 2). Tiziana Cuccia's chapter in the Towse (2003a) *Handbook of Cultural Economics*, 'Contingent valuation', chapter 14, provides a clear account of methods and problems.

7 Welfare economics and public finance

Welfare economics has been referred to in several places earlier in the book, and in this chapter its general principles are explained in the context of the economic rationale for government intervention in the cultural sector. The application of welfare economics to cost–benefit analysis and to economic impact studies is outlined and its use in cultural economics illustrated. The second part of the chapter then turns to the application of the principles of public finance to the arts and heritage and an analysis of the way subsidy works at the level of the individual arts organisation. The material in this chapter draws on the theories of production and of consumer behaviour in chapters 5 and 6; while they focused on the decision-making of individuals in the market, welfare economics and public finance examine societal decision-making. Chapter 2 introduced some of the basic points about cultural policy, and these are developed further here. The chapter therefore provides the theoretical basis for the evaluation of cultural policy that is presented in chapter 10.

Some clarification is needed about the use of terms: although cultural policy and government spending vary a great deal as to how centralised or devolved they are in different countries, this chapter ignores these differences and concentrates on general principles; therefore, the words 'government' and 'state' are used in a general way meaning any level of public administration, and the term 'public finance' applies to any level of taxation and public expenditure.

Why do governments have a policy for culture?

Culture and creativity are believed to have public good characteristics that improve the quality of life. Governments at all levels also wish to promote a certain image for their citizens, and ensuring the provision of a range of arts and heritage institutions is an obvious way of projecting that image to the rest of the country or to the world (see chapter 19). Motivations vary: the desire to promote pride in local or national identity and/or to form that identity and develop a sense of community are often held to be important; sometimes policy is motivated by economic considerations, such as attracting tourists; and it may also be motivated by less laudable reasons, such as the promotion of political power for a regime or for individuals. These public objectives are unlikely to be achieved by individual means or through the agency of the market and require concerted action by the community.

Apart from public benefits, though, there are uncovenanted private benefits, such as option demand and demand by future generations, referred to in chapter 6, that may not be met by the market, and these also require concerted action. When this is called for, established government bodies are able to supply the necessary administrative facility at a lower level of transaction costs than ad hoc bodies, and that in itself justifies government intervention. The presence of public and uncovenanted private benefits justifies state intervention and public expenditure financed by taxation. Private sources of finance, such as funds from private non-profit foundations and business sponsorship, also ensure the provision of cultural facilities and thus provide external benefits for audiences.

The concept of economic welfare

'Welfare' is a very general term and can, obviously, be interpreted in several ways; broadly, as used in economics, it means a sense of well-being or satisfaction with one's physical and mental state and quality of life. This comes from the utility that an individual obtains from his or her goods and services and from benefits that the community provides; thus, possessions, health, education, stimulation, freedom, security, and so on are productive of this broad sense of welfare. It is easy to see that some of these are collective or public goods and others are private ones that can be obtained through the market. An easy assumption to make is that greater wealth and higher personal incomes enable people and societies to enjoy more of these pleasures, and, therefore, economic welfare is a possible proxy for the broader meaning of well-being. Economic welfare can then be quantified in terms of measures of income and wealth, and their growth can be said to increase welfare. While this is convenient, it has its limitations, and economists – among others – have been critical of the elision of material wealth and welfare. In particular, the use of national income as a measure of a society's welfare has been criticised for failing to take into account untraded goods that are not priced by the market, such as external benefits (including those from the arts and heritage) and costs (such as pollution), or concepts that have little to do with money, such as people's sense of achieving their potential as individuals, or simply happiness.

Welfare economics

Welfare economics starts with the premise that the aim of society is the maximisation of welfare and that the welfare of a society is the additive function of the satisfaction or utility of each individual member of that society; thus the state itself is supposed to have no aims or objectives that are independent of those of its members. A second premise is that the individual is the best judge of his or her welfare.

Pareto optimality and Pareto improvements

Maximum welfare is achieved when there is no change possible that can make someone in a society better off without making someone else worse off. That is the definition of 'Pareto optimality', adopting the name of Vilfredo Pareto, the economist who introduced the rule, and it indicates that the economy is socially efficient. When a change could be made that would increase the welfare of society, that is called a 'Pareto improvement' (PI). These concepts provide rules for social decision-making for a government whose objective is the improvement of welfare for its citizens.

The difficulty is that nearly every policy that could lead to an improvement is likely to make someone worse off and therefore be inadmissible as an unambiguous Pareto improvement (but see box 7.1). This is because government policies mostly involve expenditure that has to be financed by taxes from citizens, who are thereby made worse off. It will be noticed that this is a very strict rule – stricter, for example, than a majority vote in which the 'losers' accept the decision of the 'winners'. While none of this may seem very helpful, it serves to show just how difficult societal decisions really are; by contrast, the majority voting rule is simple, as it requires only that a society accept the choice of the majority.

Box 7.1 Pareto improvements and honours in the arts

Vilfredo Pareto (1848–1923) was an Italian born in France and educated in Italy, where he worked for twenty years for Italian railway companies; he began to study economics only in 1890, and by 1893 he was appointed professor at the University of Lausanne in Switzerland. He is famous for both his statistical work on income distribution, developing the so-called 'Pareto distribution', and, of course, for the now well-known concept of optimal economic welfare. The concept of Pareto optimality did not enter English-speaking economics until the late 1930s, however.

Generally speaking, it is very difficult to find unambiguous Pareto improvements, since almost any change that improves one person's welfare imposes some cost, in terms of either the use of resources or a psychic cost, on another member of the society. Most policies require finance, and that means that taxes are levied to pay for them, making some people worse off even though others may be much better off as a result. Nevertheless, the award of honours to artists – being made a 'living treasure', Kammersänger(in), Chevalier d'Honneur, Commendatore, knight or lord – is an unambiguous PI, since it is costless and (presumably) adds utility to the individual, thus improving welfare (though, if other colleagues are jealous, then there is no PI!).

Prizes that are voluntarily given by philanthropists for achievements in the arts are also PIs but would not qualify if there are tax breaks for the donor, since that would mean that taxes have to be raised from others to meet public expenditure commitments.

The Hicks–Kaldor compensation principle

One way out of the problem that some people may be made worse off in a situation in which potential welfare gains can be made is to get potential losers to agree to accept compensation. The concept of compensating losers by those who stand to gain (and the converse – how much the losers would pay to prevent the action) was developed by two economists, Sir John Hicks and Nicholas (Lord) Kaldor, and it is called after them – the Hicks–Kaldor compensation principle. If there is a policy that would enable the achievement of net benefit, where the gain in welfare to some people is greater than the welfare loss to others, a potential Pareto improvement (PPI), the Hicks–Kaldor principle can be applied. According to this principle, the gainers could potentially compensate the losers because there is sufficient net benefit to society in doing so, either by actually giving them financial or other compensation (an actual Pareto improvement) or – and this was the main contribution of Hicks and Kaldor – without in fact going through the business of compensating the losers.

Cost–benefit analysis

In practice, the calculation of net benefit is done through cost–benefit analysis. CBA involves measuring the benefits of a possible policy and weighing them up against the costs. It is used at the planning stage to establish if there is a PPI – a potential welfare gain to society. This gain need not be only financial and the benefits include non-pecuniary 'public good' benefits, such as a sense of local or national pride. A form of CBA that has been much used in the arts is the so-called economic impact study, which considers, for instance, if there is a net benefit to be found from the building of a new museum or theatre that would bring in new audiences to a city and generate employment and other quantifiable economic gains, as well as providing unquantifiable cultural benefits and a sense of civic pride. CBA and economic impact studies are discussed in detail later on.

The theorems of welfare economics

Although there are difficulties with operationalising Pareto optimality, economists believe the concept is useful in providing an ideal-type decision rule. Not only that, but the conditions under which Pareto optimality can be achieved have been analysed and can be formally stated as theorems: (1) a perfectly competitive economy in which all markets are in equilibrium and in which there are no externalities or public goods will be Pareto optimal; and (2) the theorem can be stated the other way round to say that Pareto optimality requires a perfectly competitive economy. Under these conditions, there is both private and social efficiency in the economy; this is similar to Adam Smith's notion of the 'invisible hand': the idea that an individual pursuing his or her own self-interest tends to promote the good of society as well.

Nonetheless, the list of assumptions about the economy that must hold for these theorems of Pareto optimality to be valid makes it clear that this can only ever be an ideal-type economy:

- competitive suppliers in perfectly competitive markets set the prices of their goods according to marginal cost;
- suppliers of all inputs set input prices according to marginal cost, which, in the case of labour, is the marginal 'disutility' of work;
- all production takes place in the most technically efficient way and substitution of inputs and products produced takes place when relative prices change;
- there are no externalities or public goods;
- consumers make choices of what to buy based on the relative prices of goods and services, constrained by their income and in line with their 'in-

built' tastes, so that the marginal utility of the item bought is equal to the price; and

- all economic agents – buyers and sellers – are fully informed about prices both now and in the future.

Violation of these conditions can therefore point to the sources of inefficiency in the economy and points to where improvements could be made, judged by the criterion of perfect competition. For example, it immediately suggests that monopoly is socially inefficient and that competition law aimed at controlling monopoly would be welfare-improving. This is the viewpoint from which many policies and much law-making are judged.

Welfare economics and market failure

When the conditions laid out above are not met, the market is said to 'fail' – that is, it fails to maximise social welfare. Market failure is therefore taken as the main argument for government intervention.

When the 'first best' Pareto optimum cannot be reached, corrective action will produce only the so-called 'second best' outcome. This sort of action – a subsidy, tax or other regulation – inevitably prevents the attainment of Pareto optimality, as it interferes with marginal cost pricing and the allocation of resources and therefore violates the theorems of welfare economics. Copyright law provides a good example of a second best policy (see box 7.2). These interventions may improve overall social efficiency and lead to a second best solution but it is inadmissible to claim that they can lead to the achievement of 'first best'.

Box 7.2 Second best and copyright law

One of the economic arguments used to justify copyright law is that it prevents 'free-riding'; without there being an exclusive property right for works of literature, music, art, and so on that allows authors to control the use of their work, anyone could copy it, and authors would not be able to charge a cost-covering price. Unless they get a return on the investment of the time and opportunity cost of creating the work, authors would not have an economic incentive to create and so society would be worse off. The exclusive property right is a grant of monopoly that prevents a competitor from copying another's work, however. Having the monopoly, however weak, enables the copyright owner to set the price above marginal cost, which reduces welfare. Copyright law has to trade off the positive benefits against their cost to society and is therefore a second best policy. Look at box 13.2 for another way of putting this argument!

Monopoly has long been regarded by economists as one of the chief violations of the conditions for Pareto optimality, though, as is discussed elsewhere in the book, there is a case for monopoly (made by Schumpeter – see box 14.4) as a creative force. In the case of the arts and culture, it is the presence of 'unpriced' public goods and external benefits that has mostly been seen as the cause of market failure and it is their presence that justifies cultural policy measures, such as subsidies to arts organisations, to overcome market failure.

Pigovian welfare economics

In the 1930s the English economist A. C. Pigou developed what has come to be called Pigovian welfare economics, which offers a market-by-market rule for social efficiency and provides a solution for market failure in a market. Pigovian welfare economics therefore avoids the demanding requirements of perfect competition and general equilibrium throughout the whole economy, as summarised in the conditions for Pareto optimality listed above, by concentrating on one market only. The rule is simply that the socially efficient (welfare-maximising) level of output of a particular good occurs at the point where the marginal social benefit (MSB) is equal to the marginal social cost (MSC) of producing it.

MSB is the private benefit or utility to consumers plus the external benefit to others that is generated by the consumption of a good or service; MSC is the private cost of producing a good or service plus any external cost that is generated by its production. The welfare-maximising output in the market for a good is where MSB = MSC. In cultural economics, there has been much more emphasis on social benefits than on social costs (though congestion at very popular tourist sites and museums is a social cost, because one visitor imposes a cost on another – see chapters 9 and 19). In the absence of external costs, only the marginal private cost (MPC), which is the supply schedule of a competitive firm, is relevant, and this is equated to MSB to identify the socially efficient output. In figure 7.1, output Q_S is the socially efficient level of output at point B, where MSB = MPC, and that is greater than output Q_P at point A, where S = D, which is what the private market would produce. At point A there is market failure, with the market underproducing films by the quantity $Q_S - Q_P$.

In figure 7.1, the market for films is depicted. There is a market demand schedule, D, showing the level of private utility that consumers get from films; because there are external benefits to people seeing films, however, MSB is greater than demand (marginal private benefit – MPB), and it increases as the quantity demanded increases. The market supply, S, is determined by the

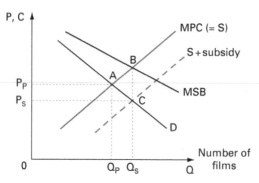

Figure 7.1   Socially efficient level of film output

MPC of producing films. The socially optimum number of films produced in the market is Q_S, and, at that level of output, MSB exceeds D (the amount consumers are willing to pay) by the amount BC. Producers will produce only Q_P at price P_P, however, because their revenue is $0P_PAQ_P$. Therefore, the market fails to produce the welfare-maximising output of films and there is a case for subsidising film producers to increase output to Q_S.

MPC is rising, however, indicating that it costs more to supply more films, and the price at which film producers wish to supply Q_S at B is higher than the equilibrium price the unsubsidised market would charge, P_P. In order to encourage producers to produce Q_S, subsidy is needed to add to their sales revenue and allow them to supply at a point on the private demand schedule D at a lower price. The lower price P_S is necessary to encourage take-up on the part of consumers of the extra output because D is downward-sloping. The subsidy to encourage Q_S should be sufficient to shift the aggregate supply S down to the right to the notional S + subsidy, so that the socially efficient price P_S at point C is charged. The area of that subsidy is the area P_PACP_S, and this is the increase in revenue needed to achieve the welfare-maximising output as defined by Pigou. Later in this chapter, we look at the impact of different types of subsidy at the level of the individual producer. Whatever form the subsidy takes, however, the principle is the same: it has to increase output to the welfare-maximising level of output in the market to the point where MSB = MSC.

Sources of market failure in the cultural sector

The main source of market failure that has been written about in cultural economics is external consumption benefits of one sort or another – 'unpriced' or 'uncovenanted' benefits – and information problems, usually about the quality of cultural goods. Market failure in the form of monopoly or oligopoly is also present in the cultural industries; the so-called 'social cost of monopoly' was demonstrated in figure 5.2 and is discussed further in chapter 14.

'Unpriced' benefits

'Unpriced' or 'uncovenanted' external benefits (introduced in chapter 6) are a source of demand-side market failure. In terms of figure 7.1, these are the 'gap' between the demand D and MSB schedules. The presence of external benefits justifies subsidy according to the extent of the unpriced benefit (also called 'unexpressed' benefits). We therefore need to know what these sources of external benefit are, in order, in principle at least, to calculate the amount of subsidy needed to achieve the socially optimal level of output and, in a wider sense, to improve social welfare.

External benefits of consumption

In general, the idea of external benefits is that there are some goods and services that give private utility to the person who consumes them but, in addition, others benefit from that consumption. Reading books and going to see films and plays that deal with social problems, for instance, makes people understand them better, and that is good for the functioning of a society. The term 'external' means that third parties benefit from a private transaction on the part of the buyer that is motivated by the consumer's private satisfaction; others benefit willy-nilly.

Public goods

The significance of public goods has already been referred to in chapters 2 and 6, and this chapter explores it further in the context of subsidy to the arts and heritage. Public goods in this context are just a stronger version of external benefits of consumption; being non-rival and non-excludable they can be shared by all, and this means that they would be underproduced or not produced at all via the market. Public goods such as shared culture strengthen ties within society (though they can also be used to exclude minorities). Such goods are a source of unpriced (or underpriced) benefits to all members of a society and are subject to free-riding, meaning that they would be overconsumed by people who avoid paying for them. Note that a difference between public goods and externalities of consumption here is that individuals pay for the goods that 'spill over' external benefits to others, because they get private benefit from them (they pay a price equal to the marginal utility or social benefit that they get from the good), whereas they have the incentive to free-ride and avoid paying for public goods.

Option demand

One of the most frequently cited sources of unpriced benefit is option demand; this means that the public are willing to pay for the existence of goods and services that they may not themselves wish to consume at present but they want them to be available for when they should wish to (a 'self-interested' motive), and they may also want them to be available to others in the society (an altruistic motive). The point is that they are willing to pay for this option but cannot do so via the prices in the market; therefore, public expenditure from taxes is mandated to finance option demand. Surveys and contingent valuation studies can establish how much people are willing to contribute through taxation to maintain option demand, as explained in chapter 6.

Demand by future generations

Unborn generations of people cannot express their willingness to pay via the market and so it is incumbent upon the present generation to express it on their behalf; this demand by future generations applies particularly to the heritage as an argument for maintaining the heritage of the arts for their future use, and this has to be done through non-market sources of finance, such as donations or subsidy. The benefits to future generations are also unknown, however, and cannot be measured.

Information problems

Lack of information

The absence of sufficient information on the part of the consumer to judge experience goods means that demand cannot truly reflect the utility the consumer could potentially have if he or she knew more about the cultural good or service in question. Indeed, all arts lobbyists firmly believe that, if people could only be persuaded to step inside a theatre or museum, they would acquire the information needed to develop the taste and knowledge (consumption capital) that would turn them into avid cultural consumers. A taste for and knowledge of the arts and heritage (as for other things, such as sports) are often cultivated in schools as part of the compulsory syllabus. While education up to the school leaving age is compulsory, however, attending cultural events in later life is not, and so audiences have to be coaxed to take part by policies that encourage demand. Public subsidy is justified according to this argument on the grounds of financing the provision of the necessary information.

Asymmetric information and supplier-induced demand

Another aspect of information problems is asymmetric information, the situation in which consumers and producers do not both possess the same information about the goods they are buying and selling. In a number of circumstances, the supplier has more information about the product than the buyer, and the buyer has to rely on that source of information in order to make his or her demand decisions, and the seller may well exploit that situation to his or her own advantage (the example of second-hand car dealers has frequently been invoked in this context). Arts and heritage experts obviously know more than audiences, and they may be able to persuade a funding organisation that subsidy is necessary to persuade potential visitors of the benefits of the arts as they see them. Merit goods are an extreme example of this way of thinking (see box 2.2).

Information problems also have to do with uncertainty about the quality of cultural products that affects demand, as discussed in chapter 6. Gate-keepers, such as critics, have a role to play here in providing information for consumers so they do not have to rely only on experts; nevertheless, there are areas in the cultural sector in which supplier-induced demand is an important factor. This is discussed at length in relation to the heritage in chapter 9.

Market failure and consumer sovereignty

The analysis of demand-side market failure provides a rationale for government intervention in the market and calls for policy to increase production beyond the level of output that results from private market signals alone; taking steps to overcome market failure increases social welfare. The problem for welfare economics with notions such as supplier-induced demand and merit goods is that they conflict with the notion of consumer sovereignty and the fundamental basis of social welfare as being based solely on individual welfare and voluntary exchange. They refute the ability of consumers to judge their own welfare, although that is fundamental to the notion of social welfare in the first place.

While there is general agreement among cultural economists about market failure, they differ somewhat in their interpretation of the implications, as box 7.3 shows. Box 7.3 shows a range of views on market failure. It is worth noting

Box 7.3 Leading cultural economists' views on market failure

Lionel (Lord) Robbins (1971: 3–4):

> Why should the taxpayer provide money for the arts? Why should not the whole business be left to consumer demand? If people want art they will buy it: if not, why should it be produced? [...]
>
> Now clearly this is not a question that can be answered by reference to scientific economics. It is a question of ultimate values, a question of what you think to be the purpose and function of the state as the authoritarian element in society, a question of political philosophy. Economics comes in only when you want to know the implications of your decisions in this respect, implications as regards proportions, incentives and machinery.
>
> On this plane therefore of political objectives, I personally have never had any difficulty in regarding some cultivation of the arts and higher learning as part of my conception of the state obligation.

(Sir) Alan Peacock (1969: 323):

> Subsidizing the Arts involves the same kind of issues as subsidizing particular industries or services in the economy, however distasteful this may seem to those who are conditioned to think in terms of a moral hierarchy in the ordering of consumption expenditure. In the analysis, attention is confined to two arguments for subsidization which are derived from the existence of 'market failure', i.e. the recognition that the strict Paretian assumptions of divisibility of goods and absence of externalities of production and consumption are not met with in practical life. A particular aspect of indivisibility which is relevant to the subsidization of the Arts is taking account of the welfare of future generations, that is to say of the welfare of those whose interests cannot be directly expressed at present through the exercise of their own preferences in the market...
>
> Cultural paternalism, which might be justified on the grounds that the community does not know what is good for it, is ruled out. Apart from any predisposition of the author to oppose paternalism, the assertion of imposed value judgements is too easy a way of deriving support for public intervention designed to give the public not what it wants but what it ought to have!

Bruno Frey (2000: 9–10):

> Each scholar has his or her basic values, even when undertaking scientific research... Consonant to the view of most modern economists, I see the advantages of using markets. They tend to be efficient and allow the different artistic preferences of the population to be met. Art is not only what (often self-defined) art experts call 'art'. Art experts have often been unable to grasp new art movements: the market has often been much quicker to respond...
>
> But I also see the limits of markets. In my view, relevant external effects and other market failures exist. These cannot simply be overcome by bargaining between the actors involved, not least because consumers are unorganised... But I do not agree that market failures in the arts necessarily mean that the government must intervene. As a political economist, I clearly see the limits of state activity, also with respect to culture.

David Throsby (2001: 140):

Moving beyond standard efficiency considerations raises the possibility that the arts might be deemed a merit good, and that, if so, this would provide normative grounds for collective action. At first glance, the arts would seem to fit the 'merit want' description rather closely: society apparently sees the arts as 'meritorious', yet people do not demand them in private markets to the extent that such a view would suggest, providing a presumptive case for corrective intervention. Closer examination, however, suggests that a number of character-istics that might be ascribed to the arts as merit goods can actually be explained as general-ised externalities or social goods. For instance, a belief that the arts are socially beneficial when held by people who do not themselves consume the arts directly, or an acceptance by some individuals of others' consumption, can be accounted for as cases of interdependent utility functions and hence explicable according to the standard theory of externalities. In such cases what appears at first sight to be 'imposed choice' turns out to be ultimately consistent with the principle of consumer sovereignty.

that all four of these prominent economists support the case for government intervention in the arts and heritage, though, obviously, to different extents. Robbins accedes to the merit goods argument, while Peacock has a strong objection to overriding consumer sovereignty, though he sees the case in terms of the protection of future generations; Frey displays caution over undue attention to experts and over state involvement, though he does recognise market failure; and Throsby tries to show that the merit goods argument is in fact an extension of externalities if people take pleasure in the enjoyment of the arts by others.

How much subsidy?

It is one thing to accept the case for government intervention, but there remains a serious problems of how much subsidy (or other non-market finance) is called for. It is all very well to draw a diagram showing the gap between private demand and marginal social benefit but how big are external effects in practice in each market? That can in principle be estimated by cost–benefit analysis or by contingent valuation of the public good/external benefit, but such studies are difficult and expensive to undertake and subject to flaws (see below). There are also moral hazard and 'principal–agent' problems that accompany negotiations with arts organisations about how much subsidy they should receive, and it is necessary to consider how the government can offer the right incentives to the arts or heritage organisation to fulfil its policy goals. All told, therefore, merely having the rationale for interventionist cultural (or any other) policy that welfare economics propounds through the analysis of market failure is a far cry from formulating specific policy measures designed to meet policy objectives. I return to this topic in chapter 10.

Cost–benefit analysis

As its name implies, cost–benefit analysis measures the costs and benefits of a specific project, and this information can then be used by the policy-maker as a guide to deciding whether or not to undertake the project. By calculating the rate of return to the project, it can be compared to the rate of return on other competing projects; a dramatic example would be that a city council has to make the choice between building a new museum or a sports stadium (or maybe a school).

The general principle of CBA is to estimate the future benefits (private and social) and to compare them with the cost of the initial outlay on the project plus the ongoing maintenance costs over its projected lifetime. It can readily be seen that all the benefits and some of the costs arise in the future, whereas the initial outlay has to be paid in the present and in advance of the project's completion; therefore, for decision purposes, the valuation of future benefits and costs must be made in 'present value' terms, so that they can be compared with the outlay or cost of undertaking the project now. Estimating the present value necessitates the use of a 'discount rate', which may be thought of as similar to an interest rate, and the process of discounting may be thought of as being the reverse of compounding interest into the future.

An example

Let us say that a city is considering building a new museum that would cost €50 million euros (or $50 million); the benefits of the museum are planned for a fifty-year period. The city council would have to borrow the €50 million at an interest rate of 5 per cent per annum; it would therefore have to pay €2.5 million a year in interest. The museum building would also have to be maintained and repaired during its lifetime. One way of making the calculation as to whether it is worthwhile building the museum is to estimate the stream of future benefits and costs and then ask what discount rate would make them equal in the present. That notional discount rate is then compared to the actual cost of borrowing; so, in this example, if the discount rate is greater than or equal to 5 per cent, the building should go ahead, because it would be socially 'efficient'. Box 7.4 explains the calculations in detail.

Box 7.4 Calculating present value

You have a principal sum of $1,000 and you can get an annual rate of interest in a bank of 5 per cent. At the end of year 1 you have $1,000 + $50 = $1,050. If you leave the interest and the initial deposit in the bank, at the end of year 2 you have $1,050 + $52.50= $1,102.50; and so on. The interest compounds at the rate of 5 per cent of an increasing amount of money over the number of years you leave the principal and the accumulated interest in the bank.

We could also ask the question the other way round: how much would you need to deposit in the bank at an interest rate of 5 per cent to earn $50 by the end of year 1? Answer: $1,000 – and this is called the present value, V_1.

We can write this as a formula: $V_1 (1+0.05) = \$1,050$.

Therefore $V_1 = \$1,050 / 1.05 = \$1,000$ is the present value.

After two years, the total value is $1,102.50; then

$V_2 = \$1,102.50 / 1.05^2 = \$1,000$.

So, this can be generalised into a present value (PV) formula:

$$PV = \sum_{t=1}^{n} X / (1 + i)^t$$

where t runs from 1 to n, and n is the number of years, i is the interest rate and X is the principal sum. Σ is the mathematical symbol used to mean the 'sum of'.

Private and social costs and benefits

CBA requires the calculation of the private and social costs and benefits; as noted earlier, social costs are private costs plus external costs, and social benefits are private benefits plus external benefits. Private costs are relatively straightforward: the estimated cost of the building project over the time it takes to build plus maintenance costs over its life; external costs, such as disruption to city life and congestion caused by the construction work, can be more difficult to quantify, but they can be calculated in terms of damage done and the value of the hours of work lost. The private benefits are the anticipated revenues from visitor entrance fees and the profits from other direct expenditures by visitors, such as on catalogues and other items in the museum shop and in the restaurant projected for the fifty-year period. Obviously, these have to be estimated, and even guessed at for the far future. The social benefits are often hard to quantify – what financial value can be given for the enhanced image of the city or sense of local cohesion? They could be estimated by a contingent valuation study but, in fact, they do not necessarily have to be quantified; it is enough to know that they would exist. This is because a social discount rate can be used that takes into account the often unspecified nature of external benefits and public goods characteristics.

Once these data have been estimated, the following equation can be applied:

$$NPV = \sum_{t=0}^{n} \frac{C_t}{(1+r)^t} - \sum_{t=0}^{n} \frac{R_t}{(1+r)^t} = 0$$

where

- NPV = net present value;
- t = the time over which each item is discounted, usually the year;
- n = the period of planning;
- C = costs;
- R = revenues; and
- r = discount rate.

The sign Σ denotes the summation of costs and revenues (benefits) over the time period n over which the project is planned.

The museum example again

Costs have to be incurred from the beginning (t = 0) but revenues do not accrue until later, when the project is completed (t = 6). Let us say the building cost of 50 million is spread evenly over the five years it takes to build it. Then, for t = 1 to 5, C_t is 10 million per year. Thereafter, the costs are the costs of any maintenance needed to the building (if the decision is only about building the museum, the costs of running the museum would not need to be taken into account). On the revenue side, there can be no revenue until the museum opens in year 6, so, for t = 1 to 5, R_t = 0, and thereafter the revenues flow in. Both costs and revenues are discounted by the discount rate (or internal rate of return) r, which makes these streams of future costs and revenues equal so that the NPV is zero at time 0, when the decision has to be made. The crucial decision variable is the value of r. If the value for r is greater than the cost of borrowing the capital outlay, then the project is profitable. So, for our city council, the museum is a socially worthwhile investment if r = 5 per cent or more. This is when the social discount rate would come into the story, however: the city council (or central government) might apply a lower social discount rate for projects, such as the museum, that have high expected external benefits; the lower the social discount rate, the more likely it is that the project will be accepted. (The reverse is true for private business undertakings: the greater the risk, the higher the discount rate needs to be, and then there will be fewer projects that reach that hurdle of acceptance).

The benefits of CBA for policy-makers

Finally, it should be pointed out that why economists favour cost–benefit analysis is because the estimated internal rate of return or discount rate for each project – a school, hospital, sports stadium or museum, for example – can be compared, thus making the choice of how to spend public money much easier. Governments usually have an agreed value for the social discount rate, which means that the value for any one project can be compared to it and the decision made on that basis. Of course, such figures do not have to be binding; if a country wants to hold the Olympic Games, it will go ahead even if the expected losses are huge (though they will probably be presented to the public as expected net benefits)!

Economic impact studies

The thinking behind economic impact studies is similar to that for cost–benefit studies and both are based on welfare economics. The main difference is that the external private effects on other *producers*, also called production spillovers, are taken into account as well as the external benefits to consumers. When a museum opens next to a café, the café owner profits from extra customers with no effort or expenditure of his or her own – a clear case of an externality in production. This café owner benefits, but it also has to be considered if these customers have been diverted from other cafés in the city or if they are additional ones brought in by increased tourism due to the museum; it is only from the latter that the city gets net benefits. In fact, as is discussed in chapter 19, if the museum were to be financed by the national government, instead of by the city, there may be no net gain nationally even if there is gain locally if it simply diverts expenditure from other parts of the national economy. Therefore, it has to be taken into consideration in doing economic impact studies how localised the planning is, who will benefit and what level of government will bear the cost of the project.

Direct and indirect expenditures

Economic impact studies measure the private benefits to visitors by their direct expenditures on the new facility as well as what they spend 'indirectly' on goods and services, such as restaurants, hotels and shops in the vicinity; they may also pay local taxes on their expenditures. These calculations may also be done in terms of extra incomes to those employed directly in the project itself, such as people working in a new museum, as well as the extra employment due to indirect spending. The important word to note in this is 'extra', because, as pointed out above, if the new project merely displaces other expenditures there is no net welfare increase. In relation to employment, the question is whether or not the project leads to employment of previously unemployed people, because if it just competes for workers already employed in other jobs it will bid up wages and could simply cause inflation instead of leading to an overall increase in welfare.

Problems with economic impact studies

An important difference between CBA and economic impact studies is that, in CBA, an internal rate of return for the project is found that can be compared to that of other potential projects or to the government's social discount rate. This is very important to economists, because they are always conscious of opportunity cost and need to be able to make comparisons between the viability of projects. Economic impact studies do not typically do this; they look only at the feasibility of an arts project without necessarily comparing it to, say, building a new sports facility.

A further problem is that non-economists often do not understand that the economic impact is supposed to be a marginal one: what would the effect be of undertaking one project – say, building a new museum? It is not valid to apply this type of study to the arts as a whole or an art form as a whole, say the whole museums sector, and it is certainly not valid to talk about its value to the national economy based on these techniques. For that, studies of value added are needed; these were discussed in chapter 2.

Unfortunately, many impact studies have not observed all the caveats that the underlying economic theory warns of, and therefore they exaggerate the net value of arts projects. There is a role for carefully constructed impact studies and they are often used for local undertakings, such as festivals and other events that attract tourists and increase awareness of a city or region and improve its image in the world (see chapter 19). Box 7.5 describes a study of the economic impact to a local economy of an arts event, a series of concerts by the Grateful Dead band.

Public finance

Welfare economics applied to the arts and culture makes a case for intervention in the market economy in order to increase output to a

Box 7.5 The economic impact of a Grateful Dead concert series in Las Vegas

The Grateful Dead pop group performed in three concerts in Las Vegas in 1995, bringing both benefits and costs to the local economy. Authors Ricardo Gazel and Keith Schwer (1997) have analysed the economic impact of the concerts. They estimated the benefits as additional expenditures from goods and services sold to non-local concert attendees plus the expected expenditures of local patrons who would have travelled elsewhere to attend the show if it had not taken place in Las Vegas. The costs included expenses for additional policing and the cost of any damage, etc.; those costs were not borne by the local economy, however, as they had been paid up front by the concert promoters.

The three concerts attracted 46,000 visitors to Las Vegas who said they came exclusively to attend the concerts, and they contributed somewhere between $17 and $28 million of additional income to the local economy. The authors estimate that the concerts created 'between 346 (conservative) and 589 (optimistic) sustained jobs' and that 'an additional impact of close to $10 million could be expected (from future visits in 1995 of fans attending the show who otherwise would not have visited the area)'.

Gazel and Schwer conclude that popular bands that can attract large out-of-town crowds can have a positive net economic impact in the local economy, depending on the size of the spillover effects. Moreover, the 'spillovers' could finance subsidies for the arts and cultural events. For that, they would have to be translated into local tax revenues, for example via higher revenues from sales taxes.

Note that the Grateful Dead were unable to capture the 'uncovenanted' benefits to the local economy, so Las Vegas got a 'free lunch'. The authors point out that such news might silence those local critics who opposed the concerts taking place on their doorstep.

Source: Gazel and Schwer (1997).

level greater than the market would achieve left to private incentives. In many situations, this means that governments undertake the task of stimulating arts and heritage organisations to produce higher levels of output, which they do by means of direct and indirect subsidies financed by taxation. The theory of public finance deals with the analysis of taxes and subsidies and lays down rules for considering both their efficiency and equity effects.

Efficiency and equity

The concepts of private and social efficiency were investigated earlier in relation to welfare economics, and they are also an important aspect of the study of public finance.

Allocative efficiency

Taxes alter the allocation of resources because they alter incentives. Income taxes reduce the consumer's income; taxes on specific goods and services increase their prices and so alter consumption patterns; taxes on business profits reduce profits; and so forth. Some types of taxes distort incentives less than others and therefore are considered more efficient (or less inefficient); for instance, if all goods and services are taxed at the same rate, as with value added tax or sales tax, this is less likely to alter consumption patterns and alter the allocation of resources – allocative efficiency.

Sometimes, certain items are exempted from taxation in order to make them more attractive relative to other goods; for example, books are zero-rated for VAT in the United Kingdom; elsewhere, theatre tickets are exempt from tax. Such 'tax breaks' or 'tax waivers' are a form of indirect subsidy, because they offer benefits to those consuming the goods and services on the one hand and, on the other, the government has to raise the 'waived' taxes elsewhere. Subsidy is subject to the same efficiency criteria as taxation, and as they are so important to the economic analysis of the cultural sector I devote a section below to them.

Equity

Equity can be used in several contexts in economics: in relation to taxation, in relation to the distribution of income and wealth, and also in relation to the distribution of benefits from public expenditure. Many policies are motivated by equity concerns, including cultural policy, in which equity or fairness is mostly connected to the distribution of resources that enable or prevent people from having access to the arts and other cultural goods and services. People on low incomes – students, the unemployed and senior citizens living on pensions – are often regarded as worthy of financial help to access the arts and are eligible for concessionary lower entry prices. Since variable costs are the same for all consumers, arts organisations offering these price concessions need subsidy to compensate for the loss of revenue due to the lower price. Many arts organisations regard it as their duty to use their subsidy for these purposes and some are required to do so as a condition of subsidy.

Equal access to financial resources is not the only equity issue, however; access to arts and heritage facilities can be difficult for people with disabilities, and equitable treatment for them has become an important (and often costly) aspect of cultural policy. Another issue is geographical distribution: some countries have (or had) very marked concentration of arts and heritage organisations and facilities in the capital city, making access very expensive for people in the regions, who, of course, pay taxes for national facilities. Greater equity in geographical distribution has been a feature of cultural policy in addition to the above.

Finally, there is also the question of equality of opportunity (equity) in access to arts training. This is discussed in chapter 11.

Taxation

The analysis of taxation can be looked at in terms of equity and efficiency. Equity underlies the case for progressive income taxation, whereby people on lower incomes pay proportionately lower rates of tax than the better off. It might also be said to underlie one of the most important 'canons' of taxation – the benefit principle of taxation, which is that those who benefit from public expenditure should contribute towards it and those who pay a tax should benefit from it. These criteria are used to evaluate equity in the distribution of taxation and subsidy in the arts: subsidy in the arts has a regressive effect, as the people who benefit most from it, as we saw in chapter 6, are on average better off while the 'burden of taxation' is spread over all taxpayers.

Direct and indirect taxation

Taxes are classified as direct or indirect: direct taxes (income and profits tax, for example) are levied directly on individual persons and businesses; indirect taxes are those levied via third parties, such as suppliers of goods and services, who charge the taxes to consumers. There are many types of tax in use by governments at different levels of government: besides income (and wealth and inheritance taxes), central and federal governments also levy taxes on goods and services (sales tax, such as VAT in the European Union), on imports (import duties or tariffs) and on business profits (profits tax, corporation tax); there are also specific (per unit) taxes on certain goods, such as tobacco or gasoline, that are designed to cut consumption. Local governments also use local income taxes, sumptuary taxes (say on hotel occupants) and property taxes. The purpose of taxation in general is to finance the activities of government, and the greater the level of public expenditure, the more tax revenue has to be levied. Then the question of the 'burden of taxation' arises: who pays the taxes and how are they distributed? Sales taxes and the like are paid by those who consume the goods, and if there is an uneven distribution of consumption between rich and poor the burden of taxation is not equally borne. An example of this is the 'specific tax' on tobacco and cigarettes, which nowadays in developed countries are consumed proportionately more by poorer than by richer people; the tax is a fixed amount per packet of cigarettes, so all consumers, rich and poor, pay the same.

From the efficiency point of view, a tax must not be so high as to displace consumption of the good. Therefore, goods with a low elasticity of demand are typically taxed. As noted above, however, some goods may be exempt from tax for 'merit' reasons, and this can be a source of imputed subsidy to the cultural sector.

Indirect tax and tax waivers

Indirect subsidy is common in the United States and applies to the arts and heritage as well as to many other types of non-profit activities: the tax system makes concessions on income or profit taxation for donations to arts or heritage organisations. Tax waivers that allow corporations to count expenditures on arts sponsorship as business expenses are a form of indirect tax expenditure. In some countries, notably the United States, private individuals can get waivers on income tax for their gifts to arts organisations, and this policy is gradually being adopted in one form or another in other countries.

This form of subsidy has an important implication for cultural policy: indirect tax giving is not in the hands of elected policy-makers but in those of the donors – the individual patrons and boardrooms of corporations. Their choice of art form or type of organisation is what decides the amount of this indirect subsidy via the amount of tax waived. If, for example, they favoured museums over the performing arts, their choices would alter the distribution of arts funding but without any responsibility to taxpayers. The significance of indirect funding is discussed in detail in chapter 8 in connection with the performing arts and the policy implications are dealt with in chapter 10.

In the United Kingdom and some other countries that have similar laws, arts and heritage organisations can register as charities, and then they benefit from a range of tax and other concessions. They also have to fulfil requirements on governance, however, and have boards of trustees with formal responsibility for financial probity and solvency. This can have considerable influence on the way the organisation is run and has implications for arts management.

Types of subsidy

Subsidies are the expenditure side of public finance and they may be analysed using the economics of public finance. In economics it is far more common to analyse the effect of various types of taxes on the markets for goods and on consumption, making a distinction between 'lump sum', 'specific' and 'ad valorem' taxes. A lump sum tax is a fixed amount of tax, like a poll tax, that every liable person pays regardless of income (and is therefore regressive). A specific or 'excise' tax, as outlined above, is a fixed payment per unit of a good, and so tax revenues increase with the number of units sold. An ad valorem tax depends upon the value of sales and so depends not only on the amount sold but also on the price; value added tax is a certain percentage, say 17 per cent, of the amount spent on a purchase. Public finance theory analyses the effects of these different taxes on economic behaviour in the market, and at the level of the individual consumer or producer and their ability to raise revenue for the government. What is less common is to apply the same kind of analysis to subsidy, but that is needed in cultural economics in order to understand the effect of direct public expenditure on arts organisations and how particular types of policy measure work.

In countries in which grants are made to private non-profit arts and heritage organisations, the funding body has the problem of inducing them to comply with the policy. This is a 'principal–agent' problem, and the funding body may use different types of subsidy to encourage compliance with its policy aims; the funding body (the principal) must set up the right incentives to the arts or heritage organisation (the agent).

In a number of European countries, subsidy is in fact direct finance through central, regional or local government (or possibly all three), and is typically in the form of a regular lump sum grant. One problem with such lump sum subsidy is that arts and heritage organisations become accustomed to receiving them and complain bitterly and publicly when they receive less than they expect, and they can force the government to restore their former level of funding by creating a lot of adverse publicity, for example by accusing the government of dirigisme and interference in the arts. One result of this kind of behaviour (which is widely reported) is that new arts organisations and art forms that have not yet got their foot in the door find it difficult to get a share of the funds available. The result is often that the well-established organisations doing more traditional work get disproportionately subsidised. This topic is discussed in chapter 10.

Lump sum grant

Lump sum grants to arts and heritage organisations would appear to be the most common form of both public subsidy and private giving. While lump sum taxes are rejected as regressive on equity grounds, a lump sum subsidy is regarded as having the benefit on efficiency grounds that it distorts incentives the least: lump sum monetary welfare payments to redistribute income are regarded as being neutral with respect to the allocation of resources (so, for example, food stamps are not neutral, as they increase the consumption of food and therefore alter relative prices). The same logic applies to a lump sum subsidy to an organisation producing arts or heritage services: a payment of a fixed amount regardless of the level of output or size of the organisation would not alter the mix of services offered. That may or may not be a good thing, however, depending upon what the policy objectives of subsidy are – whether they are to maintain the status quo or to alter the output decisions of the recipient.

Per unit subsidy

It may well be that the purpose of intervention by a private sponsor or the government is to achieve a specific aim. In that case, the subsidy would be that a certain amount was given to the organisation based on its achieving the target, for example a target number of visitors or of particular categories of visitor, such as new audiences. To get the subsidy, the arts organisation would have to show the funding body that the goal of the policy – say to bring in more people under the age of twenty-one or people from an ethnic minority – had worked and that the subsidy should be paid accordingly. Then the subsidy is awarded per unit of the chosen target.

Ad valorem subsidy

With an ad valorem subsidy, the amount would depend upon the value of the targeted item; so, for instance, the subsidy might be aimed at reducing ticket prices, and the loss of income from sales at the lower prices would determine the amount of subsidy. A policy of 'matched funding', in which the government funding body matches the amount of private finance raised by the organisation from gifts and sponsorship, would also be an ad valorem type of subsidy. Notice that the per unit and ad valorem types of subsidy involve a particular policy goal, unlike the lump sum subsidy, which just keeps the organisation afloat. One instance of the use of an ad valorem subsidy to achieve a specific target is given in box 7.6, taken from the policy statement for the Netherlands for the period 2001–4 by the then secretary of state for culture, Rick van der Ploeg.

Box 7.6 New audiences policy in the Netherlands, 2001–4, under Frederick van der Ploeg, secretary of state for culture

Professor Rick van der Ploeg is an economist who entered the Dutch parliament and became secretary of state for culture in the Netherlands between 1998 and 2002. During that time he formulated cultural policy for the period 2001 to 2004, introducing several financial incentive schemes aimed at increasing the demand for culture and reducing the dependence of Dutch performing arts organisations and museums on government subsidy.

The main thrust of his policy was directed at getting new audiences to the arts, especially young people and ethnic minorities – the 'confrontation of cultures'. Accordingly, he required cultural organisations to set aside at least 3 per cent of their grant income for new audiences, to be placed in a fund to which the organisation had to apply and demonstrate its success in meeting this target in order to have access to the money. In addition, each organisation was asked to ensure that its individual policy plans included a separate statement of how in practical terms it intended to take account of cultural diversity, both in its provision and in its relations with the public. These projects could either be activities in the field of arts education or projects run for and by young people, targeted activities in inner city areas, special tours of local theatres or introductory programmes for cultural minorities. Such activities were not to be part of the institution's mainstream activities, and the 3 per cent could include only the variable costs of provision and not the institution's normal overheads. Institutions that refused to meet this requirement or failed to do so would have 3 per cent of their subsidies withheld.

Van der Ploeg also introduced vouchers for schoolchildren to enable them to make six visits to cultural organisations of their choice.

Sources: Van der Ploeg (2004a, 2006).

Economic analysis of subsidy

The impact of different types of subsidy may be formally analysed for its effect on the market for a cultural good and for how it affects the behaviour of the individual organisation (or firm). The effect is analysed by comparing a before and after situation and the changes that are predicted for the quantity of output produced and consumed and the change in the price of the good or service.

Effect of subsidy on the market for a good or service

Taking the market for theatre performances as an example market, demand, D, depends upon their price. On the supply side, there could be many theatres competing for audiences (as in the West End of London or on Broadway) or there may only be a few; either way, there is an upward-sloping supply schedule, S, showing that the number of performances offered increases as the price rises; the market is in equilibrium at price P_1 and number of performances Q_1 – the situation that would come about in an unsubsidised market. Figures 7.2a and 7.2b demonstrate shifts in supply due to subsidies in theatres: 7.2a shows the effect of a lump sum subsidy and 7.2b shows the effect of an *ad valorem* subsidy.

A lump sum subsidy to theatres (comparable in amount to the gap between the private and social benefit modelled in figure 7.1) either encourages them to offer more performances at every price or enables more theatres to enter the market, and so it shifts S out to S', as pictured in figure 7.2a. This leads to a new lower equilibrium price, P_2, and a greater number of performances, Q_2.

What determines the increased number of performances, Q_1–Q_2, is two things: the amount of the subsidy that determines the size of the shift S–S' and the elasticity of market demand that determines the slope of D, and so the response of audiences to lower ticket prices. In this context, the amount of the subsidy is that needed to overcome underproduction due to market failure; it

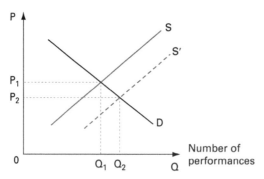

Figure 7.2a   Effect of a lump sum subsidy on the theatre market

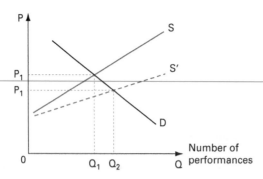

Figure 7.2b   Effect of an *ad valorem* subsidy on the theatre market

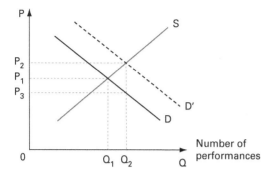

Figure 7.2c   Effect of a voucher or tax reduction on the number of performances

therefore finances a higher level of output than the market alone would achieve. An *ad valorem* subsidy (figure 7.2b) is modelled in the same way, with the difference that S shifts out proportionately more to the right as the value of the supply increases with both a higher price and a greater volume of output; the 3 per cent subsidy for new audiences in the Netherlands is an example of an *ad valorem* subsidy (see box 7.6).

Tax reductions and vouchers

A voucher scheme or the reduction of tax on a good, such as the zero-rating of VAT or a sales tax mentioned above, is modelled in figure 7.2c; with the appropriate amount of subsidy on the demand side, D shifts out to D'. Output (the number of theatrical performances) rises to Q_2 and the revenues to theatres rise from $P_1 \times Q_1$ to $P_2 \times Q_2$, giving them the incentive to produce more; the consumer pays only P_3 and the voucher is worth $P_2 - P_3$ at that level of output. $(P_2 - P_3) \times Q_2$ is the amount of the subsidy.

Effect of subsidy on an individual arts organisation

The question is: how does the organisation use the subsidy? Principal–agent problems can (and do) arise when the organisation receiving the subsidy does not share the objective of the policy-maker. Moreover, which type of subsidy is to be used? As demonstrated above, funding bodies may use different types of subsidy to achieve different outcomes. All these possibilities mean that there are many ways of analytically modelling the effect of the subsidy on the organisation's decisions about price and output. Therefore, simplifications have to be made to avoid the story becoming complicated with too many diagrams. It is important that the underlying assumptions are understood, however, with respect to the way a diagram (or an algebraic model) is constructed; for example, we need to know if the organisation is a monopoly (say the only theatre in the region) or if it has to compete with others providing very similar performances (such as Broadway or West End musicals). In what follows, it is assumed that the arts organisation is a non-profit enterprise that has a monopoly.

Comparison of a non-profit monopoly with and without subsidy

Figure 5.5 provided the basis for analysing the effect of subsidy on the non-profit theatre. To recap on that choice of how to model the effect of subsidy on the theatre: there is reason to believe that many enterprises in the creative industries have the features of a natural monopoly – that is, they have high fixed costs and relatively low marginal costs with increasing returns to scale that result in an ever-falling average total cost curve. As a non-profit organisation, the theatre does not seek to make a profit, but it must cover its total costs. A lump sum subsidy can be thought of as reducing the amount of the average fixed cost such that it shifts down from ATC to ATC′, as shown in figure 7.3; if the theatre sets its price equal to ATC, the subsidy would allow it to reduce its price from P_N to P'_N and to increase its output from Q_N to Q'_N. Notice that, in figure 7.3, the amount by which output is increased (the demand for extra performances) depends, as before, on the elasticity of demand and the amount of the subsidy.

Subsidy and marginal costs

In the above analysis, marginal costs play no role in the price and output decisions of non-profit organisations. This is because it is assumed that non-profit organisations equate ATC to average revenue (AR), which is also the same as demand (D), and that rules marginal costs and marginal revenues out of the picture. In a natural monopoly, marginal cost pricing, though most efficient from the welfare economics point of view, would not enable the theatre to make sufficient revenue to cover its fixed costs. The extra cost of

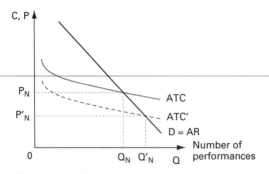

Figure 7.3   Effect of a subsidy on a non-profit theatre

producing an extra theatrical performance or of an extra visitor to a museum is an important consideration for a performing arts organisation or museum, however, and it is surely also important to know if that extra cost would be covered by extra revenue, if not from the entry fee, at least from the combination of earned income (TR) and subsidy.

Welfare economics and natural monopoly

Natural monopoly can be socially beneficial, because average costs fall as output rises and so prices may be reduced, but if the firm is a private for-profit enterprise the monopoly would be socially harmful, as it cannot be contested, as explained in chapter 5. Therefore, the welfare-maximising solution is to regulate the monopoly, and there is a well-worked-out set of rules for regulation, which are routinely applied to utilities such as gas and water: a two-part tariff with marginal cost pricing for use of the good or service (that is, the lowest possible price) plus a payment of some sort that covers the average fixed cost; in the present context, that would be achieved by a subsidy (recall EF in figure 5.4).

Natural monopoly and subsidy

Going back to the example of subsidy to a theatre discussed above, we can combine figure 7.3 with figure 5.4 to produce figure 7.4. The welfare-maximising point, E, is where P = MC, and this produces the socially optimal number of performances, Q_E. Subsidy EF would shift ATC to ATC' and give the theatre the incentive to produce Q_E. Note that the subsidy does not affect MC because its effect is on fixed, not variable, costs as we assumed a lump sum subsidy. The theatre would then charge price P_E with earned revenues from ticket sales of P_E x Q_E and subsidy of EF x Q_E. This is illustrated in figure 7.4.

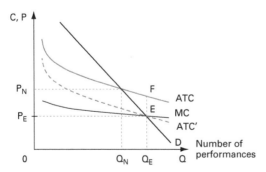

Figure 7.4   Effect of subsidy as a two-part tariff

Subsidy and objectives of arts organisations

The above analysis deals with a lump sum subsidy; the point was made earlier, however, that different subsidies can have different impacts, and they would result in different price and output combinations. Furthermore, the outcome would also depend upon the objective function of the non-profit organisation. This kind of economic theorising is adapted from the neoclassical treatment of for-profit organisations assumed to have the aim of maximising profits, but the objective function of non-profit organisations is less straightforward; it was assumed here that the theatre was maximising attendance but it could, alternatively, have the objective of maximising the quality of its productions and decide to spend the extra revenue on more lavish sets and costumes or on producing unpopular avant-garde plays; or it may do a combination of the two. In fact, unless the arts organisation is required to provide a statement of its objectives (a 'mission statement') and of how it intends to use the subsidy or donation, the funding body may not know what the management will do with it. The funding body may be happy to leave such decisions up to the management or it may set a specific objective (as in box 7.6). These topics are the subject of chapter 10.

So why, the reader may ask, do we have to go through all these diagrams only to be told that they do not always work? Is it just economic pedantry? My answer is that I believe it is instructive to take an analytical approach to an issue as important to the arts and heritage as the effects of subsidy on an arts organisation. Subsidy, after all, has an economic logic: granting extra finance to arts organisations is intended to alter their decisions about the price, quantity and quality of their output, and the rationale for granting subsidy in the first place is that reliance on the market would not achieve maximum social welfare. Asking ourselves the question 'How does it work?' reveals the difficulties in getting it to work! Moreover, it is also worth contrasting non-profit with for-profit economic behaviour, not because non-profit organisations should adopt for-profit objectives, but because the contrast shows precisely what the benefits of subsidy are.

Sources of finance to overcome market failure

Though in many countries the extra revenue needed to encourage arts organisations to produce the socially optimal level of production is provided through publicly financed subsidy, it can also come from private giving from clubs and membership organisations, sponsorship, foundations and other voluntary sources (recall box 2.1 on the National Trust). Individuals contribute to the existence of arts organisations by voluntary giving, and that is a significant source of finance, especially (but not only) in the United States. Private sponsorship by commercial enterprises may be motivated by self-interestedness or by philanthropy, just as private giving by individuals is. Philanthropy by attendees implies that the donors are willing to pay not only for the ticket but also for the external benefit; box 8.2 discusses the use of price discrimination to achieve this result. Whatever the motives, though, the effect would be the same: to increase the output of the arts organisation beyond what it would otherwise be if left to the incentive of private revenue alone.

Conclusion

This chapter has dealt with what could be called the theoretical core of cultural economics. It showed how cultural economists have adapted the theories of welfare economics and public finance that have been developed over the years in order to apply them to any area of public policy. It examined cultural policy in the same way as any kind of policy, and that is an important message to get over; there is sometimes a tendency among students of cultural economics to think that the arts and culture face unique problems – that the arts are 'exceptional'. A lot of the analysis contained in this chapter is used in the fields of environmental economics and in the economics of health and of education, as well as in regulating essential utilities that may be privately owned. There are, of course, specific problems and features of the cultural sector, and they are investigated in detail in the remainder of the book.

It is clear from the analysis of Pareto optimality that consensual public policies are hard, if not impossible, to achieve, at least through economic means that involve public expenditure financed by taxation. Voluntary giving as a form of subsidy is one way out of the problem, because any voluntary decision is consistent with the Pareto rule. It may well be that the encouragement of voluntary giving, even if it means forgoing some tax revenues due to tax waivers, is preferable to direct subsidy to arts and heritage organisations. Though that is still a second best solution, it is almost certainly less inequitable than the use of involuntary taxation.

Some economists believe wholeheartedly in the market economy, and this leads them to believe that Pareto optimality can be achieved with government policies that create the conditions for perfect competition rather than the use of subsidy. Policies such as regulation mimic what the perfectly competitive market would do, for example, in the use of marginal cost pricing. Nor is increased welfare achievable only through economic means; changes to laws could also be Pareto improvements.

These are discussions about social efficiency but it is also the case that many policies are concerned with social equity. Even if no government intervention were needed for achieving social efficiency, it can be argued that Pareto optimality is not 'fair' because income and wealth are not evenly distributed. This can also be a problem in cost–benefit analysis if the 'losers' are poorer than the 'gainers'. Particularly in the arts, moreover, it is hard to argue that there is a redistribution of welfare, because those who benefit are better off than the average taxpayer. There are many more issues that subsidy gives rise to, and they are discussed in chapter 10.

Before leaving the subject of this chapter, however, we should ask ourselves a philosophical, methodological question: is welfare economics positive economics? Is such a rule as a potential Pareto improvement, even if it could be applied, free of value judgements or not? This is indeed a controversial subject among economists. Pareto himself believed he had found a philosopher's stone that would end disputes about how to improve social welfare; unfortunately, the world is not as simple as that, and it is now accepted that some of the fundamental tenets of Pareto optimality, such as the advocacy of perfect competition and general equilibrium, and even the principle of voluntary exchange when parties have very different endowments of income and resources, involve implicit value judgements. That may also be the case for some of the underlying assumptions of the second best Pigovian market by market solutions typically adopted in cultural economics. Nevertheless, searching for a rationale for subsidy in these terms is a great deal better than accepting the so-called 'merit goods argument' and imposing the values of the ruling cultural elite on the whole population.

Applying welfare economics to the cultural sector has also shown that our analysis is different for competitive and for monopoly markets. We need more research by cultural economists on the industrial organisation of the subsidised arts sector – is there effective competition?, is it price or non-price competition?, and so on – as a guide to how to think most effectively about this very important question of how an arts organisation uses its subsidy. Cultural economics has had a great deal to say about the general welfare case for subsidy but much less to say about these microeconomic aspects.

Further reading

Welfare economics and public finance are studied at many levels, and many textbooks in economics have good introductory explanations. Some go under the heading 'public economics'. I have covered what might be called the essentials for a course in cultural economics in this chapter but I would strongly recommend that the committed student read one of the 'regular' textbooks to supplement the treatment here. John Sloman's *Economics* (2006) has a good chapter on welfare economics that I have used a lot with UK and Dutch students; now in its sixth edition, you do not need to buy it new; welfare economics at this level has not changed since the fifth or fourth editions!

My *Handbook of Cultural Economics* (Towse, 2003a) has short chapters on the following topics that connect with this chapter: 'Welfare economics', by Mark Blaug (chapter 61); 'Non-profit organisations', by Dick Netzer (chapter 43); 'Public support', by Bruno Frey (chapter 50); 'Tax concessions', by John O'Hagan (chapter 57); and 'Economic impact of the arts', by Bruce Seaman (chapter 27) are all eminently readable and provide a straightforward account of the issues and a short bibliography. 'Applied welfare economics', by William Baumol (chapter 2), is a bit more difficult but worth the extra effort. Bruce Seaman's (2004) article 'Competition and the non-profit arts: the lost industrial organisation agenda' is also recommended.

Chapters 6 and 8 in Bruno Frey's book *Arts and Economics* (2000), on government support for the arts, are clearly expressed and thoughtful statements of the main concerns.

Part II

The 'traditional' economics of the arts and heritage

Introduction

Part II consists of three chapters: chapter 8 on the performing arts, chapter 9 on the economics of museums and built heritage, and chapter 10 on the economic evaluation of cultural policy as it applies to these topics. These chapters build on the previous chapters and apply the economic analysis presented there. This part of the book could be viewed as a summary of the 'traditional' economics of the arts and heritage. There is a large literature on the topics that are discussed in these chapters, and not every topic could be included; instead, the part draws selectively on a few topics that have been most influential in cultural economics.

8   Economics of the performing arts

The performing arts – live music, opera, dance, theatre – occupy a special place in cultural economics for two reasons: they are supported by public funding in many countries and therefore attract attention and controversy; and they were the subject of the economic analysis by Baumol and Bowen introduced in chapter 1.

In the terminology of the creative industries, the performing arts occupy a position at the central core (described in chapter 14). Their activities have been defined in the United Kingdom as including content origination, costume design and making, and lighting, along with live performance. Many of these items are protected by intellectual property law; although live performance is not always protected per se until it is recorded or broadcast, authors and performers have the right to authorise any reproduction.

Economic characteristics of the performing arts

The performing arts (both non-profit and for-profit) have some common economic characteristics. A performance is ephemeral, meaning that it is supplied at a specific moment in time and, when a performance is over, the service it supplied has disappeared. Once the curtain goes up, there is no chance of selling tickets for that performance and it has to go ahead even with a high ratio of unsold seats, though the cost of the performance is the same if the theatre is full or not. Performances are supplied one at a time and the same resources must be replicated at each performance regardless of the size of the audience. There are fixed (sunk) costs to each theatrical production[1] in terms

---

[1] In this context, a 'production' means the concept of the presentation of the work being performed, and is usually associated with a particular director.

of the creation of sets and costumes, preparation and rehearsal time, and these costs can be spread over the run of performances; similarly, an orchestra has fixed costs of obtaining the music and rehearsing it for its performance. The marginal costs of each performance are determined mostly by the labour involved – the performers and stage or backroom staff. Different art forms have a different balance of fixed to variable costs but all have the same characteristic: live performance at a given point in time. Later in this chapter, the main economic features of the different art forms are analysed in turn, taking up the story from the sketches in chapter 4.

Baumol and Bowen and the 'cost disease'

Baumol and Bowen's book on the economics of the performing arts was introduced in chapter 1; it analyses the economic implications of these characteristics of the performing arts, arguing that the high proportion of labour costs in the typical performance and the upward trend in wages would inevitably drive up the costs of production and consequently, the price of performances, at a rate exceeding the rate of inflation. This would cause the performing arts to be ever more expensive, thereby endangering access by audiences. This hypothesis, which has come to be known as Baumol's cost disease or just the cost disease, has formed the basis of a large number of studies on the economics of all the performing arts.

The cost disease provides an explanation for the rise in the costs of producing the performing arts; it has also been used to argue for an increase in public subsidy to the arts, though cultural economists (including Baumol and Bowen) make the case for government intervention through welfare economics, as discussed further in chapter 10.

In many countries, the performing arts account for a significant share of direct public expenditure on the arts, especially if the expenditure per attendee is considered. It is therefore necessary to analyse the relatively high cost of the performing arts, and, in doing so, many of the economic ideas explained in the previous chapters are applied. Accordingly, topics in this chapter include the analysis of audiences for the performing arts, demand and pricing issues, the finance of the performing arts and an evaluation of the cost disease. The chapter ends with a sector-by-sector summary of each of the performing arts in which the results of empirical work by cultural economists are presented.

Table 8.1 Participation rates in the performing arts: selected countries (percentage of population that attended)

Country	Opera	Dance	Theatre	Concert
EU-27 (2007)	18[a]		32	37
Great Britain (2003/4)	7	7	25	13[b]
Spain (2002/3)	3	5	23	8
Italy (2006)			20[c]	9
United States (2002)	3	6	12	11
Australia (2002)	16[d]	10	17	9

[a] Opera, ballet and dance.
[b] Classical.
[c] Includes opera and ballet.
[d] Includes musicals.
Sources: Eurostat (2007), Council of Europe/ERICArts (2008) for the figures on individual European countries, NEA (2003) for those for the United States and Australian Bureau of Statistics (2008) for those for Australia.

Participation rates and consumer expenditure on the performing arts

Participation

Participation in performing arts events varies according to art form, with opera and classical ballet having the lowest rates and theatres the highest, and with classical music concerts coming somewhere in between. Table 8.1 gives participation rates for several countries.

Trends in participation in different art forms and in different countries are also interesting; they are important for evaluating the success of arts policy, which in many countries aims at increasing participation and attendance. Over the last few years theatre attendance was rising in Canada, Italy and Spain, remained more or less constant in Germany and Great Britain and fell in the Netherlands and Russia (in the latter probably due to the reduction in supply rather than a fall in demand). Attendance at classical music concerts stayed the same in Canada, Italy and Great Britain, rose in Spain but fell in the Netherlands and Russia. Opera attracted larger audiences in Italy and Spain while attendance at dance fell in Canada, stayed the same in Great Britain and rose in the Netherlands and Spain.[2]

---

[2] Data from www.culturalpolicies.net, accessed 15 September 2008. Note that different categorisation may be used: for example, opera is included in 'theatre' in Germany and with 'classical concerts' in Italy but reported separately in Great Britain. It is therefore impossible to make exact comparisons, even if one wished to do so.

Repeat attenders

As pointed out in chapter 6, participation surveys typically ask respondents if they have attended 'a performance' in the previous year; that does not tell us what audiences are or how often the individual attends. Audiences are usually measured by the number of seats sold, a figure known to individual arts organisations (which also know how many free tickets were issued), and these figures may be collected by an arts council or ministry of culture. Again, though, figures on audiences do not provide accurate information about how many different individuals are attending, because many members of an audience make repeat visits. Data on repeat attendance are not often published; the Australian Bureau of Statistics does provide such figures, however, and the 2005/6 survey results show that over 50 per cent of attendees attended each art form twice or more in the previous twelve months (and 11 per cent had been six or more times to classical concerts).[3]

Private consumer expenditure on the performing arts

Private consumer expenditure by individuals and households is an indicator of how much people value the arts through their willingness to pay, and official statistics in some countries identify consumer spending on the arts. The National Endowment for the Arts in the United States reports that in 2005 consumer expenditures on arts performances reached $12.7 billion; in real terms (adjusted for inflation), the figure was the same as in the previous year. According to the US Labor Bureau's Consumer Expenditure Survey for 2004, the average expenditure on admissions to movies, theatre, opera and ballet was $92 (equivalent to 41 per cent of all entertainment expenditure).[4] Consumer household expenditure in Canada on the performing arts in 2003 was C$1,170 (around US$850). In the fifteen countries of the European Union in 1999, average household expenditure on cinema, theatre, concerts, museums, galleries, and so on was €140, but no data exist for performing arts alone. The data show considerable variation in this expenditure by country, reflecting not only demand but also price differences between European countries.[5]

---

[3] Data from www.abs.gov.au/ausstats/abs@.nsf/mf/4114.0/.
[4] See www.nea.gov/research/Notes/91.pdf (accessed 21 August 2008).
[5] Calculated from Eurostat (2007: 126).

Sources of finance for the performing arts

Performing arts organisations have earned income from ticket sales and other sales (programmes, refreshments, and so on) and unearned income from public funding and private donations. In Europe, public funding is a major source of finance, though this varies from country to country; for instance, UK arts organisations tend to get less public finance than those in mainland Europe. In the United States, the proportion of income from public sources is relatively low while the proportion of private giving and business sponsorship is considerably higher than in Europe. In Japan, the performing arts are more or less supported from earned income, with public subsidy going to only a few performing arts, such as Noh theatre and Bunraku, with the purpose of preserving the performing heritage as important intangible cultural property; the Agency for Cultural Affairs also sponsors international performing arts festivals with the policy objective of promoting international exchange.[6] There is considerable variety therefore in the finance of the performing arts, and, as shown below, there is considerable variation in the sources of income in the non-profit performing arts – the for-profit sector relies entirely on earned income.

Earned and contributed income in the non-profit performing arts

In the United States, in 2004, non-profit arts organisations earned 44 per cent of their income; unearned income was comprised as follows:[7]

- 43 per cent from private sources (31 per cent from individuals, 9 per cent from foundations and 3 per cent from corporations);
- 13 per cent from public sources (3 per cent local, 1 per cent state and 9 per cent federal).

In 1992 roughly two-thirds of the income of a large sample of performing arts organisations (symphony orchestras, ballet and theatres) in the United States was earned and one-third was 'contributed' – that is, subsidy plus gifts/ sponsorship; for opera and modern dance, the figures were nearer a half.[8] In Australia, 23 per cent of the major companies' income on average came from the Australia Council, the body that supports the performing arts. Figures for thirteen major performing companies in Australia supported by the Australia

---

[6] Agency for Cultural Affairs (2006).
[7] NEA (2007a); the figures do not include tax deductions on private donations.   [8] Felton (1994).

Council show that, in 1993, 26 per cent of their total income came from subsidy and 9 per cent from sponsorship while 58 per cent was earned income. In the Netherlands in 1997, the proportion of box-office receipts to subsidy in the performing arts was 18 per cent for dance, 24 per cent for symphony orchestras, 22 per cent for opera and 14 per cent for theatre.[9]

National, regional and local public finance

The proportion of public finance in the income of performing arts organisations also varies very considerably by art form, and even within art forms, according to whether the organisation is a national, regional or local one. In countries with an 'arm's-length' funding body for the performing arts, the arts council is responsible for distributing public funds (or for advising on the distribution), and the breakdown of allocations by art form is likely to be reported by that body. It may also delegate such decisions to lower-level agencies, however. The NEA in the United States, itself an 'arm's-length' body, allocates 40 per cent of its funds to over sixty state and regional agencies. In Germany, where the states (*Länder*) and municipalities both contribute equally to 87 per cent of total public expenditure for culture (the federal government plays only a small role), 38 per cent of cultural expenditure was spent on the performing arts (music and theatre) in 2003. In Sweden in 2005, where central government expenditure on culture was nearly half the total, its expenditure on theatre, dance and music was 19 per cent, while county councils (10 per cent of government expenditure on culture) spent 41 per cent on them.[10]

A distinction may also exist between national 'flagship' organisations – the national theatre or national ballet, say – that receive subsidy from the central government and regional and local performing arts organisations that receive regional/local finance; in the United Kingdom, subsidy to the 'national companies' is centralised, but other grants are distributed on a regional basis.

Public finance for different performing arts

The distribution of public finance between art forms (ballet, opera, orchestras, music theatre, spoken theatre, and so on) can also be analysed. The Australia Council allocated 50 per cent to music (including opera), 12 per cent to theatre

---

[9] For Australia, Throsby (1996b); for the Netherlands, van der Ploeg (2006: 1193).
[10] See Council of Europe/ERICarts (2008) for Germany and Sweden.

Box 8.1 Federal, state and municipal finance of the performing arts in Austria by art form

Austria is a federal country with a population of just under 8 million that supports the arts from public finance at the federal, state (*Land*) and municipal levels. It is the home of the Vienna State Opera and to the Vienna Philharmonic Orchestra, both among the most prestigious arts organisations in the world. Opera and ballet are included in the 'Theatre/music theatre' category in the table below. Performing arts constituted a quarter of all public cultural expenditure.

Austrian public expenditure on the performing arts by level of public expenditure, 2006

	Total cult. exp.	Federal		State (*Land*)		Municipal	
	€ million	€ million	%	€ million	%	€ million	%
Performing arts	578	183	32	231	40	164	28
Music	87	9	11	30	34	48	55
Theatre/music theatre	393	153	39	165	42	75	19
Multidisciplinary	97	21	22	31	32	45	46

The table (in which the figures have been rounded) shows that 'Theatre/music theatre' dominate state and federal expenditure on the performing arts, while music accounts for the highest percentage of expenditure on the performing arts by municipalities.

Source: Council of Europe/ERICarts (2008).

and 9 per cent to dance in 2005/6. In Spain, a country in which the municipalities are responsible for more than half the public expenditure on culture, the performing arts accounted for 15 per cent of public expenditure in 2003 and, of that, music and dance took up 76 per cent. Therefore, it can be seen that there is variation in the proportion of public finance spent on the performing arts, in the source of that finance (central, regional or city) and in the amounts each spend on the various art forms in the performing arts. This variety explains why it is so difficult to generalise in connection with public finance of the arts and therefore to make inter-country comparisons.

Austria provides very detailed data on public cultural expenditures, and it is possible to see the breakdown of public finance for the performing arts both by art form and by level of government (see box 8.1).

Subsidy to performing arts organisations and to venues

The distinction between the finance of the performing arts company and the finance of the venue (whether theatre, concert hall or other type of podium) is not always made clear when the company that organises the performances is also responsible for its own performance venue. A few countries report these items separately in published cultural statistics, and they are revealing: in the Netherlands, out of a total arts expenditure of €1.3 billion in 2004, €265 million was spent on 'Performing arts' and €361 million on 'Performing arts venues', almost all of the latter being spent by municipalities.[11] Those monies typically both support the fixed costs of running the venue and also include finance for fees and other payments to the performing arts companies that perform there; thus an arts organisation that receives little or no funding can still earn fees that are financed out of public sources, and that is the case in the Netherlands for domestic and visiting foreign companies alike.

Australia also distinguishes expenditures on performing arts and on performing arts venues. Total government expenditure on the performing arts was A\$256 million in 2006/7 and A\$132 million was allocated to performing arts venues.[12]

Pricing the performing arts

Factors influencing ticket prices

A performing arts organisation has to balance commercial and non-commercial factors when setting its prices. One of the main factors that determines the price of performances is the cost of supplying them, but it is also the case that there is a lot of variation in the proportion of income in performing arts organisations that is earned: when that is relatively high in arts organisations that are heavily reliant on income from ticket sales, the question of pricing policy arises. From the analysis of demand in chapter 6, we saw that the responsiveness of attendance to prices – the elasticity of demand for tickets to the theatre or concert hall – has an important influence on revenues from sales and that many arts organisations maximise their income through price discrimination. Organisations in receipt of subsidy may be constrained by the cultural policy-maker to set a ceiling on prices or limit price rises to an amount that is within the reach of 'ordinary' people, however; in other words, admission prices are in effect 'regulated' by the funding body.

---

[11] Council of Europe/ERICarts (2008).
[12] See www.australiacouncil.gov.au/research/arts_funding/facts_and_figures/government_funding (accessed 7 October 2008).

Another factor in pricing policy is the size and layout of the venue – the theatre or concert hall. That may well depend upon the age of the building and how much it has been altered over the years. Many theatres are old buildings that are often important as built heritage in addition to their cultural importance as performing arts venues; these buildings were built with seating capacity reflecting the smaller audience sizes of their day. It is hardly surprising, therefore, that the average cost of a performance is high if fixed and variable costs can be spread only over a relatively small audience.

Price discrimination again

The theory of price discrimination was explained in detail in chapter 6; here some further aspects to it are considered. In the performing arts, there are various ways of segmenting the audience for the purposes of price discrimination: different prices may be charged by location in the theatre or concert hall or by time, for example for a matinee or evening performance; discounts may also be given for 'bulk' sales, usually of a number of different productions or programmes bundled together in season tickets (*abonnements*) but also for group bookings. Location in the theatre – how well you can hear or see the stage, or even by seat quality itself – determines the quality of the experience for different members of the audiences even though the performance is the same.

Performances are scheduled to take place over a period of time with a set number of performances per week over a 'season' or 'run' of performances. Audiences often prefer the 'first run' to later performances and 'premieres' or first nights to subsequent performances, and higher ticket prices may be charged accordingly. Prices may be reduced when 'lead' players are replaced in a production.

One limitation on the scope of price discrimination is that performance schedules have to be planned a long time in advance, as the venue has to plan its programme and the performing company has to plan its use of performers. This means that the schedule of prices also has to be posted well in advance of performances with tickets sometimes going on sale months before the date of the performance. Where season tickets are the norm, preference is often given to customers who are willing to buy a season ticket over those wishing to buy tickets for a single performance; however, some public funding bodies require subsidised organisations to sell 'single' tickets as a policy so that less well off people can attend, and also to encourage attendance by new audiences.

Box 8.2 Price discrimination and voluntary contributions in the non-profit arts

In 1981 an important article by Henry Hansmann pointed out that non-profit arts organisations maximise their revenues by using price discrimination in such a way as to encourage both ticket sales and voluntary contributions; linking the setting of prices so as to encourage private donations from attendees – that is, some people buy a ticket and donate as well – adds another dimension to the theory of price discrimination. Hansmann set out to explain this pricing strategy, and it sparked quite a discussion in the cultural economics literature (see Towse, 1997).

It is contended that only non-profit organisations can do this, as people do not voluntarily contribute to for-profit firms; moreover, tax breaks and government schemes for matching private giving do not usually apply to the latter. If the ticket price is pitched below their willingness to pay (that is, consumer surplus exists), some members of the audience may thus be persuaded to make a donation. Of course, some will free-ride, and it is also very difficult for the organisation to identify potential donors, but the fact remains that a significant proportion of income to non-profit arts organisations comes from private donations.

Source: Hansmann (1981).

Price discrimination and voluntary giving

It has been suggested by cultural economists that another aspect of price discrimination is to set prices in such a way as to attract donations from patrons – usually regular audience members (see box 8.2). Arts organisations also seek to attract members to 'Friends of' organisations to encourage loyal patrons and potential donors. One such attraction for members is that they get preferential treatment in terms of advance purchase of tickets – that is, they are able to 'jump the queue' – and this is, of course, another aspect of price discrimination.

Who sets the prices for the performing arts?

Earlier in the chapter, the point was made that performing arts organisations do not necessarily own or control their performance venues. That is obviously the case for touring companies, but it is also the case for some that regularly perform in one venue.

The question therefore arises as to which sets the prices for performances – the venue or the performing company? In most situations, there is likely to be an agreement between the two (something that no cultural economist to my knowledge has written on). When a 'national' company tours to a small town venue, however, the local venue may not wish to charge a higher than normal price. This raises interesting principal–agent problems that have not yet been addressed in the literature of cultural economics. Moreover, in cases in which the company owns its own venue, it may rent it out to other companies on tour, say during the summer break, thus providing a source of income.

Prices of 'complements'

The earned income of performing arts organisations comes from the sale of complementary goods and services, such as programmes, food and drinks, and maybe also of recordings, as well as from ticket sales. Performing arts venues have several advantages here: they have a monopoly of information about the programme and, because of the limited time of the intervals between acts, they also have an advantage in the sale of food and drinks. Performing arts organisations may use these advantages to extract maximum profits from these complementary goods and services. An irony is that some performing arts organisations claim to make more from them than from ticket sales!

Demand for the performing arts

In this section, I turn to the question of demand and discuss some of the empirical studies of demand for the various performing arts. As defined in chapter 6, demand means the quantity of an item purchased at various prices, and the analysis of demand seeks to establish the influence of prices and the consumer's income on demand; empirical studies do this using econometric techniques that capture the causal relation between changes in price and income and their effect on the quantity demanded of an item, thereby estimating the elasticity of demand with respect to price and income. Demand is also influenced by taste and preferences, but they are not observable and have to be taken as given in any empirical study.

Which price?

One of the first issues to be resolved in a demand study is how the price is to be measured, since most arts organisations use price discrimination. In theory, demand for tickets should be at every price – the demand for seats in the front rows, the balcony, and so on – but such data are very difficult to obtain and an average of all prices typically has to be used. Presumably, managers of arts venues would like to know what the effect of changing the designation of seating at various prices within the venue would be – the cross-elasticity of demand for tickets in different parts of the venue – as it influences revenue. In practice, most empirical studies of demand have not produced that information and have used average revenue data (but see the section below on ballet).

Measuring quantity in the performing arts

Similarly, an appropriate measure of quantity has to be adopted in a demand study. In chapter 5, the subject of measuring the output of the performing arts was raised – is it the number of performances or the number of attendees, and so forth? In relation to demand, the number of tickets sold is a measure of quantity, but, as with price, it is not only the location in the theatre that is the issue but also the number sold for a particular production or performance. From the discussion in the preceding paragraphs, it is obvious that 'a performance' has many dimensions – what are called in economics 'hedonic' characteristics – that affect demand. Thus, in addition to the bundle of which work is performed, the location of the seat, and so on, the time element (the time of day, the day in the week, the point in the run of the production or programme) should, ideally, be included.

Quality

Another dimension to these hedonic characteristics that is expected to have an influence on demand is the quality of the production. This is important not only for programme planning on the part of the performing arts company, but also for the public funding body – the ministry of culture or the arts council – that provides subsidy in order to raise or maintain standards of quality.

A pioneering study by David Throsby has tackled the question of how to assess the influence of quality on demand.[13] He identifies several characteristics of quality: the work itself, technical factors in the production, the benefits to audiences and to society and the benefits to the art form itself. He then analyses these characteristics by using reviews in the press of the productions of a number of theatres in Australia in order to measure their effect on attendances and willingness to buy seats for the performances at the various prices. Another study has attempted similar measures of quality: an important analysis of German regional theatres by Susanne Krebs and Werner Pommerehne finds that the theatre director has a choice of variables that he/she can use to achieve success as perceived by his/her political 'bosses' – the officials controlling the public funds that finance the theatre (typically to the tune of around 85 per cent of total income in the early 1990s).[14] This type of

---

[13] Throsby (1990).   [14] Krebs and Pommerehne (1995).

theatre in Germany typically has a mixed programme of opera, operetta/ musical theatre, spoken drama and dance. One of the variables Krebs and Pommerehne identify is 'highbrowness' or 'lowbrowness' – that is, a general quality characteristic of the programme and productions. Specifically, they consider the interaction of quality and price so that, if the director was required to achieve a minimum attendance as a measure of success, he or she would combine price increases with a greater share of lowbrow productions in the season, or vice versa; if increased funding removed the need to increase prices, the director would plan a more highbrow programme for the season and raise quality.

These studies demonstrate the very complex nature of demand for the performing arts and the interaction of artistic and economic factors. I return to the implications for cultural policy later under the heading 'principal–agent' issues.

Elasticity of demand

In an authoritative survey of empirical studies of demand for the performing arts, Bruce Seaman reports the results of forty-four econometric investigations of elasticity of demand that have been carried out since the 1960s.[15] There are technical differences between the studies; for example, some use time series data and others use cross-section data, and different statistical techniques have also been adopted. There are also different levels of aggregation; some studies look at data for individual arts organisations whereas others look at demand for all performing arts. Understanding all these features is a complex issue that calls for professional expertise; nevertheless, the general results of these studies are accessible and have considerable significance for arts policy, specifically as to whether subsidy aimed at reducing prices succeeds as a way of increasing access to the arts.

It is therefore somewhat depressing to report that, despite all efforts (at least so far), there is no firm consensus even as to whether the own price elasticity of demand is greater or less than one. While earlier studies found relatively inelastic demand and that became the established view in cultural economics, later work has cast doubt on that result; the balance of opinion is that inelastic demand is still the favoured model, however. There is some evidence that cross-elasticity is positive – that is, there is substitution between the performing arts and other goods, such as cinema – and that quality matters, though it is not yet obvious how it should be measured.

---

[15] Seaman (2006).

What seems no longer to be a firmly established fact is that income elasticity is greater than one, and that this cannot be tested without taking into account the opportunity cost of leisure time and the proportion of income that outlay on tickets represents to the consumer. In addition, the extent to which a consumer of the arts is experienced and has learned to make informed judgements about hedonic qualities has been found to influence the elasticity of demand: the more you know, the greater the elasticity with respect to price. Clearly, there is more work to be done here, but the problem is usually (as so often in cultural economics) that the relevant data are not easy to obtain in sufficient quantity or quality for doing reliable statistical analysis.

Costs of production in the performing arts

Although each art form has its own cost structure, with some having lower total costs than others, there are some general features of costs in the performing arts that can be noted. First, a performance takes place in a venue (which could be a field or park for some) and requires appropriate technical facilities, whether a stage, a sound system or a 'big top'; this is a fixed cost regardless of the number of persons who turn out for the performance (though some facilities are more durable or more flexible than others and can be altered if needed). Second, a performance uses live labour services in 'real time' that cost the same regardless of the size of the audience; as mentioned above, this is one of the defining economic features of the performing arts, and one that makes them different from other cultural services. Performers need to co-ordinate with each other in order to produce the performance at the advertised time and the performance is 'perishable', so that, once the performance has commenced, the size of the audience does not change (of course, people can leave, but they have had to pay to get in!). Third, as with many other cultural goods, the marginal cost of supplying an extra attendee, at least up to the point of full capacity at the venue, is very low. This is the 'classic' natural monopoly problem of high fixed (often sunk) costs and very low marginal costs. Marginal cost pricing therefore does not cover the fixed cost, and that has to be financed by charging a higher price that includes the average fixed cost (usual for for-profit firms); or, typically for non-profit arts organisations, the 'gap' between average total cost and marginal cost (see figure 5.4) is filled by grants and donations from public and/or private sources.

Fixed and variable costs

Fixed costs do not alter with the size of the output; in the short run the advertised programme and size of the venue are fixed but they may be altered in the long run; variable costs are incurred due to the number of units of output and, as we saw above, that could be the number of performances of a programme or the number of productions over a period of time, such as a year. It is also necessary to separate out the costs of operating the venue and those associated with the performing company. When the company owns or has control of its venue, it has to deal with both: as noted earlier, theatres and other venues are often owned by the state or municipality, and the arts organisation has little or no responsibility for them. However, in New York's Broadway and London's West End, theatres are privately owned, and they may be rented by performing arts companies for their productions or the theatre management may hire in performing companies to offer a programme of events. There has been no work by cultural economists on this topic.

Some major subsidised performing arts companies (in London, the Royal Opera House, Covent Garden, English National Opera at the Coliseum and the Royal Shakespeare Company in Stratford) own their venues. The focus of work in cultural economics on costs in the performing arts has been on the company rather than the venue, however.

Fixed and variable costs of a performing arts company

The fixed costs of a performing arts organisation can be divided into those associated with the management and those with the artistic side of the enterprise. Management costs are labour costs for personnel dealing with the business side of the arts – planning, hiring, bookings, finance, and so on – and the artistic director may also be part of the management team; office and other running costs belong to this category. In the short run, management costs are fixed, but they vary with the total size of the artistic personnel in the long run. On the artistic side, performing arts companies operate different models: some organisations work with a permanent roster of performers – 'repertory' theatre, dance and opera companies, orchestras, and so on – and others form temporary companies for the purpose of one production or run of performances. Members of the permanent company are contracted for a certain period of time while the temporary companies have short-term contracts that last for the particular run of performances.

Nevertheless, even where there is a permanent company, individual performers and other artists, such as conductors or choreographers, may be hired on short-term contracts for specific productions or programmes. Therefore what are fixed costs and what are variable costs of the performing arts company depends upon the term and conditions of the employment contract (discussed in more detail in chapters 11 and 12), and these vary considerably between countries. In Germany, any worker who has been employed for more than fifteen years has the job for life, and this applies to all performers employed in the state theatres, orchestras and choirs; thus all such artistic personnel labour costs can be viewed as a fixed cost. In the United States, as in the United Kingdom, contracts for artistic personnel can be very short term (even one performance) or permanent, but even the latter are likely to be renewable rather than fixed for life.

Fixed costs of rehearsals

Rehearsal time is a fixed cost, though the amount of time that is devoted to it can be varied, because the cost of labour time and space rental must be incurred before the performance can take place. These are likely to be sunk costs, as they are specific to particular productions. A distinction can be made between a revival of an existing production and a new production of a work or works. Every new work that is performed has to be rehearsed, and, for some art forms, that requires the long-term provision of rehearsal venues with special facilities; rehearsal periods vary according to what is going to be performed but could be six weeks for theatrical productions; revivals also need rehearsal time, though how much depends on the extent of changes, say of lead performers. The discussion about quality is also relevant here: the newer the work and the more novel the production (one measure of quality), the greater the investment in the upfront costs. 'Safe' programming of warhorses may incur less preparation time and be capable of relatively cheap revivals.

Other fixed costs

Besides rehearsal time, theatrical productions require considerable planning by the artistic director in conjunction with the set, lighting and costume designers; the sets, lighting and costumes for productions themselves require upfront investment; if they can be used for another production, they would be a fixed rather than a sunk cost. Costumes can be hired, however, at least in major centres, and such hire costs are variable costs, as they depend upon the period of time for which they are hired and so vary if the run of performances is reduced or extended. Orchestral and chamber concerts also require forward planning and research for programming, and music (orchestral parts) has to be acquired; this is usually hired from the music publisher (and is thus a variable cost).

Royalty payments for performing rights for works in copyright depend upon the number of performances and on the size of audiences; additional payments are required for recordings and broadcasts. Opera, ballet and dance companies performing to live music also have to pay royalties for performing rights on works in copyright. All these costs, some of which can be made variable but most of which are fixed, have to be incurred for the first performance of a particular production or concert.

Spreading fixed costs

The next question is how they can be spread over the run of performances. There are two questions here. First, what is the appropriate 'output' over which fixed costs can be spread to arrive at average costs (and this is also relevant to marginal costs – the change in variable costs due to another unit of output)? Second, which elements of the production process of a performing arts organisation's output, from planning through to the run of performances, can be changed if circumstances require it and which cannot?

Measures of output

Possible measures of output for the purposes of analysing average fixed cost and marginal cost are the number of performances, the number of productions (plays, opera titles, musical works, and so on), the number of attendees or the number of seats available for sale; for other purposes, for instance monitoring the use of subsidy, other measures might be used, such as cost per attendee; grant-making bodies might also be interested in the number of new productions or commissioned works. There is no economic rule that says what the 'right' measure is, and an arts organisation could well have a composite measure in mind – say a balance of attendances and works produced. Most cultural economists appear to take the number of seats available – that is, the capacity of the venue – as the unit of output, and I do so here.

Average total costs and marginal costs

With that measure in mind, the average fixed cost of a performing arts organisation is total fixed cost divided by the number of seats in the venues in which performances will take place over a given period of time (such as a year). Average total costs are the total of fixed and variable costs averaged over seating capacity, and marginal costs are the extra variable cost due to the addition of one more seat. As stated above, however, the line between fixed and variable costs may not be free of institutional constraints, such as labour contracts and laws.

Factors affecting flexibility

Once a run of performances has been announced and tickets sold in advance (as is usual, especially with sales of season tickets), the 'show must go on' and the same costs per performance have to be incurred even if losses are the result. On the other hand, if the show or run of concerts is a success and there is excess demand, it may be impossible in the short run to meet it by altering the number of performances from that scheduled. The ability to extend the run will depend upon the availability of other suitable performance venues and upon the availability of the performers themselves. Performing arts companies therefore face the difficult calculation of how much to spend up front on preparation and how many performances are needed over which to spread the fixed or sunk costs. In revivals or extensions of production runs, they may have to substitute other lead performers for the 'stars' of the first run (another quality issue) and so alter the prices they charge.

Performing arts companies that assemble for a short run of performances probably do not invest in high fixed costs, and touring is another way of spreading the fixed costs of preparing a limited repertoire of works. Nonetheless, these options do not alter the fact that a performing arts company, however small, has the same variable costs per performance whether the audience is large or small and regardless of how much box-office revenue is brought in from the performance.

Costs of the venue

A venue – a theatre, concert hall or other such performing venue – is a capital asset, and so the land and buildings have alternative uses besides catering for the performing arts. A venue needs to be maintained and serviced in order to serve its purpose and that means having backstage and front-of-house facilities. Backstage requirements are expert craftspeople to make sets and costumes, computerised management of sets and lighting, dressing rooms and wardrobes, facilities for the performers, for opera, dance and musicals an orchestra pit, and so on. Front-of-house needs are a ticketing service (again computerised), bars and restaurants, cloakrooms and other facilities for patrons. When sponsors are involved, they want a private bar for their invitees. If the venue is 'out of town', it needs a car park or garage.

All these facilities need personnel to run them, from stage managers to programme sellers and waiters. Many performing arts companies have a large number of artists: an orchestra can run to eighty plus players and an opera chorus to sixty. They probably also need a canteen, as it is not easy to go out for a snack in costume. A concert hall needs several very high-quality pianos and secure accommodation for musical instruments, which typically cost thousands of euros. These facilities need to be in place before any performances can be mounted in them.

Some of the costs are variable: for example, bar staff are not needed on 'dark' nights, when a theatre has no performance, but stage personnel may need to work to prepare the next show. Thus, as with the costs of the performing company, costs are both fixed and variable, though the theatre is undoubtedly more capital-intensive and therefore has higher fixed costs. Whether a theatre averages its total costs over the number of performances or seats sold presumably depends upon its contract with the performing arts organisation.

Efficiency of performing arts organisations

One of the abiding concerns about the performing arts on the part of arts funding bodies, both public and private, has been the efficiency of the operations of arts organisations. Indeed, it was precisely this concern that prompted the research by Baumol and Bowen that resulted in their famous book. They analysed changes in prices and costs of production over a period of time and constructed a model of unbalanced growth that compared the performing arts sector with the rest of the economy using aggregate production functions in a macroeconomic model. Other cultural economists have used a microeconomic approach and tested efficiency by looking at production and cost functions for a specific sector, such as theatres and museums. In addition to exploring this microeconomic approach, I also consider some of the later criticisms of Baumol and Bowen's work.

Economies of scale

One microeconomic topic that indicates the most efficient level of output is economies of scale; figure 5.1b shows the most efficient size of an enterprise in terms of the long-run average cost curve. In the natural monopoly model, however, there are increasing returns to scale over the whole range of output,

Box 8.3 Efficiency and costs of production in Finnish theatres

Mervi Taalas' study of efficiency and costs of the theatre sector in Finland uses panel data (combining cross-section and time series data) for thirty-seven theatres for the period 1985 to 1993. She tested for efficiency by examining relative price efficiency (RPE) – changes in the combination of capital and labour due to changes in relative factor prices – and she analysed production and cost data to see if economies of scale were present and to establish the 'shape' of the long-run cost function. Data on both physical measures of input and output quantities were needed to estimate the production function and equivalent cost data were needed for estimating the cost function. The measure of labour was the number of man-hours in full-time equivalents, and for labour costs the annual outlay on personnel. The capital costs of running the theatre (front-of-stage and backstage facilities) were calculated on a per seat basis. The measure of output used was the number of attendees instead of the number of seats available, because the theatres did not work to full capacity.

The results show that Finnish theatres were not efficient by the RPE test and that actual average costs exceeded the calculated minimum average cost by nearly 5 per cent. Both capital and labour were overemployed, with excess demand for capital being greater than that for labour; theatres were not combining inputs in economically optimal proportions in light of prevailing market prices. Taalas found that, as the number of theatre-goers increased, theatres tended to respond by increasing the size of auditorium, rather than by arranging labour-intensive reruns, and she suggests that the reasons for this were the managers' desire for large audiences, high-quality productions or large budgets – all of which are associated with subsidy to non-profit organisations.

Sources: Taalas (1997, 2003).

indicating that expansion of the enterprise will lead to lower average total costs. Thus evidence of economies of scale could be empirically tested for by constructing a production function for the activity or by analysing long-run costs. One such study on Finnish theatres is reported in box 8.3, with interesting results.

Concerns over efficiency in the use of public subsidy have led some funding bodies to develop measures of efficiency that enable them to compare the economic and cultural performance of arts organisations.

Efficient use of public subsidy

Figures on subsidy per attendance for different art forms are analysed by some public funding bodies; they show that subsidy is higher for some art forms than others and also that, in some art forms, private spending per seat is higher. Either way, such figures clearly demonstrate the cost per attendance to

Box 8.4 Subsidy per attendance in the performing arts in England

The Arts Council of England (ACE) has surveyed its client organisations and analysed figures on subsidy per attendance in different art forms for several years running over the last decade. It distinguishes the so-called 'national companies' (Royal Opera, English National Opera, Royal National Theatre, Royal Shakespeare Company and the South Bank Centre's concert halls and art gallery) from the other 'regularly funded organisations' and analyses sources of income, reporting the average per attendance.

- The national companies in 2002/3 received public subsidy of £18.88 and earned £16.98 per attendance.
- For the 'regularly funded' organisations, the figures were £7.15 and £7.00, respectively.
- 'Large-scale opera': £43.01 public subsidy and £32.39 earned income per attendance.
- Dance: subsidy £19.16, earned income £18.60 (ballet £26.48 and £25.49, respectively).
- Theatres: subsidy £9.67, earned income £10.48.
- Orchestras: subsidy £14.41, earned income £20.51.

Thus, for example, an opera attendance cost £75.40 on average, to which 57 per cent was contributed by the taxpayer and the rest from earned income – the opera-goer via the ticket price and from private giving; for theatre, the figure was 48 per cent.

Source: Joy and Skinner (2005).

the taxpayer. In the Netherlands in 1997, subsidy per visit was €48 for dance, €120 for opera and €41 for symphony orchestras; these arts organisations typically received 85 per cent of their income from public subsidy. In England, where rates of subsidy are lower, there was also considerable difference in the subsidy per attendee by art form (see box 8.4).

Performance indicators

If public subsidy to the arts is to achieve its objectives and if the funding body is to be held accountable for its decisions, it is necessary to assess the efficiency of its grants to performing arts organisations. In this context, social efficiency is the relevant concept for non-profit organisations, and performance indicators are not just ways of getting arts organisations to cut costs, as some believe. Performance indicators may consist of elementary measures, such as the number of seats sold and/or the percentage utilisation of capacity, and few are as sophisticated as those of the Arts Council of England reported in box 8.4. However simple they are, though, performance indicators must reflect the purposes for which the organisation is being subsidised. I return to the uses and limitations of performance indicators in chapter 10.

Baumol's cost disease

The single most widely known theory in cultural economics that has influenced policy-makers the world over and has been associated with claims for greater subsidy to arts organisations is Baumol and Bowen's prediction that costs and prices in the performing arts will inevitably rise over time. The analysis of what has come to be called Baumol's cost disease was introduced earlier; now it is time to go into it in more detail and investigate its significance forty years later in light of all the subsequent research that has been carried out in cultural economics.

The earnings gap

Baumol and Bowen set out to analyse the causes of the increasing difficulty that performing arts organisations were facing in covering their costs by earned revenues from ticket sales, particularly (though not only) non-profit organisations in receipt of private and public subsidy. The costs of production were rising more rapidly than revenues even though ticket prices were rising and arts organisations faced an 'income gap' (later called the 'earnings gap') as a result. Baumol and Bowen identified this as being due to the 'productivity' lag – the hypothesis that technological progress that drives up productivity in the non-arts sector of the economy cannot be applied to the performing arts. It was held that labour productivity does not rise in the arts (the 'stagnant' or 'unprogressive' sector) while it does rise in the rest of the economy (the 'dynamic' or 'progressive' sector), in which technologically enhanced capital can be substituted for labour, causing the productivity of labour to rise. This effect is exacerbated by the fact that the performing arts are anyway more labour-intensive than industries in the progressive sector.

The integrated labour market

The next step in the argument is that wages in the economy as a whole rise due to the increase in productivity. In the arts the rise in labour costs is proportionately higher than in the 'dynamic' sector, because the arts are more labour-intensive and capital cannot be substituted – the hypothesis of a fixed factor production function for performing arts.[16] Thus costs rise, and performing

---

[16] A numerical illustration of the productivity gap and rise in labour costs is provided by Heilbrun (2003), which helps those not familiar with this model to see how it works.

arts organisations have to put up prices by more than the rate at which the prices of other goods and incomes are rising, and this reduces demand.

The artistic deficit

The final point made by Baumol and Bowen concerns what has been called the 'artistic deficit': that, unless finance from other sources is found (such as public subsidy or private donations), arts organisations will be forced to cut back on quality and so audiences and society at large (where external effects are present) suffer.

Baumol's cost disease has been used by numerous arts organisations over the last forty years to make their case for higher subsidies and it persists in popularity. Baumol has extended the application of the theory to other service sectors in which labour is a key input, such as libraries, education and health, and also to the mass media, showing that the making of TV programmes was also subject to the cost disease.[17] Nevertheless, cultural economists have queried almost every individual feature of the model, and the cost disease has been tested empirically in several different ways. Studies of costs in individual art forms are discussed later. Here I first consider the theoretical objections, then turn to the empirical evidence.

Objections to Baumol's cost disease

One of the first objections to the cost disease theory was that, as the rest of the economy grows due to productivity, incomes rise, and so, even if the prices of arts performances rise above the general rate of inflation, demand can be sustained due to positive income elasticity (being greater than one). Another objection was (and is) that the case for arts subsidy cannot and should not be made on the basis of rising costs or the 'earnings' gap but requires evidence of market failure: the cost disease is all too clearly a market phenomenon and is the outcome of the way markets work, not of their failure. In fact, Baumol and Bowen made the case for subsidy using welfare economic arguments of external benefits as the market failure, and did not rest the case on the earnings gap; others have not taken heed.

Output and the artistic deficit

Several assumptions underlying the model itself have been called into question: one relates to the measure of 'output' used in the measure of productivity;

---

[17] Baumol (1996) and Baumol and Baumol (1984).

a second is the assumption of fixed coefficients in the production function; another rebuffs the underlying assumption of an integrated labour market; and, finally, the concept of 'quality' used in the artistic deficit argument has been challenged. To some extent these points overlap: it has been argued that using the number of performances as the measure of output ignores all the people who can access, say, a radio broadcast or sound recording of a concert or opera; the appropriate measure is therefore the audience size, not the performance. Moreover, the implication that only live performances 'count' for quality purposes simply ignores changes in tastes and effectively makes a value judgement that one way of experiencing art is better than another. Sound recording and other reproduction technologies are examples of technological progress in the performing arts; others relate to live performance too, such as the use of high-quality microphones, electronic instruments, computerised lighting consoles, and so on that facilitate a reduction of workers (on- and offstage).[18]

The notion of the 'artistic deficit' has also been criticised as imposing a stereotyped view of artistic quality. There is no reason to suppose that a play with a small cast is any less artistically valuable than one with a large cast, though it may indeed have been chosen for economic reasons. Audience tastes for smaller orchestral ensembles and chamber music may have changed because the prices for these performances are lower but we cannot conclude that quality is compromised. Styles of producing opera have changed – some would say improved – with minimalist sets and a greater use of lighting, which has reduced the cost of scenery, but the same operas are still being performed.

An integrated labour market?

The assumption of the integrated labour market has also been not only questioned but also disproved by studies of artists' labour markets: artists' incomes do not match those of other workers; they are lower than average and fail to rise at the same rate as those of other workers. Baumol and Bowen had themselves reported these features of artists' earnings and were aware that they diminished the impact of the cost disease (though they pointed out that even a lower rate of growth for artists' incomes is still growth and so the 'disease' would eventually appear), but they believed that artists' incomes were nevertheless influenced by the growth of incomes in the 'progressive' sector. This subject is discussed again in chapter 11.

---

[18] Cowen (1996).

It can readily be seen that these are matters of fact, and it was indeed due to the exemplary influence of Baumol and Bowen's research that cultural economists followed suit with later empirical studies. As a final word on the theory, it should be clear that no one disputes the logic of Baumol and Bowen's model; what has been questioned is the assumptions on which it rests and the policy implications that have been drawn from it, some erroneously.

Empirical evidence of the cost disease

Evidence on the cost disease and its associated problems – the income gap and the artistic deficit – is both qualitative and quantitative. Some of the qualitative points have already been mentioned above. There have been many quantitative studies of the performing arts as a sector and of specific types of arts organisations, especially orchestras, ranging from broad sectoral studies to detailed ones of individual organisations.

Sectoral evidence

Throsby's (1996b) analysis of data on the proportion of total expenditure of thirteen major subsidised performing arts companies in Australia is an example of the broad type of study: he shows that, between 1984 and 1993, expenditure on labour rose from 44 to 50 per cent; data were not available on the proportion of artistic and managerial or administrative workers employed by these Australian companies, however. Analysis of data for the 1970s in the United Kingdom on the proportion of total expenditures on artistic personnel showed only that, contrary to expectations, they were surprisingly low: just over half for orchestras in 1979/80; under one-half for the Royal Opera House; and around one-quarter for the Royal Shakespeare Company.[19]

Studies of individual organisations

The studies of the cost disease in several individual arts organisations in the United Kingdom by Alan Peacock, Eddie Shoesmith and Geoffrey Millner (1983) analyse trends in all categories of expenditure disaggregated to the level of the relevant SIC to which the item belonged, such as wood and paint used in scenery. An index of expenditures on 'capital' items and rents and of artistic and other labour categories was constructed for each performing company studied and compared with the retail price index (RPI) and the average earnings index (AEI), the latter normally being higher than the

---

[19] Shoesmith (1984).

Table 8.2 Cost and price inflation indices by art form in the United Kingdom, 1970/1–1980/1

	Dance	Music	Theatre	Opera	RPI
Cost index					
1970/1	100	100	100	100	100
1980/1	388	345	395	388	364
Price index		Cinema			
1970		63	56	56	68
1980		286	294	278	244

Source: Peacock, Shoesmith and Millner (1983).

former – that is, wages outpace prices. The result was that the source of the inflation of costs could be identified and compared to these indices. The data were then aggregated by art form, and they are presented in table 8.2.

The figures in table 8.2 are in index form, which facilitates easy comparison between the different art forms and with the RPI. Between 1970/1 and 1980/1 the RPI shows that retail prices more than trebled (they rose from 100 to 364), so if a good had had a price of £10 in 1970 the price would have been £36.40 in 1980. The upper half of the table shows that the index of costs in opera went from 100 to 388, an increase of nearly three times. The lower half of the table shows that opera prices went up from 56 to 278, an increase of almost four times, in that decade. In other words, price increases for opera outstripped cost increases, and this evidence defeats the Baumol and Bowen earnings gap hypothesis. Theatre costs and prices rose by more than those for opera; again, price increases exceeded cost increases. Table 8.2 also shows that, except for music, the rate of increase of costs exceeded the RPI – a finding that is consistent with Baumol's cost disease. For comparison, the increase in the prices of cinema tickets is also reported (those for music and dance are not).

Other studies expressed the ratio of expenditure to the income or earnings gap for performing arts organisations and analysed its trend over time, the cost disease prediction being that the ratio would tend to rise. In fact, evidence from several studies in the United States and from the United Kingdom suggested the opposite, implying that arts organisations were able to make adjustment either by reducing costs or raising prices, thus mitigating the predicted dire effects. Some of these studies are reported below in the context of the relevant art form. By the mid-1990s studies of the cost disease had dried up, and now it is no longer the talking point it used to be in arts circles. Students nevertheless continue to be interested in it (and to believe in it!) – and Baumol and Bowen's contribution to the economic theory of the arts and in setting standards for empirical research is incontrovertible.

Economic features of the performing arts by art form

The general analysis of the economics of the performing arts presented so far in this chapter sets the stage for reporting studies of the main sectors of the performing arts: the art forms included are orchestras, opera, dance and (spoken) theatre.

Orchestras

There is great variety with regard to orchestras; studies by cultural economists of orchestras have focused on 'independent', non-profit, subsidised orchestras, however, especially the US symphony orchestras, with the focus on private giving to them, the elasticity of demand for their concerts and earned income.[20] The typical size of a symphony orchestra is around 100 players, with a chamber orchestra having about forty. Orchestras tend to specialise in different repertoire, especially based on their size, though artistic trends towards 'early music' and 'historically informed performance' have tended to alter the relation between size and repertoire somewhat. The choice of repertoire can have an effect on the cost of performances, and this seems to have been a strategy in avoiding the cost disease. Symphony orchestras were generally expected to suffer the consequences of the cost disease to a greater extent than other performing arts due to their high labour intensity and assumed inability to alter the technical coefficients of their output. The evidence on balance seems to be that they did not do so, and the UK evidence in table 8.2 shows that costs did not rise in UK orchestras by as much as price inflation in the 1970s. Economic pressure on the cost side seems to have influenced the rehearsal time of orchestras and, to some extent, their repertoire, though this is hard to interpret, as artistic reasons may also have had a part to play.

Finance of orchestras

Public expenditure on orchestral concerts and 'classical' music is not always reported separately (and may include musical education). In general, orchestras

---

[20] Luksetich (2003).

seem to get a low share of state subsidy: in Sweden, government finance of 'music' was 5 per cent in 2005; in Italy, it was 2 per cent in 2000; by contrast, in Norway, it was 10 per cent in 2004. The figure for Austria presented in box 8.1 was 6 per cent, just over a quarter of the total for the performing arts. These figures may indicate the relatively low cost of running orchestras compared to other performing arts. Other measures are more telling, such as the proportion of orchestras' income from subsidy: in the United Kingdom, subsidised orchestras earned over half their income in 2002/3, with just over one-third coming from public finance; subsidy per attendance was £14.41 (approximately €20). In Germany and the Netherlands, where orchestras are supported by regional and local governments, symphony orchestras typically received over 80 and 76 per cent, respectively, of their funding from subsidy. In Japan, symphony orchestras received 20 per cent of their revenues from public funds, while those in the United States had a mere 4 per cent in the 1990s.[21] In the United States, the considerable private support for orchestras has been fostered through price discrimination with tax breaks in encouraging private donation (see box 8.2 and Luksetich, 2003).

Costs and economies of scale

As argued earlier, which costs are fixed and which are variable may depend upon labour contracts, and this would be especially important in the context of an orchestra. In European orchestras, whose musicians enjoy a civil-servant-like status in terms of salary and job security, labour costs are fixed costs. In other countries, a permanent orchestra might have annual contracts, but even so, if the orchestra is to be maintained at, say, 100 players, labour costs are effectively fixed unless salaries can be reduced by hiring younger members. 'Scratch' orchestras and loose ensembles of players that assemble for a short run of performances, on the other hand, are able to vary labour costs according to the chosen repertoire and venue.

Besides labour costs, orchestras have fixed costs of management, and of providing certain musical instruments; incidentally, an aspect of the payment to musicians that is almost never mentioned is that (with one or two exceptions) they are expected to provide their own capital equipment in the form of their instrument(s) – a true fixed combination of factors of production! In terms of economic principles, the payment to a player is both a rent for the instrument and a wage for the labour, and as musical instruments become

---

[21] Data on Sweden, Norway, Italy, Austria from Council of Europe/ERICarts (2008); for the United Kingdom, see Joy and Skinner (2005); for Germany, Japan and the United States, see Schulze and Rose (1998).

more expensive, as they are reported to be doing, one would expect musicians' incomes to rise. Touring orchestras also have to have special transport for larger musical instruments. The hire of music and royalties for performing rights for the chosen repertoire are also fixed costs in the short run.

In terms of returns to scale, again the problem of the measurement of output of an orchestra arises: is it the number of performances, the number of attendees or the number of works performed in a season? The answer would probably depend upon the context of the question, as argued above. A funding body might ask what the 'optimal' number of orchestras to support is; for example, does London need four major orchestras in receipt of subsidy, or does every provincial capital in the Netherlands need its own orchestra? If there are too many orchestras, competition for audiences can result in higher average costs per attendee and lower average revenue. These questions have been studied by cultural economists in different countries, especially the United States (see Luksetich, 2003); in Norway, Mel Gray found that fewer orchestras would increase the efficiency of the sector and reduce costs per performance.[22]

Participation and demand for concerts

Statistics on participation rates are not easy to interpret, as 'concerts' in some countries include pop concerts with classical music. Over a third of all Europeans are reported as having attended a concert (not specified), according to table 8.1, though in countries where they are reported separately the figures are lower. The greatest problem that orchestras seem to face is declining interest on the part of audiences: in the Netherlands and Sweden, attendance at classical music concerts fell during the 1990s. Festivals may offer a counterweight to this (see chapter 19). The presence of high-quality sound recording no doubt has had some impact on attendance at live performances, but this has not been studied. It is worth noting that, nowadays, many orchestras have their own record labels, and some concert halls do too (such as London's Wigmore Hall).

Turning to the revenue side, there have been a number of studies of the elasticity of demand for orchestral concerts; the consensus is that, in the United States, demand is relatively inelastic, as orchestras tend to underprice their concerts, the implication being that they could increase revenues by raising them. The results varied with the size of the orchestra and so may be difficult to generalise, however.[23]

---

[22] Gray (1992).   [23] Luksetich (2003).

Opera

Very similar topics to those for orchestras have also been studied by cultural economists researching opera. Opera has higher costs of production, however, because it requires the full facilities of a theatre with the addition of an orchestra pit, the services of a large orchestra, chorus and dancers and of principal artists – the lead singers, a conductor, stage designer and producer, the person who directs the staging – and a host of 'backroom' staff, such as répétiteurs, who coach the singers. To these are added the requirements of a theatre – the makers of costumes, wigs, props, swords and all the other paraphernalia of theatrical performance – in addition to the front-of-house staff, managers, fund-raisers, etc. The result of all of this is that some of the large national opera houses have over 1,000 personnel in their employ.

Theatre size and performance traditions

The large opera companies, the 'national' opera and important regional companies, are resident in their own theatres – the Opéra de la Bastille is home to the Opéra National de Paris, the Mariinsky Theatre for the Kirov Opera in St Petersburg, the Liceo in Barcelona, and so on. Some of these theatres are old and some new; the newer ones tend to be larger than the old ones, some of which hold fewer than 1,000 spectators. The size of the theatre and the ability of singers to sing more than a few performances a week place some of the greatest 'technical' constraints on opera companies in terms of extending their audience reach, increasing revenues, reducing costs and achieving economies of scale.

Other features also have important economic implications, however: one is the performance tradition and the other is the strong preference for nineteenth-century operas that require large casts, a large orchestra and high-quality singers. The Italian *stagione* system and the repertory system favoured in Germany were outlined in chapter 4; in the former, one opera is rehearsed and performed by one cast at a time over a period of several weeks, to be followed by the next, and the principal singers are hired for the season and then move on; with the repertory system, operas and casts alternate through the week, the resident company fills all the roles and there is little change in the roster of singers. Many opera houses now have a mixture of the two, alternating performance of several operas throughout the week over a particular performing period and reviving old productions. With a repertory system, the costs of a production may be averaged out over the total number of performances; with a *stagione* system, there is a marginal cost to each performance in terms of the fees paid to the principal singers, though the orchestra and chorus are usually on long-term contracts. Touring opera companies can avoid some of the cost problems associated with these traditions by presenting just one or two pieces in different locations, but they still face the problem that principal singers cannot perform night after night in demanding repertoire without damaging their voices.

Fixed and average costs

As with orchestras, how 'fixed' costs are depends upon a number of factors, including contractual arrangements. In the United Kingdom, the Arts Council of England in 2002/3 reported overheads, staffing and other costs for large-scale opera as constituting 62 per cent, with 31 per cent for 'artistic programme costs', the remainder being marketing costs (4 per cent) and education costs (2 per cent).[24] Artistic programme costs are likely to be sunk costs; however, with sufficient performances and revivals, they can be averaged over a number of years. Using UK data, the average total cost per performance was £127,681 in 2002/3; with 2,268 seats, the cost per seat per performance was £56.[25]

Prices, participation and revenue

Even with very high prices and the use of extensive price discrimination (in 2007 prices at the Royal Opera House, Covent Garden, in London ranged from £7 to £170 – roughly €10 to €260 – while the range was $15 to $295 at the Metropolitan Opera in 2008), it is unlikely that large-scale opera could survive without considerable support from government subsidy and private donations.

One of the difficulties for state subsidy to opera is that it is one of the least popular of the performing arts and its audiences tend to come from the highest socio-economic group in society. Participation rates for opera in Great Britain were reported in table 8.1 as 7 per cent (though a 2006 survey points to 4 per cent for the United Kingdom as a whole). Box 8.4 shows that, for large-scale opera in England, there was public subsidy of £43.01 per attendance (52 per cent), with £32.39 earned income per attendance (39 per cent) and with 10 per cent contributed income. The percentage of public subsidy is likely to be higher in other European countries, though those attending are the same high-income minority.

---

[24] Joy and Skinner (2005).   [25] My calculations from Joy and Skinner (2005).

Microeconomics of opera

Why opera seat prices are so high in opera was first analysed by Mark Blaug (1978) in a study of the United Kingdom's Royal Opera House (ROH); he calculated that, in the mid-1970s, 'average' seat prices would have had to be raised by 150 per cent if there had been no public subsidy – so a £10 ticket would have had to be priced at £25 (subsidy per attendee was higher in the 1970s than in the current decade). This study, which remains one of the few detailed microeconomic studies of an arts organisation, testifies to the complexity of these calculations due to price discrimination for different parts of the house, according to the opera being performed and according to the performers (singers, conductor, producer), whether it was a new production or a revival, and so on. Only the most popular operas fill the capacity of the house at each performance; modern or less well known operas leave many empty seats – as much as 50 per cent of capacity.

In terms of calculating how the income deficit could be reduced by higher prices and the response of audiences to them, these factors all had to be taken into account. Moreover, as discussed below, opera must share the stage with ballet at the Royal Opera House, as is also the case in many other opera houses. Blaug's main finding was that the greatest cost saving at the ROH would come from reducing the use of top international singers in opera and the greatest contribution to the net revenue of the ROH would come from reducing opera performances and switching over to more ballet performances, as ballet yielded higher revenues per outlay of expenditure than did opera.

Quality and the artistic deficit

One of the predictions of the cost disease was that, without sufficient subsidy and/or contributed income, quality would suffer, leading to the so-called 'artistic deficit'. If quality were measured in terms of the use of international singers in operatic performances, then a reduction in subsidy (or in the real growth of subsidy) would reduce quality. With an international market for opera singers, the better-financed (often meaning more subsidised) houses have the advantage in that market. The artistic deficit could also be conceived in terms of the diversity of the repertoire. Studies of operatic repertoire in the United States have shown rather mixed results: on the one hand, diversity in repertoire (the number of different opera 'titles' performed) has been found to be lower while performances of less popular works are being encouraged by public subsidy.[26]

---

[26] Pierce (2000) and Heilbrun (2001).

Dance

Dance covers a range of genres – ballet, modern or contemporary dance and ethnic dance. While they differ in popularity and in financial support, the cost structure for each is very similar and is labour-intensive. The national ballet companies typically share the theatre and orchestra with the opera company.[27] Other dance is less likely to perform with live music. A comprehensive study of dance in the United States for the National Endowment for the Arts goes into detail about the economic features of the different genres.[28]

Participation

Dance is marginally more popular than opera. Figures on cultural participation in table 8.1 indicate that, while attendance at dance performances has been rising in some countries (the Netherlands and Spain, for instance), the numbers involved are low: less than 5 per cent of the population attended a dance performance in Spain in 2002/3; 7 per cent in the United Kingdom attended a ballet in 2003/4. In Australia, however, dance performances were more popular, with over 10 per cent of the population surveyed having attended a dance performance in 2002 (two-thirds being female). In the United States in 2002, 6 per cent of Americans attended dance performances and 4 per cent attended ballet.

Earned and unearned income

In Australia, earned income accounted for 38 per cent of revenues for dance, with one-third of total income coming from government funding. In the United States, 30 per cent of the income of 'tax-exempt' dance organisations was from the box office and a further 30 per cent was from private donations, with 7 per cent from government in 1992, 1 per cent coming from the NEA. The NEA spent just 2.2 per cent of its budget on dance in 2000, a drop from 3.5 per cent in 1990, with ballet receiving more on average than other genres. In the Netherlands in 1997, the proportion of box-office receipts to subsidy was 18:82 for dance. In the United Kingdom in 2002/3, both earned income and public subsidy per dance attendance were £19; for ballet the figures were £25 and £26, respectively.

---

[27] The Blaug study referred to above found that, at the ROH in the 1970s, there was a ratio of 40:60 for ballet to opera performances despite the fact that ballet was more 'productive' in the sense of raising a higher proportion of revenue to expenditure, even though prices were in general lower for ballet than for opera performances, because ballet tended to sell a higher proportion of seat capacity than opera.

[28] Smith (2003).

Costs

In England, subsidised dance had average costs of £36 per performance. As argued previously, marginal costs depend upon the nature of labour contract, especially in highly labour-intensive art forms. Dance companies vary very considerably in size and many dancers work on short-term contracts. All dancers need to do class every day, and that requires specialised rehearsal space; in addition, choreography has to be taught 'live' – both for new works and for the classical repertoire.

Ballet

Many of the features of ballet performance mirror those of opera – the need for a theatre, orchestra, corps de ballet and leading artists in the form of dancers and choreographers, almost all of whom are on fixed contracts. It also calls for other expenses, however; ballet shoes are very costly: the New York City Ballet, for example, apparently spent half a million dollars a year on them in the 1990s. Ballet companies in England spent 34 per cent of their total costs on artistic programme costs and 61 per cent on overheads, staffing and other fixed costs (roughly similar to opera). The only microeconomic study of a ballet company, by coincidence it seems, is of the United Kingdom's Royal Ballet, which shares the ROH stage with the opera company; it concentrated on the elasticity of demand for its summer festival, finding that demand for seating in different parts of the theatre (which present different views of the stage) was relatively elastic.[29]

Theatre

Theatre, theatres and theatrical traditions

The term 'theatre' is used here to mean spoken theatre or drama. As with opera and ballet, some drama companies, especially the 'national' companies, are resident in their own theatres. Alongside subsidised theatre, there is also a strong unsubsidised theatre sector, typically in big cities with long theatrical traditions, such as London and New York. In these cities, as noted earlier, the availability of theatres for rent makes it possible for the run of a successful production, whether subsidised or unsubsidised, to be extended as long as demand is strong enough; the move may also be accompanied by a change of cast, and that is facilitated by the presence of a pool of actors available on the open labour market in these large centres (see chapter 11). Thus economies of

---

[29] Schimmelpfennig (1997).

scale may be achieved by spreading the fixed costs over a greater number of performances and costs per performance fall.

Again like opera, a distinction can be made between theatrical productions, for which the cast is hired for the run of a show that plays continuously, and the regional repertory theatre, with a company of actors on a longer-term contract, performing different plays throughout the week over the performance season. Some resident companies may have more than one performance venue, such as a studio theatre, in addition to the main stage, which allows the company to put on two (or more) productions simultaneously and thus enables it to diversify its output. This may be important in a provincial setting in which the theatre is a local monopoly and audiences are dependent upon its supply. A study of forty subsidised English repertory theatres in the 1990s found that the lowest number of productions over a three-year period was ten and the highest was sixty-five, with the average over the sample being thirty.[30]

Participation and demand

In many countries, going to the theatre is one of the most popular cultural activities, with attendance rates of around 20 per cent in Australia, Canada, Italy, Spain and the United Kingdom, albeit lower in the United States (see table 8.1). How responsive theatre audiences have been to price rises has been studied in detail by several cultural economists. The study by Louis Lévy-Garboua and Claude Montmarquette (1996) of participation in French theatre is one of the most detailed, for two reasons: first, it includes information on a range of economic, socio-economic and non-economic variables (including data on the experience of theatre-going); and, second, the survey includes attendees and persons who had attended in the previous year, enabling the researchers to analyse the influence of past learning experience on demand. Contrary to previous studies of the elasticity of demand, which found that in general demand was inelastic, this study, based on survey data in the 1990s, finds that demand for theatre in France was price-elastic; it also finds that there were substitution effects from televised theatrical performances and cinema. Satisfaction with previous visits to the theatre, the learning and taste-forming process, played an important role in demand. The study is unusual in using detailed survey data of theatre-goers; what cultural economists are more likely to have is data from theatres on sales, productions and prices – that is, box-office data.

[30] O'Hagan and Neligan (2005).

Quality/artistic deficit

In another study of French theatre, Daniel Urrutiaguer concentrated on the role of quality in influencing demand.[31] In 1995 the hundred or so theatrical institutions in the study put on 11,158 performances that attracted 2.8 million paying visitors. Like the Throsby study referred to earlier in the discussion of quality, Urrutiaguer considered the influence of critics, but he also took into account the influence of the prestigious 'director-cum-manager' and the effect that the amount of subsidy also had on demand (since that implies approval by the experts who are responsible for grant-making), hypothesising that some theatre-goers are influenced by media opinion of quality and others are instead influenced by the quality assurance of the 'director-cum-manager'. His results bear out that distinction, though he finds (like Lévy-Garboua and Montmarquette) that the two strongest influences on demand were the attendance per performance in the previous year and the size of the venue. Curiously, elasticity of demand in this study was positive, suggesting possibly that audiences judge quality by price.

On the question of the artistic deficit, the study by John O'Hagan and Adriana Neligan of English repertory theatres mentioned above analysed a 'conventionality index', defined as the number of productions per playwright as a measure of repertoire diversity (not by title, as was reported for opera), drawing the inference that increasing the proportion of subsidy in a theatre's income would marginally increase repertoire diversity.

Costs

Costs for theatre are similar to those discussed above for opera and dance. The average budget for the five national theatres in France in 1996 was Fr 87 million (around US$16 million) while the budget for the regional theatres averaged Fr 14 million (some US$3 million). The biggest theatre in the United Kingdom, the Royal National Theatre, which has three stages, employs 800 people, of whom 120 are actors; however, many theatre groups are small, with only a few actors hired for a run of performances and small management overheads. Overall in English theatre in 2002/3, artistic programme costs were 42 per cent of total costs, with 50 per cent for staffing and overheads. Table 8.2 shows that costs rose more rapidly in theatre in the 1970s than in the other performing arts. One explanation for this result contradicted the cost disease: what was driving up the costs of spoken theatrical performance was not the cost of actors, as they represent only a

---

[31] Urrutiaguer (2002).

small proportion of total costs (less than in symphony orchestras, ballet and opera), but the costs of other inputs. While costs rose by a factor of nearly three, however, prices of theatre tickets rose over four times.

Subsidy

In the French theatres studied above, subsidy amounted to 70 per cent of total income. In England, it was 50 per cent in 2002/3, with subsidy per attendance being £10, the lowest of all performing arts – perhaps not surprising, as it is the most popular and therefore able to raise a higher amount of earned income from the box office.[32]

Musical theatre

There has been no study of musical theatre to my knowledge, though one of the earliest studies in cultural economics was of Broadway theatre. Broadway and the West End of London host many musicals in privately run theatres. In addition, subsidised theatres offer musical shows and, especially in Germany and Austria, operetta. Regional theatres in the United Kingdom would not survive without the annual pantomime that opens at Christmas and runs until February, offering a vital source of work to actors at a 'low' season. There is a nice research project waiting to be done here.

Conclusion

This chapter has applied the economic analysis laid out in earlier chapters to the performing arts as a sector of the cultural economy, and has also applied it to specific live art forms – symphonic music, opera, ballet and spoken theatre – drawing on a selection of studies by cultural economists. It can be seen that, while there are significant common economic features to all the performing arts, there are also some different conditions in each market.

The analysis raises some broad questions that have been touched on but not fully investigated. Are the various art forms in the performing arts complements or substitutes – that is, do they compete with each other? If so, do they compete for audiences and/or public and private finance? Another question is the extent to which performing arts organisations compete with each other within an art form: how many orchestras or dance companies are sustainable

---

[32] Urrutiaguer (2002) and Joy and Skinner (2005).

in a country or region? A further question is: should economists treat performing arts organisations as competitive firms, monopolies or oligopolies? We know a lot about the performing arts sector in macroeconomic terms but far less about its microeconomics.

Perhaps, though, it should be said, rather, that we know a lot about the subsidised performing arts in a relatively small selection of countries that share very similar economic and artistic cultures. No mention is made here of circus, puppetry, folk music and dance or of traditional drama and the many traditional performing arts that flourish or are preserved around the world.

A considerable amount of information has been included in this chapter on public subsidy to the performing arts but there has been no discussion of the rationale for public subsidy, beyond pointing out that the cost disease does not itself make that case: how public subsidy can be justified given that there are clearly strong private benefits that people are prepared to pay for. One argument that has been made is that a heritage of performance traditions, especially in ballet, would be lost without public support, but that argument is difficult to generalise to all performing arts. Chapter 10 explores these arguments in full.

Further reading

There is a lot of literature cited in this chapter but I do not necessarily recommend it to a beginner, as some of it is difficult and technical. For readers with some experience in economics and econometrics, however, it is of course worthwhile. Chapters in the Towse (2003a) *Handbook of Cultural Economics* that relate to this chapter are James Heilbrun on Baumol's cost disease (chapter 11) and those on ballet, opera and orchestras cited in the further reading section for chapter 4. Alan Peacock's (1993) *Paying the Piper* provides the context in the United Kingdom for the study of inflation and the arts. Bruce Seaman's chapter in the Ginsburgh and Throsby (2006) *Handbook of the Economics of Art and Culture* (chapter 14) is a masterful survey of the literature on demand for the performing arts that is a very useful reference source; it is long and in places pitched at a higher level than this book, but it is well worth the effort. I like to think that my article on the Royal Opera House, Covent Garden, is worth reading (Towse, 2001a).

9   Economics of cultural heritage

'Cultural heritage' is a very broad term that covers archaeology, artefacts, buildings ancient and modern, museums, archives, works of art, and the like; besides man-made items, heritage also includes intangibles, such as inherited traditions, knowledge and skills, and the natural heritage. Cultural economics has so far mostly applied its analysis to museums and the built heritage; the principles are relevant to all aspects of heritage, however, and, indeed, cultural economists share much the same approach to built heritage as environmental economists do to natural heritage.

Heritage and public goods

What cultural heritage goods and services have in common is that they create a sense of national identity, encourage respect for other cultures and for cultural diversity, foster an understanding of the past and teach aesthetic values. These cultural values of heritage are distinguished from the asset value of heritage capital – the value of the land and buildings occupied by heritage sites, monuments and buildings and the items in museum's collections, and so on – that, at least in principle, could be realised on the market. Outdoor built and natural heritage are often true public goods, in the sense that they are mostly non-excludable and, unless there is congestion, non-rival; in general, it may be too costly to fence them off to exclude users, making charging for entry uneconomic. In the case of very popular sites, however, congestion causes rivalry that pricing policies can help to relieve: some examples of 'heritage' congestion are the excessive numbers of visitors to Stonehenge in England and to the city of Venice in Italy; besides spoiling the pleasure of a visit, they also risk damaging the fabric of the buildings.

By contrast, visitors to museums and indoor built heritage can be excluded if they do not pay, and so, in the economic sense, museum visits are not public goods (though there are external benefits of consumption). Rivalry in the consumption of museum services can be a complex question: while the objects housed in museums, such as works of art and other artefacts, can be viewed by many people without diminishing their quantity, the quality of a visit can be altered by congestion, and that may be alleviated by charging. What we see later is that museums supply multiple services. As with the performing arts, cultural economists have studied museums both as firms with costs, revenues, pricing and other such 'ordinary' microeconomic features and as non-profit cultural suppliers of public goods with the support of public subsidy.

Designation as heritage

With strong public goods characteristics, it is no surprise to find that there is considerable public intervention in the museums sector, including public own-ership as well as financial support. In the case of the built heritage, important ancient sites are usually owned by the state to protect their archaeological value, though much of the built heritage is in private ownership and subject to regula-tion to control its architectural value and use. One of the features of museum collections and built heritage is that many items now regarded as belonging to cultural heritage were not created for that purpose but were part of everyday life. Only later were they designated as part of the heritage, by experts listing them as such. A good illustration of this point is factories that were built for utilitarian industrial purposes that have been listed as being of cultural and or architectural importance by heritage authorities. Similarly, many items that are now in museums were made for use in their day and it is only subsequently that they have come to be regarded as 'museum pieces' or collectibles, through a process of certification by museum curators and other guardians of cultural value, such as UNESCO with its international listing of items of world heritage.

Moreover, what consumers view as heritage is strongly influenced by this designation, and economists call this 'supplier-induced' demand – meaning that consumer tastes and what they demand is determined by the supplier. You may think the local former gasworks is an eyesore or that your old ballpoint pen is worth nothing, but once it has been designated by heritage experts as worthy of preservation it is 'consecrated', and will be presented as a significant piece of design and preserved. This feature of regulation is dis-cussed in the context of built heritage in the second part of this chapter.

Stock and flow of supply

A further characteristic that all heritage shares is that it is non-reproducible and therefore the stock of supply of an item at any point in time is fixed or declining due to deterioration. Fixity of supply in the presence of growing demand is what drives up prices and we see this in the art market. Investment in restoration and preservation can halt the decline, and, as heritage accrues over time, the demand for this type of expenditure increases. It can therefore influence supply. Changes in the selection of items that are designated also affect the total supply. Even with a fixed supply, though, the visitor's experience can be considerably influenced by the complementary services surrounding the item, such as easy access, good information and other visitor facilities.

Digitalisation and heritage

A recent and almost revolutionary change to heritage is that museums and heritage sites are able to offer a digital guide to both potential visitors and to those who are unable or do not wish to visit them. Websites offer information on the items that can be viewed on a 'real-time' visit and intra-websites on the premises also provide guidance and information, the latter often in far more detail than would be possible at the display point.

The above points are discussed in detail in this chapter, starting with museums. One other caveat is that language varies between countries: in some, including the United Kingdom, art museums are called 'art galleries'; they should not be confused with private galleries run by art dealers.

Participation in and demand for museum services

Participation

Participation surveys provide information about museum visits. Statistics on museums have to be interpreted in the context of the way the museum sector is defined, however, as explained above, and there is also variation in the population surveyed, notably with respect to age. In Australia, 35 per cent of people over the age of eighteen visited some kind of museum in 2001. In Canada, 35 per cent of people aged fifteen and over visited a museum in 2005. According to the Eurobarometer 2007 survey (Eurostat, 2007), 41 per cent of both males and of females over the age of fifteen in the twenty-seven countries of the European Union have visited a museum once; that overall figure disguises some considerable variations: 22 per cent of the adult population in Italy and 44 per cent of the population aged nine to seventy-nine in Sweden were reported as visiting a museum. When figures on the type of museum are reported separately, visits to art museums or art galleries are significantly lower: 22 per cent of Australian males and 28 per cent of Australian females are reported as having visited an art museum; 27 per cent of the Canadian population aged fifteen and over in 2005 and 27 per cent of the US population over the age of eighteen visited an art museum or gallery in 2002; 24 per cent of the population of Great Britain over the age of fifteen in 2004 and 15 per cent of the population over the age of fifteen in Ireland in 2006 visited art museums.

Age and socio-economic background

There is considerable variation in the way museum visitor profiles are presented and this makes generalisation difficult; it seems clear from looking at details for several countries, however, that young people, especially school-age children, have higher participation rates than adults and that older adults have lower participation rates. For example, in the Netherlands, 37 per cent of the population aged twelve and over visited a museum at least once in 2003, half of whom were between the ages of twelve and seventeen. The implication is that school visits contribute considerably to museum participation; nevertheless, surveys that look at children's willingness to visit again find that it falls, as children get older, from the initially huge enthusiasm of the very young.

In terms of socio-economic background, the Eurobarometer 2007 survey shows that there was a marked difference between participation by 'managers' (68 per cent) and 'manual workers' (38 per cent); there was also a very marked difference between participation by age of completing education. In the United Kingdom, of those who attended, under a quarter were from the lowest two socio-economic groups and over a half were from the highest two groups. In the Netherlands, data on participation are also analysed by ethnic background: while 33 per cent of the population over the age of twelve visited a museum in 2003, the figure for ethnic minorities was 22 per cent.[1]

Prices and participation

As we know from chapter 6, participation studies provide profiles of audiences that are useful to the policy-maker, and over time they can also provide information on the outcome of policies intended to increase attendance or to include socially disadvantaged members of the population. Although they suggest characteristics that influence demand, however, such as education and employment status, they do not explain demand behaviour in the sense of willingness to pay for the cultural good or service. Some participation studies

[1] Eurostat (2007) and Council of Europe/ERICarts (2008).

Box 9.1 Impact of free entry to UK museums

The DCMS has monitored the increase in visits to museums and art galleries following the introduction of the policy of free entry in 2001. It has published the following figures.

- 1 December 2007 was the end of the sixth and most successful year of the free admission policy, with 7.7 million extra visits to former charging museums in this year.
- In the first six years of the free admission policy there were 37 million extra visits to DCMS-sponsored museums and galleries that had previously charged.
- In London, visits to former charging museums were up by over 94 per cent, with visits to the Victoria and Albert Museum up 151 per cent, the Natural History Museum by 117 per cent and the Science Museum by 105 per cent.
- In the regions, visits to these museums increased by 109 per cent. Visits to National Museums Liverpool were up by 188 per cent, to the Museum of Science and Industry in Manchester by 136 per cent and to the Natural History Museum in Tring by 87 per cent.

Source: www.culture.gov.uk/what_we_do/museums_and_galleries/3380.aspx

(accessed 25 August 2008).

have included questions about the role of prices in influencing participation; again, this does not say how much a person is willing to pay for a museum visit but it is a guide to the question of whether free entry would stimulate participation.

The United Kingdom provides a useful case study in the effect of free entry on participation: the government introduced a policy of free entry to museums with the stated policy objective of reducing social exclusion. After six years of the policy, it claims it has been a great success (see box 9.1); the Department for Culture, Media and Sport reported that between 2002/3 and 2004/5 there was an increase of 16 per cent in visitors from lower socio-economic groups.

The DCMS does not actually claim that free admission is the cause of the increase in visits, though this is strongly suggested. Research has shown that another factor was also at play, however: the increased facilities offered by many museums that had been awarded funds from the National Lottery for new buildings and projects; the additional visits were predominantly accounted for by museums and galleries with lottery-funded capital developments opening between April 2000 and March 2001, which coincided with the introduction of the free entry policy.[2] This important finding calls for further

---

[2] Selwood and Davies (2005).

econometric research, especially as other countries intend to institute the policy of free admission to museums.

Limitations of participation studies

Participation studies generally are concerned with a broad picture of attendance at a range of cultural events and so do not go into details about the nature of that participation. Typically, they find out if a respondent has visited a museum once in a given year. Figures on the number of visits (for example, as reported by the United Kingdom's DCMS in box 9.1) do not reveal how many visitors make repeat visits, however, or the length of their visits; with free admission, it has been claimed that people can 'pop in' for a quick visit, whereas if they had to pay that would deter the visit. Individual museums, however, do ask such questions in their own surveys; the Tate Gallery survey referred to in chapter 6 found that 40 per cent of its visitors were repeat visitors and that visitors stayed one and three-quarter hours on average.

Demand for museum visits

Demand for museum services is defined as the number of tickets that would be purchased at various entry prices for visitors wishing to view the collection. There is likely to be discriminatory pricing with different charges for children and senior citizens (free admission can be thought of as a zero entry price). Some museums offer season tickets to encourage repeat visits. Members of the museum friends may also have reduced entry prices to encourage them to join and to donate with money or voluntary labour services to the museum. Price discrimination may be practised as a policy for equity reasons to encourage access but in economic terms it is done for efficiency reasons, typically to increase revenue. Museums that normally charge for entry may have a day in the week or times of the day when entry is free; this strategy enables people with a low willingness to pay or low ability to pay to visit without charge, and it also allows the museum to charge those with a higher WTP, thus increasing revenue. Museums with free entry to the main collection charge for special exhibitions and for complementary services such as audio services, the shop and café, and therefore can still earn revenue from visitors. Museums may also ask for voluntary donations either instead of or in addition to the entry charge; and, to encourage donations, prices may be set in such a way as to encourage voluntary price discrimination, as in the performing arts (see box 8.2).

Measuring free entry

One matter that has often intrigued cultural economists is how museums with a free entry policy get their figures on visitor numbers. In some cases a ticket is offered, but the usual method seems to be that museum guards click a hand-held counter to count the number of people in various parts of the museum; the aggregation of these estimates can be problematic, however, as illustrated in a neat piece of research by David Tanner of the Indiana University Art Museum.[3] By issuing a free ticket that was then checked upon entry to the museum, it was possible to compare the methods of measuring visitor numbers, and counting by guards was shown to be very significantly overstating visitor annual numbers (32,000 were measured by the ticket method as compared to 56,000 by the counter method). This surely suggests at the very least that we need to have accurate counting of visitor numbers before concluding that demand increases considerably at a zero price or, conversely, considering what the deterrent effect of imposing entry charges is.

One guide to interest in a museum, however, is the number of visits to its website, which can be monitored accurately. As in so many other spheres, the internet opens up new services and research possibilities.

Elasticity of demand

When price discrimination is present, the quantity demanded (the number of visits) has to be related to the range of prices charged; this often has to be done in practice by taking an average of the prices charged. There have been several studies over the years by cultural economists to measure demand and to assess the elasticity of demand for admission to museums; elasticity provides two pieces of useful information at the same time: (1) the responsiveness to demand to price increases or decreases; and (2) the effect that price changes will have on revenue from ticket sales.

A study for the United States using data estimated from the 1989 Museum Survey shows that demand was inelastic in the range of –0.12 to –0.26.[4] So, if prices were raised from $10 to $20, attendance would fall by somewhere in the region of 12 to 26 per cent but, even so, revenue would rise (see chapter 6 for the relation of elasticity and revenue). Studies in the United Kingdom have also found price elasticity to be less than one and income elasticity greater than one, both of which suggest that increasing prices would increase revenue.

---

[3] Tanner (2007).
[4] Luksetich and Partridge (1997).

Box 9.2 Viewing the Book of Kells

The Book of Kells is an illuminated manuscript of the four Gospels copied and illustrated by Irish monks around 800 AD and it is regarded as the greatest example of its kind. It is housed in the Long Room of Trinity College Dublin, Ireland. John O'Hagan, a professor of economics at the university, analysed the effects of the introduction of entry charges to the Long Room and found that subsequent price rises did not at all deter visitor numbers; instead, it raised revenues that enabled Trinity College to improve the facilities considerably by adding an exhibition room and refurbishing the Long Room, thus enhancing the visitor's experience and the quality of the visit. O'Hagan also observed that, as the Book of Kells is unique, the elasticity of demand to view it is likely to be very low; moreover, many visitors are tourists whose willingness to pay is probably relatively high for such an experience.

Source: O'Hagan (1995).

One question that has been asked is: what would a museum do with the increased revenue? It is often said that, when museums are managed as part of the government bureaucracy, they do not necessarily retain any revenues for their own use. That is not the case with private museums, however. Box 9.2 provides an illustration of how a museum can increase prices, increase its revenues and use them to improve its services.

Shifting the demand for museum visits

The dramatic figures in box 9.1 show that visitors to museums respond to price; reducing prices is certainly not the only way to increase demand, however: demand can also be shifted out by altering the tastes of visitors and non-attenders, for example by educational and outreach programmes. Here the emphasis on encouraging visits by children and providing educational projects and facilities in connection with visits to the collection is designed to increase future demand for adult visits as well as to inform and educate the children. Museums can also make visitors' experience more pleasurable by having guides, tours (virtual and in real time) and other such information to make them welcome. US museums have a large force of volunteers who do just that. In the Netherlands, there is a national 'museum card' scheme that for a lump sum annual payment entitles the holder to free entry to museums throughout the country; while this no doubt encourages the number of museum visits, however, it has the undesirable efficiency effect of destroying the signalling role of prices and revenues for the individual museum.

Marginal cost pricing and congestion

Economists believe that prices play an important function not only in creating revenue that finances an enterprise, but also in providing consumers (visitors) with a means of conveying their valuation of the good or service provided by expressing their willingness to pay (and to donate). It is believed that museums that charge have a greater incentive to offer better-quality services than free museums would, especially as free museums are publicly financed and their management is influenced by government policy. As with other enterprises with high fixed costs, marginal cost pricing would not cover the fixed cost, and as the marginal cost of an extra visitor to a museum is very low, at least up to the point of congestion, the price should accordingly be very low. This argument has been used in support of free entry on the assumption that the point of congestion is never reached. That may be so in many museums, but in the world's 'superstar' museums there is certainly congestion and it is an external diseconomy that causes disutility to visitors. Prices can therefore be used to ration entry to the museum.

Congestion costs were measured by David Maddison and Terry Foster (2003) in one of the world's most visited museums, the British Museum in London, which attracts nearly 5 million visitors a year, three-quarters of whom are foreign tourists. They calculated from their survey of museum visitors that the congestion externality was £8 per person. That does not indicate that the entry price should be £8, however; for that the elasticity of demand of raising the price from zero to £8 would have to be calculated. Congestion therefore calls not just for pricing, but for discriminatory pricing based on popular days and times of the day.

Prices and demand for special exhibitions

Many museums put on special exhibitions for a limited period of time; these may be small assemblies from their own collection, based around items from the collection and including those from elsewhere, or imported works from many other museums; some are jointly curated, and the exhibition tours to those museums involved. Large exhibitions assembling items from many sources are known as 'blockbusters' and they attract large numbers of visitors. The role of these exhibitions in cultural tourism is discussed in chapter 19. Here they are mentioned because entry to these special exhibitions is usually charged for even in museums that are otherwise free. Even non-profit museums may charge a profit-maximising price for a ticket to this sort of exhibition, and visitor numbers to them suggest that high prices are no deterrent and elasticity of demand is low.

The cultural role of such exhibitions is different from that of the permanent collection, however, and the justification of charging for them and their effect on participation are different for the special exhibition from what they are for the permanent collection. Despite excess demand for these exhibitions, however, at least at certain times, as witnessed by long queues to get in and considerable congestion problems in the exhibition, museums have not yet turned to discriminatory pricing to ration entry; instead they ration quantity by limiting the number of tickets sold (at the same price) for specific entry times. This misses one of the most obvious economic solutions to excess demand that also raises revenue.

Museum finance

For many museums, ticket sales are a source of finance, but it is likely that fixed costs have to be financed by subsidy or donations. Free-entry museums have to be financed entirely by grants from foundations or from government. Typically, national museums are financed either directly or indirectly via an arm's-length body from central government funds, and regional and local museums are financed by regional and local government, though possibly with central government funds made available for the purpose.

Even for museums that charge entry, however, there is also demand that is 'uncovenanted', that cannot be expressed through the price mechanism. This consists of the option and 'bequest' demand by people who are willing to support the existence of the museum now and in the future, through taxes, even if they do not visit or donate themselves. In addition, there are external consumption benefits and public good aspects of demand that call for public finance. Later in the chapter, the finance of other museum services is also considered, such as their research and preservation activities.

Given the public good characteristics of museums and the importance placed on free entry for some or all visitors in order to maximise participation, a considerable amount of public finance is needed to support museums. For example, the national museums in the Netherlands charge an entry price that is usually around €8 for adults; even so, revenue from ticket sales constituted only 30 per cent of total income in 1997; government subsidies to museums were €408 million in 2006 (11 per cent of total public expenditure on culture). In Spain, by contrast, museums accounted for 23 per cent of total public expenditure on culture (€180 million) in 2005.[5]

---

[5] Van der Ploeg (2006) and Council of Europe/ERICarts (2008) for the Netherlands and Spain, respectively.

Figures on museum finance for England report the breakdown between revenue expenditure (ongoing expenses of running the museum) and capital expenditure – £373 million (€467 million) and £63 million (€79 million), respectively, in 2003/4 – with 1 per cent for administration; thus, 14 per cent of expenditure was on buildings. This category, however, is likely to vary widely from year to year according to the building and repair programme. In the United Kingdom, there is a considerable amount of information available to the public on the finance of museums on the websites of the DCMS and the arm's-length bodies for the museums and heritage about individual museums; in addition, the contracts between these various bodies – called funding agreements – are also published. Funding agreements set out how the institutions have agreed to use their financial aid and what they will do towards meeting government policy objectives; the agreement also stipulates how performance will be measured. In box 9.3, a few points from the agreement with the British Museum are reproduced to demonstrate the nature of these agreements and their 'businesslike' style. It can be seen that the agreement seeks to solve the principal–agent problem (which is discussed in chapter 10).

Box 9.3 Funding agreement 2005/6 to 2007/8 between the British Museum and the Department for Culture, Media and Sport

The Museum's aim is to hold for the benefit and education of humanity a collection representative of world cultures and ensure that the collection is housed in safety, conserved, curated, researched and exhibited.

The agreement:

- summarises the Museum's whole mission, strategic priorities, rationale, programme, planned output (as presented to DCMS in the Museum's plan);
- sets out the contribution the Museum will make to DCMS objectives, efficiency and public value;
- explains how the benefits of the DCMS investment will be spread geographically to the regions;
- confirms the commitment of DCMS to the Museum in terms of funding and other support;
- shows how delivery will be measured and monitored by reference to a set of key targets and performance indicators agreed with the Museum and by such other quantitative and qualitative measures that the Museum wishes to use to assess its performance and the achievement of public value in the context of its wider activities;
- provides an assessment of the risks and how they will be managed.

Source: www.culture.gov.uk/images/publications/fa_bm.pdf
(accessed 27 August 2008).

The museum as a firm

Multiple output

The first observation that has struck all cultural economists analysing museums is that they are multiple output firms, meaning that they produce a combination of visitor services (education and aesthetic enjoyment) through the display of their collections and through complementary services (shop, cafés, and suchlike), preservation services for their own collection and expertise offered to other museums, and research on the collection and on its context. (The statement of aims for the British Museum in box 9.3 above makes this clear.) Only some of these services are apparent to the public and are demanded by them. Visitors evaluate their experience without being able to value the 'backroom' activities of the museum and so their willingness to pay relates to only part of the museum's output. The digitalisation of museums' collections and information about the museum may alter that, however, as restoration work, for example, can be shown online; though online visitors do not pay for the service, their interest in visiting the museum and willingness to pay may be increased. To my knowledge, there has not yet been work on the economic effect of digitalisation on museums.

The museum has a production function that enables it to produce these various outputs whose inputs are the collection, the building (containing areas for storage, preservation, research, and so on, as well as exhibition space) and labour of various types, including the curatorial and managerial staff, research and preservation experts, education and design staff, salespeople and guards. All these inputs can be varied and combined in different quantities, and economic theory would tell us that that is done with respect to relative input prices; substitution between some inputs is possible – for example, security can be implemented with cameras and alarms instead of having a guard in each room. The one input that is rarely reduced in size, though it is added to, is the collection.

Capital value of the collection

As mentioned earlier, one aspect of museum policy that cultural economists have criticised is that museums do not treat their main asset, the collection, in an efficient way and have argued that unless a museum is willing to 'deaccession' items in its collection by selling some items or transferring them to another museum it cannot make efficient use of its resources. It is believed that the main explanation is that museum curators, who have a 'magpie' tendency to acquire more and more items, are not required to place a capital value on the collection and so the opportunity cost of holding on to it is not taken into account in costing the operation of a museum. If it were, the museum manager would be likely to sell some items from the vaults to finance the acquisition of others or to finance other activities. By contrast, a commercial firm would have to take the value of its capital assets into account and would alter its size to economise on its capital outlay. One reason for not doing so, of course, is that often it is the state, not the museum, that owns the collection and it would require government policy to sanction deaccessioning. (As mentioned above, however, museum policy in the Netherlands for the last few years has encouraged museums to share their collections, and a register of items in the collections has been drawn up to facilitate exchanges.) A stern critic of museums in this respect is William Grampp (see box 9.4).

Costs of production

Even without taking the value of the museum's collection into account, museums have high overheads and are capital-intensive. They are often

---

Box 9.4 Professor William Grampp on museum policy

William Grampp, emeritus professor of economics at the University of Illinois at Chicago, has been a scourge of art museum policy, particularly the failure to 'deaccession' items from the collection, for over twenty years, particularly in his 1989 book *Pricing the Priceless*, which advocates the use of prices to value works of art. In his article 'A colloquy about art museums', Grampp argues that art museums are inefficient by any standards and that 'if a business firm…managed its affairs as an art museum does, it would be the wonder of the western world. But its time of wonder would be brief and come to an end in a bankruptcy court' (Grampp, 1996: 221). He recognises that the sale of items from state-owned collections is prohibited in many European countries but points out that US museums behave in the same way. Moreover, he also points out that the prominent businesspeople who act as trustees on the boards of museums, who are often major donors to the museum and stand ready to assist it in time of need, also fail to 'direct their museum along the path of efficiency' (253).

Source: Grampp (1996).

located in buildings that are of great architectural importance, which may even be of more interest to the visitor than the collection; stunning new museum buildings, such as the Guggenheim Museum in Bilbao, designed by Frank Gehry, are now tourist sights in their own right (see chapter 19). Besides the initial capital outlay on buildings, older heritage buildings are expensive to maintain. Therefore, like many types of cultural organisation, museums have high fixed costs and relatively low marginal costs.

The costs of producing the various outputs are not always and perhaps cannot meaningfully be accounted for separately, though that would be what an economist would wish to see. If that were done, it would be possible to balance the costs and revenues of each activity and use the information to judge the most efficient combination of inputs and outputs. Of course, that begs the question posed previously: what unit of output is being adopted? Is it the number of visitors or the number of items on display, for example? If we take the number of visitors as the measure, then it is easy to see that the extra cost of one more visitor is low in relation to the fixed cost of running the building and displaying and maintaining the collection. In the short run, more visitors might just require extra guards and more heating or dehumidification, at least up to the point of congestion; in the long run, the museum could vary the size of the building by expanding floor space (or closing some rooms) and vary the size of the collection by buying or selling parts of it. The point at which the long–run average cost per visitor is at a minimum would then indicate the least cost or most efficient size of the museum. This does not take into account the other output of the museum, however.

A feature of the output of visitor services that can be varied up to a point even in the short run is the opening times, and this is another topic that has attracted criticism from cultural economists: that museums do not vary their opening times according to visitor demand. Some have recently begun to do so, though the 'closed on Mondays' rule still applies widely in Europe. Extending opening times can increase the efficient use of space and be economically efficient even if it increases the labour and other costs associated with more visitors, as long as the marginal revenues from ticket sales cover these marginal costs. This is the point of applying the theory of the firm to a museum.

Efficiency of museums

With museums in many countries being in state ownership, assessing their efficiency is a problem for the government. Cultural economists have studied the costs of museums to see if they are operating at an efficient level of total output by two methods: one is to look for 'efficiency frontiers' or 'best practice frontiers' and the other is to look for economies of scale, as indicated above. Efficiency frontiers can be analysed by finding the most technically efficient combination of inputs – that is, to find the best practice underlying the production function among a group of non-profit organisations against which other museums in the group can be compared. Input combinations can be altered by substituting one for another, and the museum that uses the least quantities of the various inputs will show the best practice possible. Use of this type of analysis is assessed in more detail in chapter 10 in connection with performance indicators.

Performance indicators have been developed for museums and are used by governments: they typically include visitor data (age, home or foreign visitor, ethnic minorities, number of repeat visits, workshop attendance, etc.), the number of exhibitions, learning activities, research publications, the number of objects conserved or assessed for conservation, the number and value of new acquisitions, expenditure on building maintenance, and so forth. The choice of performance indicators of course depends upon the museum's mission and on government policy for the museum sector, and performance indicators also have to take into account the practicality and cost of collecting consistent quantitative data.[6] As argued in chapter 10, however, efficiency has to be defined in relation to the wider objectives as well as narrower cost criteria.

Conclusions about museums

Free entry to museums is a very interesting illustration of the distinction between positive and normative economics: what the effect of free entry is on visitor numbers to museums is a positive matter – the increase in numbers and the frequency of visits – whereas the question of whether or not this is efficient in achieving a policy objective is a normative one. Elasticities and shifts in demand and information on participation are positive data but they can and, to an economist, should be brought to bear on the normative question too. Specifically, we can use information on the subsidy per attendee and the socio-economic profile of visitors to assess the cost of achieving a (normative) policy of making the museum more accessible to less well off and less educated people. We might also ask whether charging the typical, better-off visitor and having vouchers for first-time visitors, young persons, and so on might not achieve the same outcomes for a lower level of subsidy. Alternatively, we might be able to show that spending more public money would increase the

[6] See Paulus (2003).

target audience. Policies have to be costed directly by the responsible authority or, ultimately, by their opportunity cost. These are all standard questions in cultural economics; the one topic that is unique to the economics of museums is the matter of the deaccessioning of items in the collection.

Built heritage

The built heritage consists of a wide range of structures, from archaeological remains to contemporary architecture, including bridges, statues, memorials, churches and other religious buildings, theatres, government offices, palaces, parks and gardens, factories, even whole cities. Besides built heritage, there is also the natural heritage: areas of outstanding natural beauty, wilderness, coastlines, nature reserves and other such areas of the natural environment that have public value and require protection. Some heritage collections, such as zoos, botanical gardens and plant museums, seem to belong in part to both.

As stated at the outset, built heritage shares many characteristics with museums: it has strong public goods characteristics, it attracts public funding, it is prone to supplier-induced demand with experts playing a significant role in directing investment in restoration and upkeep, and it has multiple outputs. Built heritage also has some specific economic features that make it somewhat different from museums, however, and therefore economic analysis of built heritage has become a specialised field within cultural economics. In particular, the widespread use of regulation and its financial implications have shown up the role of bureaucratic influence in this sector, and the difficulty of controlling it has prompted the development of a political economy approach to heritage that applies public choice theory.

Visiting heritage sites is a popular activity that appeals to a broad spectrum of participants and it forms an important component of cultural tourism. Contingent valuation studies, which constitute one of the most important recent developments in cultural economics, are frequently used as a means of valuing visitors' willingness to pay for built and natural heritage.

Regulation of built heritage

Listing of heritage

A particular feature of built heritage is the significant role played by regulation by specialist authorities. The regulation of built heritage takes two forms: first, the designation of items as worthy of protection; this is typically done by

officials of a government body (local, regional or national) who are archae-
ologists, art historians, architects and other such experts. The listing of built
heritage is done individually for outstanding items but it is also done in a
blanket manner, such as designating as listed buildings all properties in a
particular part of a city or town (often the old centre), or just a rule of thumb
may be used, as in Italy, whereby every building that is over fifty years old is
'listed'. While this appears to be crude, there is an economic logic behind it of
minimising transaction costs; it is very costly to list each heritage building
individually and there would no doubt be costs of litigation over listing. In
some countries, there is a hierarchy of listing – grade 1, 2, and so on (United
Kingdom) – and of designation of local or national monuments.
Internationally, there is also the listing by UNESCO of World Heritage sites.
Lists of listed heritage sites and buildings are now available on the internet and
have considerably improved information for visitors.

Complying with listed status

The second aspect of regulation is the law that requires owners of listed
buildings to comply with requirements of style and the like laid down by the
heritage authorities. These can be very detailed and require specialist treatment and therefore impose extra costs on owners. It is due to this type of
regulation that cultural economists identify the majority of the finance of built
heritage as coming from the private sector – the property owners. Listing may
also attract sources of public money for renovation and property maintenance, however. One might suppose that, as listing imposes expenses on
owners, it reduces property prices; a study in the United Kingdom showed
that this was not the case, however: listing in fact enhanced the desirability of
properties. This fact raises the question of how necessary public grants are to
finance preservation, since private individuals (or businesses – many listed
buildings are occupied by businesses) have the incentive to finance the work
themselves and recoup the outlay via enhanced market prices.

Listing, registration of monuments and subsidy for restoration and preservation also impose a duty on owners to show certain features of their
properties to the public; in France, for instance, such buildings are supposed
to be open to the public thirty days a year. It has been argued that such
obligations can be viewed as altering property rights but that the transaction
costs of monitoring them probably inhibit effective enforcement. Moreover, if
listing automatically ensures access to public funds, there is a moral hazard
problem in that it encourages excessive expenditure on heritage preservation.

The French cultural economist Françoise Benhamou, who has done detailed research on built heritage, has made the case for the delisting of some monuments on these grounds and also because she foresees in heritage a situation analogous to the 'cost disease' in the performing arts: that the requirement imposed by official heritage experts to use specialised builders and materials drives up costs excessively, and these spiral ever higher as more and more buildings are listed.[7] Listing also has distributional effects, as it is a burden on present generations, to finance the option demand of future generations, who, however, will on the one hand be richer than the present generation and, on the other, may have different tastes. The requirement to preserve and maintain internationally important listed heritage sites can be especially hard on poor countries and justifies international financial support.

Change of use for heritage buildings

A further issue concerns changing the use of listed buildings. Many listed buildings can be preserved effectively only if their use is changed but often there are restrictions on this, thus adding to the burden of preservation. Religious buildings that are no longer in use for their original purpose present a particular challenge, and in some countries, such as Italy and France, they may constitute the bulk of listed monuments; for example, in France in the mid-1990s, over 40 per cent were religious buildings.[8] Conversions for use as university buildings, concert halls, and so on that retain them in public ownership are common. Permitting a change of use of listed heritage also raises the question of whether protected monuments can be sold as private property (albeit subject to listing and the obligations that that imposes on any property). Italy, with its overabundance of built heritage, accepted the principle of privatisation and began the process of selling it in the 1990s.

There is, however, another aspect to the extensive regulation of heritage buildings in private ownership, at least in Italy (and in particular in Sicily, which has autonomy over cultural matters and a wealth of significant built heritage): the heritage authorities have considerable powers to intervene to hold up alterations or renovations to a property both on the inside and outside, and this leads to uncertainty on the part of the owner that is a disincentive to private initiatives and even ownership. This has been called a form of 'crowding out' of private expenditure by public intervention.[9]

---

[7] Benhamou (2003b).   [8] Benhamou (2003b).
[9] Rizzo and Towse (2002); see also Rizzo and Throsby (2006).

UNESCO listing

The Convention concerning the Protection of World Cultural and Natural Heritage was adopted by UNESCO in 1972. It encourages international protection of the world heritage through a system of international co-operation and assistance designed to conserve and identify heritage in participating countries. It does so through studying the artistic, scientific and technical problems associated with the protection, conservation, presentation and rehabilitation of the cultural and natural heritage and by providing expert assistance, training and equipment. In general, the nation state is expected to finance these activities within its territory, but loans and, exceptionally, subsidies, are awarded to countries that find it hard to supply the necessary finance. There is also a reserve fund to provide financial assistance resulting from disasters or natural calamities. In 2003 the UNESCO Convention for the Safeguarding of the Intangible Cultural Heritage extended protection to cultural expressions and practices, including endangered languages and 'living treasures'.

The UNESCO list of cultural heritage consists of a range of sites, monuments and buildings of archaeological, art historical and architectural importance from Palaeolithic art to the Sydney Opera House. It is interesting to speculate on what being on the list means in economic terms. In less developed countries, the possibility of assistance, both technical and financial, is no doubt an advantage, but, in general, countries have to finance heritage maintenance themselves, so World Heritage listing may just reinforce national policy and finance and possibly ensure that the items are given priority in the event of shortages of funds. Listing may also elicit new sources of finance, such as sponsorship, by acting as a form of certification. Another advantage may be that tourism to the listed item is stimulated. This is another topic that calls for work by cultural economists to evaluate the UNESCO World Heritage listing policy.

Intangible heritage

Intangible heritage as a category is relatively new as international policy but has existed in national states for some time. Categories include oral traditions and expressions, traditional performing arts, rituals and festivals, and traditional craftsmanship. It allows recognition of 'living treasures' – artists and bearers of craft traditions of all kinds, including performance and making, and particularly folk traditions – and requires that all 'listed' intangible heritage be supported by the nation proposing them. In Japan, for example, this has resulted in support under the heading of heritage for its traditional performing arts, Noh, Kumiodori and Kabuki theatre and Bunraku puppet theatre, and the provision of a state-financed fund of ¥2 million for individuals designated as 'national living treasures'.[10]

Finance of built heritage

Much of the built heritage is in private ownership and therefore, depending upon the rules for the public subsidy of costs of heritage preservation, some proportion of the costs fall on the owners. Figures from France show that nearly a half of all listed or registered buildings were in private ownership in the 1990s. Public expenditure figures on monuments and sites in Europe range from 2 per cent of total cultural expenditure on historical monuments in Denmark to 62 per cent in Greece (€200 million spent on museums, archives, monuments and sites in 2001 in a country with a population of just over 10 million). Moreover, the data may not include expenditures on items such as theatre and museum buildings that may be reported under those categories. In Japan, for example, the Agency for Cultural Affairs, the central-government-financed body that deals with all aspects of culture, reports expenditure on 'preserving, maintaining and utilizing cultural properties' (nearly ¥35 million in 2006) separately from building a new National Arts Centre and restoring the Heijo Palace ruins (nearly ¥13 million).[11] These are just the figures for direct expenditure by the central government, and in Japan there is both considerable public expenditure by prefectures and municipalities as well as indirect tax expenditure from 50 per cent tax waivers for private spending on a range of heritage properties. Neither do the data include finance from other sources, such as trusts, private donations and sponsorship.

By contrast to its policy on arts finance, the US federal government provides considerable public funds for the built heritage as well as providing generous tax incentives for private owners, particularly for items that are listed on the National Register of Historic Places. US state and city administrations, as well as local societies, also preserve the built heritage. This is well illustrated in the case of the state of Rhode Island (see box 9.5).

---

[10] Agency for Cultural Affairs (2006). In mid-2006, the yen:euro exchange rate was 143:1 and the yen:US dollar was 113:1.

[11] Agency for Cultural Affairs (2006).

Box 9.5 Rhode Island Historical Preservation & Heritage Commission

The Rhode Island Historical Preservation & Heritage Commission is the state agency for historical preservation and heritage programmes. The commission operates a state-wide historical preservation programme that identifies and protects historic buildings, districts, structures, and archaeological sites. The commission also develops and carries out programmes to document and celebrate the rich cultural heritage of Rhode Island's people.

The Rhode Island Historical Preservation & Heritage Commission's website operates a list of 16,000 items of built heritage in Rhode Island that are listed in the National Register of Historic Places. The commission administers a Certified Local Government grant programme for municipal historical preservation activities in communities with a historic district zoning ordinance and a historic district commission; they are eligible to apply for federal 50 per cent matching grants for survey and planning projects. Projects suitable for grant funding include the identification and evaluation of significant historic and archaeological properties, the nomination of eligible properties to the national register, historic preservation plans and certain education-related activities. The state also provides State Preservation Grant funds for capital preservation projects for museums, cultural art centres and public historic sites located in historic structures; awards totalling $6 million were made in 2003–7. In addition, there are local funds for community development activities and many trusts and foundations that support Rhode Island heritage preservation projects.

Source: www.rihphc.state.ri.us (accessed 22 September 2008).

Participation and built heritage

Data on visits to built heritage – monuments, sites and heritage buildings – are not often published separately. Eurostat (2007) reports that, for the EU-27, 54 per cent of Europeans visited a 'historical monument' in 2007 and, although a significantly higher percentage of 'managers' made a visit, more than a half of every socio-economic group also did so. Some European countries publish figures on participation and there is considerable variation in the popularity of visiting built heritage: in 2006/7 34 per cent of the population of Spain visited a monument, with a similar figure for the Greek population (although there were 7.5 million visits to archaeological sites and monuments in Greece, these were in the main by foreign visitors); in Finland, in 2002, the figure was 50 per cent for historical sites and 14 per cent for archaeological sites; in the United Kingdom, in 2005, 69 per cent of persons aged sixteen and over attended at least one 'historic environment site' (from a detailed list ranging from a city or town with historic character (51 per cent) to archaeological sites (16 per cent)) with gardens being among the most popular items.[12]

[12] Council of Europe/ERICarts (2008) for Finland, Greece, Spain and the United Kingdom.

Demand

Historic city centres and other built heritage that can be viewed in public places (the outside of buildings, public statues, and so on) are non-excludable for practical purposes. Enclosed sites make entry charges possible. Though there have been no studies of demand for entry to built heritage sites and buildings, it is worth noting that entry prices for National Trust properties in the United Kingdom (see box 2.1) are relatively high (compared, say, to charging museums), and in 2007 an adult ticket for the bigger country houses was around £7–8 (some €12) including the garden and £4–£5 (€7) for the garden alone (historic gardens are very popular with UK visitors of every socio-economic background). In some properties prices were even higher, with discriminatory prices for weekends and timed tickets to reduce congestion. Congestion is evidence of rivalry in the consumption of built heritage, suggesting that, where it is present, heritage is not a public good even if it is non-excludable. Congestion at very popular heritage sites has been studied by cultural economists for some time. The city of Venice is a striking case and, at one time, it was even suggested that there could be a charge for entering the city over the land bridge. Economic solutions for dealing with congestion caused by excessive tourism are discussed in chapter 19.

Like museums, built heritage services are varied, and visitors' willingness to pay for entry is unlikely to cover total costs even when it is feasible to charge, because the visitor's valuation of his or her experience may not take into account the work on conservation, the historical accuracy of the maintenance of the property, and so on. Perhaps most important in the case of built heritage, though, is the extent of option demand and maintaining heritage for future generations, which cannot be expressed directly through entry prices. In these circumstances WTP has to be measured indirectly, and contingent valuation methods have come to be widely used.

WTP and CV studies of built heritage

Studies of willingness to pay have been extensively used in relation to built heritage and are discussed below. CV studies measure WTP and act as a guide to the public authority as to how much people would be willing to pay out of taxes for maintaining the site or property. Visiting also involves other costs, however, and the cost of travel to a heritage site has also been used as an indication of WTP.

CV was first developed for use in valuing natural heritage and damage to wilderness and it continues to be used widely in environmental economics. In cultural economics it has been used on a wide range of built heritage settings, from the restoration and maintenance of individual buildings to valuing groups of buildings, even a whole city centre, to discover the willingness to pay for items that are not priced in the marketplace on the part of both users and non-users. Thus CV studies aim to measure both what private demand would be and the value of option demand for heritage in order to produce a monetary amount that taxpayers would be willing to contribute via public finance.

The study is typically carried out with the use of questionnaires and interviews of visitors at the site while others – the non-users – are sampled by various other survey means. Participants in the survey, which may be done by telephone or face to face, are asked questions designed to elicit the value they place on an item or proposal. There is usually some information provided, such as a photograph or verbal description of the item, to ensure the participant understands the issue. Using a method that is called 'dichotomous choice', the respondent is asked if he or she would spend a stated amount of money out of taxes on the project (or have the government do so on his or her behalf) and told to give a 'Yes' or 'No' response. A variant is to inform respondents how much the government currently spends on this or other items and to ask if they agree it is acceptable; however, this does not discover if people answering 'Yes' are willing to pay more and, if so, how much more; nor does a 'No' reply inform the researcher how 'far' the respondent is from the stated amount. An alternative method is to offer a range of 'prices' – amounts of money – written on a card shown by the interviewer, say, and ask the respondent to pick one, or just to ask an open-ended question about WTP. In the latter case, checks have to be made by other questions to discover if the stated amount is feasible in terms of the person's income.

Problems with CV studies

There are a number of persistent problems with CV studies. One is the 'free-rider' problem; respondents might say what they would be willing to pay or offer an amount that they would not pay in practice, but there is no way of checking if they actually would stump up ('step up to the plate'); or, at the other extreme, they might avoid expressing their WTP altogether. A zero WTP may therefore just be an expression of unwillingness to answer questions or, equally, a statement that the item has no value to the respondent, and as a result values of zero are difficult to interpret. As a WTP of zero typically constitutes 30 per cent or more of responses by users and 60 per cent from non-users, this is a serious problem. Another problem is that respondents who are willing to pay may revise their original offer (bid) if informed what the current spending on the item is; in other words, the bid would not be realised in a practical situation. Moreover, respondents may not be aware of alternative projects that would call on their tax money.

There are problems also with calculating the 'average' WTP. The distribution is likely to be skewed, with a few richer and/or better-educated respondents having a high WTP and the majority having a low WTP; thus the median (50 per cent mark) of the distribution of WTP amounts is lower than the mean, but in order to project the total amount from the sample for the whole population the distribution of income and other socio-economic characteristics must be known. If the heritage item in question is heavily visited by foreign tourists, this adds a further complication. Despite all these problems and, by the by, the fact that carrying out such surveys is very expensive, CV studies have made an important contribution to valuing cultural heritage and will no doubt continue to be used in planning and policy-making for heritage services.

Impact of digitalisation and the internet

There has been little economic research on the impact of digitalisation on heritage, though it is clear that better information is likely to improve the quality of visits and the understanding of the value of heritage on the part of non-attendees. Use of the internet for conducting surveys online also opens up the possibility of much cheaper CV studies able to reach visitors to heritage websites.

The fixed cost of digitalising heritage collections is likely to have to be financed by public funding or private donations, and cultural economics certainly supports that, as the information on websites of heritage organisations is a clear example of a public good. Digital images of items in museums and on heritage sites enable their curators to 'propertise' them, however, by copyrighting them; as a result, access to these images could be restricted and commercialised even though the items themselves are public property. There are many interesting and challenging topics for research here.

Conclusion

This chapter has covered a range of topics about the economics of museums and the built heritage. A common feature of heritage is that the items it is concerned with were mostly produced for private purposes and they have been subject to the scrutiny of experts in cultural heritage to be recognised as important to society as well as to individuals. Certification by experts, whether of the cultural and symbolic significance of an everyday object, of the authenticity of a painting or of the architectural value of a building, affects the supply and possibly also the asset value of a heritage item as well as informing the consumer (the visitor) of its social and cultural value. Expert opinion is then used to justify intervention in the market for heritage goods, and this can take the form of public ownership of museum collections and regulation of property rights to works of art and to heritage listed buildings.

Even without the particular role played in the heritage sector by experts with bureaucratic power, the considerable public good nature of heritage would justify government intervention on public finance on standard welfare grounds of market failure. With the designation of heritage at local, national and international level leading to an ever-increasing stock of heritage items, though, the question arises as to how sustainable public and private finance is and how to protect effectively the heritage, both for the present and for future generations. This is a particular problem for built heritage of world cultural importance in poorer countries. Extensive sites such as Angkor Wat in Cambodia that have been badly damaged in war and need constant protection, restoration and maintenance are a heavy responsibility for the country in which they are located. Without international assistance, the burden may be too onerous to prevent deterioration from natural causes and from damage and theft. International co-operation to prevent the theft of art and artefacts requires finance in addition to the funding needed for national heritage protection. Besides listing tangible world heritage, UNESCO and national governments are also protecting intangible heritage – the bearers of performing arts, craft and language traditions.

The extensive public intervention in cultural heritage raises questions about public accountability in non-market situations. Particular topics that have been analysed by cultural economists are the unwillingness of museums to deaccession items of their collection, the incentives to managers of museum heritage sites and buildings to improve visitor services and the lack of response of bureaucrats to the public's preferences. In addition, there are other topics in the economics of heritage that are not treated here, such as the valuation of heritage as cultural capital or cost–benefit analysis applied to heritage. This is a growing field in cultural economics and can be expected to produce more and more varied research and publications.

Further reading

There is no shortage of interesting and accessible literature on the economics of heritage, both museums and built heritage. Top of the list has to be the recent book *The Heritage Game* by Alan Peacock and Ilde Rizzo (2008). Alan Peacock, whose name comes up frequently in this book in many contexts, pioneered the economic analysis of museums and built heritage, publishing his first articles on the subject in the 1970s; Ilde Rizzo, professor of public finance at the University of Catania in Sicily, has done important work on built heritage, particularly in Italy. Their book covers the broader economic context of heritage within the cultural sector as well as analysing heritage policy, with examples of practice in Italy and the United Kingdom.

Ilde Rizzo, Isidoro Mazza, Giacomo Pignataro and Tiziana Cuccia, all at the University of Catania, have contributed chapters on various aspects relating to heritage to the Towse (2003a) *Handbook of Cultural Economics* – Rizzo on 'Regulation' (chapter 52), Mazza on 'Public choice' (chapter 49), Pignataro on 'Performance indicators' (chapter 47) and Cuccia on 'Contingent valuation' (chapter 14). Françoise Benhamou wrote the main chapter on 'Heritage' (chapter 32) and Peter Johnson the one on 'Museums' (chapter 41). Ilde Rizzo with David Throsby wrote the chapter 'Cultural heritage: economic analysis and public policy' in the Ginsburgh and Throsby (2006) *Handbook of the Economics of Art and Culture* (chapter 28), with Bruno Frey and Stephan Meier contributing a chapter on 'The economics of museums' (chapter 29).

Bruno Frey has also made major contributions to the literature on the economics of museums with several chapters in his 2000 book *Arts and Economics*: 'For art's sake – open up the vaults' (chapter 3), 'Superstar museums' (chapter 4) and 'Special exhibitions and festivals: culture's booming path to glory' (chapter 5); chapter 10, 'Evaluating cultural property', critically evaluates contingent valuation studies, recommending instead the use of referenda for political decision-making.

Two symposia in the *Journal of Economics* are also to be recommended: issue 22, volumes 22–3, in 1998 on 'Museums' and issue 27, volumes 3–4, in 2003 on 'Contingent valuation'.

10 Economic evaluation of cultural policy

This chapter explores the way cultural economists approach the evaluation of cultural policy. It does not discuss cultural policy itself but, instead, presents the way economists assess policies in general, and it focuses on particular topics on which cultural economists have written concerning cultural policy or policies. 'Cultural policy' is a broad term that covers a range of government interventions and initiatives to achieve objectives, such as increasing participation in the arts and culture and encouraging diversity of cultural supply, which may or may not involve public expenditure; when the use of taxpayers' money is involved, that calls for accountability to voters.

Cultural policy for the arts and heritage typically has cultural aims, though, as chapter 14 shows, there can also be a strong economic motive to some policies, especially those for the creative industries, and, moreover, policy-makers and arts organisations may choose to justify projects in terms of their economic impact. Previous chapters have already discussed the way economists evaluate specific policy issues, such as charging for entry to museums. In this chapter, however, the intention is to present the analysis in general terms, using the material of all the preceding chapters. Therefore this chapter deals with applied welfare economics, principal–agent analysis, performance indicators and economic impact studies, and I revisit the cost disease as an underlying *raison d'être* for subsidy to the arts and heritage.

Cultural economics and cultural policy

It has long been the creed of economists that their role in relation to policy is to advise on ways of achieving policy objectives chosen by the political process rather than to form those objectives themselves. Many economists see economics as providing a 'toolbox' for policy. Public choice theorists regard this as naïve, however, because they consider policy-makers to be self-interested and to form policies to suit their own objectives, such as getting re-elected or gaining reputation, rather than to serve the public interest (more on this later). The other side of the coin is that economists can use their tools to evaluate policies in relation to the stated objectives and feel free to criticise the way policies work from both a theoretical and practical stance. In principle, any criticisms are scientific, but if we are honest there is also scope for some bias in any evaluation, and it should be possible to expose it.

Social efficiency

Economists use several approaches to evaluation but, essentially, the main criterion is social efficiency in maximising welfare. That said, efficiency is a complex and misunderstood phenomenon, and the view often held in the arts world, at least in the past, that efficiency simply means cost-cutting is simply incorrect; in fact, cost-cutting is more likely to be the concern of managers and accountants than of economists. Economists are concerned with social costs and benefits using the ideas of welfare economics; as has been emphasised in previous chapters of this book, externalities (the difference between private and social costs and benefits) cannot always be accurately measured, particularly when a project or policy is expected to be long-lived, and therefore there may be different views about future outcomes. Even if there were only private benefits from a policy, though, efficiency would mean using sufficient resources to produce those benefits. For example, if it is decided that a country should have an international-level opera, then the costs of producing it have to be assessed in relation to that objective, not on the grounds of comparison to other provision or that costs could be reduced by replacing international artists with local ones. In this context, cost-effectiveness analysis would be used to assess whether the policy was efficient in the sense of using the resources well for the purpose.

Efficiency in economics also means that prices reflect consumers' willingness to pay and that prices reflect the cost or opportunity cost of the resources used to produce the good. In the arts and heritage, willingness to pay may not necessarily be expressed via the market price, because some goods and services provide external benefits and may even be public goods. Cultural economists therefore use techniques such as contingent valuation to measure willingness to pay.

Cultural value and economic value

One of the main bones of contention between the arts world and economists has been that the arts are too valuable to be reduced to costs and benefits, or, at least, that such calculations cannot be made in financial terms. Some cultural economists argue that cultural and economic value should be separately identified (such as Throsby, 2001), while others maintain that the issue is that the arts are economic activities that use up resources and therefore should be subject to evaluation on economic grounds (such as Frey, 2000). For their part however, arts policy-makers and arts organisations from time to time have been reluctant to accept the validity of economic evaluation of their activities. One way that has been devised of reconciling these problems has been the development of performance indicators that enable an arts organisation to express its objectives in such a way that its success in achieving them can be evaluated. If the same performance indicators for all its clients in a particular art form are used by a funding agency, that then enables it to evaluate the efficiency or effectiveness of each in relation to the others (see below).

The funding agency and its clients

A feature of policy that is well understood by economists is that, while policy is made by one organisation, others execute it, and there can be difficulties of matching the aims of one with the efforts of the other. In economic theory this calls for principal–agent analysis, and it is particularly relevant to cultural policy, for several reasons. First, many governments wish to avoid direct provision of the arts and heritage and do so by granting funds to private non-profit organisations to manage the performing arts, heritage and museum services; though they can lay down conditions for grants, and these are increasingly clearly specified in funding agreements and the like, funding bodies cannot directly control their activities and are therefore unable to ensure that the agent fulfils the principal's objectives. Second, the central government may give the funds it devotes to culture to an intermediate body, such as an arm's-length organisation such as an arts council or heritage authority, to administer or make funding decisions, or the funds may go to local government for decisions about expenditure in their administrative area. In federal countries and those in which cultural funding is in the hands of regional and local government, policy-making may be diffused and collaboration between levels of administration will therefore be necessary. In these situations, the principal (the central government) has to offer the right kind of incentives to or controls on the agent to try to ensure that its objectives are met. The ultimate sanction is to withdraw funds, but this could lead to accusations of political interference, and could also waste scarce funds and so be unpopular with voters.

Information problems and supplier-induced demand

As we have seen in previous chapters, information problems abound in the arts and heritage because of the need for expert knowledge, and also because issues such as quality are very hard to evaluate. The problem of asymmetric information lies at the back of principal–agent problems, and can also lead to supplier-induced demand, when the buyer or the funding body has information only from the organisation that supplies the good or service; even if there were a market with competing suppliers, which would enable comparisons to be made, information problems can still make evaluation difficult for funding bodies.

It can be seen that these issues are complex, and perhaps they are nowadays understood to be more so than thirty years ago, when Karen King and Mark Blaug first sent out their clarion call 'Does the Arts Council know what it is doing?' (see box 10.1). It also has to be recognised, however, that it is at least in part because cultural economists raised these questions that evaluation of arts and heritage policy is no longer regarded as beyond the pale by arts administrators.

Box 10.1 *Policy and Planning with a Purpose or The Art of Making Choices in Arts Funding*: a presentation by J. Mark Schuster

Mark Schuster (1951–2008), former Professor of Urban Cultural Policy at Massachusetts Institute of Technology, was a public policy analyst specialising in the analysis of government policies and programmes with respect to the arts, culture and urban design. He did important work on indirect support for the arts and was also an expert in international arts policy and finance and in international comparisons of these topics.

In 2001 he gave this presentation to personnel at the Arts Council of Ireland, starting as follows:

> *'How do you know that what you are doing you are doing well?'*
> *'How does the Arts Council know that what it is doing it is doing well?'*
> *'How does the Arts Council know that what you are doing you are doing well?'*
> *'How do you know that what the Arts Council is doing it is doing well?'*
> *and*
> *'How does the government know that what the Arts Council is doing it is doing well?'*

These words echoed the 1973 paper by King and Blaug with reference to the Arts Council of Great Britain, and Schuster pointed out that these are timeless questions. His justification for asking them was this: 'Because we are discussing the deployment of public resources, we are obliged to be asking these questions. Just because we are discussing the arts and culture, we are relieved of neither the obligation nor the desirability of asking these questions. We would expect the same of any sector in which public resources are to be invested. Why should we expect less for the arts and culture?'

Sources: Schuster (2001) and King and Blaug (1973).

Theoretical underpinnings of policy and its evaluation

Applying welfare economics

As explained in chapters 1 and 7, welfare economics forms the theoretical justification for state intervention in the workings of the market economy, not only for the arts but for all sectors, and provides an underlying rationale both for the choice of policies and for their evaluation. Cultural economics makes considerable use of welfare economics as a justification for subsidy and regulation of the arts and heritage. In chapter 7, while the basic theory of welfare economics was outlined, the difficulties of applying it in practice were not discussed nor the particular problems of applying it to the cultural sector. I begin, then, with the pros and cons of welfare economics as a means of justifying and evaluating cultural policy.

The social welfare function

The underlying notion of welfare economics is that a social welfare function can be defined in terms of the utilities or satisfaction all the members of a society derive from the whole bundle of goods and services available to them; each person has individual tastes and preferences and chooses the best combination of goods and services that he or she can obtain, given the set of relative prices and constrained by his or her income and wealth. Almost every aspect of this conceptualisation has been questioned by economists, and cultural economists have added their own list of objections. The first objection concerns the possibility of meaningfully defining a social welfare function: by defining it over individual utilities, it is said that there is no room for the consideration of social or public values independent of those held by individual members. As a result, concepts such as civic or national pride or the aspirations of a society rather than just those of its members are not taken into account. This implies a highly individualistic notion of the state and of the public sphere, and many social scientists criticise this view.

Shared benefits, as with non-rival and non-excludable public goods, present problems for economists, and, as we saw in box 2.2, many economists reject the 'cop-out' of merit goods. Nonetheless, the concepts of option demand and future generations' demand that are used in cultural economics to justify government intervention in the market are deemed to be part of the individual's preference function – we derive utility from knowing that our grandchildren can enjoy our arts and culture – so they bridge the social/private preference 'gap'. Further objection to individualism has been voiced by some cultural economists on the grounds that tastes for culture and the arts are not individual but social in nature; culture is a social conception and culture in the anthropological sense (shared language and customs etc.) is a public good, and the recognition of art is a social, not an individual, process.

Other critiques by economists concern the notion of welfare itself. Some economists identify welfare just as wealth and assume that the maximisation of wealth is the aim of society; other economists define welfare in terms of people's ability to achieve their personal goals in life while others consider happiness to be the yardstick. Even if there were agreement on the aspect of welfare that is the social goal, others reject the idea of maximisation. Therefore, even before we raise the question of how applicable welfare theories are, such as Pareto optimality, there are problems with the acceptance of the notion of the maximisation of social welfare.

Problems with Pareto optimality and Pareto improvements

Pareto optimality has been and continues to be challenged on the grounds that the conditions necessary to achieve it cannot be found in the 'real world': to attain the optimum allocation of resources, there must be perfect competition, no public goods, no external effects (costs or benefits), no missing markets, and there must be futures markets that anticipate and discount future prices for inputs (especially capital) and for output. All goods must be priced according to marginal cost by profit-maximising enterprises and all markets for factors of production must be competitive, with workers and the owners of capital responding speedily to price changes. Unsurprisingly, this scenario has been rejected as unrealistic and therefore an unworkable guide by which to judge policy measures. According to the alternative 'second best' theory of welfare, every policy measure must be evaluated individually and no generalisations are possible, except that the relevant information must be assessed empirically and likely outcomes judged by their probable effects, in terms of social costs.

A deeper question is a methodological one: to what extent is Paretian welfare economics 'positive' economics and to what extent does it stray into value judgements? Pareto optimality and Pareto improvements are concerned with social efficiency, not with equity. Even if an unambiguous Pareto improvement could be found (that is, an act that raises welfare by benefiting some people without harming others), it would not take into account the distribution of income and therefore would ignore social equity implications. Social equity is also an important motive for government intervention and may well be the predominant concern of policy, and there is often a clash between social efficiency and equity, but there is no rule in economics that can determine the balance between the two. Some economists who believe strongly in the power of market forces to achieve both tend to lean too far over the 'is/ought' divide and say, for instance, that in order to achieve social efficiency government policy *should* encourage perfect competition. 'Radical right' economists (and politicians) tend to deny the importance of public goods and external effects and believe the market can deal with everything through the workings of the price mechanism. They advocate measures to increase competition in the belief that the market will work better to promote wealth and welfare; to other economists, this seems like stepping over the line from 'is' to 'ought'. On the other hand, measures to promote social equity also step over the line, because there is nothing in economics that tells us what the 'fair' distribution of income is: most economists recognise the case for progressive taxation that makes post-tax income more equal but few would advocate doing away with income (and wage) differentials, because incentives to work hard and take risks with capital would be reduced and that could lead to lower national income. Thus there is always a tug in economic policy between equity and efficiency, and the trade-off cannot be resolved theoretically.

Another of the problems of the Pareto improvement (potential or actual) is that it is impossible to devise a tax system that enables a government to give subsidies to people and organisations without making taxpayers worse off. Since financial payments to improve the welfare of some members of society mostly have to be financed by funds raised from taxes, some people are going to be made worse off. Public finance analyses the best ways of raising and spending taxation to provide benefits but there is no escaping the dilemma. Thus there are severe limitations to Paretian welfare economics as a practical policy instrument.

Public choice critique of welfare economics

Further criticism of welfare economics is to be found in public choice theory – that welfare economics ignores the process of how and why policies are made. When applying welfare economics and public finance in policy settings, many economists would take as given the objective or aim of that policy and set about analysing how best it can be achieved. Public choice theorists regard this as 'normative' because the question of why a particular policy is being adopted is not analysed. They investigate questions such as who benefits from making these policy choices in political or bureaucratic terms and see the incentive to win votes or exercise power in the administration as the motives for policy that must be taken into account in its evaluation. Public choice theorists would argue that this is 'positive' analysis because it looks at things as they are, not as what they would be in an ideal world of selfless politicians and officials. Research on the economics of heritage has shown that self-interested behaviour on the part of heritage officials can impact on heritage policy, for example. These are all aspects of the problem of replacing consumer sovereignty and the market by bureaucratic decision-making.

Government failure

Cultural economists have made much of welfare economics as the basis for government intervention due to market failure. The counterpart of market failure is government or public policy failure; whereas in the markets consumers can signal their preferences though willingness to pay, voters signal their preferences through the ballot box. Unless there is a specifically targeted electoral process, however, such as a referendum on arts spending of the type held in Switzerland,[1] choices concerning arts policy can get lost in the wider issues at general elections, particularly as the amount of public expenditure devoted to the arts and heritage is a small proportion of the government budget; therefore clear signals are not sent to policy-makers and bureaucrats are left with a free hand.

Public choice theorists favour local over national control of budgets and local over national decision-making, because they think this reduces these problems. Institutional arrangements for allocating government grants to the arts are also important and affect the distribution of expenditure: an arts council that is independent of government does not have political responsibility, but it may be responsible for monitoring the use of the funds it distributes, whereas an arts council whose role is solely to advise the ministry of culture does not have the responsibility of monitoring the way arts organisations make use of the grants they receive. It is interesting to note the observations on this topic by Alan Peacock and Rick van der Ploeg, both economists who were responsible for arts funding – Peacock as chairman of the Scottish Arts Council and van der Ploeg as secretary of state for culture in the Netherlands (see box 6.1 and box 7.6).

---

[1] See Frey (2000).

How much subsidy and for what purpose?

How much subsidy?

Though Paretian welfare economics may offer a general justification for correcting market failure on the grounds of social efficiency, it is far from providing guidance on how much subsidy is necessary to correct under-production of the arts and heritage. In chapter 7, it was shown that Pigovian welfare economics provides a decision rule in a specific market in which market failure occurs due to the presence of external costs or benefits: where there are external benefits, the socially efficient amount of the subsidy is that which would encourage producers to increase output to the point at which marginal social benefits equal marginal social costs. This guidance is qualitative, however, not quantitative. In order to assess the correct amount of subsidy, the value of the external benefit would have to be calculated. The same problem occurs with a public good for which there is no observable market demand: there is willingness to pay but that can be found out only by indirect methods, such as contingent valuation estimates and surveys of willingness to pay for benefits for which there are no market prices.

Efficiency and equity in cultural subsidy

Earlier in the chapter, the trade-off between social efficiency and equity was mentioned as posing difficult decisions for policy. One of the great conundrums of arts subsidy is whether unpopular arts should be supported in the attempt to form tastes and stimulate more informed future demand or whether taxpayers should be 'given their money's worth' by a more equitable distribution of subsidy so as to be inclusive and increase access. The conundrum takes many forms and appears in various contexts – for example, in relation to public service broadcasting (see chapter 17). The trade-off between quality and accessibility is a very difficult topic and is essentially a political question that cultural economists cannot solve, but they can contribute to it, for example by analysing the influence of quality on demand.

Efficiency relates to anything that alters the allocation of resources by affecting demand, supply and relative prices. Therefore, policies that aim to increase future demand by forming tastes and subsidies that increase output are classed as efficiency measures; regulations can also alter prices, as in the listing or control of use of built heritage and copyright law, and they are also efficiency measures. Equity relates to policies that reduce inequality between members of a society and to fairness in the distribution of resources, including tax-financed benefits. Some policies may fall into both categories; for instance, arts outreach work in schools in disadvantaged areas would constitute equity policies in the first instance, but as it may stimulate demand for the arts and encourage greater attendance it would therefore have efficiency implications.

There is a general dilemma here: when the state steps in to provide public goods or goods and services with external consumption benefits (thus justifying state intervention), should it mimic the market? Or is the rationale of subsidy to alter market behaviour? This question applies to other areas besides the arts and heritage but it is particularly fraught in the cultural arena. Moreover, it crosses the border between efficiency and equity, because the problem is essentially about the benefit taxpayers can expect to get from their taxes as they see it and the 'improvement' of tastes that would lead to changed demand patterns in the future. Of course, this improvement has to be taken up voluntarily and be reflected in consumption for there to be a welfare gain; thus merit goods provision that is imposed is not welfare-improving unless it changes consumers' choices.

Access to the arts and heritage

Access to the arts is a broad concept that has several different meanings, and in some contexts it is about equity and in others efficiency. The problem of access for provincial and rural populations to centralised cultural provision was mentioned above in the context of the private demand decisions of consumers – that is, the question was posed in terms of efficiency considerations. For the policy-maker there are also equity issues about the distribution of resources and how accessible they are to taxpayers and voters throughout the nation. Countries that are geographically large with a relatively small population – Australia, New Zealand and Norway, for instance – have to consider the costs of physical access to arts and heritage provision that do not arise in smaller and densely populated ones, such as Belgium. If outlying populations are to enjoy equal access, that may require higher subsidy per attendee; if they are to receive an equal distribution of subsidy, rural dwellers may not be able to have access to a full range of cultural provision. (Of course, these issues are not confined to the arts but apply to a range of services, and the arts and sports, for example, share the same problem.)

A similar issue arises with the question of access by people with disability of one kind or another. Physical access, in particular to old buildings, such as theatres and museums, has had to be addressed, as well as improving acoustic provision for hearing-impaired people, and heritage sites and museums have also made provision for people with impaired sight. Governments with equal opportunity policies for the disabled have used their power over the award of subsidy to require arts and heritage organisations in receipt of subsidy to provide such facilities as a condition of obtaining the full grant.

Another type of access issue is access to the arts and heritage by people from cultural backgrounds who have tastes that are not catered for by the predominant type of cultural provision. So-called 'minority cultures' or 'ethnic minorities' may be the target of cultural policy, and here, again, the question arises of whether people belonging to these groups should receive a share of the subsidy on the grounds of equity (spreading the benefits of tax revenues evenly) or whether the purpose of the subsidy is 'inclusiveness' – that is, promoting a sense of national identity with the 'majority' culture, which would be an efficiency argument for subsidy. (Note that these terms are somewhat misleading in the context of subsidised arts and heritage, since data on participation show that many art forms are 'minority' interests.) European countries with immigrant populations may set targets for increased participation in mainstream heritage and arts by ethnic minorities and may link the level of subsidy to it, as well as to first-time visitors from any cultural background. This became policy in the Netherlands (see box 7.6).

Digitalisation and digital services are likely to improve access vastly to information about cultural organisations and the output they supply. Once the investment in the fixed cost of setting up the website has been made, the marginal cost of additional information is relatively low and access to it costs the visitor almost nothing. It will be interesting to see the effect these developments have on tastes and perceptions about cultural provision.

Taste formation

Studies of demand for various art forms and participation studies in many countries have consistently shown that arts audiences have above-average levels of educational attainment; lower educational attainment would seem, therefore, to be a serious barrier to access. Arts education in schools may assist in forming tastes, and provision for outreach educational work by arts and heritage organisations is now a condition of subsidy in some countries; box 7.6 shows the incentives being offered in the Netherlands, and the Arts Council of England made educational work a requirement for a grant in the mid-1980s.

A more difficult 'access' problem in relation to the arts relates to content: should public expenditure be used to support less popular avant-garde arts in an attempt to form tastes and stimulate more informed future demand instead of responding to the current preferences and demand of present-day audiences and taxpayers? On efficiency grounds, economists would normally argue that consumers make informed choices and that welfare depends upon the satisfaction of individual demand based on given tastes. How are tastes formed, however? Consumers need information and experience to make decisions about what to consume, and subsidy can be used to provide the opportunity for people to try something new and different. The market may not support new art or art forms because they are financially risky and many cultural economists (myself included) believe that, without subsidy, consumers would not have the opportunity to experience novelty and high quality and would therefore not be able to develop informed tastes. Without new art, diversity is reduced and creativity stultified. This is a matter of dynamic efficiency, because tastes are formed over time and creativity takes place over time. The difficulty with this argument is: how long does it take for this process to work? It cannot be used endlessly for the same thing, and here again we have a dilemma: does a totally new performance of a Shakespeare play qualify for a subsidy to encourage new work? And who decides? Especially with new art forms, supplier-induced demand seems inevitable.

The observed pattern of subsidy does not appear to support the view that it targets new art, however; indeed, quite the opposite. A combination of playing safe, fear of criticism by taxpayers and bureaucratic inertia has led to a situation in which greater support goes to conventional programming by established arts organisations, especially to the large, flagship institutions, such as the national opera, ballet and theatre companies and museums, as reported in chapter 8. Studies by cultural economists have shown that, for example, few contemporary operas are performed despite the high level of subsidy.

A further problem with the efficiency of subsidy is dealt with below: subsidy encourages dependency on the part of heritage and arts organisations, especially when they are in receipt of regular grants. Instead of stimulating creativity it may, in fact, inhibit it and simply make the organisation inefficient. Before moving on to this important topic, though, I turn to a broader question of efficiency: does the presence of subsidy to the arts deter private giving?

'Crowding out' and 'crowding in'

'Crowding out' – the diversion of private finance as a result of public expenditure by the state – affects all areas of government intervention in the economy and is mostly studied as a problem in macroeconomics. Examples abound: the public provision of health and education services are held to displace private expenditure on them. In the arts, it has been questioned whether public subsidy crowds out private donors and sponsors and makes people unwilling to pay a price that covers the full cost of cultural goods and services.

There is another side to the coin, though: the existence of public support for individual arts and heritage organisations can provide reassurance to private donors that the organisation is properly run and is producing worthwhile output. Thus subsidy can act as a form of certification and assist an organisation in obtaining private finance and matched funding – what could be called 'crowding in'. Some governments encourage public–private partnership and matched funding arrangements in the arts and heritage and use tax breaks to encourage private giving; the United States is the country that places the greatest reliance on indirect support for the arts. The National Endowment for the Arts believes that this also results in 'crowding in', and on a very large scale; however, this claim has been questioned (see box 10.2 and Netzer, 2006).

Box 10.2 The NEA and 'crowding in': a case of American cultural microeconomics

The 2007 NEA publication *How the United States Funds the Arts* debunks the view that its relatively small budget ($120 million in 2006) and size of its operation make it only a marginal player on the US arts scene, especially when compared to the much larger budgets in European countries. The NEA's chairman, Dana Gioia, writes in the preface that it is the multiplying effect of its grants that makes the NEA so effective; during the 1970s and 1980s, he states, a $100,000 grant delivered $800,000 in eventual funds to an organisation – a multiplier of eight. This he calls a law of 'American cultural microeconomics'. He writes: 'The reason for this multiplying effect is obvious: NEA funding has the power to legitimate a new organization and further validate an existing one. Such endorsements attract further support. As the old saying goes, "Nothing succeeds like success"' (vii–viii).

Econometric research by Tom Smith testing such claims found limited evidence in support of 'crowding in' or leveraging of private donations by government grants. Looked at in various ways, the relationship between government grants and private donations suggests crowding in between $0.14 and $1.15, depending upon the particular art form: symphony orchestras and music companies experience a modest crowding in while dance and ballet companies experience a small crowding out.

Sources: NEA (2007a) and Smith (2007).

Direct versus indirect subsidy

The subsidy policy favoured by the United States, of encouraging private giving to the arts and heritage by private foundations, corporations and individuals by tax waivers, emphasises indirect subsidy in preference to the system prevalent in other countries, of direct grants either by a government ministry or an arm's-length body. Both are forms of subsidy, however: direct subsidy is financed from public taxation by central or local government (or both) and the amount of the subsidy is fixed by the government's allocated budget; the amount of indirect subsidy depends upon both the marginal rate of taxation of the donor and the value of the gift that is made. Thus, in the case of indirect subsidy, the policy-maker is not able to control the amount. Moreover, tax waivers are not specific to a particular art form or heritage item, and therefore the donor decides where the subsidy is spent as well as how much, taking much of the control of the finance of arts policy out of the hands of the policy-maker. Professor Dick Netzer was the first cultural economist to address this question (see box 10.3).

This is seen as an advantage by some economists, because donorship reflects the choices of private individuals and corporations, who are very likely also to be consumers of the art in question, and therefore are able to express their preferences directly not only by their willingness to pay but also by their willingness to donate. The downside would be if private donors failed to provide a balance of arts and

Box 10.3 Professor Dick Netzer and *The Subsidized Muse*

Dick Netzer (1929–2008), former Professor of Economics and Public Administration at New York University, was an expert in municipal finance and wrote on a wide range of topics including public finance, non-profit organisations and the arts and heritage. His 1978 book *The Subsidized Muse: Public Support for the Arts in the United States* was an important milestone in cultural economics, as it cautioned against excessive and untargeted subsidy. The book researched sixteen arts organisations in the United States using survey methods and found that public subsidies had encouraged large increases in the earnings of artistic and supporting personnel, kept ticket prices and admission charges from rising less rapidly than they otherwise would have, fostered some increases in output in the form of a lengthening of seasons of performances and stimulated artistic innovations of all kinds, but failed consistently to raise the representation of low-income people in audiences for the arts.

Netzer continued to write many important articles and chapters in books on the arts and heritage (see, for example, Netzer, 2006). In 1998 he was made Distinguished Fellow of the Association of Cultural Economics International and *The Subsidized Muse* was re-evaluated twenty years after its publication; in his speech congratulating him, Mark Blaug said: 'Netzer has laid the foundations for what might be called the microeconomics of cultural economics in the same way that the Baumol–Bowen book created its macroeconomics. Here is a rich research programme that has largely remained dormant for twenty years. I hope that we do not have to wait much longer before it is fully exploited' (Blaug, 1999: 32).

Sources: Netzer (1978) and Blaug (1999).

heritage provision, or favoured only conventional instead of contemporary art or tried to influence artistic policy.

Other countries besides the United States are increasingly introducing tax exemption for private giving to good causes and seeking other sources of private finance (such as lotteries). In those countries where the state (meaning central or local administrations) owns and manages cultural provision, suitable institutional arrangements had to be made for attracting private giving; one way of dealing with this has been the formation of private non-profit organisations to manage state-owned facilities, as has been done in Italy for the opera sector. Another problem is crowding out – that populations that are used to a system of direct provision or direct subsidy simply do not see the need to give over and above paying their taxes.

Principal–agent problems of cultural policy

Principal–agent analysis is concerned with the incentives and contracts that the principal can offer the agent. The agent often has the advantage in the relationship, because he or she controls information about the actions of the organisation and can hold out for a better deal. An extreme case is when a subsidised organisation deliberately overspends and threatens to reduce services or even close its doors unless more funds are forthcoming to cover the deficit. This leaves the principal (the ministry of culture or arts council) with a dilemma of being seen by taxpayers to be unable to control the size of the grant on the one hand and accused of philistinism and lack of commitment to the arts on the other. The principal, therefore, tries to get the agent to stick to an agreed budget by various means (such as a funding contract of the sort shown in box 9.3) and develops penalties for non-compliance, which could include threatening not to make a future grant. This threat is often hollow in the case of national flagship organisations, however.

When an arts or heritage organisation is managed within the government framework, the incentives the principal can offer the agent may be very limited if any 'profit' – that is, excess of income over expenditure – is clawed back by the government. In fact, these organisations have a strong incentive to overspend the budget. When this is the case, cultural economists would expect public choice issues to be prominent and the actions of agents to be difficult to control.

Opportunistic behaviour

The growth of professional training for arts management has led to improve-ments in organisations' accounting and management practices, and funding organisations may hire specialised accounting and management consultants to monitor their clients. While such measures may help to prevent bad practice, they cannot overcome the fundamental problem of asymmetry of information and the impossibility of making a complete contract that envisages all possible contingencies. Without that, however, there is scope for cheating, and therefore there has to be trust between principal and agent. This problem encourages funding bodies to concentrate on a few trusted organisations with which they have regular dealings and which do not 'cheat' ('behave opportunistically with guile', in the correct economic parlance developed by Oliver Williamson – see box 5.4). Therefore new and inexperienced organisations will always be at a disadvantage with funding bodies, especially publicly financed ones that are accountable to taxpayers.

Even reliable and proven organisations may not offer the service that is expected of them. Concern about frequent overspends of the budget was in fact one of the motives that led to Baumol and Bowen's study of inflation in the performing arts; the preface to *Performing Arts: The Economic Dilemma* well illustrates concerns in the 1960s on the part of private foundations donating to the arts in the United States over this particular problem, and the authors were at pains to reassure them that the arts organisations were not at fault. There are many ways in which an agent can behave opportunistically, however: an organisation may claim to be offering a universal service but, in fact, concentrate instead on avant-garde events or performances that do not attract audiences.[2] This can then be justified by claims that the audience needs to be educated to appreciate them, though the director may not care whether that is the case or not and it is obvious that it is very difficult to check such claims. On the other hand, the bureaucrats in the ministry may be ignorant of artistic developments and fail to understand (or not care about) their importance and hold back aesthetic progress. 'Playing it safe' may not be the right strategy if public subsidy for the arts and heritage is supposed to encourage creativity and develop tastes.

Strategies to control excess spending

One way in which the principal seeks to control the actions of the agent is by only making short-term grants, say a one-off allocation or a grant on an annual basis. While that might reassure the principal that he or she is in control, it inhibits the ability of the arts organisation or museum to plan ahead effectively. A museum may need years in which to plan and put on a major exhibition and theatrical, ballet and opera companies sometimes have to contract lead

---

[2] The study of German theatre by Krebs and Pommerehne (1995) found this to be the case.

performers years in advance. International stars, artists and museum pieces also command international rates of payment, and a national organisation has to pay internationally determined prices years ahead, which cannot be done without secure financial backing. This therefore presents the policy-maker with another dilemma: how tightly the budget should be controlled in the future as well as in the present. Of course, another problem is that monitoring and assessing the performance of the agent imposes costs on the principal, and these have to be kept to a cost-effective level; the savings gained from such activities have to be balanced against the cost of undertaking them.

I now turn to the question of whether principal–agent problems can be overcome by performance indicators and funding agreements, a solution that many governments financing independent arts and heritage organisations have adopted over the last decade or so to resolve some of these problems.

Performance indicators

Performance indicators can be thought of as a 'halfway house' between the policy objectives of the principal and the achievement of them by the agent. They put into supposedly achievable and quantifiable form ways in which the outcome of a policy can be monitored. They are essentially concerned with good practice found in organisations offering very similar output rather than with the attainment of some maximand. The simplest performance indicators relate to the number of attendees or events (performances, exhibitions, and so on), and they can reach considerable heights of sophistication, such as unit costs per activity or per attendee. What they typically aim for is to introduce accountability in non-market situations that is equivalent to the kind of discipline the market would impose, particularly over the costs of production.

The International Federation of Arts Councils and Culture Agencies (IFACCA), a global network of national arts funding bodies with members from all over the world, prepared a document in 2005 on *Statistical Indicators for Arts Policy*. Box 10.4 is an extract from that valuable document; it gives an insight into the complexity of the task of measuring arts activities, let alone setting targets for achieving policy goals (not included here), which is needed to turn an indicator into a measure of performance in reaching targets or fulfilling objectives. The document goes on to state that having effective indicators is essential both for formulating policy and for accountability to the funding body and to the public.

Performance indicators enable comparisons between similar organisations to be used by funding organisations to increase efficiency and value for money. Efficiency (as discussed above) is about achieving the objectives of the policy-

Box 10.4 IFACCA on the selection of performance indicators

Selecting the best indicators can be considered in two parts.
First, determine what factors are important in the selection process.
- How should indicators be chosen?
- Can what is trying to be measured be broken down into key dimensions?
- What level of information can usefully and sustainably be collected?
- What is it important to measure?

Second, consider possible variables and measures.
- What types of indicators are sought?
- Can the variables actually be measured?
- If a variable cannot be measured, do adequate proxies exist? If not, acknowledge that only partial indicators can be developed.
- Is an indicator really an indicator, or just a statistic?
- Indicators are not value-free. What values underlie the indicators?
- What do the indicators symbolize? The symbolic value of an indicator may outweigh its value as a literal measure.
- Is a 'composite index' (one indicator that purports to measure an index of overall perfor- mance) desirable, or multiple indicators reflecting various aspects of the phenomena being measured? If a composite index is chosen, what should be the methodology for aggregation and weighting?
- Do the indicators measure inputs, outputs, or outcomes? Be sure that there is appropriate emphasis placed on outcomes. Look for indicators that reveal causes, not symptoms.

Source: IFACCA (2005: 11–12).

maker and fulfilling the mission of the arts organisation, and each may have a different one. Therefore performance indicators need to be sufficiently flexible to allow for such differences but specific enough to enable comparison to be made. One of the most serious criticisms of the use of performance indicators is that they induce conformity, thus compromising cultural innovation and diversity as a policy aim; another is that cultural organisations are diverted from their mission and speciality in order to fulfil the list of performance indicators. A further problem is that performance indicators can be used by organisations in rent-seeking, as they reveal to the applicant for public funds what will chime with the donor institution (government or private funding body). This criticism does demonstrate, however, that funding organisations can influence the actions of arts and heritage organisations, and therefore the challenge is to find a balance of incentives between excessive control and freedom of managements to fulfil their own mission while at the same time meeting the principal's policy objectives and the requirement of accountability for public funds.

Funding agreements

When ministries and arts councils decide to award a grant to an arts or heritage organisation they need to specify the purpose of the grant and the objectives they wish to see achieved by it (as in box 9.3 with the funding agreement for the British Museum). The United Kingdom's Department for Culture, Media and Sport developed a funding agreement for the arts in conjunction with the Arts Council of England that linked the goals to be achieved with the relevant PI. This is reproduced in table 10.1.

Table 10.1 DCMS/ACE funding agreement: goals and performance indicators (arts)

Goal	Performance indicator
To encourage excellence at every level.	Assessment of artistic quality.
To encourage innovation at every level.	Number of commissions of new works by funded organisations (target for 2000/1: 2,375).
To promote a thriving arts sector and support the creative economy.	Statement of progress: quantitative indicators to be developed. Amount of commercial sponsorship (target for 2000/1: £127 million). Statement of partnership funding.
To facilitate more consumption of the arts by more of the people.	Proportion of the population attending arts events. Proportion of the population attending arts events regularly (at least twice a year); attendance at funded organisations by art form. Creation of new audiences. Attendance by ethnic minorities. Attendance by people with disabilities. Use of internet and modern communications technologies by funded organisations to broaden access.
To facilitate more participation in the arts by more of the people.	Performance indicators for participation to be developed.
To encourage more relevant training for arts sector.	ACE/DCMS support for a National Training Organisation for the arts and entertainment industry.
To encourage better use of the arts in education.	Development of quality assurance scheme for arts organisation education policies. Number of organisations with written strategy for education provision. Number of education sessions by funded organisations (target for 2000/1: 2,134).
To combat social exclusion and promote regeneration.	Impact of New Audiences Fund.

Table 10.1 (cont.)

Goal	Performance indicator
To improve public perception of the arts.	Those agreeing with statements 'The arts play a valuable role in my life'; 'The arts play a valuable role in the life of the country'.
To promote British culture overseas.	Statement progress of international role/co-operation with British Council.

Source: DCMS/Arts Council of England (1999).

Unacceptable economic arguments for subsidy

In the final section of this chapter, seemingly valid economic arguments that have been used to justify subsidy to the arts are analysed and shown not to be so: Baumol's cost disease and the economic impact of the arts and heritage. This is not to say that they are not economically sound in their own terms but, rather, that they have been used inappropriately by policy-makers and others (including some economists!) to justify subsidy to the arts and heritage.

Baumol's cost disease and the case for subsidy

Baumol's cost disease is an important and eminently valid economic theory that predicts that, under certain assumptions, costs and prices will continuously increase in the arts (Baumol and Bowen, 1966, confined themselves to the live performing arts, though Baumol has extended the application to other sectors). They themselves did not use their analysis to justify subsidy, however, making that case instead on the grounds of welfare economics (as expounded above and in chapter 6 of this book); what they did was to call attention to the growing economic problem as they saw it and paint the consequences of non-intervention. They argued that the arts could not rely on the market, as prices for performances would rise at a rate above the rate of inflation, and the gap between increasing costs and revenues would have to be filled by grants or donations if the contemporary level and quality of arts provision was to be maintained.

This is not a case of market failure, however; quite the opposite! The reason for the cost disease in the Baumol thesis is entirely due to market forces, since the argument is that it is increases in wages in the labour market that drive up wages in the non-arts sector (because of increased productivity) and in the arts sector because the labour market is integrated: as the arts are labour-intensive, and are assumed to be incapable of increased productivity, costs rise more in the arts than in the production of other goods and services, and so prices rise more. The problem is not market failure but the stagnant nature of the conditions of production in the performing arts. There is no economic argument, however, to say that industries should be supported by subsidy because they cannot adapt to technological progress, at least on the grounds of economic efficiency. 'Lame duck' industries are subsidised on equity grounds to safeguard jobs and communities (for example, in the car or steel industries) but in general the economic arguments go in the other direction; new dynamic industries are supported as 'infant industries' as an investment in the future. Thus, unless we believe that the arts and artists should be supported because the industry is dying, the cost disease on its own cannot be used to argue for subsidy. It is the welfare arguments of social benefits, and public goods characteristics are the market failure arguments.

Economic impact studies

Like cost–benefit and contingent valuation studies, economic impact studies provide useful information for policy-makers, but that information alone cannot make the case for public subsidy for an investment project, such as building a museum or theatre, independently of the welfare economic arguments. During the last decades of the twentieth century economic impact studies were frequently used by governments, central and local, to provide information on which to base policy and justify public expenditure on the arts and heritage. Some attempted to measure the economic value of the cultural sector as a whole while others were more modest and applied the analysis to a specific project. The sector-wide studies were dismissed by economists as misunderstanding the marginal nature of the analysis and the meaning of external effects at the national level, but, even when studies were carried out well and surrounded with caveats, policy-makers exaggerated the results anyway, ignored any reservations on the part of the researchers and simply brandished 'the number'.[3] Moreover, there was a tendency to assign to a cultural project external benefits that would have accrued to any other type of project with the same outlay. As a result, economic impact studies acquired a bad name, not least with government economists, and there has been a tendency recently to write them off.

[3] Van Puffeln (1996).

As we saw in chapter 7 (and box 7.5), however, local economic impact studies can be useful and may be compared to contingent valuation studies, which in some circumstances measure the same thing (in fact, CV studies can be thought of as a way of estimating benefits). In addition, like CV studies, economic impact studies do not explicitly measure costs, although, in both cases, the cost of the project is an implicit consideration; neither is an economic impact study as rigorous as cost–benefit analysis in discounting both costs and benefits into present value terms (as explained in chapter 7).

Measuring the impact

What an economist also wants to know is the net benefit of a project and whether it is possible to finance the project by a charge on those who enjoy its external benefits. Net benefits may spread well beyond the immediate beneficiaries through the spending power generated by a project. The 'additionality' aspect is important because, without it, there could be a situation in which a new project simply crowds out an existing one, thus yielding no net benefit to the area. If resources are scarce a new project would push up prices for inputs – so-called pecuniary externalities – thus reducing some of the overall net benefit. On the other hand, one of the arguments frequently advanced for using cultural projects to renew run-down inner cities is that there are vacant buildings and land prices are low and there is also unemployed labour available. In these circumstances, publicly financed investment in cultural projects has all the features of Keynesian public works policy: that economic growth can be stimulated by the multiplied effect of the initial outlay and there will be more widespread induced income.

Keynesian multiplier and induced income

The question of the use of multipliers in estimating the economic impact of a cultural facility has been a fraught one: what is the size of the multiplier, and should it in any case be used in measuring the impact of a project? The multiplier is the number by which any additional income is increased once all the stages of induced consumption spending have been completed. To give an example: if a municipality spends €5 million on a new museum, the workers and suppliers of materials for the construction have additional income out of which they spend more, thereby increasing revenues in shops, and so on and so forth. Therefore the size of the multiplier depends upon the extra consumption elicited by an increase in consumers' income – the marginal propensity to consume; say that the marginal propensity to consume is 0.75 (three-quarters of an increase in income is consumed and one-quarter saved and thus withdrawn from the flow of income), the value of the multiplier is four, and so the induced income would be four times the amount of the investment. This apparently wondrous increase would appear to justify any public works financed by government! The lower the marginal propensity to consume, the smaller the multiplier, however: at the limit, if consumers were to save all the induced extra income, the multiplier would just be one and the only addition to income would be the amount spent on the project at the outset. In fact, many economists think that the national multiplier is indeed close to one, and that claims for significant induced income are exaggerated. That may not be the case at the local level, however, especially in an economically depressed area, and this raises the question of what the appropriate geographical unit is for measuring the scope of the indirect impact. The problem for a regional or national government is what the impact is within their area of authority; if the project just displaces consumption from one place to another within that area, there is no overall net increase in income.

Geographical limits to the impact

What is tautologically the case is that the smaller the area that is considered, the greater the 'leakage' of induced income to the surrounding area, due to the need to import labour and resources from outside. Then information is needed on how far afield the impact is expected to spread. Many economic impact studies have been linked to tourism; the difficulty then is to estimate what proportion of additional spending on transport, hotels and restaurants is due specifically to the attraction of the arts or heritage project rather than to the more general attractions of the city or region. Visitor surveys are used to find out what attractions visitors wish to visit but they do not usually place a value on one item. Moreover, people have to eat and drink somewhere, and, here again, additionality is the issue: these expenditures should not be counted if they would have taken place anyway in the area being studied. Even so, of course, such expenditures would have been made somewhere, and so the issue is how to take that into account. Chapter 19 considers this question again in relation to cultural tourism.

The aggregation problem

The 'aggregation problem' is the economic term given to the question of additionality discussed above, and it means that it is not valid to generalise to the national level using local studies. This is because, within the national economy, diversion of consumer expenditure from other arts and heritage facilities, the indirect effects to other areas and pecuniary externalities that push up resource costs all take place within the national boundary. There may be net benefit to every locality considered individually in isolation but it could be a case of 'robbing Peter to pay Paul' nationally. This does not mean that a local region or city should have to take this into account when considering running a local festival or building a new museum or theatre but it does mean that the economic impact of a local project is necessarily much greater than the same project considered from the national perspective. It is precisely this problem that invalidated those so-called 'impact' studies that used regional or even local data to estimate the contribution of the whole cultural sector to the national economy. Understanding this 'fallacy of composition' is an important insight of economics; another is the recognition that if resources are not used for one purpose they can be used for another. In other words, our old friend opportunity cost is always present. If resources are used to build a theatre, those same resources cannot be used for a sports stadium, and any city, regional or national planner has to recognise this uncomfortable fact. Therefore choices have to be made between theatres and sports stadia, and economic analysis dictates that the economic impact or net benefit of each be compared. The presence of positive benefits from the economic impact of a project on its own is not sufficient to justify its provision.

Who should finance the project?

Generally speaking, economists, especially public choice theorists, favour local finance for local projects because the political support on the part of the local community can be more easily ascertained. Local finance may be levied from those likely to benefit from the project, for example by local sales or hotel taxes. If the public works aspect of the project is an important element of policy, however, national or international finance would be desirable to boost the region. As chapter 19 shows, national and European Union policies for depressed areas have financed cultural projects in various regions. Either way, the policy-maker must compare the benefits of alternative projects or use cost–benefit analysis to estimate the rate of return on one project.

Conclusion

This chapter has concentrated on the question of how economists support the case for government intervention in the arts and what economics has to say about evaluating policies. In practice, government intervention is usually in the form of direct or indirect subsidy, and each has different advantages for the policy-maker and for the consumer or voter. Principal–agent problems of ensuring that subsidy is used to achieve the funding body's policies are discussed and the usefulness of performance indicators is raised.

The theoretical underpinning of the case for government subsidy to the arts and heritage is to be found in welfare economics; applied welfare economics also underpins cost–benefit analysis and the measurement of the economic impact of cultural projects on the economy. Welfare economics makes its case through the recognition of market failure in the arts due to external benefits; the great weakness of this approach for practical purposes, however, is that it cannot tell the government the value of the external benefits so that subsidy can be gauged accordingly. It is then open to people to argue how great these benefits are – some say a lot and others a little – and so the matter has to be decided in the political rather than the economic arena.

Further reading

The chapter in Victor Ginsburgh and David Throsby's *Handbook of the Economics of Art and Culture* (2006) by Rick van der Ploeg, 'The making of cultural policy: a European perspective' (chapter 34), has the merit of being written by an economist who was secretary of state for culture in the Netherlands. Also in that handbook are chapters by Dick Netzer, 'Cultural policy: an American view' (chapter 35), and by Mark Schuster, 'Tax incentives in cultural policy' (chapter 36), which concludes with a very useful survey of international experience of tax-based incentives.

Alan Peacock, a by now familiar name and an economist who was (among other things) chairman of the Scottish Arts Council, also had 'hands-on' experience of distributing subsidy to the arts. He has written several articles on cultural policy and government intervention, and a recent one that distils his sophisticated thinking on the subject is 'The credibility of economists' advice to governments' (2004), which was reprinted in Towse (2007); his book *Paying the Piper* (1993), mentioned in chapter 8, is both entertaining and full of insights into the ups and downs of funding the arts in practice.

Part III

Artists' labour markets and copyright

Introduction

In Part III of the book, I turn to the economic analysis of artists and treat them and other creators of works of art as workers. Chapter 11 presents the theory of the supply and demand for artists in the labour market and looks at what determines incomes and employment. In studying artists' labour markets, cultural economists have used the theories of labour economics, the branch of economics that investigates topics such as the working of labour markets, employment and unemployment, rates of pay, training and education, and the effects on the labour market of institutional regulations, such as a minimum wage. Chapter 11 also looks at the question of artistic motivation and what influences creativity. Chapter 12 describes empirical research on artists' labour markets by cultural economists, showing that labour economics has to be adapted to apply to artists. Chapter 13, on the economics of copyright, goes into copyright law as an economic incentive to artists and other creators to create works of art and investigates copyright as a source of income for artists. Together, these three chapters show the key role of artists in the creative industries; the chief input of the creative industries is the creation of novel content, without which there would be no reason to distinguish these industries, and artists are the source of content creation.

11 Economics of artists' labour markets: theories

The term 'labour market' refers to the supply and demand for hours of work by workers who have similar skills; there is a labour market for hairdressers, therefore, and a labour market for electricians. In the arts, there is a labour market for classically trained singers, one for actors and another for potters. As in goods markets, what differentiates one market from another is the extent to which there is substitutability – in this case, between one type of worker and another. The ability to do certain types of work distinguishes specific occupations.

Labour markets

Supply and demand work in labour markets as they do in goods markets. Workers offer hours of work at various rates of pay; the higher the wage rate, the more hours they are in general willing to work. On the demand side of the market, employers demand more hours of work as wage rates fall. The wage rate is the price per hour of labour. At the equilibrium wage rate, the number of hours supplied and demanded is equal. This can also represent the level of employment in terms of the supply and demand for the number of workers in a labour market.

In figure 11.1, S_L represents the supply of labour (the number of workers) and D_L is the number of workers demanded at various wage rates. The equilibrium wage rate, W_e, is the one at which supply and demand are equal and the level of employment is the number of workers employed at the equilibrium wage rate. If there is excess labour supply, rates of pay will fall, and when there is excess demand for labour, they rise. In artists' labour markets it is usual to find excess supply, as discussed later. Excess supply might come about because the government or a trade union or professional association has a policy of setting a minimum wage rate, and if that is above the equilibrium wage there will be a lower level of employment as employers reduce their demand for labour.

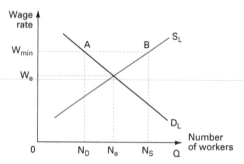

Figure 11.1 Effect on a labour market of a minimum wage

Figure 11.1 shows that, if a minimum wage rate were set at W_{min}, the number of workers employed would be N_D and N_S would be supplied, so excess supply of labour is $N_S - N_D$, or AB.

This basic theory assumes that labour is homogeneous in any given labour market and that one hour of work by any worker is as good as any other. In practice, of course, workers are differentiated by factors such as level of education and training, experience, and so on, and these factors lead to different rates of payment and incomes. In artists' labour markets, though, indefinable features that we call talent and artistic creativity apparently contribute more to success or higher rates of pay than education and training, even for people who have had little formal training. This has led cultural economists studying artists' labour markets to ask to what extent conventional labour economics applies to the arts and whether it is in fact possible to apply standard economic notions to artists' labour markets. These are the topics that this chapter investigates.

Who is an artist?

One of the first topics that necessarily has to be dealt with in the study of artists' labour markets is the question 'Who is an artist?' It is not the task of economists to make judgements about who should be regarded as an artist any more than it is to say what is art. Chapter 12 deals with this and other 'practical' questions that arise in researching artists' labour markets. A loose definition of artists, however, could be to say that they are people who create works of art. Two broad categories are frequently used in research by cultural economists on artists' labour markets: creative artists and performers. Creative artists include visual artists, literary authors, playwrights, film and TV scriptwriters, directors, composers, lyricists and choreographers.

Performing artists include musicians, singers, dancers, actors, puppeteers, circus performers, and suchlike. Of course, these are not exclusive categories: many composers are also performers, for example, and some performers write music. Artists in these two categories tend to work in somewhat different ways, with creative artists often being independent operators who are self-employed while performers are often employed by an organisation or enterprise, though many are self-employed, such as pop groups and string quartets. Even though these are not watertight categories, there is a difference between artists who can pursue their career independently of being hired by someone and those who cannot. The distinction between creators and performers also acquires significance in another context: copyright law treats each category differently, awarding full authors' rights to the creators and 'rights related to copyright' or 'neighbouring rights' to performers. This topic is explored fully in chapter 13.

Cultural workers who are *not* artists

This chapter is about artists' earnings and employment, and, as is the case with listing the creative industries (chapter 2), there is no single list of 'artists'; other workers may be included, depending upon the circumstances and purposes of the study of the labour market – architects, craftspeople (makers), designers, graphic artists, journalists, radio and TV newsreaders, announcers and show hosts, set and lighting designers have all appeared in artists' labour market studies. All these people work in the creative industries and are loosely referred to as 'artists' or craftspeople. They are also people who produce copyrightable works as creators and performers.

Besides these workers, however, there are a host of others who are employed in the creative industries, as managers and administrators, electricians, carpenters, costume makers, film operatives and many, many more, some of whom are doing jobs specifically connected to the creative industries but who are not usually thought of as artists. Generally speaking, these workers have skills that are not tied exclusively to the creative industries and they are able to find employment outside the cultural sector. The ease with which such workers can find employment in other labour markets obviously affects their rates of pay in the cultural sector, and their labour turns out to have contributed more to the rising costs of labour in the performing arts – one of the features of Baumol's cost disease – than payments to artists, as research on artists' labour markets has shown (see chapter 12).

Employment in this broad sense in the cultural sector, including both artists and other cultural workers, has been measured for the twenty-seven countries of the European Union as constituting 2.4 per cent of total employment.[1]

---

[1] Eurostat (2007).

Other research has taken an even broader view of creative workers, including accountants, lawyers and other 'knowledge' professionals in that designation. This stance has little to do with the concerns of cultural economists when studying the economic position of artists. Studies of artists' labour markets have concentrated on creative artists, craftspeople and performers.

Labour costs and Baumol's cost disease

One of the points that follows from this distinction between artistic and non-artistic labour is their relative role in the cost disease. Clearly, some types of cultural enterprises employ a higher ratio of artists to other workers (and to capital) – an orchestra has more artists (musicians) than other labour but a theatre may have far more people backstage and front of house than on-stage. It is important therefore to distinguish these two types of labour and to look separately at the rate of increase in labour costs (the mirror image of earnings) in each. Remember that the Baumol hypothesis is that the labour market is integrated and therefore a rise in wages in the economy will be passed on to arts organisations; the empirical studies referred to in chapter 8 found that it is not the costs of artists that have pushed up costs, however. Chapter 12 shows that artists' pay does not rise as quickly as that of labour in general, suggesting that the labour market for artists is not integrated with that of other workers. The labour markets for non-artistic workers in the cultural sector are integrated, however, and their earnings do rise with average earnings.

Supply of labour in the arts

In general, it is supposed in labour economics that the supply of labour is greater the higher the rate of payment, the wage rate, reflecting the fact that higher pay is required to compensate workers for the leisure they give up in order to work; in figure 11.1, this is shown as an upward-sloping line, S_L. It is believed that after a certain point, however, workers have a stronger preference for leisure than for work, and, if the wage rate is relatively high, workers will offer fewer hours of work; therefore, the supply curve bends backwards – known as the backward-bending supply of labour. To this and other qualifications of the basic theory of labour markets, cultural economists have added their own reservations about applying the theory to artists, as explained below.

It is interesting to see how Adam Smith viewed the question of the supply of professional performers in 1776; the quotation in box 11.1 is part of his

Box 11.1　Adam Smith's views on the supply of performers

There are some very agreeable and beautiful talents of which the possession commands a certain sort of admiration; but of which the exercise for the sake of gain is considered, whether from reason or prejudice, as a sort of public prostitution. The pecuniary recompence, therefore, of those who exercise them in this manner, must be sufficient, not only to pay for the time, labour, and expence of acquiring the talents, but for the discredit which attends the employment of them as a means of subsistence. The exorbitant rewards of players, opera-singers, opera-dancers, &c. are founded upon those two principles; the rarity and beauty of the talents, and the discredit of employing them in this manner. It seems absurd at first sight that we should despise their persons, and yet reward their talents with the most profuse liberality. While we do the one, however, we must of necessity do the other. Should the public opinion or prejudice ever alter with regard to such occupations, their pecuniary recompence would quickly diminish. More people would apply to them, and the competition would quickly reduce the price of their labour. Such talents, though far from being common, are by no means so rare as is imagined. Many people possess them in great perfection, who disdain to make this use of them; and many more are capable of acquiring them, if any thing could be made honourably by them (Adam Smith, *The Wealth of Nations*, bk. I, pt. 1, ch. X: 124).

To excel in any profession, in which but few arrive at mediocrity, is the most decisive mark of what is called genius or superior talents. The public admiration which attends upon such distinguished abilities makes always a part of their reward; a greater or smaller in proportion as it is higher or lower in degree (ibid.: 123).

Source: Smith (1776/1976).

explanation as to why some wages in an economy are higher than others; in the case of performers he attributed it to the 'shame' of the work, but he also considered that, if this 'public prejudice' were to disappear, the supply of performers would increase and their wages fall – and how right he was!

Stock and flow of labour supply

One of the most fundamental points with regard to supply is to distinguish between the stock of a given type of labour and the flow of labour services. The stock of labour means the number of people at any given point in time who are able to do a certain kind of work; the stock of labour in any one occupation, therefore, is comprised of those employed in it and the unemployed, and it might also include persons who are employed in other occupations but who would prefer to work in the occupation in question. To make this more concrete: the stock of actors is the number of actors in employment plus those actors who are unemployed and those who are working as waiters or taxi drivers but who are able to, and would prefer to, work as actors. The flow of labour services is the number of hours of labour or persons willing to work at any given wage rate.

Wage rates, salaries and other payments

The term 'wage rate' is used to denote payment per hour, but not everyone is paid by the hour, or even by a wage! Some artists work for an hourly wage payment, some are on a regular monthly salary, others are paid fees and/or receive royalty payments, yet others sell something for a price, such as a work of art or craft. Although these are different methods of payment, the artist has spent a number of hours working for the payment – in preparation, planning and execution, making an item or rendering a service – and the payment per hour may be calculated by taking the payment and dividing it by the number of hours of labour. This is called the 'imputed' wage rate. So, for example, if a weaver takes a week to make an item that is sold for €1,500 and, in the week, he or she worked thirty hours, the imputed wage rate is €50 per hour. Alternatively, if a dancer is paid €400 a week and spends forty hours a week practising and performing, his or her imputed hourly wage rate is €10. The imputed wage rate has been used in calculating artists' earnings, and it can be seen that the wage rate could be different for different items, depending on the price or amount of work involved.

Income and earnings

It is common in labour economics to distinguish between income and earnings. Income tends to mean a regular payment for a set number of hours of work as laid down in a labour contract; earnings are usually assumed to be income plus any payments over an above income, such as overtime payments or payments for work in another workplace. In the artists' labour markets, 'earnings' is a more suitable term to use, because many artists have payments from various sources. Thus a dancer's earnings would be the payments he or she receives for doing different jobs over a period of time, as a dancer, maybe as a choreographer and/or as a teacher and also in non-arts work. Because artists frequently work in arts and non-arts work, studies of artists' earnings usually distinguish arts and non-arts earnings (see chapter 12).

Payment may also be 'notional'; for example, if the artist has a contract for a future payment, income could be thought of as the discounted present value of that payment. Artists who produce work for which they are paid a royalty are likely to think in terms of how much they expect to earn over a lifetime from copyright royalties, and their value in the present is equivalent to an imputed wage rate. Royalty earnings are discussed in chapters 12 and 13.

Work, leisure and work preference

Usually in economics, hours of work are contrasted with hours of leisure and work is thought of as leisure forgone; thus there is a trade-off between income and leisure. Payment is therefore necessary to compensate the worker for lost leisure in order to obtain labour time; put the other way round, leisure time always has an opportunity cost of the wage that could have been earned if time were instead devoted to work. As income rises, though, the increase in utility from higher income gets less and the preference for leisure begins to predominate – hence the backward-bending supply curve.

This response to higher earnings is thought to be operative in artists' labour markets but with a different twist, and this has come to be called the 'work preference' model. It is suggested that artists do not view leisure as preferable to work in their chosen art; once they have reached a minimum income level, they are able to devote more time to arts work. The higher the wage, the fewer the hours of work that are needed to reach this minimum. The artists' work preference model has been developed and tested by David Throsby (see box 11.2). Throsby has proposed this in a 'weak' and 'strong' form, depending upon how 'driven' the artist is – something that cannot be observed directly but must be inferred from artists' supply behaviour. In fact, many people, especially young people, are willing to work in the arts even at a zero wage rate, at least at the beginning of their career. Therefore the supply of artistic labour is likely to start at a zero wage rate (the origin on figure 11.1) and rise as wage rates increase.

Arts and non-arts work

If work in the arts pays a lower wage rate than that obtainable in another occupation open to the artist, that rate of pay represents the opportunity cost of working in the arts. If artists have a preference for working in the arts, however, they may choose to do so regardless of the opportunity cost. To give an example: if an actor could earn €20 per hour as a waiter but only €15 as an actor, he or she might prefer to work as an actor, but the opportunity cost is €5 an hour. That preference has cost him or her €5 times however many hours he or she gave up as a waiter, and this has been called the 'psychic income' from the arts, or even the 'artists' subsidy of the arts'.[2]

Multiple job-holding in the arts

Many artists do both arts and non-arts work and often have more than one job at the same time. This is called multiple job-holding, the implication being that artists often need to earn income outside the arts in order to be able to earn sufficient income to meet their needs. Many artists also have arts-related work, such as teaching or judging competitions, that they do in addition to their chosen arts occupation and regard it as complementary to that. It takes up time that they may prefer to spend doing their own artwork, however, and again the issue is a trade-off of the opportunity cost of giving up that sort of work with the need to have a basic income. As we now see, this leads to a complex decision about the supply of labour to the arts.

Elasticity of labour supply

The elasticity of the supply of labour – how responsive hours of work are to increases in wage rates – is positive, at least up to the point of the desired income. Understanding this responsiveness has important implications, especially for cultural policy; without some degree of responsiveness, financial grants to artists and copyright royalties would not increase the supply of creative work as they are intended to. The real question, though, is how great is the elasticity of labour supply – that is, how responsive are workers to increases in pay? If a small increase in rates of pay elicited a more than proportional increase in the hours an artist would work, that might be very significant information for a policy-maker, suggesting that a small financial grant would bring forth substantially more output from the artist. This has to be estimated empirically, and the subject is discussed in chapter 12.

There is also the question of cross-elasticity between arts and non-arts wage rates: when non-arts wages rise, artists switch to arts work because they can 'afford' to do so once the income constraint has been met. They also do more arts work when arts wages rise, because they are able to earn the basic income they need and do their chosen arts work. That is what Throsby has referred to as 'perverse' in box 11.2.

---

[2] See Withers (1985).

Box 11.2 David Throsby and studies of artists' labour markets

David Throsby was first introduced in box 5.2, and his name has cropped up in this book in many contexts. One of his major contributions to cultural economics has been his research on artists' labour markets combining the development of theoretical models with data collection and empirical analysis. He has been responsible for four consecutive surveys of artists in Australia undertaken on behalf of the Australia Council for the Arts, starting in 1983. In the course of this research, he has developed the model of artists' work preference that explains the supply decisions of artists, suggesting that they behave differently from other workers and that this necessitates the development of a model of artistic production (Throsby, 1994).

He argues that, while the maximisation of income subject to the leisure constraint is the standard neoclassical assumption of worker labour supply, for artists, income essentially acts as a constraint that takes up labour time the artist would prefer to spend on art work that has cultural value. The need for adequate income may cause the artist to do non-arts work (multiple job-holding) in order to fulfil the income constraint, leading to the artist reacting in what Throsby calls 'an apparently perverse manner to changes in relative wages in arts and non-arts sectors, by virtue of the fact that non-arts work is simply a means of enabling as much time as possible to be spent at the (preferred) artistic occupation' (Throsby, 2001: 102).

Source: Throsby (2001).

Heterogeneous labour

In principle, a labour market is defined over a homogeneous population of workers, each of whom could easily be substituted one for the other. This might be realistic for road builders or plumbers, but it is not for artists, who are heterogeneous in terms of skills and talent and the kind of work they do. In artists' labour markets, labour can be viewed as heterogeneous in two respects: the nature of their skill and the extent of their talent. We may talk about a labour market for musicians but it is necessary to identify what instrument they play, because a guitarist belongs to a different branch of the labour market from a flute player. Moreover, some guitarists are considerably more talented than others (and most of the people who play the guitar are not professionals). In the arts, talent and innate ability (even genius) are very important in the demand and supply of artists, and the preference of consumers for 'stars' means that there is differentiation on the basis of talent, even within a tightly defined occupational group of artists. On the other hand, some workers in the arts may be relatively homogeneous, such as singers and dancers working as 'backing artists', and here, therefore, one worker may be easily substituted for another. This topic raises several important issues in the study of artists' labour markets that are dealt with later in this chapter: the demand for artistic labour and superstar theory, the role of innate ability and talent in determining incomes, and its role in relation to training and investment in human capital; the analysis of all these topics utilises the theories of labour economics, while pointing to important differences between artists as workers and workers in other occupations. Before exploring these theories, though, two other topics that relate to the supply side of artists' labour markets need investigating.

Dynamics of labour supply

Use of the word 'dynamics' in economics means that trends over time are at issue; thus the dynamics of labour supply refers to the analysis of long-term trends – including what we call 'career prospects' in ordinary speech. In the foregoing theory of labour supply, no attention was paid to a particular timescale; the only mention of the time dimension is just that the wage is the payment per unit of time (an hourly rate). Workers make long-term decisions about their occupation, career prospects and future income, however. To do this, they need to have information about probable employment and earnings in their chosen occupation and the kind of training or educational qualifications that are expected by employers. This kind of information is not easy to obtain in the arts and, even when it is available, because of the lack of homogeneity in the arts labour force and the emphasis on talent, it may not be very helpful to a young person entering an arts profession. Many new entrants therefore have to find out the hard way by personal experience.

The result is that arts occupations are characterised by the presence of many young, hopeful entrants who are learning how the market is likely to respond to them by simply getting as many opportunities as they can to show their work, either as creators or performers. As they gain experience they learn about their ranking in terms of ability and appeal, and they also get to know how much they are likely to earn, at least in the near future. It is this information that enables them to make a reasonable assessment of their chances of a worthwhile career. Many, of course, realise that they are not going to succeed as they had hoped to and drop out of that occupation and move into another, probably outside the arts (see chapter 12).

This explains why the age structure of the stock of artists is 'skewed' towards young people. It also explains the observation that there is considerable excess supply of artistic labour even at very low rates of pay, including zero earnings.

A particularly clear example of this phenomenon is in the world of pop music, in which many young 'hopefuls' abound; there, the barriers to entry are low and little training is required – just luck and talent (see chapter 15).

Excess supply

Excess supply, or 'oversupply', is an economic concept signifying that, at any given price, the quantity supplied is greater than the quantity demanded; in a labour market, this means that more people are willing to work more hours at various rates of pay than the market can absorb on the demand side. This was illustrated in figure 11.1, showing the impact of a minimum wage rate. There are many aspects to the excess supply of artists: it depresses rates of pay; it causes trade unions and professional associations to restrict entry and to impose a minimum wage by collective bargaining; it has implications for higher education institutions training artists and the role of the certificates they award; and it creates particular ways of overcoming the information problem about selecting the most talented artists. Needless to say, although there is excess supply of artists in general, there is always a shortage of 'top talent'. All these topics are discussed in the rest of this chapter.

Demand for artists' labour

Like the demand for goods, the demand for labour depends on the price of labour – that is, the wage rate – and the relationship is a negative one: the higher the wage rate, the fewer the hours of labour that are demanded (see figure 11.1). The difference between goods markets and the labour market, though, is that, while goods are purchased for the utility or satisfaction they offer, labour is hired as a factor of production or input into the production of goods and services, and demand depends upon the contribution labour makes to the value of the product. This is known as the 'marginal revenue product' of labour and it depends on both the productivity of the labour and the revenue from the sale of the product. If the product is a live performance, then the labour and the output are one and the same thing, but even then the performance is often produced in conjunction with other workers – other performers, managers, support staff, and so on – and therefore it is difficult to value the individual's contribution to the value of the output, the marginal revenue product. This is a well-known problem of teamwork in labour economics as well as in the creative industries.

Derived demand

In many situations, what the consumer demands is a particular product, and the demand for labour is derived from the demand for that product: hence the expression in economics that the demand for labour (and for other factors of production) is a 'derived demand'. Thus the demand for a particular type of labour depends upon the demand for the product that is being offered and therefore on the revenue that it generates.

Let us say that there is a trend towards reading science fiction and the demand for books in that genre increases. That would lead to an increased derived demand for authors who are able to write science fiction. Derived demand can manifest itself in many ways: when rock and roll is popular, rock artists are in demand. Here again the question of substitutability arises: can authors or pop singers easily switch genres? If not, they are at the mercy of consumer trends in taste, because, if their labour is highly specialised, once the demand for the product decreases so does the demand for their labour. If the success of a book or concert depends crucially upon one person, however, he or she would be rewarded accordingly, and, if the revenue from the sales of the book or concert tickets is high, the individual will earn a high fee for his or her work.

Organisations in the labour market: 'market-makers'

In order for the supply of and demand for labour to be 'matched', information is needed about the abilities of the supplier (the artist) and the requirements of the employer (the arts organisation). This information is necessary for markets to work efficiently, and providing this information is often done by 'market-makers' – employment agencies and other specialised agencies that specialise in matching job opportunities and vacancies with suitable workers. Matching presents particular information problems in the cultural sector, in which artistic quality is very important to producers and the supply of skills is varied. In chapter 3, it was pointed out that there are many such agencies that specialise in artists – literary agents, theatrical agents, artist management services, art dealers, and so on. In economics, these intermediaries are recognised for their 'market-making' function, of matching supply and demand in the market; they make their money by taking a percentage of the artists' payments or charge a fee for their services. This is an example of transaction costs associated with market exchange, of which there are many in the cultural sector, as in other sectors of the economy. In some countries (Germany and the Netherlands, for example), artists' agencies are regulated and need a licence in order to operate. That is not the case in the United Kingdom or the United States. In fact, there has been almost no work by cultural economists on these organisations, so it is hard to say how practices differ in different countries and in different segments of the market.

As we see later, some arts organisations go in for very expensive procedures in order to hire the right people and to match their demand with the right creative ability and talent, indicating the value and cost of information in artists' labour markets. Box 11.3 gives the example of matching procedures in opera. The need for such information is all the greater because of the excess supply of artists, which seems to be a persistent feature of artists' labour markets. In theory, artists who are unemployed or underemployed would reduce their fees or be willing to work at very low wage rates, and many do. In a world in which there is an information problem about the quality of artists, however, one piece of information that can act as a signal is price – the fee the

---

Box 11.3 Matching the supply of and demand for singers in the world of opera

The 'job-matching' role of agents is well illustrated in the world of opera singers. The labour market for trained opera singers is international and both supply and demand are global. Japanese singers sing in European opera houses and American singers sing in the Far East. Opera managements all over the world are always on the lookout for talented opera singers, and singers' agents are there to provide information and contacts between the upcoming star in one part of the world with the opera companies in another. The singers themselves cannot be forever travelling here and there for auditions (though many in fact do) and so they use the services of an agent to select the opera houses that might be interested in them. Even being accepted onto the books of an agent is already one big step up in the world for a young singer, and many well-trained singers do not even get that far, such is the excess supply.

For their part, opera companies are performing different works each year during the year, and so they need singers of varied voice types, appearance, and so on for the run of the opera, and they also need to plan the cast a long way ahead (often five years). The singer's agent or manager knows his or her singer's abilities and preferences in terms of what to sing and where and what his or her timetable and availability are. Agents therefore keep in contact with the casting department of as many opera houses as they can so as to be able to represent their singers. Without agents' services, both singers and opera houses would spend far more resources on searching for the right match.

Source: Towse (1993)

artist charges. Often, these fees are set by professional associations to make bargaining easier for artist and employer (the demand side), but there is always scope for bargaining over fees, and, when the fee is taken as information about the talent or creative ability of an artist, reducing the fee is taken as a signal that the artist is not doing well, possibly indicating low quality.[3]

The demand for superstars

The phenomenon of superstars has interested cultural economists for some time and several economic explanations have been put forward for it. Indeed, the existence of superstars is hardly a new one, and it has existed in the cultural sphere for centuries. At one level, superstardom just reflects the desire on the part of consumers to enjoy the highest-quality performance in any field, whether in sports or the arts, but a closer look at the phenomenon shows that there are deep economic reasons for the preference for top people in many 'winner-takes-all' situations. Other economists had recognised the special case of talent in the arts, but it was the analysis by Sherwin Rosen of the economics of superstars that brought the topic into the study of artists' labour markets.[4]

Like Adam Smith, the subject Rosen considered was the vastly uneven distribution of earnings in certain professions (such as medicine and the law); while there is inequality of income within most occupations due to a range of factors (age, gender and race being the main ones), Rosen notes that, in superstar professions, a few people earn very high incomes and the majority earn much less. Thus the distribution of earnings is said to be 'skewed' – there is a long tail of low earners. Rosen defines superstars as people who earn enormous amounts of money and dominate the activities in which they engage; they are highly talented and highly rewarded for their talents, and small differences in talent are magnified in larger earnings differences. By definition, there is imperfect substitution between artists with different talents, because consumers have a preference for more rather than less talent, and this would in and of itself provide a general explanation of skewed earnings distributions. Rosen argues, however, that these preferences alone do not explain the other feature of superstardom, namely the marked concentration in the market on a few superstars who have the most (perceived) talent. This is explained by the spread of mass media technology, which enables an artist to reach a huge international market while expending the

---

[3] Towse (2001b: ch. 4).   [4] Rosen (1981).

same amount of time and effort reaching that audience as he or she would for entertaining a much smaller one. It is the size of the market that is responsible for the huge multiplication of relatively small differences in talent that results in the highly skewed income distribution.

So far, this would appear to be a supply-side explanation only, but, of course, the mass market is there because of the demand for the work of the superstars. The globalisation of tastes, huge marketing campaigns and many other reasons can be given but, at bottom, the question for a cultural economist is: why do consumers have a preference for a few rather than many artists? One explanation is that, in a world of abundant supply, the costs of searching for information about quality, genre, and so on are so great that consumers save on them by following the trend and are guided by the fame of the superstar as a signal of the quality they are looking for. Thus success breeds success and the winner takes all. Moreover, the individual's enjoyment is enhanced by sharing his or her pleasure with others, and the more people there are consuming the work of an artist, the greater the individual's chance of satisfaction. This has also been called the 'bandwagon effect'; another distinct but related aspect of demand is 'conspicuous consumption', meaning that people like to be seen to buy certain goods and services and will pay more to do so. Both these motives for consuming the output of superstars reinforce market demand and 'snowball' their popularity, resulting in high incomes.

Other determinants of artists' income differentials

One of the implications of the 'winner-takes-all' aspect of superstardom is that the 'losers' join what has come to be called the 'long tail', meaning, in this context, the many artists in the tail of the skewed distribution of income. It is likely that superstar professions are associated with risk, and willingness to accept risk also explains income differentials between artists in the same occupation. Risk implies that the probability of something can be calculated, however, but the 'nobody knows' aspect of the creative industries refers to uncertainty that cannot be rationally calculated. Uncertainty about income and career prospects seems to be inherent in artists' labour markets; but, even if income in an artistic occupation were on average knowable, the individual still has to work out his or her 'ranking' in terms of talent and creative ability. This uncertainty is also to be found in relation to future earnings from copyright, and, as chapter 13 shows, copyright payments to artists vary very considerably, like their other earnings.

It is a standard assumption of neoclassical economics that economic agents are 'risk-averse', meaning that they would not accept the even chance of a fair bet or accept a bet when the probability of winning is less than fifty-fifty. Some cultural economists have suggested that artists are risk-takers by this definition, because they knowingly enter professions in which few people are really successful. Others have commented, as did Adam Smith, that 'the contempt of risk and the presumptuous hope of success are in no period of life more active than at the age at which young people choose their professions' (Smith, 1776/1976: 126). That does not necessarily mean that artists have a preference for risk, however; like everyone else, they would prefer a 'safe bet', but, as they embark on a career, that is denied to them. Even if they display a willingness to take artistic risks, they may prefer not to take financial ones!

Income and education

The economics of education has developed over the last forty years to explain the role of education and training in determining workers' incomes. As we saw above, however, innate ability (talent and creativity) poses a particular problem for the application of standard labour market theory to artists. This is also the case with the economics of education, though it has been used in cultural economics to analyse the role of training and specialised higher education in the arts. Two theories have been developed in the economics of education, 'human capital' theory and 'sorting' models, and they are explained here in relation to the training of artists. Both explain income in terms of the investment of time and expense in acquiring educational qualifications, but each has a different reasoning for that relationship.

Human capital theory

The theory that has been most widely adopted in labour economics to explain income differentials is human capital theory. The basic idea of human capital is that people can invest in themselves by means of education, training and experience and build up a stock of knowledge and skills that, like physical capital such as machinery and tools, they can use to increase their productivity and therefore earn higher incomes. Investment always involves incurring a cost in the present that yields a higher expected future income. Investment in training and education (called 'schooling') has direct costs to the individual in the form of fees for education and training courses and indirect costs in the form of earnings forgone – the opportunity cost of income that could have been earned during the training period. From the point of view of society, the investment period represents lost output in the present, but, in the future, workers who are more productive increase national income, and the investment leads to an increase in national income; there are also external benefits of education (such as being more civically minded or creative) that increase the welfare of the whole society. Like physical capital, human capital can depreciate, and it may need subsequent investment to renew its productivity. As the author of this book, I am using my accumulated knowledge of cultural economics as human capital, and hope it will pay off! I have to keep on investing time in reading new work in the field, however, or my knowledge will become out of date – that is, my human capital will depreciate and yield lower productivity: the book would be out of date.

Human capital theory has been used to analyse many topics, such as the relationship between education and economic growth, the most productive period of education and training at different levels, and why firms invest in some types of training for their employees but not others. One of its central ideas is that individuals who seek to maximise their lifetime income are prepared to make the outlay on the costs of education and training up to the point at which they expect it will pay off in terms of higher earnings. Individuals have 'age–earnings profiles' that start from the time they enter the labour market, after which earnings rise with age and experience, then fall off as they get older and by the age of retirement, earnings are zero. Those individuals who have more years of schooling earn more at every age after entering the labour market.

The theory envisages that individuals make a calculation of their expected lifetime earnings discounted into the present (see the section on cost–benefit analysis in chapter 7 for a full explanation) and also of their discounted costs (which mainly occur at the outset in this case), and assess the rate of return they expect to get from their investment in education (schooling). This is called the 'private rate of return', and it can be compared with the rate of interest that would be obtained instead from investing the sum spent on the outlay on schooling in some form of saving, for example in a savings account or in stocks and shares. Analogously, society can calculate the 'social rate of return' from its investment in educational facilities and compare that with investment in other social projects such as health care; a government would do this in making a cost–benefit calculation about subsidies to education and training.

Human capital theory recognises that some people have advantages that mean they need to invest less in formal schooling; some have greater inborn or 'innate' abilities (such as musical talent) or have a family background that already makes it easier to enter a particular profession (being a member of the Bach family). Empirical studies of artists' incomes have shown that it is these innate abilities that dominate earning power in artists' labour markets (see chapter 12).

Specific and general training

One of the topics analysed in human capital theory is the finance of training, which may take place on the job ('on-the-job training') or outside the workplace (for example, in a college or university, known as 'formal training'). Training is identified as 'general' or 'specific': general training prepares the worker to perform tasks that are general in nature and would be useful to any employer, in a variety of occupations; specific training, by contrast, relates to tasks and skills relevant only to one employer. The theory predicts that an employer would have an incentive to finance specific training, because he or she could appropriate the benefits of the trainee's greater productivity, but the employer could not capture all the benefits of general training and so the individual worker would have to pay for it. Alternatively, the state could provide general training if it is held to have strong external effects or be essential to effective membership of the society (literacy is an example).

This topic is relevant to cultural economics because it relates to arts training and the supply of trained artists; most will have received general, formal training that makes them employable in a variety of occupations; for most Europeans, that training is provided at below cost in a state-subsidised university or college. It is in fact very difficult to find examples of specific training, and even training that is apparently specific also has an element of general training about it; an example of specific training in the cultural sector is learning dances that are performed by only one dance company. This may explain why formal training predominates.

Sorting models

By contrast to human capital theory, sorting theory contends that investment in training does not raise income by raising productivity. Instead, two models – the signalling and screening models, which are always paired – constitute what is now labelled the sorting model. 'Sorting' refers to the role of a labour market in matching the supply of work and workers with employers and jobs, and sorting models see education and training as providing certification regarding workers.

In order for employers to obtain the right information about workers' ability they need some kind of certification, and the education system provides that in the form of diplomas and other evidence of qualifications. Employers 'screen' workers using this information and hire them according to the evidence the certificates provide; according to this view, the education system acts merely as a complex screen but without increasing productivity. For their part, workers 'signal' to possible employers that they have the training and skills to do the jobs the employer is offering. They do so by acquiring formal qualifications that the employer will understand as a signal of their ability. In fact, all they show is that students are prepared to 'play the game', but they do not test true ability; they just test factors such as the willingness to work hard and how well socialised the student is. These are not necessarily the features that are sought from artists, however.

A further prediction of sorting models is that students have the incentive to obtain more qualifications than are necessary to acquire the skills they need in order to try to strengthen their signalling to employers. This results in a waste of resources, including the artist's own investment of time and money. It has indeed been widely observed that artists typically are more highly educated, in the sense of having spent more years in formal education and training, than the average worker. Nevertheless, studies of artists' labour markets have found that having certificates and diplomas plays a less important role than is the case in other labour markets. Universities and colleges training artists award degrees and diplomas but they seem not to provide the kind of information that those hiring them want. Reputation, professionalism and considerable talent or creativity are what are important in artists' labour markets, and certificates from formal educational institutions are not able to provide adequate information about these characteristics (for one artist's view on this, see box 11.4).

This is evidenced by the fact that many arts-performing arts organisations organise their own systems of selection, such as auditions and the services of theatrical agents, and in the creative art forms similar screening devices are used, such as inspecting a portfolio of work. Employers may not trust colleges' certification because they produce too many graduates, not all of whom are sufficiently talented. The colleges themselves perform an initial screening function in selecting students, however, and that may carry some weight with employers. It is also worth noting that many artists are self-employed and so do not need to signal to an employer.

Box 11.4 David Hockney's views on training artists

David Hockney is one of the best-known living English artists and is one of the founders of British pop art. He was born in Yorkshire in the north of England and maintains ties there, though he has lived much of his life in California. He studied at the Royal College of Art in London and left in 1962.

I was at the Royal College of Art and 10 years later they asked me, would I go and give them some advice about things. Well I gave them advice. Ten years later they asked me again and I gave the same advice. I notice they never took any notice of it. The problem was they made it into an academic institution. My advice was to get rid of the GCE qualifications,[5] take in people who want to use their hands and eyes. But they need a bit of paper. When I was at the Royal College of Art they said to me: 'You've failed the course.' They said that to me because I hadn't attended enough lectures. I said, well that's OK, I won't say anything; nobody will know I didn't get a diploma because in painting nobody is going to ask for one, and if you are an accountant I would rely on one. But in painting, people would ask to see the painting, not the degree. They don't even look at paintings these days.

It's only dentists and accountants who give you confidence when you see their diplomas.

Source: David Hockney, quoted in Towse (1996: 303).

Competitions, prizes and signalling

Competitions and other ways of selecting prize winners are prevalent in the arts, and one reason is that they provide certification about the winner's ranking and talent as judged by independent experts. They therefore signal the quality of the winner's talent or creative ability to arts organisations and others who hire artistic labour. In chapter 18, literary awards are discussed as an important signal to both readers and publishers. Competitions are likely to carry far more weight than certificates from formal training, on account of the expert assessment and the fact that potential employers can see the artists work in a more realistically testing setting than a university or college is able to offer.

Training in the arts

Training for arts and crafts occupations is now offered widely in institutions of higher education. Historically, artists usually undertook some form of

---

[5] Former UK school examinations required as entrance for higher education.

apprenticeship and/or on-the-job training; for painters and other visual artists and craftspeople, this meant a long apprenticeship that was typically regulated by a guild working with a master, learning skills on the job; for performers, it meant studying and practising technique or just picking it up on the stage. Some crafts still have apprenticeships, even in Europe, such as pottery. Opera singers were still studying and living in with a teacher up until the Second World War.[6]

It was only with the growth of state-subsidised higher education in developed countries during the second half of the twentieth century that training became 'off-the-job' and formal, being provided in universities, drama, music and art colleges, ballet and film schools, etc. The 'upgrading' of artists' training usually implies that training becomes more academic and results in paper qualifications. This has been called the 'diploma disease' – every course must end up with a diploma of some kind (as David Hockney has noted – see box 11.4).

One of the unintended consequences of subsidised training for artists is that it encourages people to enter arts professions who would not have made that choice if they had had to pay the full cost of their training. An arts training is often expensive; it frequently involves one-to-one tuition and expensive materials, equipment and spaces, such as practice rooms and studios. If a prospective artist had to pay the full cost of his or her specialised training, it would have a positive private rate of return only in a relatively few cases of highly paid artists.[7] The concern is that talented artists might not be willing to take the risk of making the investment and so their potential creativity would be lost to the world. Such fears have prompted governments to subsidise arts training, and this is justified on efficiency grounds because it encourages higher-quality cultural output. As it is very difficult (at least in some artistic occupations) for training institutions to predict potential talent with any accuracy, however, far more artists are trained than would be justified on the above grounds. It can nonetheless be argued that, given the uncertainty surrounding success in the creative industries, it is efficient to train people with lesser talents as a form of insurance.

The number of students taking courses that train them for a creative occupation typically exceeds the number that could make a reasonable career, however, and would therefore be hard to justify on the grounds of private or

---

[6] The Italian baritone Tito Gobbi was one case in point. Tenor Placido Domingo's stage experience started almost from birth, as both his parents were zarzuela singers.

[7] See Towse (1996).

social efficiency. As pointed out in chapter 10, though, many policies are pursued not for efficiency reasons but for equity reasons: to give everyone equality of opportunity. Thus many students are admitted to arts training courses who do not stand a good chance of making a career in the arts because they want to try, and it is felt that they should have the opportunity. This is costly to society, but, as chapter 12 shows, there is not necessarily a very high financial penalty for an individual's failure, apart from the disappointment individuals experience when faced with the recognition that they are not going to succeed.

All of the above begs the question of whether sufficient training can produce talented artists and substitute for innate ability when that is lacking. If we were to take an extreme view that talent alone determines an artist's career and earnings, investment in schooling would not be worthwhile; by definition it could not raise productivity, and no certificate would be needed to 'prove' talent. Casual evidence from the biographies of artists runs counter to that view, however, as many highly talented artists have trained at an art, drama or music college. Of course, this could be for institutional reasons, and we may question whether an alternative organisation of training, such as on-the-job training or 'learning by doing', could have yielded the same results.

Artistic motivation

The economics of education presented above makes neoclassical assumptions that workers are motivated by financial reward. This may well not be the case with artists, and, indeed, the excess supply of labour in the arts and low earnings can be cited as evidence supporting this view. Nonetheless, it is important to understand what rewards artists do respond to, because, as pointed out in chapter 10, governments seeking to improve the quantity and quality of the arts and cultural output are mostly restricted to offering financial grants. The last section in this chapter on the theories of artists' labour markets is therefore devoted to what cultural economics has to say about artistic motivation.

Bruno Frey is one of the few cultural economists to have offered a theory of creativity and artistic motivation, adopting from social psychology the theory of intrinsic and extrinsic motivation, which he applies to the question of how workers, including artists, are appropriately rewarded.[8] As with motivation,

---

[8] Frey (2000: ch. 8).

reward can be either intrinsic, emphasising psychic satisfaction from peer recognition, enhanced reputation, and so on, or extrinsic, in the form of money. Frey's theory is that, unless intrinsic motivation is met with intrinsic reward, there will be 'crowding out'; incentive and reward must be matched. So, for example, an artist who is driven by inner motivation is not only *not* stimulated to produce work by monetary reward, he or she could even be *de*motivated by it. The classic example of this response is blood donorship: people are motivated by a sense of civic duty to give blood, but if there is monetary payment (an extrinsic reward) for it many civically minded (intrinsically motivated) people would feel insulted and not donate. Artists, according to this theory, are more likely to be satisfied with intrinsic reward, and this makes the task of giving them incentives to create by means of cultural policy much more difficult. Awards and honours are one way a government can offer intrinsic reward to artists.

Grants to artists

On the face of it, Frey's theory would seem to suggest that grants in monetary form would not be acceptable to artists. Many artists do take up grants if they are offered, however, and value them for 'buying time' so that they can concentrate more on their art. One explanation that is consistent with Frey's theory is that grants are often awarded by panels of artists or other experts in the field and this means that there is intrinsic reward (peer recognition). Research on grants to artists, however, has shown that those who receive them are often the ones who are doing well on the market – that is, getting extrinsic reward – already.

Finally, we might ask what the purpose is of making grants to artists. Is it to raise quality or to overcome the inherent uncertainty of creating new works of art that a market would be unlikely to reward? Market failure arguments could be evoked to show that there are serious information problems about novel art and that, without financial help advised by expert selection, there would be underproduction of creativity; in general, though, efficiency arguments are difficult to sustain in a market in which there is excess supply. There may also be an equity motive, however, and this appears to be the motivation behind one of the best-known schemes to support artists, in this case visual artists: that of the so-called WIK in the Netherlands (see box 11.5). Interestingly, the response to the scheme shows the extent to which artists respond to the prospect of higher income, even though that is the state-determined minimum income; in other words, a scheme that appears to have an equity motive can also reallocate resources and therefore have efficiency effects. Artists may not, after all, be so exceptional!

Box 11.5 Supporting artists in the Netherlands: WIK and BKR

In 1949 the BKR (Beeldend Kunstenaars Regeling – Visual Artists Scheme) was established, according to which professional visual artists who earned less than a certain minimum income were able to sell works of art to local authorities. As long as these works met minimum quality requirements, the local authorities were obliged to buy these works of art. Unsurprisingly, the scheme became increasingly expensive, and there was a problem of where to put the pieces (which were often very large, because artists had the incentive to make them so and charge a price accordingly), and the scheme was abandoned in 1987. In 1999 the BKR was replaced by the WIK (Wet Inkomens-voorziening Kunstenaars – Law for the Income Provision of Artists) for low-income artists who would otherwise be eligible for welfare benefits. Artists with below-minimum incomes are entitled to special WIK payments without the usual requirement to apply for other work and while still being allowed to earn some money in the arts.

According to Hans Abbing, the artist and economist author of *Why Are Artists Poor? The Exceptional Economy of the Arts*, while the BKR scheme was in operation the number of students in art colleges increased much more rapidly than in other post-eighteen vocational training establishments, but numbers dropped off when the scheme was run down in the 1980s; the introduction of the WIK led to another rise in students studying art, however. He argues that that increase leads to a depressing dynamic of labour supply that results in excess supply of works of art, causing prices to fall and reducing artists' incomes, and that state intervention in the market simply makes these trends worse. Abbing's hypothesis suggests that there should be empirical investigation into the effect on markets of other grant schemes for artists.

Source: Abbing (2003).

Conclusion

The question of how relevant labour market theory is to artists has long been disputed in cultural economics and the answer seems to be both 'Yes' and 'No': some theories appear to have predictive power while others do not. It is only fair to add, though, that this is also true in other labour markets. For example, the role of human capital formation versus the sorting role of training and education continues to be debated within the economics of education and in labour economics. Labour economics itself is a far more sophisticated area of research than is represented here and includes the study of incentives and reward schemes, principal–agent and moral hazard problems, contracting rules, and so forth. Richard Caves' work on the economic organisation of the creative industries (see chapter 14) relates some of these theories to the cultural sector and to artists (Caves, 2000). It has also been noted that little is known in labour economics about the demand for labour, and this is also the case in artists' labour markets.

What has frequently been thought of as exceptional in artists' labour markets is the considerable role that what we call talent plays in the earnings of artists and the demand for them, and the fact that this cannot be adequately modelled using standard earnings functions. Age–earnings profiles in artistic occupations do not behave 'normally', as artists' career paths are erratic and lifetime incomes do not obey the expectation of rising with age. It is also the case, however, that innate ability has been found to be important in other labour markets too, and the superstar phenomenon is observed in other professions than the arts. The conclusion can be drawn that cultural economists should absorb theories being developed in labour economics and in industrial organisation and apply them to the arts, but, equally, it can also be said that some features of artists' labour markets, such as flexible working on short-term contracts, seem to be appearing in other occupations, and how artists handle their careers may provide insights for the understanding of developments outside the cultural sector. The next chapter is devoted to the findings of empirical research by cultural economists applying the theory of artists' labour markets as laid out in this chapter.

Further reading

David Throsby is credited with having done most to promote the understanding of artists' labour markets: he has developed some of the most important theoretical models and been responsible for repeated surveys of artists in Australia and using the data to test these theories. This work is summarised and presented in accessible form in chapter 6 of his 2001 book *Economics and Culture*. My book *Creativity, Incentive and Reward* (Towse, 2001b) contains a survey of the main issues in artists' labour markets, written for non-specialists (chapter 3), and a chapter applying Sherwin Rosen's superstar theory to singers' earnings (chapter 4). I have also contributed a chapter to the Victor Ginsburgh and David Throsby *Handbook of the Economics of Art and Culture* on human capital theory (Towse, 2006b); this and other chapters on artists' labour markets in part 8 in that volume were written for professional economists, however, and are difficult reading. Hans Abbing's (2002) book *Why Are Artists Poor?* also presents these theories in accessible form, with the addition of his own observations.

Several chapters in my *Handbook of Cultural Economics* (Towse, 2003a) summarise research on particular topics in this field: Françoise Benhamou has done important work on European cultural employment, which she refers to in her survey chapter on 'Artists' labour markets' (chapter 7); Nachoem Wijnberg has contributed a chapter (9) on 'Awards', while Günther Schulze covers 'Superstars' (chapter 53) and Abbing writes on 'Support for artists' (chapter 55). Tyler Cowen (2000) also tackles the role of superstars in his book *What Price Fame?*

12 Economics of artists' labour markets: empirical research

Interest in the facts about artists' incomes and employment began with Baumol and Bowen's analysis of the causes of rising costs in the arts, and empirical research on artists' labour markets therefore became an integral part of testing Baumol's cost disease, with its proposition that it is labour costs that are responsible for rising costs. It seems that Baumol and Bowen themselves were the first researchers to gather data on performers' earnings and employment characteristics in their 1966 book, in which they used US Census Bureau and Bureau of Labor Statistics data. This triggered various types of data collection and analysis of artists' labour market behaviour, which are investigated in this chapter.

Data sources and research methods

In terms of the collection of data, in the United States, the National Endowment for the Arts has regularly published data on incomes, employment and unemployment of a broadly defined set of artists since 1976. In Australia the Australia Council for the Arts published the first of a series of surveys of artists in 1983 and continues to do so in collaboration with David Throsby. The Finnish Arts Council undertook a series of detailed investigations from the late 1980s and through the 1990s into the economic conditions of specific artistic occupations using tax data. Statistics on artists' earnings were collected in France by the Observatoire de l'emploi culturel from the 1980s and in the Netherlands by the Central Bureau of Statistics in the 1980s. I carried out a survey of artists' earnings, training and work conditions in Wales (the first in the United Kingdom) in 1990, which was followed by O'Brien and Feist's analysis in 1995 of employment in the cultural sector using the 1991 UK census data.[1]

---

[1] Heikkinen (1995), O'Brien and Feist (1995) and Towse (2001b: ch. 3).

This brief history shows that sources of data on artists' earnings and employment vary between official statistics and survey results. Both have advantages and disadvantages and demonstrate the difficulties of economic research into artists' labour markets. Research methods depend upon what data are available, and these data may or may not be suitable for answering the research questions posed by the theoretical analysis of artists' supply decisions presented in chapter 11. These questions include age, gender, artistic activities, how much artists earn, time spent on arts and non-arts work, sources of earnings (in arts work, non-arts work, and so on), receipt of grants and welfare payments, family income, pension provision, hours worked, educational and training qualifications, years of experience, periods of unemployment and expenses incurred in arts work. It is also the case that there is no uniformity in defining the artist population; work by cultural economists has mostly concentrated on artists supplying the 'high' arts; interest in the creative or cultural industries has recently broadened out, however, to research on workers in these industries, creative or otherwise. The situation therefore resembles that in the measurement of the size and scope of production in the cultural sector examined in chapter 2. This chapter goes into some detail about these problems and offers guidance as to how to go about research in this area; then the main findings of research by cultural economists are presented, followed by an evaluation of what we know and do not know about artists' labour markets.

Problems with official statistics

The choice of research methods depends in the first instance on the availability of data. Governments conduct various statistical surveys and censuses on population characteristics (age, gender, ethnic background, size of household, marital status, location, occupation of head of household, and so on), on labour (occupation, age, place and duration of employment, training and education, earnings), employment by sector and size of firm, unemployment, and so forth. A census takes information on basic characteristics from everyone and samples, say, one in ten to ascertain further details. Government statisticians are expert in extrapolating trends and at analysing and predicting changes, and they have relatively large samples to work with; moreover, they can require compliance by law. They classify data for their own purposes, though, and this is not necessarily in the way that cultural economists would choose, and this has led to problems for research into artists' labour markets.

Researchers on artists' labour markets have encountered the following problems with official statistics:

- many artists and craftspeople are self-employed and therefore do not appear in employment statistics because they are not employed by anyone else;
- self-employed people do not appear in unemployment statistics because someone cannot *not* employ him- or herself(!);
- workplaces with below a certain number of employees may not be included in an employment survey, thus excluding many businesses in the arts and crafts, which typically employ only a few workers;
- people who work only part-time hours or who earn below a certain amount do not qualify for enumeration;
- part-time workers or people who do not work frequently enough throughout the year do not qualify for unemployment insurance or for a state pension scheme;
- censuses or surveys may ask questions only about household income, not about individual income;
- data from tax offices, which is reliable on incomes, is often protected and confidential and not made available to any outside body, including other government departments; and
- censuses and surveys are conscious of the time it takes to complete the enquiry, and the cost too, and therefore keep questions to a minimum.

The result is that not all the information the researcher would like can be collated for specific artist occupations.

Another problem with official statistics for economic research on artists' labour markets in countries with relatively small populations is that there may not be enough individuals in any given category to ensure statistical significance. Therefore, if the researcher wishes to study the earnings of, say, authors and there are only fifty authors, a 10 per cent sample would yield only five individuals, and if one were very successful that would bias the statistical results. This can happen anyway, but the greater the number in a sample, the more reliable it is. The United States has a great advantage in this respect, because its population, including its artist population, is large enough to make numbers relatively reliable for the purposes of statistical inference. That is not the case in, for instance, the Netherlands; if the researcher wants to study, say, choreographers, there are just not that many of them to provide a sufficient sampling basis; the smaller the population of the country, the greater this particular problem is. Published official data may not identify small populations for this very reason and statisticians aggregate groups (by, for example, reporting artists with entertainers and sportspeople), thus obscuring what to a cultural economist are important distinctions.

Surveys by professional bodies

Apart from government sources, many professional associations and trade unions of artists conduct their own surveys of pay and work conditions. Respondents may or may not be motivated to reply to them, depending upon their assessment of how well the association works for them. The chief snag with these sources, though, is either that not everyone who works in those occupations joins the association or that the association has entry barriers that exclude many young or unsuccessful workers, who nevertheless identify themselves as belonging to those occupations. The actors' unions in the United Kingdom and the United States, both called Actors' Equity, admit to full membership only people who have had a certain number of weeks' work at their specified minimum rate of pay, so therefore not all actors get admitted. Once they have obtained membership, however, they can retain it whether they continue to work as actors or not. In France, membership of occupational pension schemes also provides a source of data on earnings and employment (see later in this chapter).

What all this means is that, for certain purposes, official statistics may be appropriate, but in most cases cultural economists have found it necessary to do surveys targeted on the artist population as they themselves define it. There is no hard and fast rule about what criteria should be adopted for the sample population, however.

Cross-section and time series data

Surveys provide a cross-section snapshot at a particular moment in time but researchers would also like to know how artists' careers develop over time. If a survey is truly representative and the work environment fairly stable, cross-section data from surveys can be compared over the years. The Australia Council has commissioned Throsby and colleagues to carry out a series of four surveys of artists over a period of twenty years to enable trends over time to be analysed (see box 12.2). A different kind of opportunity presents itself in the United States, where panel data – a combination of cross-section and time series data – are available from official sources. These data enable researchers to track careers and also to study movement in and out of arts occupations.[2] The results of research using these data are presented later in the chapter.

---

[2] See Alper and Wassall (2006) for a detailed account.

Defining the artist population

One of the biggest hurdles in research on artists' labour markets is to select the appropriate artist population, and the first task of a survey is to identify categories of creative occupations. As we saw in chapter 2, defining the creative sector is a complex matter; defining artists is correspondingly difficult, if not more so. An occupational category should include all who are engaged in it, just as a productive activity should include all goods and services produced that fit into the classification. Should a video artist be classified as a film- and video-maker or as a visual artist, though? Clearly, there are many problems of this kind, and in the end there is bound to be some arbitrariness. Moreover, surveys by cultural economists have found that many artists put themselves into more than one category when given the opportunity to tick more than one box in a survey to identify their artistic activity. Some examples are familiar – the composer who performs (or is it the performer who composes?) – but there are many more. A census or survey that allows only one category does not capture this variety and if all the questions relate to that one activity it can lead to underestimating arts income and time spent on arts work.

A more serious problem for classifying artists, however, is the fact that artists also work outside the arts (multiple job-holding); if a criterion for being classified as an artist is how the person spent the majority of his or her time in census week or gained the majority of his or her income in that week, that can result in him or her not being counted as an artist at all. If the person happened to spend more time working as a waiter in census week, he or she would be classified in the census as a waiter, not an actor, even though he or she is working as a waiter only because he or she is unemployed as an actor that week. This issue has been debated heatedly, because it leads to bias in census-based estimates of artists' incomes (particularly in the case of the United States), suggesting that the 'starving artist' is a myth and that there is no call for concern about artists' earnings. This was highlighted in work by Randall Filer, who drew his conclusions from US census data that artists' earnings did not differ greatly from those of other professionals, and strongly defended his position by invoking what he called the 'market test' for defining an artist: professional artists would be working in census week or any other time.[3]

Box 12.1 provides a list of criteria by which artists may be defined, and each of these has been used in one or another census or survey. It can be seen that some artists ('real' artists!) would comply with all the criteria, though not all

---

[3] Filer (1986).

Box 12.1 Criteria for defining artists according to Frey and Pommerehne

Bruno Frey and Werner Pommerehne's 1989 book *Muses and Markets* identifies eight criteria that may be applied in order to determine who is an artist:

- the amount of *time* spent on artistic work;
- the amount of *income* derived from artistic activities;
- the *reputation* as an artist among the general public;
- *recognition* among other artists;
- the *quality* of artistic work produced;
- *membership* of a professional artists' group or association;
- a professional *qualification* in the arts; and
- the subjective *self-evaluation* of being an artist.

Source: Frey and Pommerehne (1989: 47).

artists join a professional association. Many artists might fit just one or two of the criteria, however, and, especially if that were 'self-evaluation', it would present problems to a survey that wanted to research the economic conditions of professional artists. Who thinks he or she is an artist and who can be counted as a practising professional artist may be very different things. The problem is that, in many situations, the researcher is not able to make an independent assessment of how realistic the respondent's claim is – and that goes for a census as well as for a survey.

Research methods and results

In this section, some difficulties in researching artists' labour markets are explained and research methods discussed in the light of research experience.

Surveys

While an official census is likely to be more reliable than a survey by a researcher, because governments employ specialised social statisticians and may exercise powers of compulsion in getting responses, the downside is that the categories used may be inappropriate or outdated. On the other hand, surveys frequently suffer from low response rates and may be partial. Typically surveys mail a questionnaire or use telephone interviews, though nowadays e-mail surveys are also successfully used. Specialist social survey firms are expert at getting the best response rates but they are expensive; non-specialist researchers may get low response rates, and then reliable inferences cannot be drawn from data (though one all too often sees that they are).

Contacting artists

A survey requires information on the artist population to be sampled and some means of contacting individuals, such as an address or telephone number. Often this has to be secured through professional associations or trade unions, because they are the only bodies with the necessary contact information. For the reasons given above, this can introduce bias. If the direction of the bias is known, for example that only very successful artists are admitted to a particular association, then any results from a survey using its members will have an upward bias for income and other questions, such as hours of work, and this can affect the inferences that may be drawn from them.

Non-response

Some people do not reply to surveys or, more damagingly, do not receive them because they have moved away from the contact address or telephone number. This can be problematic when a mobile group is concerned, and many performers seem to be difficult to contact. This is also a problem for workplace surveys with a mobile workforce, though. Film companies and scratch orchestras, for example, often form just for a one-off production. Flexible working conditions with short-term contracts can be the cause of another problem, however: double-counting of the same people working in many different organisations can make it seem that there are more workers in the artist population than there in fact are.

It is because of these difficulties that, to date, there are few good data on the economic and social characteristics of artists.

One of the most successful accomplishments in the collection of data on artists is the repeated surveys of artists undertaken by Throsby (with various co-authors) in Australia; the main findings of the 2002 survey are reported in box 12.2. These results, apart from the actual numbers reported, are typical of all the other surveys that have been carried out into artists' labour markets.

Interpreting research findings

Having obtained the data, the next stage of research is to interpret the findings and this can be done in several ways: descriptive statistics, such as percentages; basic statistical operations, the best-known of which is probably taking the

Box 12.2 The 2002 survey of artists in Australia: main findings

- There are about 45,000 practising professional artists in Australia.
- The term 'practising professional artists' includes artists who are currently active or who have been active in the past five years; the 'professional' aspect limits the survey to those artists who operate at a level and standard of work and with a degree of commitment appropriate to the norms of professional practice within their art form. This excludes hobbyists and amateurs.
- This survey covers the following categories of practising professional artists: writers, visual artists, craft practitioners, actors, directors, dancers, choreographers, musicians, singers, composers and community cultural development workers.
- Between 1988 and 2001 the growth rate in the number of artists has been 2–3 per cent per year.
- On average, artists tend to be older than the general workforce or the total population. This is attributed to the time it takes for an artist to become established and the long careers of artists beyond the average retiring age of the workforce. The average (mean) age of artists is about forty-six years. Writers and composers are the oldest groups on average, with a mean age of forty-nine; dancers make up the youngest group, with a mean age of thirty-one.
- The numbers of practising professional artists in the survey was evenly split between women and men. This differs from the general employed workforce, in which 56 per cent are men and 44 per cent are women.
- Artists are a highly educated group. Three-quarters have had formal education in a university, college of advanced education, teachers' college, TAFE (technical and further education) or specialist artist training institution. Four out of ten have had private training.
- Almost two-thirds of all artists work at more than one job; 56 per cent hold two jobs and 7 per cent hold three jobs. Overall, 43 per cent of artists are engaged in some work in an arts-related field, and one-third do some work in an area not related to the arts.

Source: Throsby and Hollister (2003).

average of all observations; or as the basis for analysis using more sophisticated statistical techniques to estimate an equation that is drawn from theory. This could mean testing for a correlation (A and B are related) or for causation (A causes B). All these operations have been applied to data on artists' labour market behaviour, as may be seen later.

Another way of interpreting the data is by contrasting them to known characteristics from the wider population; so, the statement is often made, for instance, that artists have higher than average years of education and lower than average incomes. The 'control' group with which these contrasts are made could be everyone in the country or with a specific group, say other professional workers.

Box 12.3 Mean and median incomes: survey of artists in Wales, 1992

- Visual artists – maximum income = £60,000; minimum income = £0.
  Mean income = £4,475. Median income = £1,000.
- Writers – maximum income = £33,000; minimum income = £0.
  Mean income = £4,346. Median income = £100.
- Actors – maximum income = £60,000; minimum income = £0.
  Mean income = £7,376. Median income = £2,835.
- Musicians – maximum income = £24,500; minimum income = £0.
  Mean income = £4,514. Median income = £1,900.

Source: Towse (2001b).

One particular point refers to the reporting of artists' income data. Because the distribution of income due to the 'superstar' phenomenon is very uneven, with many low-income earners and a few very high earners, taking the mathematical average, or mean, of all the respondents' incomes would bias the results upwards. Therefore the appropriate statistic for artists' incomes is the median income, not the mean, the median being the midpoint of the distribution – the 50 per cent mark of all observations. Box 12.3 gives an actual illustration of the difference between the mean and the median. It shows the maximum reported incomes in the survey and the minimum, which were zero, though in fact all in the sample were active professional artists; the median is systematically significantly lower than the mean because of the skewed distribution of incomes.

Collectively bargained rates of pay by trade unions

As mentioned earlier, artists' professional associations and trade unions commission surveys of their members, and the resultant data provide a source of information on earnings in specific occupations. The unions may use this information to bargain with those who employ artists' services. Collective bargaining is common in the performing arts, especially in the United Kingdom and the United States, where artists are subject to market forces. The trade unions, such as those for musicians, actors, dancers, and so on, seek to ensure that a minimum hourly wage rate is paid to their members and to agree a 'closed shop' deal with the relevant employers (theatre and concert managements for live performance, and broadcasters and film and sound recording makers for recorded work), in an attempt to prevent them from undercutting the agreed minimum by hiring non-union artists.

Surveys of performers have found that, in many cases, it is only the minimum wage that is paid; this may even apply to well-known actors, including film stars, who choose to work in a live stage production. The top 'stars', often in musicals, can negotiate their own terms individually, which may well include a share of box-office receipts or of profits; it is very difficult for researchers to obtain information on this type of artist, however.

State-employed artists

When artists work for state- or local-authority-owned arts organisations there are institutionally set rates of payment and hours of work, which vary according to rank (for performers, say a principal singer, dancer, actor or instrumental soloist) and according to length of service in line with other public servants' pay and conditions. This information may be publicly available and rates of payment are certainly well known by the artists' organisations. German theatre statistics, for example, are regularly published by the Deutscher Bühnenverein and include this information. If there are well-established posts for certain types of artists – say a fixed size of the corps de ballet or positions in an orchestra for flute players – and their rate of payment is known, information on artists' earnings can be obtained direct from the accounts of the arts organisations themselves.

Finally, if the researcher has access to the tax returns of artists, as was the case with the Finnish studies referred to above (and in chapter 18), they can provide reliable data on earnings and tax-deductible costs of materials and equipment (which can be very high for some occupations, such as potters and jewellers); even so, there may nevertheless be problems with the official classification and definition of artists, as explained earlier.

Results of research on artists' incomes and employment

In this section, the results of research on artists' labour markets on incomes, employment and other features are presented, drawn from research in various countries using different research methods and data sources.

Incomes

Probably the longest-running research collecting and analysing data on artists' incomes is that done by the NEA in the United States. Table 12.1 shows median earnings for 2004 for the chosen artistic occupations, using data drawn from the Bureau of Labor Statistics. It shows that 'Art directors' were the highest-paid artist group and 'Dancers' the lowest-paid. The NEA (2008) report also provides information on the percentage of persons in the various occupations who were self-employed: 'Writers and authors' top the bill, with 68 per cent, followed by 'Artists' (fine artists, multimedia artists and animators) (62 per cent), 'Photographers' (59 per cent), 'Music directors and composers' (45 per cent) and 'Musicians and singers' (41 per cent). The report also calculates the secondary job-holding rate amongst these occupations; the overall average is 13 per cent, but this is undoubtedly biased downwards by the inclusion of architects and designers, whose rates of secondary job-holding are low; at the high end, 32 per cent of musicians and singers had a secondary job.[4] Moreover, the figures in table 12.1 are based on the census definition of the 'market test', as explained earlier; it is therefore to be expected that survey-based figures on secondary job-holding would be higher and incomes would be lower.

Table 12.1 US artists: annual median earnings, 2004 (US dollars)

Architects	60,300
Landscape architects	53,120
Art directors	63,840
Fine artists (e.g. painters, sculptors)	38,060
Multimedia artists and animators	50,360
Commercial and industrial designers	52,310
Fashion designers	55,840
Floral designers	20,450
Graphic designers	38,030
Interior designers	40,670
Actors	23,460
Producers and directors	52,840
Dancers	17,760
Choreographers	33,670
Musicians and singers	37,130
Announcers	22,130
Writers and authors	44,350
Photographers	26,080

Source: NEA (2008).

---

[4] NEA (2008).

In other countries, either census data do not exist in sufficient detail for artistic occupations to be discerned or researchers prefer their own survey to avoid the bias that census definitions introduce. Based on all these researches, the following conclusions on artists' incomes have become widely accepted:

- artists earn less than other workers when age and length of schooling are standardised;
- the distribution of artists' earnings is very uneven, with the majority earning low income from arts work, though a few superstars earn very high incomes;
- there is little relationship between age and earnings or between years of education and training and earnings;
- when there are data on trends over time, it has been found that artists' earnings do not rise as rapidly as other workers' earnings; and
- many artists are supported by other members of their household or family, by state grants and other state benefits not specifically intended for the support of artists, such as unemployment benefit.

Employment, unemployment and underemployment

The 2008 NEA report referred to above contains data on the employment and unemployment of artists and tracks the figures over the previous four-year period, showing that the rate of unemployment had fallen but that it was more or less in line with that for other workers, albeit twice as high as for other professional occupations. As with the reported income data, the NEA findings are biased upwards by the inclusion of occupational groups (architects and designers) who enjoy more stable employment conditions than other types of creative artists. Performers' rates of unemployment are especially low – in the US data, actors had a reported unemployment rate of 25 per cent in 2005. Surveys of artists in other countries have found that unemployment of artists is higher than the national rate and also that there is both voluntary and involuntary unemployment. It is important to clarify what these terms mean, because they are defined differently in different countries.

When many persons are self-employed, the concept of unemployment is not easy to characterise. Self-employment may in fact be a choice that the artist makes for his or her own advantage; in the United Kingdom, for instance, self-employed performers can offset travel expenses for tax purposes, which they could not do if they were employed. It may also suit arts organisations better to employ self-employed artists, because then they would not have to pay their pension contributions and other such expenses associated with employment – and, of course, these are considerations that vary between countries depending upon institutional arrangements, as we see below. Even for people who are employed, though, the number of hours they work may be voluntary or involuntary: many artists would like to work more hours or weeks than they are able to because they cannot find sufficient work, and this applies also to self-employed artists. Economists call this underemployment. A related further complication is that some people may choose underemployment over working more hours in another occupation because they have a strong preference to spend their time in their chosen arts occupation. Whether they can do so and still collect unemployment compensation depends upon the institutional arrangements in a particular country and the way the authorities there treat unemployment; in some, workers are permitted to work a few hours and still be eligible for unemployment benefit. There are also many types of schemes that are not specifically targeted on artists that assist them in different ways; examples are schemes to encourage rural development or depressed areas that are open to artists, and loan schemes to encourage entrepreneurship that can benefit craftspeople. Surveys of artists have turned up evidence for a variety of arrangements that support artists one way or another.

One of the main issues, therefore, is: what incentive do artists have to declare themselves unemployed and what are the consequences? In the United States, the classification of unemployment is done as part of the census and so follows the same logic as was discussed above in relation to occupational classification; it is not a voluntary choice. In the United Kingdom, workers who are eligible for unemployment benefit (compensation) register voluntarily and may then be required to apply for work outside their chosen occupation; this would increase their hours of non-arts works in relation to arts work. We saw in box 11.5 that artists in the Netherlands under the WIK income support scheme are exempted from having to take on non-arts work. There is also the matter of how long workers are eligible for unemployment benefit or other social benefit payments; in some countries it lasts much longer than others. Moreover, multiple job-holding complicates all these arrangements.

Surveys of artists by cultural economists are able to explore the question of underemployment by asking artists if they have been able to work in their chosen artistic occupation as many hours as they would like to, and many report they are not – that is, they are underemployed in the arts, even though they may be working full-time by taking arts-related or non-arts work.

Box 12.4 The Performing Artists' Unemployment Insurance Scheme in France in the 1990s

In France in the 1990s there was a special scheme of unemployment insurance for performers as part of occupational unemployment insurance provision. It was an occupational unemployment compensation scheme, financed by contributions from employees and employers in the sector. Performers who had worked for a given number of hours in the year were entitled to join and the duration of their unemployment compensation payment depended upon the number of hours per year they had accumulated. When they were employed in non- (performing) arts work, those who had spent more than half their total hours working in the performing arts were counted as performers, and it mattered not whether they were employed or self-employed. The payment during periods of unemployment was a percentage of the hourly wage that the performer had been earning plus a fixed daily amount. While receiving this compensation, the performer could take up short-term work contracts (though, during them, he or she did not get the unemployment payment) and thereby accumulate entitlement to the next round of unemployment. Not very surprisingly, the performers' unemployment scheme experienced a deficit, which had to be financed by other occupational unemployment insurance funds.

Analysis by Pierre-Michel Menger and Marc Gurgand of the data from the Performing Artists' Unemployment Insurance Scheme shows that the number of beneficiaries rose more than fivefold from 7,089 in 1990 to 38,250 in 1992, with the number of compensated days rising from 1.75 million to 11.26 million between these two years.

Source: Menger and Gurgand (1996).

Box 12.4 provides details of the unemployment scheme for performing artists in France; similar schemes are to be found in some other European countries. Having occupational schemes is a fundamentally different way of organising unemployment compensation from the universal type of scheme that pays unemployment benefit to all workers who qualify, regardless of occupation – as, for instance, in the United Kingdom. As the data from Menger and Gurgand (1996) in box 12.4 show, it has led to an interesting moral hazard problem.

Other schemes that support artists

Like France, Germany and Italy and several other European countries have institutional arrangements, such as guaranteed employment after having worked for an employer for a set period (fifteen years in Germany) or pensions that support early retirement, and these assist older artists. In the United Kingdom and some other countries, though, surveys of artists have found that a majority of artists do not subscribe to voluntary pension schemes, and, especially for self-employed artists, this can lead to problems when they retire or are incapacitated. Special schemes have been set up to encourage artists to make provision for their retirement. There are also schemes for retraining dancers, who typically do not work after their late thirties.

Hours of work

Related to the question of employment is the number of hours that artists work, and researchers have found that artists typically work harder (i.e. put in longer hours) than other workers. This seems to reflect their work preference for arts work and the need to do multiple jobs in order to make ends meet. Women artists do not work as many hours as their male counterparts, however, and this is ascribed to family responsibilities, in particular looking after children. In the next section, I discuss artists' supply functions that analyse what determines the hours of work supplied.

Gender

The survey of artists in Australia quoted in box 12.2 found that male artists' median earnings were just over twice their female counterparts from arts work, and when all income was taken into account the median income of males was one-third more than that of females. Similar findings have been reported elsewhere. Various hypotheses have been put forward to explain these observations: that females work less than males and are younger (a supply-side explanation); that they are paid less for the work they do (suggesting discrimination); and that the demand for female artists' work is lower than for males (a demand-side explanation). In the performing arts, it seems that there is less work for females than males (with the notable exception of dance), because TV scriptwriters and playwrights new and old write more parts for males. At one time, there was a strong prejudice against women musicians and orchestras were a male preserve, but this has changed and many orchestras nowadays have a large proportion of female players.

Careers and leavers

Surveys of artists ask them about their career development but a more systematic way of researching career development is to use time series and panel data. In the 1980s, Randall Filer analysed what he called 'the price of failure': persons leaving artistic occupations, presumably because they did not earn enough or succeed in other ways. He used census data to look at the earnings of former artists to see if they had incurred a penalty for their years spent in artistic occupations and concluded that they had not. Filer's other research using census data, however, was restricted to artists who passed the 'market test' and included all earnings, not just income from arts work. His sample therefore seems likely to underestimate the number of leavers, though this may not alter his results.[5]

The analysis of US panel data from the National Longitudinal Survey of Youth by Neil Alper and Grey Wassall (2006) provides some information on artists' careers and on artists who give up working in the arts. The US data show that the average age of entry into the artist labour market was twenty-five, reflecting the fact that artists have longer than average years of schooling; the sizable presence of architects, who have a long formal training period, somewhat raises the average. Because the survey started only in 1979 with fourteen- to twenty-two-year-olds, however, there is no information on the age of retirement, which varies very considerably: some artists go on working all their lives while others, notably dancers, complete their performing careers by the age of forty. What these data do show, though, is that there is significant movement in and out of arts occupations between survey years; only 2 per cent of those working as artists at some point were still artists in ten or more years. There is much more work to be done in cultural economics on artists' career paths and patterns of lifetime earnings and employment.

Analysis of artists' labour market decisions

To an economist, the importance of having data is that they can be used to test the various hypotheses posed by theories about the working of labour markets. In cultural economics, the question has always been asked if artists behave differently from other workers (for example, are they less responsive to changes in rates of pay?), and this has led to research comparing artists with other workers (or professionals) in the attempt to answer that question. To do so, statistical analysis rather than just description of the data is needed, and, in this section, empirical studies of earnings and labour supply functions are discussed.

Earnings functions

Earnings functions were developed in the economics of education in the 1960s to test human capital theory. An earnings function is a formally stated causal

---

[5] See Filer (1990).

relationship between earnings and education (years of schooling) and other variables that are expected to influence them. The hypothesis that earnings depend upon (are a function of) these variables is tested using data on artists' earnings and other variables from census or survey sources. The ideal data for estimating earnings functions would be longitudinal observations on individuals or panel data but, frequently, researchers have to use cross-section data, especially when they are using data from surveys.

The general functional form is

$$Y = A + aS + bX + u$$

where Y (earnings or income) depends on the length of schooling, S (the number of years of attending post-compulsory formal education or training), and experience, X (measured as the number of years in the workforce); variables such as age, gender and ethnic origin, marital status, number of children, and so on may also be included according to what the researcher wishes to know. A is a constant and measures innate and family background effects, and u is the error term.

If schooling and experience were important determinants of artists' earnings, the coefficients a and b would be statistically significant. Instead, what is typically found is that A is highly significant, leading researchers to conclude that innate ability, such as talent or early training, is the principal explanatory variable. Comparison with studies of earnings functions of other workers shows that innate ability is more important in artists' labour markets than it is in other labour markets, in which education and experience were found to be significant determinants of income.

One of the first estimates of an earnings function in the arts was that made by Glenn Withers in 1985, using Australian survey data, in which he compared the earnings of artists with those of other workers and concluded that, statistically, artists earn much lower incomes than other workers, which he attributed to the 'psychic' or intrinsic rewards from working in the arts. He concluded that this led to artists effectively subsidising the arts, and he calculated that this subsidy was five times as great as the government's grants to the arts in Australia at the time.[6]

Artists' supply functions

A supply function for labour essentially reverses the earnings equation by making the hours worked (the measure of the supply of labour) a function of

---

[6] Withers (1985).

earnings (and the other characteristics). An innovation in the analysis of labour markets by cultural economists was to split earnings into those from arts and non-arts work and to see what the relative role of each is in determining artists' labour supply. This enables the researcher to take account of multiple job-holding and to identify the supply of hours of work to two sectors, arts and non-arts. It obviously requires data on all these variables, and they typically come from surveys.

Throsby introduced the empirical measurement of artists' supply functions, using data from his Australian surveys; he found that an increase in the non-arts wage resulted in artists spending more time on arts work, providing confirmation of his work preference hypothesis encountered in chapter 11. He also further subdivided earnings into arts-related (such as teaching) and non-arts earnings and found that this offered better explanatory power: this division showed that 54 per cent of artists' time was spent on arts work, 28 per cent on arts-related work and 18 per cent on non-arts work in the 1993 survey.[7] An important additional finding from this research was that the role of formal training showed up as significant in relation to arts-related work as well as non-arts work (a conclusion already well established from studies of other labour markets) but not, as before, in relation to arts work itself.

This type of analysis, in which a hypothesis from an established theory is modelled and tested empirically, is very important in cultural economics (as in all other branches of economics) and can offer explanations for artists' labour market behaviour that simple descriptive statistics, interesting though they may be, cannot do.

Employment in the cultural sector

Before leaving the subject of empirical research on artists' labour markets, one more observation is in order: artists are a subsection of a wider category of cultural workers. With the growth of interest in the creative industries there has been a corresponding growth of interest in employment in the cultural sector, and, of course, artists are a part of that. The cultural sector employs far more workers from far more occupations than the people we have called artists, however. Even if we were to take a narrow definition of the 'high' arts and heritage, it would include far more 'ordinary' workers than 'artists'. For example, there are far more people working in a theatre than actors. Some,

---

[7] Throsby (1996a).

Box 12.5 US Bureau of Labor Statistics SOC and SIC

The US Bureau of Labor Statistics has this description of the occupation 'actor' (SOC 27–2011): 'Play(s) parts in stage, television, radio, video, or motion picture productions for entertainment, information, or instruction. Interpret(s) serious or comic role by speech, gesture, and body movement to entertain or inform audience. May dance and sing.'

For the category of industry, SIC 7922 has this description: 'Theatrical Producers (Except Motion Picture) and Miscellaneous Theatrical Services' includes 'Summer theaters, except dinner theaters' and 'Theatrical companies'; but it also includes 'Television programs (including commercials): live'.

Source: US Bureau of Labor Statistics.

even many, of these workers are highly skilled and specialised in theatre work but they could also use their general training to work in other sectors. It is equally the case, though, that stage actors can and do work in other types of arts work, such as film and television, in addition to working in the theatre.

If we want to know more precisely the correlation between artists' occupations and the type of work they do, it is necessary to use a classification system, such as that described in chapter 2 for classifying the cultural sector. The sector that an artist's work falls into can be classified by the Standard Industrial Classification. There is also a Standard Occupational Classification (SOC). The interesting question is the extent of overlap between SOC and SIC: if an actor is working in the theatre he or she would be under one SIC, and in film as another, though television and theatre belong to the same SIC! Box 12.5 shows these classifications and suggests some of the difficulties of arriving at a definitive description.

A major research report in the United Kingdom has also tackled the problem of matching SIC and SOC by disaggregating both and analysing the overlap. It distinguishes creative core specialists (the people we would tend to call artists) from non-creative ('humdrum') workers in the creative industries and, as a third group, creative specialists who are working outside the creative industries. This is an important step towards identifying the value added of artists and other creative specialists. It is based on the Labour Force Survey, into which, since it does not include self-employed workers, interpolations of their numbers had to be made based on census data. Average incomes are reported, which do not, however, take into account the problem of a skewed distribution of income.[8] The European Union has also struggled

---

[8] See Higgs, Cunningham and Bakhshi (2008).

with the classification problems of cultural workers for some time in an attempt to get reliable data on employment in the cultural industries through-out Europe.[9]

Manpower planning

Research by cultural economists has been undertaken for the purposes of trying to understand how artists' labour markets work and what motivates artistic supply. This is necessary for finding appropriate policy measures to stimulate the production of cultural goods and services. Some people would like to take these research findings further, however, and use the information to forecast artists' employment in the future and to ensure that there is sufficient supply of trained workers. Manpower planning has as its rationale that projections of the stock of labour in an occupation, the number of jobs and vacancies over a certain period and the schooling that existing workers have received can be combined to plan training programmes and places in formal educational establishments. It has been criticised by economists of education for many years as unrealistic and failing to understand the flexible nature of labour markets; to this cultural economists add an extra voice saying that none of these items has much meaning in artists' labour markets, which are even more flexible than those for many other occupations and industries. The problems of classifying artists, the ephemeral nature of 'jobs' in the arts and multiple job-holding, compounded by the fact that there is little evidence of a relation between training and 'success' in the creative industries, suggest that it is an impossible task to forecast the so-called 'manpower needs' of a cultural industry or sector.

In any event, in the face of oversupply in most arts occupations, there are unlikely to be shortages of artistic labour – though, as is frequently bemoaned, there is always a shortage of highly talented artists; all the same, it is doubtful if any amount of empirical research and forecasts would solve that problem!

Conclusion

This chapter has provided the empirical basis for many of the assertions in this book concerning artists' employment and occupations, earnings and other sources of income. In it, the value and difficulties of empirical research have

---

[9] See Eurostat (2007); there is no explanation of the data sources or how the data were gathered, however.

been expounded and some of its successes reported. In most countries, artists – meaning creative and performing artists and craftspeople – constitute only a small proportion of the workforce but they are vital to the creative industries, providing the content on which later stages of the chain of production depend. The many others working in these industries also depend upon the creativity of artists.

Research on artists' labour markets is not straightforward, however, and often entails the use of surveys to elicit the information that cultural economists need in order to understand artists' incentives, work patterns and careers. Understanding these factors is important for the economic health and growth of the cultural sector.

Intrinsic motivation to become and to work as an artist is believed to be strong, but it cannot be directly observed or measured and has to be inferred from artists' decisions about earnings and labour supply. It also leads to artists being easy to exploit, as Withers' estimates have shown. What is widely observed is that artists' supply behaviour suggests that they have a strong preference for working in the arts, despite the low earnings and longer hours of work, multiple job-holding, and so on. The chance of success, however small, is a great lure as well, especially to the young. Moreover, research has shown that those who give up and leave arts work do not suffer an 'earnings' penalty from having started out as artists.

Finally, it can be seen that everything in this and in the previous chapter relates to the supply side of the labour market for artists. This is because there have been no studies of the demand side. Employment data do not tell us what demand is because they do not relate the number of people employed or the hours of employment to the wage rate; nor does manpower planning have anything to do with demand in the economic sense. This failure is not peculiar to research on artists' labour markets, however, and the lack of empirical studies on the demand for labour of all kinds has been noted by labour economists. This is another area for research by cultural economists.

Further reading

This chapter deals with practical matters, and the best way to go into the issues more deeply is simply by reading studies by people who have had the experience of them! There are many such studies and you might check up on what is available in your country. I recommend the most recent of the Australian surveys, by Throsby and Hollister (2003), which can be downloaded from the Australia Council's research hub (www.australiacouncil.gov.au/Research). Equally, the survey and analysis by Alper and Wassall (2006) offers a comprehensive recent survey of empirical work by cultural economists on artists' labour markets with particular relevance to the United States. For the United Kingdom, the report by Higgs, Cunningham and Bakhshi (2008) provides much food for thought on the complexities of measuring 'creatives'' employment and incomes.

13 Economics of copyright

It is often argued that copyright is fundamental to creativity on the part of artists and other creators and to the creative industries. In fact, as we see in chapter 14, dependence on copyright is one of the ways in which the creative industries are categorised. Why, therefore, is copyright so important, and what are its effects on producers and consumers of cultural products? This chapter analyses these questions and considers the role of copyright law in markets in the cultural sector, concentrating on its economic rather than its legal aspects.

A brief history of copyright

Copyright is the creation of property rights for authors through statutory law; it gives them the exclusive right to control the use of their works and protects them from unauthorised copying; this means that anyone wanting to use the work must (with some exceptions) apply to the author or person (or organisation) who controls the right. Having these rights enables the author or creator in principle to obtain payment from anyone who wishes to copy his or her work. The first copyright law was enacted in England and had a distinctly commercial origin. The 1710 Statute of Anne[1] came about as a result of petitioning to parliament by booksellers and publishers who had lost the protection of the rights they had previously had as members of the Stationers' Company, the guild that controlled printing in earlier times. Although the statute made authors the first owners of copyright – 'for the Encouragement of Learned Men to Compose and Write useful Books' – it reflected previous practice in protecting the commercial interests of the publishers. It set the term of copyright at fourteen years with a possible

---

[1] The full text may be viewed at www.copyrighthistory.com/anne.html. The word 'copy' in this context means the 'master copy' or original, from which copies may be made.

renewal for a further fourteen years; therefore, the maximum duration of the copyright term was twenty-eight years from the date of creation of the work, after which the work (a book or map, for example) came into the public domain and could be freely copied. This effectively made the work a public good, because 'information goods' are non-rival and also non-excludable (as explained in chapter 2). Thus, conversely, copyright may be seen as a grant of monopoly that temporarily 'privatises' creative and information goods.

Throughout the late eighteenth century and the nineteenth century copyright and authors' rights came to be adopted in the national laws of many countries. Its scope was extended to include various works of art and music (and later film and broadcasts, and more recently to digital content on the internet) and its duration was also extended, with the term set in relation to the life of the author, so that now, in many developed countries, copyright lasts seventy years after the death of the author,[2] although the international standard laid down in the Berne Convention is fifty years. Although it is common to speak of 'copyright', copyright is in fact a concept of Anglo-Saxon law that is to be found in the United Kingdom, the United States, Australia, English-speaking Canada, New Zealand, India and the other countries that inherited that legal tradition. Countries with a civil law tradition have authors' rights that protect the 'moral rights' of the person of the author along with the so-called 'economic rights'; this applies in China, France, Germany, Italy, Japan, the Netherlands, Russia, Spain, French-speaking Canada and all the other countries in Europe, Africa and South America that have this legal framework.

These two traditions coexist in a world of international trade in cultural goods, and compromises have been made to achieve a workable international copyright regime. The first international agreement on harmonising copyright and authors' rights was the 1886 Berne Convention; negotiating international agreements is now the responsibility of the World Intellectual Property Organization, a United Nations agency, and there are also other international agreements that relate to copyright and world trade.[3] An international treaty with considerable significance for creators is the 1996 WIPO Copyright Treaty (WCT), discussed below. The process of harmonising authors' rights and copyright in national laws has also taken place (and continues to take place)

---

[2] Therefore, if an author or composer wrote a work (a book or musical composition) aged thirty and dies aged eighty, that work will have been in copyright for 120 years.

[3] See www.wipo.org. This website has a lot of useful information for learning about copyright and other intellectual property.

within the European Union, and copyright also features in NAFTA (the North American Free Trade Agreement).

Rights related to copyright

Alongside copyright are the related rights, or 'neighbouring' rights, as they are also called; these are the rights of performers, the producers of phonograms (sound recording makers) and broadcasting organisations. These rights are not authors' rights or copyright proper, although they are similar in many ways, and form part of the same law; one of the main differences is (or was – see below) that neighbouring rights are not exclusive rights and apply to the work from the date of its fixation, not to the life of its creator. In many cases, neighbouring rights owners have rights to remuneration only for the use of their works that is managed by collective rights management organisations or collecting societies, as explained later in this chapter. Related rights fall under their own international treaty, the Rome Convention of 1961, which has now been incorporated into and updated with the 1996 WIPO Performances and Phonograms Treaty (WPPT).

Other rights

There are some other rights that relate to creators that are not authors' or neighbouring rights, though they may be part of a country's intellectual property law. A leading example is the droit de suite, or artists' resale right, which is now harmonised throughout the European Union. It entitles visual artists to a percentage share of the resale price of their works of art when resold in public (usually in an auction). Another is the so-called 'exhibition right', which applies in some countries and requires publicly funded art galleries to pay a fee to artists whose work is displayed to the public in an exhibition for which an entry price is charged. For literary authors, there is the 'public lending right' or library compensation payment (again, not a right), which pays authors whose books are in public lending libraries for the use of their books. I return to these topics later in the chapter.

Copyright law and international treaties

The 1886 Berne Convention for the Protection of Literary and Artistic Works accorded the same protection to authors in all signatory countries.

Box 13.1 Literary and artistic works in the Berne Convention

Article 2 of the Berne Convention reads in part as follows:

The expression 'literary and artistic works' shall include every production in the literary, scientific and artistic domain, whatever may be the mode or form of its expression, such as books, pamphlets and other writings; lectures, addresses, sermons and other works of the same nature; dramatic or dramatico-musical works; choreographic works and entertainments in dumb show; musical compositions with or without words; cinematographic works to which are assimilated works expressed by a process analogous to cinematography; works of drawing, painting, architecture, sculpture, engraving and lithography; photographic works, to which are assimilated works expressed by a process analogous to photography; works of applied art; illustrations, maps, plans, sketches and three-dimensional works relative to geography, topography, architecture or science. Translations, adaptations, arrangements of music and other alterations of a literary or artistic work shall be protected as original works without prejudice to the copyright in the original work. Collections of literary or artistic works such as encyclopaedias and anthologies which, by reason of the selection and arrangement of their contents, constitute intellectual creations shall be protected as such, without prejudice to the copyright in each of the works forming part of such collections.

Source: WIPO (2000: 5).

This was an important step in the globalisation of protection offered by copyright law, because, previously, nationals had been protected only in their own countries and their works could be (and frequently were) 'pirated' (used without the authorisation of the proprietor) in other countries. At one time the Scots pirated books published in England and American publishers pirated British books; there is nothing new about copyright piracy! The Berne Convention has been updated eight times (most recently in 1979) in order to keep up with new technologies for creating and copying works of art and literature (sound recording, film, radio, TV, video, photocopying, and so on). Box 13.1 has a list of works now protected under the Berne Convention.

The Berne Convention also deals with the various rights that constitute copyright: publication and reproduction rights; the public performance right; broadcasting rights; and the right to control derivative works, such as translations into other languages, or adaptations, for example of a novel into a screenplay. As with the scope of copyrightable works, these rights also have had to be adapted to new technologies. The 1996 WIPO Copyright Treaty specifically addressed itself to the internet as a means of producing and distributing copyrightable works. It extended the Berne concept of protected works to include computer programmes and compilations of data or other material ('databases') and introduced new rights – the right of distribution, the right of rental and the right of communication to the public – that reflect the different ways in which use is made of copyright material on the internet and the business models that are used in internet trade, such as rental and licensing instead of sale. The right of communication to the public is the right to authorise any communication to the public, by wire or wireless means, including 'the making available to the public of works in a way that the members of the public may access the work from a place and at a time individually chosen by them'. The quoted expression in particular applies to on-demand, interactive communication through the internet and is often known for short as the 'making available right'.[4]

The Rome Convention has also been updated to deal with changes brought about by the internet, and, along with the WCT, there is the 1996 WIPO Performances and Phonograms Treaty. Together these treaties are known as the WIPO 'internet treaties'. The WPPT gives new individual exclusive rights to performers for the rights of reproduction, distribution, rental and making available in connection with their works. Performers therefore have rights that are now very close to those of authors. They last for fifty years from the date of the fixation of the performance, however, and are not linked to the life of the performer as copyright is to the life of the author. Under the WPPT, audio performers (musicians, singers and actors for audio media, but not audio-visual media, such as film and TV) have also been awarded moral rights (discussed later in this chapter). The United States has adopted the WPPT (though it has not signed the Rome Convention), thus now giving US performers rights in digital works; in Europe and Japan, performers had rights under the Rome Convention prior to signing the WPPT.

Limitations and exceptions to copyright law

For certain purposes, law-makers have limited the exclusive right of authors to control the use of their works and made exceptions that mean users can copy works in copyright without seeking the permission of the author or copyright holder and without payment. In legal terms these are called 'exceptions and limitations' to copyright, and they are familiar to most people because they

---

[4] See www.wipo.int/treaties/en/ip/wct/trtdocs_wo033.html.

enable private individuals to use works for educational and research purposes, for example. Under what is known as 'fair use' in US law, individuals may copy 'reasonable' amounts of the work of others without authorisation (where what is reasonable may have to be decided in court); in European law, exceptions are usually spelled out more precisely. In the United Kingdom, however, at the time of writing, there is no exception for private copying (though it is expected that this situation will change). It is these exceptions and limitations that have proved ambiguous in relation to downloading copyright material from the internet, because national laws differ and what is permitted in one country may not be so in another. This topic is discussed in chapters 15 and 16 in the context of recorded music and film.

Technological protection measures and digital rights management

The WIPO internet treaties also mandated the introduction of technological protection measures (TPMs) and digital rights management (DRM) into national copyright law, requiring signatory countries[5] to include their protection as part of copyright law. The intention is that economic rights can be enforced through technological means to prevent the unauthorised use of copyright material, and these arguments have been strongly made by rights holders (especially the highly organised music, film and computer software industry bodies) using data on piracy to push home their claims. The introduction of TPMs and DRM has been controversial, in part because these technologies can prevent the exercise of limitations and exceptions to copyright (and fair use and fair dealing) or even 'lock up' works in the public domain if they are bundled with copyright works, but also because there is no international technological standard for them. Some commentators have condemned the emphasis on DRM and TPMs in copyright law and disputed the economic arguments put forward in their defence (see below). As may be seen in the chapters on the music, film and publishing industries, however, DRM has mostly been dropped as a means of protecting copyright works, though it is used as a means of administering payments and tracking usage, including by copyright collecting societies, as explained later in the chapter. The Creative Commons and Open Source movements in particular have campaigned for freer legal arrangements to be made to encourage creativity and access through flexible licensing.[6]

---

[5] The European Union has signed these international treaties on behalf of all its members and then issued directives to each state to ensure that its national law conforms to the treaty terms.

[6] See http://creativecommons.org and www.opensource.org.

Works-made-for-hire

One of the exceptions to the rule in copyright law that the creator is granted copyright is the US 'works-made-for-hire' doctrine, which has equivalent provision in copyright law in other countries. It means that artists or other creators who are employed and directed to produce copyright works by the employer in the course of their employment are not granted copyright in these works; instead, the copyright belongs to the employer. This is justified on the grounds that the entrepreneur has invested in the wage paid to the worker and in the finance of the creation and marketing of the work(s); furthermore, if several people were to own a copyright in the same work, there could be disagreement and hold-ups about how to exploit it that would not be in the public interest of having access to works. Most of the people working on films or making music DVDs and artwork for record sleeves are hired, though film directors have copyright.[7] This is a specialised topic, and it is an important one for cultural economics because it relates to artists' labour markets; disputes can arise easily, since artists' contracts are often not entirely clear-cut as to employment status and there is ambiguity about the short-term contracts that prevail in artists' labour markets. This is a topic on which more research is needed in cultural economics; for example, we do not know what proportion of copyright works are works-made-for-hire rather than belonging to the artist.

There is another aspect to works-made-for hire: the so-called 1998 Sonny Bono Copyright Term Extension Act (CTEA) in the United States extended copyright from seventy-five to ninety-five years after publication for works of corporate authorship made after 1978 (that is, works-made-for hire) and to 120 years after creation, whichever is the earlier. This act conveniently extended copyright on Mickey Mouse, and the CTEA is sometimes pejoratively called the Mickey Mouse Protection Act. The CTEA has been strongly opposed in the United States, by leading economists[8] as well as lawyers, and has led to 'copycat' extensions (no pun intended!) in the European Union and elsewhere (where it has also been opposed by many law professors and

---

[7] See www.copyright.gov/circs/circ09.pdf for the law in the United States (remember that each country has its own law!).

[8] See the brief of George Akerlof *et al.* as Amici Curiae in Support of Petitioners at 12, *Eldred v. Ashcroft*, 537 US 186 (2003) (no. 01–618). The signatories to the amicus brief were George Akerlof, Kenneth Arrow, Timothy Bresnahan, James Buchanan, Ronald Coase, Linda Cohen, Milton Friedman, Jerry Green, Robert Hahn, Thomas Hazlett, C. Scott Hemphill, Robert Litan, Roger Noll, Richard Schmalensee, Steven Shavell, Hal Varian and Richard Zeckhauser, five of whom are Nobel-Prize-winners in economics. It is available at www.copyright.gov/docs/eldredd1.pdf.

economists). The grounds on which economists have opposed the CTEA is that it does nothing to increase the incentive to produce creative works but increases the profits of the copyright owners and reduces access by consumers. These arguments are fundamental to the economic rationale for copyright, to which we now turn.

Copyright as an economic incentive

Copyright law is a clever system for financing the creation of works of art, literature, music and the rest through the market: by granting exclusive property rights to creators it makes it possible for them to charge for the use of their work, and this gives them an economic incentive to create. In the inimitable words of the English lawyer and politician Macaulay in 1841 (see box 13.2): '[Copyright] is a tax on readers for the purpose of giving a bounty to writers.' This is indeed the basic economic principle of copyright law: it provides an incentive to creativity through the higher price that the grant of copyright protection makes possible; the 'monopoly' revenues of the sales of works of art and literature are thus the reward for creating them. The copyright monopoly is relatively weak, however, because it protects the copying of works but not the idea behind them; there is no monopoly on writing a sonnet, for instance, and anyone doing so has copyright in their sonnet; all copyright prevents is copying someone else's sonnet. This is in contrast to a patent that does protect the idea and confers to the holder an economic monopoly in the sense of a sole supplier of a good or service.[9] In economic terms, the effect of

Box 13.2 Thomas Babington Macaulay on copyright

Copyright is a monopoly and produces all the effects which the general voice of mankind attributes to monopoly... [T]he effect of a monopoly is to make articles scarce, to make them dear, and to make them bad... It is good that authors be remunerated; and the least exceptional way of remunerating them is by a monopoly. Yet monopoly is an evil; for the sake of good, we must submit to evil; but the evil ought not to last a day longer than is necessary for the purpose of securing the good. [...]

The principle of copyright is this. It is a tax on readers for the purpose of giving a bounty to writers. [...] I admit, however, the necessity of giving a bounty to genius and learning.

Source: Speech delivered in the House of Commons, 5 February 1841.

---

[9] There are many differences between copyright and patents in terms of their economic effects, and they are not always well understood. For one thing, patents have to be applied for and are more likely to cover

copyright is more like monopolistic competition: barriers to entry are low and consumers can choose between similar products, which, however, are not homogeneous.

Copyright finances the creation of works of art by charging users for the use they make of those works – the more popular the work, the greater the income it generates for the author and publisher. The higher the price and the more copies that are sold or licensed, moreover, the greater the royalty earnings are for the copyright holders. Though this and other aspects of the monopoly power of copyright holders are often deplored, that is precisely how the system is supposed to work, as Macaulay very well understood! Although in the cultural sector we are much more familiar with the use of subsidy by taxpayers to finance artistic production, it can be argued that copyright has advantages as a method of providing an incentive to create over that of public subsidy by taxpayers; taxpayers have no choice how much is spent on the arts except through the ballot box, whereas copyright law allows users to finance their chosen cultural products by paying for them.

Economics of copying

One way of understanding the economic case for copyright is to consider the counterfactual situation: what would happen without statutory property rights and their protection by copyright law? The explanation can be found in the economics of copying and in information economics. Most, perhaps all, copyright works have an economic feature in common: the fixed cost of producing them is high relative to the marginal cost of reproducing them. Quite what that ratio is depends upon the type of work and the technology of copying. Before the invention of the printing press, books had to be copied by hand, and the cost of copying came close to the cost of creating the book (manuscript) in the first place; with printing, though, once the type had been set up, multiple copies could be produced much more cheaply with economies of scale. Nowadays, a book is created in digital form and can be copied for just the marginal cost of the paper and ink and the use of the computer and printer (if it is reproduced in paper form, but it could also be read on a screen or e-book). The marginal costs of producing copies of a book have fallen but the fixed costs of authoring the book are probably more or less the same as they always were.

production processes, whereas copyright is automatically conferred to authors of works of art and literature, as explained above.

Competition between creator and copier

The economic rationale for copyright can be thought of in terms of the competition between the creator of a work and the copier and the implications that competition would have for the economic incentive to create. While the creator invests in the fixed cost of producing the work in the first place, as well as in the marginal cost of producing subsequent copies for the market, the copier has only the marginal costs of making copies; the author would not receive a royalty, and therefore the incentive to create would be reduced and fewer creative works would be produced. The creator needs to set a price and sell a sufficient number of copies to cover the fixed cost, whereas the copier has lower fixed costs (if any) but the same marginal costs and so can undersell the creator; therefore, the copier could capture the market by free-riding on the creator's investment. Once the work is in a format that can be copied costlessly it is essentially a public good, and its use cannot be controlled by the creator. Copyright therefore enables the creator to protect the investment in developing the work by awarding an exclusive statutory property right, thus providing an incentive to make that investment in creating the work. By charging a price above the marginal cost, the publisher is better able to recoup the fixed costs and pay a share to the author, thus providing an economic incentive, and that justifies granting the exclusive right of copyright. The same principles apply to every creative industry, because they all have high fixed costs and relatively low or very low marginal costs and they produce with increasing returns to scale.

The impact of digital production

Before the advent of digitalisation or production in digital format, there were two sources of protection for authors via the market: first, copies were of inferior quality to the 'original'; and, second, the original creator or publisher who was first to market had the advantage. With regard to the first point, copies were not perfect and therefore they commanded a lower price in the marketplace; some consumers preferred the original, and that offered some protection to the creator, even without copyright law. On the second point, being first to market – known as 'first-mover advantage' – gave the creator 'lead time' before the copier could copy a work and compete with the producer of the original. This led some economists to believe that market forces can protect the creator and, moreover, since copyright was not needed as an incentive, it merely raised the price to consumers. This point of view continued to be held by many economists even when copying devices (cassette recorders, VCRs, photocopiers, and so on) began to be accessible to consumers.

The digital production of works in many media (music, film, games, software, radio and TV programmes), which enables 'clones' to be made with no loss of quality, has destroyed the first of these arguments, because on quality grounds there is no reason to prefer the 'original' to a 'copy'; moreover, lead time is now seconds, not months or years. Once a work has got on to the internet it can be downloaded and stored for any number of copiers' use, now and in the future, thus turning it effectively into a public good. The justification for copyright is therefore now seen as 'privatising' what have effectively become 'public' goods (because they are non-rival in digital form and non-excludable unless there is some TPM) in order to preserve the incentive to the creator and avoid market failure. Some economists still oppose copyright, however (see 'Alternatives to copyright' later in the chapter), because they believe that digitisation benefits business models such as price discrimination and product bundling (putting several products together and charging a single price, such as a cable television package of programmes). If this is so, then copyright protection inhibits the development of market solutions to the protection of works of art and the like.

What all economists agree on is that copyright is a trade-off between the benefits of the incentive to the creation of works of art and the costs it imposes on users; these costs are not just higher prices, as discussed above, but, more fundamentally, what have been called costs of creation.

The cost of creation

Analysing copyright with the focus on the cost of creation was introduced by William Landes and Richard Posner, who are regarded as the leading writers on the law and economics of copyright; Landes is Professor of Law and Economics at the Law School of the University of Chicago, where Posner is also a senior lecturer as well as being a judge on the United States Court of Appeals for the Seventh Circuit in Chicago. In their 1989 article, they analyse the trade-off between the advantages and disadvantages of copyright and the appropriate strength of its protection in terms of the cost of creation. Copyright raises the cost of creation to later creators, who build on previous work and need to trace authors and other copyright holders (including heirs, since copyright can be inherited and can last seventy years after the death of the author) in order to check for possible infringement or to seek permission for some transformative use, such as translation, the use of excerpts, sampling in music, collages, appropriation art, and so on. These transaction costs of search and tracing – the cost of creation – have to be borne by later creators, and copyright is therefore a disincentive to creativity as well as an incentive. This trade-off depends upon the strength of copyright, its duration and the exceptions and limitations to it (fair use in the United States): the shorter the duration and the more exceptions there are, the lower the cost of creation.

In later work, Landes and Posner (2002) have come to the conclusion that copyright, which has always been a temporary monopoly, even though its duration has lengthened over the years, should become perpetual and renewable. This is a fundamental departure both from their own previous position on copyright and from the legal doctrine of copyright. They reached this conclusion following the lobbying of the US Congress to enact the Sonny Bono CTEA to copyright that introduced the seventy-year term for authors and the ninety-five years for works-made-for-hire (see above). They believe that the possibility of getting changes to copyright law through 'rent-seeking' – lobbying politicians for potential gains to give them an advantage in the market – can be stopped only by a measure as drastic as this. They propose a return to the registration of copyrights (which was the system in the United States until 1976 but which does not exist in other countries where copyright is automatic), with the copyright owner having the right to renew the copyright after a certain period. Then, like trademarks, only copyrights that are maintained by re-registration and reinvestment would be extended (and could become perpetual) and the vast majority of copyright works, which have no economic value, would not be re-registered and would then fall into the public domain, thus reducing the costs of creation.

This is one proposal for the reform of copyright, but there are now many as lawyers, economists and other commentators consider the role of copyright in the 'digital era'. I return to this theme later.

Moral rights as an economic incentive

Moral rights have been part of European authors' rights since their inception and they were introduced into the Berne Convention in 1928; they were not an aspect of the Anglo-Saxon copyright in the United States or the United Kingdom, however. The moral rights include the right to attribution (for example, being named as the artist) and integrity (for example, the artist's right to control changes to his or her work). In the United States, the Visual Artists Rights Act of 1990 gave artists moral rights; these rights do not apply to works-made-for-hire, nor do they continue after the death of the artist (as they do in European law). In Europe, moral rights cannot be waived, as they can in the United States. Under the WPPT, audio performers (musicians, singers and actors for audio media, but not audio-visual media, such as film and TV) are awarded moral rights.

The economic aspect of what are regarded as non-economic rights is an interesting question; the right of attribution is regarded by economists as important because it is a source of information or certification for consumers; knowing who the artist is, and therefore the stock of works on which his or her reputation is built, provides that information, and the same type of argument applies to the right of integrity. Furthermore, moral rights can also have economic value, as they allow the possibility of 'hold-up' by the artist, which could be used to increase his or her bargaining power; moral rights have an incentive effect for artistic production because they encourage the artistic recognition of status and professionalism and, as suggested in chapter 11, offer intrinsic motivation to supply works of art.

Copyright in the marketplace

Copyright protects the intangible creative content (the copyrightable work) that is combined with other inputs into a product, a good or a service that can be delivered to the market. These goods and services may be used in a variety of ways in primary and secondary markets alike, however, and they create value in both. Copyright holders, who may be the artists who created the work or publishers and others who exploit them in the marketplace, are entitled to payment for all the uses, and this requires some complex arrangements for collecting royalties and other payments. These topics are explored in this section.

The value of rights

As noted earlier in this chapter, copyright is not one particular right but consists of many rights in many media – the rights of reproduction, distribution, public performance, and so on – and, in any given setting, they will have very different economic value; a book that is turned into a film may earn the author far more from the screen rights than he or she would earn from royalties on sales. Moreover, the same work may be used in several media; for example, the film of the book may become a DVD, be shown on television and lead to the book being read on radio. Payment is due to the author or copyright holder for every use, each of which takes place in a different market and has different value. In view of this, it is not possible to say in general whether copyright is more valuable in the primary market or the secondary market.

Furthermore, many cultural products are complex and involve a combination of several works by different creators. An example is a sound recording, say a DVD that consists of a musical composition, the lyrics of songs, performances by principal artists and backing artists (musicians, singers, dancers), sound recording, film direction, photography and artwork. Each of these is a separate copyright work, and they combine to form another copyright work with a royalty payable for each use. Therefore, royalty contracts have to be made with each contributing creator (unless there is a works-made-for-hire contract). Complex cultural products have correspondingly complex copyright arrangements. Nevertheless, it is important to understand the mechanisms by which this value is created and transmitted to the creators.

Primary markets

Generally speaking, the primary market is the market in which the product containing the copyright work is sold to the consumer. Chapters 15 to 18 look at markets for the different goods and services, which, with digital delivery, may be real or virtual. Goods are sold at a price or a fee is paid for licences for use on electronic devices. In such markets, authors typically have a royalty contract with the publisher (including in this term any type of creative industry that markets content – record labels, broadcasters, film studios, and the rest, besides literary and music publishers).

The royalty contract

The royalty agreed in the contract between an author and a publisher is a percentage of market price of the work (typically 10 to 15 per cent), and so the author's earnings from his or her work depend on revenues from the sale of the product. As we see in more detail from the analysis of contracts in the creative industries (chapter 14), the purpose of the contract is to set out an agreement on what each party to it is expected to do and to offer terms that give each party the incentive to comply and not to 'cheat'. Thus revenue, not profit, is the key variable in the royalty contract: if the contract were based on profits (as one might well think the fairest deal to be) the publisher would have an incentive to increase the costs of production, and, anyway, it would be difficult for the author to verify profits. Therefore the author wants the publisher to market the book as well as possible and to obtain maximum revenues. As Arnold Plant demonstrated many years ago, though, the author and the publisher would aim for a different price (see box 13.3). One way that

Box 13.3 Arnold Plant and the economic aspects of copyright on books

Professor Sir Arnold Plant (1918–72), Sir Ernst Cassel Professor of Commerce at the University of London, held his chair at the London School of Economics until his retirement in 1965. He appears to have been the first economist to analyse the economics of copyright with his 1934 article 'The economic aspects of copyright in books', in which he introduced a number of concepts that are now current in economic thinking on copyright, such as lead time and the use of price discrimination – what we would now call business models; he was truly in advance of his time. Though his economic analysis remains as valid as ever, however, UK copyright law (the 1911 Copyright Act) has changed in certain features since he wrote, and this makes some of his conclusions outdated; inevitably, moreover, the technologies he was concerned with, in particular the need to typeset books, are now defunct.

Plant was a fierce opponent of copyright and believed that market solutions could be found that rendered it unnecessary (a point on which he specifically disagreed with Macaulay). Furthermore, he believed that copyright caused what we would now call 'moral hazard', by encouraging the publication of sub-marginal books that would not succeed on the market were it not for the protection of copyright enabling the publisher to charge a higher than competitive price.

One of his analytical points in particular has strong resonance today: that there is a conflict of interest between the author and the publisher over the price that it is in their respective interests to charge. The author, whose royalty payment depends on the sales revenue, would like the price of the book to be that which maximises revenues, whereas the publisher opts for the profit-maximising price. The two would coincide if costs were constant but if costs rise with the number of copies produced, as Plant assumed they do (and he based this on empirical evidence of publishing costs), the profit-maximising output is lower than the revenue-maximising output. Plant's insight is especially interesting, because present-day economic analysis of copyright generally assumes a 'harmony of interest' between author and publisher – that is, between the parties to a royalty contract – whereas Plant anticipated the conflict of interest embodied in the principal–agent problem.

Source: Plant (1934).

the author can try to ensure that the publisher does a good job (the principal–agent problem facing the author) is to get an advance on royalties, so that the publisher has to earn at least that amount back in sales.

Royalties and risk-taking

The royalty contract ties the author/creator and the publisher/producer into a risk-sharing situation. Why do artists great and small go in for sharing the risk – why not accept a buyout on the rights, take an upfront payment and put it in the bank? In principle, a 'spot' price can be computed as the discounted present value of all future royalties over the term of the copyright, but artists and their advisers rarely prefer to take that option.[10] The main reason is likely to be because 'nobody knows' how successful a work will be, but then, in principle, some will be overpaid and some underpaid. It seems that artists overestimate their chances of success and are more optimistic than the 'humdrum' people working in the industry as accountants and so on, and therefore prefer to take the risk.

One of the things that the author generally has no control over is deletion from the catalogue of his or her work by the publisher. When that happens the author or creator earns nothing from royalties – no sales, no revenue on which the royalty contract is based. Authors in some countries have the right to regain the rights they assigned to the publisher but, in most cases, the market for the work has been exhausted. In fact, the vast majority of works in copyright no longer have any market value after their first release or publication and are likely to be no longer available on the market. Of course, there are a few exceptions; works that were no longer in the catalogue can have a late revival and, for one reason or another, can suddenly become valuable again. The opposite can also happen, that works slowly build up in popularity, and, though they may not earn their creator much, the heirs benefit from the royalties. This is often the case with 'classical' musical compositions that seem very difficult to perform when first created but later become more familiar and become part of the repertoire.

Secondary markets

Secondary markets exist for cultural products, meaning that the item is used for other purposes besides sale to the final consumer. An example is the public performance of sound recordings in the many venues that this takes place, such as radio and TV broadcasts, aircraft, discos, hotels and restaurants, shops and shopping malls, sports halls and many more besides. Secondary use may be made of other types of works: literary and artistic works may be photocopied or scanned, and they may appear in films or TV programmes; broadcasts, especially in digital form, can be retransmitted on faraway television by cable companies or via the internet; and so on. These are circumstances in which a royalty contract for the author is not possible, either because the transaction costs would be very high and would probably exceed the value of

[10] On this point, see the Akerlof *et al.* brief, at www.copyright.gov/docs/eldredd1.pdf.

the use to the user or because there is no way that contact can be made between the parties concerned. Copyright holders – artists, authors, publishers, sound recording makers, broadcasters, and the rest – need some arrangement for collecting the royalties due to them for these secondary uses.

Some uses, particularly those for which there are a large number of users and the individual payment is small (e.g. photocopying), are covered by 'compulsory licences' with a right to remuneration for the copyright holder. Compulsory licences are a way of reducing transaction costs and enabling markets to exploit secondary use and thereby gain greater revenues from the product. They are essentially a waiver of the exclusive right permitting certain secondary uses as long as 'equitable remuneration' is paid by users. The term 'equitable remuneration' means that a reasonable amount of money is paid to the copyright holders of the relevant works. So, in the example of the sound recording mentioned above, a radio station playing a sound recording need not obtain authorisation to do so but must pay equitable remuneration to the composer, the performers and the sound recording maker (the record label).

These and other compensatory payments, such as 'blank tape levies' on media for copying, are administered and managed by organisations that specialise in collective rights management. These are the copyright collecting societies, and they enable rights holders to collect the reward due to them for the use of copyright works in secondary markets.

Copyright collecting societies

Copyright collecting societies go under several names: WIPO calls them collective management organisations (see box 13.4), others call them collective rights organisations and they are also called collecting societies for short. They are membership organisations that manage specific rights on behalf of their members, who are often both the authors or performers and the publishers in a particular field – for example, composers, songwriters and publishers are members of performing rights societies. Collecting societies usually specialise in particular bundles of rights, such as the public performance of sound recordings or photocopying, on behalf of copyright holders in one country (since copyright is national law and applies in the national territory). Collecting societies are mostly private, non-profit organisations regulated by the national government or by a court, although, in some countries, a collecting society may be part of the state bureaucracy. In many situations, it is only through a collecting society that neighbouring rights holders, such as musical

Box 13.4 Collective rights management

Collective management organisations most commonly take care of the following rights:
- the right of public performance (music played or performed in discotheques, restaurants and other public places);
- the right of broadcasting (live and recorded performances on radio and television);
- the mechanical reproduction rights in musical works (the reproduction of works in CDs, tapes, vinyl records, cassettes, minidiscs or other forms of recordings);
- the performing rights in dramatic works (theatre plays);
- the right of reprographic reproduction of literary and musical works (photocopying); and
- related rights (the rights of performers and producers of phonograms to obtain remuneration for broadcasting or the communication to the public of phonograms).

How does collective management work?

There are various kinds of collective management organisation or groups of such organisations, depending on the category of works involved (music, dramatic works, 'multimedia' productions, etc.) that will collectively manage different kinds of right.

'Traditional' collective management organisations, acting on behalf of their members, negotiate rates and terms of use with users, issue licences authorising uses, and collect and distribute royalties. The individual owner of rights does not become directly involved in any of these steps.

Source: www.wipo.int/about-ip/en/about_collective_mngt.html#P46_4989
(accessed 29 December 2008).

performers, sound recording makers and broadcasters, can obtain their remuneration, and revenues from levies on blank copying media, such as CDs, and taxes on computers that are remuneration for downloading music and other copyright material are paid to collecting societies for distribution (discussed later in this chapter).

Administration fees

Collecting societies deal with the licensing of members' rights to users, for which they collect fees and distribute the revenues to the rights holders based on the use made of their works; they also monitor the use made of their members' works. The collecting society charges members a fee for administering the rights (usually a percentage of the share of revenues distributed to them), and these fees can be a matter of concern on account of the monopoly the collecting society has of rights administration. In a number of countries, collecting societies also make a 'cultural deduction' of around 10 per cent that is used for communal purposes, such as training young artists or supporting older members. The cultural deduction is a source of discontent on the part of some members (though collecting societies are mostly self-governing, private membership organisations), and this has led to concern on the part of governments.

International co-operation between collecting societies

As copyright is territorial, but trade in copyright material is international, national collecting societies make mutual agreements with other national societies to perform the same functions for their members; thus a Canadian singer is a member of a Canadian collecting society that has an agreement with all other collecting societies worldwide that deal with the same bundle of rights. Then, when his or her work is played on the radio in, say, Denmark, the Danish collecting society will get the information from the radio station and co-ordinate with the Canadian collecting society; eventually, the Canadian singer is paid something for the Danish performance (minus the administration fee in both national organisations). With this arrangement, a user, such as a radio station, can obtain a licence that authorises the use not only of the 'national' catalogue of works but of an international one belonging to the members of all the collecting societies that have collaborative agreements. Without collecting societies, therefore, legal use would not be possible in some markets and, as the saying goes, the 'rights could not be cleared'. Collective rights management and the societies that organise it are therefore vital to the exploitation of copyright material and to enabling copyright holders to receive payment for the use of their work.

Blanket licensing

One of the features of collecting societies that has interested economists is that of blanket licensing, whereby an entire repertoire comprising all the works by every member of the organisation is included in a single licence by a national collecting society; as explained above, through international mutual agreements, this is tantamount to a worldwide licence. The licence fee is negotiated for all the different users, usually via their trade association; so, the association of all commercial radio stations in a country negotiates with the collecting society and they agree a tariff that depends upon their audience, measured by time or in terms of their commercial revenues. Box 13.5 shows some sample tariffs to be found on the website of SOCAN – the Society of Composers, Authors and Music Publishers of Canada – which manages their performing rights. These tariffs have had to be approved by the Copyright Board of

Box 13.5 Selected tariffs of SOCAN approved by the Copyright Board of Canada, as advertised in 2008

Description	Licence fees
Commercial radio	Monthly fee: 1.5 per cent of music station's advertising revenues for stations where SOCAN's repertoire is broadcast less than 20 per cent of broadcast time. For any other music station, 3.2 per cent on its first C$1.25 million of annual revenues and 4.4 per cent on the rest.
Commercial television	Monthly fee: 1.9 per cent of station's gross income.
Popular music concerts	Fee per concert: (a) when admission is charged: 3 per cent of gross receipts from ticket sales, exclusive of sales and amusement taxes (minimum C$20.00 per concert); (b) when no admission is charged: 3 per cent of fees paid to singers, musicians, dancers, conductors and other performing artists (minimum C$20.00 per concert).
Exhibitions and fairs	Fee based on total attendance: (a) up to 75,000 persons: from C$12.81 to C$64.31 per day; (b) attendance in excess of 75,000: (i) for the first 100,000 persons: C$1.07 per person; (ii) for the next 100,000 persons: C$0.47 per person; (iii) for the next 300,000 persons: C$0.35 per person; (iv) all additional persons: C$0.26 per person.
Motion picture theatres	Annual fee: C$1.17 per seat; minimum fee of C$117.00 per year.
Circuses, ice shows, firework displays, sound and light shows and similar events	Fee per event: 1.6 per cent of gross ticket sales, exclusive of sales and amusement taxes (minimum fee of C$61.85).
Aircraft	Fee per quarter, based on seating capacity: (a) take-off and landing music: ranging from C$40.50 to C$82.50 per aircraft;

	(b) in-flight music: ranging from C$162.00 to C$330.00 per aircraft.
Ringtones	In 2003 to 2005 6 per cent of the price paid by the subscriber for the ringtone, net of any network usage fees, subject to a minimum royalty of C$0.06 each time a ringtone is supplied in 2004 or 2005.
	In 2003, notwithstanding the previous paragraph, royalty payable for any quarter not to exceed C$7,500 per licensee.

Source: www.socan.ca/jsp/en/resources/tariffs.jsp (accessed 29 December 2008).

Canada. It can be seen from these sample tariffs that the underlying principle is to capture the value that copyright works add to the commercial undertaking and/or the number of people who have access to the works.

Distribution of licence fee revenue

Having collected the revenues for all uses, both in the domestic and foreign markets, the collecting society then distributes them to members on the basis of the use made of their works. This is done in various ways according to the type of work: for example, for sound recordings, a playlist for music is obtained from licensees (e.g. radio stations); for photocopying, it is based on a sampling of titles used, for instance, in university libraries. Thus authors and artists whose works are the most popular will receive a higher payment based on the greater use of their works. Blanket licensing has been criticised for the fact that all members receive the same per unit payment however much their work is rated by consumers, though economic logic would suggest that consumers have greater willingness to pay for popular artists and works. On the other hand, it is widely recognised that the system reduces transaction costs both to users and to creators to the lowest possible, assuming that the collecting society is efficiently run and well managed. This may not always be true, however, and the fact that, in most cases, the collecting society has a monopoly in its national territory for the bundle of rights it manages gives it less incentive to operate efficiently than if there were some competition. One source of competition is the possibility of individual rights management using DRM backed up by TPMs, and that is what the WCT and the WPPT, referred to at the beginning of the chapter, now seek to encourage. At the time of writing (early 2008) there was considerable controversy in the European Union about the efficiency of collecting societies, with the European Commission strongly promoting DRM and looking to introduce competition.

Natural monopoly of the collecting societies

The very considerable savings of transaction costs achieved by the use of blanket licensing by a single national collecting society have led to the collecting societies being characterised as natural monopolies by economists. As readers will recall, a natural monopoly is the situation when a sole supplier – in this case, of the services of managing copyright authorisation – benefits from increasing returns to scale with consequent ever-decreasing average costs and with low marginal costs. Any competitor would have difficulty entering (contesting) such a market, because his or her costs would be higher and he or she would have to charge a higher price. Therefore economists believe, in general, that a natural monopoly should not be forced to compete but, instead, should be regulated so as to gain the benefits of low costs and prices and to prevent it from exploiting its market power.

In the case of collecting societies, they have databases of information on both users and copyright holders that have taken a considerable investment to compile and manage. Moreover, the natural monopoly (which is an economic phenomenon of markets) is often bolstered in this particular case by the state that confers a statutory grant of monopoly to the collecting society, or at least tacitly accepts it; thus natural monopolies are also national monopolies, and therefore are not contestable. The benefits of the natural monopoly of rights administration, if properly regulated, seem likely to outweigh those of competition. Competition would probably increase the licence fees charged by the superstar creators and performers and raise transaction costs for users. DRM may challenge these monopolies, but the reality is still that collecting societies have advantages in the market, and it may well be that it would be very difficult for individual creators to administer their own rights and collect what is due to them without collecting societies.

Artists' earnings from copyright

Artists and other content creators receive copyright income from the royalties from sales and licence fees in the primary market and from remuneration and other sources in the secondary markets, typically via the collecting societies. Great play is made by the proponents of copyright of the value of copyright to creators and to creativity, and, as cultural economists, we wish to test these claims by looking at empirical evidence of the copyright earnings of individual creators.

It is clear from the intention of copyright law, and especially of authors' rights, that it is intended to confer benefit on creators. This is frequently invoked in claims in support of the WIPO internet treaties and in much of the material put out by stakeholder organisations in the cultural sector. The considerable hype surrounding the creative industries emphasises the role of copyright and its support for authors and performers. Authors' and performers' organisations also subscribe to this stance. There is almost no systematic evidence that proves this, however, and what evidence there is is consistent with the other data on artists' earnings – that the top superstars benefit considerably from royalty and remuneration income but the 'ordinary' artist does not.

One of the few studies of copyright earnings is by Martin Kretschmer and Philip Hardwick (2007), who compared the total earnings, earnings from writing (fees and royalties) and earnings from the respective collecting societies (VG Wort, the German collecting society that deals with the photocopying and library compensation remuneration of writers in Germany, and the Authors' Licensing and Collecting Society (ALCS), its equivalent in the United Kingdom). The German figures are shown in box 13.6; they show that the median ('typical') income from the collecting society source is relatively small; the difference between the mean (average) income and the median shows that there are a few respondents with high incomes while the majority have

Box 13.6 Earnings of German authors, 2005

Total writing income

	All	Male	Female
Mean (€)	19,368	20,072	18,092
Median (€)	12,000	12,000	10,000

Total VG Wort (collecting society) income

	All	Male	Female
Mean (€)	1,544	1,673	1,325
Median (€)	563	1,000	488

Source: Adapted from Kretschmer and Hardwick (2007: tables 8.3 and 8.4).

relatively low incomes. This study also reviews all the work on artists' earnings from copyright via collecting societies and other surveys of artists' incomes from various sources.

Droit de suite

The artists' resale right or droit de suite is a means of enabling visual artists to share in any increase (but not decrease) in the price of their works when they are resold on the secondary market. A percentage (on a sliding scale according to the resale price) of the resale price of a work of art that the owner gets when the work is sold on, usually in a public sale, is paid to the artist. Though not a copyright (because copying is not involved), it is thought of as being similar to it because it enables artists to a share of the future value of their work. For instance, if an artist sells a painting at the beginning of his or her career for a modest price, then becomes famous and his or her work commands much higher prices, he/she (or his/her heirs) does not benefit from the increase in value as he/she no longer owns the work.[11] The percentage amount (around 5 or 10 per cent) of the resale price is usually channelled to the artist via a copyright collecting society. The collecting society monitors sales and distributing the money to members, as with remuneration from copyright sources. Droit de suite has now been adopted throughout the European Union.

Droit de suite has been criticised by cultural economists on the grounds that it works like a tax on future price increases, and therefore the first buyers of a work of art take that into account in terms of the price they are willing to pay the artist in the first place; thus the resale 'penalty' reduces the prices for young artists and, in any event, only well-established artists benefit from the right. This can be tested, and this is indeed the finding that such studies have reported.[12]

Alternatives to copyright

Economists have expressed their reservations about copyright (as they have of patents) for a long time: Macaulay's comments in box 13.2 neatly sum up these doubts. So – what are the alternatives and the objections to them?

---

[11] The artist does retain the copyright on works sold, however, and can assert his/her moral rights and control copying, for which he/she is entitled to remuneration.

[12] See Ginsburgh (2005).

Grants and prizes

Historically, the most frequently suggested alternative has been state grants to creators, suggested by both Macaulay and Plant for literary authors, and some economists have suggested recently a return to the prize system of reward for creativity as an alternative to the copyright system.[13] It is interesting to consider the economic differences in incentives that these alternatives offer. A grant is an upfront, one-off payment that is awarded on the merits of the application by the artist for a specific project, typically by a committee of fellow artists or experts in the field. A grant in economic terminology is an *ex ante* payment, meaning that it provides an incentive in advance of the work being done. As we saw in chapter 11, a grant often 'buys time' for the artist to do the project. By contrast, the incentive offered by copyright is an *ex post* reward, based on the success in the market of the products to which the creator contributed (and which, as an individual author, he or she is likely to have financed). The greater the success, the higher the price, the more royalty income the artist receives and the amount is determined on the market; it is not known in advance, however, how much the copyright royalty and remuneration will be. A grant is typically a fixed amount of money and payment is certain. In fact, artists may well have it both ways, because they have copyright on works they create with the help of a grant.

There are other reward systems, such as being given honours. In former times a prince or some such would give the artist a gift as a reward for having pleased him; later on, the king or the state promised a reward for the winner of a competition – for example, to create a clock that kept time on long sea voyages. Competitions of a different sort are common in the arts, however, and many countries have prizes and awards for 'the best' violinist, novelist, film, and so on. These prizes cannot be anticipated and so are an *ex post* reward; they can be very important in artists' career development and, of course, will lead to greater fees, higher demand for their work and greater royalty payments.

Business models

Another alternative to copyright that goes back some way (for example, to Plant – box 13.3) is that businesses can adopt other means of capturing the returns from works of art, literature, music, and so forth; Plant's belief was that

---

[13] Boldrin and Levine (2002) and Shavell and van Ypserle (2001).

'lead time' or first-mover advantage was itself a monopoly sufficient to allow the publisher to recoup the fixed costs. More recently, other economists have moved away from the belief that copyright law is the solution to protecting information goods in the digital era and have expressed the view that business models are a stronger defence against copying.[14] The ability to discriminate prices in online selling is held to be the most effective business model; price discrimination can be done effectively only by a monopolist, and the argument is that this basis for monopoly is an alternative to having the exclusive copyright; for example, by offering different versions of the same item at different prices, the seller can maximise revenues by tapping into a range of willingness to pay on the demand curve. Some have argued that the presence of network economies makes it worthwhile for a firm not to enforce copyright because the more people who use a product, the greater demand becomes; then, when the product becomes the 'standard', capture monopoly profits.

Business models are discussed in more detail in chapter 14 and in connection with the various industries in chapters 15 to 18.

Copyright levy

One solution to the problem of income lost through unauthorised use is the so-called 'copyright levy'. This is a not an alternative to copyright but it is an alternative way of compensating copyright holders for the use of their work. It is a form of indirect remuneration for rights holders that is a way of compensating them for unauthorised use by private copiers, such as the downloading of music and films from the internet, that cannot be licensed or controlled. The system was adopted in the 'analogue era' with the advent of home taping devices as a tax on blank media, such as cassettes, and it therefore pre-dates the introduction of digitisation, but it has been extended to deal with the problem of unauthorised digital copying in the form of a levy on the hardware that can be used for downloading and copying. It is now widespread in the European Union and most countries (though not in Ireland or the United Kingdom, whose laws allow only very limited private copying). The levy revenue is transferred to the appropriate national copyright collecting societies and distributed to their members in the same way as other remuneration and royalties.

From an economic point of view, it is an even blunter instrument than the blanket licence or equitable remuneration schemes, because all who buy the

---

[14] Varian (2005) is a leading exponent of this point of view.

equipment have to pay the levy whether or not they use it for copying purposes, and the revenues from the levy have to be distributed in a fairly arbitrary way between the different groups of rights holders, whose work may or may not have been copied (visual artists, authors and publishers, composers, performers, record labels, and so on). Some policy-makers are concerned that the copyright levy is a disincentive to the development of digital rights management that, in principle, enables rewards to individual rights holders to be paid more accurately for the use and value of their works, but, as we saw earlier, DRM is no longer held up as the solution. Therefore the copyright levy seems to be a practical way forward as a solution to the problem of offering an economic incentive through copyright law; it also has the merit of having low transaction costs.

Conclusion

Copyright law has been established for almost 300 years and has managed to overcome the challenges faced by successive changes in technology, which now enables the copying of a wide range of works in many media. It has wide-reaching effects on the cultural economy, and it is very hard to fathom all of them. Copyright is an incentive to supply creative works and products, but does it operate evenly between the primary creators and the industries that are based on them? What is the elasticity of supply by creators of copyrightable works? Would alternative reward systems achieve the desired result? What is the impact of copyright on consumers and users of cultural products? These are questions that cultural economists ask and would like to answer. Economists have had a healthy scepticism about copyright for a long time but there are still many unanswered questions.

One problem in assessing the impact of copyright on the cultural sector is that several of the cultural industries have developed under its wing; how different these industries' business models would be without copyright protection is difficult to say. Studies of how creators worked before copyright or how industries succeed when copyright or design rights are weak or unenforceable may provide a way of trying to gain insight into the matter. There have been a number of very careful empirical studies that try to reach a conclusion on the effect of the illegal downloading of music on the music industry (discussed in chapter 15). Economists believe that carrying out such studies is the way to tackle these questions. For all the analysis by economists and lawyers on the subject of copyright, however, we still cannot say what the causal relationship is between copyright and creativity. Even though economic models of copyright are sophisticated, they are limited by the difficulty economists have in modelling effects over time – copyright's rewards are, after all, in the future; other incentives, such as grants, are given before the work is created, not afterwards.

Studying the creative industries gives us some insight into the complexity of their economic organisation in which copyright plays a significant, but not necessarily a crucial, role. Studies of artists' labour markets have demonstrated the difficulty of making clear predictions about what motivates creativity and artistic supply, and this lesson can be carried over into understanding the role of copyright, with its economic and moral rights, in the creative industries.

Copyright is what economists call a second best solution to the problem of how to increase welfare by overcoming market failure. It is also a source of market failure itself, however: it raises prices and is a barrier to entry, even though it is not a strong monopoly (see box 7.2). Digitisation and the internet have reduced barriers to entry, but in some cases have even raised prices as business models are adopted that use price discrimination. At best, the 'optimal' copyright regime is a trade-off between its beneficial incentive effects and the costs it imposes on consumers and users, but it cannot be justified in terms of first best Pareto optimality. The evaluation of copyright must therefore take place in a piecemeal fashion based on market-by-market empirical evidence.

Collecting societies are an integral part of the copyright system and constitute a solution to the problem of how to make it work in practicable terms for rights holders and users. They reduce transaction costs, but as monopolies may also bargain for higher prices, and so are regulated by the state. Again, there is a trade-off here between administrative efficiency and economic efficiency – further evidence of the second best nature of copyright. It is therefore important to consider alternative ways of achieving the objective of encouraging creativity. There is still a great deal of work to be done by cultural economists and others on the economics of copyright.

Further reading

There are a number of short chapters in the Towse (2003a) *Handbook of Cultural Economics* that are relevant to this chapter: Michael Rushton on 'Artists' rights' (chapter 8), William Landes on 'Copyright' (chapter 15), Michael Hutter on 'Information goods' (chapter 33), Joëlle Farchy on

'Internet: culture' (chapter 35) and Fabrice Rochelandet on 'Internet: economics' (chapter 36). Simon Frith and Lee Marshall's 2004 book (second edition) *Music and Copyright* is a compendium of various aspects of copyright in the music industry. Towse (2006a), 'Copyright and artists: a view from cultural economics', is a survey article that provides a more detailed overview of many of the points made in this chapter, with a detailed bibliography.

An excellent article by an excellent economist is Hal Varian's 2005 article 'Copying and copyright' in the *Journal of Economic Perspectives*; this journal is aimed at students and teachers of elementary economics, and most articles in it are accessible to people with some elementary economics training. This article is written by one of the 'copyright sceptics' in the economics profession. Also worth reading is the brief by the Amici Curiae in *Eldred v. Ashcroft*, 2003; see footnote 8 for the website at which it is available and for the list of contributors.

Part IV

The creative industries

Introduction

In Part IV of the book, chapter 14 develops the analysis introduced in Part I and discusses the definition and measurement of the creative industries and the economic rationale for treating them as a specific sector. In chapters 15–18, the profiles of the music, film, broadcasting and book publishing industries first presented in chapter 4 are expanded and research by cultural economists and others is reported. Chapter 19 covers several topics to do with spatial aspects of the creative industries: festivals, creative cities and cultural tourism.

14 Economics of creative industries

This chapter is a general introduction to the economics of the creative industries. Its purpose is to lay out a case that the creative or cultural industries can be treated, in economic terms, as a sector. In other words, what has to be shown is that there are sufficient similarities between, and common features of, a group of industries that they merit special classification and analysis. Chapters then follow on the music, film, broadcasting and book publishing industries, each containing an economic analysis of that industry, drawing upon the general points presented here, with a final chapter on festivals and locational aspects of creative industries in cities. As will become clear, these are not the only industries that are treated as creative industries but they are the ones on which there has been research in cultural economics, and they relate closely to other areas of study in cultural economics.

Structure of creative industries

The first topic in this chapter is a discussion of the ways in which creative industries have been defined and classified by international organisations and in the United Kingdom. The United Kingdom is chosen because the government officially adopted the concept of the creative industries early on and has monitored their progress over the last few years. Subsequent sections of the chapter deal with the finance and ownership patterns in the creative industries and with globalisation and international trade in cultural goods. I then turn to the economic theories that explain the organisation of these industries – the size of firms and the structure of markets for their products – and the chapter closes with a general description of regulatory policies for this sector. The chapter makes the case for a cultural economics treatment of the creative industries as a whole and demonstrates that their analysis is an integral and important area of study in cultural economics.

Classifying creative industries

In order to talk about the creative industries as forming a distinct sector in its own right, there has to be a way of classifying them. As we have already seen in chapter 2, the economist's approach to this is rather different from that of a cultural analyst for several reasons. First, the classification of industries into groups or a sector is regarded as a pragmatic matter of identifying economic features they have in common, such as the products themselves or the type of process involved in their production. Second, there is no value judgement attached to this exercise, whose main purpose is to ensure that there is no double-counting of inputs or outputs of an industry in the national income accounts. Once agreed, the classification can be used as the basis for measuring growth, productivity and the contribution of the industry to the balance of payments, and therefore comparison with other industries or sectors is made possible, as well as international comparisons.

Moreover, there is also some degree of arbitrariness as to how individual producers are allocated to an industry classification. In economics, an industry is defined by the closeness of substitutability between the products; some products are easily seen as relatively homogeneous and therefore close substitutes. Are books and newspapers close substitutes for each other, though, or even one newspaper for another and one book title for another? Unlikely – but they are lumped together in 'publishing' as an industry. It is worthwhile remembering therefore that an industry in national statistics is an aggregation of groups of firms and individual producers that are classified as producing similar but not the same goods and services. In fact, these problems can to some extent be overcome by having a more detailed classification system, for example by going to a five-digit classification, as explained below.

Creative and cultural industries

So far in this book, the terms 'creative' industries and 'cultural' industries have been used interchangeably with no explanation for doing so. In fact, there is really nothing much to choose between these terms on economic grounds, because, as was explained in detail in chapter 2, any placing of industries into one sector or another is going to be arbitrary to some extent; to give an

---

Box 14.1 From the UNESCO 2000 publication *Culture, Trade and Globalization: Questions and Answers*

(1) What do we understand by 'cultural industries'?

It is generally agreed that this term applies to those industries that combine the creation, production and commercialization of contents which are intangible and cultural in nature. These contents are typically protected by copyright and they can take the form of goods or services.

Depending on the context, cultural industries may also be referred to as 'creative industries', sunrise or 'future oriented industries' in the economic jargon, or content industries in the technological jargon. The notion of cultural industries generally includes printing, publishing and multimedia, audio-visual, phonographic and cinematographic productions, as well as crafts and design. For some countries, this concept also embraces architecture, visual and performing arts, sports, manufacturing of musical instruments, advertising and cultural tourism.

Cultural industries add value to contents and generate values for individuals and societies. They are knowledge and labour-intensive, create employment and wealth, nurture creativity – the 'raw material' they are made from – and foster innovation in production and commercialization processes. At the same time, cultural industries are central in promoting and maintaining cultural diversity and in ensuring democratic access to culture. This twofold nature – both cultural and economic – builds up a distinctive profile for cultural industries. During the 90s they grew exponentially, both in terms of employment creation and contribution to GNP. Today, globalization offers new challenges and opportunities for their development.

Source: UNESCO (2000a: 11–12).

---

example, the making of grand pianos could be classified either with furniture production or in the music industry. Choices have to be made, however, and criteria adopted for making consistent classification. UNESCO has tackled this question (see box 14.1).

Although all the industries mentioned in the UNESCO listing share some similarities, some differences can be noted between them. In particular, the performing arts are live services whereas the products of the cultural industries – sound recording, film, broadcasting, etc. – can be mass-produced, stored and then relayed repeatedly to huge audiences. This has led to the use of another term – the mass media – being applied to these industries, particularly by media economists. Another difference is that craft and designer products are usually hand-crafted and they are not produced on an industrial scale; these products are therefore more akin to the performing arts than to the mass media.

Relation to copyright

The emphasis on copyright can also present problems; for example, museums are usually thought of as belonging to the cultural sector but they do not get into the UNESCO list of cultural industries because much of their collection would be in the public domain as far as copyright is concerned; nor are they produced on an industrial scale. Museums do own the copyright on any books, photographs and catalogues they produce, however. As can be seen, there is no watertight way of drawing up a list of creative or cultural industries, and this point is reiterated in the UNCTAD *Creative Economy Report 2008*. The report adopts the UNCTAD way of defining the creative economy (reported in chapter 2 of this book) but does not use it to produce 'a list' and instead compares the definitions of creative or cultural industries that have been used in various studies, without opting for one or the other.

Creative industries in the United Kingdom

The UK government got off to an early start in the conceptualisation and promotion of the 'creative' industries; the first *Creative Industries Mapping Document* was published in 1998 by the Department for Culture, Media and Sport, using as its definition 'those industries which have their origin in individual creativity, skill and talent and which have a potential for wealth and job creation through the generation and exploitation of intellectual property'.[1] Since then there have been (at the time of writing) five more studies, and the methodology and methods of quantifying the value of these industries adopted in the United Kingdom have been refined so that they are in line with the standards of the Office of National Statistics. The DCMS defines the UK creative industries as consisting of thirteen industries: advertising, architecture, art and antiques, craft, design, designer fashion, film and video, interactive leisure software, music, the performing arts, publishing, software, and television and radio. They accounted for over 7 per cent of total UK gross value added in 2005 (excluding craft and design).[2] In 2005 the creative industries employed 1 million people directly and there were over three-quarters of a million in creative occupations outside the creative industries.[3] These figures are plugged by the DCMS and compared to those for

---

[1] By the middle of the 2000s studies and methods had developed in many other European countries, and Canada, Australia and New Zealand had already developed their own measures.

[2] There are no value added data for craft and design, only turnover figures that would inflate the final estimate. The 1998 mapping document used turnover figures for several industries. See DCMS (2007b).

[3] Figures for Great Britain, excluding Northern Ireland.

other sectors, demonstrating the leading role the creative industries play in the UK economy. It is claimed that the contribution of the creative industries so defined is the biggest in the world as a proportion of GDP, though that is not borne out by the comparative data in the UNCTAD *Creative Economy Report 2008*: the proportion of GDP contributed by the UK 'Cultural and creative sector' in 2001 was 3 per cent, compared to 3.4 per cent in Lithuania and 3.2 per cent in Sweden. Be that as it may, the real barrier to verifying such claims is that there is no comparable standard international listing of industries or their components and therefore more or less 'anything goes'.

These claims and the apparent significance of the creative industries have prompted an interest (or maybe concern) about the sustainability of their economic performance. Accordingly, the 'Creative Economy Programme' has been established by the DCMS to research various aspects of the creative industries: the collection of information and its interpretation; the size of firms in these industries and whether they are UK- or foreign-owned; the degree of concentration (that is, the percentage of the turnover in the industry accounted for by a given number of firms); and the ownership of the UK creative industries by multinational corporations.[4] Research commissioned by the DCMS as part of this programme has developed the notion of 'layers' of creative activities within the creative industry sector, corresponding to the chain of production from core content creation through the intermediary activities supporting core content and the manufacturing of products containing it, then to allied production of inputs for the production process.[5] These are pictured in figure 14.1.

Using this approach and the five-digit SIC classification changes the previous figures on contribution to GDP on the part of the creative industries for the 'core creative activities' in layer 1 in 2005 from 3.4 to 2.7 per cent. The contribution of these industries to total creative industry turnover[6] was:

(1) software and games: 41 per cent;
(2) TV and radio: 18 per cent;
(3) advertising: 16 per cent;
(4) film, video and photography: 7 per cent;
(5) music and the performing arts industry: 4 per cent;
(6) publishing: 4 per cent;

[4] DCMS (2007a).   [5] Frontier Economics (2007).
[6] The five-digit classification does not provide value added data, only turnover.

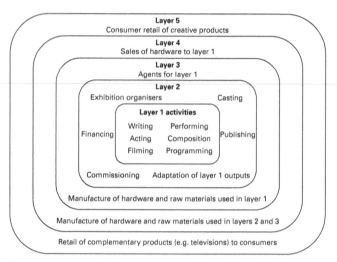

Figure 14.1   Chain of production as layers of activity

(7) architecture: 3 per cent;

(8) design: 3 per cent; and

(9) designer fashion: 2 per cent.

This research also revealed, for instance, that the 'Software, computer games & electronic publishing' industry accounted for one-third of employment in these industries, had grown more rapidly and had a higher concentration of large firms than the other industries and was typically foreign-owned, while the 'Music and the visual & performing arts' industry accounted for 13 per cent of employment, had zero growth and consisted of small firms that were mostly UK-owned.[7]

Copyright as the basis for the creative industries

Both the UNESCO and the UK concepts of creative industries refer to their connection to intellectual property for fostering the creation and exploitation of intangible content creation. Going one step further, the World Intellectual Property Organization conceives of the creative industries entirely in terms of copyright as their basis and has produced a guide for measuring the economic contribution of the 'copyright-based' industries to the economy.[8] The guide distinguishes four layers of copyright

---

[7] See Frontier Economics (2007).   [8] WIPO (2003).

'dependence': the core copyright industries, interdependent industries, partial copyright industries and non-dedicated support industries (see box 14.2). Like the 'layers' approach of the United Kingdom's DCMS, the distinction is based on the notion of a chain of production that starts with a core of creative content that then supports subsequent activities. The core can be readily connected to copyright law (and design rights that are included in copyright law in many countries) but, for the other industries, it is necessary to estimate what proportion of their production is 'dependent' upon the core and so on along the chain of production. This, of course, is intended to avoid double-counting and to correctly measure the value added of the industries involved.

In fact, identifying that part of a firm's activity that is connected to one specific output has to be done with all industries, and that is true of creative industries as much as for any other. Many firms are multi-product firms and

---

Box 14.2 The WIPO typology of copyright-based industries in its *Guide on Surveying the Economic Contribution of the Copyright-based Industries*

The core copyright industries are industries that are wholly engaged in the creation, production and manufacturing, performance, broadcast, communication and exhibition, or distribution and sales of works and other protected subject matter.

Interdependent copyright industries are industries that are engaged in the production, manufacture and sale of equipment whose function is wholly or primarily to facilitate the creation, production or use of works and other protected subject matter. TV sets, radios, VCRs, CD players, DVD players, cassette players, electronic game equipment and other similar equipment; computers and equipment; and musical instruments belong to this group. Partial interdependent copyright industries are photographic and cinematographic instruments; photocopiers; blank recording material; and paper.

The partial copyright industries are industries in which a portion of the activities is related to works and other protected subject matter and may involve creation, production and manufacturing, performance, broadcast, communication and exhibition or distribution and sales. Apparel, textiles and footwear; jewellery and coins; other crafts; furniture; household goods, china and glass; wall coverings and carpets; toys and games; architecture, engineering, surveying; interior design; and museums belong to this group.

The non-dedicated support industries are industries in which a portion of the activities is related to facilitating the broadcast, communication, distribution or sales of works and other protected subject matter, and whose activities have not been included in the core copyright industries. These are general wholesale and retailing; general transportation; and telephony and the internet.

Source: WIPO (2003).

their products have to be classified separately; if a firm makes both cat food and breakfast cereal, they are not both classified as pet food! In the case of the copyright-based industries, the WIPO guide requires that this classification process be carried out according to the extent of the copyright content in the product; a TV set is a partial copyright product because it is used entirely in connection with copyright content (broadcasts), though it is not itself a copyright good – no broadcasts, no use for a TV set! It is not hard to see that this process is difficult to carry out even in countries with sophisticated national income accounts, and probably very difficult in countries where statistics are less developed or where the creative industries themselves are not itemised in the accounts. It is also not hard to see that, as the process of separating the inputs needed to produce one output of a multi-product firm involves some arbitrary judgement, it would be easy to exaggerate the contribution of the creative industries.

This is not the chief objection, though: to an economist, the real problem is that it is very easy to slip between the use of copyright as a way of defining the creative industries and the idea that their contribution to the economy is caused by the presence of copyright. The term 'dependent' on copyright can be misread as meaning that without copyright these industries would not exist, but economists are not able to make that causal connection. Undoubtedly, copyright is an incentive to both creators and, especially, to the industries exploiting copyright content, as argued in chapter 13, but it does not necessarily follow that a stronger copyright regime would increase their contribution to GDP or a weaker one reduce their growth. Nevertheless, measuring losses to the creative industries from unauthorised use ('piracy'), which is an important undertaking for economists, requires different methods and data sources from those in the WIPO guide. This is explained in chapter 15 in relation to the music industry.

Ownership and finance of creative industries

It can be seen from the foregoing text that, while most of the cultural industries are likely to be private, for-profit firms, the addition of non-profit performing arts and contemporary visual arts in the creative industries classification makes for a mixed economy of private and public finance and also of ownership. Public sector broadcasting is mostly publicly financed (and in some countries it is also state-owned) and there is state subsidy for one or more of a range of products and producers in the creative industries somewhere or other in the world – for newspaper publishing, authorship and book publishing, film, crafts, to name a few. On the other hand, other industries, notably software and advertising, are entirely privately owned.

Research has shown that production units in the creative industries vary very much in size, from small, even one-person enterprises to large international conglomerates. This differs from industry to industry and will be discussed in more detail in the chapters that follow. There are some general points to note, however, and, as will be seen later, the size of firms and their ownership may be subject to regulation, some of which is specific to the creative industries. The large private companies are financed via stock and share issues and therefore have to compete with firms in other industries for finance on the stock markets; they have to be profitable and to make rates of return comparable to those in other industries in order to stay in business. They are subject to mergers and takeovers by virtue of this fact. The clash of art and commerce is more common in these circumstances than in smaller firms. The smaller the size of the firm, the less likely it is to be financed through the stock market and the more likely it is to rely on its own profits to stay in business. Very small enterprises, such as in crafts, visual arts, writers, and so on, may consist of just one person and, as we saw in chapter 11 on artists' labour markets, may survive on a combination of fees and revenues from sales, royalties, grants and family finance, at least until they are successful on the market. When they do succeed they may become large-scale concerns; a good example of that is successful pop groups, which may become very significant enterprises, conducting themselves like multinational corporations and moving their headquarters and residence to tax havens or countries with favourable taxation for artists (such as the Netherlands offers pop musicians and Ireland offers authors).

Start-ups and large corporations

The UK research on the size of enterprises in the creative industries referred to earlier[9] has shown that many enterprises in the creative industries are so-called 'start-ups', meaning that they are new small firms. A question that naturally arises is how long they survive. Research on entrepreneurship has shown that there is a high failure rate of start-ups in all industries and many, probably most, do not survive more than three years. The UK research suggests that start-ups are somewhat more successful in the creative industries

---

[9] DCMS (2007a).

than in other sectors; it has to be said, however, that most of these are in the software industry. Firm survival may also be a matter of choice, though, and not the outcome of malign market forces; as research on artists' labour markets has shown, short-term contracts are common, particularly with groups of artists – musicians, dancers, film-makers, and so on – getting together for specific undertakings that were never intended to be long-lasting. Such ventures may last just as long as the project grant or other finance and then disband. When that is so, the 'start-up' firm is not a failure, it has simply fulfilled its purpose.

Such comings and goings are the stuff of capitalism and especially of capitalistic cultural industries. How free are markets in the creative industries? There is entry and exit of firms, and that suggests that some markets are competitive or, at any rate, contestable (meaning that market power can be challenged). It is also the case, however, that there are large conglomerates with interests not only in one but also in several of the creative industries, and in other industries as well; for example, Sony Corporation not only owns film, sound recording and music publishing interests but also produces the hardware to go with them – CD players and burners, radio and TV sets – and financial services, banking and insurance as well. Such firms dominate many of the markets in which they operate. (Box 14.3 illustrates the size and scope of a large media corporation, News Corporation, founded in Australia by Rupert Murdoch.)

Box 14.3 Holdings of News Corporation

Chairman and chief executive officer: Rupert Murdoch.

News Corporation is a media empire consisting of film, television, cable and satellite, magazine, newspaper and book publishing companies and other assets, including interactive media (MySpace being one), sports and games. The corporation straddles Australasia, the United Kingdom and the United States of America. A selection of its subsidiaries is: film – 20th Century Fox, Fox Studios; TV – Fox Broadcasting; cable – Fox Sports, Movie and News Channels, National Geographic; satellite – BSkyB, DirecTV; magazines – specialist magazines and the largest holding in *Gemstar TV Guide*; newspapers – besides 110 Australian newspapers, in the United Kingdom – *The Times*, *The Sunday Times*, *The Sun* and *News of the World*, and in the United States the *New York Post*, book publishing – HarperCollins. It had total assets as of 30 September 2008 of approximately US$61 billion and total annual revenues of approximately US$33 billion.

Source: www.newscorp.com/investor/index.html (accessed January 2009).

Moreover, there are frequent mergers between firms and divisions of firms, indicating acquisitions of assets. The music industry by 2007 was reduced to four major firms, for example. The picture that emerges for many of the cultural industries, therefore, is that of an oligopolistic market structure in which a few large firms dominate the industry with a number of small firms coexisting with them and tolerated as long as they pose no threat. The UNCTAD *Creative Economy Report 2008* states that smaller creative firms gain from the presence of larger firms in an industry through 'subcontracting and outsourcing arrangements or joint ventures' (69) without mentioning the evidence or that the reverse is also probably true – that small firms support the large ones.

Market structure and media regulation

Understanding industrial and market structure is particularly important for regulation in these industries, because governments are concerned about the influence of ownership and finance on the range and type of information offered to the public by the media, especially the press and broadcasting. To deal with some of the less desirable offshoots of ownership patterns, there is government regulation of various kinds in this sector – ownership rules for press and broadcasting, controls on television advertising, and so on – and cultural and media policies seek to promote diverse points of view and opinion by many suppliers, which is a phenomenon usually known as diversity and plurality. Regulation and policy for the creative industries is dealt with later in this chapter. Although regulation may prevent the undesirable effects of private ownership, however, it cannot ensure that desirable ones will develop via the market, and therefore subsidy is also used to finance some of the creative industries.

State subsidy for media

State subsidy is used to support broadcasting, the press, literature, and so on, particularly in smaller countries, in which the size of the market makes it impossible to achieve economies of scale such as can be realised by private enterprises in larger countries. This often has to do with language, and here English has enormous advantages in the world market. Some products, though, do not lend themselves to global distribution: national and local news in one country is not of widespread interest in another even if it is presented in a language that is understood; there are local and national musics that do not have global appeal (though some do) and folk traditions may also not travel. Indeed, the opposite is often the case: people travel to other countries to engage with their local cultures. Maintaining national and minority languages for film, song, TV, press and literature may well require subsidy for survival purposes as well as to compete with cheaper, imported globalised products. In subsequent chapters, the role of state subsidy is examined in the context of each of the industries, while international trade and globalisation are discussed at the end of this chapter.

Economic organisation of creative industries

In this section, the market structure of the creative industries is analysed – the size of the firm and competition in markets – and this is followed by a detailed discussion of Richard Caves' approach to the economic organisation of the creative industries.

Size of the firm

The economic forces that influence the size of a firm were introduced in chapter 5; in this chapter, the basic ideas presented there are expanded and developed in more detail. The structure of the market for a particular pro-duct – whether it is competitive or not – and the so-called 'make-or-buy' decision are closely related, because, if the enterprise chooses to make all its components as a vertically integrated firm, it will typically be larger than a firm that specialises in one stage of the production process and buys in the other stages. Economists often refer to this as 'upstream' and 'downstream' activity, and it is an interesting question as to why some industries, including some of the creative industries, are vertically integrated whereas others are not.

In general, the larger the enterprise, the greater its investment in physical and human capital assets, the more integrated its chain of production is, and the more difficult it would be for a competitor to enter the market, thus increasing the tendency to oligopoly or monopoly. Some of the stages of production in a vertically integrated firm may be vulnerable to competition, however, because specialised firms may be more efficient at supplying those inputs, and, if that were the case, the firm may divest itself of those divisions or be forced to sell them off because they are uneconomic. Thus there is a dynamic process of competition through integration and disintegration, with integration often taking place through acquisitions of other firms' assets and mergers with other enterprises, and this seems to be a feature of the cultural industries, no doubt in part because they are subject to considerable technological change, as discussed below.

Besides vertical integration, horizontal integration, whereby competing firms producing the same or similar products merge, is also a threat to competition. In many countries, an excessive share of the market by one firm that threatens to damage consumers' interests is subject to competition law (antitrust legislation); even so, in the media field in particular, there is strong concentration in the hands of a few large conglomerates that are multinational corporations, due to horizontal integration across national borders (for example, see box 14.3 on News Corporation). Excessive concentration is regulated because of concerns about plurality of news and other information sources. In the case of some recent mergers, both horizontal and vertical integration were the targets of the competition authority: in the case of the Sony/Bertelsmann merger, for instance, the European Competition Authority allowed the merger of the sound recording divisions but required the music publishing arms to remain in separate ownership.

Contestability of markets and copyright

Concerns with competition in economics focus on contestability – the ability of market forces to overcome any tendency to monopoly. Markets are contestable if there are no barriers to entry, such as the need for very high outlays on sunk investment or legal impediments. In the creative industries, however, one of the most common barriers to entry is the ownership of copyrights, and the only way a competing firm can obtain existing copyrights is by buying them from the owner or acquiring a licence to use them, which the copyright owner may not grant as the new entrant is a competitor. When there are mergers in the creative industries, the main assets that are transferred are copyrights. Moreover, this can be done without the consent of the creator or performer. One instance of that was the so-called 'George Michael case'; he had signed a long-term contract with CBS that transferred the copyrights of all his songs to the record label, and then CBS and the copyrights to his works were bought out by Sony, which, he claimed, failed to market them.[10]

Anyone can enter the music industry as a composer, performer or even record label, since barriers to entry are low, and can create his or her own copyright works in competition with existing ones; in that sense, copyright does not confer a very strong monopoly or prevent market contestability. Existing copyrights can be used strategically to foil competitors until they fall into the public domain, however.

Competition and creative destruction

Competition is regarded as being as vital to the creative economy as it is to the economy in general, because it provides greater consumer choice and more

---

[10] See http://en.wikipedia.org/wiki/George_Michael#Loss_and_Court_Case (accessed 8 December 2007).

Box 14.4 Joseph Schumpeter on creative destruction

Joseph Schumpeter (1883–1950), who was born in the Austro-Hungarian Empire and was for a short time minister of finance in Austria after the First World War, moved to the United States in 1932 to a professorship in economics at Harvard. His most renowned book is *Capitalism, Socialism and Democracy*, published in 1942, which develops the idea of creative destruction. Nonetheless, his early book *Theory of Economic Development* (1912), written when he was twenty-eight years old, contains other ideas that are now evoked in the context of technological progress and dynamic competition: the distinction between innovation and invention and between process and product innovation.

Schumpeter saw the innovating entrepreneur as the driving force of progress in the capitalist economy, but that progress was not smooth but subject to business cycles (economic upswings and downturns). He believed that what drives innovation and growth are big firms with the resources and capital to invest in research and development. Their innovations provide them with a monopoly until imitators enter the market and compete away their advantage and this process takes place in waves of innovativeness – hence, creative destruction. It is creative because innovative, and destructive because technical progress sweeps away firms that do not innovate or whose technologies are obsolete. Thus capitalism ensures the survival of the fittest firms.

Source: Blaug (1986).

opportunity for creators to access markets. It is, therefore, a source of cultural diversity. Competition is not just a question of how prices are affected in a static world, though that is also important; dynamic competition as conceived of by Schumpeter (see box 14.4) is a process of suppliers jockeying with each other to get as big a share of the market as possible, only to be eventually pushed aside by a new entrant – a process he called 'creative destruction'. Many cultural and media economists see creative destruction as the driving force of the cultural sector.

Technological change

One of the main features of Schumpeterian creative destruction is the fact that enterprises need to finance technical change in products and the processes of making them, and therefore need to have monopoly profits in order to do so. Accordingly, Schumpeter argued that competition would take place dynamically through new technologies rather than through prices.

Changes in technology can catch out the incumbent firms in an industry, as Schumpeter foresaw, making way for new entrants that understand and can manage the new technologies better. The recent history of the music industry, which was unable to handle the digital delivery of music directly to customers, is an example of the inability to grasp and benefit from new technology. The term economists use for this is 'technological lock-in', meaning that, once a firm has invested in a certain technology that is embodied in its capital equipment and its human capital assets, there will be a significant cost of switching to a newer or different technology. Most of us in our own way have experienced such 'switching costs': LP-playing gramophones were made redundant by CDs, and CD players were soon replaced by Walkmans and then iPods. The high outlay of investment in many information goods industries only exacerbates the switching costs to a firm and locks it in to an older technology, which eventually makes its cost of production too high or its products too old-fashioned to compete successfully.

Technology in the means of reproducing and copying words, sounds and moving images is basic to the publishing, sound recording, film and video industries, as without it they could not have developed in the first place, and they are subject to ongoing technological progress. Even the less technologically dynamic performing and visual arts have benefited from technological progress. Process and product innovation have been very important in the development of the creative industries. The digitisation of content into what authors Carl Shapiro and Hal Varian have called 'bits and bytes' and the development of computers and the internet as means of distributing them have now radically altered many economic aspects of the creative industries.[11] Shapiro and Varian characterise the creative industries as part of the wider information economy, which displays certain economic features: high fixed or sunk costs combined with very low or even zero marginal costs reflecting economies of scale; economies of scope (as well illustrated in box 14.3 by the holdings of News Corporation) in the form of synergies between similar products, economies of scale in advertising and marketing them and the pooling of risks in similar undertakings; and besides economies of scale and scope, possible network economies that increase consumers' willingness to pay for a product. The internet enables the delivery of customised bundled services and discriminatory pricing for identical goods and services, and also the sale – or, more typically, the licensing – of different versions of the same item, a phenomenon called 'versioning' by Shapiro and Varian. Versioning in some goods was already well established before the internet – think of hardback and paperback books – but digitised information lends itself easily to it,

---

[11] Shapiro and Varian (1999); see also Küng, Picard and Towse (2008), especially chapter 3, on digitisation and the internet.

especially as marketing can be targeted to the individual (and recall from chapter 13 that Varian is one of the most prominent economists opposing the economic case for copyright on the grounds that these business models render it unnecessary as an economic incentive).

Shapiro and Varian have famously said: 'Technology changes, economic laws do not,' and the question of whether a new economics is called for to deal with the 'new economy' has certainly been asked by a number of economists. All Shapiro and Varian are prepared to concede to the digital age is that new business models may need to be adopted, but the basic rules of supply and demand and the underlying economic incentives still function. Thus Shapiro and Varian adopt a neoclassical approach to the information economy, with a strong emphasis on the power of the market to adopt new technologies and use them for economic gain.

Caves' analysis of the creative industries

In contrast to Shapiro and Varian, Richard Caves has applied contract theory to understanding the economic organisation industries, and, unlike them, he specifically addresses the creative industries. In the preface to his book *Creative Industries: Contracts between Art and Commerce*, Caves explains that he uses 'the theory of contracts and the logic of economic organisation – the question of why and how some transactions are internalised within the firm while others take place between independent economic agents or firms' (Caves, 2000: vii). In other words, he wants to explain the make-or-buy decision in firms in the creative industries: is the firm a single entrepreneur in a back room who is contracting to buy in all the inputs he or she needs on the market, or a huge conglomerate that tries to produce all stages of the output in-house?

Caves sees the firm as a 'nexus of contracts' and he seeks to explain the nature of contracts between artists and business firms that provide what he calls the 'humdrum' inputs in the creative industries. These are the contracts between art and commerce of the book's subtitle. The humdrum firm (say a record label) needs creative content provided by artists for its production and marketing of a commercial product, and the artist (say a singer) needs the humdrum inputs to get his or her work (a recording) to market; therefore there is mutual benefit to be had. The firm must pay the artist for his or her work, and that is an investment by the firm; therefore each party's commitments are contained in the contract between them.

'Contracts between art and commerce'

In the book, Caves successively examines each of the creative industries ranked according to the complexity of the chain of production in that industry, and then he analyses the contracts between the 'humdrum' inputs (the commercial side of the firm) and the suppliers of the creative content, the 'artists'. To give an idea of how the analysis proceeds: the first industry Caves examines is the contemporary art market, in which artists are producing work that is sold via an art dealer or gallerist. The artist has a contract with the gallery, which may be no more than a loose arrangement sealed by a handshake; on that basis the artist hands over his or her work(s) to be put on display and sold at a price determined by the gallerist, from which the gallery will deduct (typically) 50–60 per cent as a commission for displaying and marketing the work and arranging the sale. An alternative deal could be that the gallery buys the work from the artist outright and then sells it on, but that is likely to happen only when the gallery knows the artist's reputation and the value of his or her work on the market. Caves describes these arrangements and explains the economic organisation of the industry in terms of the type of contract that is made between the artist and the commercial enterprise. He then proceeds to analyse more complex deals, such as book and music publishing, sound recording, film, and so on. In what follows, it can be seen that Caves uses the ideas of transaction cost economics (box 5.4), principal–agent theory and the property rights approach outlined in chapter 5 and in the appendix to chapter 1.

Contracts lay down the terms of the transaction, such as a description of the good or service that is to be supplied, the delivery date and the price (or fee) that is to be paid; the contract then stipulates the transfer of property rights. Contract theory has shown that contracts are never 'complete', however, because it is impossible to anticipate all future events and conditions. 'Incomplete', therefore, the contract tries to get the best mutually agreed deal, while attempting to anticipate possible contingencies, but, because bargaining over and writing contracts have transaction costs, they set a limit to the bargaining process. It also has to be possible to monitor the contract for what Caves calls 'contract fealty' – that is, truly fulfilling the contract – and, in addition, the contract has to be able to deal with conflict resolution, which ultimately could be in a court of law.

Incomplete contracts

Given that no contract can ever be complete, Caves argues that contract incompleteness is even greater in the creative industries than in the rest of the economy: there is too much uncertainty about the outcome of artistic

Box 14.5 Economic properties of the creative industries according to Richard Caves

- Nobody knows: there is uncertainty surrounding the production and consumption of creative products.
- Art for art's sake: the utility that artists derive from their work.
- Motley crew: the diversity of skills required for producing the good or service.
- A list/B list: the vertically differentiated skills of creative workers.
- Infinite variety: the wealth of differentiated products.
- *Ars longa*: the durability of creative products.
- Time flies: the problem of co-ordinating the 'motley crew' to deliver the good on time.

Source: Caves (2000).

plans, and creative artists and performers cannot work to order; in addition, the reception by consumers of newly created works is unpredictable. Nobody knows with sufficient precision how things will work out in the production and consumption of cultural products and there will therefore always be some gaps in the contract, ones that may be exploited by one or another party. Caves has summed up the features of the creative industries that make them especially susceptible to problems of contract incompleteness (see box 14.5).

Features of the creative industries and contract incompleteness

The features listed in box 14.5 start with one of the most famous statements in the movie industry, attributed to Samuel Goldwyn: 'Nobody knows anything' about Hollywood. The typical problem in contract theory is asymmetric information, when one party to the contract knows more than the other; Caves adapts this for the creative industries to the pervasive problem of 'symmetric ignorance', because 'nobody knows' – creativity is an uncertain business. These problems are exacerbated, however, by the fact that artists are not doing routine jobs, they care about their work ('art for art's sake') and may make that a priority over commercial (humdrum) concerns; moreover, many creative undertakings need co-ordinated work by many different artists, especially in the performing arts (the 'motley crew') and these artists cannot be substituted one for another, at least not easily (the 'A list/B list' property), because they have different levels of talent. The creative industries supply an 'infinite variety' of products, and some of them may last a long time ('*ars longa*'), meaning that revenues from them can take many years to flow in. As most products of the creative industries are protected by copyright law, royalties on authored works can last as long as seventy years after the death of the author, and films and sound recordings are now protected in the United States for ninety-five years after they were produced (see chapter 13). Finally, the problem of co-ordinating production is subject to the pressure of time ('time flies'), especially in the live performing arts, in which opening nights and concert schedules are advertised long in advance, but also, for example, in film production, when shooting schedules require the 'motley crew' to be in the same place at the same time.

Types of contracts

Caves identifies several different types of contracts: implicit, incentive, relational and option contracts. Each has different features and is appropriate to different economic conditions; all are made use of in one or another of the creative industries.

Implicit contract

The implicit contract is not a formal written contract but, rather, an understanding based on custom. It relies on trust and reputation rather than formal arrangements. Such deals are common in the art and antiques market but could be found in any small-scale community, even a worldwide one, in which individuals know, or know of, each other. The handshake contract between an artist and dealer or gallery discussed earlier is of this type. Pop groups are notorious for not making formal contracts when they start out, which can lead to serious problems later on, especially if they are very successful.

Incentive contract

In an incentive contract, the payment ('reward') is linked to the contribution each party brings to the deal, and is designed to encourage both parties to perform their best and to overcome principal–agent issues. An example is a royalty contract on a copyrighted work, such as a book; the publisher agrees to pay the royalty based on the retail price of the book to the author in exchange for the right to publish and sell the book. Both share the risk of its success or failure, and that ties them together in the undertaking (as explained in chapter 13). The author can easily check on the price but needs to be able to verify the sales to find out if the publisher is paying him or her the right amount of royalty. Copyright royalties are not predictable, however, because 'nobody knows' how successful the product will be. In many situations, though, the contribution of the individual artist to the economic success of the deal cannot be identified, especially in a 'motley crew'.

Relational contract

A relational contract is used when there is complementarity between partners who produce 'transaction-specific assets' – for instance a partnership between musicians in a pop band or string quartet, in which each member invests in a joint venture. If one member threatens to leave – to hold up the performance or a recording – the others experience 'switching costs', as they have to search for a replacement member. If all the members 'commit' equivalent resources, such as their time and experience to the group, they produce an asset that has value to each member over and above that which each individual would be able to produce on his or her own.

Option contract

Caves regards the option contract as being the most common type used in the creative industries. An option contract gives one party the right to control decisions about sequential activities, when one decision has consequences for the next stage in the chain of production. So, for example, a record label finances a pop group for several months to create a sound recording; if it is no good, the investment is wasted, but 'nobody knows' that in advance. In the event that it is good, though, the record label binds the pop group into a contract that gives the group the option to continue working on it. The record label that has sunk the investment wants the decision rights – the option to decide – over what to do with the sound recording and the right to make another recording with the group if the first is a success, and the label probably also wants to keep the option open to future collaboration. These decision rights and the way the record label rewards the pop group (usually with a royalty contract of a percentage of sales revenue) are all written into the contract.

Thus the option contract gives the entrepreneur an opportunity to assess the qualities of a piece of work before laying out any further investment on the project. This is partly because the products of the creative industries are complex and require investment at various stages of the chain of production (think of what goes into making a sound recording or film) and partly because of the incompleteness of contracts. Such a contract gives one party control over unanticipated payments ('residual rents') or other things that the (incomplete) contract did not specify.

Transfer of property rights

Whichever type of contract is used in any given situation, the outcome is the transfer of property rights of one sort or another between the parties to the contract. Contract incompleteness reinforces the need of the humdrum side of the firm (the 'suits' – the accountants, managers and investors in charge of the finances of the enterprise) to control property rights. Bargaining is not even-handed, however, because, typically, the industry side has the money and the artist has only his or her human capital and experience and also has to compete with others, unless he or she is a 'superstar'. Moreover, the more artists are involved (the 'motley crew' feature), the more difficult the bargaining process will be and the higher the contracting costs.

The main contribution of Caves' analysis is his proposition that the transfer of property rights typically follows the investment in sunk costs, which he recognises as being particularly high in many of the creative industries; the party with the greatest sunk costs will insist upon having control of the property rights over that stage of the chain of production. As a complex production process involves several distinct stages, there are sequential stages of investment in sunk costs, and the investor requires control over the decisions to be made about that stage and therefore acquires the property rights needed to proceed from one stage to the next. A well-known example of contracting that attempted to be complete by controlling all aspects of production is the Hollywood studio system, whereby a studio controlled every stage of film production and distribution (see box 4.3).

Gate-keeping

Caves has also noted in his analysis of the structure of the creative industries that they perform an important function in reducing search and information costs for both consumers and for producers by undertaking what sociologists call 'gate-keeping' and media analysts call 'intermediation'. Given the abundant, even excessive, supply of creative content by artists and other creators, not all of which can be produced and marketed by the creative industries, elements in those industries filter out the better material and people. This is typically done in the first instance by people such as literary agents, managers and talent scouts, who act as middlemen between the bigger firms and the individual creators whose work they assess. Trusted middlemen (many are in fact women!) act as intermediaries. Intermediation means more than that, however; it also means that what actually reaches the marketplace, and therefore the consumer, is the result of the selection made by the enterprises in the creative industries.

Economists explain gate-keeping in terms of the costs that firms would otherwise have to incur to search out and evaluate the quality of creative products. It seems that independent specialist firms are better able to do this and that the bigger media conglomerates therefore buy in their services rather than provide them in-house. This interesting economic aspect of creativity and quality assessment is discussed in more detail in the subsequent chapters on the industries in which this happens, especially with books and music. The internet has opened the door for artists to avoid this gate-keeping process, however, and approach the consumer directly – a topic Caves does not explore.

To sum up Caves' analysis of creative industries, several points can be noted. Although he emphasises the property rights approach of contract theory, he also uses what might be called more 'traditional' economic notions, such as returns to scale, that are essentially neoclassical concepts. He also adopts the view that there is excess supply in the creation of content and that this weakens the bargaining power of creators in these industries. He explains that weakness by arguing that decision rights and property rights will follow the economic logic of sunk investment – given that some investment is sunk, the entrepreneur can try to avoid further sunk costs by acquiring the decision rights to the next stage in the inevitably complex and uncertain environment that is faced by these industries. These are powerful ideas that go a long way to explaining the structure of firms and of markets throughout the creative industries, and they are explored in the subsequent chapters of this part of the book.

International trade, globalisation and cultural diversity

One of the claims of the United Kingdom's DCMS is that cultural goods and services are an important source of export earnings and this is part of the contribution of the creative industries to economic growth. In other countries, a concern of cultural policy is the domination of markets for cultural products via international trade by a few large-scale producers and the resulting loss of cultural diversity. Inevitably, this often means rejection of US hegemony and of the English language because cultural products in English are most easily and cheaply traded internationally to global markets due to economies of scale. International trade is market-driven and is the vehicle for the globalisation of all goods, services and technologies, including culture; although economists speak of trade taking place between countries, those who transact it are typically private enterprises. Concerns over globalisation through international trade in cultural goods have given rise to exceptions in international trade treaties and to special regulations for the creative industries. In this section, statistics on international trade in cultural products are presented first and the scene set for discussing the question of globalisation and cultural diversity. In the next section, regulation in international trade is examined.

International trade flows

As with statistics measuring the contribution of the output of the creative industries to national GDP, so the appropriate way of collecting international trade statistics is also subject to much debate, and the matter is made the more complex by the aim for universality in the data on the products traded by the 192 member countries of the United Nations. Trade is a basis for economic development, and UN agencies report trade statistics according to development categories (developed countries, developing countries, economies in transition, and so on). The established basis for collecting trade data for goods is by product type but services present problems, not least due to the fact that many countries do not collect such data; according to the *Creative Economy Report 2008*, only fifty-seven UN member states report trade in services. Furthermore, there is no standardised way of collecting the data, and the figures that are collected include items, such as royalty payments for patents, that do not relate to the creative industries, thus inflating those figures, but they do not include items such as box-office revenue from cultural tourism, thus understating the value of international trade in creative services. These problems pertain to the data presented in tables 14.1, 14.2 and 14.3. The classification of both goods and services for international trade purposes differs from that used in domestic production, and it is a specialised topic.[12]

In chapter 2, the point was made that trade is unevenly distributed throughout the world and, in fact, most trade takes place between a relatively small number of countries; this is also the case with international trade in creative

Table 14.1 Percentage of world trade in creative goods by product group, 2005

Arts and crafts	7
Audio-visuals	0.2
Design	65
Music	4
New media	4
Publishing	13
Visual arts	7

Source: UNCTAD (2008).

[12] See UNCTAD (2008: table 5.1).

Table 14.2 Top exporters of creative goods,[a] 2005

Rank in 2005	Market share[b] (%)	Growth 2000–5 (%)
China	18	18
Italy	8	6
Hong Kong (China)	8	1
United States	8	4
Germany	7	14
United Kingdom	6	10
France	5	9
Canada	3	2

[a] All creative industries.
[b] Share of world total (rounded).
Source: UNCTAD (2008: 260).

Table 14.3 Imports and exports of audio-visual services, and royalties and licence fees for leading countries, 2005 (million US dollars)

	Imports	Exports
Audio-visual and related services		
World total	16,392	17,518
Canada	1,773	444
China	154	134
Japan	903	82
Germany	2,809	705
United Kingdom	1,090	2,499
United States	915	7,060
Royalties and licence fees		
World total	134,548	123,842
Canada	6,649	3,471
China	5,321	157
Japan	14,654	17,655
Germany	6,589	6,828
United Kingdom	9,069	13,303
United States	24,501	57,410

Source: UNCTAD (2008: 303–4, 313–15).

goods and in creative services.[13] In addition to this pattern, the type of product traded internationally is also very uneven, as table 14.1 shows.

Table 14.2 shows the top exporting countries of creative *goods* (such as TV sets and CDs) in 2005. China is the leading exporter and also has the highest rate of growth of exports, so it can be expected to pull even further ahead in the future. The issue for the income from foreign trade, however, is the balance of payments and the value of net exports – the excess of the value of exports over imports. By 2005 the European Union (treated as a single entity in some recent trade statistics) and Canada were importing and exporting the same value of creative goods – that is, they had an almost zero balance of payments for goods – but the United States and Japan were net importers. When the data on international trade in *services* are analysed, however, there is a very different story; then it can be seen that the United States is a huge net exporter of audio-visual services (film, broadcasting, and so on) and of royalties and licence fees, and the only other net exporter in this category is the United Kingdom (table 14.3).

The picture underlying these international trade figures was one of a marked concentration of firms producing the exported cultural products. In 1993 36 per cent of the companies were based in the United States, 36 per cent in the European Union and 26 per cent in Japan, but only four years later over 50 per cent were based in the United States. Now around 85 per cent of worldwide screened films are made in Hollywood, and Hollywood earns a half of its revenues from overseas markets, compared to 30 per cent in 1980, even though more films were actually made in India and in Europe each year than in Hollywood and Asia produces as many films as it imports (see chapter 16).

Globalisation and cultural diversity

Cultural economists and cultural policy-makers are in two minds about the pros and cons of globalisation. On the one hand, free trade reduces the prices of cultural goods as countries specialise in producing those goods in which they have a comparative advantage, introduce new goods to some countries and transfer new technologies and ideas; on the other hand, though, cheap products may be lower in quality and lacking in cultural diversity; moreover, imports may undermine the development of markets that could supply material that is more specifically targeted to individual countries' cultures and identities. There are both economic and cultural arguments here, and cultural economists cannot separate them.

---

[13] The term 'creative' is now applied to every aspect of the creative economy in UNCTAD (2008).

It is argued, however, that the internet – a strong force for globalisation – enables the development of niche markets that make specialised and esoteric cultural goods available to consumers all over the world, thus increasing cultural diversity. Furthermore, with a wide offering of cultural products available, no one is forced to consume the globalised products decried by critics; indeed, it is one of the difficulties that cultural policy-makers have to overcome that even with trade restrictions, such as the screen quotas and content rules for TV programmes discussed later on, consumers do not show a preference for the products of a national or regional industry fostered by such policies, as evidenced in chapters 16 and 17.

Concentration of ownership, especially in the hands of US companies, is one of the elements of the fears that free trade reduces rather than increases cultural diversity. This is a matter of concern to national policy-makers and to supranational bodies, such as UNESCO, and gives rise to policies to protect national and regional markets in contravention of the aim of international regulatory bodies such as the WTO to liberalise international trade.

International regulatory policies

The main body that regulates – or, rather, seeks to *deregulate* – international trade is the World Trade Organization. It aims to promote free international trade by removing barriers such as tariffs, the preferential treatment of national products, quotas and import restrictions. With its GATS (General Agreement on Trade in Services), this includes cultural services. The WTO is also responsible for the TRIPS agreement, which is concerned with copyright and other intellectual property in world trade and therefore has important implications for international trade in cultural goods and services.

Like other international treaties, TRIPS and GATS are agreements between nations to extend an agreed minimum level of protection of IP rights to the producers and traders in all signatory countries. Some countries offer protection above the minimum requirement (for example, the international treaties on copyright, the Berne Convention and TRIPS require protection of authors' rights for fifty years after the author's death, whereas the law in many countries now gives protection for seventy years after death). When trading countries offer the same conditions for trade, this is called most favoured nation (MFN) status. There are some exceptions to the exact terms of MFN offered and several of these relate to cultural products – the so-called 'cultural exception' to MFN. The doctrine of cultural exception was applied to GATS, with the result that the European Union refused to liberalise services in broadcasting and film or on services related to libraries, archives or museums; other countries in the negotiations did so too, with the outcome that only a minority of countries agreed to free trade in all cultural goods and services. Trade in some sectors of the creative industries is free, however, for example in publishing and architectural services.[14]

The doctrine of cultural exception allows the EU countries (and those other countries that applied it, such as Canada) to adopt a protectionist audio-visual policy, while its member states enjoy MFN status for other goods and services. It recognises the symbolic significance of cultural products in the life of a nation (and region, in the case of the European Union) and the desire to protect and promote cultural diversity and sets limits to the globalisation of culture through international trade. It remains to be seen how these trade agreements and rules withstand the so far unregulated and transnational nature of the internet. Audio-visual policies that concern film and television are dealt with in chapters 16 and 17.

There are several points of significance in this. The WTO enables countries to apply trade sanctions to other signatory countries that fail to honour the treaty conditions; for example, the United States can apply restrictions on the imports of clothing goods from China if China does not sufficiently protect copyright material produced in the United States (such as software and CDs). In this, the WTO differs from UNESCO and its Convention on Cultural Diversity, which does not have those powers of enforcement. There is also international co-operation in controlling trade in illegal products, such as counterfeit and 'pirated' goods, which are increasingly produced and traded internationally, especially via the internet.

Conclusion

This chapter demonstrates that the analysis of the creative industries can be treated in an integral way and that it links up with topics that have long been studied in cultural economics. Moreover, viewing the arts and heritage as well as the cultural industries as a sector in the economy in their own right has become part of the political economic scene not only in those countries that have championed the creative industries but also in international organisations. Even if we wanted to ignore this as hype, it has become impossible to do so. Nevertheless, it is important that economists continue to be sceptical of

---

[14] See http://ec.europa.eu/avpolicy/ext/multilateral/wto/index_en.htm (accessed 4 January 2009).

claims made for the size and growth of these industries, at least until the data are collected and analysed on an appropriate standardised basis. In addition, it always has to be remembered that charting and mapping these industries does not say anything about causality; for example, the use by WIPO and the WTO of words such as 'dependence' suggests that the underlying cause of growth in the creative industries is well understood.

This chapter also serves as an introduction to the topics that are investigated in subsequent chapters in this part of the book in an industry-by-industry treatment, reporting on the empirical and theoretical research by cultural and other economists on each industry. In surveying the scope of the creative industries as a field of study in cultural economics, the chapter has covered a range of theoretical and practical topics. In it, we have seen the role that the rhetoric of creativity plays in advocating the concept of the creative industries as a sector of the economy, and also that of copyright law as being necessary to protect and promote creative production. The implication is that, without copyright, these industries would fail, though, as the discussion in chapter 13 showed, this dependence is not proven.

Nevertheless, it can be accepted that the cultural products of the creative industries are mostly protected by copyright law (or have come out of copyright and passed into the public domain) and that this can be a legitimate way of defining the creative industries, given that any definition is arbitrary and the greatest need is for consistency in classifying and reporting data.

In addition to the general problems of properly measuring the value added by the creative industries to GDP and the balance of payments, which are an indication of the economic role of these industries, there is also the problem of measuring their qualitative aspects in the context of policy on cultural diversity and global international trade. Many nations worry that their distinctive cultures and cultural products could be wiped out by the cheaper products of large international corporations that are freely traded around the world. This has led to national, regional and international policies to protect cultural identity and promote diversity and the regulation of free markets in cultural goods and services. The pros and cons of these policies are an important topic in cultural economics and are an extension of the discussion on the role of government in the cultural sector that was the subject of chapters 7 and 10 in this book. The supply of new and diverse cultural products is important for the success not only of cultural policy but also of other policy objectives, such as consumer choice, access to information and freedom of expression. In addition, cultural products have symbolic importance that may make the case for specific regulation, for example of broadcasting.

As cultural economists, we need to understand the underlying economic incentives that determine the structure of these industries – the tendency to competition or monopoly, mergers, vertical and horizontal integration – and the contracts that are made between artists and other creators and the 'humdrum' side of the industries, as analysed by Caves. Regulation through competition law and other laws specifically dedicated to the media industries requires that these aspects of economic organisation be understood. The study of the creative industries is not just the domain of cultural economists, however, and other social scientists bring a different approach to understanding them. Cultural sociologists are credited with having done the bulk of the empirical studies on cultural industries well before economists came to terms with them. The concepts of intermediation and the role of gate-keeping have been very influential in under-standing the socio-cultural implications of concentration and globalisation in the sector, and these are themes that are also studied in media economics. There is much to be gained from a multidisciplinary approach to the study of the creative industries and of policies directed at them.

Further reading

There is no shortage of reading on the topics covered in this chapter! All students of cultural economics should read Richard Caves' (2000) book *Creative Industries*; Shapiro and Varian (1999) is still pertinent and gives a good idea of how business economists approach the information economy, particularly in respect of digitalisation. Chapter 7 of David Throsby's book *Economics and Culture* (2001) is on 'Cultural industries'. There are several chapters in the Towse (2003a) *Handbook of Cultural Economics* that provide introductory over-views of topics discussed here: Towse on 'Cultural industries' (chapter 20), Keith Acheson on 'Globalization' (chapter 31), Michael Hutter on 'Information goods' (chapter 33) and Günther Schulze on 'International trade' (chapter 34).

Gillian Doyle's 2002 book *Media Ownership* covers the regulation of media in Europe well, while the 1999 book by Keith Acheson and Christopher Maule, *Much Ado about Culture*, has a particular emphasis on Canadian protectionist policy. Acheson and Maule have also contributed a chapter, 'Culture in international trade', to the Ginsburgh and Throsby (2006) *Handbook of the Economics of Art and Culture* (chapter 33) and the main article to an issue of the *Journal of Cultural Economics*, volume 28 number 4 (November 2004), on the UNESCO Convention on Cultural Diversity, with comments by Rick van der Ploeg, Françoise Benhamou and Lelio Iapadre.

The many professional publications cited in the chapter are also accessible; in particular, the UNCTAD (2008) *Creative Economy Report 2008* is worth reading. There are creative industries reports in many countries and a quick search will unearth one for your country or region. A nice critical article reviewing recent government reports from several countries is by Anne Kolmodin (2008).

Economics of the music industry

This chapter concentrates mainly on music publishing and sound recording, as I have elsewhere touched on many of the other segments of the music industry: composers and performers were included in the analysis of artists' labour markets in chapters 11 and 12 and the role of copyright in chapter 13; chapter 8 discussed music, dance and opera as performing arts. The topics of the general introduction to the creative industries in chapter 14 all apply to the music industry and are investigated in further detail here.

Technical change and copyright

Music was one of the first of the cultural industries to be afforded protection through copyright law: as early as the nineteenth century composers were protected by authors' rights under the Berne Convention, and in the early years of the twentieth century music publishers and composers were granted so-called 'mechanical rights' in the mechanical reproduction of music, initially using piano rolls and, later, sound recording, and composers' so-called 'synchronisation' rights enable them also to control the use of their music on TV and in film and video. With the spread of radio ownership, the public performance of music led to copyright legislation that enabled composers and publishers to collect remuneration for the public performance of music from broadcasting, and this right was later extended to sound recording makers and performers. Other public performance of music also requires a licence, which is issued by a collecting society (see chapter 13).

The development and spread of the home ownership of record players and the development of shellac records started the post-Second-World-War consumer boom for sales of sound recordings in the United States, which spread to all developed countries, so that most households came to own several sound carriers of one sort or another, fuelling sales of sound recordings to a mass market. Meanwhile, music became a vital part of the emerging teenage culture in the 1950s, and pop stars surfaced as cultural icons, promoted on radio and television, often through disc jockeys, a new occupation of people specialised in selecting and playing sound recordings on radio and in clubs and discos; there was a dubious practice known as 'payola' – payment to a DJ to push a certain recording or artist.[1] Music videos also came on the scene, originally as promotion for records but soon becoming an integral part of the music experience. Cassettes enabled consumers to play music outside the home and to record music from the radio themselves, and the playing of recorded music in public became part of almost every activity, from travel to shopping. The story was the same for CDs, but it was not until the 1990s that the development of digital technology and the internet enabled consumers to access and record music 'on demand' for themselves. DVD as a format gained in popularity and DVD music sales rose in the 1990s, while sales of cassettes and CDs began to fall.

The question that has now been addressed by economists, among others, is the extent to which the new technologies that enable the unauthorised use of music without payment have been the cause of the decline in the sales of the sound recording industry, and what the overall welfare effects might be. After all, historically all technological progress has harmed some established industries and their workers but brought increasing wealth and well-being to society at large. Sound recording itself displaced thousands of live musicians, who even in the 1970s were waging a 'Live Music' campaign in the United Kingdom with broadcasters to limit 'needle time' – the use of recorded instead of live music. It is a well-attested fact in the economics of innovation that the adoption of new inventions is rarely achieved by incumbents in the industry and it is newcomers who demonstrate their wider uses; the recent history of the sound recording industry has demonstrated this par excellence, and the Schumpeterian 'creative destruction' model appears to apply to it. As a result, the music industry, especially in the 2000s, has attracted the attention of cultural economists and others interested in the economic effects of technical change wrought by the internet.

Primary and secondary markets

In the sound recording industry, two markets operate side by side: the primary market, for sales of sound recordings and printed music, and the secondary market, for these products to reach the consumer in conjunction with another

---

[1] Coase (1979); see also Connolly and Krueger (2006).

service, such as broadcasting or as background music, in discos and so on. Both markets are important sources of revenue for composers and performers, though the secondary market is less important for sound recording makers. In almost all European countries (with the exceptions of Ireland and the United Kingdom) music rights holders also receive income from a levy on blank recording media (cassettes, CDs, computers) – that is, remuneration for the loss of sales that are displaced by home recording. These streams of income arise from the array of rights accorded to composers, performers and sound recording makers under copyright law. As explained in chapter 13, royalties on sales of recorded music are paid to contracted artists by the record label, while licence fees from the secondary market are mostly collected and distributed by collecting societies.

In this chapter, these various aspects of the music industry are analysed, starting with the overall picture of consumption and production.

Consumption and production in the music industry

The varied nature of the music industry makes it difficult to give an overall picture of consumption and production for the whole industry. It is necessary to consider the different sectors in turn, using several sources of information to build up a picture of the different markets for music.

Consumption and participation

Consumption implies that a good is purchased on a market (real or virtual), but this is not always the case, as many people make music for their own pleasure; even amateur activity usually involves payment for some items, however, such as sheet music or musical scores, musical instruments and, in the case of amateur bands, orchestras and choirs, the services of professional musicians as accompanists and conductors. Tickets are often sold for performances by unpaid amateurs (choirs, orchestras, bands) just to cover costs. Consumption in the form of attendances at live performances of all kinds (concerts, musicals and opera, clubs, festivals, and so on) can be measured by ticket sales; and sales revenue and licence fees for the use of published music and of recorded music provide information on their consumption. I return to these later.

There are also data on participation that are indicative of the popularity of music as a cultural activity. In addition to attendances at classical concerts reported in chapter 8, some countries provide data on broader participation in music. A 2006 survey of participation in Ireland showed that 28 per cent of the population participated in rock or popular music and 19 per cent in traditional Irish or folk music, and that 8 per cent played a musical instrument for pleasure. In Sweden in 2003, 58 per cent attended concerts (type unspecified), 17 per cent played instruments and 4 per cent sang in choirs. Canada collected information in 2005 on 'listening to recorded music on CD or other format' (84 per cent) and 'listening to downloaded music on a computer, MP3 player' (29 per cent).[2] In the United States, the average American spent forty-five minutes a day listening to music and almost three hours listening to the radio in 2000 (the data do not, however, distinguish the music content of radio listening).

Figures on CD sales per capita show the variation in consumption patterns between countries: in 2006 per capita sales were 2.7 in the United Kingdom, 2.1 in the United States, 1.9 in Australia, 1.5 in Canada and Japan, and 1.4 in Germany (IFPI, 2007). Demand for CDs is discussed in the section on piracy below.

Production

There are several stages in the production of music, starting with its creation and proceeding through to its marketing and reception by consumers, and many different individuals and organisations are involved at each stage. At the initial stage of content creation are the creative artists – composers, songwriters and performers (singers, instrumentalists, conductors); as described in chapter 11, they are assisted by agents, managers, promoters and the like, who act on their behalf. Music publishers handle musical compositions; they both publish the music and manage its copyrights, dealing with the array of public performance, mechanical and synchronisation rights with record, film and broadcasting companies. Sound recording ('phonogram') makers make and distribute records in various formats (cassettes, CDs, music videos, DVDs – generically called 'sound carriers') and supply them to retail outlets for sale to the final consumer and to the many other organisations in the secondary market that use music as part of their own production (restaurants, sports halls and the rest; see chapter 13). The copyright collecting societies that administer the musical rights of artists, publishers and record companies are

[2] Arts Council (2006) for Ireland, Swedish Arts Council (2003) and results of General Social Survey 2005 for Canada, reported in Council of Europe/ERICarts (2008).

Table 15.1 Estimated value added of UK music industry, 1995 (million pounds)

Live performance: rock, pop, etc.	300.0
Live performance: classical, etc.	146.0
Other artists' earnings[a]	525.0
Opera and music theatre	120.0
Recording[b]	415.4
Music publishing	85.5
Collection societies	23.3
Retailing and distribution	334.1
Musical instruments: production, retailing and distribution	319.0
Managers, agents and promoters	132.0
Education and training[c]	100.9
Total	2,501.2

[a] Estimates by Cliff Dane.
[b] Including manufacturing and majors' distribution.
[c] Excluding mainstream schooling.
Source: Dane, Feist and Laing (1996: table 68).

another feature of the music industry (again, see chapter 13). Then there are the various businesses providing a range of services, such as musical instrument makers and music providers, venue operators and ticket agents, who depend upon the various branches of the music industry. Table 15.1 provides a breakdown of the value added of all the sectors in the chain of production in the music industry in the United Kingdom. Although its source is somewhat out of date now, it is unique in having data on artists' earnings. We may suppose that, even with the advent of P2P in 1999, these proportions will have remained more or less the same.

In the DCMS typology explained in chapter 14, these activities can be thought of in layers in descending order of creativity, with composition and the creation of performances in layer 1. Another typology is that of WIPO (see box 14.2), in which the composition and performance as well as the creation of sound recordings are core copyright activities. Either way, an important feature of the music industry, in common with other information goods industries, is that at its core is the intangible, copyrightable content that is packaged in the different media for communication to the consumer. A CD is just a piece of plastic and, without the bits and bytes that are embodied in it, it has little value; the value is in the content, not the medium. It is precisely the intangible nature of music that makes it so vulnerable to misappropriation and necessitates the apparatus of copyright law and collective rights management organisations to appropriate the rewards for those who created and produced it. The other economic activities of the music industry that rely upon the success of the content build on that core or layer activity.

The establishment of property rights in music via copyright law is significant for the internal organisation of the music industry, because licensing arrangements at various stages of the production process make subcontracting of some of the production processes possible, and they also enable the sale of catalogues and artists between record labels, which is what takes place in a merger between record labels or the transfer of artists from one label to another. As we saw in chapter 14, Caves' analysis of the economic organisation of the creative industries rested on contracting over property rights and the investment made by the humdrum side of the industry (the so-called 'suits'). This provides the framework for analysing the structure of the different sections of the music industry and their implications for copyright law.

Sectors of the music industry

Composition/songwriting

The starting point for the production of music is the musical composition, and, as with many artistic activities, there is an excess supply of musical composition, leading to what has been called a 'Malthusian nightmare' for composers of contemporary classical music – the creation of compositions proceeds at a rate that vastly exceeds opportunities for getting them performed and therefore paid for. In some countries there is state subsidy for composition, and, to ensure that subsidised compositions are performed, grants are often made to the performing organisation, such as the orchestra or band, for them to commission a work on the condition that it is performed (and that more than once). Composers typically supply works for a range of purposes besides live performance: music for films and TV programmes, advertising jingles and arrangements of existing music. They usually have an agent, who makes contacts for them with publishers and other music users.

Composers may also conduct and perform their own music in concerts and recordings; this is also typical of the way many pop groups and bands work, with composition and songwriting taking place experimentally in a studio. Formally composed music can easily be created on a computer using standard software and printed off by the composer in a performing version. This is a tremendous change from the days when the original score had to be copied and all the parts[3] produced separately. It also removes from the music publisher the function of printing music, although, like literary publishers, they assist with editing. Music cannot simply exist in the composer's computer or on paper, however; it needs to be performed, and, in order to get the composition to market, composers and songwriters seek the services of a music publisher.

Music publishing

Music publishing, besides the selling and renting of printed music, is concerned with managing rights for composers and making deals for them with users of music. Publishers may require the assignment of rights from the composer in order to exploit the market for the composition, as predicted by Caves' contract theory. The composer or songwriter has a contract with the music publisher, who traditionally receives the so-called 'publisher's share' – 50 per cent of the royalty income from mechanical and synchronisation royalties. Royalties from public performance are typically collected by a rights management organisation (collecting society) and the music publisher usually receives 25 per cent of that income. Bearing in mind that copyright on a musical work (song title or other composition) lasts seventy years from the death of the composer, the nearly US$7 billion worldwide in revenues from music publishing are not so surprising (see table 15.2). The table provides data for 2000 for revenues from music publishing in the main world music markets – the United States, Japan, Germany, France and the United Kingdom – as well as the world total. It can be seen that mechanical royalties are the biggest single source for the four countries that have a sizable sound recording industry and synchronisation royalties reflect the dominant position of film music in the United States and the United Kingdom.

In terms of the market structure of the music publishing industry, the major publishers are arms of the 'major' record companies, though there are several notable smaller firms in the industry. For example, Sony Entertainment Inc., an arm of the Sony Corporation of America, has a 50 per cent ownership of Sony BMG Music Entertainment as well as 50 per cent of Sony/ATV Music Publishing (in a joint venture with Michael Jackson at the time of writing).

---

[3] As mentioned in chapter 2, each instrument of an orchestra or ensemble has its own part, with only the conductor and sound engineer having the full score. These parts can be controlled by the publisher as an elementary form of protection against misappropriation.

Table 15.2 World revenues from music publishing, 2000 (million US dollars)

	United States	Japan	Germany	France	United Kingdom	Other	World total
Public performance revenue							
Radio	291.8	108.9	50.8	23.0	60.3	179.3	714.1
TV/cable/satellite	317.0	16.1	84.3	122.2	64.4	465.1	1,069.1
Live performance	203.1	158.2	180.9	174.6	126.0	450.4	1,293.2
Subtotal	811.9	283.2	316.0	319.8	250.7	1,094.7	3,076.3
Reproduction revenue							
Mechanical royalties	691.5	311.3	258.7	105.8	195.9	432.1	1,995.3
Synchronisation royalties	156.7	80.5	67.8	50.8	124.6	189.5	669.9
Other	–	16.1	16.0	17.0	–	23.8	72.9
Subtotal	848.2	407.9	342.5	173.5	320.5	645.5	2,738.1
Distribution revenue							
Sheet music sales	316.1	19.9	140.2	58.3	69.2	125.2	728.9
Rental/lending rights	n.a.	30.9	6.6	–	–	2.4	39.9
Subtotal	316.1	50.7	146.8	58.3	69.2	127.6	768.8
Other	30.4	78.9	28.8	49.7	26.2	80.1	294.1
Total	2,006.5	820.7	834.0	601.2	666.6	1,948.2	6,877.3

Source: Throsby (2002: 6); figures may not sum precisely due to rounding.

Sony/ATV Music Publishing owns or administers copyrights and catalogues of the Beatles, Bob Dylan, Jimi Hendrix, Joni Mitchell and Hank Williams, to name a few.[4] Sony/ATV in the United Kingdom publishes songwriter Mike Batt, whose work is widely recorded by many different performers. Although they are known to run into millions, there are no figures on the number of song titles in copyright or figures on royalty payments to them.

Sound recording

By 2007 production in the record industry worldwide was dominated by four major companies, EMI, Sony BMG (SBMG), Universal Music Group (UMG) and Warner Music Group (WMG); that year the share of each by volume in the US domestic market was UMG 32 per cent, SBMG 25 per cent, WMG 20 per cent and EMI 9 per cent. Independent labels had 14 per cent of the market.

Unit sales in the United States (including online paid downloads and physical sales, but excluding mobile) totalled 1.37 billion, an increase of 15 per cent over the previous year. The pattern differed by type of sound carrier:

---

[4] See www.sony.com/SCA/outline/atv.shtml (accessed 10 January 2009).

- CDs 449.2 million, down by 19 per cent;
- digital albums = 50 million, up 54 per cent (10 per cent of the album market in the United States);
- single tracks = 844.1 million, up 45 per cent.[5]

The main source of information on world sales of sound recordings is the International Federation of Phonographic Industries (IFPI), the industry lead body. According to IFPI data, the retail value of sales of recorded music (physical, digital and performance rights revenues) in 2007 was just under US$30 billion; the United States and Japan accounted for half of the total, the United Kingdom, Germany and France a further quarter.[6] As is well known, sales of sound recordings fell during the first years of the twenty-first century, attributed by the industry to 'piracy' – unauthorised use – brought on by the development of P2P and MP3 file-sharing technologies available on the internet and made accessible by various file-sharing services, starting with Napster. The development of legal downloading services, mainly by new firms unconnected to the sound recording industry, such as iTunes and the accompanying iPod hardware, has led to an increase in downloads. The topic of piracy is discussed in more detail below. Legal downloads and sales of digital music were rising in 2008, according to the IFPI (see box 15.1).

International trade

In 2005, according to the UNCTAD *Creative Economy Report 2008*, music exports (which were 99 per cent CDs – that is, physical goods, not services) were valued at nearly US$15 billion, of which 75 per cent were from Europe and 10 per cent from the United States. The top exporter was Germany, with 23 per cent of total world exports, followed by the United Kingdom and the United States, both with 10 per cent. Nevertheless, 84 per cent of all imports of CDs were also by developed countries: Germany was the biggest importer, with 15 per cent of the world total, followed by the United Kingdom with 10 per cent, the United States with 8 per cent and France with 6 per cent, attesting both to the imbalance in international trade in the music industry and to the fact that major exporters are also major importers.[7]

Taken together, all these data on the music industry paint a picture of a highly concentrated industry whose production and consumption are concentrated in developed countries, generating revenues through sales of sound

---

[5] See www.ifpi.org/content/section_statistics/index.html (accessed 10 January 2008).
[6] See www.ifpi.org/content/library/Recorded-music-sales-2007.pdf.   [7] UNCTAD (2008).

Box 15.1 IFPI statistics for the first half of 2008

The International Federation of Phonographic Industries collects data worldwide on the market performance of sales and licensing of sound recordings.
- Global digital sales increased by 25 per cent in the first half of 2008.
- Sales through digital platforms now account for 20 per cent of the world market, compared to 15 per cent in 2007.
- The global overall market decline is slowing: trade revenues to record companies were down by 5 per cent, compared to an 8 per cent fall in 2007.
- UK digital music sales were up 45 per cent to US$116 million, well above average and the highest digital growth among the top five markets.
- There was overall market growth in trade revenues to record companies in thirteen countries.
- Global sales of music in physical formats were down by 12 per cent.
- The United States and the United Kingdom together account for 60 per cent of the global decline in CD sales.
- Japan's overall market for recorded music was up by 6 per cent.
- There was double-digit growth in performance rights income worldwide.
      Source: www.ifpi.org/content/library/First-Half-2008.pdf (accessed 04 January 2009).

Box 15.2 Music in Jamaica

Home to the legendary Bob Marley and many other successful musicians past and present, music is a vital part of the Jamaican image and culture at home and abroad. Shaggy, Jamaica's only living Diamond-plus selling artist, has sold over 20 million albums, has had five no.1 hits and eleven top ten singles worldwide and has won a Grammy. The Jamaican government has recognised its music industry as part of its development strategy and has introduced tax measures to assist Jamaican artists and producers. Even so, Jamaica ranked only seventy-first in world music sales in 2000 and the music industry employed just 1 per cent of the employed labour force.
      Sources: www.bigyardmusic.com/index.php?option=com_bigyard&artist=
                  1&show=biography&Itemid=20 and Throsby (2002).

carriers to both domestic and international markets but also through royalties from licences and downloads.

Music is being promoted by various international organisations as a creative industry that could foster economic growth in less developed countries. Jamaica is a country with a long history of world-renowned music that is supported by the government; as box 15.2 shows, however, it is a considerable challenge to reap economic benefits from world-class music.

Economic organisation of the sound recording industry

This section applies the economic analysis of previous chapters to the economic organisation of the sound recording sector of the music industry. It reviews the recording deal, contract and transfer of property rights in the light of Caves' theory of the industrial structure of the creative industries.

The recording deal

The sequence of events that takes place in popular music is that a band forms to perform music live and makes demo tapes; it may write its own music, but if it uses music by other composers and songwriters it will have to pay public performance royalties for live performances and mechanical royalties on any sound recording. It starts playing as many gigs as it can in clubs and pubs, gets a manager (who works for between 15 and 30 per cent of the revenues of both concerts and record deals) and moves on to bigger venues, while trying to get a recording contract; early on it creates a website, and may make some of its music available on the internet. Through the manager, a lucky or highly talented band gets a record and publishing contract (and so needs a lawyer), is promoted on radio and TV, adopted by disc jockeys, plays the opening number for a well-established band, and so forth; there are various ways all this happens, but it is not necessary to go into them all here.

The contract

In terms of Caves' analysis, the point for economics is that every deal involves a contract, an agreement between the parties concerned to do certain things, often with a performance or delivery date (Caves' 'time flies'), involving outlays of time and investment in the pertinent activities – creating its repertoire, rehearsing and publicising its image for the band, management, publishing, recording, production and marketing – that require contracting between artists and the humdrum business side. From the record label's perspective, a new band is a step into the unknown ('nobody knows'); it will give the band an advance on future royalties up front on signing the record deal (usually for an album) but in only one in eight deals will the record label recoup its outlays. It needs a few big successes to finance its losses on unsuccessful albums, which is essentially a system of cross-subsidisation and risk-pooling by the label. This explains the strategy on the part of the sound recording industry of focusing on superstars.

The contract aims to stipulate the terms of agreement and may run into many pages but, however detailed it may be, it will inevitably be incomplete and cannot foresee all contingencies; for example, the band may not be able to create sufficient music for an album or it may not meet deadlines. Caves' property rights approach tells us that the record company will therefore defend its investment, which has been sunk (perhaps literally too!) in the band in several ways. First, it will want a risk-sharing deal with the band receiving a royalty rate, which is usually between 10 and 15 per cent on sales (superstars get more – the Beatles eventually got 25 per cent);[8] this gives the band the incentive to engage in publicity events, concert tours and the like to promote the album. Second, the record company pockets all the sales revenue until the advance on royalties has been 'paid back'. Third, the contract is likely to be an option contract giving the record label the option on the band's next album, as an insurance for the record company should the first album be successful or sufficiently promising to suggest future success. If the sales on the first album still have not been sufficient to pay off the advance, the outstanding amount is passed on to the next album as a form of collateral to increase the incentive. It has been calculated that an album needs sales of 1 million to clear all liabilities fully, and only the superstars achieve that. This may act as a deterrent to the band to spend an excessive amount on the recording of the album and DVD. The typical recording contract gives the record label a deal over a period of five or more years and specifies the number of albums to be made over which it has an option; in the 1980s and 1990s that was an eight-album deal, but this seems to have been reduced. The 'option' also allows the record label not to publish an album if it does not think it will sell.

Transfers of property rights

If the band is signed with a smaller independent label and has a big success, it may choose to move on to one of the majors, or the 'indie' label might sell it on. When there is a merger of sound recording companies (and there were two between major companies in the first few years of the twenty-first century), artists are transferred via their contracts to the new company. The other side of the coin is that, if the band breaks up, property rights have to be reassigned within the band, and this can lead to bitter fights over ownership, made all the

---

[8] This is in principle, but, regardless of the royalty rate, there are various stipulations that mean the band gets royalties on only 75 per cent of sales; see Caves (2000: 3); see also Vogel (2001).

worse if the band has failed (as many do at the outset) to allocate property rights between the members. Then the record label is unlikely to be able to enforce its contract, although it will still have earnings from sales and copyright on existing recordings, which it has to share with the manager under the usual terms of the deal.

Microeconomic analysis of firms in the music industry

Besides applying contract theory to understanding the economic organisation of the sound recording industry, the theory of the firm can be applied to other branches of the music industry. It can safely be said that the 'humdrum' side of the industry is motivated by profit maximisation, but is that true of the creative side – the composers, songwriters and performers? Studies of artists' labour markets suggest that they are more concerned with artistic success and reputation (Caves' 'art for art's sake'); it cannot be ignored, however, that, at least in the commercial music sector, the two go hand in hand. It should also be noted, by the way, that national statistics count composers and songwriters, who are self-employed, as firms (and they may also be thought of as entrepreneurs). Content creation, whether motivated by the desire for art, fame or profit, is an economic activity.

In a now familiar manner, economists ask why some of the inputs to the production process are bought in and others supplied within the firm – the make-or-buy decision; what are the economic forces that govern the size of the firm and lead to the observed mergers and oligopoly in music publishing and sound recording? In answering these questions, well-known neoclassical economic concepts, such as economies of scale and scope, barriers to entry, and so forth, can be applied and, later, the theory of transaction cost economics is applied. These ideas can be applied to all branches of the industry, including live performance by non-profit organisations (classical concerts, opera) and for-profit companies (musicals), but the analysis here relates mostly to the world of unsubsidised recorded music.[9]

Barriers to entry

Composing music has a low entry barrier and, depending on the level of sophistication the genre requires, it can be done by anyone with the creative

---

[9] There are in fact subsidies in some European countries for pop music, which are chiefly used in training and getting started.

drive and time available. Though nowadays computers and music keyboards are used, composition can be done equally well with a pencil and paper. Similarly, the formation of a band (or a solo performer) has no barrier to entry other than the opportunity cost of the individuals' time, and even that may be low if creating and performing is a leisure activity or if the individuals would otherwise be unemployed. The size of the band or ensemble, at least at the start-up phase, is probably determined by personal and artistic motives rather than economic ones; once it begins to get a name, it has the incentive to maintain its image and brand name (which can be trademarked).

Recording music at one time required a considerable investment in capital and human capital assets but technological developments in capital equipment have made it possible for almost anyone to make a reasonable demo tape at home using equipment available to every consumer (hence the term 'garage music'); the barrier to entry into sound recording is therefore also low. The same technological progress in sound recording has similarly made entry to supplying professional sound recording services relatively easy, and the emphasis has switched to skilled use of the equipment by expert sound engineers and producers from the ownership of the capital equipment (a good example of human capital assets). Bands, orchestras and other performers can therefore shop around in a competitive market for these services and for the equivalent professional services of making the music video. Moreover, as mentioned in chapter 11, pools of skilled musicians, singers and dancers are available in some centres of the music industry (London, Los Angeles) who can be hired on short-term contracts to make the recording and video. The pressing and packaging of CDs and other sound carriers has long been a specialised business (China specialises in it, as we saw in table 14.2) and a band can easily commission artists to design the artwork. Where barriers to entry exist, therefore, are in the marketing of music by publishers and record labels, which requires access to considerable amounts of financial capital, and in the property rights – the exclusive contracts the record company makes, the copyrights to the composed work, its performance and the sound recording, and the trademark of the band – which are used to exclude competition; these barriers can be overcome only by the acquisition of the rights by licence or by takeover until the copyrights enter the public domain.

Economies of scale and of scope

The discussion in chapter 14 on mergers in the cultural and media industries pointed to the role of economies of scale and scope in horizontal and vertical integration. The merging of music publishing and sound recording activities into the same ownership is vertical integration, and there has been horizontal integration within the sound recording sector with the many acquisitions and mergers over the years, resulting in there being at the time of writing (2008) only the four 'majors' coexisting with a number of small independent labels. The latter mostly supply niche markets, and so they are no threat to the majors; if they were, they would be vulnerable to being taken over. There has also been vertical disintegration within the sound recording industry, as record companies no longer need to own their own recording studios or to produce the recordings in-house.

The majors supply the international mass market with superstar performers and popular genre music, which they are able to market efficiently through economies of scope; they can advertise and promote several records side by side. In having a stable or roster of artists, they are able to turn the inherent uncertainty ('nobody knows') of the individual's success into a somewhat more manageable risk by spreading it across artists at different stages of their careers and over different genres. This risk-pooling is not a traditionally recognised source of economies of scale but it amounts to the same thing in the music industry. A new record label would not have this advantage in the market; it may have other advantages in respect of its ability to spot new talent and trends, however, and it has been suggested that the majors cannot handle this due to inflexible management procedures and bureaucratic problems that come with size – clear-cut examples of diseconomies of scale. These shortcomings can be described in relation to the artist and repertoire function of the sound recording firm, always known as A&R (discussed below). Similar problems apparently prevented the record industry from adapting its business models soon enough to the internet and to the demand by consumers for interactive services to download music (also discussed later in this chapter).

Transaction cost economics and the music industry

Chapter 5 sketched the implications of transaction cost economics for the firm and contrasted it with the neoclassical notion of the firm based on a production function determined by the underlying technology. The theory assumes that people act in their own self-interest and that, in the event of a conflict, self-interestedness leads to various types of behaviour, such as 'opportunism' – exploiting situations from which you can gain, ranging from honest disagreements to cheating ('guile') or 'hold-up' problems (one party can hold up the other's production, for example by refusing to supply until previously agreed prices are altered to the advantage of the party supplying a vital input). These problems are present when the firm buys in the resources it needs for its production, which it does when that is more efficient than making them in-house, but this lays it open to this kind of trust problem. When the resources in question are highly specialised 'specific' human capital assets – people with special talents and skills, as they are likely to be in the creative industries – they have the power to act opportunistically and hold up production. The implication for economic organisation is that firms attempt to control these specific assets through property rights and with contracts offering appropriate reward schemes. This theory explains the 'governance' of the firm – how it is organised to control property rights through partnerships, joint-stock companies or holding companies. Transaction cost economics has been applied to the music industry, highlighting the role of one specific resource, namely the A&R function.[10]

Artist and repertoire

A&R is the equivalent of the research and development (R&D) arm of a manufacturing company and is concerned with product development; in the case of the record industry, the product is a catalogue of sound recordings by a diverse roster of artists in various musical genres – pop, rock, punk, reggae, country and western, jazz, classical, and all the rest. The A&R department is concerned with the creative side of the record industry and therefore performs the gate-keeping role. The function of A&R staff is to develop and use their knowledge of the market, trends in music genres and tastes to search for new talent and sign up the artists; the team of A&R personnel consists of individuals with highly specific assets – networks of relationships with artists, managers, club owners, and so on – that cannot be transferred at all easily between members of the A&R team.

One of the important decisions a record label has to make, therefore, concerns the size and composition of the A&R department and whether to do all the work in-house or to use outside agents, which might be independent record labels, to spot talent. Either way, it may be considerably dependent on a few individuals with a track record of success. How to monitor their performance, however, is very difficult in a situation in which 'nobody knows'. As

[10] See Gander and Rieple (2004).

with other creative industries, one of the most serious problems of insufficient information (called 'bounded rationality' in transaction cost theory) in the music industry is predicting the success of a sound recording – another topic that has been researched by cultural economists.

Predicting success

The success of an album or single can be gauged in two ways: entering the charts (top thirty, *Billboard* or its equivalent) and, secondly, how long it stays in the charts. Both mean artistic and financial success for the artists and record label, and the longer the record stays in the charts, the greater the success. The question is, though: can any factors that predict success be identified? Demand studies have found that the main predictors of sales are the size of the population of young people and seasonality (particularly Christmas). These factors do not get at the role of taste in the face of frequent product differentiation in experience goods about which consumers have little prior information, however; moreover, there is also a 'snowballing' effect on demand by buyers who are highly influenced by the tastes of their peer group. What studies by economists of success in the charts have shown is that the distribution of success in terms of staying in the charts is highly skewed and is experienced by a few top artists in line with superstar theory (discussed in chapter 11). This is, perhaps, not particularly surprising; one study of the UK charts in the 1990s, however, was able to identify that film sound tracks and 'greatest hits' albums were a recipe for success.[11] Chapter 16 discusses the problem of predicting success in film, which has attracted more interest in cultural economics than it has in the music industry.

Commercial success is, of course, crucial to any enterprise: the point about the success of specific albums in the record industry, as we saw earlier, is that they cross-subsidise the less successful albums, and the longer they remain popular, the greater their ability to generate finance for future artists and recordings. Copyright on sound recordings lasts for fifty years in many countries (and ninety-five years in the United States; see chapter 13) and highly successful artists and recordings continue to generate royalties and remuneration for the artists, publisher and record label long after the initial chart success (Caves' 'ars longa').

---

[11] Strobl and Tucker (2000).

Table 15.3 Distributions from UK performances: PRS writer members, 1994

Band of net domestic distributed revenue (pounds)	Number of writers	Percentage of all members	Million pounds	Percentage of total revenue
< 25 not distributed	4,182	31.0	0.04	0.19
25 – 49	1,624	10.5	0.06	0.29
50 – 74	1,001	6.5	0.06	0.30
75 – 99	800	5.2	0.07	0.34
100 – 149	920	5.9	0.11	0.56
150 – 199	632	4.1	0.11	0.54
200 – 249	460	3.0	0.10	0.50
250 – 499	1,481	9.6	0.53	2.6
500 – 749	750	4.8	0.46	2.2
750 – 999	452	2.9	0.39	1.9
1,000 – 2,499	1,130	7.3	1.79	8.8
2,500 – 4,999	590	3.8	2.11	10.4
5,000 – 9,999	389	2.5	2.75	13.5
10,000 – 19,999	255	1.6	3.50	17.2
20,000 – 49,999	164	1.1	4.98	24.5
50,000 – 100,000	30	0.19	2.04	10.0
> 100,000	10	0.06	1.26	6.2
Total	14,870	100.00	20.35	100.00

Source: Monopolies and Mergers Commission (1996); figures may not sum precisely due to rounding.

Secondary markets

So far, this analysis has concentrated on sales, the primary market for musical goods and services; secondary markets are also important in the music industry, however, and royalties and remuneration are collected on behalf of copyright holders by collecting societies (rights management organisations). The basis of this was explained in detail in chapter 13.

Table 15.3 shows the distribution of incomes to the composer and lyricist ('writer') members of the UK Performing Rights Society (PRS); although the data are for 1994, the pattern of skewness in the distribution is likely to remain very similar in the present. It shows that over 40 per cent of the writers received £49 or less, with 31 per cent earning below the minimum amount distributed of £25, while ten writers received more than £100,000. Table 15.4 shows a very similar pattern of distribution of copyright incomes to performers in Japan by Geidankyo, the performers' professional association that is also a collecting society for remuneration from rental (renting CDs was widespread in Japan) and secondary use (radio and TV and the rest). Both

Table 15.4 Remuneration of Japanese musicians for rental and secondary use of commercial phonograms, 1998

Band of distributed remuneration (yen)	Rental fee		Secondary use fee	
	Number	Percentage	Number	Percentage
< 1,000	475	19.5	1,102	25.22
1,000 – 4,999	474	19.5	1,224	28.02
5,000 – 9,999	235	9.6	496	11.35
10,000 – 49,999	473	19.4	927	21.22
50,000 – 99,999	197	8.1	250	5.72
100,000 – 499,999	374	15.4	334	7.64
500,000 – 99,999,999	108	4.4	27	0.62
1,000,000 – 4,999,999	97	4.0	9	0.21
> 4,999,999	4	0.2	0	0.00
Total numbers	2,437	100.00	4,369	100.00
Amount of remuneration	33,720,132		115,774,661	
Median	10,276		4,513	

Source: Matsumoto (2002).

tables attest to the superstar feature of the music industry for composers, songwriters and musical performers.

Impact of the internet

There is no doubt that the combination of cheaper computers, laptops and other electronic devices, the spread of broadband and the internet has had a major influence on the economics of the music industry. Commentators have pointed out, however, that it is only another in a series of major technological developments – sound recording, radio, digitisation – that in turn have fundamentally altered the patterns of the consumption of music and its production, each with consequences for artists and the commercial side of the business. Some economists have made an analogy between the impact of radio and the impact of the internet on the music industry; in any event, it is important to remember that the existence of new technologies goes for nothing unless they are adopted, and, in this case, adoption by consumers far outstripped adoption and adaptation by producers.

The internet is essentially a means of delivery and communication, although it is growing as a source of content and much of its content is available in other formats; digitisation enables electronic delivery, and it has probably had more impact than the internet itself, although trying to separate out their individual effects is very difficult.[12] It is also worth noting that previous means of copying music had developed in the 1970s and 1980s using tape recorders and cassettes, and, in many European countries and elsewhere, concern about their effect on the music industry led to the introduction of the levy on recording media, whose proceeds were used to compensate artists and record labels. A similar solution for the present day in the form of a 'copyright levy' was discussed in chapter 13 (on this, see more below).

Much of the analysis presented earlier in this chapter preceded the incursion into the music market in the developed world of mass computer ownership and the internet, with their facilitation of 'burning' CDs and downloading music files legally or illegally. It took the record industry several years to make files available with the copyright clearance of royalties to all parties, so, in the first few years, most downloading was illegal and dubbed as 'piracy'. Napster, which offered the first commercial service for downloading music files via the internet in 1999, was closed down in 2001 following the court case brought in the United States by the Recording Industry Association of America, which judged it to contravene copyright laws. 'Burning' a legally purchased CD onto computer equipment for one's own private use was not illegal in many countries, however (although it still was in the United Kingdom at the time of writing), as it was regarded as falling into the category of exceptions and limitations to copyright law. Indeed, the levy on blank media is deemed to remunerate rights holders for some of these uses. The development of online music services has reduced illegal downloading somewhat, and they are growing rapidly (as shown in box 15.1), but they are far from eliminating it.

Besides illegal downloading, piracy also takes the form of counterfeit and bootlegged copies that are sold in sound carrier form: counterfeit copies mimic the whole bundle of sound recording, sleeve and notes and therefore cheat all the artists and the record label of incomes; bootlegging is the illegal recording of performances. The international sound recording industry wages a fight against this type of piracy: the IFPI reports that it is estimated that some 37 per cent of all CDs purchased (legally or otherwise) in 2005 were counterfeit – 1.2 billion pirate CDs in total. Pirate CD sales outnumbered legitimate sales in 2005 in a total of thirty markets.[13] This has nothing

---

[12] See Küng, Picard and Towse (2008).

[13] See www.ifpi.org/content/library/piracy-report2006.pdf (accessed 13 January 2008). Siwek (2007) provides figures for physical piracy as a percentage of the total market in 2005: 88 per cent in China, 63 per

to do with the internet per se, however, though sales may be advertised online; what has been most researched by economists (mostly ones specialising in the economics of copyright rather than cultural economics) is illegal digital downloading.

Internet and piracy of music

The question that has exercised economists is whether illegal downloading was the sole cause of the reported fall in record (mostly CD) sales. Record sales had already begun to fall in the late 1990s so the first reaction was that there was another cause. Another early reaction was that downloads were a complement to sales, not a substitute for them (and there still is some credence in this hypothesis): people sample a CD online then go out and buy it; indeed, this was formalised using the theory of network effects to suggest that record companies could stimulate sales by allowing downloads even if they were illegal, because they would start the snowball of demand (and that strategy is certainly adopted by some of the artists trying to market their work themselves online). Empirical investigation revealed that so-called unit sales figures put out by the IFPI were in fact deliveries to retail outlets of CD albums and they did not fully reflect consumption patterns, especially given the downturn in consumers' incomes and expenditures in the late 1990s. Moreover, it was subsequently shown by Stanley Liebowitz (see box 15.3) that the much-touted 10 per cent downturn in unit sales of CDs caused only a 2 per cent drop in revenues – an example of how data are used for advocacy and of the importance of checking exactly which data are being used.

Another line of argument in relation to demand was that the value of so-called piracy was being overestimated, because there was the implied assumption that every 'lost' sale could be valued at the retail price, whereas many consumers of pirated tracks would not have paid for them anyway – in other words, their demand would not have been effective at those prices. It was argued that piracy reflected the fact that CDs were overpriced (this argument may still apply to markets in less developed countries) and, in any event, consumers did not want all the tracks bundled together but just a few favourite tracks. Although there were good series of data on sales, and soon also on downloads, it took some time before these hypotheses could be tested rigorously. Now, however, it is possible to say that there have been repeated empirical tests showing that the case has been made that illegal downloads

cent in Mexico and Russia, 38 per cent in Brazil and Italy, 5 per cent in France, Germany, the United Kingdom and the United States.

Box 15.3 Stan Liebowitz's tests of the impact of downloading on record sales

Stan Liebowitz began working on copyright issues in 1979, and he is probably the world expert on empirical testing of the effects of copying (legal and illegal) on markets for music; he has carried out a number of tests of the hypothesis that MP3 downloads damage the legitimate music market. His research results are all the more persuasive in that, in the early days of downloading, he was sceptical of the claims of the record industry and even suggested at the beginning that file-sharing might be good for sales. In his 2003 working paper *Will MP3 Downloads Annihilate the Record Industry? The Evidence so Far* (Liebowitz, 2003), he examines various determinants of demand in order to understand the causal relationship between downloads and sales; after all, if it were possible to explain the fall in sales by ordinary economic variables such as price, incomes, demographic changes and the quality of the music, then there would be no case to answer. Having tested all this very carefully using various measures, and trying all the time to fault the analysis, he finally concludes that downloading is harming record sales to the tune of 20 to 25 per cent. Is that a large number? Liebowitz says 'Yes'; but is it enough to annihilate the industry? Who knows?! Read for yourself on www.utdallas.edu/~liebowit, where you can download his articles (for free!).

have damaged and do damage sales of music carriers; it should be pointed out, however, that many of these studies look solely at the United States.

The IFPI's *Digital Music Report 2008* discloses that tens of billions of illegal files were swapped in 2007, with the ratio of unlicensed tracks downloaded to legal tracks sold being about twenty to one; the IFPI concludes that even the 40 per cent growth in digital sales will not offset the fall in CD sales.

A copyright levy

Given the acknowledged damage to royalties and revenues for artists and the sound recording industry and the difficulties of enforcing copyright with digital rights management (see chapter 13), it has been proposed that a 'copyright levy' be adopted along the lines of a blank tape levy – that is, a form of indirect remuneration for rights holders that is raised to compensate them for unauthorised use. A fixed-rate levy would be made on the hardware that can be used for downloading and copying or on some other service involved in internet use, such as broadband. The levy revenue would be transferred to the national copyright collecting societies and distributed to their members on the same basis as royalties and other remuneration (including the blank media levy that has existed for some years in a number of countries), after deductions for administration charges and cultural purposes.

The cultural levy is what economists call a second best solution: the first best is to pay artists what they are due for the use of their works through fees and royalties. It is very difficult to find any sound economic rule for setting the rate of the levy (although this is also the case with several of the copyright remuneration schemes currently in use), and how much a levy would add to musicians' earnings can only be guessed at. It was calculated in 2005 that a €5 per month charge on broadband connection would fully compensate all stakeholders in the record industry in Finland.[14] Despite the economic short-comings, a levy offers a solution, with low transaction costs, to the problem of remunerating copyright holders, and, as there are already blank media levies in place in many European countries, it seems likely to be adopted throughout the European Union.

Internet and digital music services

Music can be accessed in a variety of ways via the internet: by online sales and through digital services such as streaming and downloading to computers and mobile phones and other electronic devices.

Online sales

It is a matter of interest to economists that online digital delivery of music that was authorised and paid for was offered first not by the record industry but by other service providers that have made deals with the record labels and the collecting societies to pay royalties to them and to the artists. This conforms to Schumpeter's ideas about innovation and entrepreneurship – that new entrants see and seize opportunities for adopting new technologies that sclerotic incumbent firms are unable to adapt to. Initially, tracks supplied digitally were protected by DRM to ensure that they could not be passed on, and in some cases they were time limited. DRM is not secure, however, and has moreover caused problems for consumers and producers, so that, at the time of writing (2008), most record labels had given up on their use of DRM. By 2006 there were reported to be 500 online music services in forty countries, of which iTunes was the market leader, selling 2 billion tracks in 2006.

The demand for these services by consumers is linked to the development of hardware, particularly of a mobile nature, such as portable players, notably the iPod, and 3G (third generation) mobile phones. Worldwide, there is considerable variation in the provision of broadband and wireless services,

---

[14] Oksanen and Välimäki (2005).

Table 15.5 Global music market, 2006

Category	Sales, downloads, subscriptions (million US dollars)	Percentage growth, 2005–6
Broadband	280	34
Song catalogue online	4	100
Single tracks downloaded	795	89
Subscription service users	3.5	25
Mobile subscriptions	2,017	11
3G mobile subscriptions	137	52
Portable player sales	120	43

Source: IFPI (2007).

and these complementary services, which are not controlled by the recording industry, are significant determinants of demand for digital music. Some countries are far ahead with 3G mobile phones, particularly Japan and South Korea: over a half of Japanese mobile subscribers had 3G and over one-third in South Korea, compared to under 10 per cent in the United States, Germany and France. This was reflected in demand for digital music: mobile music accounted for 90 per cent of digital sales in Japan in 2006, and in South Korea digital sales outstripped physical sales. Sales of digital singles were growing rapidly that year, as were music videos. In an individual innovative move, the UK act Keane and the Island record label released a limited edition single for sale on a USB stick along with the track's video.[15] The worldwide picture is presented in table 15.5, which shows the considerable rates of growth of music available online and the platforms consumers choose for accessing it.

Streaming

Music streaming services are also developing, with Sony BMG's Musicbox reportedly being the first. Streamed music is also increasingly available from public and private broadcasters. Companies such as AOL, Napster and Yahoo! offer the free streaming of music of various kinds to a PC or to other devices, such as the iPod. The BBC has been active in this field: in 2007 it launched the iPlayer, which uses P2P and DRM technology to deliver both radio and TV

---

[15] All information taken from IFPI (2007), available at www.ifpi.org/content/library/digital-music-report-2007.pdf (accessed 6 January 2009).

content of the last seven days for offline use for up to thirty days. As part of the iPlayer music offerings, BBC Radio Three offered a cycle of all the Beethoven symphonies, which were downloaded 1.4 million times. This was a 'free' service, meaning that there was no charge for it, as it is covered by the BBC licence fee. In an even bolder move, the Berlin Philharmonic Orchestra (Berliner Philharmoniker) now streams its concerts live with its 'Digital Concert Hall'; this is a service that charges for the online concert.[16]

Business models and digital music

One of the aspects of the internet that has intrigued economists is the change in the type of business models it has both facilitated and made necessary. Analysis of business models has been one of the contributions of Shapiro and Varian (1999) outlined in chapter 14. The term 'business model' is not often defined, but to economists it essentially means how a product is marketed and the revenues from it captured. The internet may be used in various ways for accessing goods and services, as table 15.5 demonstrates, and different business models are appropriate to each; it is also clear that these may change quickly as new technologies offer consumers new choices.

The internet may be used like a shop for buying cultural goods and services: you order your books and records and get your concert and cinema tickets through it, and then you pay a price for the item and it is yours. You can also obtain digital content directly when you access music through one of the digital music sites, and business models vary on these services: you pay either a price per unit or a subscription fee for a period of time that may or may not limit the quantity you can download or you can pay a rental that time-limits access to the music; on some services, access is free, being financed by advertising, or even, as with some public service broadcasting, by subsidies. The IFPI now sees the future for online music delivery as being paid for by subscriptions. Product bundling and presentation combined with price discrimination are also an aspect of business models, and there has been innovation in that in the record industry; for instance, Madonna's 2007 album was released digitally in three bundles with three different prices (an example of Shapiro and Varian's notion of versioning).

There are many different ways of accessing digital music (and whatever is written here is bound to be outdated by the time you read it) and different conditions for the licence – either you can sample or play the whole track before ordering it (a way of overcoming the experience good problem) or the

---

[16] See http://dch.berliner-philharmoniker.de/#/en (accessed 6 January 2009).

music is given away with something else you buy; either way, these are business models – ways that commerce accesses your money.

At the time of writing, one noteworthy aspect of digital music services was that the price per track in iTunes had been set at a standard 0.99 in several currencies (dollars, euros, pounds sterling) even though these currencies had very different nominal and real values – the pound was worth more than twice the dollar! This had attracted the attention of the EC competition authorities, and changed in 2008. Even in the United States and Eurozone countries, however, the download price of a single track, which was set by the record industry, exceeded the equivalent on a full-price CD, although the record companies did not have the same production, delivery and marketing costs. Nor did there seem to be price competition. Nevertheless, the artists did not seem to receive a bigger royalty payment, and many appear to have become dissatisfied with their record label, to the extent that they now market their own recordings, enabled by the internet to control their own distribution.

Before moving on to that topic, though, one other aspect of business models in the music business can be noted: the switch to concerts as a source of revenue, effectively to compensate for the lost royalties on sales sound recordings due to illegal downloads and other piracy.

Live concerts

By 2007 a number of old bands had re-formed and made extensive concert tours, and new and well-established bands were also doing the rounds. Concert tours are hard work, however, and require a great deal of organisation, so the expected returns must also be great! A recent study has calculated the revenues accruing to various bands and acts that had a concert tour in the United States in 2002: top of the list was Paul McCartney, who grossed $72 million, followed by the Rolling Stones ($44 million) and Dave Matthews Band and Celine Dion (both $31million).[17] The first three made 90 per cent of their estimated income for that year from concerts. The Rolling Stones' 'A Bigger Bang' tour took $437 million and Madonna's 'Confessions' tour grossed almost $200 million – $3 million per concert (these were world tours, not just in the United States).[18] Concert prices have been rising in the United States, and hearsay evidence confirms this for Europe too. Moreover, depending upon contracts with concert organisers, managers and publishers, bands seem to get a greater proportion of concert revenues and they keep the revenues from merchandising. In recognition of that, Madonna left her record

---

[17] Connolly and Krueger (2006). [18] *International Herald Tribune*, 28 September 2007.

Box 15.4 Madonna's new deal, 2007

Los Angeles, 16 October 2007: Live Nation's president and chief executive officer, Michael Rapino, officially confirmed today that Madonna has entered into an unprecedented global partnership with Live Nation and will become the founding artist in its Artist Nation division.

'The paradigm in the music business has shifted and, as an artist and a businesswoman, I have to move with that shift,' commented Madonna. 'For the first time in my career, the way that my music can reach my fans is unlimited. I've never wanted to think in a limited way and, with this new partnership, the possibilities are endless. Who knows how my albums will be distributed in the future? That's what's exciting about this deal – everything is possible. Live Nation has offered me a true partnership and, after twenty-five years in the business, I feel that I deserve that.'

The first-of-its-kind partnership between Madonna and Live Nation encompasses all Madonna's future music and music-related businesses, including the exploitation of the Madonna brand, new studio albums, touring, merchandising, fan club/website, DVDs, music-related television and film projects and associated sponsorship agreements. This unique new business model will address all Madonna's music ventures as a total entity for the first time in her career.

Artist Nation was created to partner with artists to manage their diverse rights, grow their fan bases and provide a direct connection to fans through the global distribution platform and marketing proficiencies that have made Live Nation the world's largest live music company. Artist Nation has significant infrastructure in place to execute additional revenue streams, including recorded music, merchandise, studios, media rights, digital rights, fan club/website and sponsorship divisions.

Source: www.madonna.com (accessed 15 January 2008).

---

label and joined Live Nation in 2007, the organisation that had arranged her three previous worldwide tours (see box 15.4).

Own promotion

Madonna is not the only artist to leave her record label; others have done so, in popular and classical music alike. In classical music, a number of well-known orchestras and individual artists now produce their own recordings and market them via the internet; these are mostly artists who have already made their reputation, however. At the other end of the market, new entrants also hope to attract publicity and market their music through their own websites and through social network sites, such as MySpace, which the record industry is now using for A&R purposes. Singer-songwriters Kate Nash, Lily Allen and Amy Winehouse are examples of stars who have been hurtled to fame via MySpace and YouTube.[19] Inevitably, though, as is the way with all

---

[19] *International Herald Tribune*, 8 January 2008.

performers, we get to know only about the huge successes, not the millions of failures nor of the thousands of artists who enjoy no more than modest success throughout their careers.

One of the economic explanations for own promotion of recordings and other aspects of an artistic career is the principal–agent one. We saw from the analysis of record contracts that artists are treated by the record label as their agent in the business of making money. Artists get a relatively low share of royalties, although a few superstars get more than the average. Superstars may well think of themselves as the principal and the record label as their agent, however, and it has become increasingly easy for them to contract themselves for the services of promotion, production, marketing and distribution. In other words, the artist can also decide whether to 'make or buy'.

Conclusion

The music industry has attracted the attention of cultural economists and sociologists because it plays a significant role in the cultural life of a society. Music has always been a vital aspect of cultural expression, for enjoyment, ceremony and personal identity. Live music continues to attract audiences while sound recording delivers international and local music alike in the globalised world market. The industry worldwide is dominated by the four 'majors', with a long tail of small, independent record labels, and the majors favour the superstar artist as a strategy for financial success. Mergers have been a common feature of the record and publishing sectors of the music industry over the last century and there have also been concerns on the part of competition (antitrust) authorities about both vertical and horizontal integration. This has raised questions about the loss of cultural diversity as well as about the loss of consumer choice and prices of sound recordings. The music industry has been significantly affected by the internet and the digitalisation of recorded music, and at the time of writing it was only starting to become possible to analyse the outcomes; almost certainly, there are more changes ahead as the technologies of receiving recorded music continue to be developed.

The sound recording industry and its component parts – composers, artists, music publishers, record labels – are all protected by copyright, and the main issue in the industry in the first years of the 2000s was the extent to which it was feasible and desirable to continue to enforce copyright. Many other specialised sectors of the music industry, such as sound studios, online music services and instrument makers, who do not have copyright, depend upon the success of the sound recording industry. Meanwhile, live concerts of popular music are an important source of income for the superstars, and probably also for other musicians too. The biggest changes are coming through new technologies, however, via the internet and mobile platforms; online music and streaming are a means of access for consumers, and for artists they offer an opportunity to reach an audience that could (maybe) enable them to make a living as musicians.

Further reading

My *Handbook of Cultural Economics* (Towse, 2003a) has three expert articles on the subjects of this chapter: the chapters by Michael Einhorn on 'Digitalisation' (chapter 26), by Fabrice Rochelandet on 'Internet: economics' (chapter 36) and by Andrew Burke on the 'Music business' (chapter 42). The book edited by Simon Frith and Lee Marshall (2004), *Music and Copyright*, is as relevant to this chapter on music as it was on copyright. Peter Tschmuck's *Creativity and Innovation in the Music Industry* (2006) deals with all aspects of the music industry and is easy to read; Einhorn's *Media, Technology and Copyright* (2004) is an expert treatment that relates to music in an uneven but at times brilliant book. It is also time to introduce readers to Harold Vogel's *Entertainment Industry Economics*; this regularly updated compendium (the sixth edition appeared in 2004) does not deal with analytical economics, although it refers to important economic work in the creative industries, but it does contain a wealth of institutional material on their economic organisation, including financial facts and figures on all the industries in Part IV of this book, including music, focusing particularly but not exclusively on the United States.

16 Economics of the film industry

In this chapter, I analyse film production and distribution as well as the cinema industry. The film or motion picture industry has many component parts, and its economic organisation is accordingly complex. Film production requires the sequential co-ordination of many people with artistic and technical skills, often working to a fixed time schedule (Caves' 'motley crew' and 'time flies' features; see box 14. 5); greater co-ordination problems and higher sunk costs mean more contracting and therefore higher transaction costs. Although many of the economic principles are the same as for other creative industries, the huge outlays of investment that are associated with feature film production make for some significant differences in the way the film industry is organised. Nevertheless, a similar framework to that for the music industry is used to analyse the structure of the film industry from film production to cinema (movie theatre) exhibition, which is the primary market, and then move on to consider the secondary market for film on television and in video and DVD formats, as well as the impact of digitalisation and the internet.

Technical change

The film industry is more or less 100 years old and was international from the start, with the development of and competition between technologies and ideas flowing between Australia, France, England and the United States. Like other new industries, it took some time before the content and delivery technologies of moving pictures settled into a standard pattern, and at first films were exhibited in temporary spaces. Soon special theatres (nickelodeons – they charged 5 cents for a ticket) were built, and many of the music halls and variety theatres that film competed with were turned into cinemas, first showing silent films that were accompanied by live music, then the 'talkies'. Eventually, purpose-built theatres were built in lavish style in every city and these theatres had to be adapted to accommodate subsequent technological innovations in sound and cinematographic developments.

In the interwar and early post-war years, before television spread to every home, cinema-going was extremely popular; it was a whole 'night out', with a B movie followed by the Pathé news, trailers for coming programmes and probably also a cartoon, then the A movie; in the intervals an organ appeared from the pit, complete with organist, who entertained the audience while they bought ice creams and popcorn. Some cinemas specialised in relaying only cartoons, and it was usual in all cinemas for the programme to be shown continuously so that audiences could come in when they wished to and leave when the film came round again. Cinemas were owned by the film studios in the heyday of what was called the Hollywood studio system from the 1920s until 1948, when the US antitrust authorities broke up the vertical integration of the two in the famous 'Paramount case' (see box 4.3 and later in this chapter). Audiences in the West declined in the 1970s and 1980s and the huge cinemas were turned into other uses or carved up into multiplexes. Now films are made digitally and can be beamed by satellite to specially equipped theatres anywhere in the world.

National film culture

Films can have international appeal or strictly local interest, and language plays a role in this; language can be changed by dubbing or with the use of subtitles, which overcome some of the barriers to international trade in film. Preferences for particular styles and genre may mean that some films have only national or regional appeal, however. Diaspora communities have influenced the exports of films made in India and China, for instance, and some have achieved world distribution. 'Bollywood', the term often erroneously used to suggest that the films are made in Mumbai, is in fact shorthand for the huge Indian film industry producing films in Hindi, other Indian languages and English as well. The typical film has stock characters and a large cast of singing and dancing actors. Over 1,000 films were made in 2002, with ticket sales of 3.6 billion, making Bollywood the biggest producer of films in the world and India the biggest domestic market. Japan has the third largest output of feature films and a significant home market. China is home to the fourth biggest film industry; films using the Cantonese dialect have long been made in Hong Kong, and China is now also producing film; the content mirrors that of Chinese opera and song, and, with pop stars an important ingredient, it is strongly linked to the music industry. Nigeria became a major film producer of 'home video' movies in the 1990s, though its output is not yet

---

Box 16.1 'Nollywood'

Nollywood, the name given to Nigeria's film industry, is now regarded as the world's third largest producer of feature films, with around 300 producers making some 1,000 films a year (estimates vary) using video and digital cameras and selling them on disc. Editing, music and other post-production work is done with ordinary computer-based systems. It is estimated that the average production takes just ten days and costs approximately $15,000. Starting from the mid-1990s, Nollywood has grown into an industry with revenues of $250 million a year. Thirty new titles are delivered to shops and market stalls every week, not only in Nigeria but in other English-speaking African countries, where an average film sells 50,000 copies at a price of $2 each.

Source: www.thisisnollywood.com/nollywood.htm (accessed 22 January 2008).

---

included in international statistics (see box 16.1). France is the leading European producer of feature films. This is a world industry, therefore, with strong regional markets; Hollywood nevertheless continues to hold sway, and much of the economic analysis of the film industry is concerned with the hegemony of Hollywood.

Audiences and consumption of film

A distinction can be made between cinema attendance and viewing films on television and via DVD. Table 16.1 shows cinema attendance – the number of visits – per capita based on 2003 UNESCO data and ranked by frequency.

The Motion Picture Association of America (MPAA), the industry lead body, provides detailed information on audiences for film relayed in theatres, home videos and on television in the United States.[1] For theatres, movie-goers and admissions are distinguished, the latter reflecting frequency of attendance. In 2006 the average US movie-goer saw 7.6 movies in the theatre; one-third of movie-goers were in the twelve to twenty-four age group, but older people were increasingly attending, with 12 per cent being sixty or over; the balance between male and female movie-goers was more or less equal. In total, 1.45 billion tickets were sold in 2005/6, at an average price of $6.55, with prices rising somewhat. Box-office receipts grossed $9,487.8 million in 2006.

Besides going to a movie theatre (cinema), Americans also viewed films in several other ways, as shown in table 16.2, of which the predominant platform was television.

---

[1] MPAA (2007).

Table 16.1 Cinema attendance per capita by country: top ten, 2003

Iceland	5
United States	4.8
New Zealand	4.2
Georgia	4
Australia	4
Singapore	3.8
Canada	3.4
Spain	3.3
Ireland	3
Lebanon	2.8

Source: Collated by www.nationmaster.com/graph/med_cin_att_percap-media-cinema-attendance-per-capita, based on data from the UNESCO Institute for Statistics (accessed 8 January 2009).

Table 16. 2 Consumption of filmed entertainment, United States: hours per person, 2002–6

	2002	2003	2004	2005	2006
Cable and satellite TV	828	886	909	980	989
Broadcast TV	744	729	711	679	684
Consumer internet	138	155	165	172	177
Home video[a]	57	60	67	63	63
Box office	14	13	13	12	12
In-flight entertainment and mobile content	4	5	8	10	12

[a] Includes playback of pre-recorded VHS cassettes and DVDs only.
Source: MPAA (2006).

Consumer spending on TV, video and box office in the United States ran to around $450 per person in 2006, according to MPAA data. In terms of film industry revenues: 38 per cent came from video viewed in the home, 30 per cent from theatrical distribution (of which a half was from foreign distribution), 16 per cent was from TV (of which 7 per cent was foreign TV) and 12 per cent came from films made for TV.[2] The US data therefore show that home consumption of films far outweighed cinema visits.

Participation in film and cinema

Going to the cinema and watching film are among the most popular cultural activities in many countries. In Australia, 65 per cent of all nationals over the

[2] Vogel (2004).

age of fifteen visited the cinema, of whom over 47 per cent went more than five times in 2006; there were 83.6 million admissions, resulting in gross box-office revenues of A$867 million (approximately US$747 million). Canadians spent sixty-one hours a year going to a movie theatre and drive-in theatre, which between them sold 120.3 million tickets in 2005, and, in addition, they spent seventy-nine hours viewing a movie, bought or rented (VHS or DVD format) – in all, 2.7 hours a week. In Europe, data are collected on cinema: Germans made 178 million visits to the cinema in 2002; 49 per cent of Italians attended cinema in 2006; 62 per cent of Swedes did so in 2002; and 65 per cent of UK citizens did so in 2003/4 (cinema admissions were 171.28 million in 2005). UK and Ireland box-office revenue was £840.35 million in 2005.[3]

Domestic and imported film consumption

→ Hollywood = 93% us

In the United States, domestic films constitute 93 per cent of the market, but the story is very different everywhere else. In Australia in 2000, 14 per cent of all films exhibited were domestic, 51 per cent from the United States, 11 per cent from India and 8 per cent from the United Kingdom.[4] In 2004, domestic films accounted for 13 per cent of the market in the Netherlands; 75 per cent of films exhibited were from the United States and a mere 5 per cent from other European countries.[5] These figures demonstrate the dominance of Hollywood and, essentially, reflect consumer choice.

One of the key themes in audio-visual policy, especially in the European Union and in Canada, is the proportion of domestic films in the national market, and concern over diversity of supply, often measured in terms of the country of origin of a film, has become a dominant policy issue. Hollywood films dominate world markets and are the butt of protectionism in Europe and Canada and elsewhere.

→ Subsidy, Tax breaks, etc? when your film in other
(states or places
[Simpsons & kids and Harry)
↳ Consider Co-productions ; Are they from diff countries?

Film production and costs

It is customary to identify the country of origin of a film according to where the production company is based; this is not always an accurate guide for audio-visual policy purposes, however, since film production is a global

---

[3] Australia Film Commission (www.afc.gov.au/gtp/cinema.html – accessed 20 January 2008) and www. culturalpoliciesnet (accessed 20 January 2008).

[4] As footnote 3.

[5] See www.hollandfilm.nl/facts/pdfs/staalkaart_06.pdf (accessed 20 January 2008).

industry and a film may be set in one country, filmed in another with an international cast and direction, financed elsewhere, and so on. In addition, there are co-productions that cross national borders. Nevertheless, data on output and costs are collected on a country basis and details of numbers and types of films and costs of production are published by industry bodies and governmental organisations in countries where film production is encouraged by cultural policy measures (subsidy, tax breaks, and so on). As with other cultural products, it is necessary to clarify a suitable measure of output. In the case of films, a distinction is made between feature films and other films, such as documentaries, animated films and cartoons, and suchlike, made for television. Films are produced and then rated in terms of their suitability for audiences (the PG – parental guidance – rating indicates that there may be some scenes that are unsuitable for young children) before being released for distribution, and there may be a time lag between these procedures; rating is done on a national basis by different national bodies – some by the industry regulating itself and some by a government board of censors – and rating may also be subject to local adjustment. In addition to new productions, some films are reissued. Table 16.3 lists film production in the leading countries in 2006 for the previous ten years. It can be seen from the table that the United States is not the greatest producer of feature films; nevertheless, Hollywood dominates international film markets, with an 85 per cent share of all films exhibited.[6]

Production costs by country

[handwritten annotations: why does Hollywood have such big Market shares? · Domestic Revenue is High · Easier Finances · Access to Variety of rich cultures]

With Hollywood dominating world markets, one of the questions that cultural economists have asked is: what economic advantages does Hollywood have over film-makers in other countries? The most common explanations are the size of the domestic market in the United States as a major source of revenue and the advantage of English as a world language that enable economies of scale. In addition, flexible organisational and managerial techniques of production and access to finance have also been offered as explanations as has the global mix of people working in Hollywood, producing a globally attractive product.[7] It is interesting therefore to contrast information on film production and costs in different producing countries.

Hollywood

Information on Hollywood is provided by the MPAA, whose members are the 'major' studios – the Walt Disney Company, Sony Pictures, Paramount

---

[6] UNCTAD (2008: 125).   [7] Acheson and Maule (1994).

Table 16.3 Number of films produced, ranked by 2006 output: top ten countries, 1996–2006

Rank	Country	Number of feature films produced					
		1996	2002	2003	2004	2005	2006
1	India	649	1,200	877	934	1,041	1,091
2	United States	735	543	593	611	699	480
3	Japan	278	293	287	310	356	417
4	China	110	100	140	212	260	330
5	France	134	200	212	203	240	203
6	Commonwealth of Independent States	21	62	68	120	160	200
7	Spain	91	137	110	133	142	150
8	Brazil	40	48	50	81	90	142
9	United Kingdom	111	119	175	132	131	134
10	Germany	64	116	80	87	103	122

Source: Australian Film Commission (2008).

Viacom/Dreamworks, Twentieth Century Fox, Universal Studios and Warner Brothers – and subsidiary and affiliates, such as Fox Searchlight, Miramax, New Line and Sony Pictures Classics, identified as studio classic and speciality divisions. Besides representing the interests of its members, the MPAA also provides a voluntary rating of films in conjunction with the National Association of Theater Owners. In 2006 MPAA members produced 480 new feature films, rated 853, released 599 new features and reissued eight – a total of 607.

The MPAA also reports the average cost of making a theatrical film in two categories: its member companies – that is, the main Hollywood studios – and its subsidiaries and affiliates. The average cost for the majors in 2006 was $100.3 million and for the others $48.5 million.[8] These costs were broken down into marketing costs (approximately one-third) and 'negative' costs (two-thirds). Negative costs are the costs of producing the negative and include production costs, studio overheads and capitalised interest on finance. The chain of production costs in turn consist of: story acquisition and development into the screenplay; pre-production – script development, location choice, cast and crew selection, set and costume design; principal photography costs, divided into 'above-the-line' (actors, directors, producers, writers) and 'below-the-line' (set construction, soundstage, wardrobe); and post-production – editing, scoring and soundtrack, titles and credits, dubbing and special effects.[9] Marketing costs consist essentially of: production/creative

[8] MPAA (2006).   [9] Vogel (2004). The credits of a film give a detailed picture of what is involved!

Box 16.2 Anatomy of film costs (US dollars): *Spider-Man 2*

- Story rights: $20 million.
- Screenplay: $10 million.
- Producers: $15 million.
- Director (Sam Raimi): $10 million.
- Cast: $30 million (Tobey Maguire, $17 million; Kirsten Dunst, $7 million;
  Alfred Molina, $3 million; rest of cast, $3 million).
- Production costs: $45 million.
- Visual effects: $65 million.
- Music: $5 million (composer, Danny Elfman, $2 million).
- Total: $200 million.

Source: *Guardian* 11 June 2004 (http://arts.guardian.co.uk/fridayreview/story/
0,12102,1235533,00.html (accessed 8 January 2009)).

---

services, exhibitor services, promotion and publicity, and market research (22 per cent); advertising on cable TV, radio, magazines, billboards (24 per cent); network TV (21 per cent); spot TV (14 per cent); newspaper (11 per cent); trailers (4 per cent); and internet/online (1 per cent).[10] The studio overheads are the fixed cost of maintaining the studio, and interest on capital is a significant item, because the studio borrows finance for the film, which can take up to two years to produce (and maybe longer to release) before it begins to earn any revenue. Box 16.2 contains a breakdown of the estimated costs of $200 million for producing *Spider-Man 2*, a film that made $821 million worldwide. Film finance is discussed below; in the next section, the economic aspects of Hollywood are analysed.

India

It is not easy to find official information about the Indian film industry; the government's Central Board of Film Certification provides figures on the number of films (celluloid) passed for release: in 2003 2,564 films were passed, of which 877 were Indian feature films and 282 were foreign features films, 1,177 were Indian short films and 228 were foreign short films. The board refused permission for forty-five Indian 'long' films. It reported that there were 13,000 cinemas. One of the interesting questions is whether Bollywood has mimicked Hollywood in its financial and managerial organisation and this has led to its success. Bollywood films in the twenty-first century have large

---

[10] MPAA (2006).

budgets and typically call for large casts of singing and dancing stars and a chorus. Finance seems to come from private distributors and studios. The domestic Indian film market is vast, with cinema attendance of some 2,860,000,000; in terms of attendance per capita, however, India (with 2.6) did not enter the top ten in table 16.1.[11]

Japan

Japan ranked third in world production in 2006. It produced 417 feature films and showed 821 films that year, so over half the films exhibited were domestically produced. There were 3,062 screens and 164.3 million admissions; Japanese films grossed ¥107,752 million (approximately US$950 million).[12]

Australia

Australia produced twenty-nine Australian feature films and five co-productions in 2007/8; foreign sources accounted for 47 per cent of the total funding available, 28 per cent came from government, 17 per cent from Australian private investors and 8 per cent from the Australian film/TV industry.[13] In 2007 58 per cent of the 388 films screened in Australian cinemas were from the United States, 10 per cent were from the United Kingdom and 8 per cent were Australian; Australian films earned 4 per cent of total box office in 2007.[14]

Canada

Canada produced seventy-six feature films in 2006 (122 in 2005) and was among the top ten world producers in some years of the previous decade. Statistics Canada provides data on sources of revenue from Canadian and foreign film for 2002/3: total revenue from Canadian content was C$356 million (approximately US$231 million). Of this, one-third was earned by domestic distribution (12 per cent was from theatrical distribution, 76 per cent from TV distribution and 6 per cent from home video) and two-thirds from distribution outside Canada.[15] Movie theatres, excluding drive-ins, recorded 118.5 million visits in 2004/5 and attendance at drive-ins was 1.8 million.

European countries

Table 16.4 shows the leading film-producing countries for feature films in Europe and the shares they have of their domestic markets in 2005. In fact,

---

[11] www.nationmaster.com/country/in-india/med-media (accessed 8 January 2009).
[12] Motion Picture Producers Association of Japan (www.eiren.org/history_e/index.html).
[13] Screen Australia (2008).   [14] Australian Film Commission (2008).
[15] www.statcan.ca/english/freepub/87F0010XIE/2004001/data.htm (accessed 24 January 2008).

Table 16.4 Film production and market shares in Europe by leading producers, 2005

Country	Number of films produced	Market share domestic films (%)	Market share European films (%)	Market share US films (%)
France	240	37	14	49
Germany	103	14	7	77
Italy	98	26	25	46
Spain	142	14	21	63
Sweden	54	21	16	60
United Kingdom	131	30	n.a.	66

Note: Numbers do not always sum to 100 per cent due to rounding errors.
Source: MEDIA Salles (2006).

"Feature films may account for a nation's Cultural diversity"

figures for any one year can be misleading on account of year-on-year fluctuations in production (as can be seen table 16.3), and market shares reflect this. Unsurprisingly, the larger the country by population, the greater the number of films produced; that said, however, there are some countries with small populations that produce a considerable output when that is taken into account: Denmark (with a population of 5.4 million) produced twenty feature films and Norway (with 4.5 million) produced twenty-one in 2005.

Table 16.4 also shows the share of US films in these countries' markets, reflecting the concern about cultural diversity discussed in chapter 14. France and Italy were the only countries in 2005 in which US films had less than half the market; Italy and Spain showed a higher proportion of European films. The financing of films in European countries is explained in the section below.

Film finance

Film production requires considerable outlays of finance for the sunk costs made many months, even years, before recoupment begins with the release of the film. Hollywood excels in the private financing of films, and obtaining finance is one of the main tasks of the studio. In countries with smaller domestic markets, however, film finance is often problematic, and many countries support their film industry directly with financial subsidies and/or indirectly with tax breaks, as well as using regulation by quotas to protect the domestic market, usually on TV distribution. Film finance can therefore be looked at in terms of private and government sources of investment.

Hollywood

The financial arrangements for Hollywood feature films are an object lesson in the ways of capitalism! In the days of the Hollywood studio system the studios dealt with every aspect of film production, distribution and theatrical exhibition, and this allowed them to internalise some of the problems of finance, such as the need for collateral (an asset with financial value that can be sold to cover any loss of the capital outlay); their ownership of theatres, usually situated in city centres on high-value land, was adequate collateral. Over the last fifty years, however, other ways of financing the production and marketing of films have evolved, which seek to reduce the risk of loss in the familiar setting of 'nobody knows'. Of course, once the film is made (at least the negative) investors can view it and obtain some information about quality, but, by then, much of the investment has been sunk (as can be seen from box 16.2).

Following the logic of specialisation and the division of labour, the studios (both majors and the independents) now mostly concern themselves with the finance and distribution of films made by one-off teams of creative and humdrum personnel – the system called 'flexible specialisation'. To obtain finance, the producer assembles the screenplay and screenwriters, principal actors and director (the 'talent') and gets their commitment to participate in the film; there is a catch, though, because, in order to secure their services, there has to be sufficient finance to offer them a contract and pay them or they will not want to sign. The task of the producer, therefore, consists of getting one or other of the talent and the finance to make a deal in order to persuade others to jump on board.

Sources of finance include commercial banks and other financial institutions that are prepared to lend money to an established studio (which can offer collateral and experience to reassure the lender and also, like a record label, is involved in several projects at once and therefore can to some extent pool risk); the stock market; and internal industry sources. One type of internal industry arrangement is the 'negative pick-up deal', in which the studio agrees to distribute the film when it is made and advances money to the producer with a claim on future returns. In case the film runs over budget, however, or experiences other problems, such as the withdrawal of a key individual (maybe due to illness), there is another layer of financial security available, in the form of the completion guarantee, which is essentially a type of insurance or hedge.

The complexity of these financial arrangements and the scale on which they are conducted (the 'thickness' of the market) is what makes Hollywood the centre of film-making it is. The locational advantage afforded by the

California sunlight that originally attracted the early pioneers of film has transformed into agglomeration economies of financial deal-making, and this makes it very hard for other centres to compete; it forms an industrial 'cluster' (see chapter 19). In smaller national markets, some type of government guarantee is needed to stand in for the market-based Hollywood system. Even Hollywood has benefited in its time from favourable tax treatment, however.[16]

European countries

There are several schemes and sources of finance for film at the supranational level in Europe. The European Union has adopted a new programme to support the European audio-visual sector, called MEDIA 2007, with a budget of €755 million over seven years (2007–13).[17] The programme provides finance and training to support the promotion of European film and other audio-visual works, particularly through festivals and trade fairs, and contributes to European Film Promotion, a network of twenty-six European national export and promotion organisations that promotes and markets European film throughout the world; it has a budget of around €1.5 million, half from MEDIA 2007. The Council of Europe's European Cinema Support Fund Eurimages supports co-productions throughout Europe; in 2007 it supported fifty-six feature films and five documentaries with €21.5 million.[18]

Individual countries also have national support schemes, and each country does it in its own way; it is not possible to go into them all, or even many of them, but some generalisations may be made. Basically, there are three means of financial support from governmental schemes: direct financial subsidy from public expenditure; indirect subsidy by tax exemptions; and finance from the market controlled by governmental measures, particularly taxes on users, especially with regard to television. Some countries effectively operate all three together. Overall in Europe, it has been estimated that the biggest single source of public funding for film production is not public finance but, rather, the taxes on television and cinema and similar taxes (such as cable) and the obligatory contribution of public and even other broadcasters required under the conditions of their licence. There is, therefore, a strongly symbiotic relationship between these media for film distribution and the finance of film

---

[16] See Vogel (2004: ch. 4).   [17] Hoefert de Turégano (2006).
[18] Council of Europe (www.coe.int/t/dg4/eurimages/History/Coproduction/2007coproductions_EN. asp#TopOfPage (accessed 8 January 2009)).

production. Three countries' arrangements are sketched out below, those of France, Denmark and the Netherlands, each representing a somewhat different combination of the different types of schemes.[19]

France

France is one of the world's largest film producers and the biggest in Europe, and has a history of public support for film going back to 1946. Its central government agency, Centre National de la Cinématographie (CNC), supports a range of film and television programme production, with funds levied mainly from television channels and also from cinema tickets and video and DVD distribution; in 2005 the CNC had revenues of €510 million, of which around 30 per cent was spent on feature films (and two-thirds on TV productions). In addition, there are tax incentives to encourage private investment in CNC-approved productions and tax credit schemes that allow producers to write off up to 20 per cent of their production costs incurred in France (with a limit of €500,000). There is also a system of financial guarantees through the Institut de Financement du Cinéma et des Industries Culturelles, a partly government-owned financial body that encourages private finance from the banks by sharing around a half of the risk on loans for film production – essentially offering collateral for loans to producers who have already obtained a distribution or other deal. Thus film finance in France, though organised by state agencies, relies on the market for sources of finance and there is no system of direct public subsidy.

Denmark

In Denmark, public support is provided almost entirely with public finance by the Ministry of Culture and is mainly channelled through the Danish Film Institute, with some regional funds and with finance from the Nordic Film and Television Fund (financed by the five Nordic countries: Denmark, Finland, Iceland, Norway and Sweden), which had a budget of €35 million in 2005. The two national Danish broadcasters are required to contribute to feature film production through the Danish Film Institute (and they also finance other film projects). In 2005 Denmark had no specific tax incentive scheme. Box 16.4 has more details on Danish film subsidy.

The Netherlands

The Netherlands has both direct subsidy and a tax incentive scheme (the so-called 'CV') to encourage private finance of film. The Dutch Ministry of

---

[19] Based on Blaauw (2006).

Culture had expenditure on film of €14.8 million in 2005, with its grant to the Film Fund (Filmfonds) as its national agency responsible for supporting film production. The Film Fund had a budget of €15.5 million, with finance also from broadcasters. In 2005 thirty-one feature films were released, of which twenty were supported by the Film Fund. They had known production costs of at least €47 million, of which €7.8 million was contributed by the Film Fund and €6.1 million came from the market due to special tax regulations (the CV) for film finance. In all, around half the total production costs of new releases were supported by direct or indirect subsidy.[20] Since 2007 producers with 65 per cent of their production financing in place can apply for the final third of their film's budget; 25 per cent of the film's total finance must come from private investors.

What transpires from research on European film finance is that the arrangements the film funding bodies have made essentially mimic the Hollywood system of private finance for film production; instead of free market production-financing-distribution Hollywood-style deals, the distribution companies (TV, cinemas, and the rest) are required by taxation or regulation to put the finance up front into the hands of state-run organisations, which then pass the funds on to the film producers. We need to ask ourselves, therefore, what implications these financial arrangements – which are to be found not only in Europe but also in Canada, Australia and elsewhere – have for the economic organisation of the film industry.

One of the major differences between Hollywood and European film production, though, is that film subsidy in the latter has cultural rather than financial goals, and therefore the financial profitability of European films is not regarded as the only measure of success, as it is in Hollywood. Box-office success also means that audiences respond to the film, however, and if they do not there is the question of how to measure success. As with other subsidised arts, the questions we want to answer are: what difference did subsidy make and did it achieve its aims? Without subsidy, would European cinemas and TV screens just be showing Hollywood films? And, if that is what audiences want, why should governments try to change their taste? I return to these questions later.

---

[20] See www.hollandfilm.nl/facts/pdfs/staalkaart_06.pdf (accessed 20 January, 2008). An interesting comparison is with Canada, where the Canadian Feature Film Fund contributed C$48 million (around €32.5 million) to the production of thirty-one feature films with budgets totalling, C$147 million in 2005/6. Canada produced seventy-six films in 2006. Reported on www.cftpa.ca/newsroom/pdf_profile/profile2007-english.pdf (accessed 20 January 2008).

Economic analysis of film production

The description of film production and finance in the preceding sections of this chapter call for an analysis of the underlying economic logic of the structure of the industry. Like the music industry, the US film industry, depicted as Hollywood, is highly concentrated, with a few dominant studios surrounded by a host of smaller producers. There is obviously a distinction to be made between the film industry in countries where the market rules (Hollywood and Bollywood) and the European, Australian and Canadian industries, where there is state support. Throughout the film industry, though, work for artists and craftspeople follows the flexible specialisation model, whereby individuals are contracted for the duration of making the movie and then move on to the next one. Research by cultural economists on the film industry has tended to focus on Hollywood but it is also important to ask if and to what extent the different institutional arrangements alter these conclusions.

What also interests us in cultural economics is whether cultural outcomes are determined by economic forces and, when those outcomes are not consistent with the aims of cultural policy, what measures can be taken to alter them. Film is regarded as an important influence on cultural identity and social cohesion as well as providing entertainment; moreover, it is an industry that generates income and employment for thousands of people; where that money is earned and the resources are employed has an influence on GDP and on the balance of payments.

Industrial organisation

As with other industries, the economic organisation of an industry is studied by looking at the structure of firms and how much of the chain of production of the final product they produce – what is made in the firm and what do they buy on the market? The answer has significant effect on the size of the firm and on the degree of concentration in the industry. In chapter 15, the effects of the major record companies on diversity and national interests in the music industry were discussed; here the same line of analysis is followed, especially as expounded by Richard Caves (2000). Caves' treatment of the film industry is presented as a general analysis and therefore should apply regardless of the institutional arrangements in one country or another, but, as he relates it only to Hollywood, it is interesting to enquire whether different incentives are at work in the state-supported film industries.

The Hollywood studio system

As is now well documented, the Hollywood studio system was the last word in organising every element of production within the firm. Every worker in all stages of production, from screenwriter to cinema attendant, was on contract to the studio, with either a contract for employment or an option contract that controlled the freedom of the individual to work elsewhere. This restricted the ability of the 'talent' to work on other projects or to increase earnings by moving to a competitor. The advantage to the studio was that it could control costs and establish a 'brand' with its contracted actors and other artists, and by owning cinemas as well as production studios it could control the distribution of its films and thereby keep out those of potential competitors. It was the latter that caused studios to fall foul of the antitrust authorities in the United States under the Sherman Act, because they restricted competition to the detriment of the film-going consumer's choice. In the so-called 'Paramount case' of 1948 the court issued a consent decree requiring the company to cease from monopolising control over distribution in its cinemas; the studios sold off their cinemas, thus opening up the distribution market and making it necessary for them to deal with distributors to get the films they produced to market. The decision did not succeed in the long run in altering the number of distribution firms or their integration with the producers, however, and nor did it control the tendency to oligopoly in ownership of movie theatres by later entrants, as discussed later in the economics of cinema.

In retrospect, it has been argued that the 'Paramount case' was not the only trigger for these changes in the economic organisation of the film industry in Hollywood, as cinema-going in the United States at that time had also begun to be threatened by the spread of television. Either way, the rigid vertical integration of the film industry disintegrated and gave way to what has come to be called 'flexible specialisation', with films being made by one-off production units contracting all non-production matters to specialised firms or individuals, as described above. This system relies on the presence of (or, at any rate, easy access to) a pool of artists and craftsmen who are available to form a team to make a film, the team being, as we saw, assembled by the producer. With globalisation, these personnel, especially on the technical side, might come from anywhere in the world that has a film industry. This type of economic organisation, as Caves has shown, entails multiple contracts and both gives rise to considerable scope for opportunistic behaviour and raises transaction costs. The effects of hold-ups, one type of opportunism, involving specific human assets are well illustrated in the example of the Hollywood writers' strike of 2007/8 (see box 16.3). As noted in the context of the music

Box 16.3 US Writers' Guild strike, 2007/8

A strike represents the ultimate hold-up weapon, and there have been some notable strikes in the cultural sector over the years. The more 'specific' the skill and human capital involved in the profession that strikes, the more effective the strike, because, apart from employing non-union labour and blacklegging, there is no good substitute for that skill. The Writers' Guild of America (both West and East) represents 12,000 movie and television writers, and the strike particularly affected Hollywood's film and television programme production, demonstrating both the crucial role of the writers in the chain of production and their problems in bargaining with the producers, represented by the Alliance of Motion Picture and Television Producers.

The strike lasted from the beginning of November 2007 until mid-February 2008 and was about residual payments for the digital distribution of movies and TV shows and compensation for advertisement-supported TV programmes streamed over the internet. This was a case, therefore, of new technologies altering long-standing agreements about the distribution of revenues, the payment of creators and the business models of the enterprises they work for. For the writers, the increasing use of the internet and other new media distribution channels threatened their revenue streams from sources that seemed likely to be displaced by the new technologies. It was not only the writers and producers who suffered from the strike, however; it put many others in the film business out of work as production ceased, reflecting the type of contracts many work on in Hollywood's so-called 'flexible specialisation' model.

industry, the radical uncertainty of financial success surrounds every stage of production, and every contract reflects that.

'Nobody knows'

Unsurprisingly, the original 'nobody knows' quote originated in the film industry. What predicts a hit? If one knew the answer, it could be used to increase revenues at all stages of production, distribution and exhibition; price discrimination could be used to maximise revenue and costly mistakes could be avoided. Moreover, revenues are not profits, and small-budget films can be profitable. Detailed analytical exploration of the 'nobody knows' problem has been rigorously pursued by Arthur De Vany.[21] In a significant body of work using sophisticated statistical methods, he has shown that success is a wild card in a winner-takes-all context familiar to cultural economists; neither the presence of stars nor big budgets predict success at the box office. He makes the point that, for its own purposes in trying to read the tea leaves of

---

[21] See De Vany (2006) for a summary of his work.

information about the progress of any one film, the movie industry produces huge data stocks and many sources for statistical analysis. This is because it can use the information even at a late stage to mount some kind of rescue operation for a film that 'bombs' or adopt a revenue-maximising strategy when signs of success reveal themselves in the reception of a film. The film industry is an information industry par excellence, in which information about the initial reception of a film and its success unfolds dynamically over time. With very low marginal costs of multiplying copies of a film and also of extending both its run and frequency of exhibition (assisted in the latter by multiplexes that can show a smash-hit movie on several screens simultaneously), success can be made to breed success.

That can happen only after the film has been produced and released however, and so the economic organisation of production and distribution have to anticipate the uncertainty in the contracts that are made at the planning stage, in order to be able to capture the benefit of the unpredictable success (and no doubt being made to bear the consequence of failure too). Despite De Vany's scientific reinforcement of the old industry adage that 'nobody knows', the belief nevertheless persists against all the odds (or, to be more precise, even when there are no odds) that some people know more than others, and the industry seeks to profit from that.

Caves' analysis of contracting in film production

As we saw in chapter 14, Caves (2000) bases his general theory of the economic organisation of the creative industries on the type of contract between principal and agent that results from a situation in which the principal has sunk financial capital into a project or enterprise and secures property rights to the agent's assets (human or physical capital) so as to control and protect the investment. The greater the amount of the financial outlay and the longer it is invested, the greater the incentive the principal has to control the agents at each stage, and the more stages there are to the production and marketing process involving specialists (specific human assets), the more contracts will have to be made to protect earlier sunk costs. Underlying this whole business, though, is the impossibility of writing a complete contract, which in the creative industries is further exacerbated by the fact that 'nobody knows'. Not only that, but, when artists are involved ('art for art's sake') whose quality of work cannot be assured, when many such people have to be co-ordinated sequentially (the 'motley crew'), when there are people of different levels of reputation and ability (the 'A list/B list') who cannot easily be substituted one for another, and, to cap it all, when the project is essentially unique because each is a one-off creation of a novel product ('infinite variety'), there is no formula that exactly guides the principal in the undertaking. This is an obvious depiction of the film industry, and Caves uses all his analytical tools to explain the type of contracts and deals that are made in it. The figures in box 16.2 show the sort of outlay that is made at the various stages in a big-budget movie.

Contracts and incentives

The succession of creative decisions and contracts starts with the story and screenplay; the producer takes an option on a story from an existing source on which there is copyright (the option being secured with a payment of around 10 per cent of the agreed price); this is insurance against the screenplay not working out. If the story is a best-seller, however, there is likely to be an auction for the price and no option. Caves points out the difficulties in offering the best incentive to the screenwriter: payment by the hour would encourage spending too much time on the job but, if the producer can veto the script by having decision rights, then the producer has the incentive to try for the best script by asking for rewrites. The compromise is, therefore, to divide the task into stages at each of which there is an option that can be exercised; for example, the 'treatment' or summary of the plot is one stage; if accepted, the dialogue can be written by a dialogue specialist, with an option to take it then to the next stage of completion, and so on.

The contract with the director is likely to pay him or her a fixed fee so as to reduce the incentive to drag out the time schedule, which would increase the costs of the assorted personnel, who are working on weekly pay (often under standard union contracts). The contract with the A-list actors has to ensure they are all available at the dates, times and locations required by the shooting schedule; it may also involve haggling over who gets precedence in the screen credits. The director and stars may want a contract – a participation deal – that gives them a share of the receipts as well as an upfront payment; and so on and so forth.[22] These are just a few illustrations of the issues involved, but it is clear that there is an underlying economic logic of contracting as Caves postulates. Transaction costs are very high – much higher than with the Hollywood studio system – and therefore it can be assumed that the gains from specialisation outweigh the greater costs (though it has to be kept in

---

[22] Vogel (2004).

mind that it was legal intervention, not market forces, that ended the studio system).

It also seems very likely this economic logic applies to the flexible specialisation model of film production wherever it takes place. It is driven by the profit motive, however, and that may not predominate in circumstances in which film production is supported by a government in order to achieve its cultural policy aims. Government support often presents opportunities for moral hazard, when incentives or regulations induce unwanted reactions from economic agents.

Principal–agent problems with European film subsidy

European film is heavily subsidised, both as a defence against Hollywood domination and to promote European cultural values. The economic arguments put forward for subsidy are that US film is 'dumped' (sold at below cost) in European cinemas, and European countries with a small market size are unable to achieve economies of scale that would reduce costs and enable prices to become competitive; it is argued, therefore, that subsidy is needed to reduce costs – the same argument for film as for performing arts.

As with public subsidy to the performing arts, there is often a tension between improving artistic quality and box-office success. 'Art for art's sake' motivates directors to lobby governments for subsidies to make films that satisfy them and their peers but the results do not always, or even often, attract either national or international audiences, with the consequence that only a very few of the 700 or so films subsidised each year in Europe earn sufficient at the box office to cover their costs. The European industry has become reliant on subsidy to survive, and, it is claimed, this leads to oversupply of films that are able to attract subsidy but not good enough or are not sufficiently well marketed to generate revenues.[23] The problem for the funding body in film, as with the arts, is how to avoid the moral hazard problem and promote viable film production in the presence of asymmetric information, given that even in Hollywood, success cannot be predicted. The Danish Film Institute, which is the national Danish agency responsible for supporting and encouraging film and cinema culture, clearly places emphasis on both box-office success in comparison to US films and on international recognition (see box 16.4).

It is not only at the stage of production that the European film industry is subsidised, but also with distribution to which I now turn.

---

[23] Danish Film Institute (2006).

Box 16.4 Danish film industry: the 'Danish wave' still has its momentum

In terms of the basic market indicators, 2007 confirmed the long-term success of Danish films, according to the Danish Film Institute's *Facts and Figures 2008*. The figures also reflect the long-term sustainability of Danish films in a marketplace otherwise dominated by American releases. Denmark is a country with 5.5 million inhabitants. There were a total of 12.1 million cinema admissions in 2007, with 2.2 tickets sold per inhabitant. There are 167 cinemas in Denmark with a total of some 59,000 seats. Twenty-seven Danish films were released in 2007, representing just over a quarter of the national market share, with 108 American feature films being released. The market share of American films was 58 per cent. The DFI provided subsidy to seventeen feature films in production in 2007, with eight feature films for children and young people. The average budget for a Danish feature film was €2.6 million and the average DFI subsidy was 31 per cent.

Danish films have been successful in both the domestic and foreign markets: for the years 1999 to 2007 the share of Danish films in the national market was 26 per cent, with six Danish feature films in the 'top twenty' every year since 1999. Danish films also took over half the national DVD market. Danish films have won ninety-two awards at international festivals, and they represented one-third of the share of tickets bought in other EU countries between 2002 and 2006.

Source: Danish Film Institute (2008).

Film distribution

The distributor is responsible for marketing and advertising films and making rental deals with cinemas, television companies, DVD and video distributors and other users, and ensuring that they receive prints of the film for the contracted opening date. As noted above, film distribution in Hollywood is integrated with the majors, though, as with film production, there are also independent distributors, and distributors may have invested in the finance of the film. Box-office shares of the top six distributors – Warner, Twentieth Century Fox, Universal, Buena Vista (owned by Disney), Sony and Paramount – accounted for 72 per cent of the total in 2005. The same integration is to be found elsewhere; for example, in South Korea, a country with a vibrant film industry that released seventy-three feature films for theatrical distribution in 2004, three theatrical distributors controlled over three-quarters of the total, amounting to over 20 million admissions.[24]

---

[24] Korean Film Council, cited in Choi (2006).

The contract between the distributor and the cinema shares the box-office revenues, making allowance for the overhead costs of running the theatre, and this is done on a sliding scale that takes account of the 'run' of the film – that is, its success with consumers following the typical release strategy, or 'window'.

Market 'windows'

There is a standard strategy for releasing and marketing films into the various 'windows': domestic theatrical exhibition in first-run, and later, in second-run, cinemas, followed by international release, then pay-per-view television, pay TV, foreign TV, domestic and international home video, network TV and syndication. For many years there was also a standard time lag between the different window release dates; for example, pay-per-view release was six months after the date of the first release; movie piracy, or its threat, has speeded up this sequence, however. The timing and place of first release is determined by the distributor according to supposed audience demand – children's films, for example, are released in school holidays.

The distributor also tries to influence the admission price at cinemas: cinemas (like other theatres and museums) make money from selling food and drinks and seemingly make a higher profit on that than on exhibiting movies. Therefore the theatre management has the incentive to have a low ticket price, because that will increase sales of refreshments, whereas the distributor would like to have a high price because his or her revenues depend upon box-office takings.[25] If the price at a first-run theatre is too high, however, this will inhibit sales (assuming that demand for cinema is price elastic – see below), and that would interfere with the signalling system of transmitting information to potential audiences about the quality of the film – the network or snowball effect. If the box-office takings exceed the figure anticipated in the contract with the distributor, the exhibitor can appropriate the extra amount; alternatively, cinemas sometimes have to pay up if they fail to achieve the anticipated box office. Again, these deals are based on guesswork about a film's success, though, once the film is ready, the distributor shows it to exhibitors.

Economies of scale and scope in film distribution

Vertical integration between producers and distributors is a means of overcoming the uncertainty of 'nobody knows'. The business of film distribution requires the distributor to advertise a film title in advance of its release and to

---

[25] See Vogel (2004) on all the above.

supply titles to a large-scale domestic and international network of cinemas, TV companies and others who will market the film. These activities have high set-up costs and, because the marginal costs of supplying one more cinema with any given title and of supplying more titles are low, economies of scale and scope can be exploited, causing barriers to entry to exist, thus making it difficult for new entrants to contest the market. It is therefore not surprising that the EU MEDIA 2007 programme spends over half its budget on film distribution, as the distribution of European films has been seen as a problem. European Film Promotion is the official supranational film promotion agency in Europe and it has successfully managed to bring together twenty-seven countries, even though film promotion still varies between them in terms of the amount of finance available and how it is administered.

In addition to the efforts of the European Union, individual countries also have programmes for promoting and distributing film.[26] For example, the German Films Distribution Support programme was started in 2005 for the support of German films abroad. A maximum support of €50,000 per film per country can be granted as a conditionally repayable loan, whose repayment depends on the success of the film in the cinema. Funding of up to €10,000 may also be granted as a subsidy. Foreign distributors can apply to German Films Distribution Support for funding for additional promotion measures for the theatrical release of a German feature film or documentary. The budget for 2008 was €570,000 plus repayments. In 2007 German Films Distribution Support provided funding for a total of fifty-eight projects.[27] Other European countries provide similar aid for distribution.

DVD and home video

By the 1990s the spread of VCRs and then DVD players reached high levels of penetration in North America, Japan and Europe, and this was both a threat and an opportunity for the film industry. As table 16.2 shows, consumers in the United States spent five times as many hours watching films on video as going to the cinema in 2006. Home consumption of film by these means competes with cinema exhibition and reduces box-office takings but it has also opened up a market in the rental and retail sale of videos and DVDs, with DVDs growing and video declining. By 2006 68,000 film titles were available on DVD in the United States, with an average price to the consumer of $22,

---

[26] Hoefert de Turégano (2006).
[27] See www.german-films.de/app/support/news_list.php (accessed 8 January 2009).

and 85 per cent of US households had a VCR and DVD player.[28] The price is significant for two reasons: first, retail sales compete with rental outlets; and, second, if home viewing of DVD is a substitute for going to the cinema, the price of the DVD will affect the demand for cinema tickets; there has been no work on the cross-elasticity of demand for cinema tickets and DVDs by cultural economists, however.

The European Audiovisual Observatory presented an array of statistics on video on demand (VoD) at a workshop in Cannes in 2007.[29] By 2006 there were 142 VoD services in Europe, 60 per cent of which were streamed over the internet and 30 per cent were part of a TV channel package; penetration was greatest in France and the Netherlands, where broadband is highly developed and providers are a mixture of telecom and cable operators, aggregators and broadcasters. Content (40 per cent of which was film) could be rented or purchased, with rental being the most popular business model in 2006. Again, there seem to be no studies of cross-elasticities between cinema attendance and the other ways of accessing film; this is clearly an area for econometric research.

Digitisation and piracy of film

Digitisation means that a movie may be created using digital images for content as well as for storing the whole movie in digital form for distribution; distribution may also be to a digital cinema via satellite. Digitised films are also available through online rental and streamed over the internet, and increasing access to broadband has considerably increased demand for this way of viewing films. By 2008 Apple had initiated an online movie rental service in collaboration with the major Hollywood studios, and it was reported that 1,000 titles would be available via iTunes, with prices of $2.99 for older movies and $3.99 for new releases.[30] With computers becoming ever more portable and mobile phones acquiring the ability to access film, film could become as mobile as music. It remains to be seen what effect this will have on the demand for cinema viewing and theatrical distribution, and potentially also on the type of films that are produced.

Film is protected by copyright law and, as with music, digitisation has enabled unauthorised copying to take place; at first, copies were crude and due to the length of time it took to download by the internet via P2P only the most popular movies were copied. The same technological developments that enable legal

---

[28] MPAA (2007).
[29] See presentation by André Lang www.obs.coe.int/online_publication/expert/vod_presentation.pdf (accessed 9 January 2009).
[30] *International Herald Tribune*, 16 February 2008.

access to films also empower illegal copying, however. It has been estimated that MPAA member studios lost $6.1 billion to movie piracy in 2005.[31]

Economics of cinema

Whereas the production and distribution of film is a typical creative industry that supplies a mass audience, cinema is more like a performing art: films are shown at specific times and, if the theatre has unsold seats during the showing of the film, that revenue cannot be rescued. Unlike live theatre, however, cinema is much more flexible, in both the short run and the long run. In the short run, it can easily substitute another film for one that is not doing well at the box office and it can easily put on more performances of popular films, either by extending the run or, nowadays, by using multiplex cinema screens to extend capacity. As with earlier technological developments in screening films, this required long-term capital investment, but, once made, multiplexes have offered flexibility in theatrical exhibition that the live performing arts typically lack; so, instead of measuring the supply of exhibition facilities by the number of movie theatres, the number of screens is now the relevant measure of output. Multiplexes enable cinema managers to differentiate the product by showing the same film at different times, and, at least in principle, this facilitates price discrimination (a feature we know to be common in live performing arts theatres); films are often shown in the afternoon at lower prices for children and senior citizens, reflecting the low marginal cost of exhibiting a film. Now, digitisation calls for cinemas that can exhibit digital films, and there are capital investment programmes under way to respond to these technical requirements.

As the antitrust consent decree following the 1948 'Paramount case' is still in place, US film studios are banned from owning cinemas. Nevertheless, as in other creative industries, the advantages of economies of scale and scope, for example in advertising, have led to integration, so the intention of creating competition between exhibitors has been eroded over time and one oligopoly has replaced another. Movie theatres in the United States are now owned by a few chains that account for over 80 per cent of exhibition revenues from cinema attendance, and a similar picture is to be found in Canada. Small independent cinemas exist side by side with these giants (a feature typical of oligopolies, as we saw in the music industry), controlling 35 per cent of US screens.[32]

---

[31] Siwek (2007).   [32] Vogel (2001).

In Europe, Europa Cinemas was created in 1992 with financing from the MEDIA programme and the Centre National de la Cinématographie in France as an international network for the circulation of European films in cinemas. In 2004 the MEDIA programme contributed approximately €6 million to Europa Cinemas. Its aims are to increase European programming in film theatres and to raise attendance, particularly of young people; it also supports the transition to digital projection in cinemas. Europa Cinemas is active in 404 European cities and supports 704 cinemas, totalling 1,765 screens in thirty-one countries.[33]

Other sources of revenue and finance

So far in this chapter, film production, distribution and exhibition, DVD sales and rental, online and offline, have been discussed as sources of revenue via the market, and various subsidy and other such schemes have been mentioned. It would be impossible to give a full account of these schemes throughout the world as they are so many and varied. There are other sources of revenue and finance that should also be noted, however. Merchandising is an important source of revenue for some films, particularly children's films, that use trademarks to protect the merchandise in addition to copyright; Disney is well known for this. Some studios operate their own retail outlets for the sale of merchandise based on films. There are many schemes for co-productions between film-makers and producers from different countries, encouraged by subsidy. Besides earnings from the distribution of domestic films, there is also inward investment from film production in a country by a foreign film studio, and some countries actively encourage the promotion of locations. Several countries (Australia and Canada, for instance) publish figures on this inward investment. Figures are also published on the contribution of the film industry to GDP and on employment directly and indirectly associated with the film industry.

Conclusion

The film industry is complex and complicated with a long chain of production, from the creation of a film to the consumer, who may view it in a cinema or at home. This does not mean, however, that the economics of the film

---

[33] See www.europa-cinemas.org/en/programmes/media/index.php (accessed 8 January 2009).

industry are particularly complex; just that there are many stages at which investments have to be made, often of large amounts of money, and involving many highly skilled workers with specific abilities (human capital assets) and, accordingly, many contracts. The most difficult economic problem in the film industry is on the demand side – how the film will be received and whether it will earn sufficient revenues from all sources to cover the sunk costs. If 'nobody knows', every production has to deal with uncertainty, and the economic organisation of the industry, as Caves (2000) has shown, is set up to minimise potential losses.

Caves' theory covers the supply side from an analytical point of view and relates to an industry that is essentially market-orientated and unregulated except for the protection of copyright. His theory gives clear insights into the economic organisation of Hollywood. The rest of the world has a hard time competing with Hollywood and deals with it in several ways, on both the supply and demand sides: one on the supply side is for countries to produce their own films reflecting their own language and culture, and this mostly requires some form of direct government financial assistance or tax breaks; another form of support is schemes to assist with film distribution and marketing; on the demand side, some countries set quotas for the exhibition of Hollywood films on television with the intention of stimulating the viewing of domestic films (or European-made films within Europe). It has to be said, however, that, despite the many schemes in various countries, and especially within the European Union, very few films succeed in competing with Hollywood in world markets. At bottom, though, it appears from the data on consumer choice that the underlying explanation is that, for whatever reasons, consumers simply prefer Hollywood films. This presents an aesthetic challenge (and one that cultural economists are sympathetic to) but, as long as consumers have had exposure to a range of alternatives, consumer sovereignty has to be respected. Films are experience goods but consumers have sufficient information to make their own judgements. It is easy (and glib) to blame globalisation when consumers repeatedly make consistent choices. Nor should it be forgotten that part of Hollywood's success is that it attracts top film-makers of all kinds (directors, actors, craft workers such as camera operators) from all over the world.

The film industry has benefited from technological change throughout its 100-year existence and continues to do so with the adoption of digitisation. Having had advance warning from the music industry about the need to respond to consumer demand for home viewing and now mobile viewing, it has adopted business models to supply that demand, although, like music, it will probably never fully appropriate all potential revenues in the face of piracy. A question that is interesting to cultural economists is whether these new distribution channels will elicit new film content – say a return to more short films – as the combination of technological change and economic incentives generate new tastes and opportunities.

Further reading

Caves' (2000) book, so frequently referred to in this book, is authoritative on film, which is analysed in several chapters. Chapters 2 and 3 of Vogel (2001) are on the movie industry and are an invaluable source of information. My *Handbook of Cultural Economics* (Towse, 2003a) has two chapters that are recommended reading: Darlene Chisholm on 'Motion pictures' (chapter 40) and Sam Cameron on 'Cinema' (chapter 13); Cameron carried out one of the first studies of the demand for cinema and the cross-elasticity with television, so his interest in the subject is long-standing. Besides these chapters on the film industry, the further reading recommended in chapter 14 on globalisation is also relevant, such as Keith Acheson and Christopher Maule's book *Much Ado about Culture* (1999). Acheson and Maule's (1994) article 'Understanding Hollywood's organization and continuing success' in the *Journal of Cultural Economics* is also worth reading.

Economics of broadcasting

In this chapter, the broadcasting of television and radio are analysed from an economic point of view. Broadcasting has public goods characteristics that shed light on public policy in the sector. The state typically has been involved in its provision and, in many countries, broadcasting has been provided and financed exclusively by the state – and it still is in some countries. In addition to economic reasons, however, because broadcasting is so important as a means of mass communication, the state has typically regulated it to promote acceptable standards of reporting news and events, to give equal opportunities to all political parties and to minority communities and languages, and to ensure there is sufficient public service element to broadcasts. These and other reasons also lie at the back of the strong state regulation of broadcasting that is observable in all countries, and has been there since the beginning. A feature of particular interest to cultural economists is the question of the finance of public service broadcasting (PSB), which, in some ways, shares similar features to the discussion of subsidy to the arts.

Radio and television supply programmes to an audience and, as mass disseminators of cultural content, they are creative industries; as such, they share economic properties with other creative industries, and are closely linked in the case of radio to music and to film in the case of TV. Watching TV and listening to the radio are the most popular of all cultural participation activities and people spend more hours 'consuming' them than any other cultural product.

Technical developments

Radio is the older broadcast medium, and it has retained a universal and popular appeal despite the introduction of television. Access to radio (or the 'wireless', as it was often called) grew during the 1920s, and by the 1950s 95 per cent of American households owned a radio receiver (a 'radio'), with

Europe gradually catching up; at the turn of the twenty-first century the same percentage owned a TV set, and, by now, many households in developed countries own multiple TV sets and radios. Before the 1950s and the spread of TV, radio provided most people's news and entertainment, both high- and lowbrow. When TV came along and gradually replaced radio, it survived as a background to many other activities at work and in the home and was particularly successful as a purveyor of music and news. With transistorisation (an earlier technological revolution) and batteries, radio became a mobile medium and could be used in the open air and in cars. Digitisation has meant that radio and TV programmes can be consumed in several other ways: streamed via the internet and accessed through PCs, laptops and various electronic devices, and time-shifting, formerly done with a VCR, can be done digitally (for example, the BBC's iPlayer). At the time of writing, digital radio and TV were spreading, and in some countries had reached around a half of all households as consumers purchased digital sets. This picture is certain to be transformed by further technological developments during the lifetime of this book!

At the beginning, and for many subsequent years, broadcasting was transmitted over the air in 'wireless' form, using specific bands of the electromagnetic spectrum, from stations with a certain geographical reach, typically part of a national network; local stations were mainly concerned with the transmission of national programming. Later, other technologies – cable, satellite and broadband – came into use that expanded the reach of a 'broadcaster' and the number of delivery channels, and this increased the number of programmes available to audiences.[1] The economic analysis of broadcasting originated at a time in which over-the air broadcasting was the only technology in use and the focus of economic interest was on the finance of broadcasting. Later developments in technology and the advent of advertiser-financed broadcasting have altered that and prompted economic debates about broadcasting policy. The chapter focuses mostly on public service broadcasting, because it shares a number of analytical features with the arts and has attracted most attention from cultural economists. Besides analysing the finance and regulation of broadcasting, this chapter also considers the consumption by audiences of radio and TV programmes as well as programme-making and diversity.

---

[1] Cable and satellite are not 'broadcast' but, as a convenience, I shall refer to all types of transmission and delivery as broadcasts.

Consumption of radio and television

Television and radio are supplied to consumers by various means, only some of which require payment. PSB requires the household to pay a tax or licence fee while commercial radio and TV are free to the consumer. Cable and satellite delivery is charged for by subscription, often for a bundle of channels, regardless of actual consumption, and pay-per-view charges a price for viewing a specific programme. It is customary to measure television viewing by participation and time budget surveys for government policy purposes and by audience numbers and characteristics for commercial services supplying information to radio and TV stations and advertisers.

As with other data on participation and time use, there is considerable variation by country, and it is not possible to give even a representative overview; there is one constant, however: watching television is the most popular leisure time activity, even though viewing hours are falling in some countries. Instead, some selective statistics are included here to illustrate the issues involved. One thing that differs is what is reported; for instance, Austria reports the number of TV and radio licences issued. Other data on participation report the proportion of the population that listened or viewed; for example, in Spain, 98 per cent of the population are reported to watch TV daily and 60 per cent to listen to the radio daily. Measurement in terms of time use seems to be the most common: table 17.1 reports use by minutes per day for a sample of countries.

The data also reveal details of TV use. In Canada, where per capita average weekly television viewing was 24.3 hours in 2006, women aged eighteen and over watched 26.5 hours, adult men (eighteen plus) watched 25.4 hours and

Table 17.1 Time spent on radio and TV usage, 2005 (minutes per day)

Country	Radio	TV
Canada	114	115
China	n.a.	150
Spain	110	222
Sweden	105	96
Switzerland	94	88
Taiwan	51	188

Source: Küng, Picard and Towse (2008).

children aged two to eleven years watched 17.3 hours. In the Netherlands, time spent on watching television dropped somewhat from 12.4 hours a week in 2000 to 10.8 hours a week in 2005, the fall being attributed to increased use of the internet by Dutch teenagers. In Germany, the average viewer in 2000 spent 190 minutes per day actually watching television and had the television set switched on for a total of 251 minutes. Germany also reports the breakdown of viewing habits by category, with the following percentages for public versus private broadcasters, respectively, for specific types of programme: information, 84:16; sports, 23:77; entertainment, 58:42; feature films (fiction), 32:68; and advertising, 2:98. In 2000 the market share of the eleven public television broadcasting corporations was 43 per cent and the market share for private (commercial) broadcasters was 57 per cent.[2]

A report by Ofcom (the UK regulator of broadcasting) showed that, in 2005, the United Kingdom had the highest digital penetration of any country in the world and that take-up had not exceeded 50 per cent in any other European country. At the end of 2005 digital TV was viewed by 70 per cent of all UK television households. Sales of set-top boxes needed for digital access are an indicator of demand for digital TV. Digital satellite had become the United Kingdom's most popular television platform; by 2005 there were more digital satellite subscribers in the country than homes watching analogue terrestrial-only TV. More households were watching the private BSkyB subscription services on their principal TV set than were watching any other form of television service. Cable served 13 per cent of television homes with digital services.

Finance of broadcasting

To economists, broadcasting has presented one of the most interesting examples of a public good: the signal is non-rival (non-exhaustible) and, with over-the-air broadcasting, it is non-excludable, since anyone with a radio or TV set can pick up the signal. This, of course, raised the question of how broadcasting would be financed, as the potential for free-riding would make it unattractive to a private supplier. Moreover, like film and music production, radio and TV programmes and transmission have features of natural monopoly – high fixed or sunk costs while marginal costs are practically zero. The solution in most countries was state finance or state-organised finance and direct state

---

[2] See www.culturalpolicies.net for Austria, Canada, Spain and Germany.

Box 17.1 Finances of the British Broadcasting Corporation

The BBC was in the first place a private company, the British Broadcasting Company Ltd, formed in 1922; it was given a royal charter and made a state-owned corporation in 1927. It had a monopoly of TV broadcasting until 1955 and of radio broadcasting until the 1970s, and since then it has been the chief public service broadcaster in the United Kingdom. The royal charter, which is renewed every ten years, lays down the mission of the BBC as a quasi-autonomous, 'arm's-length' body (meaning that it is independent of the state and government) and provides for the appointment of what in 2007 became the BBC Trust, the organisation whose members (appointed by the government) represent viewers' interests.

The BBC is financed by a licence fee that is levied per household possessing one or more television set(s); the amount of the licence fee is set by parliament and its renewal is the opportunity for re-evaluation of the BBC's role as a public service broadcaster and of the quality and efficiency of its operation. The annual licence fee in 2007/8 was £135.50 for colour TV (£45.50 for black and white) and there is no charge to people over the age of seventy-five. The BBC reported in 2008 that the licence fee is spent as follows: 69 per cent on the eight national and regional TV channels; 18 per cent on ten national and forty local radio stations; 9 per cent to broadcast all radio and TV output plus the cost of collecting the licence fee from 25 million homes; and 4 per cent on its websites.

Source: www.bbc.co.uk/info/licencefee (accessed 21 February 2008).

provision or a state-regulated monopoly. In the United Kingdom, the BBC was an early model of a monopoly regulated by the state but at 'arm's length', with finance raised by a licence fee based on the possession of a receiving set (see box 17.1). Nowadays, only the United Kingdom, Sweden and Japan out of the developed countries have licence-fee-only finance for public service broadcasting. In other countries, the state broadcaster was financed by taxation.

The first American network, the National Broadcasting Company (NBC – formed in 1927 at more or less the same time as the BBC), was and is a private company, eventually becoming NBC Universal in 2004; Universal Entertainment GE (General Electric) owns 80 per cent of NBC Universal and the remaining 20 per cent is owned by Vivendi, the French media conglomerate. Unlike European countries and Australia, Canada and New Zealand, the United States did not go down the route of national publicly financed broadcasting and adopted a model based on advertising. Thus broadcasting in the United States has always been almost entirely a for-profit, commercial competitive industry, with some non-profit PSB financed in part by federal and local taxation but mostly by sponsorship and voluntary contributions (see below).

By the last quarter of the twentieth century most countries that had had only a state monopoly broadcaster acceded to the other main source of finance for free over-the-air broadcasting and allowed commercial stations financed by advertising to compete with the former monopoly through a programme of deregulation. As discussed below, however, regulation of the broadcasting sector by government organisations, such as the Federal Communications Commission (FCC) in the United States, is still a dominant feature of broadcasting markets (detailed in box 17.4).

In some countries, the state ownership and provision of broadcasting have not been seen as a barrier to commercial advertising on public stations, and state finance is supplemented by commercial advertising. In the Netherlands, for example, advertising is permitted on PSB stations: commercial and state finance also co-exist in Canadian PSB, and Channel Four in the United Kingdom is an entirely commercially financed TV channel with a public service remit – interesting examples of privately financed public good provision.

Public service broadcasting

In the days of monopoly state-run or -financed broadcasting, there was no distinction to be made between PSB and other broadcasting as they were one and the same, but nowadays it is necessary to make that distinction, as PSB has to compete for viewers with commercial broadcasting. It is necessary therefore to define what the purpose of PSB is and how it is to be regulated and evaluated. Curiously, the progression from public to private was reversed in the United States, with the Corporation for Public Broadcasting (CPB) being created by Congress in 1967 and its operating arm in charge of programme creation and distribution, Public Broadcasting Service, being established in 1969, long after the development of market-based broadcasting. To use the wording of the CPB website:

The fundamental purpose of public telecommunications is to provide programs and services which inform, enlighten and enrich the public. While these programs and services are provided to enhance the knowledge, and citizenship, and inspire the imagination of all Americans, the Corporation has particular responsibility to encourage the development of programming that involves creative risks and that addresses the needs of unserved and underserved audiences, particularly children and minorities.[3]

---

[3] See www.cpb.org/aboutcpb/goals (accessed 26 February 2008).

Box 17.2 UNESCO's mandate on PSB

Strengthening public service broadcasting for education, cultural awareness and civil society, Public Service Broadcasting (PSB) is broadcasting made, financed and controlled by the public, for the public. It is neither commercial nor state-owned, free from political interference and pressure from commercial forces. Through PSB, citizens are informed, educated and also entertained. When guaranteed with pluralism, programming diversity, editorial independence, appropriate funding, accountability and transparency, public service broadcasting can serve as a cornerstone of democracy.

Source: http://portal.unesco.org/ci/en/ev.php-URL_ID=1525&URL_DO= DO_TOPIC&URL_SECTION=201.html (accessed 15 February 2009).

Similar mission statements are to be found in other countries, and UNESCO has summarised them in its PSB mandate (see box 17.2).

While these goals expressed by UNESCO are worthy ones, they do not easily lend themselves to evaluation. It is also notable that neither the CPB nor the UNESCO mission statements make any reference to the quality of broadcasting, even though that is one of the issues that has concerned many people. What these goals do suggest is that for-profit, commercial broadcasting is not likely to achieve society's public service goals and programme diversity.

Both PSB and commercial broadcasting (with the exception of pay-per-view TV) do share a common feature, however: the absence of direct price signalling between viewer and broadcaster. This is due to the public good nature of broadcasting, which necessitates the finance of broadcasting by an intermediary – the taxpayer or licensee in the case of PSB or commercial advertisers in the case of commercial broadcasting – that severs the direct link between producer and consumer. Pay-per-view services do have that link, however. In the absence of the price mechanism, which would enable the viewer to communicate his or her tastes to the broadcaster, there is tremendous attention to ratings in order to estimate audience size and reaction. Ratings, though, do not measure strength of preferences as does willingness to pay a price. Even with increased choice of channels, programming is determined by the broadcaster and the advertiser, and both have an incentive to provide programmes that appeal to the widest possible 'median taste' audience, with the result that programming is similar on all channels, PSB and commercial. When the public broadcaster has to consider ratings and compete in the market, moreover, this is likely to push PSB programming in the same direction as commercial programming. One solution (discussed later) is to undertake contingent valuation studies to discover how much the public is willing to pay for PSB.

The 'underserved' audience referred to in the CPB mission statement includes anyone who has a different taste from the 'typical' viewer. This is an unusual type of market failure, though to cultural economists it is easy to recognise, because it bears a strong resemblance to information problems in the arts and the case for arts subsidy based on taste formation. Catering for minority tastes inevitably makes PSB more expensive per viewer, however (because by definition there are fewer viewers over whom to average out costs); the achievement of the aims of PSB do not have wide appeal (CPB's prime-time audience in 1999 was 3 per cent of the total), and this leads to difficulties in justifying public finance.[4] In the case of PSB in the United States, the CPB has received less federal finance over the years and has had to rely increasingly on sponsorship and a more commercial attitude. In the United Kingdom, the PSB rationale of the BBC is repeatedly scrutinised for its appeal, efficiency, and so on every ten years as its charter is renewed and each time the licence fee is renewed in parliament. More is said about this later, but first I consider the more usual market failures connected with commercial broadcasting as typically analysed by media economists.

Commercial broadcasting and advertising

Commercial firms with products they wish to advertise pay for advertising slots between TV and radio programmes that they believe will maximise the response of viewers to consume their products. The broadcaster in turn 'delivers the audience' to the advertiser. Thus radio and TV stations act as intermediaries between the advertiser, who pays for advertising time, and the viewer, and the broadcaster therefore offers programming that it hopes will maximise the amount of advertising expenditure it attracts. Children's toys are accordingly advertised on children's programmes and sports goods on sports programmes, and, in general, the advertiser will pay more for prime-time advertisement slots, and so on: demand by advertisers is for time slots and programme types. These are the predictable incentives of commercial broadcasting. If more time is devoted to advertisements than viewers are prepared to tolerate, they do not watch the 'ads' and the company will not sell sufficient quantities of its goods; on the other hand, advertisers have other

---

[4] Caves (2005).

competing media to exploit, such as billboards, magazines and newspapers, and now the internet.

These considerations lead to incentives to broadcasters on the demand side to maximise audiences to 'deliver' to advertisers. On the supply side, the broadcaster faces virtually zero marginal costs of delivering radio and TV services to the audience but high fixed costs of acquiring programmes. These features of increasing returns to scale lead to incentives for the large-scale production of TV and radio and so to monopoly. To combat these tendencies, as well as for other reasons, broadcasting is highly regulated, particularly with respect to media ownership, as discussed below.

The greater dependence on commercial TV in the United States is reflected in figures on expenditures on advertising per TV-owning households, which was $443 in 1996, compared to Japan's $336, Australia's $254 and the United Kingdom's $239.[5] Figures for the United States in 2003 show that the average household watched eight hours of TV a day (around four hours per individual) and that prime-time commercials lasted nine to ten minutes per hour, with a further five minutes of non-programme time taken up with promotions and suchlike. Between them, broadcast TV and cable spent $61,000 million on advertising and radio $19,000 million in 2003.[6] This represents the 'shadow price' paid by viewers, at least those who watch the ads; it can be avoided by time-shifting devices (the oldest being VCR) and by simply using the remote control to turn them down. The European Union lays down detailed limits on advertising breaks in programmes (see box 17.3).

Finance of TV programme-making

In economic terms, the making of TV programmes is similar to film-making (though there are fewer 'windows' for recouping outlays), and several of the big Hollywood studios are active in programme production; smaller producers and companies also produce TV programmes, however. What has encouraged independent production in the United States and elsewhere, such as in the United Kingdom, is that regulators have required broadcasters to include independently made programmes or banned the big studios from a financial interest in TV prime-time programming in an attempt to prevent the vertical integration of production and distribution. In the United States, from 1970 to 1995, that was forbidden by law, but, once the law was revoked,

---

[5] Vogel (2001).   [6] Anderson and Gabszewicz (2006).

Box 17.3 European Union's Audiovisual Media Services directive on TV advertising

The European Union has a history of regulating broadcasting, starting with the 1989 Television without Frontiers (TVWF) directive, which laid down common rules about broadcasting to allow the free movement of TV services across national borders within the European Union. The Audiovisual Media Services (AVMS) directive was adopted in 2007 and updated (and replaced) the TVWF (see text below). One of its clauses refers to TV advertising:

Advertising must be recognisable, separated by acoustic and visual means. Isolated ads must stay the exception. Subliminal techniques and surreptitious advertising are prohibited.

Generally, advertising must be placed between two programmes. Besides that, there must be a minimum of 20 minutes of programming in a row. Sport events can only be interrupted in the pauses foreseen. News, religious programmes, documentaries and children's programmes of less than 30 minutes duration shall not be interrupted. Religious services shall never be interrupted.

For all other programmes, the number of interruptions permitted depends on the length of the programme. Here are the provisions for the most common cases:

longer than 45 minutes – one interruption.
longer than 90 minutes – two interruptions.
longer than 110 minutes – three interruptions.

The overall limit of 20% of any given one-hour period of broadcasting time has been altered to 20% of any given clock hour. Self-promotion is assimilated to advertising and subject to most of the same provisions. Public service messages and charity appeals, in contrast, are not to be included for the purposes of calculating these maximum periods.

Source: http://ec.europa.eu/avpolicy/reg/tvwf/advertising/index_en.htm, ch. 4, articles 10–11 (accessed 7 February 2008).

vertical integration has reasserted itself.[7] In the United Kingdom, the BBC is required to buy in independently made programmes.

Where TV programme production differs from that of films made for cinema distribution is that soap operas and miniseries (which dominate TV content) require the same team of writers and actors to produce them sequentially, leading to different types of contractual arrangements.[8] While movies focus on star actors, TV series are more likely to hire less starry casts on longer contracts. The Writers' Guild of America strike (see box 16.3) revealed just how important the role of writers is not only in dramas but also in a wide spectrum of TV programmes. In his 2005 book on broadcasting, Caves reminds us that Baumol's cost disease applies as much to TV programme-making as to the live performing arts and that the Baumols (Will

---

[7] See Caves (2005).   [8] Caves (2005).

and Hilda) have researched the topic.[9] Though Caves states that he does not (yet) see the effects, he does warn of the ever-increasing tendency to programme cheaper reality shows in preference to dramas and soaps.

PSB and film production

A number of countries in Europe have a policy of requiring or encouraging the financing of film-making by public service broadcasters, partly to provide European content to comply with the Television without Frontiers directive (see box 17.3) on European programming and partly also to prevent vertical integration. Arrangements differ by country, so only a few examples are cited: in France, there is a statutory obligation on broadcasters that broadcast over fifty-two films per year to invest at least 3.2 per cent of their annual turnover in European films (and 2.5 per cent in the French language); this resulted in €315 million being invested in the European film industry in 2004. In Germany, there is a voluntary system for the public service and commercial broadcasters that has yielded over €27 million. In Italy, there is a statutory requirement for public broadcasters to spend at least 20 per cent of their licence fee on European audio-visual productions; one outcome has been the foundation of RAI (Radiotelevisione Italia) Cinema as both a producer and distributor of (mostly) Italian films. In Spain, both PSB and commercial broadcasters have the statutory obligation to spend 5 per cent of their income on European films for both TV and cinema, of which 60 per cent has to be in Spanish (or an official Spanish language) film production; in 2004 broadcasters exceeded the requirement and spent nearly €100 million this way. The United Kingdom has no such requirements, though the PSB Channel Four is a co-producer of films.[10]

Radio programme production

There is little mention in the cultural or media economics literature of the role of radio in producing performing arts programmes. Public service radio channels carry a considerable amount of live performances by their own orchestras and choruses as well as commissioning radio dramas and employing actors for sound performances, such as plays and book and poetry readings, in addition to their playing of recorded music and transmission of live performance from theatres and concert halls. The 'Met' (Metropolitan

---

[9] Baumol and Baumol (1984).
[10] A full description is to be found in European Audiovisual Observatory (2006); see also Blaauw (2006).

Opera of New York) broadcasts have become as much a part of European listening as well as that throughout the United States. There are also some commercial classical music stations.

A number of the German public radio stations finance orchestras, increasingly employing high-profile international conductors, and offer employment to a considerable number of orchestral players and professional singers in their choirs. These activities are financed by a levy on radio and TV sets.[11] This pattern is repeated in other European countries. In the United Kingdom, the BBC has five orchestras and a big band; it also supports the BBC Singers, a professional choir and the BBC Chorus (unpaid). In addition, it runs what it claims to be the biggest music festival in the world, the Proms. This model is not unknown in North America, though the Canadian Broadcasting Corporation (CBC) Radio Orchestra seems to be the only one remaining. The orchestras and radio stations promoting them are now streaming live broadcasts of concerts that can also be downloaded.

Regulation of broadcasting

The regulation of broadcasting takes place for three basic reasons: technical, economic and cultural (in the widest sense of that word). As technology changes, the original technical rationale for regulation has become less compelling, but the need remains to ensure that there is no interference with the signal. The economic case for regulation, which is done through media ownership rules, is to guarantee market contestability and plurality of provision. Regulation for cultural purposes, to achieve diversity of content, is accomplished by stipulating conditions for the licence.

Spectrum regulation

The electromagnetic spectrum, sections of which are utilised by radio and TV, is limited and it is also needed for other purposes, such as police and ambulance communication, air traffic control and military purposes, and overlapping use causes interference. There are therefore good technical reasons for a central authority to co-ordinate use and allocate spectrum to individual users. That authority (the Federal Communications Commission in the United

---

[11] See www.nytimes.com/2006/10/29/arts/music/29midg.html?n=Top/Reference/Times%20Topics/Subjects/C/Classical%20Music.

States, Ofcom in the United Kingdom, Industry Canada, and so on) allocates spectrum by issuing a licence for broadcasting; how that is done varies, however. Traditionally, spectrum was allocated on a 'beauty contest' according to the perceived merits of the broadcaster, and it is still done that way for over-the-air broadcasting in many countries; an alternative is for the regulating authority to retain control of the spectrum and offer licences for parts of it by auction; alternatively, the parts of the spectrum may be auctioned without the authority retaining ownership, thus allowing secondary markets to develop. This latter course is increasingly recommended by economists, who are convinced that well-established property rights will find their most efficient use via a free market. In many cases, a combination of licence auctions and beauty contest is adopted as the chosen means of allocation, ensuring that a spread of socio-cultural interests and financial strength is accommodated.

Technological advances have increased the ability to use the spectrum and therefore reduced spectrum scarcity while other delivery technologies – satellite and cable – have increased modes of access for viewers, again reducing the impact of scarcity. Now digitisation and increased bandwidth have opened up vastly increased possibilities for the delivery and access of broadcasts, narrowcasts (such as cable), pay-per-view, streaming and downloading of radio and TV on the internet, reception on mobile devices, and so on. These developments do not require the same type of regulation as in the days of limited spectrum.

Media ownership regulations

The regulation of media ownership has little to do with spectrum regulation, though the licensing system associated with it has enabled broadcasting authorities to control licence fees and set limits on ownership. It is likely that media ownership regulations will persist even with a free market in licences, because the reason for them is cultural and political: they promote plurality of view and diversity of provision, and this is seen as best achieved by preventing domination by a few large corporations. Media ownership regulations cover the national market and, under some circumstances, cross-border markets (as in the European Union). Box 17.4 gives an idea of what these regulations look like: it contains excerpts of the US FCC rules on media ownership in 2006 (which were being reconsidered for possible revision). It can be seen from the precise and very detailed wording that such rules have to be capable of standing up in a court of law, and, in fact, they have been so challenged. Besides dealing with ownership within one medium, they also deal with cross-media ownership between TV and radio, TV and newspapers and

Box 17.4 US Federal Communications Commission media ownership rules under review in 2006

- Local television ownership limit – A single entity may own two television stations in the same local market if (i) the so-called 'Grade B' contours of the stations do not overlap or (ii) at least one of the stations in the combination is not ranked among the top four stations in terms of audience share and at least eight independently owned and operating commercial or non-commercial full-power broadcast television stations would remain in the market after the combination. The FCC in 2003 voted to revise the local TV ownership rule to permit an entity to own up to two television stations in markets with seventeen or fewer television stations, and up to three television stations in markets with eighteen or more television stations
- Local radio ownership limit – As a general rule, one entity may own (i) up to five commercial radio stations, not more than three of which are in the same service (i.e. AM or FM), in a market with fourteen or fewer radio stations; (ii) up to six commercial radio stations, not more than four of which are in the same service, in a market with between fifteen and twenty-nine radio stations; (iii) up to seven commercial radio stations, not more than four of which are in the same service, in a radio market with between thirty and forty-four (inclusive) radio stations; and (iv) up to eight commercial radio stations, not more than five of which are in the same service, in a radio market with forty-five or more radio stations.
- UHF discount used in calculating the national television ownership limit – In 2004 Congress enacted legislation that permits a single entity to own any number of television stations on a nationwide basis as long as the station group collectively reached no more than 39 per cent of the national TV audience.
- Newspaper/broadcast cross-ownership ban – The current rule prohibits the common ownership of a full-service broadcast station (television or radio) and a daily newspaper if the station's service area completely encompasses the newspaper's city of publication. In an order in 2002 the FCC relaxed this rule and the separate radio/TV cross-ownership restriction by replacing both regulations with a set of 'cross-media limits.' The new limits were tiered according to the size of the local market: (i) in those with three or fewer TV stations, all newspaper/broadcast and radio/television combinations were prohibited; (ii) in markets with between four and eight stations, an entity could own a combination that included a newspaper and either (a) one television station and up to 50 per cent of the radio stations that may be commonly owned under the applicable radio cap, or (b) up to 100 per cent of the radio stations allowed under the applicable radio cap; and (iii) in markets with nine or more television stations, cross-media combinations would be permitted without limit as long as they complied with the applicable local television and local radio caps.
- Radio/television cross-ownership limit – The current rule allows an entity to own one TV station (or two, if the market is large enough to trigger the 'duopoly' provisions of the local television ownership rule) and a varying number of radio stations in a local market, depending on the number of independently owned media 'voices' that are left.
- Dual network ban – The current rule permits the common ownership of multiple broadcast networks but prohibits a merger between or among the 'top four' networks – i.e. ABC, CBS, Fox and NBC.

Source: www.fcc.gov/ownership/rules.html (accessed 15 February 2009).

other communication media. The same principles of regulating ownership are to be found in other countries, though smaller jurisdictions do not necessarily have the need for such complexity.

Audio-visual policy in the European Union

The objective of the Television without Frontiers programme, which began in 1989, was to enable viewers to watch TV channels from all over Europe and to enable broadcasters to reach larger audiences. This would make European productions more competitive in world markets and promote cultural diversity. Common rules apply to the production of audio-visual programmes, television advertising (see box 17.3) and the protection of minors. The directive requires member states to comply by establishing suitable regulatory arrangements in each country. The TVWF was updated in 1997 and, among other things, required broadcasters to reserve a majority proportion of their transmission time (excluding the time appointed to news, sports events, games, advertising, teletext services and teleshopping) for European works and to reserve at least 10 per cent of their transmission time to 'recent European works' (created within the preceding five years) created by independent producers. The Audiovisual Media Services directive was adopted in 2007 and updated (and replaced) the TVWF; it covers all EU audio-visual media services, including on-demand services, in the digital age and must be transposed to national law by 2009. As the AVMS directive (2007/65/EC) states: 'Audiovisual media services are as much cultural services as they are economic services. Their growing importance for societies, democracy – in particular by ensuring freedom of information, diversity of opinion and media pluralism – education and culture justifies the application of specific rules to these services' (article 3).[12]

Whatever technological changes come about, it seems unlikely that broadcasting will be entirely deregulated and left to the free market. What is still an open question, however, is the role of public service broadcasting and how it should be financed and provided.

Welfare economics and public service broadcasting

The remainder of this chapter is devoted entirely to the economics of PSB. There are many similarities between the discussions in cultural economics

---

[12] See http://ec.europa.eu/avpolicy/reg/avms/index_en.htm.

about subsidy for the arts and those about the finance of PSB and how it should be provided – by a state-owned or state-financed organisation[13] or by subsidies to or regulations on commercial broadcasters for including PSB programming in their schedules; non-profit broadcasting financed by subscription is another model. Apart from the United States, where broadcasting was financed by advertising from the start (and PSB was developed from that basis), the typical situation seems to be the one in which the national state monopoly broadcaster has gradually had its monopoly eroded by deregulation and competition from commercial broadcasting and other entertainment sources, so that PSB now has to make its case and justify the finance it receives from or via the state. It is also believed (though data are hard to come by) that audiences for PSB are falling relative to those of commercial broadcasters. Welfare economic analysis has been evoked in making the case for retaining PSB and public finance for it.

Market failure and PSB

As we know, welfare economics can make a case for state intervention in a market on the grounds of market failure, meaning that the free market would not produce the socially optimal level of output or, in the presence of public goods, could fail to work at all. These are the well-known efficiency arguments for government policy; policy is also frequently called for on equity grounds, in order to ensure equality of opportunity, which in the case of broadcasting could mean equal access to affordable news and other information and entertainment, and also that broadcasting would be geographically accessible and provided to far-flung rural areas or places where there are technical problems with delivery. As supply to these locations usually costs more, people living in them otherwise could be at risk of social exclusion.

Market failure can be overcome by regulation, the community pooling of costs, direct subsidy from taxes or state-organised finance through a licence fee. Regulation as described above typically reallocates costs; in the case of broadcasting, it can force broadcasters to provide programmes that profit-maximising behaviour would not support. Community-based finance by voluntary subscriptions and sponsorship, popular in the provision of PSB in the United States, may now be spreading, especially with micro radio broadcasting, but it has not so far been adopted to finance national PSB networks,

---

[13] The BBC and other 'arm's-length' PSBs are, strictly speaking, neither but, they can be included in this categorisation as the state is involved in organising their finance.

Box 17.5 Sir Alan Peacock on the 1986 'Peacock Report' – *Report of the Committee on Financing the BBC*

Sir Alan Peacock was chairman of the Committee on Financing the BBC set up to review the licence fee, which produced the so-called 'Peacock Report' in 1986. The committee also considered the question of competition in the light of new technological possibilities that were beginning to present themselves as alternatives to over-the-air broadcasting. It was argued that some of these technologies removed the public good characteristics of broadcasting and enabled broadcasting to be treated like any other market. Nevertheless, Peacock and the committee recommended the retention of the BBC and its finance through the licence fee regulated by parliament, the status quo for PSB in the United Kingdom.

Peacock subsequently revisited his thinking in the report (Peacock, 1986a). One of his main concerns had been equity of access, both in geographical terms and on the grounds of income. He noted that he had toyed with the idea of trying to subsidise the viewers and listeners directly, possibly by the issue of vouchers in the form of a card for insertion in a receiver that could reduce the price for viewing PSB programmes, realising that new technologies might permit such a system. He restated his view that the public finance of PSB should be continued, though all programming, scheduling and transmission of PSB content did not have to be done by the BBC. He was also concerned about the 'cosy duopoly' that existed at the time between the BBC and the Independent Television Commission, which licensed commercial TV and held back free entry into broadcasting.

Finally, it is worth noting in the light of the earlier discussion of Peacock's views on heritage that he considered a governance system for a privatised BBC along the lines of the National Trust – that is, a private non-profit organisation controlled by members.

Sources: Peacock (1986a) and Towse (2005).

---

leaving subsidy from taxation or licence fees mandated by the government as the model for financing PSB. As Alan Peacock has observed, however (see box 17.5), a PSB such as the BBC does not have to do all the scheduling, programming or transmission itself.

Market failure exists in broadcasting on three counts. First, over-the-air broadcasting has the characteristics of a public good, being non-rival and non-excludable. Second, broadcasting tends to natural monopoly, with high fixed costs, acting as a barrier to entry, and almost zero marginal costs, requiring the broadcaster to cover its fixed costs by means other than marginal cost pricing. Third, there are sizable external effects of broadcasting for various reasons, ranging from the fundamental nature of broadcasting as a source of public information to so-called network effects of sharing common experiences. Closely related are the merit good arguments of the inherent value of diversity. It is argued in this context that a broad range of programmes may not be produced by commercial broadcasters because they all aim for the median viewer's taste instead of catering to niche markets.

Quality and taste formation

In addition to these static arguments, there is the dynamic argument, laid out in chapter 6 in the context of the arts, that perceptions of quality are developed over time in a personal and social learning process of taste formation. Without some standard of excellence, which the market is unlikely to produce from commercially motivated supply, consumers do not have the chance of learning what quality (of the arts or broadcasting) they could demand and cannot act in the informed way required for consumer sovereignty. This argument is on the face of it close to the paternalistic one of the merit good argument, but it is in fact different because its focus is the effect of an information deficit on the working of markets that could lead to market failure of quality. Information about quality is not saying what is good for people. Knowledge of quality may, in fact, be treated as a public good in its own right. In this context, it is worth reiterating that there are several meanings to the term 'information' in economics: lack of information is a problem, as mentioned above; then there is the problem of asymmetric information, when one party to a transaction has more information than the other and uses that to his or her advantage; the extreme case of that is supplier-induced demand, in which the seller informs the buyer about his or her needs. Information is a good in its own right. Information goods, and specifically knowledge, are public goods.

In discussing information externalities, it is said that an objective such as the desire to live in a well-informed and therefore well-functioning civil society cannot be met by individual choice alone, because the individual cannot exert enough influence over whether the whole society is well informed.[14] Nor can property rights in information, such as news, be fully established, and therefore revenues cannot be appropriated in full by the supplier. Another feature that is particularly important in relation to news is the question of trust, a subject that is clearly crucial in the context of news provision. 'Informed consumers' need information but it costs time and money to acquire; trust and reputation save on these costs. Surveys have shown that people have greater trust in PSB news than in that provided by commercial broadcasters. There are also negative consumption externalities, such as the legitimation of violence, that require control (though that can be regulated by the state independently of broadcasting), and some people believe it is easier to achieve this control with

---

[14] See, on this and subsequent points, Hargraves Heap (2005).

PSB than with commercial broadcasting. Finally, the familiar 'nobody knows' problem of all creative industries applies to TV and radio programme-making, and radical uncertainty can lead to market failure.

Before leaving this topic, a study by Richard van der Wurff (2005) is particularly valuable as a piece of empirical testing of the popularly held belief that PSB provides greater programme diversity than does commercial broadcasting. He analysed the role of PSB in ensuring programme diversity by studying broadcast programme provision in a number of European countries. He shows that diversity requires plurality of provision, including PSB, but that PSB alone does not provide the answer. His conclusion is based on an empirical study of programming of both commercial and public service broadcasters and does not, as he points out, deal with other performance indicators such as programme quality. He found that, in the countries studied, audiences were broadly satisfied with their choice of programmes from the mix of commercial and PSB programmes and there was no evidence that competition between the two resulted in similar, low-cost programmes. Thus empirical evidence goes against the arguments put forward above.

Governance of PSB providers

One of the issues that has been discussed in relation to PSB is how to make it sufficiently accountable to the public and responsive to public tastes. This raises a familiar conundrum in cultural economics: should subsidised arts and heritage providers do something different with their subsidy from that which the market would produce, with the risk of not having popular appeal, or should they just provide more or less the same output as the market would – in this case programmes? This is a perpetually unresolved problem and leads inevitably to tension between PSB and commercial broadcasting, with the latter complaining that the PSB providers have the advantage because they have subsidy or licence fee revenues. Related to this problem is the question of how a national PSB, such as the BBC, should be governed so as to achieve the objectives set for it by the government; again, the question of governance did not arise in the days of state monopoly broadcasting, as the state was itself responsible. This also raises questions about how independent of the state a PSB is and to what extent it is free to criticise the government of the day.

As we saw in Peacock's reflections on financing the BBC (box 17.5), the functions of PSB can be split off from their provision, and he favoured a model of governance that more closely involved the public, such as a membership organisation. One proposal in the United Kingdom has been for an 'Arts

Council of the Air' – that is, an 'arm's-length' body that independently administers public finance for a specified type of PSB activity. This would make a dedicated PSB broadcaster unnecessary, as any broadcaster may apply for subsidy to such a body to produce a PSB programme. An obvious advantage of such a system would be that there is competition for PSB programme supply. Experience of arts councils, however, is that they tend to elitism and the favouring of insiders and have a preference for merit goods. Another danger is that having the subsidy and making the programme do not guarantee that it will be broadcast – something the arts council cannot control. Moreover, there is also the familiar principal–agent problem, which cannot easily be overcome since complete contracts cannot be drawn up. Shaun Hargreaves Heap (2005) has analysed these options and rejects the idea in favour of a dedicated PSB provider, asking to what extent there is a difference anyway between an 'Arts Council of the Air' and the dedicated PSB; if the PSB (he refers specifically to the BBC) is required to buy in products, it must act as a gate-keeper in the way the arts council would.

An interesting and seemingly unique model of PSB governance is that found in the Netherlands (box 17.6), in which membership of broadcasting associations determines the allocation of PSB licences.

Finally, the other subject considered by Peacock (boxes 6.1 and 17.5) is the possibility of having vouchers for PSB that new technologies may make feasible. That would be a means of solving one of the oldest problems in cultural economics: supplier-induced demand, whereby the supplier has more information than the consumer and uses that to extract subsidy (so-called 'rent') that is then spent according to the preferences of the arts manager, not the consumer. With a voucher, the consumer can signal his or her tastes and assert his or her consumer sovereignty; if he or she does not like what an arts organisation offers, that person does not attend and there is no subsidy. If it were feasible to supply PSB using digital means, the household could be given a voucher and offered a choice of 'taste-forming' programmes and use the vouchers in a pay-per-view setting. This way, consumers' preferences as well as their willingness to pay for particular programmes could be elicited.

Contingent valuation studies of PSB

It is widely acknowledged that the argument for PSB is much weaker with digital technologies; nevertheless, there is a consensus in a number of countries for retaining PSB on various grounds, and contingent valuation methods have been used to estimate the willingness to pay for it. There is also the matter

Box 17.6 Governance of PSB in the Netherlands

The Netherlands has a unique governance arrangement for PSB that has its origins in the time when Dutch society was organised along partisan lines (known as pillars) – Protestant, Catholic, liberal, conservative, and so on – and this was reflected in the finance of the press, radio and, eventually, television. PSB is financed from taxation (there was a licence fee until 2000). This is how it is governed. Quoting from the English-language version of *Cultural Policy in the Netherlands* – OCenW (the Netherlands' Ministry for Education, Culture and Science), 2006: 94–5:

Broadcasting time on public radio and television channels is shared by a large number of broadcasting associations and several other non-profit organisations, which are granted broadcasting licences either because they are deemed representative of a particular section of population, or on the basis of a specific programme remit. For many years, these organisations operated under a self-appointed general management. When commercial television entered the market and the audience share of public television declined, this organisational structure failed to produce an effective answer. Dutch governments responded by altering the *Media Act* several times, gradually changing the organisation of public service broadcasting. On the whole, the autonomy of the separate broadcasting organisations was reduced, whereas more power was vested in a central body, i.e. an independent Board of Directors. This Board was installed in 1998 to coordinate and oversee programming and ensure common interests. In 2000, the *Concessions Act* ... was introduced to further improve the responsiveness of public service broadcasting. The duty to provide public service radio and television has been entrusted to the Board of Directors, whose job is to ensure that the broadcasters together – as participants in the concession – comply with the statutory remit to provide a high quality, varied range of programmes that reach large and small sections of the Dutch population. Over the years, the Board of Directors has gained power over spending, production and programming within the system. For some years, the broadcasting associations kept seats in the supervising Board of Governors, but since 2005 this Board is entirely made up of independent members (appointed by the Crown).

Subsequent changes in the *Media Act* have not changed the basis on which the public system operates. Various broadcasting associations representing various schools of thought and groups within Dutch society are still at the heart of the Dutch public broadcasting system. They can get a licence every five years. The *Media Act* lays down that new broadcasting associations entering the system must represent an ideological school of thought. To be assigned a licence for the first time, a new broadcasting association must have at least 150,000 paying members and demonstrate that it will add a new kind of programme to the public channels. Associations which are already part of the public broadcasting system need at least 300.000 paying members to keep their licence. In 2006, eight broadcasting associations shared responsibility for public radio and television: KRO (Catholic), NCRV (Protestant), EO (Protestant), AVRO (neutral), TROS (family viewing), BNN (the young), VARA (progressive) and VPRO (progressive).

Source: OCenW (2006).

of the appropriate method of charging – should it be a licence fee, financed out of general taxation, or by subscription? From an economic point of view, a licence fee is not an efficient method of charging for PSB programmes, because it is a flat-rate payment independent of how many hours of viewing take place or what viewers choose to watch. Moreover, the public good nature of broadcasting would mean that there is no price that is efficient. Non-rivalry of broadcasts means there is no scarcity, so there is no reason to ration viewers, and the efficient price set according to marginal cost would be zero. In the absence of pricing, however, institutional and non-market means have to be employed to estimate what people want to see (it cannot be called 'demand' in the absence of prices). Thus the only way of setting the price is according to consumers' willingness to pay.

Several CV studies of willingness to pay for broadcasting have been undertaken, and here I mention those by Franco Papandrea (1999) for domestic TV regulation in Australia and by Adam Finn, Stuart McFadyen and Colin Hoskins (2003) for PSB in Canada.[15] Papandrea measured WTP for the cultural benefits of domestic regulation requiring 55 per cent of free-to-air commercial broadcasters to provide Australian content. The survey was administered as part of a national government statistical survey dealing with a range of issues and asked respondents to say whether they were willing to pay the amount of the estimated average per household cost of supplying domestic programming or if they valued it more or less than that amount and, additionally, the maximum they would pay if costs were to increase. Summed over all households, he estimated the net benefit to Australian society of retaining domestic regulation. The outcome of the exercise was that WTP was slightly lower than the stated cost, but other questions established that there was broad support for the regulation.

Finn, McFadyen and Hoskins estimated the value Canadians place on the Canadian Broadcasting Corporation, the Canadian PSB. This included both the value households place on their own use and what they would pay to make it available to others. They also assessed the non-use value to Canadians of the CBC; without such a survey, there is no way (other than through a referendum) to place a figure on the external benefits derived from the existence of a good that others are willing to pay for. In the survey, Finn, McFadyen and Hoskins found that half the Canadian households surveyed were non-users. Again, they found that the estimated total valuation of benefits was slightly

---

[15] The UK government also commissioned a study of willingness to pay for the BBC: see Fauth, Horner and Bevan (2006).

lower than the cost of running the CBC. These studies demonstrate that the presence of public goods and externalities does not rule out a monetary valuation of PSB, even in the absence of prices, and that this may at least supplement political decision-making.

Conclusion

Broadcasting is a particularly fine example of a cultural industry, with its complex interaction of economic and cultural aspects, and understanding the workings of the market for broadcasting presents an interesting topic in welfare economics and the economics of regulation. It is also an industry that has experienced changes in technology over the last few decades. It is therefore a true topic for cultural economics, with its combination of economic analysis and concern with cultural outcomes. Broadcasting supplies a service that is vital to the cultural well-being of the community and one that governments have a special interest in protecting; that alone would be sufficient to justify government intervention. In addition, though, over-the-air broadcasting, the technology that was in use for generations, necessitated regulation for technical reasons, and its public good nature also required finance by means other than direct payment between buyer (viewer or listener) and seller. That finance came in two versions: state (or state-organised) funding and finance via the market, in the form of advertising with the broadcaster acting as intermediary. The co-existence of these two types – PSB and commercial TV and radio – has been a source of friction about the purpose of PSB and the balance that is needed between them, a balance that the state can achieve by regulation through its control of the allocation of broadcast licences but not if it sells licences on the market as property rights that can be resold in a secondary market.

The broadcasting industry, broadly defined, shares with other creative industries the combination of content creation (programme-making) and delivery (transmission and scheduling), and these two activities have very different economic features: programme-making is very similar to film-making and even shares some features in common with the live performing arts, while transmission is a natural monopoly and requires some form of two-part tariff to cover its high fixed costs supplied by subsidy or commercial advertising. Regulation has brought about disintegration between these two sides of the broadcasting industry, so that broadcasters buy in programmes. This in turn has led to regulation in the European Union and some other countries to prevent TV being swamped by American programmes and films, along with government incentives to encourage the rise of independent 'national' programme-makers.

No mention has been made of copyright issues in broadcasting in the chapter. Broadcasts are themselves protected works in the sense of copyright law, and all the material they carry is also copyrighted, either as a work of an author or a performer (though performers do not have full rights in their audio-visual performances in the way that musical performers do). The syndication of broadcasts makes for a complex business of licensing and royalty collection, and studying it is a relatively new area in the economics of copyright. More complex still is the licensing of broadcasts with new technologies and interactive use. These are topics that require advanced specialist analysis and therefore they have not been part of the treatment here.

The onset of new technologies over the last twenty or so years that vastly reduced, even removed, spectrum scarcity has had several consequences for broadcasting: first, it strengthened the hand of those in favour of deregulation; second, it enables broadcasters to provide a far greater array of services, and this has called for greater creative content as well as innovation in delivery; third, it has introduced competition for viewers' time from other sources of news, information and entertainment from the internet, with its blogs and games, and mobility has been achieved through mobile devices. The regulation of broadcasting is now often combined with the regulation of telecommunications – in some cases, a return to former times: the BBC in the United Kingdom was regulated along with telegraph and telephones in the 1920s! In this context, it is also interesting to note that observers of the turbulence caused by the internet boom regard radio as its true precedent as a medium for mass communication and its creative destruction of existent media, such as the music industry and newspapers.[16] Broadcasters now use the internet as an integral part of their service for both content and distribution purposes, and media ownership regulations and audio-visual policy now take that into account. This is another specialised field that cultural economists have yet to explore.

This chapter has touched on this mixture of technical, financial and cultural regulation in broadcasting, which has been studied in depth in a considerable literature of media economics and by other economists with an interest in the economics and practice of regulatory issues. In the main, the chapter has concentrated on PSB because of its affinity to the economics of the arts, and it

---

[16] See Küng, Picard and Towse (2008).

has shown that welfare economics can throw an interesting light on the subject. Studies of willingness to pay for PSB show an affinity between the valuation of broadcasting and that of other heritage. All in all, then, the chapter demonstrates that cultural economics has a specific contribution to make to the economics of broadcasting as well as much to learn from it.

Further reading

As ever, Harold Vogel's *Entertainment Industry Economics: A Guide for Financial Analysis* (now in its sixth edition – 2004) is a terrific source of information and institutional data for a researcher on any of the cultural industries, mostly but not only on the United States. Also on the United States, Richard Caves' (2005) *Switching Channels* is a follow-up to his earlier book in terms of methodology, but now with the focus on the television industry. On Europe, Jürgen Heinrich and Gerd Kopper's (2006) compendium *Media Economics in Europe* covers economic policy and institutions from every corner of the continent, including the television industry, with chapters by experts from all over Europe. Chapters in my *Handbook of Cultural Economics* (Towse, 2003a) by Glenn Withers on 'Broadcasting' (chapter 12) and by Christopher Maule on 'Television' (chapter 58) give a broad, expert overview of the economics of these topics. Richard van der Wurff's (2005) article 'Competition, concentration and diversity in European television markets' shows how empirical research challenges conventional views.

18 Economics of book publishing

This chapter first looks at international data on the publishing industry and then at the production of trade books, including authors' contracts, and after that at consumption – both the demand for books and for library services – and at various schemes for stimulating reading. Authors may be supported by state subsidy and awards, and these schemes and evidence on authors' earnings from copyright round off the chapter.

Background

Publishing covers a wide range of print material that is distributed in various ways. There is considerable product diversity within the categories of publication, such as books, journals, magazines and newspapers; books may be fiction or non-fiction, textbooks or manuals; fiction may be a great classic or a trifling tale. Until recently publication was on paper, but now electronic books and other publications are emerging and digitisation is under way in the industry. Book publication is divided into several categories: the biggest distinction is between trade books and educational and professional books. The latter, which constitute around a half of the publishing market, are aimed at schools and colleges; our interest here is in the market for 'trade' books, meaning adult fiction and non-fiction and children's books.

Books are some of the oldest cultural products and reading is an essential means of accessing knowledge and entertainment, and authorship – the creation of content – is one of the oldest creative activities. Book publishing has been a creative industry for centuries and has been a private enterprise for as long. Copyright law was initiated to support the book trade and to enable authors to control the use of their work for economic and artistic reward. It is interesting to note that so vital a cultural activity as publishing is largely unsubsidised, and its chief form of state support is through copyright; in many European countries and in Japan, however, the 'fixed' book price is government policy, allowing publishers to prevent price competition. In addition, authors may be supported by state subsidy. Reading, although enforced at school, may not endure the competition with other entertainment sources, however, and a lack of reading skills has become a matter of concern in some countries, which have been initiating schemes to remedy the situation.

International trade and value added

International trade

According to the UNCTAD (2008) *Creative Economy Report 2008*, the global market for internationally traded goods from the publishing and printed media industries was $44 billion in 2005; the most traded subsector was 'Other printed materials' ($16 billion), consisting of catalogues, brochures, advertising material, posters, calendars, maps, greeting cards, and so on – the joys of international trade data! Newspapers accounted for $15 billion and world trade in books was $13 billion. These are data for trade in goods and do not include copyright payments, licences and other 'services'. There was a very strong bias towards domination of the international trade in books by a few developed countries, with over a half of all exports of books from the top five countries – the United States, the United Kingdom, Germany, Spain and France – and the top five importers of books were the United States, the United Kingdom, Canada, France and Germany, together importing 44 per cent of the world total.

Contribution to value added in the European Union

The publishing industry in the twenty-seven European Union countries has a value added of some €44 billion: newspapers contribute 42 per cent, periodicals 33 per cent and books 25 per cent. The value of the publishing industry for the leading five countries in the European Union are presented in table 18.1, which also shows the number of enterprises and the number of employees. Table 18.1 shows that the United Kingdom had the highest value added (almost one-third of the EU total). In fact, publishing was the second largest creative industry in the United Kingdom, contributing nearly £10 billion in gross value added to the UK economy in 2006. These figures are for all types of publication, not just books.

Table 18.1 Publishing sector in leading five EU countries, 2001

	Production value (billion euros)	Value added at factor cost (billion euros)	Number of enterprises	Number of employees
United Kingdom	28.9	13.1	9,694	165,430
Germany	27.9	10.1	6,709	185,307
France	19.1	5.9	12,223	88,992
Italy	11.6	3.5	6,934	36,692
Netherlands	7.1	2.9	2,620	38,659
Total EU-15 countries	116.6	43.5	54,102	672,805

Sources: Kretschmer and Hardwick (2007); data from Eurostat.

Production of trade books

The number of titles and sales figures are the typical indicators of output. For example, the 2,000 plus publishers in the United Kingdom (which produces around 45 per cent of all books published in the English language) produced 119 million titles in 2001, just under a half being trade books: 11 per cent were adult fiction, 9 per cent were children's books and 26 per cent were non-fiction; 60 per cent were sold on the home market and 40 per cent exported. Over 120,000 new book titles were published in the United Kingdom in 2004, with the annual production of new titles more than doubling in the last fifteen years. Box 4.2 provides a full profile of the UK book market. Trade books constituted just over one-quarter of all book sales in the United States in 1999.[1]

Books may be published in hardback, paperback, audio- or e-book format. Each has its associated production and delivery costs for producer and consumer: for bound books on paper, the cost of printing and binding is borne by the publisher; the purchaser buys the book and may use the book as he or she wishes (for example, lending it or reselling it). Audiobooks and e-books have to be put into those formats by the supplier, and the consumer needs equipment to access them; and, as with sound recordings, consumers may be restricted in what they can do with the book by some form of digital rights management technology.

[1] Vogel (2004).

Books on paper

Hardback and paperback are price-discriminated versions of the same title, which may be released sequentially or simultaneously, printed on similar paper but bound differently; traditionally, the hardback is priced significantly higher than the paperback and is aimed at libraries and high-income purchasers and, if published in advance of the paperback, also at consumers who want the book quickly. The hardback recoups the fixed (or sunk) costs of publishing the book and the paperback can then be released and sold at a much lower price.

A breakdown of the cost of producing a trade book in a paper version is indicative: manufacturing (10 per cent), distribution (8 per cent), marketing (7.5 per cent), publisher's overhead (8 per cent), author's royalty (average 10 per cent), retail discount (average 47 per cent), cost of returns (3.5 per cent), publisher's profit (6 per cent).[2] These costs would be different for other formats.

Audiobooks

Audiobooks began on cassettes, often in abridged versions so as to cope with the length. The books are read out ('performed'), often by well-known actors (although their names are not overtly advertised), and recorded like music. Nowadays they are more likely to be on CD or in MP3 format for downloading for purchase or rental. Until recently audiobooks have been protected by DRM, but, like musical online supply, this protection is gradually being withdrawn to increase sales and distribution outlets. There are several big specialised audiobook suppliers whose catalogues include a range of genres, and a considerable number of titles are supplied.

E-books

E-books require a reading device, such as a personal computer or e-book reader, which, though available for some time, have not proved popular. E-books are simply scanned from the text, and some books are now published in both paper and e-book formats. They may also be converted into audio-books and put on an iPod. In Japan, sales of mobile-phone books that are downloaded and read, usually in instalments, on the screen of a mobile phone are reputed to be increasingly popular. There are now dedicated e-publishers and e-book sellers; eBooks.com offers around 102,000 popular, professional and academic e-books for sale.

---

[2] Vogel (2001).

Online access to books

There are various schemes to scan and upload books. One is Project Gutenberg, a non-profit organisation that makes (mostly) public-domain books available in long-lasting, open formats that can be used on almost any computer. Project Gutenberg claimed to have over 24,000 items in its collection in 2007: most releases are in English but non-English languages are also represented: French (1,053 files), German (451), Finnish (396), Dutch (279) and Spanish (155). In 2004 Google began to scan and upload books that were out of print in the United States, even though many were in copyright. As a result of a threatened class action lawsuit by the Authors Guild and the Association of American Publishers, Google agreed in 2008 to compensate them at a minimum of $60 per word in a deal worth $120 million.[3] By the end of 2008 the full text of some 7 million books could be accessed through Google Book Search, and partnerships were being formed with libraries.[4]

Economic organisation of book production

Like many other creative products, books in Caves' terminology have 'infinite variety' and titles are not perfect substitutes, though some characteristics, such as being by the same author, make substitution possible (as online booksellers know very well). The market for books is therefore monopolistically competitive: there is product differentiation, which gives the supplier some monopoly power, but there is also possible substitution, so price competition is limited. In many respects, book publishing is very similar to the record industry: it includes the stages of development, acquisition, copy-editing, graphic design, production (printing or putting in another format), marketing and distribution to retailers – bookshops, other retail outlets, such as department stores and supermarkets, online bookshops – and to book clubs and libraries. Only the first two of these stages of production and marketing are done in-house nowadays and the other specialised services are bought in, quite a few of which are outsourced to various countries – India, China, Slovenia come to mind (this book will probably have been printed, and possibly edited, in one of them!). Graphic design, printing and other production techniques are crafts that benefit from specialisation; distribution is also a specialised function, because books are bulky to store and transport to the retailer or consumer. As a result, there is little vertical integration in book publishing, and these services are bought in by publishers.

---

[3] *The Guardian*, 29 October 2008.   [4] See http://books.google.com/googlebooks/agreement.

Unlike the film and record industry, though, there seems not to have been the incentive to publishers to own their own retail outlets. There has been a strong trend to horizontal integration, with over 600 mergers and acquisitions of trade book publishers taking place in the United States in the 1990s; these mergers are not thought to have raised entry barriers, however, and there was contestability in the industry; nor did book prices rise due to increased concentration.[5] It seems likely that economies of scale and scope in marketing are the incentive for mergers. Therefore, the main function of trade book publishing is the commissioning and contracting of authors.

Gate-keeping and market intermediaries

In common with other creative industries, book publishers fulfil the role of gate-keepers, selecting for publication a small proportion from a huge excess supply of offerings by potential authors. British publishers receive something like 200 unsolicited manuscripts per week. In order to get the attention of a publishing house, authors employ literary agents, who in turn have contacts with editors employed by the publisher; the agent works on a commission of 10 to 15 per cent of the author's revenues, which are in turn royalties of 10 to 15 per cent of the retail price of the book. Agents play an important co-ordinating role in the market (as market-makers) and aim to develop a long-term relationship with both authors and editors. Agents may also advise authors on improvements to a work.

Editors are the equivalent in book publishing to A&R in the record industry: they are in charge of acquiring manuscripts and seeing them through to publication. The editor selects potential books and works with the 'humdrum' side of the business to get the author signed up. Editors are examples of 'specific human assets', people who are knowledgeable about the market and are believed to be able to recognise talent and potential success – where 'success' means paying off the sunk costs in the book (the advance to the author, the production and marketing costs). One feature of the publishing industry is that editors frequently move between publishing houses and thereby obtain a lot of information about the industry, and this is the source of their asset specificity and their reputation for selecting good authors.[6] As employees, however, they earn relatively little and seem unable to capture the benefits of their knowledge without changing jobs.

Editors listen to literary agents because they are well informed about the market and have the incentive to pick winners. Still, this is another industry in

---

[5] Greco (2000).   [6] For this paragraph, see Caves (2000).

which 'nobody knows', and success with a blockbuster book is both rare and very lucrative. Best-seller books sell in the millions and are likely to be translated into other languages, and may possibly be made into a film. The agent of an author with a track record will probably hold an auction for the author's next book, carried out on the basis of a prospectus. J. K Rowling's title *The Tales of Beedle the Bard* was bought at auction at Sotheby's for £1.95 million by Amazon in 2007.

The publishing contract

The author as the creator of the book automatically has copyright on the work and owns all the rights that copyright law accords to it – the bundle of publication, reproduction, translation, public performance (if it were read on radio, for example), broadcasting, making available (for online delivery) and adaptation rights. In order to publish the book, the publisher has to obtain the relevant rights from the author, and in so doing the publisher will often also require other rights in order to exploit the work fully, often far in excess of what is actually needed. In exchange, the publisher agrees to pay the author a royalty on the price of each unit of the book sold; the royalty varies according to the type of use; for example, the royalty rate is lower on book club sales. The royalty on sales is typically 10 per cent. If the book is translated, the publisher and author split the translation fee fifty-fifty, and similar arrangements relate to film and other such contracts. The author usually has no control over the price of the book (see box 13.3) and therefore cannot anticipate the royalty revenue; in addition, of course, he or she does not know (and nor does the publisher) how many copies will be sold. The contract ties the author and publisher into a risk-sharing arrangement. The author will therefore try to minimise the risk by getting an advance on future royalties. The author has also had an expense in terms of the time taken writing the book and may well have to make corrections and alterations as required by the editor; these are sunk costs for the author. The publisher has the outlay on the sunk costs of publishing the book. Bargaining power is, for the most part, strongly on the publisher's side.

Authors' earnings by genre

The outcome of the publication results in revenues for the publisher, out of which the author is paid his or her share as a royalty. Table 18.2 presents data for the United Kingdom on professional authors' earnings from writing, where 'professional' means that the respondent to the survey spent over 50 per cent of his/her time writing. The differences between the mean (average) and median income are due to the presence of a few very high earners and many relatively

Table 18.2 Writing income of UK professional authors by genre and media, 2004/5

Genre/media	Mean writing income (pounds)	Median writing income (pounds)
Books		
Fiction	35,187	13,000
Children's fiction	23,249	15,531
Non-fiction	19,294	8,000
Academic/educational	24,322	10,000
Translations	8,756	5,000
Newspapers/magazines	22,542	13,195
Theatre/film writing	40,527	20,000
TV writing	43,591	39,419
TV soaps	73,863	73,000
Audio, internet and other	35,584	13,500

Source: Kretschmer and Hardwick (2007).

low earners (see chapter 11). The figures in table 18.2 show the variation in incomes by genre of books and other writing; it can be seen that writing for TV is the most lucrative source of income. The same study found similar results for German writers (whose royalty earnings were reported in box 13.6).

Consumption of books

Book consumption takes various forms: consumers buy books from book-shops (in physical and online form), download them in electronic form, buy and share books in book clubs and reading groups and borrow them from libraries and friends. Data on reading habits and expenditure on books and libraries are collected by national statistics offices and by international orga-nisations, especially UNESCO. Many factors affect the demand for books. Books are purchased not only by individual consumers but also by libraries. Demand by individuals depends upon book prices, prices of alternative cultural products, income and tastes. Before discussing demand, reading habits and other factors that influence taste for books are analysed.

Reading for leisure

Apart from concerns about literacy, many developed countries have noted a decline in the reading for pleasure – or 'leisure reading', as it is sometimes

Table 18. 3 Percentage of young Americans who read a book not required for work or school

Age group	1992	2002	Rate of decline
18–24	59	52	−12
25–34	64	59	−8
35–44	66	59	−11
All adults (18 and over)	61	57	−7

Source: NEA (2007b).

called – of books, magazines and newspapers. The decline is believed to be due to increasing use of the internet, on which it is, of course, possible to read a great deal of material that was previously available only in print form. Another decline that has been observed is in the use of public libraries, and this has led to a discussion about the respective roles of books and electronic media in public (and school) libraries. Governments are concerned about the decline in reading, as it is regarded as fundamental to effective citizenship as well as having strong external benefits for social cohesion. In the United States, concern about these trends has led to policy initiatives to encourage reading (outlined below). Table 18.3 shows the extent of the decline in the United States of reading for leisure. In 2004 only 22 per cent of seventeen-year-olds read for pleasure; in 2006 the younger groups spent between seven and nine minutes on average on weekdays and ten to eleven minutes on weekends reading for pleasure (as compared to average reading times of seventeen and twenty-four minutes on average, respectively, for forty-five- to fifty-four-year-olds).[7]

Data from other countries are based on participation studies. In the Netherlands, 81 per cent of people aged twelve and over were reported in 2005 to read print media (down from 89 per cent in 1995): in 2008 they spent 3.8 hours per week reading; the reading of magazines, newspapers and books was reported to have declined, with book reading declining more than reading other media.[8] In Canada in 2005, 87 per cent of Canadians read a newspaper, 78 per cent read a magazine and 67 per cent read a book ('not for paid work or academic studies'). In the United Kingdom, 63 per cent of the population in 2005 read for pleasure (excluding newspapers, magazines or

---

[7] NEA (2007b).   [8] SCP [the Netherlands' Institute for Social Research] (2008).

comics) and 45 per cent bought a novel, or book of stories, poetry or plays for themselves. In France, a fall in the quantity of books read has been noted, but that contrasted with a rise in the success of libraries. In Germany, the number of people visiting public libraries fell from 9.4 million in 1995 to 7.5 million in 2006.[9] A very detailed survey of reading, book buying and library use in Australia conducted under the auspices of the Australia Council and connected to the 'Books Alive' programme (see later) provides insight into socio-economic aspects of these activities: some of the many results of research on reading and book buying are reported later in box 18.2. As may be seen from box 18.1, readers are not necessarily buyers of books; they borrow from libraries but also read books already in the house, borrow books from friends and get them as presents.

Consumer expenditure on books

Measured in per capita terms by country, there are substantial differences in consumer expenditure on books. In the United States in 2005, consumer expenditure on trade books was $24,571 million, roughly $70 per head of population; average annual household spending on books dropped 14 per cent, when adjusted for inflation, from 1985 to 2005.[10] Per capita expenditure was more or less the same in Japan, though in Australia it was half the US figure; table 18.4 shows the variation in per capita expenditure on books (value of sales) in a selection of EU countries; for all but the Scandinavian countries, the average book price was reported by Miha Kovac and Mojea Kovac Sebart (2006) to be the same (€14).

These differences in consumer expenditure might also be explained by the use of public libraries by readers: Denmark and the Netherlands, for instance, had high rates of library loans per capita – 13.4 and 12.1, respectively, in 2002 (see table 18.4). On the other hand, the highest number of loans per capita was in Finland (19.0), a country with relatively high book sales, and Belgium also had relatively high loans per capita (7.1). These data do not necessarily show that Finns and Belgians read a great deal more than other people, however: Finns do (76 per cent) but Belgians do not (42 per cent)![11] The story is, in fact, complex and seems to reflect taste differences rather than the effect of economic variables.

[9] Data from www.culturalpolicies.net (accessed 11 March 2008).
[10] NEA (2007b).   [11] These data are from Kovac and Kovac Sebart (2006).

Box 18.1   National survey of reading, buying and borrowing books for pleasure: Australia, 2001 (selected results)

- Three-quarters of the adult population (78 per cent) read for pleasure every day or on most days of the week.
- The most frequent readers for pleasure are likely to be females, over sixty-five years old, educated to tertiary standard and of upper socio-economic status. Their interest in reading is above average, and they tend to have more books in their homes.
- The incidence of reading books for pleasure (72 per cent) is lower than for newspapers (91 per cent), but well ahead of magazines (63 per cent) and reading for work or study (44 per cent). For many, reading papers is only a weekend activity, while reading books for pleasure occurs across the week, so the average number of days per week on which reading occurs is actually higher for books than for newspapers (4.6 days versus 4.2 days).
- Among those who had read for pleasure in the previous seven days, there was wide variation in the time spent, but the average time spent reading over the week was 8.1 hours.
- In the previous week: 67 per cent of adults had read for pleasure; 35 per cent had gone into a bookshop; 21 per cent had read a book borrowed from a friend; 17 per cent had gone to a library; 16 per cent had read a book borrowed from a library; 16 per cent had bought a book for themselves; 6 per cent had bought a book as a gift; 4 per cent had received a book as a gift; 73 per cent of parents with children under thirteen years had read to their child in the previous week; 19 per cent of parents had bought a book for their child in the previous week.
- Among those who had read for pleasure in the previous week, the average number of books being read or referred to was 3.4.
- One in five readers (21 per cent) had not bought any books. On average, purchase activity was highest among males thirty to forty-four years old, who were working, well educated, with higher incomes and living in state capital cities.
- The origins of all the books read were as follows: 29 per cent bought new; 20 per cent borrowed from the library; 19 per cent in the house for a long time; 13 per cent borrowed from a friend; 10 per cent received as a gift; 5 per cent bought second-hand; 2 per cent borrowed from someone in the house; 2 per cent other sources.
- The majority of adults (57 per cent) were members of a public library. Library use shows a strong bias to the over-sixty-fives. Library use is well below average among those aged thirty to forty-four, and those in rural locations.

Source: www.australiacouncil.gov.au/−data/assets/pdf_file/0007/1987/ national_survey_reading.pdf (accessed 14 January 2009).

Demand for books

Consumption and survey data are indicative of what influences book buying and reading but, in order to understand demand, it is necessary to specify the relationship between the number of books purchased and their price, as well as other economic determinants, especially income. From these demand

Table 18.4 Per capita sales of books and library loans: selected EU countries, 2002

Country	Value (euros)	Number of books	Library loans
Austria	80	5.7	1.8
Belgium	110	7.9	7.1
Denmark	90	4.0	13.4
Finland	130	5.9	19.0
France	50	3.6	5.2
Germany	80	5.7	3.7
Greece	20	1.4	0.2
Ireland	60	4.3	3.2
Netherlands	35	2.5	12.1
Portugal	65	4.7	0.3
Spain	40	2.9	0.6
Sweden	45	3.1	9.1
United Kingdom	85	6.0	6.9

Source: Kovac and Kovac Sebart (2006).

functions, price and income elasticities of demand can be estimated. As with other cultural goods, measurement of the elasticity of demand provides information for understanding markets and also for any policy intervention that is deemed necessary. In the case of books, there is government intervention in the market, and there are also policies to encourage authorship and reading; knowing the extent to which consumers respond to price and income changes can, therefore, inform these policies. A curious reversal of the usual government policy for the arts of giving subsidy to arts organisations in order to reduce prices (in the belief that attendance is price elastic) is to be found reversed in the case of books: the fixed book price policy (discussed in detail below) is intended to raise or maintain prices above the competitive level in order to provide an incentive to publishers and bookshops to increase the range of titles they supply.

Studies by cultural economists have shown that demand for books is price elastic and also income elastic; people buy more books at lower prices and when their incomes rise (indicating that books, like other cultural goods and services, are a luxury item). An important question is: what is the interaction between the two? As people's incomes rise, as they do on average with economic growth and with age, they will purchase more books, and that could swamp the negative effect on demand of any price rises, as demonstrated by the numerical example in box 18.2. As we shall see in discussing the policy of the fixed book price in many European countries, price elasticity is an

---

Box 18.2 Relative effect of price and income elasticities: an illustration

The price of a book rises from €10 to €11, a 10 per cent increase; consumers buy 15 per cent fewer books (elasticity of demand is −1.5) and weekly sales fall from 115 to 100; weekly sales revenue falls from €1150 to €1100.

If, at the same time, income rises by 10 per cent and consumers buy 115 (a 15 per cent increase) books per week (income elasticity of 1.5), sales revenue at the higher price of €11 goes from €1100 to €1265.

Overall, therefore, the effect of the rise in sales revenue due to increased income is €165, and that exceeds the fall of €50 that was due to the increase in the price.

---

important piece of information, as it tells us that raising the price of books will result in lower numbers of books being purchased.

Other influences on the demand for books

Tastes and best-sellers

Positive income elasticity means more books being bought at every price – in other words, income shifts the demand curve for books upwards and to the right. The same effect can also be achieved through an increased taste for books, or, indeed, for one title. It is interesting to know therefore what influences tastes for book titles. Books are experience goods, in the sense that the reader cannot be sure he or she will enjoy the book until he or she has read it, though readers do know the pleasure they get from reading and many have had the experience of reading many books and are therefore prepared to try out new titles and authors. It is the publishers who face the 'nobody knows' problem of predicting success. Publishers spend considerable amounts of money on advertising books and attending book fairs to promote books, but these efforts may not be very significant in attracting buyers. The survey conducted in Australia, some of whose results were reported in box 18.1, also enquired as to what influenced the selection of books that people made, and over half the respondents said 'word of mouth', followed by information from the book itself 'on the cover' (over one-third), and 30 per cent said that reviews had influenced their choice; best-seller lists had very little influence. Perhaps best-seller lists are more interesting to sellers than buyers.

It is worth recalling the discussion in chapter 6 about taste formation and demand and the tendency of all markets for cultural products to focus on 'superstars' and 'blockbusters'; the explanation offered there was that consumers, faced with a great variety of goods to choose from, economise on their search and information costs by using best-seller lists and the like as a form of certification of quality in making their choices. It is often thought that the focus on superstars is due to supply-side factors, such as the strategy of large corporations in publishing and other creative industries to go for winners that satisfy the 'average' taste at the expense of cultural diversity; while that may be part of the explanation, consumers' 'bandwagon' behaviour also plays a role in the preference for best-sellers and other manifestations of superstardom. Word of mouth acts in a similar way, as people know their informants' tastes and can question them about a book. Oprah Winfrey seems to fulfil the same function: Oprah Winfrey's Book Club, her advice on organising book clubs and her choice of books, with her opinions about books expressed on her TV show and available on her website, can be very influential on book sales. These effects on taste may exert a strong effect on demand and swamp the effect of price.

One of the greatest publishing successes of all times is the *Harry Potter* series by J. K. Rowling. By 2008 the first six books in the book series had sold more than 400 million copies worldwide and had been translated into more than sixty-seven languages. The seventh and last book in the series was released in 2007, and publishers announced a record-breaking 12 million copies for the first print run in the United States alone. Worldwide sales of the *Harry Potter* books have topped 325 million copies. The film series, from which Rowling also enjoys royalties and merchandising, has already grossed $3.5 billion, with a possible three more movies to come.

Book clubs and reading groups

Book clubs have always been a feature of the market for books. In 1999 they accounted for 18 per cent of US adult sales. That figure is probably higher now, as book clubs and reading groups have increased in popularity. Book clubs offer books at reduced prices as they are able to get discounts for bulk buying on behalf of their members. In Europe, book clubs are also significant in sales: they account for around 20 per cent of sales in France, Germany, the United Kingdom, the Netherlands and Sweden.[12] Reading groups are a different matter, and reflect the external benefits of sharing cultural experiences; they also act as an information source. Even quite small reading groups are increasingly being used by publishers as focus groups for informing marketing strategies.

[12] Vogel (2001) and Rightscom (2004).

Promotion of books

Book fairs

International trade fairs for the music, film, broadcasting and publishing industries are regular (usually annual) events, some being self-standing and others forming a part of other fairs and festivals (see chapter 19). The Frankfurt Book Fair dates back some 500 years and is probably the biggest such event in the publishing industry, playing host to exhibitors from 108 countries all over the world in 2007; top of the bill in terms of the number of exhibitors that year was Germany, with 3,358 (the United Kingdom had 816, the United States 653 and Spain 383), with many countries having a collective exhibition that enabled smaller publishers to participate; in all there were 7,448 exhibitors and seventy-two national exhibitions, and it attracted over a quarter of a million visitors.[13] So important are these fairs to publishers that there is subsidy available from many national governments to enable publishers to participate. The business conducted at fairs is important for sales of rights. Though they are primarily for people working in the book trade, however, many also are open to the public or have open days, including readings and signings by authors.

UNESCO World Book Capital

Every year UNESCO, in conjunction with the International Publishers Association, the International Booksellers Federation and the International Federation of Library Associations and Institutions, selects a city for the designation as UNESCO World Book Capital, for one year from 23 April (UNESCO World Book Day) until 22 April the following year. During its tenure the city is required to organise events around books, literature and reading (for a detailed account, see chapter 19).

Bookshops and retail outlets

Bookselling has tended to concentrate into the hands of horizontally integrated chains. By 1999 in the United States, 25 per cent of sales were in chain bookstores and 11 per cent in independent bookshops. In France, most sales were made through retailers, divided between bookshops (18 per cent), hypermarkets (18 per cent) and multimedia stores (20 per cent); in Italy

---

[13] See www.buchmesse.de/imperia/md/content/pdf/pressepr/pressemappen/eroeffnungs_pk_2007_katalan/ eroeffnungs_pk_2007_de/eroeffnungs_pk_091007_de/ausstellerstatistik_2007.pdf (accessed 4 April 2008).

70 per cent of sales were though bookshops, and 75 per cent were in Sweden; in the United Kingdom, 43 per cent of retail sales were in large chain book-shops.[14] It is to preserve independent local bookshops and the diversity of titles that many countries in Europe and elsewhere have a policy of permitting the retail price maintenance of books.

Other government policies on books and reading

Besides the kind of policies discussed above to encourage reading, there are several types of government policy that have considerable impact on the market for trade books. The most direct of these is the so-called 'fixed book price', which is an exception to the ban in competition law on price-fixing as unfair trading. Another very important government policy, this time usually at the level of local government, is the provision of and public expenditure on public libraries.

The fixed book price agreement

The fixed book price policy enables publishers to set the retail price of books and requires retailers (bookshops and other outlets) to charge it. Its purpose is twofold: to assist publishers in increasing the number of titles they publish, especially of less popular books, thereby increasing cultural diversity and offering a greater choice to consumers; and to encourage the survival of smaller, neighbourhood bookshops that are well stocked with a good choice of books (not just the best-sellers the chain bookshops and other outlets are expected to supply) and so make book buying more accessible to the public. The arrangement of price-fixing may be a voluntary one, as in Japan and Belgium, and it may operate for only a restricted period for a title (six months in Belgium, two years in the Netherlands). Austria, Canada, Denmark, France, Germany, Hungary, the Netherlands, Portugal and Spain all have a statutory fixed book price agreement. Finland, Sweden and the United Kingdom aban-doned retail price maintenance on books along with that on other products well over ten years ago.[15]

Several cultural economists have studied the fixed book price and tested its efficacy. Measures of diversity have to be found and explained by the presence of the fixed price policy: the number of titles per capita and the number of

[14] Vogel (2001) and Rightscom (2004).   [15] Rightscom (2004).

Box 18.3 Le Loi Lang: protecting the book market in France

Jacques Lang as minister of culture in France in 1981 introduced, among many other initiatives, the law known as the Loi Lang to protect the diversity of the French book market by specifying a maximum discount on the price of books of 5 per cent. Books occupy a very significant role in French cultural life, and this is reflected in the fact that they account for nearly a half of all cultural product sales by value and two of every three items purchased.

French consumers are not so prone to buying best-sellers as are other consumers: sales of the top twenty book titles attracted only 20 per cent of all sales. In 2003 the value of book sales was €3,181 million; book prices rose by 1.5 per cent, below the inflation rate of 2 per cent, so books became proportionately cheaper despite the protection of prices offered by the Loi Lang, and this posed a threat to smaller bookshops.

In terms of where they buy, the French buy 78 per cent of their books in bookshops (57 per cent of them in chains – FNAC and Hachette effectively dominate this category – and 21 per cent in independent bookshops, and 22 per cent in other retail outlets). FNAC has over half the market for retail books and Hachette 8.6 per cent. With small bookshops under pressure and being bought up by the chains, the Loi Lang seems not to achieve the aim of protecting them.

Source: www.pch.gc.ca/progs/ac-ca/progs/padie-bpidp/reports/
rapport-report_2007/tdm_e.cfm (accessed 10 April 2008).

---

bookshops in a country are used and related to GDP, levels of schooling, loans from public libraries and other items (per capita figures are used to standardise for the different sizes of national populations and therefore of the number of consumers in the various countries); no indication has been found to support the role of the fixed book price policy in stimulating diversity, however.[16] In fact, the United Kingdom, Finland and Sweden all achieve a high output of book titles per capita without the fixed price policy.

The fixed book price works like copyright: it maintains higher prices than a competitive market would bring about, in order to provide an incentive to publishers and bookshops to increase diversity, and, like copyright, it is a trade-off between the hoped-for benefits to suppliers and the costs to consumers in terms of higher prices. As studies have shown that the demand for books is price elastic, the higher price cuts out some consumption, so reading suffers; as suggested in box 18.3, though, as demand for books is income elastic, the number of books bought may not fall.

There are other criticisms of the policy, however; one is that it is indiscriminate and affects all books regardless of whether they are of good quality or of

---

[16] See Canoy, van Ours and van der Ploeg (2006).

literary merit – just having more titles of any sort of book (such as *How to ...* books) is not in itself the aim of the policy. The second criticism is that the policy does not necessarily encourage bookshops to stock a wide range of books, as they have only to charge the price the publisher determines. Third, although publishers may have higher profits, they are not obliged to invest them in books or authors that would otherwise fail to get published – the cross-subsidisation that is envisaged by the policy. There are other ways of achieving the same aims without preventing price competition: publishers in the 'free' countries, like record labels, cross-subsidise anyway; grants to authors and/or publishers would target quality much more precisely; and bookshops would benefit from greater sales and revenue at lower prices (remember that, if demand is relatively elastic, a fall in the price increases revenues); US and UK publishers have a policy of 'sale or return' on unsold stocks that encourages small bookshops to stock books they otherwise might not risk doing; finally, book prices can be reduced by being zero-rated for sales tax or value added tax, as they are in the United Kingdom. Just to show how this can influence demand: when Sweden reduced VAT on books from 25 per cent to 6 per cent in 2002, book sales rose by 20 per cent (so what was the elasticity of demand, reader?). In France, the so-called Loi Lang (see box 18.3) is intended to protect diversity of book titles.

Other public policies and subsidy for literature and reading

Although many countries allocate funds to literature, they are mostly a tiny proportion of total subsidy. Some countries have a strong programme of encouraging literature, however. Australia is an example: the Australia Council invested more than A\$7.8 million (roughly US\$5 million) in Australian literature in 2006/7 to finance grants to writers and publishers, residencies and touring grants, support for writers' centres, literary journals and literary festivals, and other initiatives to develop the sector. The 'Books Alive' programme is an Australian government initiative, managed by the Australia Council, with an annual budget of A\$2 million that aims to encourage the reading of Australian books. The programme lasts for one month each year and provides a list of recommended books, some of which are given away free. A similar programme is the 'Big Read' in the United States, an initiative of the National Endowment for the Arts 'designed to restore reading to the center of American culture' by encouraging people to read and discuss a single book within their communities. The programme is concerned with stimulating reading rather than with book production or distribution. It provides lists of books and organises reading programmes of those books, and has a website offering information on the authors and their works.[17]

Public spending on public libraries

Public libraries originated as early as the seventeenth century in the United Kingdom and the United States and have become a feature of cultural life in most communities. They are widespread in major cities and small towns alike; in a small town the library is probably the focus of a number of cultural activities, and libraries may also have a space for art exhibitions, possibly a theatre or cinema and other cultural facilities. Many school-children visit the public library with their class as part of the school curriculum. In rural areas there may be a mobile library reaching small communities and people, especially the elderly people who are not them-selves mobile. Libraries supply not only books, newspapers and documents but also a wide range of information services, and many provide internet links and IT facilities.

Public libraries are significant purchasers of books and other reading material. For some people, reading library books is a substitute for buying their own books, and therefore libraries can have the effect of reducing sales; the same copy of a book is lent out repeatedly, thus displacing demand. In order to compensate authors and publishers for this loss of revenue, govern-ments operate public lending right arrangements or library compensation schemes (see below).

Entry to public libraries is usually free – hence the term *public* library! A library is not a public good in the economic sense, however, and private circulating libraries have existed for many years. Public libraries do not charge for entry because they are regarded as a vital service to the public; reading and being well informed are essential to civic life and are therefore financed by the community as a service to all. The 'Big Read' programme, which addresses low rates of reading in the United States, is justified on precisely these grounds. Some public libraries may make a small charge for book loans but in general the full cost of the facility is financed from public expenditure. Table 18.4 showed the considerable variation in library loans per capita in EU countries. This may reflect different levels of provision of public libraries.

The public library is typically financed by local or regional (state) expendi-ture, and an inspection of the data on spending on libraries shows that public

[17] See www.neabigread.org.

expenditure on them is very varied: in some countries they account for a relatively high proportion of public expenditure on culture while in others that is not the case. The data do not always distinguish the finance of national libraries and archives from public libraries. Finland appears to top the bill in terms of the percentage of the total public expenditure on culture spent on libraries: it was 30 per cent in 2001; next came Denmark (23 per cent), followed by Germany, Hungary and the United Kingdom (all 16 per cent), the Netherlands and Italy (15 per cent), Ukraine (14 per cent), Switzerland (10 per cent), France (includes 'Books'), Norway (includes 'Literature') and Spain (all 7 per cent), Ireland (4 per cent) and Sweden (3 per cent). Of course, these percentages belie the actual amounts spent, and a small percentage could indicate a large absolute amount of expenditure. In some countries, public library expenditure exceeds that on heritage.[18]

All this makes it especially strange that cultural economics has entirely ignored libraries. Work in the United States on the costs and benefits of public libraries was begun in 1999 with a study of the St Louis public library, however, showing that the benefits of public spending exceed the costs by a factor of four, and plans were reported to undertake a study of middle-sized and small public libraries.[19] It is clear that there should be research by cultural economists on public libraries – a nice subject for a thesis!

Support for authors

There are various ways in which authorship is supported other than through the market; these include government grants, publicly funded writer-in-residence schemes and awards and prizes. These topics are dealt with in this section: in the next section, library compensation schemes and remuneration for photocopying are discussed in connection with copyright for authors.

Grants to authors

Grants are made to authors (and to other creative artists) in several ways, as discussed in chapter 11: direct grants of stipends and guaranteed income support and grants and scholarships for travel for specific projects such as research, study and promotional purposes, as well as to cover the cost of preparing manuscripts for publication, and in some cases also for publishing

---

[18] All data are taken from Council of Europe/ERICarts (2008), for various years 2000–5.
[19] Holt, Elliott and Moore (1999) and Holt and Elliott (2003).

costs; in some countries, there are translation funds. Indirectly, authors may be supported by state grants to special funds and artists' organisations. Copyright collecting societies also have funds for assisting authors from their cultural deductions (see chapter 13).

There are many and varied grants for authors, and it is not possible to summarise them; instead, a few examples are given to indicate their scope. Norway has possibly the most generous schemes: under its guaranteed income scheme, authors and other creative artists receive a guaranteed annual income equal to the lowest level of the salary scale of the civil service, minus a percentage of the artists' own income, that lasts until pension age is reached. The aim of the scheme is to give individual artists security and peace to work. An alternative is the 'work stipend', which lasts from one to five years for creative artists working on a defined project or who want to devote all their working hours to artistic work; the stipend is similar to the guaranteed income. Finland has a comparable system. In France, the National Book Centre, a public body under the supervision of the Directorate of Books and Readership, allocated 281 grants to authors and publishers in 2001 (a total of €2.27 million); in the Netherlands, the Dutch Foundation for Literature aims to stimulate the quality and availability of Dutch and Frisian literature, as well as literature translated into Dutch and Frisian. With a budget of €5 million, the foundation offers professional literary authors and translators work and travel grants, and fees to writers and translators of fiction, poetry, non-fiction, children's books and drama. Approximately 200 authors per year and 100 translators of literature into Dutch or Frisian receive a grant.[20] Other countries, by contrast, offer little in the way of financial support to authors.

Awards and prizes

Awards and prizes are offered by state organisations, by foundations and by the publishing industry itself through the publishers' or authors' societies and the like. As with grants, there are so many different awards and prizes, varying considerably in value, that it is impossible to give more than a hint of their scope. Most awards and prizes pay some amount of money but others are honorary; Russia, for example, has honorary degrees for artists and cultural workers – a system inherited from the Soviet period (Artist of the People, Honorary Artist, Honorary Master of the Arts, Honorary Cultural Worker) – and they provide some additional social support or privileges to the recipients. Other countries have similar non-financial awards.

[20] Council of Europe/ERICarts (2008).

The world's largest literary prize is likely to be the Nobel Prize in literature, which is worth over €1 million (10 million Swedish kronor or US$1.5 million). France has several hundred literary prizes, of which the most famous are the Prix Goncourt for the best imaginary prose work of the year, the Femina, with its exclusively female jury (both dating from 1903), and the Renaudot, Interallié and Médicis prizes. Other famous literary awards are the Man Booker Prize (worth £50,000), for the best novel of the year written by a citizen of the Commonwealth or the Republic of Ireland; the Pulitzer Prize, for American fiction; the PEN/Faulkner Award, which each year recognises the best published works of fiction by contemporary American writers; the David Cohen Prize for Literature, which is an award for a lifetime's achievement in British literature (£52,500); and the IMPAC Dublin Literary Award, which is offered by Dublin City Council (€100,000) annually for writing in English (in 2007 it was awarded to a Norwegian author, Per Petterson, and his translator, Anne Born). These are only a few of the large number of prizes for authors, translators and books, including poets and poetry, some for young writers, others for themes and so on, that exist all over the world.[21]

Prizes are an *ex post* reward for the creation of literary works (or other works of art) and cannot be anticipated. They do not provide a direct incentive to the effort of producing them, therefore, though a sufficiently high-value prize would enable the author to finance work on future output. Prizes are often awarded by a jury of peers, however, and the recognition this brings to an author has a very high value as intrinsic motivation. Prizes also provide publicity and influence demand for the prize-winning book and stimulate interest in the author's other works.

Copyright remuneration schemes

Copyright law, as we saw in chapter 13, is intended as a way to stimulate authorship and publishing by protecting the rights of authors and publishers to control the use of their works and enable them to obtain financial reward via the market. That reward comes from the sales revenues of books and other published material that accrue to the publisher, and a percentage (typically 10 per cent) is then distributed as a royalty to the author. As noted above, use by readers of public libraries can displace demand for buying books and deprive authors and publishers of some revenues; photocopying can also displace

---

[21] The Christchurch (New Zealand) Public Library publishes a list of literary prizes.

buying. To compensate for these losses of sales, governments have created the public lending right (PLR) and set up statutory bodies to administer it. Publishers and authors are also compensated for photocopying that is not for personal use – that is, use that is not covered by an exception to copyright law – through separate arrangements.

Public lending right

The public lending right, sometimes called library compensation, works in a similar manner in the various countries that have adopted it (most developed countries). In Canada, for example, the federal government's 'arm's-length' PLR programme was established in 1986 to increase the revenues and improve the financial situation of Canadian writers. It is administered by the Public Lending Right Commission, comprised of representatives of national writers', librarians' and publishers' associations, and operates under the administrative aegis of the Canada Council for the Arts. The PLR consists of payments to Canadian writers, translators and illustrators based on the holdings of their books by a representative sample of libraries across Canada. In 2006/7 15,417 Canadian writers, translators and illustrators received just over C$9 million (US$8 million) in PLR payments. In Spain, the Intellectual Property Act established a PLR levy on the loans made by cultural institutions such as libraries, museums and archives. Libraries will have to pay €0.02 for each book copy acquired for loan; public libraries in municipalities of fewer than 5,000 inhabitants and those integrated in educational institutions are exempted. Payment to the authors is made through the copyright collecting societies. The UK government administers its PLR scheme itself with a fund that totalled £7.6 million in 2006/7. Payment is made according to the number of times an author's books are borrowed (the rate per loan was £0.0557 in 2005/6). Over 34,000 authors are registered for PLR. The maximum yearly payment an author can receive is £6,600 from 2006/7. In 2005/6 £6.5 million was paid out to 18,500 authors. In Finland, besides the PLR grants for writers and translators (totalling €2.6 million), there are also PLR grants for illustrators (€50,000).[22]

Generally speaking, the PLR is expensive to administer, with the now familiar feature that many authors receive small payments and a few top authors get relatively high amounts, reflecting library borrowers' predilection for best-sellers and other popular titles; thus the administrative cost per

---

[22] All data are taken from www.culturalpolicies.net (accessed 17 March 2008).

payment can easily exceed the amount due to an individual author. When the PLR scheme is administered by a government or 'arm's length' body the administrative costs are borne by the government; this is in contrast to the costs of administering royalties and remuneration by the copyright collection societies, which the members have to pay.

Photocopying

The right to remuneration for photocopying is embodied in copyright law and is administered by the authors' and publishers' collecting societies in a manner very similar to those already described in chapter 13 for the public performance of recorded music through a collecting society. In the United Kingdom, the Copyright Licensing Authority operates on behalf of the authors' and publishers' collecting societies and issues a blanket licence making photocopying legal for schools, universities and other large-scale users whose use is not private (that is, covered by the exceptions to copyright for individual study purposes); it then hands over the revenues to the collecting societies (on a fifty-fifty basis), and they in turn distribute them to the authors and publishers on the basis of the use made of their books and articles. Other countries have a levy on photocopying machines that is distributed through collecting societies; in Germany, an arrangement is made for lump sum compensation for educational purposes. The data in box 13.6 from the survey of German authors' copyright earnings include monies from foreign public lending rights as well as the payments for photocopying.[23]

Impact of digitalisation and the internet

Digitalisation and the internet have had their effect on book publishing, as on other creative industries, but the effect here has been somewhat different. Rather than posing a threat to the publishing industry of losses through piracy, the internet has posed a threat to bookshops through the huge success of online retailing, and it has also enhanced the operation of second-hand markets, which pose something of a threat to sales of new books. The internet has benefited both consumers and producers: consumers have benefited from better information (reviews and customer ratings, for example) on a wider range of individual titles, including backlist titles that are increasingly

---

[23] See Kretschmer and Hardwick (2007) for details.

neglected by mainstream retailers; and authors and publishers have benefited from what has been called the 'long tail' phenomenon – the fact that (in the case of books) a 'small title' can reach a very wide market via the internet that would never have been possible with 'physical' bookshops. This is the superstar experience all over again but in a different guise: the size of the market leads to multiplicative revenues, but this time it works for non-star authors as well as the superstars.

Digitisation has affected the actual production of books: authors now have to prepare manuscripts in pristine condition, but they can also avoid publishers and issue their work as books on demand via their own website or via an online distributor. This can be done in electronic or paper versions. Books, like other cultural products, are vulnerable to piracy on a large scale only when in electronic form (and let us not forget that books always have been pirated; indeed, US copyright law in the nineteenth century favoured the piracy of English authors!). Scanning can put a printed paper version into digital form and manuscripts can be released on the internet, but, so far, they have not apparently been a major threat to sales. Audiobooks are vulnerable to copying, though some audiobook sellers have already dropped digital rights management on the grounds that it inhibits demand. E-books remain a possibility, and may grow in popularity as better reading devices are developed, and that could unleash copying. To date, though, the internet seems to have been a force for good in book publishing, though it has had very different effects on markets for newspapers and magazines.[24]

Conclusion

Book publishing appears to be in a healthy state; the number of titles being published, at least in English, is rising and the market produces an enormous variety and quality of books, justifying belief in the ability of the market to cater for a range of special tastes and niche markets. Consumers/book readers are well served not only by the private market for books, which is assisted by government intervention of various kinds to encourage diversity and protect national languages and identities, but also by the provision by the state of public libraries. Increased international trade in books (often 'intra-industry' trade, meaning that exporting countries also import as well) increases the globalisation of culture, and use of the internet allows increased economies of

---

[24] See Küng, Picard and Towse (2008).

scale and scope that reinforce the capacity of the global book market to produce diversity and variety and to reduce prices. Barriers to entry for both authors and publishers are relatively low and the internet has led to increased competition in the market for books. As the demand for books is income elastic, we may expect the increased incomes and increased leisure that come with economic growth to sustain the demand side of the market, although this could reverse in a recession; competition from other leisure activities and a diminished taste for reading could pose the most serious threat to book publishing. Economic forces cannot always combat cultural trends!

Further reading

As mentioned in this chapter, there is very little work in cultural economics on books, libraries and reading schemes. Media economists have written a great deal on newspaper publishing, however; Gillian Doyle's (2002) book *Media Ownership* is a good introduction. Cultural economists have taken an interest in translations and in the fixed book price, and there are three chapters in the Towse (2003a) *Handbook of Cultural Economics* that are relevant: Marja Appleman on the 'Fixed book price' (chapter 29), Christian Hjorth-Andersen on 'Publishing' (chapter 51) and Nachoem Wijnberg on 'Awards' (chapter 9). The chapter by Marcel Canoy, Jan van Ours and Frederich van der Ploeg (2006), 'The economics of books', in the Ginsburgh and Throsby, *Handbook of the Economics of Art and Culture* (chapter 21), is also recommended reading. We can expect considerable developments in the digitalisation of books, and Lucy Küng, Robert Picard and Ruth Towse (2008) provide an overview of the issues, including those affecting books and newspapers.

19 Economics of festivals, creative cities and cultural tourism

This final chapter of Part IV attempts to pull together a rather scattered literature on several related topics on which cultural economics has something to say: festivals, creative cities and cultural clusters, and cultural tourism. While they are not new topics in cultural economics – in fact, festivals were a relatively early topic[1] – they have not been analysed together in a textbook treatment, and lately they have been more the concern of economic and cultural geographers and urban planners than of economists. They call on some of the most basic concepts of cultural economics, however: the social benefits of the arts and culture, their economic impact, the evaluation of cultural policy, and so on.

As with all economic topics, there is a supply side and a demand side, and each calls for its own analysis. On the supply side, festivals provide a city or other location with an image and cultural identity, often fostered by the local or regional administration and subsidised by them, and they cause external production economies (spillovers) for the tourist trade by attracting visitors. Cultural facilities may also attract non-cultural businesses, and the facilities and aura of cultural activity attract creative people and enterprises; there may also be a policy of promoting cities as creative hubs in line with this image. The European Union's policy of designating Cities of Culture (now European Capitals of Culture), for which cities compete, and UNESCO's cultural heritage listing, which includes 'heritage' cities, attract tourism. UNESCO also has a Creative Cities Network.

In all this, creative industries are promoted and producers of cultural products, including live performance, heritage and firms in cultural industries, are able to increase their markets and probably obtain extra public finance for putting on special events. On the consumption side, people living in places with festivals and in creative cities benefit from the excitement of events such

---

[1] Edinburgh Festival (Vaughan, 1980); Salzburg Festival (Frey, 1986); Wexford Opera Festival (O'Hagan, 1992).

as festivals and trade fairs and the increased choice of cultural products they offer, though residents may also suffer external costs of excessive tourism.

One of the challenges of this chapter is to find a common economic logic for these various topics rather than to review the diverse literature in this field, and I begin with some general theoretical points before looking at each of the applications – festivals, creative cities and cultural tourism – in turn.

Spatial economics

In general, economists have completely ignored the spatial or locational aspects of economic life and there has been little interest in where activities take place and what economic factors determine their location. Economists have been much more concerned with the nation state as the focus of economic activity and with trade on an international scale, taking place between nation states, not with the geographical pattern of trade within a country. Nonetheless, German economists already had well-developed spatial economic theories by the 1930s, which had originated in the early nineteenth century. These theories analysed the choice of location of the place of production that required the assembly of inputs from different locations and the delivery of the product to a market; the location of production was analysed in terms of the relative costs of transport for producing and getting goods to market, and also dealt with the geographical distribution of market and city sizes.

Land use

The growth of urban and regional economics and of city planning in the 1960s prompted the recognition of these theories and led to an understanding that the location of production and consumption, and hence of land use, is determined by interaction between transport costs and property prices or rents within specific geographical areas, particularly cities. Although the physical dimensions (such as weight) of inputs and output have little relevance in service economies, there are still some fixed locations of inputs, such as potters' clay and sculptors' marble, that attracted production to these sources in the first place, and, even though substitutes for such raw materials later became available, the place could still have an advantage in the market due to its reputation for producing certain goods and the presence of specialised skilled labour and know-how. Cities with their cultural facilities of theatres, museums and festivals are in specific locations, and visitors must go there to participate in them, but it is also the case that cities can invest in these facilities in order to create facilities for its citizens and to attract visitors.

Agglomeration economies

The concept of what came to be called agglomeration economies in urban economics is also an old idea in economics: recognition of the external economic benefits of production to firms of a shared location due to economies of scale and scope in production and the increased specialisation that market size in cities and other conglomerations offers for both producers and consumers. The proximity of a number of people with specialist skills (the 'pool of skilled labour', as it used to be called) is beneficial for producers, who have easy access to a flexible supply of their labour, and it is beneficial for the skilled workers themselves to have abundant work opportunities. They also have the necessary support services and other inputs at hand, such as specialised supplies of capital equipment and repairs.

The Hotelling principle

On the consumption side, the so-called 'Hotelling principle', named after the economist Harold Hotelling, explains the locational clustering of suppliers in terms of the minimisation of travel costs for consumers: finding a choice of all the shoe shops in one place is an advantage to consumers, who have to travel to access them – the well-known principle of 'minimum differentiation'. Consumers can spread the fixed cost of travel over a range of purchases. In addition, agglomerations of producers and retail outlets result in lower prices due to economies of scale, and that feature alone would encourage consumers to go to specific locations to shop. It was in 1929 that Hotelling published his article 'Stability in competition', in which he developed the principle of minimum differentiation, which was applied later to a range of concepts from political parties to TV programmes and airline schedules, but its origin was explaining spatial competition and locational choice in terms of firms maximising their market share.

Creative clustering

In relation to the arts, the size, level of income and education of the population in cities provides a viable audience that is able to support regular live

Box 19.1 MuseumsQuartier in Vienna

The MuseumsQuartier is one of the ten largest cultural complexes in the world, where baroque buildings, new architecture, cultural institutions and various disciplines of art are united.

The Leopold Museum and the MUMOK (Museum of Modern Art Ludwig Foundation Vienna) are large art museums. Additional highlights include the TanzQuartier, an international, state-of-the-art centre for dance, the Architektur Zentrum Wien, production studios for new media, artist studios for artists-in-residence, outstanding art and cultural facilities designed for children and a variety of other events and festivals, such as the renowned Viennale film festival, the ImPulsTanz Festival and many others.

The MuseumsQuartier also aims to attract a 'younger and hipper clientele' with Musiktank, offering a wide selection of Austrian popular music, and an ice curling rink with DJs and a play area for children.

Source: www.aboutvienna.org/museums/museumsquartier.htm
(accessed 15 January 2009).

performances and sufficient visitors for libraries, museums and art galleries. It has also been observed that artists and other creative workers mostly live and work in cities, and this seems to be explained partly by the fact that there is more work for them but also because, especially for freelance and self-employed artists, networking is an important way of obtaining work, and this is a feature of agglomeration. It is generally more expensive to live in cities, however, and that in itself would be a disincentive. Run-down inner cities with old buildings, such as factories, have nevertheless proved popular with creative enterprises, especially visual artists, because they provide cheap and suitable studio space, and this trend has been encouraged by city administrations, which have converted some of these spaces for artists. Creative clusters, which offer strong agglomeration economies, may also be encouraged in this way. An example is the MuseumsQuartier in Vienna, the former barracks and stables of the Austrian cavalry, which combines museums with studio spaces, restaurants and cafés and other entertainment facilities (see box 19.1).

Urban regeneration

Spatial economic theory is closely allied to economic development, or, to be more precise, differential economic growth within a region or country. The use for cultural purposes of decayed areas and buildings for urban and regional regeneration has become a standard tool planning and development since the 1980s. Many of the early economic impact studies in cultural economics had as their rationale the potential for economic regeneration and growth. The same thinking also applies to the encouragement of cultural tourism; buildings such as the Bilbao Guggenheim Museum (see box 19.6) attract people to the area and produce spillovers, as does tourism to heritage sites, which by their nature are in a fixed location.

The economic analysis of festivals, creative cities and cultural tourism uses one or another of these concepts from spatial economics.

Economics of festivals

Athens in the fifth century BC held theatrical festivals to accompany its games. Interestingly, these festivals were state-run and -financed and attendance was obligatory![2] Nowadays there is every sort of cultural festival, from the most rarefied operatic festivals all along the line to folk festivals, including on the way festivals dealing with all sorts of music and theatre, dance, mime, film, literature and books, art and crafts, which may specialise in one type of cultural offering or a mixture, possibly with a theme that changes year by year. They may last anything from a day or so to several weeks or even months and they may be celebrations of local culture or have international participation; some are more like trade fairs, with events for the public, and others are aimed at a specialised client audience. Although many festivals are held in the summer, others take place at different times of the year; a festival tends to be held at a set time of the year, however, to assist with planning for audiences and producers.

With such a huge variety of festivals all over the world, is it possible to offer any economic explanation as to why there are festivals and why there are so many of them?

Supply side

On the supply side, it has been argued that performing arts festivals overcome Baumol's cost disease by enabling greater flexibility in hiring performers and offering lower wage payments and lower overheads for venues.[3] This picture would certainly fit the Bayreuth opera festival or the Salzburg Festival, which hire singers and instrumental players when the German and Austrian opera

---

[2] See Baumol (1971).   [3] See Frey (2003a).

houses are closed, thereby enabling the festivals to assemble very high-quality musicians who would normally be on a fixed contract with one or another of the many opera houses spread over the German-speaking world. Similar arguments could be made for festivals in other countries with similar institutional arrangements (for instance, Italy with its Arena di Verona opera festival, the Rossini Festival in Pesaro and the Avignon and Aix-en-Provence Festivals in France). This model does not fit the Edinburgh International Festival in Scotland or the Wexford Opera Festival in Ireland, however, or any of the US festivals, for the simple reason that there is a much more flexible labour market for performers in these countries (see chapter 11). What is the case, though, is that many festivals arrange spin-offs such as recording contracts or radio transmissions that help to finance the event. Bruno Frey also makes the point that festivals can be more adventurous in their programming than a regular theatre or concert hall is able to. Moreover, they give local politicians scope for proving that they support culture and provides them with a forum for publicising the achievements of the city administration in a specific forum.

Demand side

In general, the demand-side explanation offered by Frey (2003a) seems more persuasive: the growth of incomes has raised demand for festival attendance, as it is income elastic; this is also the case, as we see later, with the demand for cultural tourism, which is connected to festival attendance. Given that festivals often take place in holiday periods (or that people attending festivals choose their holiday dates accordingly), the opportunity cost of travel is lower than it would be in work time; in some countries, moreover, travel charges are reduced over holiday periods as a form of price discrimination. The search and other transaction costs of obtaining tickets for festivals are lower as one box office deals with all performances, and, if visiting the festival involves travel arrangements, both may be purchased as a package, reducing costs further. These arguments would also apply to special 'blockbuster' art exhibitions, which may themselves be the main attraction for the visitor or just be a part of the festival offering.

Economies of scope

The Edinburgh International Festival is regarded as one of the oldest and largest of the summer season festivals and it has expanded in scope from the original

Box 19.2 Edinburgh International Festival

The Edinburgh Festival (as it is commonly known) is regarded as one of the oldest international festivals of performing arts; it was started in 1947 and is now probably the largest arts festival in the world. In fact, it could be described as a compendium of festivals that take place in Edinburgh at the same time (three weeks in August). The Edinburgh International Festival presents a full daily programme of classical music, theatre, opera and dance in its several major theatres and concert halls; that is the 'official' festival. Allied to it is the Edinburgh Festival Fringe, which started spontaneously in 1947. It has now grown to enormous proportions, with well over 1,000 acts of every description (amateur and professional) crowding into every conceivable venue all over the city. The Fringe is now professionally organised, with ticketing services, and also some large venues running professional shows for almost twenty-four hours a day, but the Fringe retains some of its former sense of spontaneity and fun.

Other festivals that take place during the Edinburgh Festival are:
● Edinburgh International Book Festival;
● Edinburgh Jazz Festival;
● Edinburgh Film Festival;
● Edinburgh Television Festival;
● Edinburgh International Internet Festival;
● Edinburgh Mela (Asian arts); and
● Edinburgh Annuale of contemporary art.

This is not to forget the Edinburgh Military Tattoo, apparently the most popular of all, which takes place nightly in the spectacular setting of Edinburgh Castle.

performing arts festival to an array of specialised festivals held at the same time as the international festival, and others, that take place throughout the year (see box 19.2). It was started in the aftermath of the Second World War to 'provide a platform for the flowering of the human spirit' and has now taken place annually for over sixty years. Besides the so-called 'official' festivals, there is a huge, spontaneous 'fringe' that also takes place at the same time, which has acquired its own centralised programme and box-office arrangements. There has often been a controversial relationship between the city and the festival over finance, and also because of the disruption to normal life in the city during the festival. It is interesting to note that citizens apparently need to be persuaded of the value in both cultural and economic terms of a festival or other such event – something that has been observed in relation to other city image-building projects, such as those in Bilbao and Liverpool (discussed below).

Economic aspects of specialist festivals

Can the above economic explanations be applied to film and other types of specialist festival, such as a book or film festival? Take the example of film festivals; they combine both economic and cultural motives. On the one hand, they are very important showcases for the industry and offer the facilities of a trade fair to exhibitors; they may specialise in certain types of film, and most films being exhibited are new. Prizes and awards are also significant features of film festivals and they are used as certification devices with distributors and audiences and also for publicity purposes. Film is also regarded as an art that cannot survive without some form of subsidy, however, and this explains why film festivals are supported by public subsidy; the Venice Film Festival, for example, which was the first of its kind, dating from 1932, is held in conjunction with the Venice Biennale contemporary art exhibition (not called a festival), signifying the connection between the two art forms. On the other hand, film (and other such) festivals also offer an attraction for consumers on account of the much greater choice of films on show at one time and the experience of new content that is different from the normal run of films that is available. The selection of films by juries prior to exhibition also act as information about quality to film-goers, and they may find it exciting to be present when awards are made. It therefore seems that specialist festivals do share the same economic features as those of the performing arts festivals and those with mixed offerings. These features explain the incentives for the supply of and demand for festivals.

Festivals and city image

There is another aspect to festivals: they are frequently promoted by a city or other place in order to promote an image and to encourage tourism, and in order to do so the festival is subsidised from taxes. The subsidy is justified in different ways: it is regarded as investment if it attracts tourists who spend money not just on entry tickets for attending festival events but also on food, accommodation, and so on. If the intention is to build the image of the city, though, this has a public goods rationale in terms of increasing the sense of citizenship and identity; in other words, the investment justification is a means to an economic end whereas image-building is an end in itself. A city that has set itself this latter task is Barcelona, which offers a large number of festivals with the purpose of building its image at home and abroad (see box 19.3).

Box 19.3 Festivals in Barcelona

Two of the city of Barcelona's aims are: to consolidate culture as a basic strategy in the development of the 'city of knowledge'; and to assist Barcelona in becoming a centre for the production of cultural content. Its programme of festivals is intended to meet these objectives as well as to honour the tradition of religious and secular festivals in the city.

Among the regular festivals held in Barcelona are the Sónar Festival of Advanced Music and Multimedia Art, the Festival of Contemporary Musics, the Barcelona Guitar Festival, the Festival of Early Music, the LEM Festival of electronic music, the Cuitat Vella Flamenco Festival, the Festival of World Musics, the Butxaca Opera Festival, the Barcelona International Jazz Festival, the International Festival of Visual Theatre and Puppets and the Alternativa 2000 International Festival of Independent Film.

The majority of the city's festivals are privately run but receive public sector support. The Barcelona Institute of Culture organises the Barcelona Grec Summer Festival. The Grec is regarded as the cultural highlight of summer in the city, with its in-house productions and its international scope.

Source: http://w3.bcn.es/V01/Home/V01HomeLinkPl/0,2460,7610_52619_3,00.html
(accessed 10 April 2008).

City of Culture/European Capital of Culture

The European Union initiated the programme of annually designating a European City of Culture in 1985, with Athens being the first; by 2008 thirty-two cities had been selected. In 1999 it was renamed European Capital of Culture, with two cities being designated annually. The Culture 2000 programme ran from 2000 to 2006 and provided grants to cultural co-operation projects. It has been followed up by the EU Culture programme, whose aim is to celebrate European culture and to encourage cross-border collaboration between cultural institutions; running from 2007 to 2013, it has a budget of €400 million euros.[4] The Americas adopted a similar designation of City of Culture in 1997; so far, all the cities have been in Central and South America.[5]

In order to apply for designation, a city must make an application in a manner similar to that for major sporting events, and doing so involves considerable investment by the city. The European Union announces years in advance the countries in which the cities are to be selected, and the choice of cities in those countries is then left to the national governments. In 2008 it was

---

[4] See ec.europa.eu/culture/our-programmes-and-actions/doc413_en.htm (accessed 15 January 2009).
[5] See www.cac-acc.org/present.php?lang=en (accessed 15 January 2009).

the turn of Norway and the United Kingdom, and Stavanger and Liverpool were designated European Capitals of Culture. Stavanger 2008 had a budget of 300 million Norwegian kroner (€37 million or US$58 million). The municipalities of Stavanger, Sandnes and Rogaland County contributed a total of 100 million kroner; income also came from sponsors, licensed products, supplier agreements and various other projects, and, in addition, the Norwegian government contributed another third of the total budget, with a top limit of 100 million kroner.[6] The Liverpool bid started in 2001 with the formation by Liverpool City Council of the Liverpool Culture Company. Liverpool won the UK nomination in 2003, and the Liverpool Culture Company was then responsible for the celebrations for Liverpool's 800th birthday as a city in 2007 and for the cultural programme for being European Capital of Culture in 2008. It was estimated that the programme for the cultural capital and associated improvements to infrastructure (including Liverpool's football club and some transport facilities) would require an investment of £2 billion of public and private money and would bring an additional £50 million each in expenditures to the city and to the region from an additional 1.7 million visitors for 2008.[7] Increased tourism was not the only or main objective of the bid, however: the objectives were to achieve a sustainable improvement to the cultural infrastructure, to increase local and regional participation in cultural consumption and in the cultural industries and to be perceived as a 'premier European city'.

These calculations are typically made in connection with economic impact studies based on cost–benefit analysis. The benefits consist of both marketable benefits, such as expenditures by visitors, and the so-called 'uncovenanted' or social benefits to citizens and the city's image with its residents, visitors and the world beyond. The European Capital of Culture designation is widely publicised throughout Europe and this helps to build the image as well as encouraging visitors. Liverpool explicitly stated that it wanted to become a competitive, 'creative city' and saw being the European Capital of Culture as achieving that.[8] Notions such as 'sustainable infrastructure' do not carry with them a planning timescale over which the present value of the benefits can be calculated, however. By contrast, the costs must be financed in the present before any of the benefits can be obtained, and this fact alone necessarily stacks the chips against the undertaking: the present value of

---

[6] See www.stavanger2008.no/?event=about.showElement&id=503&catId=12 (accessed 12 October 2008).
[7] See www.08businessconnect.com/content/AboutLiverpool20082.aspx (accessed 12 October 2008).
[8] See ERM Economics (2003).

costs is likely to outweigh the benefits for years to come but the present value of future benefits at normal discount rates renders them relatively low (see chapter 10). In other words, the benefits must come quickly and be very great in order to make the undertaking economically viable. This is not to say the policy might not be desirable anyway, but it can be misleading to justify such a project as a 'profitable' investment.

The direct costs are the outlays on the building projects, programmes and administration; there could be external costs due to extra traffic congestion and pollution and disruption during any rebuilding and renovation pro-grammes. One danger of economic impact studies, noted in chapter 10, is that they are frequently undertaken by individual cultural organisations and then aggregated without taking into account the fact that, to some (unknown) extent, these organisations are in competition with each other for local and incoming visitors, though each one cannot expect to attract all 'new' visitors. It is also the case that one city or region does not take into account the 'substitution' effect of attracting visitors away from neighbouring cities. One city may well benefit at the expense of another but need not take that into account; it is then up to the central government to view the overall picture within the country.

All in all, it seems likely that the economic rationale for becoming a European Capital of Culture is the same as that for festivals.

Economics of creative cities

By contrast to the European Capital of Culture status, which lasts for a year, the creative city is perceived as a long-term, self-sustaining undertaking, which may, of course, be assisted by policies such as designation as a capital of culture and by organising festivals. It is also conceptually different from earlier concepts of cities of culture or cities of art; the last term is derived from the Italian città d'arte, as typified by Venice, Florence and Rome – that is, cities with an enormous heritage of architectural beauty and significance and with a unique historical character and artistic traditions – and other cities (for instance, St Petersburg and Kyoto) can be described in the same way. These cities all attract tourists, but there is not the focus on generating creativity as in the concept of the creative city. The notion of the creative city is linked to the economic growth of the creative industries and the observation that this takes place in an urban setting. The creative economy and creative cities have

Box 19.4 Creative New York, 2005

The city's 'creative core' consists of 11,671 businesses and non-profit enterprises (5.7 per cent of all employers in the five boroughs) and provides employment for 309,142 people (8.1 per cent of all city workers). In recent years creative industries have added jobs at a considerably faster rate than the overall city economy: between 1998 and 2002 employment in New York's creative core grew by 13.1 per cent (adding some 32,000 jobs) while the city's overall job totals increased by 6.5 per cent. Among the city's nearly unparalleled concentration of creative core enterprises, New York has more than 2,000 arts and cultural non-profit organisations and over 500 art galleries, roughly 2,300 design services businesses, more than 1,100 advertising-related firms, nearly 700 book and magazine publishers and 145 film production studios and stages. No other place in the United States even comes close to matching the city's creative assets. In fact, 8.3 per cent of all creative sector workers in the United States are based in New York. The city is home to over a third of all the country's actors and roughly 27 per cent of the nation's fashion designers, 12 per cent of film editors, 10 per cent of set designers, 9 per cent of graphic designers, 8 per cent of architects and 7 per cent of fine artists. The entities that comprise the creative core range from mega-corporations such as Time Warner and vaunted institutions such as the Metropolitan Museum of Art to small organisations and individual entrepreneurs throughout the five boroughs. It includes non-profit and for-profit enterprises, full-time workers and freelancers. Indeed, 28 per cent of all those in the city's creative workforce – roughly 79,000 people – are self-employed.

Source: Center for an Urban Future (2005).

become inextricably intertwined, even though the central idea of creativity is still evolving.[9]

The underlying economic concepts of the creative city are the agglomeration economies and spin-offs, or external benefits, analysed above. It is not simply the fact that many creative enterprises co-exist side by side in the same place but the fact that there is a synergy between them that leads to an atmosphere of creativity and scope for network economies, with their public goods characteristics. New York and London can lay claim to being creative cities but many other cities look to generate economic growth through fostering creativity, such as Shanghai.[10] Box 19.4 lists the creative enterprises and people in New York taken from an exercise in mapping the creative industries of the city.

[9] UNCTAD (2008).   [10] UNCTAD (2008).

Creative cities and economic growth

Following Richard Florida's sweeping endorsement of the role of the creative class (consisting of a very broad swathe of the professional labour force) in city profiles, many cities have evaluated their position as creative cities and drawn up mapping documents with copious data to show their strengths and weaknesses in this context.[11] As with other such mapping undertakings, however, no causal relationship is specified, and therefore they offer little guidance for policy purposes. Just knowing that, for example, the presence of immigrants in a city is associated with the growth of the creative industries in a city does not explain why they are there. Early studies in the 1980s of the economic size of the cultural sector investigated the location decisions of firms to see if the presence of cultural facilities was a 'pull' factor for senior executives, but found that sports and other recreational facilities had a stronger attraction. This comes back to the question we considered earlier in this book: do greater cultural production and consumption cause economic growth or does economic growth facilitate greater cultural consumption and production? These questions have to be answered if policies for economic development or city regeneration are to be adopted on economic grounds. It could also be argued, however, that growth, at least as measured by increased GDP, is not what is meant by development and that creativity has as much to do with human values as with economics. Be that as it may, economic growth and development have been allied with creative industries and the cultural sector, utilising various concepts of locational advantage, including creative clusters and cultural districts, and using the concept of creative cites as a basis for urban regeneration.

Creative clusters

The concept of industrial or business clusters is an old one and led to the development of industrial estates and the like, including 'brain parks' linking universities and industry. Hollywood is often cited as an example of an industrial cluster, and Silicon Valley has been hailed as a prime example of a business cluster in the knowledge economy. This concept has been adapted to the creative cluster, in which creative enterprises (non-profit and for-profit) in the same industry or closely related industries locate close to each other and benefit from networking and external economies. Some firms benefit from

---

[11] Florida (2002).

economies of scale and scope, though clusters are often of small or medium-sized enterprises, which in the creative industries are believed to be the true source of innovation, even if it is the large international corporations that eventually capture the ideas or fruits of their knowledge. Small innovative enterprises may well not be able, or wish, to expand and compete with the global giants, and are more efficient as innovators in a small-scale setting in which individuals come in frequent contact with each other and are thus motivated to work imaginatively. By clustering, they can specialise and interact with other firms that buy in their products, while reducing the transaction costs of contracting and marketing.

An important question concerning clustering is whether it is a spontaneous market outcome and, if so, whether the intervention of a city or regional authority can achieve these economic benefits by policy: perhaps even more to the point is the question of whether clustering can be socially engineered by state intervention. One aspect that the state or local authorities can deal with is to ensure that planning permission for zoning purposes permits such developments; they may also encourage the development by waivers on property taxes or start-up subsidies and the like. The question then is whether the clusters are self-sustaining in the long run. This is one of the aspects of creativity that attracts support for creative clusters from policy-makers.

UNESCO is one of many organisations that evidently believes that creative clusters can be fostered, at least by shared experience, and its Global Alliance for Cultural Diversity programme includes the Creative Cities Network (see box 19.5). This network has identified the following industries in which cities should specialise in order to be eligible for participation: literature, cinema, music, folk art, design, media arts and gastronomy. It will be noted that the list conforms to the UNESCO listing of creative industries as presented in box 14.1, with the notable inclusion of gastronomy. At the time of writing the following cities had been designated for their achievement in one industry or another: Aswân, Egypt (UNESCO City of Folk Art), Buenos Aires, Argentina (first UNESCO City of Design), Santa Fe, New Mexico (UNESCO City of Folk Art), Popayan, Colombia (first UNESCO City of Gastronomy) and Edinburgh, Scotland (first UNESCO City of Literature). UNESCO asserts (see box 19.5) that there is a benefit from the exchange of ideas (though it does not explain why a successful city – or, more to the point, the entrepreneurs located in the city – would have the incentive to tell others how it achieved success, always supposing it knows) but it does not suggest any underlying causal relationship that could be harnessed. Many of the publications in this field use case studies and generalise from them inductively, but there does not

Box 19.5 UNESCO and the Creative Cities Network

In October 2004 UNESCO's Global Alliance for Cultural Diversity launched the Creative Cities Network. The network connects creative cities so that they can share experiences, know-how, training in business skills and technology on a global level. This facilitates local capacity-building that encourages diversity of cultural products in domestic and international markets, employment generation and social and economic development.

The network has focused on cities because they are increasingly playing a vital role in harnessing creativity for economic and social development. Cities harbour the entire range of cultural actors throughout the creative industry chain, from the creative act to production and distribution.

As breeding grounds for creative clusters, cities have great potential to harness creativity, and connecting cities can mobilise this potential for global impact. Cities are small enough to affect local cultural industries but also large enough to serve as gateways to international markets.

Creative cities have managed to nurture a remarkably dynamic relationship between cultural actors and creativity, generating conditions whereby a city's 'creative buzz' attracts more cultural actors, which in turn adds to a city's creative buzz. This virtuous cycle of clustering and creativity, which is shaping the foundation of creative cities, is also perpetuating the evolution of the 'new economy'.

The new economy is rapidly taking shape, giving rise to the mass production and consumption of unique experiences, and cities that can effectively harness human creativity are at the heart of this evolution. Cities play an integral role in the transition towards a new economy because they harbour clusters that are essentially hubs of creativity with the potential to shape global demand for a city's local offering.

Sources: http://portal.unesco.org/culture/en/ev.php-URL_ID=29032&URL_DO=DO_TOPIC&URL_SECTION=201.html (accessed 15 January 2009) and UNCTAD (2008).

appear to be a general theory, apart from the ones outlined earlier in the chapter. The subject calls for more rigorous economic analysis and empirical testing for causal relationships.

Cultural districts or geographical indicators

The term 'cultural district' can be used in two distinct ways. One is to denote a specific geographical part of a city as its cultural district, an example of which is the Fort Worth Cultural District, with its concentration of art galleries; this meaning is close to that of the cultural or creative cluster. The second use of the term is in connection with collective intellectual property rights (IPRs) or 'geographical indicators'. Geographical indicators protect producers in an area or cultural district that has an established reputation for producing a particular product or that is a source of a particular natural resource; examples abound from the field of gastronomy, and perhaps two of the best-known examples are the related products from the region near the city of Parma – Parmesan cheese and Parma ham. The geographical indicator is of the nature of a trademark that relates to the cultural district and prevents producers from other areas from calling their products champagne or Parma ham and so on. To do so is regarded in law as 'passing off' and can give rise to a lawsuit. Particularly in the case of wines and similar drinks, geographical indicators are protected under TRIPS (see chapter 14). Passing off would also incur the notice of trading standards officers, who check in addition for counterfeit and other unlawful copies of trademarked and brand products. Similar schemes, such as the appellation d'origine contrôlée in the wine industry in France, are self-regulated.

In economic terms, the IPR creates a monopoly for all the producers within the cultural district, raises the prices of the products for all producers (who nevertheless compete with each other) and probably also raises land prices within the district.

Sustainability and competition in creative clusters

Creative clusters and creative cities programmes are intended to foster sustainable economic growth in both developed and less developed countries, regions and cities. To an economist, the term 'sustainable' implies that supply will be supported by demand in a market, otherwise the scheme would require endless financial support from public sources; true, the market may be assisted by various forms of state intervention, such as the establishing and protection of property rights, but, essentially, the result of these programmes is expected to be that the enterprises are able to survive in a market economy. It is useful therefore to consider how competitive the markets are expected to be, given the emphasis on co-operation and collaboration in the programmes.

Some business economists have observed a phenomenon they call 'co-opetition', meaning that there is co-operation co-existing with competition: firms within an industry collaborate in order to gain some mutual benefit, but once this is obtained they compete with each other for customers.[12] Registering a cultural district geographical indicator is an example of something that requires co-operation, but once that is achieved each firm or farm

---

[12] See Küng, Picard and Towse (2008).

within the district competes in the market (unless, of course, there is a co-operative marketing arrangement); hence this is an example of co-opetition. Note that this does not contravene competition law, because the firms are not forming a cartel for the purpose of price-fixing, though it is also the case that such action is likely to raise prices. This may be acceptable to consumers if there are substitutes in the market – say goods from other sources – at lower prices, and they may be prepared to pay higher prices for high-quality goods that are certified by the geographical indicator because a firm so protected defends its reputation in the mutual interest of all producers in the cultural district.

Again, it seems that there are welfare gains to both producers and consumers from the encouragement of creativity in cities, in creative clusters and also in geographical indicators that are similar in economic terms to those obtained from festivals. These welfare gains are compounded by the extent of synergy between these various developments.

Cultural tourism

In one sense, all tourism has a cultural aspect to it, because tourists see how other people live in different places; by 'cultural tourism' here is meant tourism that is in some way connected to cultural facilities, such as heritage sites, historic cities and arts attractions, such as festivals. Cultural tourism started centuries ago with ancient Greeks visiting Egypt to marvel at the pyramids, Romans visiting Greece and Egypt, and so on. Pilgrimages to the Holy Land for Christians and Jews, to Mecca for Muslims, to Varanasi for Hindus and to Kapilavastu for Buddhists are some examples of religious tourism that began centuries ago and continues to this day. As chronicled in the *Canterbury Tales* by the English writer Chaucer, religious observance was not the only aspect of pilgrimages, and the festivals and fairs at present-day Indian temple cities testify to their continuing attractions for visitors.

Tourism for whatever purpose entails travel within a country or abroad, and making the necessary travel arrangements long ago became the specialisation of travel agents, who continue, along with travellers' own use of the internet, to facilitate travel to the far corners of the Earth. Some of this travel is directed solely or mainly at visiting cultural sites, and there are travel agents who specialise in arranging tickets to events such as art exhibitions, opera festivals, and so on, as well as for travel to them, often in 'package deals'. In fact, tourism may often have mixed motives, and cultural attractions may not always be predominant motives but secondary ones: besides sitting on the beach, tourists like to visit cultural events occasionally as well. Many countries and regions welcome tourism as part of a development strategy, though tourism can also have serious cultural and economic disadvantages – as UNESCO puts it: 'It is a well-known fact that tourism can be a deadly foe as much as a firm friend in the matter of development.'[13]

Cultural heritage sites are recognised for their cultural significance and are not located because of policy on tourism. They may be very difficult to get to, as are Machu Picchu in Peru and Hampi in India, and become accessible to tourists only with investment in transport and nearby accommodation. For such sites, visiting them is the main purpose of the tour, and the visitor has to make a considerable outlay in travel costs in order to reach them. By contrast, a visit to the Statue of Liberty can easily be fitted into a 'general purpose' visit to New York with little extra expenditure. Other cultural attractions, such as festivals, are located in a specific place and offer a range of events for the same outlay of travel costs. Cultural tourism thus competes with other types of tourism, and within the category of cultural tourism there is also competition for visitors and their expenditures.

Economic aspects of cultural tourism

From the economic point of view, there are some differences between 'ordinary' tourism and cultural tourism. On the demand side, cultural tourists are likely to have higher levels of income and education than the average tourist and are probably willing to pay more for their experience. According to the Massachusetts Cultural Council, in the United States cultural tourism is the fastest-growing sector of the travel industry. Cultural tourists spend $62 more per day and $200 more per trip than other travellers and have higher levels of income. Cultural tourists include multiple destinations during a visit and stay one half-day longer at each destination. In Massachusetts, cultural tourism generates $11.2 billion in direct spending, which contributes an additional $751 million in state and local taxes and supports 124,800 jobs in a variety of industries.[14]

These figures show the combination of direct and indirect spending that is typically taken into account when measuring or projecting cultural tourist

[13] See http://portal.unesco.org/culture/en/ev.php-URL_ID=11408&URL_DO=DO_TOPIC&URL_SECTION= 201.html (accessed 15 January 2009).
[14] See www.massculturalcouncil.org/services/tourism.html (accessed 15 January 2009).

revenues. Tourism has costs and benefits, however, and they must also be taken into account to estimate the overall economic value; as discussed in chapter 7, cost–benefit analysis includes external costs and benefits, which could be cultural as well as purely economic ones.

Foreign tourism is a form of export: tourists from abroad must pay in local currency for the services they demand, thus selling their own currency in order to do so. For some countries, earning foreign currency is an important aspect of tourism. In the case of foreign tourists, rates of exchange are an important influence on their demand for a tourist destination and on their spending there.

Net revenues from tourism

How valuable the visit is to the 'owners' of the tourist site depends upon entry prices, whether it is feasible to make charges (the direct revenue) and the ability to capture indirect economic benefits from associated services, such as hotels, restaurants, shops and travel services. Foreign tourist expenditures are a net inflow; some proportion of expenditures by tourists from within the country or region add to the regional or city income only by diverting expenditure they would have made at home to the tourist destination, however – that is, spending by tourists in Massachusetts comes at the expense of spending in their home state. The impact on the local or regional economy will be greater the more 'local' are the products on which tourists expend their money; if goods or labour services have to be imported from other regions or from abroad to satisfy tourists' demands, that weakens the impact of their spending in the locality. The impact may also depend upon the ownership of hotel chains and so on, as a foreign chain of hotels would remit its profits abroad, weakening the contribution that tourist expenditures make to the local economy.

External costs

Tourism can also damage the environment and cause pollution and congestion. As these are external costs, tourists do not pay for them directly, and a way of charging them for compensation to internalise the costs has to be found. This may be done by a tourist tax in hotels and restaurants in tourist districts or as a charge on travel facilities for which local residents can get concessions; this is the case in the city of Venice, one of the world's most popular destinations for cultural tourism, where tourists pay a higher price for travelling on the canals by the vaporetti than do Venetian residents. Venice has another problem, though: many tourists have a day's excursion to the city and walk around without spending money on food or lodging in the city, making it impossible for the city authorities to charge them for their external costs, which therefore must be financed by residents or charged to tourists who do consume taxable services.

Damage from pollution or just from walking has made it necessary to close some famous cultural sites to visitors: the Lascaux caves in France were closed many years ago because peoples' breath was causing humidity and nurturing a fungal growth that damaged the prehistoric cave paintings; instead, a site nearby with reproductions of the paintings is open to the public. Entry to Stonehenge in the United Kingdom is also closed to visitors, because the stones were becoming loose due to the pressure of feet on the surrounding ground. Congestion from tourists in Venice and Bruges in Belgium makes life difficult for residents, who move out to other areas to live, surrendering the city to tourists in a negative vicious cycle. Tourism can also damage local culture by encouraging the trivialisation of handicrafts or folklore. Some of these external costs can be assigned a monetary value and could be charged for in ticket prices or taxes, and they must be taken into account in a cost–benefit or economic impact study.

Cultural tourism and economic development

Tourism, including cultural tourism, is often a source of net income to a city, region or country, and cultural tourism is often linked to policies for urban and regional regeneration schemes (including creative city and cultural cluster policies) and to the generation of income and employment in developing countries. The economic impact of tourism in fostering economic growth is greater when there are unemployed resources, because the net inflow of expenditures sets up a multiplier effect on incomes and consumption in the locality, which could spread beyond to the whole country provided that there is no diversion of resources. This may be the basis for investment in cultural and associated facilities to attract tourists. Economists would then counsel that cultural investment be compared to other forms of investment, however, to see which is likely to produce a higher return. It needs to be kept in mind that any publicly financed expenditure that employs labour and other resources that were lying idle will increase incomes in a locality, even if that investment simply involves digging holes and filling them up again! If there are no unemployed resources, such investment projects result only in inflation.

Cultural investment therefore often has to compete with investment in sports events, such as hosting international competitions and games, the

Box 19.6 Cultural investment in Bilbao

The city of Bilbao in northern Spain is the capital of the Basque region; the city itself has a population of just over 350,000 and Greater Bilbao just under 1 million. In the 1990s the city embarked on a huge investment in various buildings designed by world-famous architects, with the intention of attracting tourists and leading to the regeneration of the city. First was the Guggenheim Museum, designed by Frank Gehry, which opened in 1997. There then followed a new pedestrian bridge, linking the museum with hotels, and a new airport terminal designed by Santiago Calatrava, a new metro system designed by Norman Foster, the Euskalduna Convention and Music Centre, with an opera house, concert hall and exhibition space designed by Federico Soriano and Dolores Palacios (opened 1999), and several other major renewal and architectural schemes.

The outlay on the museum building and its surroundings was €84.14 million and €48.08 million was spent for the collection – in total €132.22 million. The museum attracted 1.36 million visitors in its first year, of whom 80 per cent went to Bilbao with the express purpose of visiting the museum. Visitor expenditure in the first two years was €433 million, of which €23.4 million was spent in the museum itself. The Basque regional authority recouped its investment in the museum in the first year, with an increase in GDP of €144 million. Overall, by 2000 the museum had generated regional income of €600 million.

Source: Cooke (2008).

Olympic Games being the biggest project. Cultural investment may or may not involve outlays on large capital projects, such as sports stadia. There are cases in which considerable investment in cultural projects has taken place in order to attract tourists as a sustainable source of income in the future. A striking example of this is the city of Bilbao in northern Spain (see box 19.6), which adopted a policy of cultural investment for urban and regional regeneration, with the focus on buildings and other facilities designed by leading architects, that has proved very successful in cultural and economic terms by increasing tourism.

Cultural tourism and cultural development

Finally, an interesting twist to the story of cultural tourism is the policy adopted in Abu Dhabi, capital of the emirate of the same name that is part of the United Arab Emirates. Like Bilbao, it also plans a Guggenheim Museum designed by Frank Gehry, due for completion in 2011, and, like Bilbao, the intention is to encourage cultural tourism. Unlike Bilbao, however, this policy is not motivated by the need for economic growth, as GDP per head in this state with fewer than half a million inhabitants (the majority of whom are expatriates) was $63,000 in 2007, ranking it third in the world; with an estimated $25 million per day in oil revenues and between forty and 100 years of oil reserves, this would seem to be sustainable. This wealth is the basis of the plan to make Abu Dhabi the cultural hub of the Arab world, combining Eastern and Western art. Besides the Guggenheim Museum, there is to be a branch of the Louvre, a maritime museum and a performing arts centre, with five theatres, a music hall, an opera house and other spaces to seat over 6,000 people. The performing arts programme had already begun at the time of writing, with a festival and recitals by world-famous performers. Despite low prices, the audience had not yet filled the auditorium, but it is expected to take time to do so.[15] This is surely an interesting experiment in taste formation, and, for cultural economists, it could throw light on the question often asked: can expenditure on the arts by itself stimulate tastes?

Conclusion

This chapter has dealt with several topics that concern the location of the production and/or consumption of creative products. In the case of festivals, there is multiple output of cultural supply, and this attracts visitors from home and abroad. Most festivals, though not all, take place in cities, and these cities, besides holding festivals, may also be creative cities, with policies for urban development through creative industry clusters and tourism; some will have been or plan to be capitals of culture. In other words, the different categories analysed here could coincide in any one place.

One of the main questions for cultural economics is whether there is a general theory of spatial location that can be invoked in explaining the location of cultural facilities. This is an important matter for cultural policy, whose aim is not just to obtain the greatest value from the production of cultural goods and services but also to increase their consumption and the access that consumers have to them. Travel costs must be added to entry costs in determining the willingness to pay for cultural events, and this is as much the case for local offerings as it is for ones that involve overnight stays and other tourist expenses. The concept of agglomeration economies is clearly a powerful one in explaining the clustering of the supply of creative products as well as the demand for them. Clusters offer network and other external benefits as well as internal ones to artists and other producers of creative

---

[15] *The Guardian*, April 2008: 11.

products; festivals offer producers a forum for expanding their cultural supply in qualitative and quantitative terms and they offer local and tourist consumers an expanded choice of events and experiences as both private and social benefits.

It is also the case, however, that locations can become overcrowded with producers and consumers; this manifests itself through the market as higher prices (rents, hotel prices, space for workshops, and so on), but there are also external costs, which means that the net increase in economic welfare from growth has to be assessed. The presence of public goods characteristics means that price signals do not work, as argued in chapter 9 in relation to heritage sites; in addition, planning restrictions and other such regulations may prevent the market from working and obscure price signals. There are also dynamic effects over time with the possibility, already a problem in Venice, of the cultural experience being spoiled in a downward spiral by congestion or pollution, including cultural degradation. For these reasons, the calculation of benefits and costs of festivals, cultural tourism, and so on are necessary on an individual basis. Such exercises are themselves costly and, to be done correctly, require considerable amounts of information. These costs and benefits must also be discounted into present value terms (as explained in chapter 7).

There is a considerable emphasis in policy statements and in the literature on these topics on sustainability. In economic terms, sustainability is achieved through market forces with revenues covering costs for non-profit enterprises and events and sufficient profits being made by for-profit entrepreneurs. Due to the presence or possibility of external effects, however, intervention is required to attempt to internalise costs and benefits, through taxes and subsidies, as economic solutions. There is a strong suggestion in these literatures that planning is necessary to control external effects and stimulate improvements, particularly with respect to spatial design. It is indeed an interesting matter if government intervention is needed to stimulate creative cities and clusters in view of the observation that they are a response to market incentives. Evidence from the innovation literature suggests that appropriate policy interventions can offer extra incentives. For other topics covered in this chapter – capitals of culture, cultural districts and geographical indicators – government action is necessary to set them in motion.

These topics are well understood by cultural economists but policy-makers and others with an interest in promoting them do not always care to recognize the problems. Living up to its name in this context, the dismal science cautions for careful and objective analysis of the economic costs and benefits, including the cultural benefits, in evaluating projects and adopting these policies. This has not always proved popular. What is often lacking is consideration of that most basic of economic ideas, the opportunity cost.

Further reading

UNCTAD's (2008) *Creative Economy Report 2008* offers a straightforward introduction to these diverse topics, with boxes by experts such as Charles Landry that give a good insight into the way other disciplines look at these matters. David Throsby's (2001) book *Economics and Culture*, recommended earlier, also offers a broad view of sustainable development with the focus on economics. My (Towse, 2003a) *Handbook of Cultural Economics* has several introductory chapters: Lluís Bonet on 'Cultural tourism' (chapter 23), Bruce Seaman on the 'Economic impact of the arts' (chapter 27) and Bruno Frey on 'Festivals' (chapter 28). Frey also has a chapter on special exhibitions and festivals in his 2000 book *Arts and Economics*. Jen Snowball's work on the National Arts Festival in South Africa is the basis of Willis and Snowball (2009). Xavier Greffe's (2002) book *Arts and Artists from an Economic Perspective* provides a thoughtful insight into the role of art in cultural districts and creative industries, and Walter Santagata's chapter (31) in the 2006 Ginsburgh and Throsby *Handbook of the Economics of Art and Culture* covers cultural districts and clusters and geographical indicators and considers policy issues for both developed and developing countries. This is complemented by Trine Bille and Günther Schulze's chapter (30) in the same volume, 'Culture in urban and regional development'.

Part V

Conclusion and exercises and problems

Introduction

The conclusion includes a summary of the main points made in the book and an assessment of the theories and research in cultural economics that are used in the various chapters. It draws together various strands of thinking developed through the book and considers how the ideas presented here could be used in possible future scenarios.

The problems and exercises are those I have used in my years of teaching cultural economics; some are topics for discussion in seminars, some are homework assignments and others are examination questions. A short multiple choice test is also included.

20 Conclusion

A conclusion could mean different things: one would be a summary of the main points made in the book as a fairly routine piece of writing (common in student essays!); another would be an assessment of the theories and research, in this case in cultural economics, that are discussed throughout the book; a third could be the author's thoughts upon completing the book – what works, what does not, omissions, and so on; finally, the conclusion could point the way forward to how the ideas presented in the book could be used in possible future scenarios. I attempt all of these in this conclusion.

Writing this book has been a journey through familiar and unfamiliar territory. Much of the material is based on that which I have used over the last ten years or so in teaching courses on cultural economics, the economics of cultural industries and the economics of copyright (some, such as welfare economics, I have taught for much longer). My intention in this book was to bring it all together and make it accessible to readers with little or no previous experience of economics. Of course, the book has ended up longer than was intended! Over the two and a half years in which I was writing it, however, I discovered that there were a lot of things I did not know about (and there still are) and that this is a very fast-moving area: new literature and research results are coming out all the time; technologies and consumer and producer behaviour are changing under our noses; and the conceptual framework of the creative economy seems to have shifted gear perceptibly – what was once an exploration of the idea of combining what were previously called the cultural industries with the creative and performing arts and heritage (plus other industries until very recently not considered part of the arts economy), to form a 'creative economy', has now become an accepted and widely recognised term in government circles and beyond. That necessitated some rewriting, in particular to include reference to the UNCTAD *Creative Economy Report 2008* and recent data.

The main claims in the book

One of the main strands running through the book is that cultural economics is a field of study in its own right and that it has explanatory power for the topics treated here. These topics may be summarised as follows.

- Analysis of the economic organisation of the production and delivery of content of all kinds (visual art, literature, performing arts, film, broadcasting, heritage), starting with the artist and through the chain of production to the final consumer.
- This organisation is influenced by market forces and by government intervention; intervention may be direct provision or finance or regulation. Regulation includes copyright law, which applies to all content and much of the delivery of creative goods and services, and sector-specific regulation, as for broadcasting and built heritage. Regulation originates at the international and national levels, with the European Union, UNESCO, UNCTAD and WIPO increasingly active in the area of the creative industries; international trade is also regulated, among other reasons to protect cultural diversity.
- There are specific features of some creative goods and services that make their consumption somewhat different from that of other products: particularly for the more esoteric arts, such as ballet and opera, and recently produced art, such as contemporary music, visual art and literature, consumers have to learn to appreciate them and form a taste for them. This can be exaggerated for cultural products such as film and recorded music, however, for which tastes are more readily developed. Tastes for the new are unpredictable, though, and this influences the behaviour of firms producing such goods and services. Related to this is the question of quality: consumers need to be well informed to evaluate quality, as do the bureaucrats and others dispensing public finance to the cultural sector.
- Economics provides a disciplined way of analysing and evaluating policy on the creative industries.

Cultural economics as a field

Cultural economics relies greatly on the broader discipline of economics with added attention to the public goods and externality aspects of the consumption of creative goods and services, to taste formation and uncertainty ('nobody knows') and the problems that are associated with government intervention, such as principal–agent issues and rent-seeking, that other sectors experience as well as the creative industries. Cultural economics also recognises the particular role that culture and creativity play in social life as well as in the economy.

Economics has adapted to huge changes in technologies, pre-dating as it does the Industrial Revolution, and our journey through time and technologies has taken place with much the same economic laws at play (for example, the ideas of opportunity cost, supply and demand and response to incentives). At the same time, economics itself has changed in emphasis over the centuries, sometimes in response to the changing environment of the economy: economic laws may be the same but the economist's toolbox for applying them has changed; a relevant example here is information economics, which has changed the way economists look at a whole range of issues, from job contracts to government regulation.

The same is also claimed for copyright law – that it has coped with a succession of technological changes with the same principles intact. As we have seen, copyright is intimately connected with the creative industries, and it has been part of my mission to show that cultural economics throws a particular light on the economics of copyright, especially as it affects primary creators or artists. Questions are now being asked if the same experience of adapting to new technologies applies to the digital era or if it is different in kind (rather than in degree) from its predecessors: do we need a new economics to deal with digitisation and do we need a new type of copyright law? Most economists are fairly sanguine that the basic laws of economics apply to the creative industries as to other industries, and that new business models apply to new services, but they are not so sure that this is the case with copyright law.

Cultural economics shares with economics its methodological approach, in particular the need to express theories in testable form and to measure economic relationships. Economists have a strong predilection for looking for causality where other disciplines may be more interested in correlations between variables. As we have seen, this aim is frequently stifled in cultural economics by a lack of appropriate data, although one of the things that has changed greatly even over the time of writing this book is the increasing supply of official statistics on the creative economy.

Developments in cultural economics

I would say that there have been three areas in which developments in cultural economics have taken place: in the scope of the topics studied; in the range of economic theories used; and in the increasingly sophisticated empirical research that has developed, partly due to the availability of better data and of statistical packages but also because there is greater recognition that this is part of professional economics. In is probably fair to say that the econometric analysis of art prices has gone furthest in this last respect – a topic that has only been touched on in this book because of its complexity.[1] Cultural economics has changed, therefore, and that leads to the question of whether it has made progress as a discipline. A survey of cultural economics by Blaug (2001) applied the criteria of economic methodology to cultural economics, methodology being the study of scientific method, investigating, for example, how we establish that propositions are true or not. Blaug suggests that there has been considerable progress in empirical terms and that much has been achieved in understanding the economics of cultural production and consumption without there having been any real theoretical progress since the publication of Baumol and Bowen's book in 1966. I would dispute that now; in my opinion, the introduction into cultural economics by Caves (2000) of contract theory and the property rights approach, along with transaction cost economics, has made for theoretical progress. Other changes are afoot: cultural economists, such as Frey and Peacock, emphasise public choice theory and the role of institutions; Throsby and others seek to reconcile the notion of cultural value with economic value; Baumol (2006) has argued that the 'new economy' has revolutionised the arts. In my own work, as evidenced by this book, I have sought to extend the scope of cultural economics by integrating the economics of copyright and by embracing the notion of the creative industries as an all-encompassing view of the cultural sector. I am confident that cultural economics has made progress and will continue to do so as it attracts more young economists to it.

The creative industries 'paradigm'

In methodological terms, a paradigm is a philosophical or theoretical framework that advances a particular analytical outlook, and people speak of a 'paradigm shift' taking place when a new way of investigating a set of problems or phenomena is adopted. It is probably too strong a term to apply to the creative industries 'movement' but it is certainly the case that a shift has occurred, for better or worse, over the last few years in conceptual thinking about the creative industries. There has undoubtedly been a lot of hype about

[1] See Ginsburgh (2003) for an introduction to this topic.

creativity and the creative industries, and this has put many social scientists, me included, off the idea, but researching and writing this book has persuaded me that, at least from the economic point of view, the concept is valid. To say that the concept is valid implies acceptance of a satisfactory listing of the creative industries, however, and, as we have seen, this is fraught with problems; while I am prepared to accept the notion of creative industries, I am not comfortable with the broad lists we see being promoted and the items that get put into each category. I return to this topic below but, first, I go through the economic features that make the case to my mind for having the concept of the creative economy, paradigm or not.

Economic features of creative industries

The first step is to accept that all stages in the creation of cultural content and its delivery form part of an industry. This is anathema to some thinkers but, to an economist, an industry merely comprises the stages of production of a good or service from its inception as an idea or a plan through to its delivery to the final consumer in the market. Artists and other creators of ideas or 'information' (to use the language of the information economy) who supply their creations in the form of works that can be disseminated (notice the 'copyright' way of expressing this) are part of what will be measured statistically as an 'industry'; primary content creation is the first layer or stage of what may be a lengthy business of getting it to audiences or buyers, or it may very simply be sold or licensed direct to the consumer. As long as some financial transaction takes place that is reported as income by the seller, the seller is part of an industry. This is no value judgement, just a fact of economic life. It does not raise the question if the price truly valued the work or if the work was art or not. Material put on blogs and on YouTube and Facebook and the rest that does not form part of a financial transaction, however worthwhile or valuable to society, does not contribute to the economy in terms of value added.

One way of identifying creative industries is to look for their common economic features. These are:

- on the supply side, the feature of natural monopoly/increasing returns – the high sunk cost of producing the 'original' combined with the much lower, and in some cases virtually zero, marginal cost of delivering subsequent copies;
- still on the supply side, that the original work falls under the scope of copyright or other intellectual property law – that is, it is a work of art, literature, and so on – or it would have been so protected before entering the public domain (so old master works of art and the like are included);

- that the resources used in the stages of the chain of production in the industry have no alternative use except in connection with the production of creative goods and services;
- on the demand side, there are information issues to do with quality and taste formation because the goods and services contain an element of novelty that make consumer reception uncertain (rather than unpredictable) – that is, 'nobody knows';
- these information problems take the form of asymmetric information as far as regulatory bodies and grant-giving organisations are concerned, providing the opportunity for rent-seeking.

It is clear to me that all these features apply to all the creative and performing arts, museums and art galleries, the music, film and video, broadcasting and publishing industries (that is, those included in this book) and to advertising, architecture, crafts, design and designer fashion, the games and computer software industries. I did not include these other industries in this book for two reasons: first, they have not (yet) been much written about by cultural economists, and, second, I do not know enough about them!

Not every feature in the above list apparently applies to every activity we would surely call creative, however: visual artists, fashion designers and craftspeople making one-off items and musicians performing a work only one time do not make copies and therefore do not fit the natural monopoly category, but it can be argued that their human capital accumulates with each experience and that this is equivalent to increasing returns to scale (falling average total costs).

This leads to one further economic feature: that Baumol's cost disease applies at the initial content creation phase, whether that is in the hands of an individual artist or in a large firm. There is no escaping the input of human creativeness, even if it is assisted by capital equipment, such as digital technologies and a computer. This might be regarded as the essential aspect of Baumol's idea – that the labour input cost of creation is irreducible; we might (and I do) criticise the view that there is no technical progress in the arts and heritage but it does appear inescapable ('ineluctable', as Baumol phrases it) that time has to be taken to create the new, even taking into account the point made above that experience and human capital accumulation could reduce it. The cost of that time depends upon the opportunity cost of alternative uses of the creator's time, which would be rising in a growing economy, though, as we have seen, that might be something an artist ignores. Copyright may come into play here: as we saw, Landes and Posner (1989, 2002) have argued that the cost of creation rises with increased copyright scope and duration.

Humdrum inputs

What bothers me about the creative industries 'paradigm' is not the underlying conception but the exaggerated inclusion of what Caves has aptly called the 'humdrum' inputs. Humdrum inputs are necessary for the processing and delivery of creative content to the next stage in the chain of production or to the consumer but they have alternative uses, whether they are capital or labour. One of the findings of research on Baumol's cost disease was that the costs of management and other non-arts workers in an arts organisation rose precisely because, unlike artists, they were not trapped in the arts and therefore their reservation payment was determined in the non-arts economy. They appear to get the same treatment in the 'creative industries paradigm' as the creators of original content, however. There is a tendency to ignore the very different footing that the creators are on from the business side of the industries, and this diminishes the vital distinction between artists or creators and the humdrum inputs. It could be reduced to this: without new creative works, the creative industries would eventually wither away, exhausting their back catalogues; without humdrum inputs, artists would find some way of reaching their market (maybe not so efficiently) and consumers would find some way of obtaining the work they want to experience; moreover, that day is approaching in some respect with the internet. The point is: the humdrum depends on content but it has alternative uses; content does not – content *is* 'king'!

My complaint is that definitions and measures of the creative industries include far too much of the humdrum. Ideas of a creative class that include accountants and lawyers as creative just play into the hands of those who want to hype up the scale and economic size of the creative industries. This applies in reverse too: studies that look at how many former art students are working in humdrum businesses diminish recognition of the role of creativity in the creative industries. I return below to the question of the size of these industries.

Copyright law

You would think that copyright law would recognise the distinction between 'art and commerce' and give pride of place to the content creators. In principle, it does, but it does not distinguish the 'small' from the 'large' creator, affording the same treatment to large corporations as to individual artists. That is the nature of law. What it does not do is to protect the creator from contracts that reduce the protection it initially offers. The author (creator) is frequently required under a contract to assign the copyright, or, at any rate, the valuable economic rights, to the humdrum end of the industry that is going to invest in processing and marketing the work. Of course, as publishers invest in authors by getting their works to market, they get copyright protection, and Caves has offered a very plausible economic explanation for this transfer of rights; but that may not be a consolation to the author. Combine this with the pressure of excess supply of artistic/creative content, and the author is in a weak bargaining position unless he or she is a superstar. Despite this widely recognised scenario, all concerned clamour for greater copyright protection, despite evidence that it mostly favours the industries more than the authors.

I have two proposals for righting the balance. First, that some sort of investment fund be set up to lend financial capital to artists to exploit their work themselves; it is very difficult for creators (or inventors) to get a bank loan because they have only their human capital as collateral. Such a fund could work like a student loan scheme, and successful artists/creators would pay back, say, a proportion of any copyright royalties. Second, that copyright law be changed so that it automatically reverts to the original creator after a reasonable period, say twenty years, at which point the contract with the industry would then have to be renewed and the new contract would reflect the success or otherwise of the work on the market. There are, in fact, many ideas for the reform of copyright being discussed by government advisory groups as well as by academics.

Another way of righting the balance is for more effective use of competition law to regulate the undesirable effects of natural monopoly in the creative industries.

Subsidy to creators

Copyright law works through the market by establishing property rights that enable trade to take place, and revenues to creators and the creative industries are determined by success on the market. Subsidy works against market trends, in the sense that it is used to counteract market failure and adverse market conditions, but, even so, it ultimately works in the context of a market economy. Subsidy is one of the alternatives to copyright that have been proposed. Subsidy is used to encourage creativity by individual creators and cultural organisations, and cultural economics has paid a great deal of attention to various aspects of public expenditure, mostly in the arts (so film and broadcasting subsidies have not attracted much attention), and has analysed in detail principal–agent, moral hazard and governance problems connected to subsidy. The experience of arts councils and similar cultural policy-makers is that they tend to elitism and the favouring of insiders and have a preference for merit goods, and these tendencies show themselves as much in relation to subsidies to film and broadcasting as with those to writers and visual artists. Copyright, by contrast, has the advantage of mediating creativity via neutral market forces.

Evaluating cultural policy

There is also the question of how to evaluate cultural policy, especially when its aims are fuzzy and not clearly stated; a current policy objective that has these characteristics is 'promoting diversity', which has proved difficult to pin down for research purposes. In this context, a particular conundrum in cultural economics has always interested me: should subsidised cultural organisations do something different with their subsidy from that which the market would produce, taking the risk of not having popular appeal, or should they just provide more or less the same output as the market would, such as time-honoured plays, ballets and TV programmes?

Cultural economics should apply the same criteria to evaluating copyright and creative industry policies as it uses for the subsidised arts, treating them as part of cultural policy. One fact of life should make the case for that: of the measured output of the creative industries, that due to subsidy represents only a small proportion, as can be seen from looking at the statistics on the creative industries; software and computer games are by far the leading sector – they represent almost a half of all value added by the creative industries in the United Kingdom, for instance, and completely dwarf music and the performing arts. One has to ask if supporting the 4 per cent contribution to GDP of software and games industries is a major objective of cultural and copyright policies.

A necessary precondition for evaluating the emphasis of policy on the creative industries, and the claims that are made for them as a leading sector of the economy, is to have reliable, official data. As with measures of the economic 'importance' of the subsidised arts in the 1980s, we see a familiar process at work with the creative industries in the 2000s: exaggerated claims about their economic contribution to the economy, achieved by overstating their size and constituent parts. In the 1980s measuring the cultural sector began as an exercise by consultancies and similar organisations; that prompted government interest, leading to the involvement of national statistical offices and international agencies, and resulted in improved data. The same process is now taking place with data on the creative industries.

Measuring the creative industries

The point has been made repeatedly throughout this book that defining and measuring the creative industries is, to a considerable extent, an arbitrary exercise. Which slot to use for any particular product or activity is governed by an overall design but that cannot eliminate subjective decisions about what goes where. This is a common problem in national income accounting, and there is no single correct answer – just an agreed way of doing it; furthermore, process and product innovation quickly outdate categories, but revising them is costly in terms of consistency. International trade figures seem to suffer from these problems more than those on domestic trade in developed countries.

There has been considerable discussion about the criteria for defining the creative industries at the international level and by national governments. The UK evaluation of measurement methodologies was highlighted in this book; using one set of measures can reduce the size of the creative industries compared to another. Instead of the matter resting there as a straightforward matter of national income accounting for government statisticians, however, the size and growth of the creative industries has become a highly charged political matter, and one, moreover, that is used to justify other policies, especially copyright law. This encourages lobbying and rent-seeking by industry bodies – in the United States the Intellectual Property Alliance is a case in point – whose claims are constantly reinforced by the belief that, without stronger copyright protection, economic growth would be under threat. Unfortunately, it is all too easy to slip from recognising copyright as a constituent feature of creative industries to asserting its causal effects and then tagging every industry that supplies the creative sector as 'dependent upon copyright'. What should be a positive exercise of measurement has become a normative undertaking, in part connected with pressure to control the 'piracy' of intellectual property.

What has been achieved by having creative industry policy?

In my opinion, the value of the notion of creative industries is that it removes the artificial boundary between the notions of 'high' subsidised arts and 'low' commercial culture. I believe this book has shown that we truly have a mixed economy of the cultural sector, with all sorts of activities being subsidised by government one way or another and many elements of cultural production being left to private for-profit commercial firms. It has led to an understanding of the similarities of the economic aspects of cultural production and consumption, of the respective roles of content creation and delivery and of the importance of copyright law in balancing the interests of society in financing creativity and diversity, on the one hand, and the cost in terms of prices and access on the other. It has also highlighted the tremendous effect and potential of new technologies for all aspects of cultural production and consumption for even the most traditional arts; for example, new technologies have offered far improved access to opera performances by transmitting live performances to cinemas via satellite, as well as access to museums, which as a result can have far wider appeal. This is bound to alter perceptions of the arts and culture. There is no research that I am aware of on these topics, though they clearly have important implications for cultural policy and for the finance of the arts, whether public or private.

What we know and what we do not know

Here and there in the book, I have indicated topics that could well be researched by students of cultural economics. There are a lot of things we still do not know, although, as the book has shown, there is also a lot that we do know; for instance, I think I have answered the ten questions posed at the beginning of chapter 1. We still do not know the response of creators to changes in copyright law or how lawmakers should respond to the clamour for stronger copyright protection. In addition to the usual difficulties of research, it would take place in an environment of huge changes in technology and financial uncertainty.

The big question, though, is what effect the internet/digitalisation will have on the creative industries – or perhaps I should say what effect these industries will have on the use of digital technologies and the internet. We know of some of the economic changes that it has already brought about – the greater use of price discrimination, subscriptions for licences replacing prices for goods, and so on. The issue, though, is whether property rights in digital material can be established and enforced while at the same time allowing reasonable access for the public to information, freedom of expression and other vital societal values; this will presumably involve something akin to digital rights management. What is clear is that cultural economists will have to be knowledgeable about these issues, which, sadly, is very difficult for the older ones such as me.

The future

The effects of digitisation were the biggest question for the future when I started to write this book but, as I finish it, the developed economies, and probably also the entire global economy, has entered the most serious recession of our lifetimes, with uncertainty hanging over the whole financial system. The so-called 'credit crunch' will surely be a crunch for the arts and creative economy. It will certainly divert government attention away from the creative industries, and it is likely to answer one of the big claims for the creative economy: are the creative industries what used to be called 'the icing on the cake' or real drivers of economic growth? With cultural goods being income elastic we would expect demand for them to fall as national incomes fall, but, at the same time, prices are likely to fall, which would normally encourage consumption. Consumption of the arts takes time, and the greater enforced leisure that a recession brings with greater unemployment reduces the opportunity cost of time, therefore stimulating consumption. Does all this send more people to the theatre, though, or do they stay at home and watch TV? Or does it encourage people to be more creative? The opportunities for that with the internet are greater than ever, and my guess is that the recession will encourage a great deal more 'amateur' activity via the internet and have a negative effect on the 'professional' creative industries. What is your guess?

Further reading

It may somehow seem inappropriate to have further reading following a conclusion but this is a chance to remind readers that I have my own interests and other writers have theirs!

William Baumol's (2006) thoughtful chapter 11 in the Ginsburgh and Throsby *Handbook of the Economics of Art and Culture* is a very good way of rounding off thinking about the impact of the 'new economy'. Mark Blaug's (2001) article provides an overview and assessment of cultural economics up to 2000; what makes it particularly worth reading is that he assesses cultural economics from the point of view of a methodologist. Tyler Cowen's (2008) article in the *Journal of Cultural Economics*, 'Why everything has changed: the recent revolution in cultural economics', is, like all his work, full of zest and catches your attention; its focus is more on technological developments and their economic implications than on cultural economics, and none the worse for that! My rather more sober piece in the same issue advocates more emphasis in cultural economics on the economics of copyright (Towse, 2008).

Exercises and problems

Multiple choice test

This test can be used as a mid-term test for a beginners' course in cultural economics (assuming no previous course in economics) or as a diagnostic test for entrance to an 'intermediate-level' course.

Test

Choose the best answer from the point of view of economics to each one of the following questions.

(1) An artist earns half the income of a person of the same age and with the same level of education. What would you call this income difference in economic terms?

(a) The opportunity cost of being an artist.
(b) Evidence that the arts are not sufficiently valued by the market.
(c) Evidence that the demand for art is too low.
(d) Evidence that the supply of art is too high.

(2) The government gives artists income support to enable them to concentrate on producing art. What is the expected effect on the market for works of art?

(a) Artists are able to reduce their prices.
(b) The demand schedule for works of art shifts out to the right.
(c) The supply schedule for works of art shifts out to the right.
(d) The supply schedule for works of art shifts in to the left.

(3) Instead of giving income support to artists, the government decides to buy works of art from artists. What is the expected effect on the market for works of art?

(a) Artists increase their prices.

(b) There is a movement up the demand schedule for works of art.

(c) The demand schedule for works of art shifts out to the right.

(d) The supply schedule for works of art shifts out to the right.

(4) In order for the market for works of art to function efficiently, there must be which of the following?

(a) Efficient production of works of art.

(b) Well-developed tastes in art on the part of consumers.

(c) Prices that are controlled at a fair level.

(d) Prices that reflect the cost of producing a work of art.

(5) A theatre wants to increase its revenue from ticket sales by raising prices. It will succeed if which of the following statement is true?

(a) Demand for theatre seats is elastic.

(b) Demand for theatre seats is inelastic.

(c) The theatre usually sells out all its seats.

(d) It is the only theatre in the region.

(6) Pop music is said to be highly competitive because of which of the following?

(a) Everyone wants to have a go at being a pop musician.

(b) It is cheap and easy to start up a band and get dates.

(c) You can make a lot of money with a successful band.

(d) Pop musicians are prepared to work for very little money.

(7) In order to protect their incomes, orchestral musicians join a professional association that sets a rate of payment for a three-year period that is greater than the going market rate. The result is which of the following?

(a) Demand for musicians' services rises.

(b) There is excess demand for musicians' services.

(c) There is excess supply of musicians' services.

(d) The government has to give a greater subsidy to orchestras.

(8) Orchestral musicians usually have to borrow money from the bank to buy their instruments. If the rate of interest on bank loans rises, which of the following would happen?

(a) The price of musical instruments would rise.

(b) The price of musical instruments would fall.

(c) Orchestral musicians would have to borrow more money.

(d) The price of concert tickets would immediately rise.

(9) If DVDs and going to the cinema are substitutes, what is the effect on the market for cinema seats of a fall in the price of DVDs?
   (a) Cinema ticket prices will fall.
   (b) The number of cinema seats demanded will fall.
   (c) The number of cinema seats demanded will rise.
   (d) New cinemas will open.

(10) Some museum services are called a 'public good' by economists, for which of the following reasons?
   (a) There are public benefits from learning about national or local history and identity.
   (b) Museums are open to the public.
   (c) Museums do not charge an entrance fee that covers the full cost of a visit.
   (d) Museums are owned by public authorities.

End of test

Exercises/examination questions

(1) Answer all parts of the question.
   (i) A museum raises its entry price by 10 per cent and attendance falls by 4 per cent. How would you characterise the demand for museum visits?
   (ii) What do you expect to happen to the revenue from the museum's ticket sales after the price rise?
   (iii) The government decides to give a voucher to everyone from the age of eighteen to twenty-five. Draw a diagram to illustrate the effect of this on the price charged by the museum. What determines the extent of the effect the introduction of the voucher has on the price?
   (iv) The government decides to subsidise museums directly by giving them a grant of €5 per visitor. Draw a diagram to illustrate this. With the grant, museums are able to reduce prices. What determines how much the price will fall?
   (v) Explain in brief how the museum could use price discrimination and what it would achieve by so doing.

(2) Answer all parts of the question.
   (i) What are appropriate measures of the output of arts and heritage organisations?
   (ii) Discuss possible performance indicators a ministry of culture or arts council might adopt for assessing a cultural organisation's efficiency. Give an example from your country.
   (iii) Do you think performance indicators can adequately assess the success of cultural policy?

(3) Answer all parts of the question.
   (i) What is meant by the term 'market failure'?
   (ii) Give some examples of market failure in the arts and heritage.
   (iii) Explain why market failure in the cultural sector is used as an argument for subsidy to the arts and heritage.

(4) Answer all parts of the question.
   (i) What affects the supply of artists' labour?
   (ii) Define the term 'labour-intensive' and explain why the performing arts are said to be labour-intensive.
   (iii) Explain what is meant by the 'productivity lag' in the performing arts and say what its implications are for the costs of production.
   (iv) Do you think that schemes to give subsidies to artists have the desired outcome? Give reasons for your answer.

(5) Answer all parts of the question.
   (i) Using a diagram, compare the output of a for-profit and a non-profit organisation, each of which has a local monopoly of supplying a cultural service, and the price that each would charge.
   (ii) The government gives a subsidy to the non-profit organisation that takes the form of a voucher worth €10 per attendance given to young people. Analyse the effect on price and output of that subsidy. What determines the extent of the effect?
   (iii) What is the economic explanation for the predominance of non-profit organisations in the arts and heritage sector?

Topics for discussion or essay topics

(1) What historical evidence is there that markets work in the creative industries?

(2) Is willingness to pay a good measure of demand for creative goods and services?

(3) Direct or indirect subsidies: what difference do they make (a) for the funding organisation and (b) for the arts organisation?

(4) Why do principal–agent problems arise in relation to cultural subsidies? Give some examples.

(5) Do you think subsidy encourages innovation in the creative industries?

(6) Why do cultural economists place so much emphasis on taste formation? To what extent do you think cultural subsidies succeed in developing tastes?

(7) Is free trade always a 'good thing' (as it is typically assumed to be by economists)?

(8) What are the pros and cons of the globalisation of culture?

(9) What are the problems of compiling national cultural data? Give some examples of problem areas. What are the problems of making international comparisons? Give some examples of problem areas. What do international comparisons achieve?

(10) Students are asked to choose a creative industry they are interested in and to answer the following questions about it.

  (i) Give examples of the following in your industry:
     (a) an author's right;
     (b) a neighbouring right;
     (c) fair use/exceptions and limitations to copyright.

  (ii) What are the primary and secondary markets for products from this industry?

  (iii) What royalty and/or remuneration payments are there? How are the payments administered?

  (iv) What has the effect of digitalisation been in this industry?

  (v) What business models have developed to accommodate digitalisation?

  (vi) Give some examples of the A list/B list ranking.

  (vii) Who are the gate-keepers in this industry?

  (viii) Who are the 'certifiers' in the industry? What is their economic role?

  (ix) Are there economies of scale/scope in this industry?

  (x) What are the sunk and fixed costs in this industry?

  (xi) What are the variable costs in this industry?

  (xii) What are the transaction costs in this industry?

  (xiii) What determines the size of firms in this industry?

  (xiv) What are the assets of firms in this industry?

  (xv) Identify the various property rights in this industry. What limitations are there (if any) to these property rights?

(xvi) Give an example of a contract in this industry. Why is it likely to be 'incomplete'?

(xvii) Give an example of asymmetric information in this industry.

(xviii) Give examples of vertical or horizontal integration in this industry. How does contract theory explain their presence or absence?

(xix) Give some examples of technical progress in your industry that succeeded and some that failed. Who bears the cost of the failures?

(xx) Give some examples of network effects from your cultural industry.

References

Abbing, H. (2002) *Why Are Artists Poor? The Exceptional Economy of the Arts*, Amsterdam, University of Amsterdam Press.

(2003) 'Support for artists', in R. Towse (ed.) *A Handbook of Cultural Economics*, Cheltenham, Edward Elgar: 437–44.

Acheson, K. (2003) 'Globalization', in R. Towse (ed.) *A Handbook of Cultural Economics*, Cheltenham, Edward Elgar: 248–54.

Acheson, K., and C. Maule (1994) 'Understanding Hollywood's organization and continuing success', *Journal of Cultural Economics*, **18**(4): 271–300.

(1999) *Much Ado about Culture: North American Trade Disputes*, Ann Arbor, University of Michigan Press.

(2004) 'Convention on Cultural Diversity', *Journal of Cultural Economics*, **28**(4): 243–56.

(2006) 'Culture in international trade', in V. Ginsburgh and D. Throsby (eds.) *Handbook of the Economics of Art and Culture*, Amsterdam, North Holland: 1141–82.

Agency for Cultural Affairs (2006) *Administration of Cultural Affairs in Japan*, Tokyo, Bunka (available at www.bunka.go.jp).

Ala-Fossi, M., P. Bakker, M.-K. Ellonen, L. Küng, S. Lax, C. Sádaba and R. van der Wurff (2008) 'The impact of the Internet on business models in the media industries: a sector-by-sector analysis', in L. Küng, R. Picard and R. Towse (eds.) *The Internet and the Mass Media*, London, Sage: 149–69.

Alper, N., and G. Wassall (2006) 'Artists' careers and their labor markets', in V. Ginsburgh and D. Throsby (eds.) *Handbook of the Economics of Art and Culture*, Amsterdam, North Holland: 815–64.

Americans for the Arts (2005) *Creative Industries 2005: The Congressional Report*, Washington, DC, Americans for the Arts (available at www.americansforthearts.org/information_services/research/services/creative_industries/default.asp).

(2008) *Creative Industries 2008: The 50 City Report*, Washington, DC, Americans for the Arts (available at www.americansforthearts.org/information_services/research/services/creative_industries/default.asp).

Anderson, S., and J. Gabszewicz (2006) 'The media and advertising: a tale of two-sided markets,' in V. Ginsburgh and D. Throsby (eds.) *Handbook of the Economics of Art and Culture*, Amsterdam, North Holland: 567–614.

Appelman, M. (2003) 'Fixed book price', in R. Towse (ed.) *A Handbook of Cultural Economics*, Cheltenham, Edward Elgar: 237–42.

Arts Council (2006) *The Public and the Arts 2006*, Dublin, Arts Council (available at www.artscouncil.ie/Publications/PublicandtheArts2006.pdf).

Ashenfelter, O. (2003) 'Art auctions', in R. Towse (ed.) *A Handbook of Cultural Economics*, Cheltenham, Edward Elgar: 32–9.

Australian Bureau of Statistics (2008) *Arts and Culture in Australia: A Statistical Overview*, 2nd edn, Sydney, Australian Bureau of Statistics (available at www.abs.gov.au/ausstats/abs@.nsf/Products/05C3AEC1302AC24ACA2574E90012F06C?opendocument).

Australian Film Commission(2008) *Get the Picture*, Canberra, Australian Film Commission (available at www.afc.gov.au/policyandresearch/policy/film_industry.aspx).

Baumol, H., and W. Baumol (1984), 'The mass media and the cost disease', in W. Hendon, D. Shaw and N. Grant (eds.) *Economics of Cultural Industries*, Akron, OH, Association for Cultural Economics: 109–23 [reprinted in R. Towse (ed.) (1997) *Cultural Economics: The Arts, the Heritage and the Media Industries*, Cheltenham, Edward Elgar, vol. II: 304–18].

Baumol, W. (1971) 'Economics of Athenian drama: its relevance for the arts in a small city today', *Quarterly Journal of Economics*, **85**(3): 365–76.

(1996) 'Children of the performing arts, the economic dilemma: the climbing costs of healthcare and education', *Journal of Cultural Economics*, **20**(3): 183–206.

(1997) 'On the career of a microeconomist', in R. Towse (ed.) *Baumol's Cost Disease: The Arts and Other Victims*, Cheltenham, Edward Elgar: 3–28.

(2003) 'Applied welfare economics', in R. Towse (ed.) *A Handbook of Cultural Economics*, Cheltenham, Edward Elgar: 20–31.

(2006) 'The arts in the "new economy"', in V. Ginsburgh and D. Throsby (eds.) *Handbook of the Economics of Art and Culture*, Amsterdam, North Holland: 339–58.

Baumol, W., and A. Blinder (2006) *Essentials of Economics: Principles and Policy*, Mason, OH, Thomson South-Western.

Baumol, W., and W. Bowen (1966) *Performing Arts: The Economic Dilemma*, Hartford, CT, Twentieth Century Fund.

Benhamou, F. (2003a) 'Artists' labour markets', in R. Towse (ed.) *A Handbook of Cultural Economics*, Cheltenham, Edward Elgar: 69–75.

(2003b) 'Heritage', in R. Towse (ed.) *A Handbook of Cultural Economics*, Cheltenham, Edward Elgar: 255–62.

(2004) 'Comment', *Journal of Cultural Economics*, **28**(4): 263–6.

Bille, T., and G. Schulze (2006) 'Culture in urban and regional development', in V. Ginsburgh and D. Throsby (eds.) *Handbook of the Economics of Art and Culture*, Amsterdam, North Holland: 1051–1100.

Blaauw, J. (2006) 'When film met television. Film industries in western European countries and the role of television broadcasters in them: a cultural economic approach', MA thesis, Erasmus University Rotterdam.

Blaug, M. (1978) 'Why are Covent Garden seat prices so high?', *Journal of Cultural Economics*, **2**(1): 1–20.

(1986) *Great Economists before Keynes*, Cheltenham, Edward Elgar.

(1999) 'A tribute to Dick Netzer and *The Subsidized Muse*', *Journal of Cultural Economics*, **23**(1): 31–2.

(2001) 'Where are we now on cultural economics?', *Journal of Economic Surveys*, **15**(2): 123–43.

(2003) 'Welfare economics', in R. Towse (ed.) *A Handbook of Cultural Economics*, Cheltenham, Edward Elgar: 476–82.

Boldrin, M., and D. Levine (2002) 'The case against intellectual property', *American Economic Review, Papers and Proceedings*, **92**(2): 209–12.

Bonet, L. (2003) 'Cultural tourism', in R. Towse (ed.) *A Handbook of Cultural Economics*, Cheltenham, Edward Elgar: 187–93.

Burke, A. (2003) 'Music business', in R. Towse (ed.) *A Handbook of Cultural Economics*, Cheltenham, Edward Elgar: 321–30.

Cameron, S. (2003) 'Cinema', in R. Towse (ed.) *A Handbook of Cultural Economics*, Cheltenham, Edward Elgar: 114–18.

Canoy, M., J. van Ours and F. van der Ploeg (2006) 'The economics of books', in V. Ginsburgh and D. Throsby (eds.) *Handbook of the Economics of Art and Culture*, Amsterdam, North Holland: 721–61.

Caves, R. (2000) *Creative Industries: Contracts between Art and Commerce*, Cambridge, MA, Harvard University Press.

(2005) *Switching Channels: Organization and Change in TV Broadcasting*, Cambridge, MA, Harvard University Press.

Center for an Urban Future (2005) *Creative New York*, New York, Center for an Urban Future (available at www.nycfuture.org/images_pdfs/pdfs/CREATIVE_NEW_YORK.pdf).

Chevalier, T. (1999) *Girl with a Pearl Earring*, New York, Dutton Adult.

Chisholm, D. (2003) 'Motion pictures', in R. Towse (ed.) *A Handbook of Cultural Economics*, Cheltenham, Edward Elgar: 306–14.

Choi, S.-H. (2006) 'Monopolization of the Korean film industry: a focus on vertical integration', MA thesis, Erasmus University Rotterdam.

Coase, R. (1937) 'The nature of the firm', *Economica*, new series, **4**(16): 386–405.

(1960) 'The problem of social cost', *Journal of Law and Economics*, **3**(1): 1–44.

(1979) 'Payola in radio and television broadcasting', *Journal of Law and Economics*, 22(2): 269–328.

Connolly, M., and A. Krueger (2006) 'Rockonomics: the economics of popular music', in V. Ginsburgh and D. Throsby (eds.) *Handbook of the Economics of Art and Culture*, Amsterdam, North Holland: 667–719.

Cooke, P. (2008) 'Culture, clusters, districts and quarters', in P. Cooke, and L. Lazzeretti (eds.) *Creative Cities, Cultural Clusters and Local Economic Development*, Cheltenham, Edward Elgar: 23–45.

Council of Europe/ERICarts (2008) 'Compendium of cultural policies and trends in Europe', 9th edn, www.culturalpolicies.net.

Cowen, T. (1996) 'Why I do not believe in the cost-disease', *Journal of Cultural Economics*, **20**(3): 207–14.

(1998) *In Praise of Commercial Culture*, Cambridge, MA, Harvard University Press.

(2000) *What Price Fame?*, Cambridge, MA, Harvard University Press.

(2002) *Creative Destruction: How Globalization is Changing the World's Cultures*, Princeton, NJ, Princeton University Press.

(2005) *Markets and Culture Voices: Liberty vs. Power in the Lives of the Mexican Amate Painters*, Ann Arbor, University of Michigan Press.

(2006) *Good and Plenty: The Creative Successes of American Arts Funding*, Princeton, NJ, Princeton University Press.

(2007) *Discover Your Inner Economist: Use Incentives to Fall in Love, Survive Your Next Meeting, and Motivate Your Dentist*, New York, Plume Books.

(2008) 'Why everything has changed: the recent revolution in cultural economics', *Journal of Cultural Economics*, **32**(4): 261–73.

Cuccia, T. (2003) 'Contingent valuation', in R. Towse (ed.) *A Handbook of Cultural Economics*, Cheltenham, Edward Elgar: 119–31.

Dane, C., A. Feist and D. Laing (1996) *The Value of Music*, London, National Music Council.

Danish Film Institute (2006) *Film*, **50**, Copenhagen, Danish Film Institute (available at www.dfi.dk/tidsskriftetfilm/50/thinktank2.htm).

(2008) *Facts and Figures 2008*, Copenhagen, Danish Film Institute.

DCMS (1998) *Creative Industries Mapping Document*, London, DCMS.

(2007a) *The Creative Economy Programme: A Summary of Projects Commissioned in 2006/7*, London, DCMS.

(2007b) *Creative Industries Economic Estimates*, statistical bulletin, London, DCMS (available at www.culture.gov.uk/images/research/CreativeIndustriesEconomicEstimates2007.pdf).

DCMS/Arts Council of England (1999) *Funding Agreement between the Department for Culture, Media and Sport (DCMS) and the Arts Council*, London, DCMS.

De Marchi, N., and J. Greene (2005) 'Adam Smith and the private provision of the arts', *History of Political Economy*, **37**(3): 431–54.

De Vany, A. (2006) 'The movies', in V. Ginsburgh and D. Throsby (eds.) *Handbook of the Economics of Art and Culture*, Amsterdam, North Holland: 615–60.

Doyle, G. (2002) *Media Ownership: The Economics and Politics of Convergence and Concentration in the UK and European Media*, London, Sage.

Einhorn, M. (2003) 'Digitalisation', in R. Towse (ed.) *A Handbook of Cultural Economics*, Cheltenham, Edward Elgar: 214–23.

(2004) *Media, Technology and Copyright: Integrating Law and Economics*, Northampton, MA, Edward Elgar.

ERM Economics (2003) *European Capital of Culture 2008: Socio-economic Impact Assessment of Liverpool's Bid*, Manchester, ERM Economics (available at http://image.guardian.co.uk/sys-files/Society/documents/2003/06/10/finalreport.pdf).

European Audiovisual Observatory (2006) *Broadcasters' Obligations to Invest in Cinematographic Production*, Strasbourg, European Audiovisual Observatory.

Eurostat (2007) *Cultural Statistics: 2007 Edition*, Luxembourg, European Communities (available at http://epp.eurostat.ec.europa.eu/cache/ITY_OFFPUB/KS-77-07-296/EN/KS-77-07-296-EN.PDF).

Farchy, J. (2003) 'Internet: culture', in R. Towse (ed.) *A Handbook of Cultural Economics*, Cheltenham, Edward Elgar: 276–80.

Fauth, R., L. Horner and S. Bevan (2006) *Willingness to Pay for the BBC during the Next Charter Period*, London, Work Foundation.

Felton, M. (1994) 'Evidence of the existence of the cost disease', *Journal of Cultural Economics*, **18**(4): 301–12.

Filer, R. (1986) 'The starving artist: myth or reality? Earnings of an artist in the United States, *Journal of Political Economy*, **94**(1): 56–75.

(1990) 'The arts and academe: the effect of education on earnings of artists', *Journal of Cultural Economics*, **14**(1): 15–38.

Finn, A., S. McFadyen and C. Hoskins (2003) 'Valuing the Canadian Broadcasting Corporation', *Journal of Cultural Economics*, **27**(3–4): 177–92.

Florida, R. (2002) *The Rise of the Creative Class: And How It's Transforming Work, Leisure, Community and Everyday Life*, New York, Basic Books.

Frey, B. (1986) 'The Salzburg Festival from the economic point of view', *Journal of Cultural Economics* **10**(1): 27–44.

(2000) *Arts and Economics: Analysis and Cultural Policy*, Berlin, Springer Verlag.

(2003a) 'Festivals', in R. Towse (ed.) *A Handbook of Cultural Economics*, Cheltenham, Edward Elgar: 232–6.

(2003b) 'Public support', in R. Towse (ed.) *A Handbook of Cultural Economics*, Cheltenham, Edward Elgar: 389–98.

Frey, B., and S. Meier (2001) *Museums between Private and Public: The Case of the Beyeler Museum in Basle*, Working Paper no. 116, Institute for Empirical Research in Economics, University of Zurich.

(2006) 'The economics of museums', in V. Ginsburgh and D. Throsby (eds.) *Handbook of the Economics of Art and Culture*, Amsterdam, North Holland: 1071–47.

Frey, B., and W. Pommerehne (1989) *Muses and Markets: Explorations in the Economics of the Arts*, Oxford, Basil Blackwell.

Frith, S., and L. Marshall (eds.) (2004) *Music and Copyright*, 2nd edn., Edinburgh, University of Edinburgh Press.

Frontier Economics (2007) *Creative Industry Performance: A Statistical Analysis for the DCMS*, London, Frontier Economics (available at www.culture.gov.uk/images/research/statistical_Analysis_of_the_creative_Industries_Frontier_Economics_2007.pdf).

Galbraith, J. (1958) *The Affluent Society*, Harmondsworth, Penguin Books.

Gander, J., and A. Rieple (2004) 'How relevant is transaction cost economics to inter-firm relationships in the music industry?', *Journal of Cultural Economics*, **28**(1): 57–79.

Gazel, R. and K. Schwer (1997) 'Beyond rock and roll: the economic impact of the Grateful Dead on a local economy', *Journal of Cultural Economics* **21**(1): 41–55.

Ginsburgh, V. (2003) 'Art markets', in R. Towse (ed.) *A Handbook of Cultural Economics*, Cheltenham, Edward Elgar: 40–56.

(2005) 'The economic consequences of droit de suite in the European Union', *Economic Analysis and Policy*, **35**(1–2): 61–71 [reprinted in R. Towse (ed.) (2007) *Recent Developments in Cultural Economics*, Cheltenham, Edward Elgar: 384–93].

Goldstone, L. (2003) 'Cultural statistics', in R. Towse (ed.) *A Handbook of Cultural Economics*, Cheltenham, Edward Elgar: 177–82.

Goodwin, C. (2006) 'Art and culture in the history of economic thought', in V. Ginsburgh and D. Throsby (eds.) *Handbook of the Economics of Art and Culture*, Amsterdam, North Holland: 25–66.

Grampp, W. (1989) *Pricing the Priceless: Art, Artists and Economics*, New York, Basic Books.

(1996) 'A colloquy about art museums: economics engages museology', in V. Ginsburgh and P.-M. Menger (eds.), *Economics of the Arts: Selected Essays*, Amsterdam, Elsevier: 221–54 [reprinted in R. Towse (ed.) (2007) *Recent Developments in Cultural Economics*, Cheltenham, Edward Elgar: 119–31].

Gray, M. (1992) 'Art costs and subsidies: the case of Norwegian performing arts', in R. Towse and A. Khakee (eds.) *Cultural Economics*, Heidelberg, Springer: 267–73 [reprinted in R. Towse (ed.) (1997) *Cultural Economics: The Arts, the Heritage and the Media Industries*, Cheltenham, Edward Elgar, vol. II: 337–43].

Greco, A. (2000) 'Market concentration levels in the U.S. consumer book industry: 1995–1996', *Journal of Cultural Economics*, **24**(4): 321–36.

Greffe, X. (2002) *Arts and Artists from an Economic Perspective*, Paris, UNESCO and Economica.

Hansmann, H. (1981) 'Nonprofit enterprise in the performing arts', *Bell Journal of Economics*, **12**(2): 341–61 [reprinted in R. Towse (ed.) (1997) *Cultural Economics: The Arts, the Heritage and the Media Industries*, Cheltenham, Edward Elgar, vol. II: 393–413].

Hargreaves Heap, S. (2005) 'Television in a digital age: what role for public broadcasting?', *Economic Policy*, **20**: 112–57.

Hart, O. (1989) 'An economist's perspective on the theory of the firm', *Columbia Law Review*, **89**(7): 1757–74.

Heikkinen, M. (1995) 'Evaluating the effects of direct support on the economic situation of artists', *Journal of Cultural Economics*, **19**(3): 261–72.

Heilbrun, J. (2001) 'Empirical evidence of a decline in repertory among American opera companies 1991/2–1997/8', *Journal of Cultural Economics*, **25**(1): 63–72.

(2003) 'Baumol's cost disease', in R. Towse (ed.) *A Handbook of Cultural Economics*, Cheltenham, Edward Elgar: 91–101.

Heinrich, J., and G. Kopper (2006) *Media Economics in Europe*, Berlin, Vistas Verlag.

Higgs, P., S. Cunningham and H. Bakhshi (2008) *Beyond the Creative Industries: Mapping the Creative Economy in the United Kingdom*, London, National Endowment for Science, Technology and the Arts.

Hjorth-Andersen, C. (2003) 'Publishing', in R. Towse (ed.) *A Handbook of Cultural Economics*, Cheltenham, Edward Elgar: 399–407.

Hoefert de Turégano, T. (2006) *Public Support for the International Promotion of European Films*, Strasbourg, European Audiovisual Observatory.

Holt, G., and D. Elliott (2003) 'Measuring outcomes: applying cost–benefit analysis to middle-sized and smaller public libraries', *Library Trends*, **51**(3): 424–40

Holt, G., D. Elliott and A. Moore (1999) 'Placing a value of public library services', *Public Libraries*, **38**(2): 98–108.

Hotelling, H. (1929) 'Stability in competition', *Economic Journal*, **39**: 41–57.

Hutter, M. (2003) 'Information goods', in R. Towse (ed.) *A Handbook of Cultural Economics*, Cheltenham, Edward Elgar: 263–8.

Iapadre, L. (2004) 'Comment', *Journal of Cultural Economics*, **28**(4): 267–73.

IFACCA (2005) *Statistical Indicators for Arts Policy*, IFACCA, Sydney (available at www.ifacca.org/files/statisticalindicatorsforartspolicy.pdf).

IFPI (2007) *Digital Music Report 2007*, London, IFPI.

(2008) *Digital Music Report 2008*, London, IFPI.

Johnson, P. (2003) 'Museums', in R. Towse (ed.) *A Handbook of Cultural Economics*, Cheltenham, Edward Elgar: 315–20.

Joy, A., and M. Skinner (2005) *A Statistical Survey of Regularly Funded Arts Organisations 2002/03*, London, Arts Council of England.

KEA European Affairs (2006) *The Economy of Culture in Europe: A Strategy for a Creative Europe*, Brussels, KEA European Affairs (available at www.keanet.eu/Ecoculture/Study%20new.pdf).

King, K., and M. Blaug (1973) 'Does the Arts Council know what it is doing? An inquiry into public patronage of arts', *Encounter*, **12**(3): 6–16 [reprinted in M. Blaug (ed.) (1976) *The Economics of the Arts*, Boulder, CO, Westview Press: 101–25].

Klaes, M. (2008) 'Transaction costs, history of', in S. Durlauf and L. Blume (eds.) *The New Palgrave Dictionary of Economics*, 2nd edn, vol. VIII, London, Palgrave Macmillan: 363–6.

Kolmodin, A. (2008) 'Creative industries: a growth sector?', *Growth Policy Outlook*, 6 (Sep) (available at www.itps.se/Archive/Documents/Swedish/Publikationer/Tillv%C3%A4xtpolitisk%20utblick/TpU_nr6_2008_eng_webb.pdf).

Kovac, M., and M. Kovac Sebart (2006) 'Reading and book usage in the European Union', *Publishing Research Quarterly*, **22**(2): 55–63.

Krebs, S., and W. Pommerehne (1995) 'Politico-economic interactions of German performing arts institutions', *Journal of Cultural Economics*, **19**(1): 17–32.

Kretschmer, M., and P. Hardwick (2007) *Authors' Earnings from Copyright and Non-copyright Sources: A Survey of 25,000 British and German Writers*, Bournemouth, Centre for Intellectual Property Policy and Management (available at www.cippm.org.uk/publications/alcs/ACLS%20Full%20report.pdf).

Küng, L., R. Picard and R. Towse (eds.) (2008) *The Internet and the Mass Media*, London, Sage.

Landes, W. (2003) 'Copyright', in R. Towse (ed.) *A Handbook of Cultural Economics*, Cheltenham, Edward Elgar: 132–42.

Landes, W., and R. Posner (1989) 'An economic analysis of copyright law', *Journal of Legal Studies*, **18**(2): 325–66.

(2002) *Indefinitely Renewable Copyright*, Olin Working Paper no. 154, University of Chicago Law School (available at www.law.uchicago.edu/Lawecon/index.html).

Lévy-Garboua, L., and C. Montmarquette (1996) 'A microeconomic study of theater demand,' *Journal of Cultural Economics*, **20**(1): 25–50.

Liebowitz, S. (2003) *Will MP3 Downloads Annihilate the Record Industry? The Evidence so Far*, working paper, School of Management, University of Texas at Dollas.

Luksetich, W. (2003) 'Orchestras', in R. Towse (ed.) *A Handbook of Cultural Economics*, Cheltenham, Edward Elgar: 349–55.

Luksetich, W., and M. Partridge (1997) 'Demand functions for museum services', *Applied Economics*, **29**(12): 1553–9.

Maddison, D., and T. Foster (2003) 'Valuing costs in the British Museum', *Oxford Economic Papers*, **55**(1): 173–90.

Matsumoto, S. (2002) 'Performers in the digital era: empirical evidence from Japan', in R. Towse (ed.) *Copyright in the Cultural Industries*, Cheltenham, Edward Elgar: 196–209.

Maule, C. (2003) 'Television', in R. Towse (ed.) *A Handbook of Cultural Economics*, Cheltenham, Edward Elgar: 458–64.

Mazza. I. (2003) 'Public choice', in R. Towse (ed.) *A Handbook of Cultural Economics*, Cheltenham, Edward Elgar: 379–88.

MEDIA Salles (2006) *European Cinema Yearbook 2006*, Milan, Media Salles (available at www.mediasalles.it/yearbook06_fin.pdf).

Menger, P.-M., and M. Gurgand (1996) 'Work and compensated unemployment in the performing arts: exogenous and endogenous uncertainty in artistic labour markets', in V. Ginsburgh and P.-M. Menger (eds.) *Economics of the Arts: Selected Essays*, Amsterdam, North Holland: 347–81.

Monopolies and Mergers Commission (1996) *Performing Rights*, Cm 3147, London, HMSO.

Montias, J. M. (1982) *Artists and Artisans in Delft: A Socio-economic Study of the Seventeenth Century*, Princeton, NJ, Princeton University Press.

(1989) *Vermeer and His Milieu: A Web of Social History*, Princeton, NJ, Princeton University Press.

MPAA (2006) *Entertainment Industry Market Statistics, 2006*, Washington, DC, MPAA (available at www.mpaa.org/USEntertainmentIndustryMarketStats.pdf).

(2007) *Entertainment Industry Market Statistics 2007*, Washington, DC, MPAA (available at www.mpaa.org/USEntertainmentIndustryMarketStats.pdf).

Musgrave, R. (1959) *The Theory of Public Finance: A Study in Public Economy*, New York, McGraw-Hill.

(1987) 'Merit goods', in J. Eatwell, M. Milgate and P. Newman (eds.) *The New Palgrave: A Dictionary of Economics*, London, Macmillan: 452–3.

Musgrave, R., and P. B. Musgrave (1973) *Public Finance in Theory and Practice*, New York, McGraw-Hill.

NEA (1995) *Effects of Arts Education on Participation in the Arts*, Report no. 36, Washington, DC, NEA (available at www.nea.gov/pub/Researcharts/Summary 36.html).

(2003) *2002 Survey of Public Participation in the Arts*, Note no. 81, Washington, DC, NEA (available at www.nea.gov/research/notes/81.pdf).

(2006) *Consumer Spending on Performing Arts*, Note no. 91, Washington, DC, NEA (available at www.nea.gov/research/notes/91.pdf).

(2007a) *How the United States Funds the Arts*, 2nd edn, Washington, DC, NEA.

(2007b) *To Read or Not to Read: A Question of National Consequence*, Report no. 47, Washington, DC, NEA (available at www.nea.gov/research/ToRead_ExecSum.pdf).

(2008) *Artists in the Workforce: 1990–2005*, Report no. 48, Washington, DC, NEA.

Netzer, D. (1978) *The Subsidized Muse: Public Support for the Arts in the United States*, Cambridge, Cambridge University Press.

(2003) 'Non-profit organisations', in R. Towse (ed.) *A Handbook of Cultural Economics*, Cheltenham, Edward Elgar: 331–41.

(2006) 'Cultural policy: an American view', in V. Ginsburgh and D. Throsby (eds.) *Handbook of the Economics of Art and Culture*, Amsterdam, North Holland: 1223–51.

Oates, M., and W. Baumol (1972), 'On the economics of the theatre in Renaissance London', *Swedish Journal of Economics*, **74**(1): 136–80 [reprinted in R. Towse (ed.) (1997) *Cultural Economics: The Arts, the Heritage and the Media Industries*, Cheltenham, Edward Elgar, vol. II: 3–27].

O'Brien, J., and A. Feist (1995) *Employment in the Arts and Cultural Industries: An Analysis of the 1991 Census*, London, Arts Council of England.

OCenW (2006) *Cultural Policy in the Netherlands*, Amsterdam, Boekman Studies.

O'Hagan, J. (1992) 'The Wexford Festival: a case for public funding?', in R. Towse and A. Khakee (eds.) *Cultural Economics*, Heidelberg, Springer: 61–6.

(1995) 'National museums: to charge or not to charge?', *Journal of Cultural Economics*, **19**(1): 33–47.

(2003) 'Tax concessions', in R. Towse (ed.) *A Handbook of Cultural Economics*, Cheltenham, Edward Elgar: 451–7.

O'Hagan, J., and A. Neligan (2005) 'State subsidies and repertoire conventionality in the non-profit English theatre sector', *Journal of Cultural Economics*, **29**(1): 35–57.

Oksanen, V. and M. Välimäki (2005) 'Copyright levies as an alternative compensation method for recording artists and technological development', *Review of Economic Research on Copyright Issues*, **2**(2): 25–39.

Papandrea, F. (1999) 'Willingness to pay for domestic television programming', *Journal of Cultural Economics*, **23**(3): 147–64.

Paulus, O. (2003), 'Measuring museum performance: a study of museums in France and the United States', *International Journal of Arts Management*, **6**(1): 50–63 [reprinted in R. Towse (ed.) (2007) *Recent Developments in Cultural Economics*, Cheltenham, Edward Elgar: 269–82].

Peacock, A. (1969) 'Welfare economics and public subsidies to the arts', *Manchester School of Economic and Social Studies*, **4**(December): 323–35 [reprinted in R. Towse (1997a) *Cultural Economics: The Arts, the Heritage and the Media Industries*, Cheltenham, Edward Elgar, vol. II: 501–13].

(1986a) *Report of the Committee on Financing the BBC*, Cmnd 9824, London, Stationery Office Books.

(1986b) *Making Sense of Broadcasting Finance*, Robbins Lecture Pamphlet, University of Stirling [reprinted in R. Towse (ed.) (1997) *Cultural Economics: The Arts, the Heritage and the Media Industries*, Cheltenham, Edward Elgar, vol. II: 427–34].

(1993) *Paying the Piper: Culture, Music, and Money*, Edinburgh: Edinburgh University Press.

(2004) 'The credibility of economists' advice to governments', in V. Ginsburgh (ed.) *Economics of Art and Culture: Invited Papers at the 12th International Conference of the Association of Cultural Economics*, Amsterdam Elsevier: 165–78 [reprinted in R. Towse (ed.) (2007) *Recent Developments in Cultural Economics*, Cheltenham, Edward Elgar: 60–73].

Peacock, A., and I. Rizzo (2008) *The Heritage Game: Economics, Policy and Practice*, Oxford, Oxford University Press.

Peacock, A., E. Shoesmith and G. Millner (1983) 'Measuring the extent of cost inflation', 'The study's main results' and 'Conclusions and recommendations', in A. Peacock (ed.) *Inflation and the Performed Arts*, London, Arts Council of Great Britain: 7–48 [reprinted in R. Towse (ed.) (1997) *Cultural Economics: The Arts, the Heritage and the Media Industries*, Cheltenham, Edward Elgar, vol. II: 319–60].

Pierce, J. (2000) 'Programmatic risk-taking by American opera companies', *Journal of Cultural Economics*, **24**(1): 45–63.

Pignataro, G. (2003) 'Performance indicators', in R. Towse (ed.) *A Handbook of Cultural Economics*, Cheltenham, Edward Elgar: 366–72.

Plant, A. (1934) 'The economic aspects of copyright in books', *Economica* (new series), **1**(2): 167–95.

Publishers Association (2006) *UK Book Publishing Industry Statistics Yearbook 2006*, London, Publishers Association.

Rightscom (2004) *Publishing Market Watch Sectoral Report 2: Book Publishing*, Brussels, European Commission (available at www.rightscom.com/Portals/0/European%20Book %20Publishing%20Report.pdf).

Rizzo, I. (2003) 'Regulation', in R. Towse (ed.) *A Handbook of Cultural Economics*, Cheltenham, Edward Elgar: 408–415.

Rizzo, I., and D. Throsby (2006) 'Cultural heritage: economic analysis and public policy', in V. Ginsburgh and D. Throsby (eds.) *Handbook of the Economics of Art and Culture*, Amsterdam, North Holland: 983–1016.

Rizzo, I., and R. Towse (2002) *Economics of Heritage: A Study in the Political Economy of Culture in Sicily*, Cheltenham, Edward Elgar.

Robbins, L. (1971) 'Unsettled questions in the political economy of the arts', *Three Banks Review*, **91**(September): 3–19 [reprinted in R. Towse (ed.) (1997) *Cultural Economics: The Arts, the Heritage and the Media Industries*, Cheltenham, Edward Elgar, vol. II: 347–63].

Rochelandet, F. (2003) 'Internet: economics', in R. Towse (ed.) *A Handbook of Cultural Economics*, Cheltenham, Edward Elgar: 281–6.

Rose, M. (1993) *Authors and Owners: The Invention of Copyright*, Cambridge, MA, Harvard University Press.

Rosen, S. (1981) 'The Economics of Superstars', *American Economic Review*, **71**(5): 845–58.

Rosselli, J. (1989) 'From princely states to the open market: singers of Italian opera and their patrons 1600–1850', *Cambridge Opera Journal*, **1**(1): 1–32 [reprinted in R. Towse (ed.) (1997) *Cultural Economics: The Arts, the Heritage and the Media Industries*, Cheltenham, Edward Elgar, vol. II: 37–68].

Rushton, M. (2003) 'Artists' rights', in R. Towse (ed.) *A Handbook of Cultural Economics*, Cheltenham, Edward Elgar: 76–80.

Sagot-Duvauroux, D. (2003) 'Art prices', in R. Towse (ed.) *A Handbook of Cultural Economics*, Cheltenham, Edward Elgar: 57–63.

Santagata, W. (2006) 'Cultural districts and their role in developed and developing countries', in V. Ginsburgh and D. Throsby (eds.) *Handbook of the Economics of Art and Culture*, Amsterdam, North Holland: 1101–19.

Scherer, F. M. (2001) 'An early application of the average total cost concept', *Journal of Economic Literature*, 39(3): 897–901.

   (2006) 'The evolution of music markets', in V. Ginsburgh and D. Throsby (eds.) *Handbook of the Economics of Art and Culture*, Amsterdam, North Holland: 124–43.

Schimmelpfennig, J. (1997) 'Demand for ballet: a non-parametric analysis of the Royal Ballet summer season', *Journal of Cultural Economics*, **21**(2): 119–27.

   (2003) 'Ballet', in R. Towse (ed.) *A Handbook of Cultural Economies*, Cheltenham, Edward Elgar: 85–90.

Schulze, G. (2003a) 'International trade', in R. Towse (ed.) *A Handbook of Cultural Economics*, Cheltenham, Edward Elgar: 269–75.

   (2003b) 'Superstars', in R. Towse (ed.) *A Handbook of Cultural Economics*, Cheltenham, Edward Elgar: 431–6.

Schulze, G., and A. Rose (1998) 'Public orchestra funding in Germany – an empirical investigation', *Journal of Cultural Economics*, **22**(4): 227–47.

Schumpeter, J. (1912) *Theory of Economic Development: An Inquiry into Profits, Capital, Credit, Interest and the Business Cycle*, Leipzig, Duncker and Humblot.

(1942) *Capitalism, Socialism and Democracy*, New York, Harper & Brothers.

Schuster, M. (2001) *Policy and Planning with a Purpose or The Art of Making Choices in Arts Funding*, working paper, Cultural Policy Center, University of Chicago (available at http://culturalpolicy.uchicago.edu/workingpapers/Schuster10.pdf).

(2006) 'Tax incentives in cultural policy', in V. Ginsburgh and D. Throsby (eds.) *Handbook of the Economics of Art and Culture*, Amsterdam, North Holland: 1253–94.

Scitovsky, T. (1976) *The Joyless Economy: An Inquiry into Human Satisfaction and Consumer Dissatisfaction*, Oxford, Oxford University Press.

SCP (2008) *Facts and Figures of the Netherlands; Social and Cultural Trends 1995–2006*, The Hague, SCP.

Screen Australia (2008) *National Survey of Film and TV Drama Production 2007/8*, Woolloomooloo, Screen Australia.

Seaman, B. (2003) 'Economic impact of the arts', in R. Towse (ed.) *A Handbook of Cultural Economics*, Cheltenham, Edward Elgar: 224–31.

(2004), 'Competition and the non-profit arts: the lost industrial organisation agenda', *Journal of Cultural Economics*, **28**(3): 167–93.

(2006) 'Empirical studies of demand for the performing arts', in V. Ginsburgh and D. Throsby (eds.) *Handbook of the Economics of Art and Culture*, Amsterdam, North Holland: 416–72.

Sedgwick, J. (2000) *Popular Filmgoing in 1930s Britain: A Choice of Pleasures*, Exeter, University of Exeter Press.

Selwood, S., and M. Davies (2005) 'Capital costs: lottery funding in Britain and the consequences for museums', *Curator*, **48**(4): 439–67.

Shapiro, C., and H. Varian (1999) *Information Rules: A Strategic Guide to the Network Economy*, Boston, Harvard Business School Press.

Shavell, S., and T. van Ypserle (2001) 'Rewards versus intellectual property rights', *Journal of Law and Economics*, **44**(2): 525–47.

Shoesmith, E. (1984) 'Long-term trends in performing arts expenditures', *Journal of Cultural Economics*, **8**(2): 51–71.

Shubik, M. (2003) 'Dealers in art', in R. Towse (ed.) *A Handbook of Cultural Economics*, Cheltenham, Edward Elgar: 194–200.

Siwek, S. (2007) *The True Cost of Piracy to the US Economy*, Lewisville, TX, Institute for Policy Innovation.

Sloman, J. (2006) *Economics*, 6th edn, Harlow, Pearson Education/FT Prentice Hall.

Smith, A. (1776/1976) *An Inquiry into the Nature and Causes of the Wealth of Nations*, eds. R. H. Campbell, A. S. Skinner and W. B. Todd, 2 vols., Oxford, Clarendon Press.

Smith, T. (2003) *Raising the Barre: The Geographical, Financial, and Economic Trends of Non-profit Dance Companies*, Report no. 44, Washington, DC, NEA.

(2007) 'The impact of government funding on private contributions to nonprofit performing arts organizations', *Annals of Public and Cooperative Economics*, **78**(1): 137–60.

Stigler, G., and G. Becker (1977) 'De gustibus non est disputandum', *American Economic Review*, **67**(2): 76–90.

Strobl, E., and C. Tucker (2000) 'The dynamics of chart success in the U.K. pre-recorded popular music industry', *Journal of Cultural Economics*, **24**(2): 113–34.

Swedish Arts Council (2003) *Cultural Barometer 2002 (Kulturbarometern 2002)*, Stockholm, Swedish Arts Council.

Taalas, M. (1997) 'Generalised cost functions for producers of performing arts – allocative inefficiencies and scale economies in theatres', *Journal of Cultural Economics*, **21**(4): 335–53.

(2003) 'Costs of Production', in R. Towse (eds.) *A Handbook of Cultural Economics*, Cheltenham, Edward Elgar: 151–60.

Tanner, D. (2007) 'Innovation and teamwork: a modest ticketing project yields accurate attendance figures', www.aamus.org/pubs/accurateattendance.cfm.

Tate (2005) *Tate Modern: The First Five Years*, London, Tate.

Throsby, D. (1990) 'Perception of quality in demand for the theatre', *Journal of Cultural Economics*, **14**(1): 65–82.

(1994) 'A work-preference model of artist behaviour', in A. Peacock and I. Rizzo (eds.) *Cultural Economics and Cultural Policies*, Boston, Springer: 69–80 [reprinted in R. Towse (ed.) (2007) *Recent Developments in Cultural Economics*, Cheltenham, Edward Elgar: 397–408].

(1996a) 'Disaggregated earnings functions for artists', in V. Ginsburgh and P.-M. Menger (eds.) *Economics of the Arts: Selected Essays*, Amsterdam, North Holland: 331–46.

(1996b) 'Economic circumstances of the performing artist: Baumol and Bowen 30 years on', *Journal of Cultural Economics*, **20**(3): 225–40.

(2001) *Economics and Culture*, Cambridge, Cambridge University Press.

(2002) *The Music Industry in the New Millennium: Global and Local Perspectives* (paper prepared for the Global Alliance for Cultural Diversity, UNESCO), Macquarie University, Sydney.

Throsby, D., and V. Hollister (2003) *Don't Give Up Your Day Job Yet: An Economic Study of Professional Artists in Australia*, Sydney, Australia Council.

Throsby, D., and G. Withers (1979) *The Economics of the Performing Arts*, New York, St Martin's Press.

Towse, R. (1993) *Singers in the Marketplace: The Economics of the Singing Profession*, Oxford, Clarendon Press.

(1996) 'Economics of training artists', in V. Ginsburgh and P. Menger (eds.) *Economics of the Arts: Essays*, Amsterdam, North Holland: 303–29.

(ed.). (1997) *Cultural Economics: The Arts, the Heritage and the Media Industries*, 2 vols., Cheltenham, Edward Elgar.

(2001a) 'Quis custodiet? Or managing the management: the case of the Royal Opera House, Covent Garden', *International Journal of Arts Management*, **3**(3): 38–50 [reprinted in R. Towse (ed.) (2007) *Recent Developments in Cultural Economics*, Cheltenham, Edward Elgar: 219–31].

(2001b) *Creativity, Incentive and Reward: An Economic Analysis of Copyright and Culture in the Information Age*, Cheltenham, Edward Elgar.

(ed.) (2003a) *A Handbook of Cultural Economics*, Cheltenham, Edward Elgar.

(2003b) 'Cultural industries', in R. Towse (ed.) *A Handbook of Cultural Economics*, Cheltenham, Edward Elgar: 170–6.

(2003c) 'Opera', in R. Towse (ed.) *A Handbook of Cultural Economics*, Cheltenham, Edward Elgar: 342–8.

(2005) 'Alan Peacock and cultural economics', *Economic Journal*, **115**(June): F262–F276.

(2006a) 'Copyright and artists: a view from cultural economics', *Journal of Economic Surveys*, **20**(4): 567–85.

(2006b) 'Human capital and artists' labour markets', in V. Ginsburgh and D. Throsby (eds.) *Handbook of the Economics of Art and Culture*, Amsterdam, North Holland: 867–94.

(ed.) (2007) *Recent Developments in Cultural Economics*, Cheltenham, Edward Elgar.

(2008) 'Why has cultural economics ignored copyright?', *Journal of Cultural Economics*: **32**(4): 243.

Tschmuck, P. (2006) *Creativity and Innovation in the Music Industry*. Dordrecht, Springer.

UNCTAD (2008) *Creative Economy Report 2008: The Challenge of Assessing the Creative Economy: Towards Informed Policy-making*, Geneva, UNCTAD.

UNESCO (2000a) *Culture, Trade and Globalization: Questions and Answers*, Paris, UNESCO (available at http://unesdoc.unesco.org/images/0012/001213/121360E.pdf).

(2000b) *International Flows of Selected Cultural Goods 1980–98*, Paris, UNESCO.

UNESCO Institute for Statistics (2005) *International Flows of Selected Cultural Goods and Services, 1994–2003: Defining and Capturing the Flows of Global Cultural Trade*, Montreal, UNESCO Institute for Statistics.

Urrutiaguer, D. (2002) 'Quality judgements and demand for french public theatre', *Journal of Cultural Economics*, **22**(3): 185–202.

van der Ploeg, F. (2004a) *Culture as Confrontation: Principles on Cultural Policy 2001–2004*, Zoetermeer, OcenW (available at www.minocw.nl/english_oud/internat/english/).

(2004b) 'Comment', *Journal of Cultural Economics*, **28**(4): 257–61.

(2006) 'The making of cultural policy: a European perspective', in V. Ginsburgh and D. Throsby (eds.) *Handbook of the Economics of Art and Culture*, Amsterdam, North Holland: 1183–221.

van der Wurff, R. (2005) 'Competition, concentration and diversity in European television markets', *Journal of Cultural Economics*, **29**(4): 249–75.

van Puffeln, F. (1996) 'Abuses of conventional impact studies in the arts', *Cultural Policy*, **2**(2): 241–54.

Varian, H. (2005) 'Copying and copyright', *Journal of Economic Perspectives*, **19**(2): 121–38.

Vaughan, D. (1980) 'Does a festival pay?', in W. Hendon, J. Shanahan and A. MacDonald (eds.) *Economic Policy for the Arts*, Cambridge, MA, Abt Books: 319–31.

Velthuis, O. (2003) 'Visual arts', in R. Towse (ed.) *A Handbook of Cultural Economics*, Cheltenham, Edward Elgar: 470–83.

Vogel, H. (2001) *Entertainment Industry Economics: A Guide for Financial Analysis*, 5th edn, Cambridge, Cambridge University Press.

(2004) *Entertainment Industry Economics: A Guide for Financial Analysis*, 6th edn, Cambridge, Cambridge University Press.

Wijnberg, N. (2003) 'Awards', in R. Towse (ed.) *A Handbook of Cultural Economics*, Cheltenham, Edward Elgar: 81–4.

Willis, K., and J. Snowball (2009) 'Investigating how the attributes of live theatre productions influence consumption choices using conjoint analysis: the example of the National Arts Festival, South Africa,' *Journal of Cultural Economics*, **33**(3): 167–83.

WIPO (2000) *Basic Notions of Copyright and Related Rights*, Geneva, WIPO (available at www. wipo.int/copyright/en/activities/pdf/basic_notions.pdf).

(2003) *Guide on Surveying the Economic Contribution of the Copyright-based Industries*, Geneva, WIPO.

Withers, G. (1985) 'Artists' subsidy for the arts', *Australian Economic Papers*, **25**(December): 290–5; reprinted in R. Towse (ed.) (1997) *Cultural Economics: The Arts, the Heritage and the Media Industries*, Cheltenham, Edward Elgar: 269–74.

(2003) 'Broadcasting', in R. Towse (ed.) *A Handbook of Cultural Economics*, Cheltenham, Edward Elgar: 102–13.

Index